CASES FOR
STRATEGIC MANAGEMENT

CASES FOR STRATEGIC MANAGEMENT

John H. Barnett

University of New Hampshire

William D. Wilsted

University of Colorado

PWS-KENT PUBLISHING COMPANY
Boston

PWS–KENT
Publishing Company

Acquisitions Editor: Rolf Janke
Production Editor: Wanda K. Wilking
Interior Design: Outside Design
Cover Design: Sally Bindari, Designworks
Manufacturing Coordinator: Margaret Sullivan Higgins
Composition: David E. Seham Associates, Inc.
Cover Printer: Lehigh Press, Inc.
Text Printer and Binder: The Maple-Vail Book Manufacturing Group

PWS-KENT Publishing Company is a division of Wadsworth, Inc.

Printed in the United States of America
1 2 3 4 5 6 7 8 9 — 93 92 91 90 89

Library of Congress Cataloging-in-Publication Data

Barnett, John Hayes.
   Cases for strategic management / John H. Barnett, William D.
Wilsted.
     p.   cm.
   ISBN 0-534-91742-9
   1. Strategic planning — Case studies. I. Wilsted, William D.
II. Title.
HD30.28.B3678   1989
658.4′012 — dc19
                                    88-25535
                                       CIP

for Vasilka and Karen

*The survival of any firm depends upon the generalities of economics;
the success of any firm depends upon the particularities of its strategy.*

PREFACE

This preface presents the rationale, structure, and content of Barnett and Wilsted's *Cases for Strategic Management*. This book is composed of cases that allow you to apply your skill at the art of strategic management to a variety of specific examples of strategic management.

The Cases

The authors wrote six of the twenty-five cases. Current significant managerial dilemmas such as disinvestment in South Africa, Japanese competition, and hostile takeovers are combined with strategic management problems in these cases.

Contributed cases include some favorites and cover issues such as high technology, small businesses, manufacturing and service industries, and a few nonprofit enterprises. Furthermore, the international business environment makes up a significant part of seven cases.

Several cases are devoted to two industries, lodging/entertainment and alcoholic beverages, that are currently experiencing significant changes. These changes include the increasing popularity of wine, the decreasing market share for traditional "brown" whiskeys, anti-alcohol trends, the marketing and competitive revolution in the beer industry, and new entertainment technologies, such as VCRs, and lodging segmentation strategies. The student takes a look at the industries, both over time and from different managerial perspectives — such as the production view of Coors, the survival perspective of Schlitz, and the leader view of Marriott.

In many of the cases the focus is on personal values, and in particular, on ethics. Ethics is central to the Polaroid and South Africa cases.

Introductory sections include financial tools for strategic analysis, a general approach to preparing cases, a sample case, and an illustrative analysis of that case.

Materials accompanying this text include the videotape program, Strategic Insights, to support some of the cases in this book. Also, two data discs containing five computer programs that utilize Lotus 1-2-3 to study specific strategic problems and to extract strategic information from a ten-year, industry-wide data base for the beer industry.

Acknowledgments First in our acknowledgments must be Carol True. In addition, we are fortunate to have benefited from the comments and criticisms of many excellent reviewers:

William E. Burr
University of Oregon

Robert W. Carney
Georgia Institute of Technology

Edward S. Dyl
University of Arizona

David P. Gustafson
University of Missouri, St. Louis

Frederick C. Haas
Virginia Commonwealth University

William D. Kane, Jr.
Western Carolina University

Michael D. Lucas
Western Illinois University

Richard R. Merner
University of Delaware

Michael C. White
Louisiana State University

We would like to acknowledge the important case contributions of

Sexton Adams, North Texas State University; Larry Agranove, Wilfred Laurier University; Larry Alexander, Virginia Polytechnic Institute and State University; Steven Anderson, Austin Peay State University; Peter Asp, University of South Carolina; Edgar Barrett, Southern Methodist University; Paul Beamish, University of Western Ontario; James Chrisman, University of South Carolina; Joseph Durocher, University of New Hampshire; Jonathan Foster, London School of Economics; Joseph Fry, University of Western Ontario; Tim Furey, Harvard University; Kim Goates, University of South Carolina; Adelaide Griffin, Texas Woman's University; Frederick Haas, Virginia Commonwealth University; Charles Hinkle, University of Colorado; Jay Horne, University of South Carolina; Jeffrey Miner, Virginia Polytechnic Institute and State University; Rowland Moriarty, Harvard University; Christopher Nussbaumer, Austin Peay State University; John Oliver, Valdosta State College; Robert Palmer, University of Massachusetts; Christine Perkins, University of South Carolina; Ken Sarris, University of South Carolina; Arthur Sharplin, McNeese State University; Dean Schroeder, University of Massachusetts; Esther Stineman, Yale University; Charles Stubbart, University of Massachusetts; Albert Taylor, Austin Peay State University; Julian Vincze, Rollins College; Jeanne Whitehead, Austin Peay State University.

We also want to thank the North American Case Research Association, at whose 1986 and 1987 meeting two of the text cases were reviewed.

Finally we would like to thank the editorial staff at PWS-KENT Publishing Co., especially Wanda Wilking and Rolf Janke.

John Barnett
William Wilsted

CONTENTS

THE CASE METHOD

The primary teaching method used in strategic management is the case method. Cases allow you to apply the art of the strategic process in real-life situations.

Two basic principles apply to case work. First, the cases are not designed to prepare you for a specific incident you may meet in your business career; they are simply vehicles that force you to practice systematic analysis and decision making. Second, there are no school solutions to the cases. Your job is to analyze the situation, define the major problem(s), decide on appropriate courses of action, and logically and rationally present and defend your recommendation. Recommendations to the cases may differ considerably, and many recommendations might be creditable alternatives. Your work will be evaluated in terms of how clearly, precisely, and logically you think the problems through and defend your recommendations.

The following outline provides a very broad, general checklist. In any specific case used in this course, only parts of this outlined analysis will be appropriate. Make sure you use this checklist only as a general reminder, not as a "cookbook" appropriate to every situation.

GENERAL APPROACH

Case analysis generally proceeds through the following seven stages or steps.

1. Sizing up the situation
2. Evaluating the present strategy
3. Identifying issues and options
4. Evaluating options
5. Making recommendations
6. Implementing strategy
7. Monitoring results

Sizing up the Situation

What is the enterprise doing at present? In what circumstances? With what results? As you answer these questions, you are getting a feel for the situation. You are obtaining the facts in a meaningful order and placing dimensions upon them.

1. Analyze the economics of the situation.
   1.1 Attributes of products and of the demand for them (the demand curve)
   1.2 Attributes of the technology, including the productive and distributive processes

1.3 The input mix, the cost mix, the unit (average) cost curve
1.4 The competitive situation both in the market for the inputs and in the market for the finished products
1.5 The price-cost-volume-profit relationships resulting from 1.1 through 1.4
2. Analyze opportunities and constraints, and strengths and weaknesses relative to them.
3. Identify the strategy of the enterprise, which refers to established company policy concerning
    3.1 Mission, objectives, and goals
    3.2 Strategy being employed
        3.2(1) to improve opportunities
        3.2(2) to overcome constraints
        3.2(3) to meet competition
        3.2(4) to gain access to markets, both as buyer and as seller, on favorable terms
    3.3 Basic decisions concerning
        3.3(1) products and markets
        3.3(2) technology
        3.3(3) make-or-buy
        3.3(4) resource procurement
        3.3(5) location
        3.3(6) scale
        3.3(7) standards

From the outline you should derive insight into what the enterprise is trying to do — its "game plan" — and the circumstances in which this effort is being made. You will assemble and order the available facts, analyze them objectively, and withhold a decision until the size-up has been completed.

As you attempt to identify the strategy of an organization, you may study (1) its pronouncements as to its purpose, (2) its resource allocation, (3) its products and markets, and (4) its method of competition.

Pronouncements. Often you will come across a statement of strategy, such as "We want to be the General Motors of XYZ industry"; "We want constantly rising earnings"; or "We want to be on the cutting edge of technology." You should look for statements about what a company wants to be or what it wants to do.

Resource Allocation. Strategic pronouncements might be too general to be of help, or they might be contradictory or misleading. Assuming that the company has a logical procedure for allocating monies for capital expenditures, you may be able to deduce what the company's strategy is by where it spends its money. Unfortunately, a company might not have a logical procedure for capital budgeting. Certainly political and bureaucratic processes might outweigh strategic considerations, especially in a huge bureaucratic company.

Products and Markets. What is the company selling and to whom? Reduce the product to its essential nature, if possible, in order to understand where the company's skills lie: Does a cruise line transport people or entertain them? Does a technical school train people or place them in jobs? The answer often varies, and you need analytical and judgmental tools to answer questions about the product.

The market may be described geographically, or as a customer or consumer group, or as one or more segments within customer groups. Again, use a very broad definition of markets; neat and tidy definitions may not work for many companies. What is Sears, Roebuck's market? Catalog and store customers? Financial consumers? Real estate purchasers and sellers?

Competitive Focus. The nature of a company's competitive thrust reveals a lot about a company's strategy. Does the company compete on the basis of price, quality, technology, and/or marketing skills? Is it a leader or a follower in product research? How important is service? A firm often competes on the basis of what it believes is the most significant resource in its internal environment.

Summary. To begin analyzing a company's strategy, identify critical aspects of the strategy by asking

What does the company say its strategy is?

How does the company spend its resources?

What does the company sell and to whom?

How does the company compete?

Analyzing the individual answers and the relationship of each answer to the sum of all four answers should move you beyond the identification of strategy to the more demanding evaluation of strategy.

Evaluating the Present Strategy

A company's game plan may or may not make sense or work well. Evaluate a game plan in terms of the following criteria.

1. Are the separate elements that make up the strategy consistent with each other and mutually supportive?
2. Is the strategy appropriate considering the surrounding circumstances (externalities) and the internal situation (resources, purpose)?
3. Are these policies and strategies likely to enable the enterprise to meet not only short-term goals but long-term objectives as well?
4. Have considerations of ethical and social responsibility been properly taken into account?
5. How satisfactory are the results?
6. Is the strategy practical and workable?
7. Does the strategy adequately consider risk?

Identifying Issues and Options

Against the background of the size-up and evaluation that you have made, what policy/strategy issues are most important? What are the alternatives to these issues — the realistic options open to the enterprise?

Try to distinguish between primary and secondary issues, the latter being either derived from and dependent upon the first, or of lesser importance. Concentrate on *one*, or, at most, *a few* primary issues. You will analyze more effectively by narrowing your field and sharpening your focus. Carefully and thoroughly considering a small number of important issues is far preferable to an extensive and, therefore, more superficial coverage. Cases often contain an "action" question which is only symptomatic of the real problem(s).

Evaluating Options

Develop the arguments for and against each option, including the option of making no change from the present course of action. Remember to consider *costs* and implications for *organization* and *personnel*. At a minimum, consider the following criteria for each option.

1. *Appropriateness*: Will the option allow us to achieve our objectives?
2. *Feasibility*: Do we have the resources — tangible and intangible — to achieve our objectives?
3. *Reality*: Do we want to go with this option? Will or does top management buy into it?
4. *Workability*: Can we gain corporate-wide organizational committment?

Making Recommendations

What would you recommend for change in the present strategy? And how should these recommendations be accomplished? Useful policy/strategy recommendations are specific, making explicit the *rate* of change and any scheduling or phasing being recommended; the additional resources, if any, to be procured; and any organizational and personnel changes involved.

Implementing Strategy

A proposed strategy is useless unless the organization commits to its adoption. When implementing a recommendation you must consider (at a minimum): *Who* will be in charge of its implementation? What *time* frame is involved in its implementation? Does the organization need to restructure, or is the present structure appropriate? Why? How will people be affected by its implementation? Will a new motivation or compensation system be necessary? How will you know if the plan is not working?

Monitoring Results

Timely and accurate information assists the strategic manager in determining if the proposed recommendations are working. The ongoing nature of the strategy process entails a constant monitoring and appraisal of results. Any variances must be quickly identified and corrected, so that operating remedies may be identified, evaluated, and implemented.

By following these seven steps to analyzing a case study, you will more quickly develop a logical approach to strategic problems. Nonetheless, since each case is unique, some aspects of some or even all of these steps may not be appropriate, given the nature of the case issues and alternatives.

INDUSTRY ANALYSIS

Since a company's success depends in part on the economics of its industry, you should look for information about the industry in general. Ideally, you would like to be able to answer the following four questions about the industry.

1. How does the general economy affect the industry?
2. How does the industry affect the economy?
3. What is the general trend of industry sales?
4. What are the characteristics of the industry?
   — number of companies
   — percentage share of industry sales
   — barriers to entry
   — capital versus labor intensity
   — value added
   — level of competition
   — method(s) of competition
   — rate of technological change
   — research and development expenditures
   — international factors
   — regulatory factors

Industry trends and industry characteristics will have important strategic implications. The strategic manager in a declining industry may be very reluctant to make major capital investments. The manager in an increasingly competitive industry may revise marketing promotion and pricing policies.

In addition, the performance of a specific company versus the performance of the industry as a whole can tell you a great deal about the success of a company's strategy and its strength relative to that of the industry.

CLASS PARTICIPATION

The primary role of the instructor is to facilitate discussion. Generally, the instructor will try to direct the discussion only when critical issues are being ignored or the discussion is not progressing. Occasionally the instructor may intervene in order to make sure your analysis is complete or to give you practice in defending your recommendations. These occasional interventions should be viewed as ultimately helpful, even if they may prove somewhat stressful. Since there is not one correct answer, the instructor will serve as a listener for reasonable suggestions and logical analyses.

Exhibit 1 includes some general guidelines for effective versus ineffective class participation.

EXHIBIT 1
Class participation factors

Positive Factors/Effective Participation

1. A complete analysis of one or more important case issues and problems
2. A well-reasoned conclusion following logically from a complete analysis
3. A reasonable recommendation for action while recognizing the consequences of that action
4. Constructive criticism of another student's comments
5. The integration of concepts and theories from other courses and/or from other cases
6. Effective communication

Negative Factors/Ineffective Participation

1. Repetition of case facts without analysis or conclusion
2. Irrelevant comments
3. Lack of participation
4. Poor communicative ability

STRATEGIC FINANCIAL ANALYSIS

The strategic manager must use the financial reports prepared by the organization's accountants as one source of strategic signals. Using financial reports aids both in analyzing one's own organization and in studying competitive businesses.

Two major kinds of strategic signals are contained in financial reports; namely, profitability signals and viability signals.

PROFITABILITY

Whether looking at a competitor or at our own company, we want to know how profitable the business is. The specific data and ratios that might contain strategic information include

I. Total profits (What is the general picture?)
  1. Net profits in absolute terms
  2. Net profits as a percentage of sales
II. Operating profits (How profitable are operations, disregarding financial and tax costs?)
  1. Operating profits (sales minus cost of sales and operating expenses) in absolute terms
  2. Operating profits as a percentage of sales
III. Costs (What are the critical cost elements?)
  1. Cost of goods sold as a percentage of sales
    (a) materials
    (b) labor
    (c) overhead
  2. Selling costs as a percentage of sales
  3. Administrative costs as a percentage of sales
  4. Financial, interest costs as a percentage of sales
  5. Depreciation as a percentage of sales
  6. Taxes as a percentage of sales
  7. Research and development as a percentage of sales

Because the strategic manager is concerned with the long term, these profitability measures provide strategic significance if they are viewed over a number of periods, preferably at least three to five years. The strategic manager really is looking for positive and negative signals contained in the *trend* of these measures. The direction in which the measures are heading is of more strategic importance than a single measure.

The strategic manager must consider not only profitability trends within the company, but also competitor-to-competitor trends. The strategic manager can put quantitative measures on the relative strength of the company versus the competition, and can begin to predict competitive strategies. For example, lower profits probably indicate a lower chance of price competition; higher research costs probably indicate a higher chance of new product innovations. Profitability measures are always a potential source for strategic signals, and often they will contain essential data for strategic judgments and decisions.

VIABILITY MEASURES

Profits indicate how well a firm is performing; viability measures depict the strengths or weaknesses of the firm's resources. The specific data and ratios that might contain strategic information include

    I. Return on investment (How satisfactory are the profits?)
        1. Operating and net profit as percentages of stockholder's equity
        2. Operating and net profit as percentages of total assets
   II. Value added (How important is the function performed?)
        1. Sales minus costs paid outside the firm to suppliers
  III. Sources of capital (Where are resources coming from?)
        1. Funds provided by net income and depreciation
        2. Changes in net working capital (current assets minus current liabilities)
        3. Changes in net "quick" assets (current assets minus inventories and minus current liabilities)
        4. Debt as a percentage of total capital (total liabilities and equity minus current liabilities)
        5. Equity as a percentage of total capital
        6. Inventory turnover (cost of goods sold divided by average inventory)
  IV. Uses of capital (Where are resources being allocated?)
        1. Dividends as a percentage of earnings
        2. Dividends as a percentage of total funds used
        3. Plant and equipment expenditures as a percentage of total funds used
   V. Stock prices (How does the stock market view the firm's prospects?)
        1. Stock market prices
        2. Volume of stock traded
        3. Price earnings ratio

As with profitability measures, these viability measures, describing how "healthy" a firm is, should be examined from both the long term and the competitor-to-competitor viewpoints. What measures point to problems, and what measures show a firm's relative strength in comparison to its competitors?

Specific financial ratios measure specific abilities of a firm. Liquidity ratios measure a firm's ability to pay short-term debts. A common liquidity ratio is

$$\frac{\text{Current assets}}{\text{Current liabilities}} = \text{Current ratio}$$

Many liquidity ratios suggest a ratio of about 2 to 1. Leverage ratios measure long-term debt, as follows:

$$\frac{\text{Total debt}}{\text{Total assets}} = \text{Leverage ratio}$$

A leverage ratio greater than 0.5 may indicate a debt repayment risk and/or inadequate profits and stockholder investment.

Activity ratios measure turnover of inventory (sales ÷ inventory), accounts receivable (sales ÷ accounts receivable), and asset turnover (sales ÷ fixed assets). These activity ratios may indicate that management successfully or unsuccessfully employs resources.

Finally, not all measures will be strategic signals. Viability and profitability measures must be viewed as potential sources of strategic information, not as having any intrinsic value. There is no right or wrong debt ratio, inventory turnover, or price earnings multiple. The strategic manager uses these measures as a signal of strategic problems or advantages. Financial measures thus indicate an issue that will require further strategic analysis and conclusion. The next step for the strategic manager is to analyze those factors and characteristics that resulted in a favorable or unfavorable indicator. Financial data provide input for strategic decision making; they are not ends in themselves.

FOOD, LODGING, AND ENTERTAINMENT: AN INDUSTRY OVERVIEW

INTRODUCTION

The growth of restaurant, lodging, travel, and entertainment facilities in America stems from the growth of the American economy and accompanying social trends. These trends include increasing levels of family income, increasing business travel, increasing leisure time, reduced travel costs, population changes, and the promotion and development efforts of the industry participants. Exhibit 1 highlights the growth of this industry.

The strategist needs to understand and forecast not only the demographics and psychographics that especially affect the demand for food, lodging, travel, and entertainment, but to foresee the internal forces affecting the industry. Market/product segmentation in both the food and lodging industry has increased competition. Strategists have chosen the product segmentation strategy to expand the sales of individual units.

This is particularly true of the lodging industry where some franchise chains offer willing investors a choice of up to five different "chains within a chain" which ostensibly appeal to differing market segments. Such segmentation has led to rapid expansion of some franchise companies.

Franchise businesses represent about one-third of all U.S. restaurant business or close to $600 million, according to *Restaurant Business Magazine* (3/20/88, p. 2). Investors will pay for franchises in order to (1) reduce the perception of risk (assuming current successful franchises exist), (2) increase marketing clout, and (3) minimize operating problems through franchiser's packages of systems, control, and procedures. Franchisers, of course, get maximum market impact for minimized capital requirements.

On the downside, franchising segmentation has led to some end consumer confusion over what to expect from a given product line, and in several cases has led to litigation from franchisees who feel that the parent company has taken unfair advantage by

This case was prepared by John Barnett and Joseph Durocher, both of University of New Hampshire. © 1988 by John Barnett and Joseph Durocher. Reprinted by permission.

EXHIBIT 1
Industry trends

Air Passengers

1960	52,400,000
1970	155,100,000
1980	292,500,000
1986	418,500,000

U.S. Vehicle Miles Traveled (in billions of miles)

1960	718
1970	1,114
1980	1,521
1986	1,861

Hotel and Motel Revenue[a]

1969	$ 8,200,000,000
1978	18,900,000,000

Eating and Drinking Places

	Number		Revenue in billions	
	Single Units	Chains	Single Units	Chains
1967	323,700	24,200	$19.5	$4.4
1972	320,500	39,000	$25.9	$9.4

Fast Food Sales in Millions

	Hamburger	Pizza	Chicken
1972	$3,800	$300	$1,000
1975	$6,500	$700	$1,300

[a]Note: The sales in 1987 of *all* lodging and all food service companies (593,000) was almost $200 billion, and these units employed eight million people in the United States.

constructing a "competing" property in their geographic area. The retort of the parent company has continually been that the new product appeals to different markets and thus does not directly compete.

The U.S. Department of Commerce (*Franchising in the Economy, 1986–1988*) reported that discontinued franchises increased from 1,200 (200 company owned and 1,000 franchisee owned) in 1976 to 2,000 in 1986 (600 company and 1,400 franchisee owned).

Barriers to entry for new franchisers arise because major product markets are exploited by dominant companies. Chicken, hamburger, and coffee shops are dominated by successful chains, although niches, such as gourmet burgers and ethnic foods, exist.

Capital costs have heightened the barriers to entry every bit as much as a shortage of suitable locations and dominated product markets. In the early 1970s the per room cost of lodging construction was well below $75,000 per unit. Today the cost has risen to above $250,000 per room in many markets. The standard lodging industry rule of thumb of setting room rates as $1 per thousand dollars of construction costs means that average room rates in some markets have moved up to $250 per night. On the other end of the spectrum, some operators have sought out fringe locations and employed bare bones construction and interior design treatments which yield a per room cost of less than $29,000. Again, with the same rule of thumb, this translates to a $29 room rate, which recalls the roadside motel rates of the early 1960s.

Market segmentation strategy has not been realized as greatly in the restaurant end (versus lodging) of the hospitality industry. Nonetheless, competition is increasing. The large chain operators once set a minimum population density level of 100,000 persons before they would consider selling a franchise. Today, there are market areas with fewer than 35,000 persons that contain as many as three units of a given franchise chain.

It is harder for firms to pursue economies of scale, through purchasing power or spreading marketing costs, as competition heightens. One response has been to oversaturate the market with a product to create a brand awareness. Further, lodging industry magnates have identified key destination city locations and developed marketing programs aimed at developing brand loyalty among business travelers. In the food service arena, most loyalty is built around promotional programs and mega-advertising programs. The leader of the fast food industry spends in excess of $900 million in advertising to create maximum awareness and to try to create brand loyalty.

The hospitality industry has borrowed concepts from the airlines. Airline traveler loyalty was built around "cheap fares" in the early 1980s. With the advent of airline deregulation, the cheap fares and the discount airlines disappeared as the entire industry kept rates high. In their place, frequent flyer programs were developed as an effort to build customer loyalty. Hotel and motel chains recently have introduced frequent guest programs of free second or third night stays.

Niche and differentiation options (bed and breakfast lodging, music videos) are increasing, especially with the new technology in entertainment (compact discs) and in lodging (the commercial traveler centers with personal computers; retirement villages).

Within food service, the 1980s witnessed trends toward spicy food and toward lighter eating, referred to as grazing. Grazing consumers chose several appetizers and salads rather than a full course meal. This trend toward lighter eating can be seen in single serving portions, whether a single slice of pizza, premium wine by the glass, or salad bars. And on the beverage side of the food service industry the trend was also toward light drinks. Light beer along with light wine and wine cooler sales took over a major portion of total sales. Along with this, the sale of "white" liquors — gin and vodka — increased while "brown" liquors such as bourbon and Scotch sales decreased.

An increased concern over drunk driving, bartender liability, and the efforts of SADD and MADD, along with increased publicity and police check points led to an overall decrease in spirited beverage sales. During a twelve-month period, one major chain realized a 34 percent decrease in the sale of spirited beverages.

Who is the restaurant consumer? Exhibit 2 shows the weekly expenditures for food away from home in the mid-1980s.

Mexican, Cajun, and spicy Asian food grew in importance during the 1980s. As an example, many non-Mexican restaurants offer nachos. Consumers ate more of the ultra-hot Thai cuisine, as consumer taste buds became conditioned to more spices. Some customers even complained to one hot sauce manufacturer that it was watering down its product. After extensive testing it was discovered that the product was the same but the customers' perception of what was hot had changed.

The focus on nutrition continues, although the vegetarian craze seems to have subsided into increasing vegetable and starch and decreasing red meat demands. Yet, while consumers sought out foods with decreased amounts of fat and salt, sales of desserts — especially ice cream and cookies — grew rapidly.

The "brewpub" is one outlet phenomenon of the 1980s. Hopland Brewery's first U.S. brewpub (an outlet selling the draft and bottled beer output of a small microbrewery) opened in Mendocino, California in 1983. The number of brewpubs grew to almost one hundred by the mid-1980s, including The New Amsterdam Brewery's Tap Room in New York City and the Hillside Brewery and Public House in Portland, Oregon.

EXHIBIT 2
Weekly expenditures for food away from home

Household Size	Weekly Amount Spent for Food Away From Home	
	Total	*Per Capita*
1	$15.87	$15.87
2	20.94	10.47
3	24.05	8.01
4	26.16	6.54
5	25.93	5.19

Age and Income	Per Capita Weekly Expenditure Household Income ($000)				
	10–14.9	*15–19.9*	*20–29.9*	*30–39.9*	*40+*
Under 25	$9.34	$10.60	$12.00	$ NA	$ NA
25–34	5.40	7.68	8.28	9.40	12.25
35–44	4.62	5.48	7.33	8.04	12.14
45–54	5.08	6.62	7.22	9.89	13.48
55–64	6.20	6.48	7.15	11.56	14.97
65–74	6.57	7.25	8.90	NA	14.41
75+	5.62	NA	NA	NA	NA

Source: "Consumer Expenditure Survey, 1985," Bureau of Labor Statistics, 1987.

As businesses pursued the 60 million single adults, technology played a role. Relatively simple plumbing adjustments allowed a Texas entrepreneur to open a Barwash, half saloon and half laundromat. Dating services interview clients on camera; VCRs allow other clients to decide whether or not to meet the video date in person.

This case describes the specifics of food, lodging and entertainment. It should be understood that there are several alternative ways of categorizing and classifying food, lodging, and entertainment facilities. To date the industry uses very imprecise definitions. For example, does the addition of a swimming pool or a miniature golf course change a "motel" to a "resort"?

When is a store entertainment? Tower Records chain stores are "a real scene. It's fun to shop in a place like this," says Tower's founder (*Fortune* 12/24/84, p. 91) of the stores with rock video monitors, lots of glass, chrome, red and yellow neon, and mirrored ceilings.

Thus, the student must keep in mind that these categories have vague definitions; they are clearly not mutually exclusive.

This description includes (1) the fast food industry, (2) institutional food, (3) lodging, (4) entertainment and (5) the accompanying cases.

THE FAST FOOD INDUSTRY

Hamburgers, pizza, and specialized fast foods underlie the offerings of companies such as McDonald's, Burger King, Wendy's, Hardees', Kentucky Fried Chicken, Dunkin' Donuts, Ponderosa, Bonanza, Roy Rogers, Dairy Queen, Baskin Robbins, Pizza Hut, and Domino's Pizza.

McDonald's, number one in the industry, began selling 15-cent hamburgers in San Bernadino, California in 1949. By the mid-1980s the company approached $10 billion in sales and in 1988 opened its 10,000th outlet. The outlets were comprised of company-owned and franchised locations in over thirty countries. McDonald's focused on a standardized product sold within minutes with low prices, supported by heavy international advertising that reached nearly a billion dollars per year. Increased profitability was achieved by opening for breakfast (Egg McMuffin), and a combination of new product offerings and competitive responses manifested in Chicken McNuggets and Filet-O-Fish.

McDonald's market share, in excess of 40 percent of the fast-food hamburgers sold, has increased steadily. Its outlet at the Marines' Camp Pendleton grossed $3 million its first year. McDonald's executives see its success as being due to the company's commitment to founder Roy Kroc's QSCV motto: "quality, service, cleanliness, and value." Company directors explained:

If [a new product or concept] doesn't improve Q, S, C, or V, it doesn't fit.

I don't think there's a religion in the world that has such a level of commitment.
(*Fortune*, 11/12/84, p. 35–6)

Competitive strategies vis-a-vis McDonald's, the industry leader, included higher price-points (Wendy's), full menu (Ponderosa), comparison advertising (Pillsbury's Burger King and its "Battle of the Burgers" or its flame broiling as opposed to frying), and specialized food offerings. R. J. Reynolds' Kentucky Fried Chicken did not sell hamburgers, nor did PepsiCo's division, Pizza Hut.

The privately-held Domino's Pizza is the world's largest privately owned chain with 1984 revenues of more than $1.5 billion. Its owner, Thomas S. Monaghan, was on the verge of bankruptcy in 1970, but Monaghan turned the company around, relying on employee incentives and a simple concept of limited selection, takeout only, and guaranteed delivery service.

Strategic operating issues in the fast food business include service variables (layout, equipment), efficiency (output per employee), purchasing economies, portion and labor cost control, labor shortages (especially given the decreasing supply of teenagers), and franchise management. A longer term strategic issue is the stimulus to restaurant acquisitions that network television advertising represents. Economies of scale suggest that chains should expand in order to spread television promotion costs over a larger base. Acquisition efforts and concentration on sales growth, however, should not obscure another essential strategic factor, per unit profitability, and its surrogate, average volume per restaurant.

A competitive threat of increasing strategic importance to the restaurant chains is the prepared food offered by grocery and convenience stores, magnified by the increasing use of microwave ovens in homes to heat up gourmet meals prepared by groceries, delis, and specialty stores. The invention of the term "couch potato" — one who rents a movie to play on the VCR and eats a meal heated up in the microwave — was emblematic of a growing threat to conventional food service operators. The threat was exacerbated by the "mini baby boom" in the mid-1980s. The yuppies began having babies and started staying home rather than dining out. In response, many operators expanded their take-out and home delivery offerings which also appealed to the couch potato.

The accounting firm of Laventhol & Horwath produced restaurant industry data for the National Restaurant Association in 1985, displayed in Exhibit 3.

INSTITUTIONAL FOOD

Components of the institutional food industry include hotel and motel restaurants, educational, employee, health care, military, transportation, and recreational food-service. The National Restaurant Association (NRA) estimated sales of these categories as shown in Exhibit 4.

These institutional sales growth rates can be compared to the 8 percent 1983 to 1986 growth rate for nonlodging eating places (excluding bars and taverns). *NRA News* estimated sales for eating places as $95.3 billion in 1983 and $120.0 billion in 1986.

EXHIBIT 3
Restaurant industry data

Food and Beverage Restaurant Statistics

	1983	1985
Revenue		
Food	72.0%	74.5%
Beverage	25.6	24.3
Other	2.4	1.2
Total	100.0%	100.0%
Costs		
Food	27.9%	26.8%
Payroll	25.4	24.7
Beverage	6.6	6.3
Employee benefits	3.8	3.6
Operating	5.8	5.5
Music, entertainment	1.0	0.8
Advertising	2.2	2.1
Utilities	3.1	2.9
Administrative	4.0	5.2
Repairs	1.8	1.9
Rent	5.8	6.6
Depreciation	3.3	3.1
Interest	1.5	1.6
Insurance	0.8	1.3
Taxes	1.4	1.5
Other	1.4	1.2
Net income before tax	4.2	4.9
	100.0%	100.0%

Source: "Restaurant Industry Operations Report '85," National Restaurant Association and Laventhol & Horwath.

EXHIBIT 4
Institutional food sales estimates

Sales in billions 1983–86

	1983	1986	Annual Growth
Lodging (hotel and motel)	$9.4	$11.7	7.8%
Educational	7.8	8.7	3.9
Employee	4.9	5.9	6.3
Health care	11.2	11.8	1.7
Military	0.8	0.9	6.8
Transportation	1.4	1.8	10.0
Recreational	4.5	5.6	7.7

The National Restaurant Association (*NRA News,* December 1985), commented that increased travel should support increased motel and hotel food service sales, while educational sales will slow due to declining enrollments. Employee foodservice will see increasing competition as contractors expand their efforts, while transportation foodservice will decrease as commercial airlines move from meals and beverages to snacks, according to *NRA News.*

THE LODGING INDUSTRY

Twenty-five chains controlled 50 percent of the 2,600,000 rooms in the United States in 1986 for lodges, hotels, and motels with 25 rooms or more. The industry concentration has led to segmentation strategies, with significant growth in the economy and middle market segments. In addition, the all-suite segment catering to the business traveler was a growing one in the mid-1980s.

Further industry trends are increasing emphasis on marketing, including emphasizing amenities as a competitive tool, relatively lower rates or upgraded facilities for the same rate, and expansion around convention facilities.

Laventhol & Horwath publishes extensive data on the lodging industry. Selected statistics from Laventhol & Horwath's U.S. lodging industry reports for 1984 and 1987 are given in Exhibit 5 and Exhibit 6.

Holiday Inns

Annoyed by high prices and cramped quarters that he and his family had to endure on an automobile trip, Kemmons Wilson decided to open a hotel on the outskirts of Memphis, Tennessee in 1952. By the mid-1980's Holiday Corporation operated 20,000 hotels, was opening just under 200 hotels a year, and had revenues of $1.6 billion; the industry leader anticipated offering over 400,000 rooms to the public by 1990.

The acknowledged hospitality leader, Holiday Corporaton has expanded its hotel product offerings to include an all-suite hotel brand, Embassy Suites, a limited service brand, Hampton Inn, and an extended-stay product, Residence Inn. Further, the company expanded into gaming, acquiring Harrah's and other casino companies in Atlantic City, Reno, Las Vegas, and Lake Tahoe.

Holiday's aggressive product and competitive strategies is clear in its market segmentation actions to offer a breadth of products from gaming to long-term lodging. Services that are today expected as part of the normal lodging package that were pioneered by Holiday include computerized reservation systems, free ice and parking, color television, swimming pools, and in-room movies. Holiday Inn University in Memphis tries to instill marketing and service improvement attitudes in its classes for Holiday managers.

EXHIBIT 5
Lodging industry
statistics

	1983	1986
Source of Business		
Leisure	27.4%	30.0%
Business, government	43.8	42.1
Conference	22.0	18.9
Other	6.8	9.0
Sales Revenue		
Guest room	59.0%	52.4%
Food	24.6	22.2
Beverage	9.5	8.4
Other	6.9	17.0
Costs		
Payroll	36.2%	36.6%
Department	12.2	13.9
Interest	6.6	8.0
Depreciation	6.1	7.9
Food	7.7	7.2
Administration	4.3	5.1
Rent	7.4	6.9
Energy	5.1	4.3
Marketing	3.5	5.3
Other	10.9	4.8
Occupancy		
Total	NA	64.9%
Northeast	NA	68.0
Southern	NA	62.8
North Central	NA	63.0
Western	NA	67.5
Room Rates		
Total	NA	$56.29
Northeast	$52.55	63.43
Southern	41.68	51.56
North Central	40.36	54.88
Western	49.27	57.81

By the end of 1986, Holiday Corporation's plan of selling hotels and retaining management contracts had resulted in the following overnight room availability:

	1984	1986
Company owned	15,400	12,900
Company managed	4,900	11,400
Franchised	95,500	104,600
Total	115,800	128,900

EXHIBIT 6 Lodging industry per room statistics

Property Location

	Center		Suburban		Airport		Highway		Resort	
	1983	1987	1983	1987	1983	1987	1983	1987	1983	1987
Food sales	$4,880	$6,780	$3,080	$5,470	$3,530	$4,890	$3,100	$3,630	$7,260	$6,670
Beverage	$1,740	$2,450	$1,450	$2,490	$1,510	$1,940	$1,850	$1,890	$2,410	$2,120
Occupancy	64.2%	63.9%	69.7%	64.9%	67.5%	69.9%	64.6%	61.5%	63.6%	67.6%
Food, beverage profit	6.4%	4.6%	7.9%	6.5%	9.1%	6.5%	12.9%	7.0%	12.8%	4.0%
Room profit	40.0%	42.2%	44.7%	44.1%	44.7%	43.7%	45.8%	48.8%	43.4%	47.4%

Source: Laventhol & Horwath, "U.S. Lodging Industry," 1984, 1987.

Holiday Corporation's income mix also changed.

| | *Revenue (millions)* | |
	1984	*1986*
Hotel	$1,004	$ 952
Gaming	644	690

| | *Operating Income (millions)* | |
	1984	*1986*
Hotel	$169	$140
Gaming	123	113

| | *Occupancy (Owned/Managed)* | |
	1984	*1986*
Holiday Inn	71.0%	65.2%
Embassy Suites	76.3%	71.5%
Hampton Inn	91.8%	69.1%
Residence Inn	NA	73.3%

| | *Average Room Rate* | |
	1984	*1986*
Holiday Inn	$50.89	$57.03
Embassy Suites	66.97	72.69
Hampton Inn	30.59	34.26
Residence Inn	NA	66.96

The company had disposed of earlier acquisitions (Trailways, Perkins Cake and Steak) and faced the competitive hospitality industry "hav(ing) been through these (extremely competitive) cycles before, we know that the strong invariably prosper while the weaker competitors fall away," as Michael Rose, Holiday's CEO wrote in the 1986 Annual Report.

Marriott Corporation

A mere root beer stand in Washington, D.C. in 1927, Marriott is now the largest operator of hotel rooms in the United States. It also is a leader in the food service industry, serving 5 million meals a day by the mid-1980s and being the leading airline caterer. Its fast food operations include Hot Shoppes, Big Boy, and Roy Rogers.

Further, Marriott began market segmentation strategies similar to Holiday, opening moderate price Courtyard lodgings, and testing quality suite hotels and economy motels in the mid-1980s. Marriott's CEO, J. W. Marriott, Jr., described a four part corporate strategy in the firm's 1986 report:

1. Providing outstanding customer service,
2. Taking care of employees and investing heavily in recruiting and training,

3. Carefully selecting growth market segments, and

4. Aggressively expanding through internal development and acquisitions.

Marriott's income data follows:

	Sales (millions)	
	1984	*1986*
Lodging	$1,640	$2,230
Contract Food	1,070	2,240
Restaurants	810	800
Total	$3,520	$5,270

	Operating Income (millions)	
	1984	*1986*
Lodging	$160	$220
Contract Food	90	150
Restaurants	80	80
Total	$330	$450

Hilton Hotels

Hilton owned 7,500 rooms and had a 50 percent partnership interest in another 14,000 rooms in the mid-1980s. Hilton was also active in the gaming industry, with financial results as follows:

	Revenue (millions)	
	1984	*1986*
Hotels	$350	$330
Casino Hotels	340	410
Total	$690	$740

	Operating Income (millions)	
	1984	*1986*
Hotels	$110	$ 80
Casino Hotels	70	90
Total	$180	$170

ENTERTAINMENT

Certainly, aspects of the food and lodging industry overlap with the entertainment industry. The thin line separating the lodging and entertainment business becomes totally blurred at the Walt Disney Company. In the mid-1980s Disney was completing a 900 room, $120 million Grand Floridian Beach Resort, a moderate-priced hotel at

Walt Disney World, and four EPCOT Center resort and convention hotels. Disney's income shows the importance of the hospitality industry to Disney.

	Revenue (millions)[1]	
	1985	1987
Theme parks, resorts	$1,260	$1,830
Filmed entertainment	320	880
Consumer products	120	170
Total	$1,700	$2,880

	Operating Income (millions)	
	1985	1987
Theme parks, resorts	$260	$550
Filmed entertainment	30	130
Consumer products	60	100
Total	$350	$780

[1]Note: Food and lodging sales were approximately $265 and $170 million in 1987.

The top tourist parks in the United States in 1987 were (1) Walt Disney World and EPCOT Center, Orlando, Florida, 26 million visitors; (2) Disneyland, Anaheim, California, 14 million; (3) Sea World of Florida, 5 million; (4) Universal Studios, 4 million; (5) Knott's Berry Farm, California, 4 million; and (6) Sea World of California, San Diego, 4 million.

Disney's strategy, as explained by Michael Eisner, CEO, in the 1987 report, is twofold. First, "continued dramatic growth and success of our existing business," plus "selective expansion into new related business areas." Elements of Disney's corporate culture could be seen in remarks quoted in "Do You Believe In Magic," *Time*'s cover story about Eisner and Walt Disney (April 25, 1988).

> *When it comes to Disney, there are two camps in this industry: extreme jealousy and admiration.*
>
> David Matalow, President, Tri-Star Pictures

> *You see guys like Eisner as a little crazy . . . but every great studio in this business has been run by crazies. What do you think Walt Disney was? The guy was off the goddamned wall. This is a creative institution. It needs to be run by crazies again.*
>
> Stanley Gold, Disney Board of Directors, President, Shamrock Holdings

> *If you don't come in on Saturday, don't bother coming in on Sunday.*
>
> Jeffrey Kutzenberg, Chief Executive, Walt Disney Studios

The entertainment industry thrives on change, as yesterday's fad gives way to today's hot item. Underlying these changes are often technological changes. Entertainment technology has seen video games and home computers in the early 1980s, cable television and VCRs, music videos and the compact discs (CDs). Tomorrow's opportunities may include pay-per-viewing cable, which would require two-way cable communication. In the wings is digital audio tape, comparable to CDs, but capable of recording.

During the mid-1980s cable TV surpassed the revenues of the three national TV networks. Almost half of American households have cable. Further, the growth of cable has added indirectly to the major networks' problem. The underfinanced and underequipped independent stations, especially the UHF channels — 14 through 83 — have over-the-air quality difficulties, but these difficulties disappear when they are brought into the home by cable. Independents can build viewers with old movies, reruns, and syndicated shows.

Fads and technologies represent dangers as well as opportunities. For example, Warner purchased Atari for $28 million, and rode a Pac-Man, Space Invaders ride that had 62 percent of Warner's $522 million of operating income coming from the Atari division in 1982. In 1983 the roller coaster turned downhill. Customers were tired of video games, and Warner's operating income fell from $338 million to $184 million. Net earnings were negative in 1983 and 1984.

A central strategic issue in the entertainment business is the product life cycle. What is hot in the entertainment business can be as cold as ice in a short time, so that entertainment strategists must plan for very short life cycles and very different rates of growth and decline depending on the appeal of the entertainment offering.

Further, the definition of product poses a major strategic issue. What, for example, makes up the product of Harlequin, the romance novel publisher? If Harlequin management defines the product as standardized publications, it might try, as it did, to grow through the addition of science fiction and Western novels. After failures in nonromance fiction, Harlequin tried romance motion pictures, deciding that its product was romance and escape for women.

Similarly, had RCA defined the home video market in terms of a playing and recording product, it might have avoided more than $500 million in losses. Instead, RCA's ''priority of the decade'' (*Fortune,* 12/24/84, p. 129), the video disc player, costing half as much as videocassette recorders and with disc prices lower than cassette prices, became ''one of the decade's mangiest dogs'' (*Fortune,* op. cit.) because it could not record programs.

THE CASES

Three cases represent the foodservice industry. Bill Armbruster looks back over his two years of operating a restaurant in rural Virginia. The Pizza Delights case presents the manager with an option of purchasing a Pizza Delights franchise he has managed for five years. The five founders of the Roxy Dinner Theatre review their first month of being in the dinner theatre business.

The Roxy Dinner Theatre is, of course, also an entertainment industry case. In the Grand Theatre Company case the nonprofit agency's board of directors must decide whether to hire a world-class director, Robin Phillips.

Finally, the Marriott Corporation 1984 presents a lodging industry giant just finalizing a divestiture out of entertainment parks and cruise lines. Where will Marriott next turn to in its quest for growth?

ARMBRUSTERS AT BLACKSTONE

Mr. William (Bill) Armbruster, owner and manager of Armbrusters at Blackstone, and his wife Betty were having mixed emotions in the early spring of 1986 as they reviewed the financial results of fiscal 1985, their first full year of operations, in Blackstone, Virginia. (See Exhibit 1, 1985 Income Statement by Month; Exhibit 2, Balance Sheet, December 31, 1985; and Exhibit 3, Income Statement, December 31, 1985, 1984.) A total sales of $193,911.58 had resulted in a $5,302.22 net loss for the year. They could see some notable achievements and some things which they felt urgently needed improvement.

EARLY HISTORY

Bill Armbruster, age fifty-one, was in the restaurant business because he wanted to be. Early on during college days he had tried the business and liked it. Now, after a 26-year career in the Navy and being retired with the rank of captain, he was giving it a try. Betty, while not as drawn to the business as her husband, was nonetheless totally involved with it. She had been born in Blackstone and educated there. Although Bill's career had taken them to many places within and outside of the United States, they had agreed to return to Blackstone when he retired because that was where they wanted to be. They had had their eyes on the two houses now occupied by their doll museum and restaurant for several years prior to purchasing them.

Armbrusters had begun operation with an open house on October 10, 1984 in a building where a restaurant had previously failed to achieve a profitable volume of business. Despite this bad omen, the Armbrusters had had the courage to follow an unsuccessful operation because they believed they could avoid the problems it had encountered. One of these was the limited kitchen space which simply had not been adequate to prepare food in sufficient volume. Prior to opening, Bill had

EXHIBIT 1 Armbrusters at Blackstone, income statement, 1985 (by month)

	Month ended 1/31/85	Month ended 2/28/85	Month ended 3/31/85	Month ended 4/30/85	Month ended 5/31/85	Month ended 6/30/85	Month ended 7/31/85	Month ended 8/31/85	Month ended 9/30/85	Month ended 10/31/85	Month ended 11/30/85	Month ended 12/31/85
Sales												
Food	$7,628.67	$7,594.89	$ 9,940.29	$11,764.38	$15,270.38	$16,096.59	$18,719.93	$27,761.08	$14,571.06	$14,342.20	$14,464.73	$16,534.22
Liquor	480.25	329.25	631.25	474.25	1,029.25	917.25	1,358.85	2,079.00	835.75	528.75	678.80	1,371.00
Beer	66.75	31.00	99.50	61.50	119.00	206.75	194.50	477.75	194.75	80.25	109.50	63.50
Wine	303.00	326.75	612.75	419.36	588.03	580.50	703.75	1,429.25	386.00	432.25	490.25	532.25
Total	$8,478.67	$8,281.89	$11,283.78	$12,719.49	$17,006.29	$17,801.09	$20,977.03	$31,747.08	$15,987.56	$15,383.45	$15,744.28	$18,500.97
Food costs												
Food	$2,914.40	$3,101.70	$3,695.02	$ 5,075.42	$ 4,341.20	$ 5,426.75	$ 7,133.27	$ 8,129.65	$ 7,109.41	$ 5,307.55	$ 5,288.24	$ 6,117.02
Liquor	78.00	138.70	140.60	113.95	251.40	99.75	236.45	332.25	278.55	0.00	109.40	(103.85)
Beer	71.05	20.25	51.95	36.60	46.80	107.75	92.95	246.65	67.30	31.55	31.55	25.85
Wine	229.38	117.64	265.19	195.64	287.18	295.18	396.54	583.03	146.24	443.00	347.85	(367.00)
Total	$3,292.83	$3,378.29	$ 4,152.76	$ 5,421.61	$ 4,926.58	$ 5,929.43	$ 7,959.21	$ 9,291.58	$ 7,601.50	$ 5,782.10	$ 5,777.04	$ 5,672.02
Gross profit	$5,185.84	$4,903.60	$7,131.02	$ 7,297.88	$12,079.71	$11,871.66	$13,117.82	$22,455.50	$ 8,386.06	$ 9,601.35	$ 9,967.24	$12,828.95
Other expenses												
Salaries & wages	$2,604.28	$3,010.87	$ 4507.85	$ 3,522.46	$ 3,418.04	$ 3,880.41	$ 3,986.07	$ 8,589.91	$ 4,419.89	$ 4,192.53	$ 4,033.98	$12,996.79
Travel	0.00	0.00	0.00	0.00	0.00	0.00	0.00	0.00	0.00	0.00	0.00	$ 1,544.00
Rent	67.55	67.55	135.10	67.55	67.55	67.55	67.55	67.55	67.55	94.49	67.55	67.55
Linen	222.84	191.16	224.71	293.27	237.25	240.52	287.26	235.99	231.08	412.30	241.95	304.21
Supplies	62.79	528.53	306.14	510.83	179.27	362.15	430.21	48.42	354.97	904.37	96.78	301.99
Utilities	766.67	585.81	1,126.08	546.40	711.21	643.15	453.53	675.16	742.31	768.00	506.84	562.34
Telephone	230.37	0.00	242.26	142.29	114.84	119.63	136.89	112.59	128.25	119.10	142.85	133.61
Taxes	864.23	702.32	330.10	1,286.12	1,037.04	615.74	2,234.42	700.00	815.00	3,395.72	1,645.28	(7,230.05)
Replacements	130.40	148.51	26.00	0.00	0.00	44.20	79.30	0.00	24.23	0.00	0.00	150.00
Repairs & maintenance	508.95	53.51	74.62	32.60	0.00	104.68	235.00	118.98	482.63	126.20	25.00	52.25
Advertising	190.40	15.00	30.00	118.22	175.56	10.00	0.00	0.00	116.00	140.40	75.00	232.71
Legal & professional	0.00	0.00	0.00	800.00	0.00	0.00	250.00	0.00	0.00	0.00	0.00	0.00
Dues & subscriptions	0.00	0.00	0.00	0.00	60.00	90.00	0.00	0.00	0.00	0.00	0.00	0.00
Interest	523.56	0.00	0.00	0.00	0.00	0.00	523.56	0.00	529.31	0.00	0.00	15,692.37
Employee discounts	1.88	7.95	24.47	17.54	17.33	9.39	11.99	19.15	18.33	11.03	3.00	4.25
Miscellaneous	319.16	90.10	(53.00)	0.00	0.00	111.00	58.05	137.27	(36.46)	67.52	17.00	473.68
Credits	57.81	20.02	33.04	51.72	35.19	237.56	49.01	116.92	308.29	(87.66)	99.38	220.06
Over/short	16.66	24.92	22.37	(7.60)	0.78	22.60	48.75	15.61	17.13	(0.72)	(48.41)	(14.11)
Wages—other	0.00	0.00	100.00	50.00	0.00	0.00	0.00	50.00	50.00	0.00	50.00	0.00
Insurance	0.00	0.00	600.00	1,200.00	0.00	1,076.00	0.00	0.00	0.00	0.00	0.00	1,593.00
Bank charges	71.38	46.47	121.69	76.75	154.34	5.39	94.94	143.47	287.74	188.90	104.40	151.85
Depreciation	0.00	0.00	0.00	0.00	0.00	0.00	0.00	0.00	0.00	0.00	0.00	$14,500.00
Dining Club	0.00	0.00	0.00	0.00	0.00	0.00	12.30	25.70	65.64	35.12	24.75	24.65
Total	$6,638.93	$5,482.72	$ 7,851.43	$ 8,708.15	$ 6,208.40	$ 7,639.97	$ 8,958.83	$11,056.72	$ 8,102.47	$10,896.71	$ 7,085.37	$41,761.15
Total other income	0.00	0.00	0.00	$ 23.72	$ 0.00	$ 133.12	0.00	0.00	0.00	0.00	$ 47.30	57.26
Net operating income (loss)	($1,453.09)	($ 579.12)	($ 720.41)	($ 1,386.55)	$ 5,871.31	$ 4,364.81	$ 4,158.99	$11,398.78	$ 283.59	($ 1,295.36)	$ 2,929.17	($28,874.94)

EXHIBIT 2 Armbrusters at Blackstone, balance sheet, December 31, 1985

	Assets		Liabilities and proprietor's capital	
Cash				
Bank	$ 8,723.00		Sales tax payable	$ 720.00
Register	128.00	$ 8,851.00		
Deposits		$ 1,203.00		
Inventory		1,990.00	Notes payable	$150,510.00
Property and equipment				
Building	$ 24,683.00		Proprietor's capital ($31,861.00)	
Building improvements	59,686.00			
Equipment	37,314.00			
Automobile (personal)	13,158.00			
	$134,841.00			
Less accumulated depreciation	(27,516.00)	107,325.00		
Total assets		$119,369.00	Total liabilities and proprietor's capital	$119,369.00

a new, larger wing added to the building after having the old kitchen removed. The new kitchen was equipped with all of the cooking, baking, and crockery-handling equipment needed to support the volume of business they calculated was needed to provide an adequate cash flow. Well-cooked, consistent-quality meals were their prime consideration. Only fresh meats and vegetables cooked for the meal were served.

They anticipated two kinds of restaurant business. The primary customer would come to the restaurant for lunch or dinner, hopefully, on a repeat basis. Table seating from two to six persons were provided in four downstairs rooms. There would also be parties: birthday, retirement, christenings, holidays, and whatever else, served on the second floor, in a separate banquet room which provided tables for large groups. Betty Armbruster was optimistic that they could build both types of clientele because, as she explained, "There are lots of places to eat in Blackstone, but there is nowhere to dine." Armbrusters was to have the atmosphere and the menu that would qualify it as a place to *dine* rather than be just another place to eat.*

THE DOLL MUSEUM
AND RESTAURANT BUILDINGS

In addition to the restaurant itself, there is a doll museum, housed in a separate building next door, run by Bill's mother, Mrs. Margaret Armbruster. Now eighty-two years old but still active and outgoing, she had been collecting dolls for several decades and had an outstanding collection. The doll museum, which had been

*See note at the bottom of p. 28.

EXHIBIT 3 Income statement, December 31, 1985, 1984

	For the year ended 12/31/85	Percent of total sales	Food cost %	For the 3 months ended 12/31/84	Percent of total sales	Food cost %
Sales						
Food	$174,688.04	90.09%		$31,598.84	90.02%	
Liquor	10,714.65	5.53%		2,111.23	6.01%	
Beer	1,704.75	0.88%		252.86	0.72%	
Wine	6,804.14	3.51%		1,139.94	3.25%	
	$193,911.58	100.01%		$35,102.87	100.00%	
Food costs	$ 63,639.63	32.82%	36.43%	$14,580.58	41.54%	46.14%
Food	1,675.20	0.86%	15.63%	1,180.14	3.36%	55.90%
Liquor	830.25	0.43%	48.70%	138.40	0.39%	54.73%
Beer	2,939.87	1.52%	43.21%	816.29	2.33%	71.61%
	$ 69,084.95	35.63%		$16,715.41	47.62%	
Gross profit	$124,826.63	64.38%		$18,387.46	52.38%	
Other income	$ 261.40	0.13%			0.00%	
Other expenses						
Salaries and Wages	$ 59,463.08	30.67%		$12,246.02	34.89%	
Depreciation	14,500.00	7.48%		8,141.00	23.19%	
Equipment Rental	905.09	0.47%		67.55	0.19%	
Linen	3,122.64	1.61%		975.25	2.78%	
Supplies	4,086.35	2.11%		1,567.14	4.46%	
Utilities	8,087.50	4.17%		1,014.34	2.89%	
Telephone	1,622.68	0.84%		366.08	1.04%	
Taxes	5,820.92	3.00%		806.25	2.30%	
Licenses	575.00	0.30%		540.00	1.54%	
Repairs & maintenance	1,814.42	0.94%		1,847.09	5.26%	
Insurance	4,469.00	2.30%		0.00	0.00%	
Advertising	1,291.45	0.67%		935.75	2.67%	
Travel	1,544.00	0.80%		865.00	2.46%	
Legal & professional	1,050.00	0.54%		544.55	1.55%	
Dues & subscriptions	150.00	0.08%		30.00	0.09%	
Interest	17,268.80	8.91%		7,718.17	21.99%	
Replacements	602.64	0.31%		0.00	0.00%	
Employee discounts	146.31	0.08%		29.59	0.08%	
Miscellaneous	1,149.32	0.59%		976.02	2.78%	
Credits	1,141.33	0.59%		247.61	0.71%	
Contributions	25.00	0.01%		0.00	0.00%	
Bank charges	1,447.34	0.75%		117.76	0.34%	
Over/short	107.98	0.06%		77.06	0.22%	
Total other expenses	130,390.85	67.28%		39,112.23	111.43%	
Net income (loss)	($ 5,302.82)	−2.77%		($20,724.77)	−59.05%	

The Blackstone Chamber of Commerce Business Directory for 1986–87 listed six restaurants: Armbrusters at Blackstone, Traditional Fine Southern Dining; Blackstone Restaurant, Try Blackstone's Favorite Eating Place; Brother's Pizza Restaurant, New York Style Italian Restaurant; Dairy Freeze, Fresh All-Beef Hamburger; Slaw's Restaurant, Restaurant & Sporting paraphernalia; and Sullivan's Restaurant and Tavern, Steaks, Seafood, and Mixed Drinks.

operating in Florida for several years, was transferred to Blackstone when the Armbrusters found that they could obtain the building adjacent to the restaurant to house it. This building required extensive renovation. The doll museum was opened in November 1983, about a year prior to the restaurant. People dining at Armbrusters are invited to visit the museum. A fee of $1.50 is charged to cover operating expenses, which include a carefully controlled climate. Conversely, people coming to the museum frequently dine at the restaurant. Thus, the two businesses complement each other.

The building housing the restaurant is a large, two-story colonial-revival–style brick structure with six massive white columns supporting the roof of the front porch. A former elegant residence, it provides an ideal setting for the restaurant. On the first floor, there is an entry foyer of heroic proportions. Four dining rooms open off the foyer. A bar (crafted from two massive pocket doors salvaged from a Victorian home now demolished) is located in one of these. The new kitchen is located to the rear. On the second floor is a large hall. The banquet room opens off to one side and the restrooms are to the rear. There is an apartment on this floor also.

In a separate, two-story frame building next door to the restaurant, the doll museum occupies all nine rooms on both floors and the entrance hallway and stairwell as well. The several thousand dolls, doll houses, carriages, and doll furniture plus a collection of antique items fill all of the available space to overflowing.

THE NEIGHBORHOOD

The two buildings are located on Church Street in Blackstone, Virginia. U.S. Highway 460 runs east-west in southern Virginia, connecting Richmond and Petersburg with Appomattox, Lynchburg, and Roanoke. Route 460 bypasses the town of Blackstone (population 3600), but a Business 460 runs through the town and Church Street is a residential part of that Business 460.

Bill and Betty believe they have a very suitable location in a desirable part of town. The street is called Church Street because there are two churches across the street from Armbrusters plus churches on the same side of the street one block away. The downtown section of Blackstone is a few blocks away, and there is a well-established traffic flow past the restaurant.

Armbrusters does not have a parking area for off-street parking. Street parking is adequate for casual traffic but is not sufficient for large parties. There is a paved parking lot located behind a church directly across the street from the restaurant which can be used except when services are being held.

Parking is one problem disturbing Bill and Betty, but there is another thing annoying them even more. The doll museum and the restaurant are two of three houses sharing a city block. There is a third house, which is now unoccupied. All three had once been elegant buildings. The two structures owned by the Armbrusters still are. The other privately owned house is not. It has deteriorated to the point of being an eyesore. It is owned by an elderly widow, a semirecluse, who is not having any maintenance done on it. The Armbrusters view it as a potential safety and health hazard. Town authorities have not taken action requiring maintenance of this property. Bill and Betty had once envisioned this house as a potential bed-and-breakfast facility which would complement both the restaurant and the museum (if it could be obtained before it deteriorates beyond restoration) or it could be torn down for a parking lot for the restaurant. They have not given up on the bed-and-breakfast idea although they cannot justify the added investment at this time. Its owner will neither sell it nor make any effort to maintain it. As Betty remarked, it had not even been painted in over 10 years. There is no question that it detracts from the atmosphere the Armbrusters are trying to create. If Bill is unable to buy the property, he'd like to see it cleaned and fixed up, or torn down.

OPERATING RESULTS

As the Armbrusters reviewed their first 3 months and their first full-year results, they noted several things. Breakeven had been briefly achieved in May 1985, but subsequent monthly cash receipts showed some very obvious variations and for the year they experienced a net loss. Bill noted that an important factor in their customer traffic is the officers and enlisted men and women of the National Guard training at Fort Pickett. The fort, which lies immediately adjacent to the town, hosts Guard units during much of the year by providing a place for training exercises. Officers and enlisted men and women of the units apparently find Armbrusters' atmosphere to their liking. It was military customers primarily who caused the 50 percent increase in sales in August 1985. However, since they had had only one year's results, Bill and Betty felt they would need at least one more year to see any strong patterns. Still, February had been so slow in 1985 they closed up for 2 weeks during February 1986. The restaurant was given a thorough cleaning and some deferred maintenance was done while they took a much-needed vacation.

THE CUSTOMER MIX

Another pattern they had observed was that while a loyal local patronage had developed, approximately 25–35 percent of their customer traffic was from out of town. Particularly on Saturdays and Sundays, out-of-town patrons were likely to outnumber locals. Helped by some favorable publicity in the Richmond press and the Virginia Automobile Association's newsletter, Armbrusters at Blackstone had begun to attract out-of-town customers almost immediately after it was opened. A Richmond reporter described Sunday dinner at Armbrusters as "dinner at Grandmother's house." People were coming from as far as 60 miles away. They came from Richmond, Petersburg, South Hill, Farmville, Crewe, Burkeville, and other towns. Many had become regulars. The original story in the Virginia Automobile Association's journal had accidentally placed the restaurant in Blacksburg instead of Blackstone. A correction in a subsequent issue gave it doubled publicity.

ADVERTISING

Bill described Armbrusters' advertising as primarily word-of-mouth. The guiding philosophy of treating diners as though they were houseguests resulted in first-time diners returning again. Quite frequently they brought guests; many first-time visitors said Armbrusters had been recommended by a friend.

Some advertising was done primarily in newspapers in Richmond and the principal towns in a 60-mile radius of Blackstone. Promotions consisted primarily of special menus, particularly on holidays or during town events in Blackstone.

Because the Armbrusters had been invited to place their advertising brochures in the Virginia Visitors' Welcome Centers near the state borders, they were also getting customers from out of state who were driving through Virginia. Bill noted that the personnel from the Automobile Club and also from the Visitors' Centers had personally "checked them out" by dining at Armbrusters before agreeing to recommend it and to encourage people to patronize the restaurant and the museum. He felt that that was entirely appropriate. Spurts in customer traffic were observed, some of which Bill felt could be the result of these favorable publicity events.

THE MENUS

The luncheon menu included Soup of the Day (bowl, $1.35; cup 75¢) or Brunswick stew with ham biscuits ($3.25). The main fare, served with vegetable and salad, included Our Special Quiche of the Day ($3.65), petit steak ($4.75), or chicken pie from an old Virginia recipe ($3.85). Croissants, other sandwiches, and desserts completed the luncheon offering.

Dinners included soup or juice appetizer, salad, entree, vegetables, and homemade rolls and muffins. They featured Chicken Old Virginia (chicken breast with Virginia country ham topped with white wine sauce for $7.75), Southside country pot roast ($6.75), sliced Surry County ham with redeye gravy ($7.25), southern fried chicken ($6.75), and broiled lamb chops ($11.95). Desserts included peanut pie and chocolate mousse pie, both with fresh whipped cream. The menu noted under beverages that wine and spirits are available.

SPECIAL EVENTS

Party bookings had risen steadily since their opening and offered substantial revenue. Certain organizations also provided profitable bar business in addition to their dinner bookings. The 1985 pre-Christmas party business had filled almost all available evenings. Because these events were preplanned and held on a separate floor, these bookings caused little disruption to the regular customer traffic. Additional personnel were always assigned to handle these large parties which gave the employees welcome added income. During the parties, designated cooks, waiters, and waitresses served the casual diners so they would not be neglected.

EMPLOYEE RELATIONS

Keeping a steady staff had been a continuing vexation to both Bill and Betty. Prior to opening, they had advertised the positions they planned to fill and selected what seemed like very suitable employees by picking carefully from a large number of applicants. All employees were hired as part-time help. Many of those hired first were still employed in early 1986, while others had lasted only a few days or weeks. All through the first year, there had been a constant process of replacing personnel who either had quit or been released for not meeting the standards the Armbrusters were trying to maintain. To keep a staff of sixteen for the first 12 months, they had hired a grand total of thirty-seven! As Bill observed, constantly training new employees was both disruptive and expensive. After a year and a half of operation, Armbrusters had acquired a sufficiently stable employee group to permit a smooth operation. They were now holding a list of potential employees, but were not actively seeking anyone to add to the staff.

SUMMARY

Despite these problems, they felt that all of their hard work and long hours had paid off. Income had risen steadily. Their debt was being promptly serviced. Much of the required additional improvements and maintenance had been done and all accounts payable had been handled promptly; the Armbrusters had established excellent credit standing with all of their suppliers. Not being dependent on the business because of income from other sources, they had not paid themselves any salaries. Net income was committed to helping the business grow.

The Armbrusters were hoping that customer traffic would grow enough to permit them to hire a manager for supervision of the day-to-day operations. This would given them an opportunity to begin doing some longer-range planning and to try to resolve some of their persistent problems instead of just living with quick fixes. They were well aware that their good start could be wasted if these problems were not resolved.

Approaching their second anniversary, Bill and Betty had some reasons to be optimistic. The restaurant had become well enough known throughout a 60-mile radius of Blackstone to have a regular, repeat clientele. There were forces in motion that could greatly increase the number of people visiting Blackstone, many of whom would be potential diners. One of these was an organized effort to have the city's business district, basically several blocks of one street, declared a historic area. Along with the request for historic designation, a restoration effort was underway to return the storefronts to something near their original, early 1900s appearance. Bill Armbruster was directly involved in both of these initiatives. Many out-of-town visitors to Armbrusters had remarked on the obvious historic value of some of the buildings and the desirability of preserving them.

The Armbrusters felt that as these efforts moved from planning to reality, restaurant traffic would increase along with that of the other businesses. They felt that if they could acquire the unoccupied third house on their block and make it into a bed-and-breakfast, an antiques sales outlet, or a combination of the two, the businesses would complement each other.

Despite his optimistic outlook, Bill Armbruster put his concerns into some pertinent questions:

The restaurant business was what I wanted to do, and Betty has been a good sport about going along with it. It's not her first choice by any means, although she was born and raised in Blackstone.

My son is also involved, he is doing the accounting statements for us. It's sort of a sideline for him, but he's been invaluable for us in terms of putting the numbers together and giving us a readout each month.

Further, Mother is involved through the doll museum. The best month has been July 1985 with almost 500 visitors. She now averages between 100 and 200 visitors per month.

What should we do now? We've made a substantial cash and time investment here. Including all the pre-opening arrangements, renovations and such, we've worked very hard here for over 2 years. What possibility is there that we will get a payoff for all of this? Can we hold out until it happens? When can we expect to be profitable, if we will be? What must we do now to make 1986 a profitable year? What about the future, say, 5 or 10 years from now?

THE ROXY DINNER THEATRE

Tom Thayer sat alone in the dark of the empty stage. "I really love this business," he thought, "but some changes have to be made if we are to survive." Tom was president of South Stage Theatre Corporation, owners of the Roxy Dinner Theatre. He had just left the cast party that celebrated the first full month of operation at the Roxy. The cast was still celebrating its artistic success when Tom left. Now he must consider the business side of the Roxy's first month.

The Roxy Theatre is located in downtown Clarksville, Tennessee. Constructed in the 1930s, the Roxy enjoyed many years of profitable operation as a motion picture theatre showing first run cinema classics like *Casablanca, Gone With the Wind,* and Roy Rogers Westerns. In 1974, the Roxy was forced to close its doors due to a lack of business. Shopping center cinemas had taken most of the old theatre's patrons. The Roxy lay dormant and fell into a state of disrepair until June 1980, when a minor renovation was attempted by a community theatre group. This attempt failed and the Roxy once again closed its doors in January 1981. It seemed there was little hope for the Roxy, and it was slated for demolition to make room for parking in the downtown area. It was then that a group of young entrepreneurs decided to establish a theatre in Clarksville, saving the old building in the historic downtown location.

SOUTH STAGE THEATRE CORPORATION

In July 1981, a group of five young people from varied theatrical backgrounds formed the South Stage Theatre Corporation and leased the Roxy building. Each of the five owners held an equal $2,000 share in the corporation and occupied a seat on the board of directors. Each had unique qualifications and played a personal role in the operation of the Roxy.

Tom Thayer, age 27, was the president of the corporation. He was selected to

This case was prepared by Steven J. Anderson, Christopher Nussbaumer, Albert J. Taylor, and Jeanne Whitehead, all of Austin Peay State University, and John E. Oliver, of Valdosta State College. This case was designed for classroom discussion only. It was not meant to depict effective or ineffective handling of administrative situations.

serve in this role by his colleagues only because officers were necessitated by the articles of incorporation. Tom graduated from Clarksville Northwest High School in 1975, attended the American Musical and Dramatic Academy in New York on scholarship, and studied acting with Sally Welch, a protege of Lee Strasberg. He had been in the theatre since age 12 both locally and in New York. Tom taught dramatic arts at the Rhodes School in Maine. He functioned as primary director, choreographer, designer, writer, coach, carpenter, and general business manager.

Carmello Roman, age 27, also graduated from Clarksville Northwest High School in 1975, attended Austin Peay State University briefly, then studied graphic arts at Stephens College, Missouri, on scholarship. Like Tom, Carmello studied acting with Sally Welch and performed extensively in local area productions. When not working in New York as a graphic artist, Roman designed makeup and costumes for the Roxy and assisted in direction, acting techniques, and choreography. Roman did all the graphics, brochures, and posters for the Roxy.

Ginger Mulvey, age 28, was vice president for marketing and general house manager. Ginger graduated from Clarksville High School in 1974. She had extensive acting experience in the Clarksville area and worked as an actress sporadically for five years in New York. Ginger returned to Clarksville to open the Roxy. Her duties included the hiring of staff, inventory, serving as hostess, reservations, some accounting and marketing, and publicity photos.

Tom Griffin, age 26, was the technician. A native Clarksvillian, Tom graduated from Clarksville High School in the mid-1970s. He was the son of a long time theatre professional who taught at the local state university. Tom did a stint in the U.S. Air Force in Germany where he handled lighting for the oldest English speaking theatre in that country. Griffin was in charge of all the technical aspects of the Roxy, including the design of lighting for plots and sets, construction of sets, lighting of performances, inventory and procurement of set materials, directing, and performing.

John McDonald, age 38, was a native of Memphis, Tennessee. John had acting experience in soap operas and off-Broadway shows. He taught acting at the American Academy of Performing Arts and at the Rhodes School in Maine where he met Tom Thayer. McDonald was primary director of the children's theatre and workshops, selected plays, helped design sets and directed about one-third of the shows.

The Roxy group was tightly knit with a great cumulative drive to make the Roxy a success. The group's primary objective, as evidenced by the statement of purpose in Exhibit 1, was to bring the performing arts to Clarksville and the surrounding community. Profit was necessary, but was not the primary motivation of the group.

PERFORMING ARTS IN THE MIDDLE-TENNESSEE AREA

Clarksville, Tennessee is a town of about 60,000 people located in Montgomery County which adds another 30,000 people to the available market population. The primary employer in the area is Fort Campbell, the home of the U.S. Army's 101st Airborne Division where 20,000 military personnel plus additional civilian support

EXHIBIT 1
Roxy Theatre
statement of
purpose

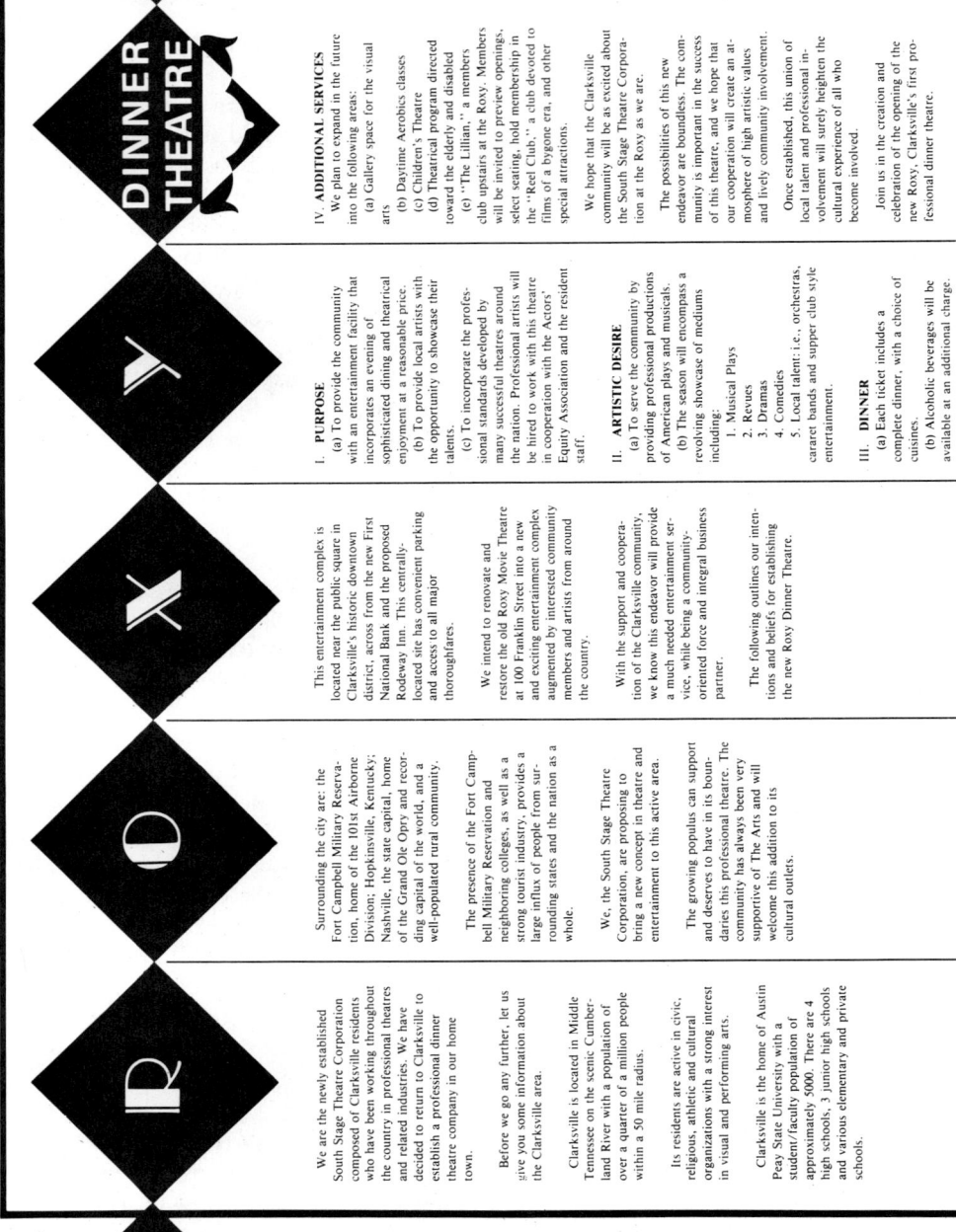

We are the newly established South Stage Theatre Corporation composed of Clarksville residents who have been working throughout the country in professional theatres and related industries. We have decided to return to Clarksville to establish a professional dinner theatre company in our home town.

Before we go any further, let us give you some information about the Clarksville area.

Clarksville is located in Middle Tennessee on the scenic Cumberland River with a population of over a quarter of a million people within a 50 mile radius.

Its residents are active in civic, religious, athletic and cultural organizations with a strong interest in visual and performing arts.

Clarksville is the home of Austin Peay State University with a student/faculty population of approximately 5000. There are 4 high schools, 3 junior high schools and various elementary and private schools.

Surrounding the city are: the Fort Campbell Military Reservation, home of the 101st Airborne Division; Hopkinsville, Kentucky; Nashville, the state capital, home of the Grand Ole Opry and recording capital of the world, and a well-populated rural community.

The presence of the Fort Campbell Military Reservation and neighboring colleges, as well as a strong tourist industry, provides a large influx of people from surrounding states and the nation as a whole.

We, the South Stage Theatre Corporation, are proposing to bring a new concept in theatre and entertainment to this active area.

The growing populus can support and deserves to have in its boundaries this professional theatre. The community has always been very supportive of The Arts and will welcome this addition to its cultural outlets.

This entertainment complex is located near the public square in Clarksville's historic downtown district, across from the new First National Bank and the proposed Rodeway Inn. This centrally-located site has convenient parking and access to all major thoroughfares.

We intend to renovate and restore the old Roxy Movie Theatre at 100 Franklin Street into a new and exciting entertainment complex augmented by interested community members and artists from around the country.

With the support and cooperation of the Clarksville community, we know this endeavor will provide a much needed entertainment service, while being a community-oriented force and integral business partner.

The following outlines our intentions and beliefs for establishing the new Roxy Dinner Theatre.

I. PURPOSE

(a) To provide the community with an entertainment facility that incorporates an evening of sophisticated dining and theatrical enjoyment at a reasonable price.

(b) To provide local artists with the opportunity to showcase their talents.

(c) To incorporate the professional standards developed by many successful theatres around the nation. Professional artists will be hired to work with this theatre in cooperation with the Actors' Equity Association and the resident staff.

II. ARTISTIC DESIRE

(a) To serve the community by providing professional productions of American plays and musicals.

(b) The season will encompass a revolving showcase of mediums including:
1. Musical Plays
2. Revues
3. Dramas
4. Comedies
5. Local talent: i.e., orchestras, cararet bands and super club style entertainment.

III. DINNER

(a) Each ticket includes a complete dinner, with a choice of cuisines.

(b) Alcoholic beverages will be available at an additional charge.

IV. ADDITIONAL SERVICES

We plan to expand in the future into the following areas:

(a) Gallery space for the visual arts
(b) Daytime Aerobics classes
(c) Children's Theatre
(d) Theatrical program directed toward the elderly and disabled
(e) "The Lillian," a members club upstairs at the Roxy. Members will be invited to preview openings, select seating, hold membership in the "Reel Club," a club devoted to films of a bygone era, and other special attractions.

We hope that the Clarksville community will be as excited about the South Stage Theatre Corporation at the Roxy as we are.

The possibilities of this new endeavor are boundless. The community is important in the success of this theatre, and we hope that our cooperation will create an atmosphere of high artistic values and lively community involvement.

Once established, this union of local talent and professional involvement will surely heighten the cultural experience of all who become involved.

Join us in the creation and celebration of the opening of the new Roxy, Clarksville's first professional dinner theatre.

personnel work bringing the total area market population to 110,000. Austin Peay State University has approximately 5,000 students, faculty, and staff. Forty different plants employ approximately 5,000 people in manufacturing. Agriculture is a major contributor to the economy with beef and dairy cattle, dark-fired tobacco, corn, wheat, and soybeans leading the list of commodities produced in the area. The rest of the population is employed in either government or retail establishments serving the military, education, manufacturing, and agricultural communities. Nashville, Tennessee is forty miles away.

The Roxy faced competition from primary as well as secondary competitors. The following is a list of these:

1. The Barn Dinner Theatre was located in Nashville, Tennessee, 40 miles from Clarksville. For $17.25 patrons were provided with a catered meal similar to those offered by the Roxy. The schedule was similar to the Roxy's, but nationally known talent was sometimes featured.

2. The Fort Campbell Cabaret Dinner Theatre charged $11 for a ticket that included a meal. They were open year round on Friday and Saturday nights and showcased local Fort Campbell talent in modern plays similar to the Roxy's fare.

3. The Soldier Show Theatre at Fort Campbell was a motion picture cinema that charged $2 per ticket.

4. The Tennessee Performing Arts Center in Nashville was usually open on Friday and Saturday evenings featuring Broadway shows with the original casts like Mickey Rooney in *Sugar Babies*. Five shows per year-round season were usually offered at prices that varied from $10 to $25. No meals were served, but cocktails and other beverages were offered during intermissions.

5. The Austin Peay State University Theatre and Music Department offered free performances with no meals or refreshments. Shows were offered year round usually featuring student talent, but occasionally featuring a professional Shakespearean group or other special talent.

6. The Kiwanis Club Community Theatre offered four performances each of three different plays per year at a cost of $8 to $10 per ticket. No meals or beverages were available.

7. The high school drama club offered three free performances of two modern plays each year.

8. The Capri Twin and Martin 4 motion picture theatres charged $3.75 per ticket.

THE ROXY OPENS

Before the Roxy could be opened, an extensive physical renovation of the building was necessary. In fact, the doors could not be opened until they were replaced by fire doors. The proscenium (the area located between the curtain and the orchestra) of the original stage was struck, the theatre seats were removed, and platforms for new seating were built. The neon green and red interior was repainted and a projected stage was built. After much work, planning, and training, the Roxy opened its doors on 3 November 1981 as a fully operational dinner theatre.

OPERATING THE ROXY

The Roxy staff established a production schedule of 144 performances per year based on 12 performances per month of 12 different shows per year. Six of the 12 shows were to be musicals. Each show would run three weeks with four performances per week. This left one week per month between shows to prepare for the next show's three week run.

A Thursday night show was available without dinner for $8 a person. On Friday and Saturday nights, patrons could dine or not as they wished. The price was $8 without a meal and $13, $15, or $17 with a meal depending upon seating. On Sundays, a brunch performance was featured for $11. Dinners were catered by a local restaurant. Waiters were hired to serve all meals. While the Roxy had a bar and maintained a bartender, it did not have a liquor license and sold only beer and soft drinks. "Brownbagging" by patrons was permitted. Seating was highly flexible consisting of small tables and chairs which could be clustered to create many different seating arrangements.

Open auditions were held and performers, selected from the community, donated their time and talents. The supply of talent was entirely dependent upon those persons in the area willing to volunteer their time to rehearsals and performances. This would limit the types of performances the Roxy could present in the future, especially musicals.

The primary promotional tool for the Roxy was advertising in the entertainment section of the local newspaper. This advertising was "donated" in exchange for tickets. There was no other charge if the finished copy was provided. Very little additional advertising was available or sought by the staff. Limited funds were a major constraint. An example of an ad is shown in Exhibit 2.

The five members of the Roxy staff performed a variety of tasks that were often rotated and shared. Specialization was not possible due to the mercurial nature of theatre operations. One day might require intensive work on costumes or choreography, while another might require greater attention to sets or rehearsal. The flexibility of the members was a plus, and the feelings of cohesiveness and comraderie were strong within the group. Members worked in the cold of winter to save on utility bills and often relied on "happy hour" at a nearby hotel for food.

The freewheeling, flexible style of the group, while positive in most respects, caused problems in some areas of operations. For instance, there was often confusion concerning reservations, advertising, and cash disbursements. In fact, accounting records for purchases, bills to be paid, receipts, and disbursements were not kept on a regular basis. Check stubs often showed amounts with no explanations or explanations with no amounts. The Roxy operated on a shoestring budget. Often, when bills were due, funds were not available to pay them. The Roxy staff discovered,

EXHIBIT 2 Roxy advertising example

by accident, that it was less expensive to bounce a check at the bank than to pay a reconnection fee for utilities. It became their unwritten policy to write checks on insufficient funds to pay bills. This allowed the Roxy to continue operations while they scrambled to produce funds to cover the check. Funds were provided from several sources — the sale of tickets, meals, and beverages; cash donations of patrons, who were noted in the programs as angels and saints according to the size of the donation; and donations of old clothes, furniture, rugs, etc., by concerned friends.

Expenses for a performance consisted of costumes, sets, script rentals, royalty payments, advertising, printing, food, labor costs, musicians (for musicals), and overhead items such as utilities. Cash was limited so expenditures were made only for the most necessary items. Often, old sets were cannibalized to create new ones. Additional props or parts were sometimes borrowed from local businesses in exchange for tickets, sometimes donated by concerned patrons, or, if absolutely necessary, purchased at the lowest possible cost often with tickets proffered to sweeten the deal.

For musicals, the Roxy staff made a verbal agreement with a pianist to provide music for $600 per show. Royalties for musicals were expected to average $975 per show while royalties for a play averaged $250. The first production was a play, not a musical.

Labor expense included the cost of a bartender at $75 per week and four waiters who worked approximately 16 hours a week at $2.05/hour plus tips during the run of the show (three weeks). The cost of a catered meal was $6.50 per plate.

The fixed costs associated with operating the Roxy included a $910 monthly lease payment, $540 per month to repay a renovation loan (half of which was interest), and $150 per month for insurance. The principals paid themselves a total of $1,175 per month. This included the $235 rent for two of the members' apartment. In addition, they retained an attorney to keep track of royalties, entertainment taxes, and other required record-keeping and reporting. Entertainment taxes were 6.75 percent of ticket sales.

Utilities expenses included telephone, gas for heating, and electricity for lighting. The telephone bill was expected to average $220 per month. Gas expense would probably average $1,000 per month during the four months of winter and $50 per month during the warmer months. Electricity averaged $400 per month.

Because of the informality of the Roxy staff, two of the owners have elected to have the corporation pay their rent of $235 per month rather than draw salaries.

THE FIRST MONTH

November 1981 had been an exciting time for the members of the Roxy group. Ticket sales amounted to $10,734, even though an average of only 118 of the 200 available seats were filled at most performances. However, Tom was concerned about a number of things. He could not tell how many of the seats at a performance were filled by free-ticket holders. He also had no record of how many meals were sold, given away, or spoiled. He also did not know how many tickets of each price had been sold.

He had a cigar box filled with notes, receipts, bills, and canceled checks. Upon examination of the contents, Tom found the following information:

1. A bill for $303.33 for graphic design of advertising and programs.
2. A bill for $460.00 for the printing of programs.
3. A receipt from the U.S. Post Office for $88.

4. A bank statement indicating monthly service and nonsufficient funds charges of $57.75.
5. A note from Tom that the corporation owed him $33.37 for the use of his personal auto for business trips.
6. Receipts totaling $331.74 for props.
7. A laundry receipt for $300.28 for cleaning costumes.
8. Several bills from plumbers and electricians for repairs to the old building totaling $893.45. Tom wasn't sure whether such expenses might be incurred every month.
9. Canceled checks indicating several purchases of supplies (napkins, cleaning supplies, etc.) totaling $391.82.
10. Other miscellaneous items totaling $312.50.
11. Canceled checks to the caterer totaling $4,722.92.
12. A bill for $115 for attorney fees.

Tom believed that he could construct an Income and Expense statement and that he could find out the number of tickets the Roxy must sell to break even. But he was more concerned about how to control disbursements, free tickets, meals, and other operational problems. More importantly, Tom was concerned about filling the house with a paying audience. When audiences didn't just appear, Tom had begun questioning whether the market for the Roxy's productions was as rosy as the group imagined in its statement of purpose in Exhibit 1. An economics professor from the university had mentioned something about regional node theory to Tom. According to the professor, people from small towns would travel to larger regional population centers for shopping and entertainment, but it was questionable whether people from the larger city would travel to the smaller town for the same purposes. Since the Roxy had not advertised outside Clarksville, it was difficult for Tom to know whether audiences would travel from Nashville to the Roxy.

In his discussions with friends, Tom found that many believed that the majority of area residents were apathetic toward the arts and support of the arts, especially the performing arts. The statement that, "If it's in Clarksville, it can't be very good," was expressed by more than one acquaintance. One person responded that there was a limited audience for anything more intellectually stirring than a tractor pull and an inherent distrust of any form of entertainment out of the norm. Others expressed a hesitancy to spend more than the price of a movie ticket for any form of entertainment. Some thought the transient population with wide cultural backgrounds afforded by Fort Campbell was unaware of cultural events in the local community.

Tom wondered whether serving meals was a good idea, and whether serving alcoholic beverages might increase the audience size. He had obtained some information from the State Alcoholic Beverage Commission indicating that, following an inspection of a business's premises, a liquor license could be granted under the following constraints:

For businesses seating 75 to 125 persons, the minimum fee per year was $600, which was paid to the Alcoholic Beverage Commission. The business must also procure business tax licenses from the city and county which would equal the fee paid to the Alcoholic Beverage Commission ($600) and put up a $10,000 bond. The fee for a business seating 126 to 175 persons was $750 in addition to the $10,000 bond.

Once the liquor license was secured an outlay of up to $5,000 would be necessary to stock liquor and mixers. An experienced bartender would be required at a wage of $5 an hour.

A study of some local restaurants which served both dinner and liquor showed 25 to 30 percent of their total profits came from business at the bar. Bars usually earned a 70 percent profit per dollar on liquor sales. This was an after-tax profit estimate.

Tom was perplexed as he wondered what needed to be done to operate the Roxy profitably, fill the house, solve the money problems, and keep the group together. One thing was certain though. The Roxy team had never enjoyed life as much as they had in the last thirty days. They all agreed that they wanted to continue their poor — but fulfilled — artist lifestyle even if the Roxy didn't return a profit.

PIZZA DELIGHTS, INC.: THE ST. GEORGE STREET RESTAURANT

Earnest Outbanks, manager of the St. George Street Pizza Delights in Roebuck, South Carolina, hung up the phone after a two-hour conversation with Leonard Lloyd, owner of three Pizza Delights in Greer, South Carolina. It was 11 P.M. on the night of 5 April 1986, and soon it would be time to close. It occurred to Outbanks as he glanced around the restaurant he had successfully managed for five years that both he and Lloyd were on the verge of a major decision, the outcome of which was certain to shape the rest of their careers. He tried to concentrate on the job at hand, but his thoughts kept returning to Lloyd's proposal.

Outbanks' career in the pizza business had started some ten years earlier, in 1976, when he became a cook for Pizza Delights during high school. Lloyd's involvement began in 1981, when he bought his first Pizza Delights restaurant in Greer, South Carolina. By 1986, at the tender age of 25, Outbanks had become well established as the manager of the St. George Street Pizza Delights in Roebuck, a small community approximately five miles to the southeast of Spartanburg, South Carolina. Lloyd, on the other hand, had by 1986 established a chain of three successful Pizza Delights franchise restaurants throughout the rural Greer area, which was approximately 20 miles from Spartanburg.

Since Outbanks had taken over the company-owned restaurant on St. George Street in 1981, he had managed to change a sluggish, break-even operation into the second most profitable Pizza Delights in the greater Spartanburg area (see Exhibit 1 for income statements for 1983–85). His achievements had not escaped the attention of many fellow businesspeople in the fast-growing communities which surrounded the restaurant. Leonard Lloyd had learned of Outbanks' achievements too, as he was always on the lookout for a way to enter the more lucrative Spartanburg market.

Lloyd had contacted Outbanks on several occasions during the spring of 1986 in hopes of persuading Outbanks to join him in buying the restaurant from Pizza Delights.

This case was prepared by Jay Horne, Christine Perkins, Kim Goates, Peter Asp, and Ken Sarris under the direction of Dr. James J. Chrisman, University of South Carolina, and associate editor, *Case Research Journal*. This case was prepared for classroom discussion and was not intended to illustrate either effective or ineffective handling of administrative situations.

EXHIBIT 1
St. George Street restaurant income statements, 1983–1985

A. The St. George Street location income statements, 1983–1985

	1985	1984	1983
Gross food sales	$557,278	$478,603	$422,375
Less: Allowances	7,869	7,547	7,038
Sales promotions	34,394	32,982	31,651
Net food sales	515,015	438,074	383,686
Plus: Vending machines	1,734	2,103	1,923
Game machine	1,582	1,661	1,843
Total revenue	518,331	441,838	387,452
Cost of goods sold	144,406	133,225	117,486
Gross profit	373,925	308,613	269,966
Operating costs:			
Management salary	54,373		
Crew labor	56,445	111,391	108,476
Other labor	12,979		
National advertising	7,544		5,637
Co-op advertising	12,652	22,880	7,629
Local advertising	9,001		8,538
Operating costs	12,795		13,330
Utilities cost	19,531		16,343
Maintenance	9,749	40,464	9,019
Uniforms	349		1,113
Other	2,474		2,110
Premiums	5	1,110	210
Operating profit	176,028	132,778	97,981
Plus: TJTC credit	4,435	0	0
Less: Fixed costs	47,467*	33,985*	35,647
Total profit	$132,996	$ 98,793	$ 62,334

*See fixed cost schedule.

B. Fixed cost schedule for 1984–1985 income statements

	1985	1984
Fixed costs	$47,466	$33,985
TJTC expense	161	54
Bank charges	570	615
Personal property tax	221	254
Real estate taxes	3,939	3,939
Licenses and fees	269	289
Equipment depreciation	10,149	7,774
Leasehold amortization	2,618	2,768
Building rental	17,417	15,813
Contingent lease rent	8,442	502
Insurance	2,441	1,909
Abandonment and property	1,236	65
Goodwill amortization	3	0

Although Lloyd's idea sounded quite attractive to Outbanks, who had had visions of owning his own franchise for several years, he was reluctant to give an answer right away. Outbanks' career with Pizza Delights had been quite successful, and he believed that his future with the firm was bright. However, he knew that Lloyd could not be kept waiting forever and was determined to make a decision in the near future.

The remainder of this case will describe the history, environment, and operations of the Pizza Delights Corporation, the restaurants on St. George Street and in Greer, as well as Lloyd's franchising plans for Outbanks' restaurant.

PIZZA DELIGHTS, INC.:
COMPANY BACKGROUND AND STRUCTURE

The Pizza Delights chain was established in the greater Omaha, Nebraska, area in the late 1960s. The restaurants offered the customer a limited range of Italian dishes including pizza, spaghetti, and cavatini. The restaurants proved to be very successful. They offered something the public wanted — a high-quality pizza with a high level of personal service. The original restaurants enjoyed immediate success, since it was one of the first chains in the area to offer strictly pizza and other Italian dishes.

Due to its early successes, Pizza Delights was an attractive acquisition candidate. It caught the attention of a large food manufacturing corporation, which purchased the company as well as the rights to its secret recipes in the late 1970s. With the corporation's financial backing, Pizza Delights restaurants began to spring up all over the United States at an even faster rate than before. Throughout this period of national expansion, the high degree of quality and service that were Pizza Delights' trademark were maintained.

Since 1983, Pizza Delights had introduced several new products, which were "big sellers." These products included a small pan pizza (1983), the double-decker pizza (1984), and the Italian turnover pizza (1985). All of these products required a great deal of refrigerator space for storage. However, according to restaurant managers, Pizza Delights had not provided the additional freezer capacity needed to store these items.

Additionally, as Pizza Delights was owned by a large food corporation, all the supplies used at company-owned restaurants had to be obtained from the parent company. These items included everything from straws and napkins to pizza dough and pepperoni. If an emergency situation occurred, such as a shortage of green peppers, the restaurants were allowed to make purchases from outside suppliers as long as these purchases, in total, did not exceed 1 percent of yearly sales for the individual restaurant. However, this practice was not generally encouraged by the corporation.

Franchised restaurants had more flexibility in this respect. To ensure standardization, certain items, such as printed napkins and pizza ingredients, still had to be purchased from the parent corporation. However, other items (such as pizza cutters) could be purchased from outside sources. This was important for possible cost reductions as purchasing solely from the corporation tended to inflate costs. For example, ladles to dip pizza sauce currently cost $8 when purchased from the corporation. Outside suppliers offered this item for a lower price, sometimes as much as 10 to 20 percent less than charged by the corporation.

In 1986, the headquarters of Pizza Delights remained in Omaha. The chain had grown to nearly 1,500 restaurants. Management planned to open 100 to 200 new restaurants per year over the next decade. To accommodate this growth, six regional offices, located in the population centers of the United States, had been added since the 1970s. These regions were subdivided into areas, which were further subdivided into districts (see Exhibit 2). Each region, area, and district had a full-time staff of managers, accountants, inspectors, and other personnel to ensure that each individual restaurant fulfilled its duties to the corporation.

This hierarchical maze created some problems for the individual restaurants, however. For example, any purchase exceeding $500 had to be approved by the area supervisor, the district manager, and the regional vice president before the restaurant manager could proceed with the investment. This situation sometimes created a time lag of several months between requests and implementation. As a result, many of the restaurant managers had given up trying to solve certain problems and, instead, merely tolerated them.

HISTORY OF THE
ST. GEORGE STREET RESTAURANT

The St. George Street Pizza Delights was built in 1974 primarily to serve customers in Roebuck, a small community five miles southeast of Spartanburg, South Carolina. It also served commuters who traveled on Interstate 85, a major traffic artery into Spartanburg.

EXHIBIT 2
The Pizza Delights hierarchy

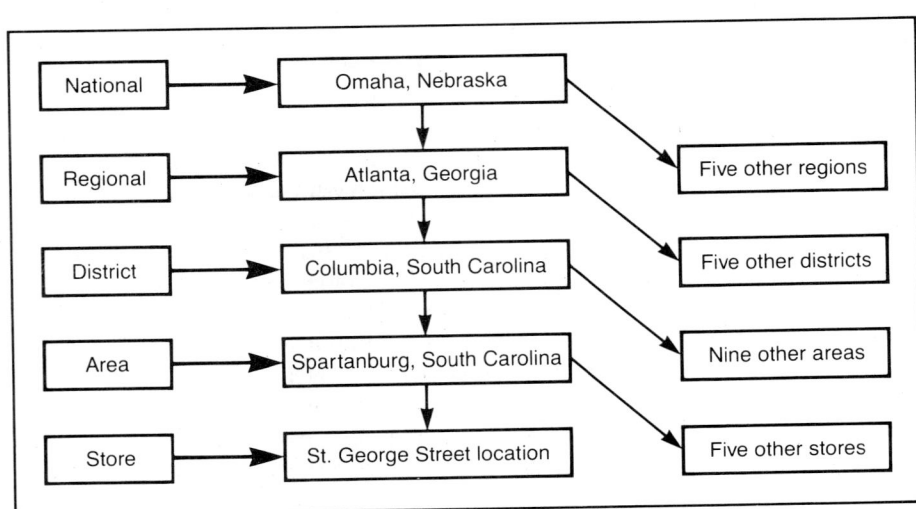

The restaurant was modestly successful from the start, showing low to moderate profits during its first few years. As the populations of Roebuck, Spartanburg, and the surrounding areas grew, so initially did the restaurant's profits. With this population growth, however, came increased competition (and lower profits) as other fast-food chains began to appear along a strip of St. George Street for several miles. By 1981, when Outbanks became manager, there were a total of three direct pizza competitors within one mile of the restaurant, not to mention the numerous other fast-food competitors which did business in the area.

Outbanks had inherited a restaurant which had many problems. First of all, the crew at the restaurant had been described by the district manager as probably the "most lazy and inhospitable bunch he had ever met." Second, food costs at the restaurant had been astronomical. Cheese costs in particular were extremely high. High food costs were partially attributable to the fact that many of the employees were either taking home free pizzas or giving them away to their friends. In addition, the cooks were not preparing the pizzas according to Pizza Delights standards. None of the ingredients were weighed, which often resulted in more ingredients being used on the individual pizzas than were needed.

As a result of the increased competition as well as the inefficiencies in operations, the restaurant's net profits before taxes had dipped to their lowest level since 1975 ($42,680) when Outbanks assumed control in 1981. Outbanks attempted to alter these problems by replacing most of his staff and training the new employees himself. He also began to implement new policies to improve the efficiency of operations. Due to his extensive experience in the pizza business, as well as his ability to deal effectively with high school- and college-age employees, most of the more obvious problems had been solved, and the restaurant's profits rose steadily under his stewardship.

THE GREATER SPARTANBURG ENVIRONMENT

Located in northern South Carolina, Spartanburg was a city of approximately 45,000 persons. Situated in an agricultural region that produced crops such as cotton, peaches, melons, and feed crops, the city was the seat of Spartanburg County and was part of the tri-county region (Spartanburg, Greenville, and Pickens counties) that made up the Greenville–Spartanburg SMA (standard metropolitan area). Spartanburg boasted a variety of employment opportunities for its residents in manufacturing industries, such as textiles, metals, rubber, paper, chemicals, clothing, and plumbing supplies. In addition, it was the site for several colleges and universities (see Exhibit 3). Unfortunately, the area had not shared equally in the growth experienced in other parts of South Carolina and the South Atlantic region (Delaware, District of Columbia, Florida, Georgia, Maryland, North Carolina, South Carolina, Virginia, and West Virginia) in recent years.

For example, the populations of the surrounding SMA and county were growing at a rate exceeding the average for the United States. However, between 1978 and 1984 this growth rate had not kept pace with the population growth experienced in

EXHIBIT 3
Colleges and
universities in
Spartanburg
County:
Enrollments

Institution	Enrollment
University of South Carolina–Spartanburg	2,778
Spartanburg Technical College	1,813
Converse College	1,078
Spartanburg Methodist College	1,067
Wofford	1,034
Rutledge College–Spartanburg	447

Source: *South Carolina Statistical Abstract, 1984.*

the rest of South Carolina or in the South Atlantic region. In fact, the population in the city of Spartanburg had actually declined (see Exhibit 4).

Despite lackluster population growth, the Spartanburg area was relatively prosperous in comparison to the rest of South Carolina. Even so, the effective buying incomes of area inhabitants lagged behind both the total United States and the South Atlantic region. To make matters worse, Spartanburg was falling further behind national and regional averages and had recently lost some of its advantage over the rest of South Carolina (see Exhibit 5).

The outlook for retailing, particularly eating-and-drinking establishments, was not exceedingly bright either. Sales did increase for retailers between 1978 and 1984 in Spartanburg and the surrounding area. And as Exhibit 6 shows, this growth rate compared favorably overall to that experienced on average in the United States. Unfortunately, Exhibit 6 also shows that the rate of growth in retailing for the Greenville–Spartanburg SMA did not compare favorably to average growth rates in South Carolina and the South Atlantic states. Additionally, contrary to trends in South Carolina, the South Atlantic states, and the United States in general, eating-and-drinking establishments' share of total retail sales in the Greenville–Spartanburg SMA had declined substantially in the 1980s. The outlook for eating-and-drinking places in the city was the least favorable. Eating-and-drinking-place sales had increased only 5 percent since 1978, while they had increased 73 percent on average in the United States and had more than doubled in the rest of South Carolina during the same period. There were greater opportunities outside the city, though, as the migration to the suburbs provided increased demand for restaurants in these locations.

COMPETITION IN THE SPARTANBURG AREA

The pizza industry had rapidly expanded in the 1980s. With this trend came increased competition for the St. George Street Pizza Delights from nationally owned pizza

EXHIBIT 4 1978 and 1984 population statistics (population and households in thousands)

Year	Total population	Percent of U.S.	Total households	Percent of U.S.	Median Age	Percent of population by age group				
						0–17	18–24	25–34	35–49	≥50
Spartanburg										
1978	46.9	.02%	16.7	.02%	31.2	26.8%	14.2%	14.6%	16.3%	28.1%
1984	44.9	.02	17.4	.02	32.2	24.5	13.3	17.0	16.0	29.2
Percent change	−6.2%		+4.2%							
Spartanburg County										
1978	196.7	.09	67.8	.09	30.6	28.0	12.6	16.7	17.2	25.5
1984	213.5	.09	78.3	.09	32.1	26.6	11.1	17.2	19.6	25.5
Percent change	+8.5%		+15.5%							
Greenville–Spartanburg SMA										
1978	541.4	.25	184.5	.24	29.8	27.9	13.9	17.1	17.1	24.0
1984	605.0	.25	222.1	.26	31.3	26.2	12.6	17.8	19.5	23.9
Percent change	+11.7%		+20.4%							
South Carolina										
1978	2,934.8	1.3	933.8	1.2	27.7	31.2	14.5	15.9	16.0	22.5
1984	3,353.4	1.4	1,172.0	1.4	29.8	28.2	13.3	17.6	18.1	22.7
Percent change	+14.3%		+25.5%							
South Atlantic Region*										
1978	34,981.7	15.9	12,186.8	15.9	30.3	28.2	13.4	15.7	16.3	26.4
1984	39.904.5	16.8	14,612.2	16.8	32.3	25.4	12.1	17.2	18.5	26.8
Percent change	+14.1%		+19.9%							
United States										
1978	219,768.5	100	76,904.7	100	30.1	28.8	13.2	15.7	16.4	26.0
1984	238,274.7	100	86,926.6	100	31.7	26.3	12.2	17.4	18.3	25.9
Percent change	+8.4%		+13.0%							

*Includes Delaware, District of Columbia, Florida, Georgia, Maryland, North Carolina, South Carolina, Virginia, and West Virginia.
Source: "Survey of Buying Power," *Sales and Marketing Management,* 1979 and %1985.

chains and even from companies producing frozen pizzas sold in grocery stores. In addition to being in fierce competition with seventeen local and nationally owned pizza places, the St. George Street restaurant competed with a total of 170 restaurants of other types and with several other Pizza Delights restaurants in the greater Spartanburg area. One of these Pizza Delights restaurants was within a few miles of the

EXHIBIT 5 Effective buying incomes (EBI) in 1978 and 1984

	Total EBI ($000s)	Per capita EBI	Average household EBI	Median household EBI
Spartanburg				
1978	$ 308,625	$ 6,580	$18,481	$14,721
1984	410,214	9,136	23,576	18.782
Percent change	+32.9%	+38.8%	+27.6%	+27.6%
Spartanburg County				
1978	1,127,798	5,734	16,634	14,702
1984	1,943,381	9,102	24,820	21,828
Percent change	+72.3%	+58.7%	+49.2%	+48.5%
Greenville–Spartanburg SMA				
1978	3,203,011	5,916	17,360	15,349
1984	5,434,481	8,983	24,469	21,540
Percent change	+69.7%	+51.8%	+41.0%	+40.3%
South Carolina				
1978	15,425,876	5,256	16,519	14,047
1984	28,550,182	8,514	24,360	20,969
Percent change	+85.1%	+62.0%	+47.5%	+49.3%
South Atlantic region				
1978	212,961,331	6,088	17,475	14,681
1984	408,218,168	10,230	27,937	23,576
Percent change	+91.7%	+68.0%	+59.9%	+60.6%
United States				
1978	1,439,815,449	6,552	18,722	16,231
1984	2,576,533,480	10,813	29,640	25,496
Percent change	+78.9%	+65.0%	+58.3%	+57.1%

Source: "Survey of Buying Power," *Sales and Marketing Management,* 1979 and 1985.

St. George Street operation. Exhibits 7 through 9 provide average common size income statements, balance sheets, and financial ratios, respectively, for traditional and fast-food restaurants with less than $1 million in sales for 1985. Exhibit 10 provides a map with the locations of competitors in the St. George Street area. Pizza Delight's major pizza competitors are described below. Exhibit 11 summarizes the product, service, and pricing strategies of these competitors.

EXHIBIT 6 Total retail and eating-and-drinking-place sales in 1978 and 1984

	Total retail sales	Sales per capita	Eating-and-drinking places		
			Total sales	Sales per capita	Percent of total retail
Spartanburg					
1978	$ 417,207	$ 8,896*	$ 41,507	$885*	9.9%
1984	526,485	11,725*	43,625	972*	8.3
Percent change	+26.2%	+31.8%	+5.1%	+9.8%	
Spartanburg County					
1978	635,084	3,229	58,911	299	9.3
1984	1,015,451	4,756	79,688	373	7.8
Percent change	+59.9%	+47.3%	+35.3%	+24.7%	
Greenville–Spartanburg SMA					
1978	1,911,506	3,531	175,057	323	9.2
1984	3,117,321	5,153	257,667	426	8.3
Percent change	+63.1%	+45.9%	+47.2%	+31.9%	
South Carolina					
1978	9,243,104	3,149	670,142	228	7.3
1984	15,484,516	4,618	1,343,043	401	8.7
Percent change	+67.5%	+46.6%	+100.4%	+75.9%	
South Atlantic region					
1978	129,343,686	3,697	11,434,037	327	8.8
1984	220,144,917	5,517	19,950,436	500	9.1
Percent change	+70.2%	+49.2%	+74.5%	+52.9%	
United States					
1978	817,461,457	3,720	71,602,628	326	8.8
1984	1,296,659,715	5,442	124,035,013	564	9.6
Percent change	+58.6%	+46.3%	+73.2%	+73.0%	

*Retail sales per capita for the city are higher than for the county, SMA, state, region, and nation due to the large number of noncity resident sales.
Source: "Survey of Buying Power," *Sales and Marketing Management,* 1979 and 1985.

Domino's

Domino's, Inc., was the leading competitor for delivery pizza. The company's strategy was to offer its customers fast delivery service (usually less than 30 minutes) for a medium-priced pizza. Domino's sold only pizza; the firm did not include other Italian dishes on its menu. Domino's pizza was of reputedly low to medium quality, however.

EXHIBIT 7
Average common size income statements for United States restaurants (less than $1 million in 1985 sales)

	Traditional* (n = 481)	Fast-foods[†] (n = 301)
Sales	100.0%	100.0%
Cost of goods sold	43.8	39.3
Gross profit	56.2%	60.7%
Operating expenses	52.6	55.0
Other expenses	1.6	2.7
Net profit before taxes	2.1%	3.0%

*Includes restaurants selling prepared foods and drinks for consumption on the premises. Caterers and industrial and institutional food service establishments are also included (SIC 5812).
[†]Includes franchise operations (SIC 5812).
Source: Robert Morris Associates, *1986 Annual Statement Studies.*

EXHIBIT 8
Average common size balance sheets for United States restaurants (less than $1 million in 1985 sales)

	Traditional* (n = 481)	Fast-foods[†] (n = 301)
Assets		
Cash and equivalents	12.1%	14.9%
Trade receivables (net)	4.3	1.9
Inventory	7.6	4.8
All other current assets	2.6	2.6
Total current assets	26.6%	24.2%
Fixed assets (net)	56.3	53.0
Intangibles (net)	4.5	6.2
All other noncurrent assets	12.6	16.6
Total assets	100.0%	100.0%
Liabilities and owners' equity		
Current liabilities	40.0%	38.6%
Long-term debt	32.8	35.6
All other noncurrent liabilities	2.9	2.1
Total liabilities	75.7%	76.3%
Owners' equity (net worth)	24.3	23.7
Total liabilities and owners' equity	100.0%	100.0%

*Includes restaurants selling prepared foods and drinks for consumption on the premises. Caterers and industrial and institutional food service establishments are also included (SIC 5812).
[†]Includes franchise operations (SIC 5812).
Source: Robert Morris Associates, *1986 Annual Statement Studies.*

EXHIBIT 9 Financial ratios for traditional and fast-food restaurants in the United States with less than $1 million in sales for 1985

	Traditional restaurants*			Fast-food restaurants†		
	Upper quartile	Median	Lower quartile	Upper quartile	Median	Lower quartile
Ratios						
Current	1.3	0.7	0.3	1.2	0.6	0.3
Quick	0.8	0.4	0.2	0.9	0.4	0.1
Sales/receivables	INF	451.0	74.9	INF	INF	507.1
Cost of sales/inventory	46.1	27.4	16.1	59.6	42.7	28.2
Sales/working capital	51.0	−38.5	−12.1	56.2	−31.4	−11.8
Times interest earned	4.9	2.0	0.4	5.9	2.5	1.0
Cash flow/current portion of long-term debt	4.5	1.6	0.7	5.4	2.4	1.2
Debt/equity ratio	1.0	3.2	−26.2	1.2	3.8	−14.5
Asset turnover	5.2	3.5	2.2	5.1	3.3	2.4
Return on equity (percent)	62.1%	23.1%	4.6%	81.6%	36.7%	−15.9%
Return on assets (percent)	17.1%	5.3%	−3.1%	20.0%	9.6%	1.0%

Note: INF = Infinite.
*Includes restaurants selling prepared foods and drinks for consumption on the premises. Caterers and industrial and institutional food service establishments are also included (SIC 5812); 481 establishments studied.
†Includes franchise operations (SIC 5812); 301 establishments studied.
Source: Robert Morris Associates, *1986 Annual Statement Studies.*

Little Caesar's This was a chain restaurant located in Perkins Plaza off White Rock Road and St. George Street. Little Caesar's catered to the take-out customer; it did not make deliveries or provide facilities for eat-in dining. Its pizza was of medium quality and was medium priced. The chain also offered customers special Greek and Italian salads, sandwiches, and sliced pizza. To get volume, Little Caesar's frequently placed two-for-one coupons in local newspapers.

Pizza Factory Located in the nearby Stephenson Plaza, this national chain restaurant provided take-out services as well as eat-in dining facilities for customers. Its customer service was low, however, as the restaurant had no waitresses. Pizza Factory offered customers a low-priced, medium-quality pizza as well as a variety of sandwiches, a salad bar, and alcoholic beverages.

Showbiz Pizza Showbiz Pizza was a national chain restaurant catering to small children. Its dining room decor included dancing bears, games, and other attractions for children. Showbiz offered customers a medium-quality pizza at a medium to high price.

Pizza Hut Pizza Hut was the largest and most important competitor of Pizza Delights. Its strategy was to be a full-line pizza competitor, offering a medium- to high-priced product

EXHIBIT 10 Locations of the St. George Street Pizza Delights and its competitors

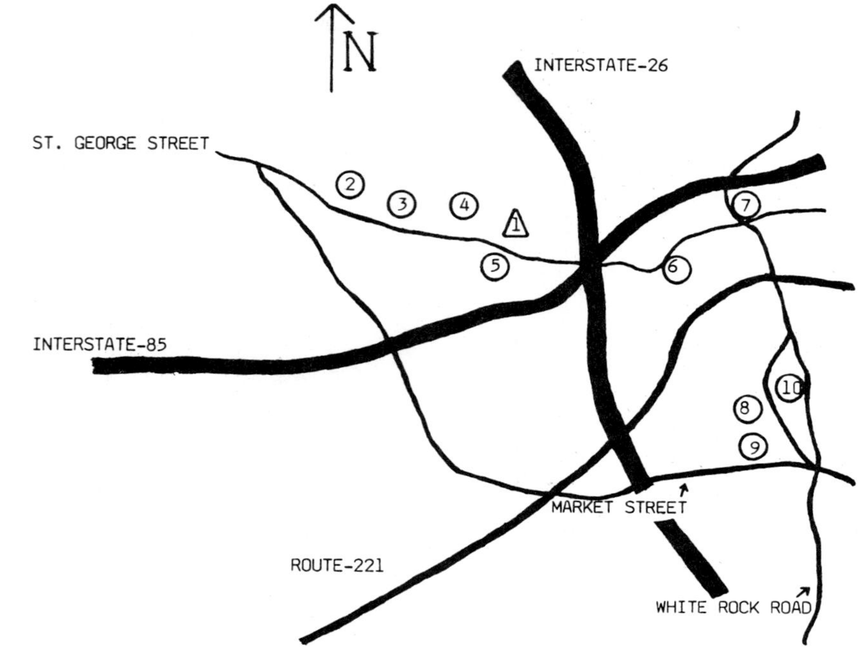

KEY:

1. PIZZA DELIGHTS
2. St. George Cinema & Video Arcade
3. PIZZA FACTORY (Stephenson Plaza)
4. DOMINO'S
5. SCHIANO'S (St. George Plaza)
6. SHOWBIZ PIZZA
7. LITTLE CAESAR'S (Perkins Plaza)
8. PIZZA HUT
9. Competing PIZZA DELIGHTS
10. PIZZA INN

LEGEND:

one mile

with correspondingly high levels of service and product quality. The company had been quite successful in introducing new pizza products, which it advertised heavily.

Although Pizza Hut did not operate a restaurant on St. George Street, its White Rock Road location was only a few miles to the east of the St. George Pizza Delights. It had been more successful than the other Pizza Delights restaurant located nearby. Moreover, the growing population in the area had caused the Pizza Hut Corporation to consider building a new restaurant on St. George Street. Such a move would have a direct impact on Pizza Delights because 30 to 35 percent of its customers were

EXHIBIT 11 Comparisons of product, service, and pricing strategies of pizza competitors

	Pizza Delights	Domino's	Little Caesar's	Pizza Factory
Services				
Eat-in	Yes	No	No	Yes
Take-out	Yes	Yes	Yes	Yes
Delivery	No	Yes	No	No
Buffet	No	No	No	No
Luncheon menu	Yes	No	No	Yes
Salad bar	Yes	No	No	Yes
Service level	High	High (delivery only)	Low	Low
Products (dinner only)				
Quality	Medium/ high	Low/ medium	Medium	Medium
Number of pizzas on menu	6	2	6	6
Types of pizzas	2	1	1	1
Sizes	3	2	3	3
Slices	No	No	Yes	No
Meat/fish toppings	6	4	6	9
Vegetable toppings	6	7	7	10
Italian dishes	Spaghetti	No	No	No
Sandwiches (number × sizes)	4	0	3 × 2	4
Salads (excluding bar)	No	No	3 × 3	No
Alcoholic beverages	Beer	No	No	Beer
Other beverages	Soft drinks, tea, milk, coffee	Coke	Soft drinks	Soft drinks, tea
Prices				
Medium cheese pizza	$ 7.45	$ 6.02	$ 6.78	$ 6.70
Medium 5–7 toppings (#)	10.00 (6)	—	10.29 (5)	9.55 (6)
Medium 8–11 toppings (#)	10.80 (9)	$11.12 (9)	—	11.25 (11)
Large cheese pizza	9.85	8.17	9.28	8.00
Large 5–7 toppings (#)	12.70 (6)	—	13.52 (5)	10.95 (6)
Large 8–11 toppings (#)	13.55 (9)	15.42 (9)	—	13.25 (11)
Toppings—medium/large	.85/.95	1.02/1.45	.77/.96	.85/.95
Italian dishes	1.99–3.39	—	—	—
Sandwiches	2.89	—	2.25–2.69	2.49
Salads	2.49	—	1.20–4.69	2.59
Alcohol (glass)	.95	—	—	.75
Other beverages	.50–.75	.65	.48–.87	.55–.75

	Showbiz	Pizza Hut	Pizza Inn	Schiano's
Services				
Eat-in	Yes	Yes	Yes	Yes
Take-out	No	Yes	Yes	Yes
Delivery	No	No	Yes	No

EXHIBIT 11 (continued)

EXHIBIT 11 (continued)

	Showbiz	Pizza Hut	Pizza Inn	Schiano's
Services (continued)				
Buffet	No	No	Yes	No
Luncheon menu	Yes	Yes	Yes	No
Salad bar	No	Yes	Yes	No
Service level	High	High	High	High
Products				
Quality	Medium	Medium/ high	Low/medium	High
Number of pizzas on menu	5	10	12	6
Types of pizzas	1	3	2	2
Sizes	3	3	4	3
Slices	No	No	No	No
Meat/fish toppings	4	7	6	5
Vegetable toppings	6	8	7	6
Italian dishes	No	Spaghetti	Spaghetti, lasagna	Parmigiana, calzone, lasagna
Sandwiches (number × sizes)	5	3 × 2	4	6 × 2
Salads (excluding bar)	1	No	1	2
Alcoholic beverages	Beer	Beer	Beer, wine	Beer, wine
Other beverages	Soft drinks, tea, milk, coffee	Soft drinks, tea, milk, coffee	Soft drinks, tea, milk, coffee	Soft drinks
Prices				
Medium cheese pizza	$ 8.09	$ 7.05–7.25	$ 5.80–7.80	$ 4.95–6.45
Medium 5–7 toppings (#)	10.99 (6)	9.80 (6)	9.35–9.75 (7)	9.20–10.70 (6)
Medium 8–11 toppings (#)	—	10.60 (9)	10.20–10.70 (9)	10.20–11.70 (8)
Large cheese pizza	9.99	9.45–9.65	9.00–9.50	7.20–8.70
Large 5–7 toppings (#)	12.99 (6)	12.50 (6)	11.85–12.35 (7)	12.20–13.70 (6)
Large 8–11 toppings (#)	—	13.35 (9)	12.80–13.40 (9)	13.20–14.70 (8)
Toppings—medium/large	.90/1.00	.90/1.00	.85/.95	.85/1.00
Italian dishes	—	2.09–4.49	1.89–3.89	3.29–6.95
Sandwiches	1.39–2.69	2.79–3.79	.79–2.59	2.15–4.55
Salads	2.29	2.79	1.99	1.79–3.49
Alcohol (glass)	.99	1.00	1.00	.95–1.60
Other beverages	.50–.79	.50–.80	.45–.80	.65

from the Roebuck area. However, after conducting a market survey, Pizza Hut decided not to build a new restaurant in Roebuck in 1986, although this possibility was still under consideration for the future.

Pizza Inn   Besides Pizza Hut, Pizza Inn was Pizza Delights' most formidable competitor. Pizza Inn offered customers a variety of services including eat-in dining, take-outs, home delivery (started in early 1986), a salad bar, a luncheon buffet during the weekdays, and a dinner buffet every Tuesday. Its pizza was low to medium priced, with corresponding levels of quality.

Schiano's   Schiano's was an example of the expanding pizza competition in the St. George Street area. This restaurant was, in 1986, under construction directly across the street from Outbanks' restaurant. Schiano's was planning to offer a dining room with extensive service in the new St. George plaza. This chain restaurant offered a high-quality, high-priced "New York"-style pizza.

Grocery Stores   The grocery stores in the area stocked a diverse line of pizzas and pizza products, including microwave pizzas, store-made pizzas, and national brands of frozen pizzas. For the do-it-yourself customers, grocers also offered prepackaged pizza ingredients, such as instant pizza crust, sauces, grated pizza cheese, sliced pepperoni, and so on. These take-home products were generally of lower quality than the pizzas served in restaurants. They were, however, also much lower in price (prices generally ranged from 79 cents to $4).

DELIVERY

One trend in the fast-food industry, especially for pizza, had been to increase speed and efficiency. This trend was responsible for the opening of several delivery pizza stores in the greater Spartanburg area, such as Domino's. In an attempt to penetrate this market for delivered pizza, Pizza Delights had opened a delivery store in August 1984 in Arcadia, South Carolina, just outside of the Spartanburg city limits. This store only produced pizzas that were to be delivered. The delivery area included only those areas within a 10-mile radius of the store, excluding approximately 30 percent of the Spartanburg-Roebuck area. Since there was only one Pizza Delights delivery location, many problems had deveoped. In order to save transportation and delivery costs, the Arcadia store held orders until a large number of pizzas could be delivered to one area. This practice helped lower costs, but it hurt customer relations since delivery time sometimes exceeded one hour, and pizzas were frequently delivered cold. According to market research, approximately 75 percent of the customers were dissatisfied with the current delivery service offered by the Arcadia Pizza Delights.

PRODUCTS AND MARKETS OF THE
ST. GEORGE STREET RESTAURANT

The St. George Street restaurant did not have a specific target market, according to Earnest Outbanks. All types of individuals frequented the restaurant. In addition to regular customers, which composed 58 percent of the customer base, this store was convenient to shoppers of the two nearby plazas, commuters, and theater-goers. Almost 50 percent of the St. George Street restaurant's customers drove between three and five miles to the restaurant. Market research suggested that customers frequented the St. George Street restaurant fairly often, usually on a monthly basis.

Although pizza was the primary product, other menu items (such as sandwiches, spaghetti, and a salad bar) were available to offer diversity to the customer. Exhibit 12 lists the menu items and prices for the St. George Street restaurant. Exhibit 13 provides

EXHIBIT 12 The St. George Street location—menu items and prices

	Small	Medium	Large*
Pizza			
Double decker (3 varieties)	$8.00	$10.80	$13.55
Pan pizzas			
Cheese	5.05	7.45	9.85
Delight (6 toppings)	7.30	10.00	12.70
Super Delight (9 toppings)	8.00	10.80	13.55
Additional toppings	.75	.85	.95

(pepperoni, ham, pork, beef, Italian sausage, mushroom, onion, green pepper, black olive, jalapeno pepper, anchovy, extra cheese)

	Small	Regular
Spaghetti		
Meat sauce	$1.99	$ 3.19
Meatballs	2.39	3.39
Salad bar		
As a meal		2.49
With a meal		1.99
Children under 12		.99
Sandwiches		
4 varieties		2.89
Drinks		

Soft drinks

Pitcher	2.25	Coffee	.50	Beer	
Large	.75	Milk	.55	Glass	.95
Medium	.70	Ice Tea	.65	Pitcher	3.95
Small	.65				

Luncheon specials:
Monday–Friday

	Pizza only	Pizza/salad bar (one trip)
Italian turnover[†]		
Cheese	$2.49	$3.88
Sausage	2.49	3.88
Small pan pizza		
Pepperoni	1.79	3.18
Supreme (6 toppings)	2.19	3.58

*Small pizzas serve one–two people; medium, three–four people; large, five–six people.
[†]Guaranteed to be ready in 10 minutes or your lunch is free.

EXHIBIT 13
The St. George Street location—gross profit by product line

	1985	1984
Pizza		
Eat-in pizza	$204,886	$168,174
Carry-out pizza	215,806	181,774
Net pizza	$420,692	$349,948
Plus: Pizza allowances	$ 5,772	$ 4,806
Coupon sales	31,213	30,241
Total promotion/advertising sales	$ 36,985	$ 35,047
Gross pizza sales	$457,677	$384,995
Cost of pizza dough	$ 20,530	$ 17,793
Cost of toppings	38,066	30,666
Cost of cheese	47,944	41,698
Cost of paper—pizza	6,580	5,663
Freight	99	1,157
Total pizza cost	$113,219	$ 96,977
Gross profit on pizza	$344,458	$288,018
Beer		
Sales	$ 13,747	$ 13,236
Costs	4,453	4,004
Gross profit on beer	$ 9,294	$ 9,232
Drinks		
Sales	$ 39,599	$ 33,200
Costs	8,162	6,584
Gross profit on soft drinks	$ 31,437	$ 26,616
Other		
Salad sales	$ 26,295	$ 27,012
Pasta sales	9,069	9,873
Sandwich sales	5,615	4,805
Other promotion/advertising revenue	5,278	5,482
Total other sales	$ 46,257	$ 47,172
Cost of other sales	18,572	20,649
Gross profit on other sales	$ 27,685	$ 26,523

a per-item breakdown of food and beverage sales and costs for 1984–85. Studies indicated that the quality of the pizza was the most important reason customers visited the St. George Street location, with service being high on their list as well.

SALES FLUCTUATIONS

Over any 12-month period, sales at the St. George Street restaurant were lowest in January, February, and March. Sales in these months accounted for only 13 percent of yearly revenues. April through June sales accounted for 24 percent of yearly sales, while 31 percent of annual sales occurred between October and December. The highest sales period was between July and September, where 32 percent of annual sales were realized. September, which accounted for 18 percent of annual sales alone, was typically the best month for the restaurant. The high sales levels in September were due to Roebuck High School's weekly football games. After the games spectators and students often meet for an evening snack at Pizza Delights.

Sales fluctuations also occurred during the week (see Exhibit 14). Monday was the slowest day, accounting for 8.5 percent of weekly sales. Friday's sales were the highest (23.4 percent).

Lunch sales were always low. The best day for lunchtime sales was Friday, but even on this day lunch sales averaged only 3.3 percent of weekly revenues. The slowest day for lunch was Tuesday, which accounted for a mere 1.8 percent of weekly sales. When the Italian turnover pizza was introduced as a strictly lunchtime item, the Pizza Delights Corporation felt that sales for lunch would increase. However, this situation did not occur at the St. George Street location; sales simply shifted from the small pan pizzas to the Italian turnovers.

ADVERTISING AND SALES PROMOTION

Pizza Delight's advertising could be divided into three types: national, co-op, and local ads. National advertising was done countrywide, targeting mass markets to familiarize people with the Pizza Delights name as well as its products. Co-op advertising was done on a district-by-district basis and included mention for the individual restaurants and products. Both types of ads were financed by the restaurants on a percentage-of-sales basis. This arrangement applied to company-owned and franchised restaurants. Neither company-owned nor franchised restaurants had any input into these decisions and basically just implemented whatever campaign the corporation recommended.

EXHIBIT 14 Daily sales breakdowns

	Lunch		Dinner	
	Dollars	Percent	Dollars	Percent
Monday	$198	1.9%	$ 692	6.6%
Tuesday	186	1.8	716	6.8
Wednesday	191	1.8	874	8.3
Thursday	260	2.5	1,390	13.3
Friday	350	3.3	2,105	20.0
Saturday	308	2.9	1,761	16.8
Sunday	205	1.9	1,277	12.1
Sales per week	$1,698		$8,815	

Local ads were paid for by the individual restaurants and placed in local papers. Franchise owners had greater discretion than managers of company-owned restaurants concerning the types and amounts of local promotions used. The St. George Street restaurant's advertising expenses amounted to over $29,000 in 1985. As shown in Exhibit 1, this represented a substantial increase over advertising expenses for 1983 and 1984.

All national and co-op advertising for the St. George Street location was coordinated by an advertising firm in Washington, D.C. A sample announcement of a new national promotional campaign for the Italian turnover is provided in Exhibit 15. The main

EXHIBIT 15 Promotional announcement to Spartanburg Pizza Delights

---

HOT NEWS FROM YOUR FRIENDS AT BEAUMONT GREEN ADVERTISING

To: Pizza Delights managers and employees/Spartanburg
Date: February 26, 1986
Subject: Advertising for the Italian turnover

Background

Many of you will recall the tremendous success that the introduction of the small pan pizza had on our business in 1983. In 1986, the opportunity to stimulate both trial and frequency at lunch lies mainly in the area of menu expansion. Therefore, the Italian turnover has been developed. This new product will increase your sales and profits at lunch. You have all shown your operational strength with the double-decker pizza introduced in 1984. Let's make the Italian turnover the success story of 1986!

Television

Starting March 14, 1986, and running through May 1, 1986, three new TV commercials focusing on the Italian turnover will be run.

Radio promotions

A radio promotion has been developed and implemented. This promotion is provided free of charge in exchange for Italian turnovers for give-aways. Details of the promotion are provided below.

WASQ-FM will encourage listeners to be the X number caller that spotted the WASQ logo on one of the Italian turnover outdoor billboards. Winner receives two Italian turnovers and two medium soft drinks. There to be three give-aways per day, Monday thru Friday, for a total of 60 give-aways.

Outdoor

There will be #18 outdoor boards strategically placed in the area. The message will be "Turn over a New Lunch with the Italian Turnover," which is the main print advertising theme for the introduction of the Italian turnover. These boards will be posted from March 26, 1986, to May 10, 1986.

component of the co-op advertising for the greater Spartanburg area restaurants was a monthly four-color, free-standing insert in the city newspaper. This ad usually was accompanied by coupons for selected items, allowing customers a 15 to 20 percent discount off regular prices. The bulk of the greater Spartanburg area co-op advertising was done in the fall, when sales tended to be the highest.

The St. George Street location also did a variety of sales promotions. If a child read five books in one month, he or she would receive a free small pan pizza. The restaurant also did birthday parties and allowed participants the opportunity to create their own pizzas in the kitchen. Two other promotions which the St. George Street restaurant ran in the past were "family night" and "football night." Family night was a dinner promotion in which a family could buy a large pizza and a pitcher of soft drinks for $9.95. This was a companywide promotional effort which was discontinued because of low response on a national level. However, this promotion was a huge success at the St. George Street restaurant. The football promotion involved taking small pan pizzas to the Roebuck High School game and selling them with a soft drink for 99 cents. This promotion was also discontinued because the district office felt that it would ruin Pizza Delight's high-quality/high-service image. Despite the district office's concerns, the football night promotion received tremendous consumer response, usually producing sales of around $800 per game.

INTERNAL OPERATIONS

Order Processing

As shown in the work flow diagram of the St. George Street restaurant provided in Exhibit 16, when an order was punched into the computer terminals located at the waitress station and the cash register, it was printed out on a printer located over the cook's make table and at the waitress station. If the order was for a pan pizza, the cook had to walk 20 feet to the walk-in cooler and get a dough shell. If the order was for a double-decker pizza, the dough was rolled out on the table at that time. The pizza, whether it was regular, double decker, or pan, was then made on the table and placed in the oven.

Next, the ticket was placed on an order stand at the end of the make table, where an employee in charge would place it on a ticket holder. When sales volume was extremely high (for example, on the weekends), the movement of the ticket led to problems and lost pizzas.

After the pizza was cooked, it was given to the customer at the cash register, where payment was also received in the case of to-go orders. For in-store orders, the waitress would take it and the ticket out to the customer.

Operating Concerns

Outbanks realized that there were several major problems at his restaurant that needed to be corrected. All of these problems troubled him, but none had yet been solved.

Most of Outbanks' concerns stemmed from the physical facilities at the restaurant itself. Cooler space at the restaurant was inadequate. Frequent opening and closing of the cooler kept items from staying cold. This led to several problems in trying to

EXHIBIT 16
Work flow diagram

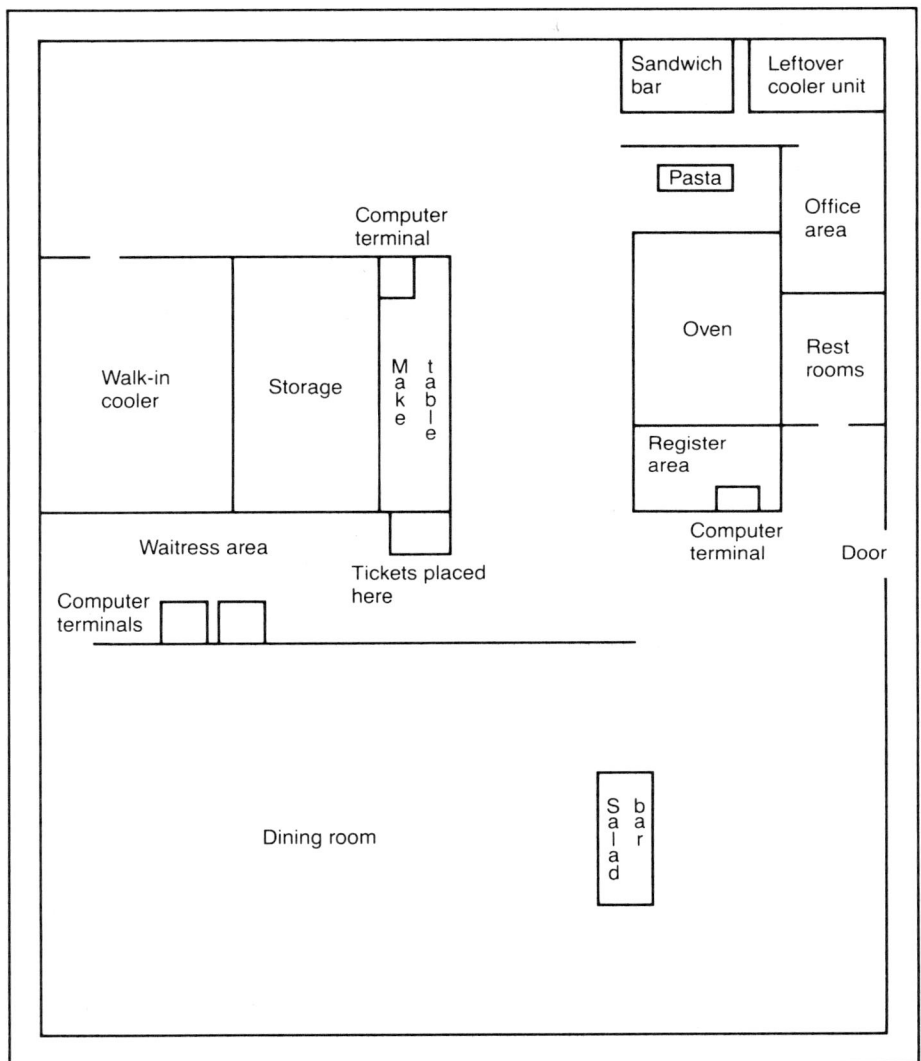

maintain high-quality products. For example, customers consistently complained that the beer was too warm, perhaps explaining why beer sales had not increased like other items had. Keeping beer cold was not the only concern. According to Outbanks, because pizza ingredients and other foods were not kept cold enough, inventory spoilage was very high ($175–$200 per month) and was increasing. To make matters worse, each Friday and Saturday when sales reached their weekly peak, employees had to shuffle other items around in the walk-in freezer to make room for the dough shells. This situation often caused older stock to be used last, leading to an even larger amount of spoilage.

Outbanks had spoken to the district manager about purchasing a new walk-in cooler for the restaurant but had no idea how long it would take for the Pizza Delights hierarchy to approve the purchase. The new walk-in cooler was estimated to cost approximately $11,000.

Outbanks' restaurant had several other capacity problems which needed to be corrected. In 1986, the restaurant used a conveyor-type oven in its operations. The oven was only two years old and was in good repair. It had two conveyors. The upper conveyor was kept in operation at all times; the lower conveyor was used only during peak periods. Both conveyors were 10 feet long. Up to four uncooked pizzas could be loaded on the first 2 feet of each conveyor. The oven itself was 6 feet long and could accommodate up to 12 pizzas at a time, 6 per conveyor. The last 2 feet of the conveyors were used to allow the pizzas to cool off before serving. The conveyor oven allowed a more uniform-quality pizza than the traditional oven. However, for preparing other items (such as spaghetti or hot sandwiches), the traditional oven had an advantage over the conveyor oven.

Another limitation was that the speed of the conveyors which passed through the oven could not be adjusted up or down. As a result, the pizzas and other products could not be cooked any faster than the conveyor allowed. Although cooking time for the conveyor-type oven was faster (eight minutes for cooking and one minute for cooling) than traditional pizza ovens under normal circumstances, it limited the number of products which could be produced on an extremely busy night. With traditional ovens, on the other hand, it was possible to ''stack'' cook the pizzas. This procedure, while lowering the quality of the final product (e.g., burnt pizzas) and sometimes creating confusion among the workers, did allow many more pizzas to be cooked during the course of an evening. Outbanks had considered purchasing another conveyor oven at an installed price of $12,500 but had not discussed this idea with the area supervisor or with Leonard Lloyd. By contrast, a traditional oven would cost $8,200 installed.

Limited dining room and parking capacity also constrained sales. The dining room consisted of 22 tables, which could seat 88 customers. During peak sales nights, customers were forced to form a line out the door while waiting for an empty seat. Furthermore, the parking lot had only 30 spaces, which created havoc on Friday and Saturday nights as take-out customers tried to rush in and out, while families and friends slowly ushered their way into the line for dining in. Due to the limited parking, employees were required to park in a dirt field behind the restaurant. Outbanks estimated paving the field would allow 15 extra parking spaces for customers at a cost of $8,000.

EMPLOYEES

Outbanks' staff included two assistant managers, Pete Gorman and Betty Franks. Gorman, a 36-year-old ex-high school teacher, had been an assistant manager at another Pizza Delights for several years prior to joining Outbanks' staff. He was considered a stringent, rule-oriented manager, who was trying to do everything in his power to gain a head-manager position. Franks was a recent graduate of Clemson University. She had brought many innovative ideas to the restaurant, including the idea to weigh out the cheese instead of using cheese cups as had been done previously. Outbanks had not totally accepted this idea, but since he knew of a manager in another location who had cut his cheese costs by 10 percent using this technique, he decided it was worth a second look. The assistant managers were responsible for supervising the restaurant when Outbanks was not working and for helping him with other managerial chores, such as purchasing, inventory, scheduling, and so on. Both assistant managers were required to work a minimum of 55 hours per week. Assistant managers were paid $5.80 per hour for the first 55 hours worked and time-and-one-half for any additional hours after that.

In addition to Outbanks, Gorman, and Franks, the St. George Street restaurant employed 17 hourly workers, including 6 waitresses, 7 cooks, 2 dishwashers, and two "employees in charge" (EICs). The majority of these employees worked on a part-time basis. All employees were evaluated every six months, and they automatically received a 10-cent raise regardless of performance.

The waitresses were paid on an hourly basis, below the minimum wage. Nonetheless, with tips included, their overall wage usually amounted to well above the hourly minimum wage of $3.35. The waitress was responsible for seating customers, taking orders, and presenting the product to the customer. Since waitresses were continuously in contact with the consumer, they played a vital role in providing the excellent service that Pizza Delights was famous for.

The cooks were hired at, or slightly above, the minimum wage. Their duties included doing the prep work, cooking the food, and ensuring the cleanliness of the facility. They also played a vital role in the business by ensuring that the food prepared was of the highest quality possible.

The dishwashers were usually hired at minimum wage and were usually promoted to cook after a few months. Besides washing dishes, their duties included keeping the dining room and other work areas as clean as possible.

The EICs were those cooks or waitresses that, through experience and expertise, had shown that they could handle additional responsibilities. Paid in excess of $4 per hour, they were responsible for the supervision of the cooking processes and the daily bookkeeping. They were, thus, instrumental in ensuring product quality.

Commenting on his employees, Earnest Outbanks once said, "The St. George Street Pizza Delights is a quality restaurant because everyone from me to the dishwashers works as a team to provide the best product, with the best service to our customers." This was in stark contrast to the way the restaurant had been operated prior to Outbanks assuming the manager's position in 1981. Despite the improvements made in this area, Outbanks also realized that, in general, employee commitment was low due to the fact that the cooks and waitresses were generally young college or high school students who often had conflicting responsibilities, such as school or another job.

LABOR COSTS

By company policy, all labor costs were computed daily. Pizza Delights had established a labor grid, which stipulated how many employees were needed each hour the restaurant was open based on normal per-hour sales. One labor grid was used during lunch hours (11 A.M. to 4 P.M.), and another was used for dinner hours (4 P.M. to closing). These grids are provided in Exhibit 17. Outbanks also used the average break times of employees to compute his daily labor costs. At the end of the day, the actual number of hours was compared to the suggested labor grid hours. Any variances had to be explained to the district manager.

The number of employees needed per sales dollar was higher during lunch hours because of the lower per-item price of lunchtime products and because of the extra

EXHIBIT 17 Projected labor schedule—lunch and dinner

Lunch		Dinner	
Projected sales per hour	Projected labor needs (number of workers)	Projected sales per hour	Projected labor needs (number of workers)
$ 0– 41	2	$ 0– 95	2
42– 61	3	96–143	3
62– 87	4	144–190	4
88–119	5	191–211	5
120–156	6	212–255	6
157–180	8	256–295	8
181–202	9	296–338	9
203–245	10	339–379	10
246–298	11	380–423	11
299–342	12	424–461	12
343–387	13	462–507	13
388–450	14	508–547	14
451–519	15	548–589	15
520–614	16	590–631	16
615–695	17	632–673	17

Notes to labor schedule:

Average total hours of breaktime per week:

Monday	Tuesday	Wednesday	Thursday	Friday	Saturday	Sunday
2.6	2.6	2.9	3.5	4.6	4.2	1.9

Average hourly pay scale per position:

Assistant managers	$5.80
Employees in charge	$4.10
Cook	$3.45
Waitresses	$2.30 plus tips
Dishwasher	$3.35

demands in providing a 10-minute guarantee for serving the small pan and Italian turnover pizzas.

Since the introduction of the Italian turnover pizza, Pizza Delights required that a minimum of 10 employees be present during the guaranteed hours of 11 A.M. to 1:30 P.M., Monday thru Friday, in order to better promote the new product. No minimum was specified for the weekends, however. Before it was introduced, the St. George Street restaurant was operated quite efficiently with a total of 28 employee-hours between 8 A.M. and 4 P.M. on Monday, Tuesday, Wednesday, Saturday, and Sunday; 33 total employee-hours on Thursday; and 38 total employee-hours on Friday. These hours had increased to almost 55 hours per day on average during the weekdays, due to Pizza Delight's new policy after the Italian turnover pizza was introduced. Since Outbanks had not realized any additional profits from the Italian turnover, he wondered if he could operate the restaurant as profitably as he did before it was introduced.

LLOYD'S GREER AREA
PIZZA DELIGHTS FRANCHISE OPERATIONS

With a population of approximately 10,000 persons in 1985, Greer, South Carolina, could be categorized as a typical small southern town. The inhabitants of this small community were very family oriented. The town was custom made for a restaurant providing a high level of customer service, as Lloyd's original Pizza Delights franchise did.

Eating out was not very common in Greer in the early 1970s, partly because there were only two places in town to eat (a diner and a truck stop) and partly because the residents generally preferred to eat at home. However, in the mid-1970s the attitudes of the population began to change as several fast-food restaurants were opened. Grabbing a hamburger or some chicken after church or after a Little League game became fashionable and convenient.

Lloyd's Pizza Delights restaurant was the last fast-food restaurant built in the community, although it was company owned during the first three years of operations. Recognizing the potential of the restaurant, Lloyd, an area businessman, purchased the franchise from Pizza Delights in 1981 for $375,000 plus $1.2 million for the right to use the company's brand name.

In his first year of operation Lloyd succeeded in increasing the seating capacity at the restaurant from 65 to 150 people. He felt that the demand for pizza in the Greer area could easily accommodate a dining area of that size. Sales revenues increased 7 percent that year. However, the restaurant did not operate at full capacity.

In 1982, disenchanted by the slow growth in sales, Lloyd decided to offer customers more specials and new dining options. Two-for-one coupons were placed in the local newspapers on a regular basis. Taking advantage of his two ovens and massive dining area, Lloyd also began to offer a lunch buffet during the weekdays to attract students from a nearby community college. Sales revenues increased by 10 percent almost overnight, and many customers began inquiring about the possibility of a Sunday buffet. Lloyd's decision to extend the buffet to Sundays allowed him to capture a significant share of the after-church market, increasing sales during a time of the week when sales had traditionally been low.

The first Greer franchise restaurant was very successful, with sales increasing by about one third since 1982. The only direct pizza competitor for the Greer restaurant was Papa Joe's. This restaurant offered relatively little service and relied almost entirely on take-out business.

Due to his success at the Greer location, Lloyd had purchased the franchises to two additional Pizza Delights restaurants in two small rural communities, both approximately 5 to 10 miles outside of Greer, in 1983 and 1984. Both of these restaurants followed the same strategy as the Greer restaurant, and both were profitable. Lloyd had been able to retain the managers who had previously worked for the Pizza Delights Corporation by giving them a minority ownership position in these restaurants.

LLOYD'S PLAN

Although Lloyd had not worked out all the details of how the St. George Street restaurant should be operated, he had made some initial inquiries at the Pizza Delights' district office in Columbia, South Carolina, to determine if purchasing the restaurant would be feasible. The district office quoted Lloyd a price of $725,000 for the physical facilities plus an annual payment of 12 percent of the restaurant's net profits before taxes. The Pizza Delights brand name was valued at over $1 million. However, Lloyd knew he would not have to pay this fee since he had already purchased the brand rights for the Greer restaurants.

Lloyd hoped that many of the same strategies he had used at the Greer restaurants would be feasible at the St. George Street location. He wanted to offer a buffet-style dinner or lunch to customers at least once or twice a week. He also wanted to try to offer more in the way of coupon and promotional gimmicks to attract more customers and balance out sales. Outbanks had wanted to attempt such a move for several years but had been constrained by the corporation's policies. Franchising would at least partially solve this problem.

All these policies had been quite successful in Greer, and Lloyd saw no reason why these successes would not be transferable to the Roebuck/Spartanburg area despite the differences between the two locales. In addition, Lloyd toyed with the idea of setting up a delivery service at the St. George Street location. Spartanburg was a college town, and Lloyd expected that such a service would be welcomed by students in the area. If a delivery operation was started, it would require two half-time employees (paid at the minimum wage) plus the purchase of two used cars for approximately $5,000 apiece. Gas, maintenance, depreciation, and other related operating expenses associated with the vehicle were estimated at 20 cents per mile.

Lloyd felt that these proven strategies, combined with new ideas and Outbanks' managerial abilities, would ensure success for the St. George Street location.

FRANCHISE OWNERSHIP AND FINANCING ARRANGEMENTS

Lloyd was prepared to invest $250,000 in the St. George Street restaurant and planned to borrow the rest of the needed capital from one of the financial institutions in the area. In 1986 the prime rate for commercial borrowing was 7.5 percent. However, Lloyd realized that he would probably be required to pay a premium of at least 1.5–2.5 percent over prime.

After talking with a Spartanburg banker, Lloyd learned that he would need a minimum of 25 percent equity to back the franchise and would be required to give the bank a first mortgage on the restaurant, as well as pledge all his personal assets as security. The loan itself would probably be a term loan amortized over 15 years, with a balloon payment after 3 to 5 years. Lloyd figured that payments for a straight 15-year amortized loan of $500,000 at 10 percent interest would amount to $5,373 per month or almost $65,000 per year.

The Spartanburg banker also informed Lloyd that franchise loans were not frequently approved by her bank, citing an example of another Pizza Delights franchise in Greenwood, South Carolina, that was recently denied a loan. Exhibits 18 and 19 provide the income statement and balance sheet for the Greenwood Pizza Delights franchise.

Lloyd was not particularly worried by the banker's pessimism, however, as the types of loans sought differed (the Greenwood franchise wanted capital for equipment purchases and for building a new restaurant), the local area environments differed (Greenwood was a rural community more like Greer than Spartanburg in terms of population and area demographics), and the financial performance of the St. George Street restaurant was stronger. Lloyd also had a successful track record in business and had never experienced problems obtaining financing in the past; he saw no reason why it would be different this time around.

Although all the details had not been discussed, as part of the proposed franchising plan, Outbanks was expecting to receive a one-quarter to one-third interest in the store, plus his normal salary, for services rendered. Outbanks also expected to have complete control over the day-to-day operations of the restaurant. In respect to strategy and policy matters, Outbanks believed that both he and Lloyd would have an equal voice. Such an arrangement, Outbanks felt, was similar to the deal Lloyd had made with the managers at his franchise restaurants in Greer.

Outbanks also expected to be required to cosign the note and pledge his personal assets as collateral. His financial commitment to the franchise would be considerably less than Lloyd's, though, as Outbanks had only around $25,000 to $30,000 to invest.

EARNEST'S DILEMMA

After turning over the pros and cons of current operations in his mind, Outbanks still was not sure whether he should join Lloyd in the franchising venture or stay with the company and try to progress up the corporate ladder. Outbanks did understand

EXHIBIT 18

1985 income statement for the Greenwood Pizza Delights

Sales		$638,284
Food in	$322,928	
Food out	239,260	
Food delivery	14,064	
Food subtotal	$576,252	
Beverages in	$ 61,612	
Beverages delivery	120	
Beverages subtotal	$ 61,732	
Premiums	$ 300	
Cost of goods sold:		
Food cost	167,600	
Beverage cost	16,800	
Premiums	0	184,400
Gross profit		$453,884
Operating expenses:		
Advertising	$ 22,000	
Auto and delivery expenses	600	
Payroll	198,325	
Repairs	19,403	
Utilities and telephone	30,504	
Operating supplies	10,320	
Other operating expenses	22,408	303,560
Operating profit		$150,324
Administrative expenses:		
Royalty fee	19,000	
Insurance	12,450	
Interest	7,770	
Depreciation	27,250	
Rent	42,000	
Taxes and licenses	4,000	
Other administrative expenses	18,610	131,080
Net profit before taxes		$ 19,244

that his restaurant was currently making hefty profits (Exhibit 1), profits that he was not sharing in. He also understood that he was responsible for most of the restaurant's current successes. Moreover, he admired Lloyd for his success with the Greer Pizza Delights franchises. Nonetheless, Outbanks wondered if Lloyd's plans, which had worked so well in Greer, would achieve comparable levels of success in the St. George Street restaurant. He also knew that Pizza Delights was growing rapidly and that there might soon be an area supervisor position open for a young, energetic manager with a proven track record.

EXHIBIT 19
1985 balance sheet
for the Greenwood
Pizza Delights

Assets		
Cash in bank	– $ 14,200	
Cash on hand	1,000	
Investments	2,700	
Accounts receivable	1,500	
Inventory	$ 7,500	
Total current assets	– 1,500	
Automobiles	$ 17,500	
Less: Depreciation	– 9,500	
Net automobiles	$ 8,000	
Equipment	$150,000	
Less: Depreciation	– 70,000	
Net equipment	$ 80,000	
Leasehold improvements	$ 10,200	
Less: Depreciation	– 3,000	
Net leasehold	$ 7,200	
Total fixed assets	$ 95,200	
Deposits	$ 220	
Insurance reserve fund	1,700	
Prepaid insurance	3,000	
Prepaid rent	4,200	
Franchise fees	17,000	
Total other noncurrent assets	$ 26,120	
Total Assets		$119,820
Liabilities		
Accounts payable	$ 650	
Other current liabilities	13,300	
Total current liabilities	$ 13,950	
Long-term liabilities	$ 50,000	$ 63,950
Equity		$ 55,870
Total		$119,820

Personal problems also caused Outbanks to wonder whether he would continue to have the time, money, and motivation to devote to such a venture. A major dispute with his now-estranged wife had greatly taxed Outbanks' mental and physical endurance. This dispute, which Outbanks expected to end in divorce, was also likely to deplete his financial resources once it had been settled.

Despite all the problems Outbanks had to contend with, as he began to prepare for closing time he knew it was time to fish or cut bait. He resolved that he would give Lloyd his decision before the end of the following week.

THE MARRIOTT CORPORATION, 1984

J. W. Marriott, Jr., president and CEO of Marriott Corporation, glanced at the calendar clock on his desk and reminded himself that the date was 7 January 1985. But his mind really wasn't on this day's events. Instead he was thinking about the future. He wondered what lay ahead for Marriott in the next five years, and especially in 1985.

J. W. was principally concerned with the overbuilding in the lodging industry and the provisions of the proposed 1985 Tax Act. He could readily recall grimacing at the headline "U.S. Lodging Industry Is Staggered by Room Glut and Building Boom" in *The Wall Street Journal*. The article had confirmed Marriott's own market research. He vividly remembered the quote attributed to Tom Herring, Sr., the president of the American Hotel and Motel association: "We're on a collision course with disaster if we don't do something about the overbuilding." J. W. had chatted with Tom several times recently and knew that Tom meant what he said. Perhaps more ominous were the proposals by the U.S. Treasury Department to virtually eliminate business deductions for travel. A lot of empty hotels would result. (Exhibit 1 contains the proposed changes in the tax laws.) J. W. did not really believe that the proposed revisions would pass, but he felt that you never could tell about such things. He wanted his firm to be prepared for the most likely scenarios.

THE MARRIOTT CORPORATION

The Marriott Corporation is a diversified company organized into four divisions: Hotels and Resorts, Contract Food Services, Restaurants, and, until 1983, Theme Parks/Cruise Ships. Annual sales surpassed $3 billion in 1983 and exceeded $3.5 billion in 1984, as Exhibits 2 and 3 indicate. Marriott has facilities in forty-nine U.S. states and twenty-five countries and employs more than 109,000 people, who make an estimated 6 million customer contacts yearly.

Prepared by Julian N. Vincze, Crummer Graduate School of Business at Rollins College. This case represents neither effective nor ineffective administrative decisions. Rather, it is to be used as a basis for classroom discussion. All rights reserved to the author.

EXHIBIT 1 Lodging industry braces for tax changes

The U. S. Treasury has proposed limiting deductions for out-of-town business trips and for business meals. In addition the Treasury would completely eliminate entertainment expense deductions for such items as club dues, cruise ship travel, and tickets to professional sports events.

If the Treasury's plan becomes law, the proposal is to limit out-of-town business travel expenses to a maximum of $150 per day, and for some areas (cities) of the country this would be a maximum of $100 per day. These maximums do not include the costs incurred in traveling to the destination city from the traveler's home base of business. Instead the limits per day are for lodging, meals, and other business expenses incurred at the destination city.

These limits are very restrictive, says a spokesperson for the restaurant industry. For example, the Florida Restaurant Association says that the meal limits proposed by the Treasury at $10 for breakfast, $15 for lunch, and $25 for dinner, aren't realistic because they "don't take regional differences into account."

Source: Vick Vaughan, "Industry Braces for Tax Overhaul," *Central Florida Business,* January 7–13, 1985, pp. 10–15.

EXHIBIT 2 Marriott Corporation and Subsidiaries Income Statements, 1981–1984 (in thousands of dollars except per share amounts)

	1984	1983	1982	1981
Sales				
Hotels	$1,640,782	$1,320,535	$1,091,673	$ 860,134
Contract food services	1,111,300	950,617	819,824	599,050
Restaurants	772,855	679,375	547,403	446,475
Theme parks	—	86,176	82,453	94,655
Total sales	$3,524,937	$3,036,703	$2,541,353	$2,000,314
Operating Income				
Hotels	$ 161,245	$ 139,706	$ 132,648	$ 117,561
Contract food services	90,250	73,300	51,006	45,552
Restaurants	76,220	61,634	48,492	38,533
Theme parks	—	13,041	20,004	17,714
Total operating income	$ 327,715	$ 287,681	$ 252,150	$ 219,360
Interest expense, net	48,691	55,270	66,666	52,024
Corporate expenses	42,921	34,309	31,801	28,307
Income before income taxes	$ 240,613	$ 198,102	$ 153,683	$ 139,029
Provision for income taxes	100,848	82,857	59,341	52,893
Net Income	$ 139,765	$ 115,245	$ 94,342	$ 86,136
Earnings per share				
Primary	$ 5.18	$ 4.15	$ 3.46	$ 3.21
Fully diluted	$ 5.18	$ 4.15	$ 3.44	$ 3.20

Source: Marriott Corporation annual reports.

EXHIBIT 3 Marriott Corporation and subsidiaries balance sheet, 1982–1984 (in thousands of dollars)

	1984	1983	1982
Assets			
Current assets			
Cash and temporary cash investments	$ 22,656	$ 92,279	$ 89,811
Accounts receivable	242,341	169,630	167,173
Inventories, at lower of average cost or market	111,722	95,806	89,071
Prepaid expenses	53,330	43,655	35,617
Total current assets	$ 430,049	$ 401,370	$ 381,672
Property and equipment, at cost			
Land	$ 141,714	$ 171,984	$ 153,528
Buildings and improvements	245,367	373,593	419,634
Leasehold improvements	658,815	716,461	564,284
Furniture and equipment	415,634	475,003	446,133
Property under capital leases	77,566	86,539	89,297
Construction in progress	668,845	388,025	200,808
Total property and equipment	$2,207,941	$2,211,605	$1,873,684
Depreciation and amortization	(375,108)	(419,823)	(379,457)
Total property and equipment less depreciation and amortization	$1,832,833	$1,791,782	$1,494,227
Other assets			
Investments in and advances to affiliates	$ 268,177	$ 68,412	$ 42,961
Assets held for sale	230,760	81,312	27,979
Cost in excess of net assets of businesses acquired	26,742	26,380	26,929
Other	116,058	132,172	88,880
Total other assets	$ 641,737	$ 308,276	$ 186,749
Total assets	$2,904,669	$2,501,428	$2,062,648
Liabilities and shareholders' equity			
Current liabilities			
Short-term loans	$ 7,486	$ 8,895	$ 9,155
Accounts payable	252,806	194,499	183,043
Accrued wages and benefits	129,452	111,420	91,145
Other payables and accrued liabilities	152,654	149,308	116,903
Current portion of debt and capital lease obligations	31,588	29,799	27,898
Total current liabilities	$ 573,986	$ 493,921	$ 428,144
Debt			
Mortgage notes payable	$632,923	$491,999	$182,455
Unsecured notes payable	420,860	509,144	627,854
Total debt	$1,053,783	$1,001,143	$ 810,309
Capital lease obligations	$ 61,504	$ 70,468	$ 79,016
Other long-term liabilities	259,694	60,009	61,420
Deferred income taxes	280,142	247,683	167,754

EXHIBIT 3 (continued)

EXHIBIT 3 (continued)

	1984	1983	1982
Shareholders' equity			
Common stock	$ 29,419	$ 29,422	$ 29,424
Capital surplus	145,756	140,882	135,589
Deferred stock compensation and other	3,141	4,160	6,671
Retained earnings	622,283	494,585	389,524
Treasury stock, at cost	(125,039)	(40,845)	(45,203)
Total shareholders' equity	$ 675,560	$ 628,204	$ 516,005
Total liabilities and shareholders' equity	$2,904,669	$2,501,428	$2,062,648

Source: Marriott Corporation annual reports.

Founded in 1927 by J. Willard Marriott, who is still chairman, the company began as a small root beer stand. Marriott is dedicated to taking special care of people away from home. The primary objective of Marriott is ''to be the premier company in lodging, food service and related areas.'' 1984 had been one of Marriott's most memorable years of operation, filled with major events that had made it a very successful year, as Exhibit 2 reveals.

DISTINCTIVE ASPECTS

One reason for Marriott's success is the relationship between guests and employees. The company provides an environment which stimulates pride and performance. Employees are encouraged to have the hospitable and friendly spirit that has become a Marriott trademark.

The Marriott Corporation became the largest chain of company-operated hotel rooms in America in 1984. It has strong management training and development system and controls that help maintain an unsurpassed reputation.

The strategic planning, market research, and business development staffs work closely with senior operating executives to develop new opportunities. These new opportunities include the Host and Gino's acquisitions, as well as the internal developments. (See Exhibit 4.)

Marriott is one of the largest developers in the country utilizing another key skill — real estate expertise. Each year it develops hotels and restaurants valued at over $1 billion. These are designed and constructed through a fully integrated internal department.

Marriott's management is characterized as strong, stable, and aggressive. The top 100 executives average 12 years of experience with the company.

EXHIBIT 4 Acquisition of Host and Gino's

Host International, Inc.
Purchase date: March 3, 1982.
Purchase price: Reported at $204,725,000.
Type of business: Operator of bars and shops in airports (nationwide).
Base of operations: California.

Gino's, Inc.
Purchase date: February 5, 1982.
Purchase price: Reported at $112,725,000.
Type of business: Restaurant operations with a total of 308 locations.
                      108 Rustler Steak Houses included in purchase (resold in 1983).
                      180 of the units acquired were updated and turned into Roy Rogers units
                        (this conversion began in May 1982 and was estimated to take 20
                        months).
Base of operations: Mid-Atlantic market (Baltimore north to northern New Jersey).

Sources: *Marriott Corporation Annual Report*, 1983; *Business Week*, February 1, 1982.

Financial Policies

Creative, sophisticated financial skills have been used to repurchase the company's stock, to dispose of nearly $200 million in underproductive assets, and to finance $3 billion in hotels since 1978.

Marriott's financial policies of importance to shareholders involve cash flow, cost of capital, debt maturity, and working capital. These financial policies are important because Marriott's ambitious capital investment and acquisition programs are financed by a combination of retained discretionary cash flow, incremental debt on an expanding asset base, and sales of hotels with management agreements. Careful management of Marriott's highly liquid hotel assets and debt structure has enabled the company to maintain targeted leverage and to minimize capital costs. (Exhibit 5 details discretionary cash flow.) Marriott bases target debt levels on cash-flow coverage of four times interest expense. Marriott's coverage objective is reported to be what lenders require to provide the company with debt financing at prime rates.

Despite aggressive expansion, Marriott financing techniques maintained coverage

EXHIBIT 5
Discretionary cash flow vs. net income, 1979–1984 (in millions of dollars)

Year	Cash Flow	Net Income
1984	$278	$140
1983	246	115
1982	192	94
1981	157	86
1980	125	72
1979	118	71

Source: Marriott Corporation annual reports.

at targeted levels. Today capital spending of $800 million in 1984, $499 million in 1983, and $667 million in 1982 (including the Gino's and Host acquisitions) was financed primarily from internal cash flow and hotel dispositions.

The ability to grow aggressively yet maintain planned coverage demonstrates that Marriott's high discretionary cash flow ($8.85 per share versus EPS of $4.15 in 1983), combined with the declining capital intensity of the company's hotel business, has allowed Marriott to expand hotel rooms 20 percent annually without commensurate capital requirements. As a result, investment capacity has been released to fund additional corporate growth, such as the 1982 Host and Gino's acquisitions.

Marriott's objective is to minimize the cost of capital by optimizing a mix of fixed and floating interest rate debt obligations. Marriott believes operating cash flows have a high correlation with inflation and short-term interest rates. Therefore the desired optimal debt structure requires a significant quantity of floating-rate debt to minimize capital cost and risk. In addition, the company requires that construction in progress be financed in the traditional manner with floating-rate debt. Excluding construction financing, long-term debt with floating interest rates averaged 58 percent of total debt capitalization in 1983, compared to 60 percent in 1982.

Marriott has followed a policy of avoiding new commitments of nonprepayable, fixed-rate, long-term debt since 1980. Rather than speculate on fixed interest rates at relatively high levels, the company has matched capital costs with cash flows, thus attempting to minimize capital cost and risk.

Debt maturity remains within Marriott's conservative policy limits, which require that total debt amortizing in the subsequent five-year period not exceed funds provided from operations of the prior year. The company has met this policy constraint by wide margins since 1979, as Exhibit 6 indicates.

Marriott has no requirement for positive working capital, since it principally sells services (rather than goods) for cash. Therefore, the company maintains relatively low receivable and cash balances. Negative working capital is a source of interest-free financing. As a result of a company-instituted program to aggressively reduce

EXHIBIT 6 Debt maturity schedule, 1979–1984 (in millions of dollars)

Year	1984	1983	1982	1981	1980	1979
1	$ 26	$ 25	$ 23	$ 16	$ 9	$ 9
2	36	36	28	17	18	18
3	50	43	36	22	18	24
4	58	50	42	40	34	27
5	72	62	48	43	38	35
Total	$242	$216	$177	$138	$117	$113
Funds provided from operations	$330	$294	$231	$187	$150	$141

Source: Marriott Corporation annual reports.

current asset investment, Marriott increased its negative working capital to $93 million at year-end 1983 and $144 million in 1984.

Lodging

The Hotels and Resorts Division, with annual sales in excess of $1.5 billion, continues to be Marriott's largest and fastest growing. The lodging operations include locations in the United States, Mexico, Central America, the Caribbean, Europe, and the Middle East.

In 1983 sales increased by 21 percent and the trend continued with a 24 percent increase in 1984. Occupancy rates also continued to be among the highest in the industry (up 3 percent in 1983), while average room rates increased by approximately the same rate as inflation.

Marriott is noted for its aggressive marketing program. This program, begun in 1982, stresses strong ties with the airlines' frequent-flier programs but also utilizes extensive promotions at the individual hotel level, the keystone of which is the emphasis on selling skills in customer-contact employees at all levels.

The corporation has excellent employee relations. Marriott reinforces its employees' positive attitudes with recognition and development programs, but also believes in internal promotion/advancement opportunities and the need for strong technological support systems. In 1983 approximately one-third of all new managers were originally hourly paid personnel.

Marriott concentrates ownership of its hotels among outside investors while retaining long-term management contracts. In fact, over 75 percent of Marriott-operated hotels are owned by outside investors. Marriott is also a leader in financing hotel growth by various methods, including private syndications, management agreements, and traditional financing. In fact, it has developed and financed more than $4 billion in hotels since 1970, $800 million in 1984 alone.

Contract Food Services (CFS)

Contract Food Services revenues amount to approximately one-third of Marriott's annual sales. CFS sales increased 16 percent in 1983 and 17 percent in 1984, while operating profit rose 30 percent in 1983 and 23 percent in 1984. CFS is the world's leading airline caterer, serving more than 150 airlines (from 80 flight kitchens located in the United States and abroad).

Since 1982, through its Marriott/Host facilities, CFS has been a major operator of airport terminal cafeterias, snack bars, full-service restaurants, gift shops, and newsstands. These airport operations at 39 domestic locations are viewed as complementing CFS's airline catering business and thereby broadening Marriott's ability to serve airline passengers.

A third area of CFS's activities involves the provision of quality meals and food-service assistance to more than 275 business, educational, and health-care facilities nationwide. CFS's services range from management supervision to facilities design and turnkey operations. CFS also manages educational facilities and conference centers for corporate clients.

In addition CFS operates a few nonairport merchandise shops and turnpike restaurants. However, CFS's strategic growth is attributed primarily to these factors:

its relatively large size and depth of experience; its productivity (low costs); and its reputation for quality in operations management, procurement capabilities, and organizational depth.

Restaurants

Marriott's Restaurants Division operates or franchises over 1,800 popularly priced restaurants in 47 states, Canada, and Japan. In 1983 a sales gain of 24 percent was reported with a 27 percent increase in operating income. The sales increase was attributed to gains in both customer counts and average amount of checks, plus the addition of 100 company-operated and franchised units. The increased income was attributed to relatively stable food and labor costs throughout the year. The two largest restaurant chains are Roy Rogers and Big Boy.

The Roy Rogers (RR) chain was founded in 1968 and provides premium-quality fast food at more than 500 locations, primarily in the Middle Atlantic region. RR has a varied menu featuring roast beef sandwiches, burgers, chicken, salad, and breakfast items. Approximately one-fourth of RR's locations are franchised.

The Big Boy (BB) chain includes more than 1,200 restaurants, making it larger than any of its direct competitors. Although founded in California more than 40 years ago, BB now is located nationwide. Most BB restaurants are franchised but more than 200 — operating under the name Bob's Big Boy — are company-owned. During 1983 the Big Boy franchise system received new emphasis via cooperative national programs in marketing, menu development, and procurement, in order that Big Boy might retain its company-perceived leadership in family restaurants.

In addition to Big Boy and Roy Rogers, Marriott operates several other theme restaurants. Over 50 specialty restaurants are in operation in California and the East Coast under the Charley Brown's/Charley's Place dinner house concept or the Casa Maria Mexican restaurant concept.

Theme Parks and Cruise Ships

Marriott's fourth division until 1983 included two Great America theme parks and three Sun Line cruise ships. In total about 5 million people annually were customers of this division. The 1983 sales revenues increased about 5 percent over the prior year but operating income declined some 35 percent.

Located in Gurnee, Illinois (between Chicago and Milwaukee), and in Santa Clara, California (near San Francisco), the theme parks were designed to have strong family appeal. Thrill and family rides, as well as games, stage shows, and restaurants, were offered. Attendance rose 9 percent in 1983 in response to lower admission prices and aggressive marketing. However, 1983's attendance was still 10 percent below the 1981 figure. Both parks were sold during 1984.

The city of Santa Clara purchased the California park for $101 million. The Gurnee park sold for approximately $114.5 million. Neither park will be operated by Marriott in the future.

The three Sun Line ships — the *Stella Oceanis,* the *Stella Maris,* and the *Stella Solaris* — offer a combined total of about 140 cruises per year. Cruises are offered on the Caribbean, Aegean, and Mediterranean seas.

By the end of 1984 Theme Parks and Cruise Ships was no longer considered a separate operating division or a "primary business line."

REMARKS TO SHAREHOLDERS — 1984 RESULTS

J. W. had asked his secretary to bring him a copy of his "Remarks to Shareholders" from the 1983 annual meeting and, as he held the document up to look at it, his memory focused on that day (10 May 1984).

He remembered beginning his remarks by noting the construction of the New York Marriott Marquis, which, at 1,900 rooms, will be Marriott's largest hotel. However, the construction list included Boston's Copley Place and Fort Lauderdale's Beach Resort (both of which opened in 1984) as well as the Atlanta Marriott Marquis (which, with the New York Marquis, was due to open in 1985), the Orlando World Center Resort (1986), and the San Francisco–Yerba Buena Center (1988). These five added a total of over 6,000 more rooms. In fact, by including the international expansions and acquisitions, especially the Vienna, Austria, 1984 opening, the planned additions to hotel rooms totaled 26,000 by 1988.

The real theme of his remarks, however, had been Marriott's "five special strengths," which "are the basis for our growth strategy." J. W. scanned the copy and recalled these five distinctive strengths as:

First, our values and systems.
Number two is our leadership position.
The third strength is our business synergy.
The fourth strength is our technical skills.
Number five, we have a strong management team.

But here J. W. paused. In his own mind the question formed: Are these still our special strengths? Or does Marriott have more than five special strengths? He didn't want to take the time now to answer these questions, but J. W. knew he would have to come back to them very soon.

Instead J. W. scanned his copy to recall how he had worded the "strategy for growth." After noting the most visible growth mechanism — "the expansion of our existing business" — which was exemplified in hotel room additions, he had highlighted other operations' "selective expansions" in general terms. But perhaps the most important major growth strategy was "acquisition and development of new businesses . . . to develop, test, and expand a number of new, yet related business opportunities."

Two specific new opportunities for 1984 had been cited, Courtyard Hotels and American Resorts Group.

Courtyard Hotels

In fact, the decision to move forward from a testing of the Courtyard concept into a major expansion mode had occurred in June of 1984, shortly after the annual shareholders' meeting. A statement had been released that Marriott planned to expand

Courtyard nationwide. Over the next 18 months between 20 and 30 Courtyards in New Jersey/New York; Washington, D.C./Baltimore; Chicago/Milwaukee; and northern California were planned. The total investment over five years would be between $1 and $2 billion. The statement also noted that by the 1990s Marriott could have more than 300 Courtyard locations with more than 5,000 rooms.

The Courtyard hotel concept had developed from Marriott's research over several years into the moderate-price segment of the lodging market. The moderate segment's current price range was considered to be between $30 and $60 per night and was referred to as the "largest part of the lodging market." Marriott had found that these customers viewed the following factors as important:

1. An attractive, comfortable, and functional room.
2. A relaxed, secure environment.
3. A relatively simple restaurant with good food.
4. A well-managed operation.
5. Friendly, helpful staff.
6. All of the above at "affordable" prices.

To meet these customer needs, Marriott had designed a small 130- to 150-room operation that required "very few employees." The targeted customer group was focused "on the transient guests . . . not the group business of a traditional hotel."

Testing of Courtyard had occurred in Atlanta, Augusta, and Columbus, Georgia, and because of the favorable results, expansion into states adjoining Georgia was planned as well as the eventual nationwide expansion noted above.

American Resorts Group

The second example of new opportunities, American Resorts Group, was viewed as an extension of Marriott's lodging and management skills. American Resorts Group is a leading developer of vacation condominiums in the time-share industry. Marriott's initial venture into the time-share industry was a 120-unit resort on Hilton Head Island in South Carolina named Monarch at Sea Pines.

J. W. knew he would have to explain carefully to the shareholders why Marriott had moved into the time-share industry. He was well aware of the many negative stories about the time-share industry which had appeared in the press recently. J. W. recognized that some shareholders were likely to have a poor opinion of the time-share industry and perhaps even the basic concept of time-sharing. It was even probable that some shareholders could have personally experienced a less-than-successful time-share investment, or at least have close relatives or friends who were unhappy about one. He knew he had to think through this "new opportunity" explanation with more than ordinary care for shareholders' sensitivities.

RECENT DEVELOPMENTS

As J. W. was pondering the ways of explaining these already-announced new opportunities which Marriott had acted upon, he also realized that other more recent developments had not yet received full disclosure. Three items immediately came to mind.

First there was the sale of the 24-unit Casa Maria restaurant operation to El Torito Restaurants, Inc., a subsidiary of W. R. Grace and Company. This divestiture was expected to be completed in early 1985 and was generally viewed as consistent with Marriott's longer-term strategy related to the purchase of Host in 1982. Casa Maria had been acquired as a part of Host in 1982, and since Host's acquisition, many locations which were considered peripheral to the Restaurant Division's main activities had been sold.

A second development related to a new approach to financial management of Marriott's assets. In August 1984 a wholly owned partnership subsidiary had been established to purchase nine existing Marriott hotels for $305 million. The new company would continue to operate these hotels as an integral part of the Marriott Hotels and Resorts Division (via management agreement with Marriott). Interests in Chesapeake Hotel Limited Partnership were offered in private placement to accredited investors in 440 units of $100,000 each.

The third development concerned a recent decision that Marriott would build all-suite hotels. Construction of the first Marriott Suites hotel was announced to begin in the spring of 1985, with about a dozen expected to open in 1988. This new hotel product was designed to compete directly with companies already in the all-suite market. Marriott Suites would be located in suburban areas, and possibly in downtown areas of medium-sized cities. Each would contain 200 to 250 suites as well as limited meeting space.

A few other developments also had occurred. For example, during 1984 Marriott had bought substantial numbers of its own shares on the open market, 1,475,000 shares during the first six months of the year. Also Marriott had reported "exploring entry into the life care community development." In an approach similar to that used for the Courtyard hotel concept, Marriott had issued a statement that the concept would be tested by the establishment of "two or three life care communities over the next four years." A decision about proceeding on a larger scale would then be made. A typical Marriott life care development was expected to accommodate approximately 300 to 400 people in a complete retirement community. Services offered would include lodging, food service, recreational facilities, and limited health-care facilities.

SUMMARY OF ITEMS TO BE EXPLAINED

At this point J. W. paused and mentally summarized the items he felt needed to be explained to shareholders:

1. Full expansion of Courtyard hotels concept (moderate-price customer segment).
2. Movement into time-share vacation ownership — American Resorts Group.
3. Continued expansion of major hotels with ongoing construction program.

4. Sales of the two Great America theme parks.
5. The sale of Casa Maria Mexican restaurants and the continued expansion of Big Boy and, to a lesser extent, Roy Rogers restaurants.
6. The testing of the Marriott Suites concept in hotels.
7. The purchase on the open market of Marriott's own stock.
8. The continuation of funding the hotel expansion program through creative financial arrangements, such as the Chesapeake Hotel Limited Partnership.

In addition to these eight items, J. W. knew he also had the traditional explanation of operating results for 1984 to offer. He knew the stockholders would be pleased with the 1984 financial results but the future role of Marriott in the lodging industry was the key issue.

REFERENCES

"Bill Marriott's Grand Design for Growth: Upscale and Down in the Lodging Market," *Business Week* (October 1, 1984), pp. 60–62.

Carmichael, Jane, "Full Speed Ahead," *Forbes* (July 5, 1982), 90–94.

Celis, William, III, "U.S. Lodging Industry Is Staggered by Room Glut and Building Boom," *Wall Street Journal* (November 26, 1984), p. 37.

"Expansion at Marriott Hits a Financial Snag," *Business Week* (June 7, 1982), p. 28.

Form 10-K, Marriott Corporation, Securities and Exchange Commission.

Gamrecki, John, "The 'New Breed': Marriott Design Transformed," *Hotel and Motel Management* (June 1982), pp. 22–23.

Karmin, Monroe W., and Robert J. Morse, "Higher Taxes? Who Would Pay?" *U.S. News & World Report* (December 10, 1984), pp. 20–24.

Marriott Corporation annual reports, 1983 and 1984.

"Marriott's New Deals Defy the Recession," *Business Week* (February 1, 1982), pp. 21–22.

Mikesell, Lillie A., "Marriott International Headquarters," *Buildings* (August 1980), pp. 35–39.

Moody's Handbook of Common Stocks (Fall 1984).

Travel Weekly 42, no. 46 (May 31, 1983) (25th anniversary issue).

Vaughan, Vicki, "Industry Braces for Overhaul," *Central Florida Business* (January 7–13, 1985), p. 15.

APPENDIX A: THE LODGING INDUSTRY

Total receipts for the lodging industry approximately $29.4 billion in 1983. This represented a 6 percent increase over the 1982 figures. For 1984 the industry was expected to top $31 billion.

WHAT THE INDUSTRY DOES

In very basic terms the lodging industry takes care of travelers' housing needs while they are away from home. The needs of today's travelers are very different from those of 1794, when the City Hotel opened in New York City. The City Hotel was purported to have been the first building constructed in the United States specifically for hotel purposes.

Business travelers typically occupy more than 60 percent of all lodging rooms, with the remaining 40 percent split almost equally between personal and convention travelers. Business travelers' needs include basic lodging plus meal services and communication facilities. However, additional services — meeting rooms, special stenographic, duplicating, and communication services, and, recreation and entertainment — are also frequently desired.

The convention travelers' needs also include the basic lodging, meal services, and communication facilities. Obvious additional needs are meeting rooms (both small and large), exhibit halls, and banquet rooms; appropriate social gathering facilities as well as significant leisure and recreational amenities may also be expected.

The personal travelers' needs are often limited to lodging and meal services, unless the location is a destination resort. Destination resorts are expected to provide extensive facilities for leisure, recreation, and socializing. Personal travel has grown steadily in recent years. Several factors which have encouraged the growth in personal travel include rising disposable personal income, stable gasoline prices, expanded leisure time, and increasing numbers of single-person households. The deregulation of the airline industry, with the resultant fare reductions and the establishment of no-frills regional carriers, has also increased personal travel.

Personal travel is generally viewed as being quickly affected by changes in the economy, whereas business travel more typically follows the turns in the economy by three to six months.

Food and beverage sales account for approximately one-third of total lodging revenues. Gross profits are usually about 20 percent, a substantially narrower margin than that of room rentals, and although food and beverage sales per room have risen over the last ten years, this rise has been at a slower pace than room rates.

INNOVATION IN THE INDUSTRY

Rather than travel to a central location, business people in different cities may now hold conferences by means of satellite communication. Because an estimated 40 percent of hotel revenues come from corporate business meetings, many hotels originally feared this development. Recently, however, more than one-eighth of the nation's largest hotels have been linked to a teleconferencing system. These hotels are expecting teleconferences to attract new customers and to increase the bar, catering, and meeting room revenues, although they may indirectly hurt the primary room revenues.

Another innovation consists of in-room computer terminals that provide the occupant with access to a computer that can receive telegrams and telexes and supply economic news, shopping information, entertainment tips, and even job listings. Users gain access to the computer through a credit card number and are charged for their time at the terminal on the basis of sliding rates similar to those for long-distance phone calls. Some industry observers predict that within the next few years thousands of rooms may be equipped with these terminals.

MAJOR SUBDIVISIONS

More than 50,000 lodging locations are currently operating in the United States. However, the industry is fragmented, its offerings ranging from small roadside motels to mammoth resort hotels containing 3,000 or more rooms. The lodging industry is usually subdivided into four distinct categories: convention/commercial, resort, roadside, and airport.

Lodging chains may operate through a management contract of a franchise system or may own their properties outright or in part. In a franchised system the properties are neither owned nor managed by the lodging company — the company receives an initial fee and a percentage of gross room receipts in exchange for the use of its name, reservation services, and national advertising, and other considerations. Most of the national chains are franchise operations.

The management contract method has grown in importance over the years. With this method, the facility is managed for its owners for a fee based on gross room rentals.

FACTORS IN SUCCESSFUL LODGING ENTERPRISES

Although a variety of factors influence the operation of every lodging enterprise, the following six are considered the key success factors: an effective reservation system, actual locations chosen, the amenities/facilities available at each physical location, friendliness/efficiency of staff, pricing policies, and aggressive marketing, including customer groups targeted plus advertising and special promotional activities.

It may seem unnecessary to detail the importance of an effective reservation system; however, no other single factor can cause so much ill will in potential customers as lost reservations, incorrect dates, errors in requested room types, and so on. Even if adjustments at the check-in registration can be made in order to accommodate the customer, the impact is still the same: a negative start to the guest's stay at that location — a negative which may never be overcome.

In a similar manner it seems intuitively logical that the actual physical location chosen for a lodging enterprise would be extremely important to the success of its operations. For example, a resort hotel in Florida located on the beach would be expected to have a more advantageous location than one situated three or four blocks inland. However, locational factors are much more complex than this simplistic example. Various factors must be included in the location decision analysis process. These factors include, but are not limited to, the following: (1) the type of lodging enterprise planned (airport versus midtown commercial); (2) the physical amenities to be included in the actual operation (lounges, cafes, swimming pool, exercise facilities); (3) the types of customer groups expected to be chosen as the dominant group targeted for marketing efforts (business versus personal versus convention traveler); (4) the proximity of the physical location to other desirable amenities and services (for example, golf courses, gourmet restaurants, or after-hours social activities), including proximity to business centers, transportation facilities, convention centers, exhibition halls, and so forth.

A third success factor includes the actual facilities available at each location site: such in-room facilities as beds, configurations of bath and dressing rooms, cable and color television, and desks and furnishings, and such overall facilities as swimming pools, tennis courts, exercise rooms, cafés, restaurants, lounges, meeting rooms, recreational and duplicating services, computer hookups, and so on. The list can be very lengthy and is continuing to expand with changing lifestyles and technology.

Several lodging chain operators have suggested that the friendliness and efficiency of the lodging staff is an extremely important success factor. Friendliness and efficiency must be a pervasive staff attitude. It must begin at the initial guest/staff contact point, be it the doorman or reception desk clerk or wherever, and continue through all other guest/staff contact situations for the duration of the guest's stay.

The final few success factors of pricing policies, advertising, and special promotional activities are all related to an aggressive marketing program as an important key to success. Pricing has recently become far more segmented and competitive than in the past. Convention and business as well as other group pricing is only the beginning of the pricing policy variables currently practiced at many enterprises. A basic variable of room amenities and location becomes much more complex when factors related to the type of guest, the length of stay, the days of the week in residence, the frequency of visits, and so forth are included in a pricing formula approach. In addition, these pricing policies must be established to be compatible with and coordinated with other marketing activities such as advertising themes and special promotion programs and activities. To summarize, what is necessary for success in today's highly competitive lodging industry is a well-designed and coordinated aggressive marketing program which stresses promotional activities such as media advertising in conjunction with a relatively sophisticated approach to multiple pricing policies.

In the future all segments of the lodging industry are expected to become more aggressive as they compete in the market. Special promotions will be offered to encourage short stays during holiday periods and weekends. Hotels that cater to a balanced mix of business, convention, and pleasure travelers are expected to fare better than others.

MAJOR COMPETITORS IN INTEGRATED HOTELS

Listed below are a number of organizations that operate multiple locations and have thousands of lodging rooms available nightly:

Best Western, Inc.

Friendship Inns

Budget Motels and Hotels

Days Inn of America

TraveLodge International/Trusthouse Forte, Inc.

Quality Inns

These organizations are either specialized or concentrated in their types of operations and therefore are not considered major competitors in the integrated hotel segment of the lodging industry.

The major competitors operating in the integrated hotel segment are such firms as:

Holiday Inns, Inc.

Ramada Inns, Inc.

Sheraton Corporation

Hilton Hotels Corporation

Hyatt Hotels Corporation

Marriott Corporation

These firms are integrated from the standpoint of operating several types of lodging destinations, from resorts to airport to convention to business and commercial locations. In addition, a number of these firms have also moved into such new areas as all-suite and mid-price locations. All are diversified in their operations. Exhibits A1 and A2 provide details regarding some of these major competitors.

EXHIBIT A1
Competitors in integrated hotels, 1983

Company	Number of Hotels	Number of Rooms	Occupancy Rate (percent)
Hilton Hotels Corp.	N/A	88,864	60.0%
Holiday Inns, Inc.	1,707	310,337	70.2
Marriott Corp.	131	55,000	69.5[a]
Ramada Inns, Inc.	593	93,592	63.0

[a]Estimated by author.
Source: 1983 annual reports.

EXHIBIT A2 Financial highlights of integrated hotels (in thousands of dollars)

Company	Revenues	Net Income	Earnings per Share	Return on Equity (percent)	Main Businesses
Hilton Hotels Corp.	$ 682,928	$112,637	$4.20	18.7%	Hotels and casinos (international)
Holiday Inns, Inc.	1,585,080	124,399	3.28	12.5	Hotels, restaurants, and casinos (international)
Marriott Corp.	3,036,703	115,245	4.15	20.0	Hotels, contract food services, and restaurants (international)
Ramada Inns, Inc.	573,831	12,597	.38	5.2	Hotels and casinos (international)

Source: 1983 annual reports.

OCCUPANCY RATES

The economic downturn in 1982 adversely affected occupancy levels and lowered profit margins. However, despite an increase in the number of rooms available, economic recovery in 1983 and 1984 boosted pleasure and business travel.

An important factor in determining the profitability of any lodging enterprise is the occupancy rate. The break-even occupancy level for a hotel is determined by the property's initial cost, the manner in which the initial cost was financed, the ability of management to control operations costs, the actual occupancy rate, and the average price per room. The average industry occupancy rate in 1983 was 66.5 percent, up approximately 6.6 percent from 1982. With economic recovery 1984 was expected to have an even stronger showing.

The average price per occupied room was just over $56 in 1981. In 1982 it rose to $62, and fluctuated around $68 in 1983. In 1984 room rates continued to rise; however, the increase was less than the double-digit rises of previous years, when several lodging chains boosted rates in line with changes in the Consumer Price Index.

CONSTRUCTION

The construction rate of new hotel facilities is not expected to grow in the near future, mainly because interest rates remain high. In the latter part of the 1970s and the early 1980s, most lodging chains curtailed construction programs. The reasons included rising building costs, high capital costs, an oversupply of rooms stemming from overbuilding in previous years, and declining occupancy rates for many hotels brought about by unfavorable economic conditions. In recent years the emphasis has been on renovation of older rooms and elimination of marginal locations. When new construction resumes, airport and downtown locations are predicted to have top priority.

INDUSTRY OUTLOOK

As the lodging industry enters the mature phase of its life cycle, several analysts believe that major market segmentation strategies will be utilized by the national chains. These segmentation strategies, which have been identified as budget-priced operations, all-suite operations, premium full-service operations, and so forth, are necessary if the national chains are to retain their market share percentages and ensure future profits. Meanwhile, the smaller industry competitors are intent on creating a market niche for themselves — a niche that separates their operations from the other competitors in the industry. In fact, the all-suite hotel and the budget-priced operations were started by small competitors searching for a market niche to give themselves a competitive advantage.

REFERENCES

Moody's Handbook of Common Stocks (Fall 1984).
Standard & Poor's Industry Surveys (1984).
Travel Weekly (May 31, 1983).
U.S. Industrial Outlook (1984).
Value Line Investment Survey (1984).

THE GRAND THEATRE COMPANY

"There is no better director than me. Some may be as good, but none better." [1]

In December 1982, the board of directors of Theatre London (see Exhibit 1) were considering a proposal to hire Robin Phillips as artistic director, to replace Bernard Hopkins. The hiring decision was complicated by Phillips's ambitious plans for the theater, which included a change from a subscription theater to repertory, an increase in budget from $1.9 million to $4.5 million, and even changing the organization's name. The board had to act quickly as plans had to be made, and actors hired, for the next season.

THEATER IN ONTARIO

Theater is big business. In Toronto alone (including cabaret, dinner theater, and opera) some 3.5 million people attended 120 productions in 1982, in twenty-eight locations. There are twenty-four nonprofit professional theaters in Toronto, and eighteen in the rest of Ontario.

Most theater organizations are nonprofit (with rare exceptions such as Ed Mirvish's Royal Alexandra) and are subsidized by local, provincial, and federal grants. Thus theaters compete for funds with charitable, educational, and health care organizations. As shown in Exhibit 2, a third of revenue typically comes from government sources and half of this comes from The Canada Council. Another 10 percent comes from individual and corporate donors, and the balance from the box office. Because of

---

[1] Robin Phillips, quoted in the Toronto *Globe and Mail*, Dec. 31, 1983, p. E1.

This case was prepared by Dr. Larry M. Agranove with the assistance of Dr. J. Peter Killing from published sources and interviews with numerous people in theater, government, and arts organizations. It was prepared as a basis for class discussion rather than to illustrate correct or incorrect handling of an administrative situation. Copyright © 1986 by Wilfrid Laurier University. Reprinted by permission.

EXHIBIT 1
Grand Theatre
Company board of
directors, December
1982

J. Noreen De Shane (president).	President of a stationery firm
Peter J. Ashby.	Partner, major consulting firm
W. C. P. Baldwin, Jr.	President, linen supply firm
Bob Beccarea.	Alderman and civic representative
Art Ender.	Life insurance representative
Ed Escaf.	Hotel and restaurant owner
Dr. John Girvin.	Surgeon
Stephanie Goble.	Representative of London Labour Council
Elaine Hagarty.	Former alderman, active in arts community
Barbara Ivey.	Active board member of various theater groups
Alan G. Leyland.	Entrepreneur
John F. McGarry.	Partner, major law firm
C. Agnew Meek.	Corporate marketing executive
Robert Mepham.	Insurance company executive
Elizabeth Murray.	Board member of theater groups and Ontario Arts Council
John H. Porter.	Vice-president and partner, major accounting firm
Peter Schwartz.	Partner, major law firm
Dr. Tom F. Siess.	University professor
Dr. Shiel Warma.	Surgeon

EXHIBIT 2 Major arts organizations in Canada

Arts organizations	Total revenue 1982–1983	Box office and earnings	Government grants	Private donations	Accumulated surplus (deficit), end of 1982–1983
1. Stratford Festival	$12,314,300	$9,678,285	$1,405,939	$1,230,076	(1,731,492)
2. Toronto Symphony	9,480,503	6,020,112	1,893,100	1,567,291	(149,391)
3. National Ballet	7,271,616	3,233,810	2,943,856	1,093,950	(675,096)
4. Orchestre Symphonique de Montreal	7,071,886	4,048,749	2,164,350	858,787	(857,662)
5. Canadian Opera Company	5,969,077	2,668,698	2,029,100	1,271,279	(290,168)
6. Vancouver Symphony	5,189,041	2,488,690	1,784,315	916,036	(818,951)
7. Shaw Festival	4,801,700	3,848,200	586,000	367,500	(45,167)
8. Royal Winnipeg Ballet	4,021,263	1,884,339	1,611,463	525,461	343,639
9. Centre Stage	3,483,020	1,923,312	1,316,000	243,708	(212,108)
10. Citadel Theatre	3,541,911	2,097,096	1,117,733	327,082	(177,821)
.					
.					
18. Grand Theatre	1,990,707	1,277,625	390,000	323,082	0[a]

[a] Reduced by Wintario Challenge Fund.
Source: Council for Business and the Arts in Canada.

the pressing need for box office revenues, most theater companies sell subscriptions of five or so plays from October to May.

In 1982–1983, audience size was 570,000 for the Stratford Festival, the largest arts organization in Canada, and 268,000 for the Shaw Festival, the second largest theater company. According to a Stratford audience study, audiences break down into: (1) committed theater goers (27 percent) who see a number of plays each year and who tend to be older and more educated and live in Ontario, (2) casual theater goers (53 percent) who attend a theater every year or two to see plays of particular interest, and (3) first-timers (20 percent). The challenge for these theaters is to develop these first-timers to be the audience of the future.

Theater audiences tend to be well educated, with most having university education and slightly over 50 percent having attended a graduate or professional school. Those aged thirty-six through fifty make up 35 percent of the Stratford audience, and the twenty-one–thirty-five and fifty-one–sixty-four age groups each make up 25 percent. Visitors from the United States account for 35 percent of box office receipts at the Stratford Festival, Toronto residents account for 25 percent, and the remaining 40 percent come from elsewhere in Ontario. Twice as many women attend as men. It is understood that Shaw's market is similar, with slightly fewer coming from the United States.

A recent study showed that, while 42 percent of Ontario residents attended live plays and musicals in 1974, this grew to 55 percent by 1984.[2] Some 24 percent of the Ontario population are "frequent attenders" (at least six times a year). They come from all age groups, but many are "singles," and many are university educated and affluent. In fact, while only 63 percent of Ontarians without a high school education attended live theater, 94 percent with university degrees have attended live theater.

There is some price sensitivity: 73 percent said they would attend more often if tickets were less expensive. However, 77 percent (which included young adults and lower-middle-income families) said they would accept a tax increase of up to $25 to support the arts.

THE ORGANIZATION OF A THEATER COMPANY

The Board of Directors

The Board of Directors is fiscally and legally responsible for the theater. They may determine the theater's artistic objectives and then delegate the fulfilling of these objectives to the artistic director. However, any artistic plan has financial objectives, and the board's responsibility is essentially financial. Artistic directors generally demand, and are generally granted, a great deal of autonomy in such matters as programming and casting; to a large extent the board "bets" on the

---

[2] Special Committee for the Arts, *Report to the Honourable Susan Fish, The Minister of Citizenship and Culture, Province of Ontario,* Spring 1984.

artistic director's ability to put on a season of theater, subject to his accountability in meeting budgets and providing an appropriate level of quality.

Board members are typically expected to assist in fund raising and to set an example by contributing generously themselves.

Board members often have business backgrounds. As a result, they may be — and are certainly often perceived to be — insensitive to the unique needs of an artistic organization. Artistic boards often include lawyers and accountants, who are often recruited to serve a specific function, but who tend to remain on long enough to achieve positions of power.

Busy business people serve on boards for a number of reasons. They may perceive their serving as a civic responsibility. Others may see it as an opportunity to wield power at a board level, something they are not allowed to do in their own organizations. Membership on a board allows people to widen their social and business contacts; this can be important to professionals who are limited in their freedom to advertise. One common motivation for business people to join arts boards is the opportunity to mingle with luminaries in the arts. Here is one view of their performance:

> *It has often been charged that many a hard-headed businessman loses his business sense on entering a meeting of an arts board. Lacking a profit motive to guide the affairs of the organization, businessmen who serve on arts boards sometimes feel unsure of themselves and their expertise. Compounding this problem is the inclination on the part of arts organizations to consider themselves a breed apart, outside the realm of normal business practice. But whether a company manufactures widgets or mounts exhibitions, the basic business concerns remain the same: strategic planning, good marketing, adequate financing, and competent management are essential to any enterprise.*[3]

Theater Management

In addition to the artistic director, there is usually a general manager who is responsible for the business affairs of the organization. Since artistic directors strive for maximum quality, which is expensive, and since business managers have to find and account for the money to run the theater, conflicts often occur. Not surprisingly, boards often side with the business manager because of their similarities of culture and values. Typically both artistic director and general manager report directly to the board.

MOUNTING A PRODUCTION

The theater company selects "products" to suit its objectives and audiences. For example, a theater might select a playbill of classics or children's plays. A regional theater might select a Canadian play (to satisfy government grant-giving agencies),

[3] "Developing Effective Arts Boards," undated publication of The Council for Business and the Arts in Canada, pp. 28–29.

a classic (to satisfy the artistic aspirations of the artistic director), a resounding hit from Broadway or England (to help sell the series), and one or more plays that have been successful elsewhere.

Each production requires a producer (who may be the artistic director) to act as the "entrepreneur" to put the show together. The producer acquires the rights to the play, if it is not in the public domain, for a fee of 7 to 10 percent of the box office revenue, and also retains a director, who may be on staff or who may be a freelance director retained for the run of the play. In the latter case, minimum scale would be $6,174.80 for a run of 3 weeks of rehearsal and 3 to 4 weeks of performance.

Casting is done, beginning with the major parts, on the basis of a uniform contract, which sets out fees (minimum of $416.27 per week for a major company), starting date, billing, working time, and "perks" (e.g., dressing room, accommodation).

Finally, a stage manager is contracted, as are designers for sets, costumes, and lighting. It is essential, of course, that all these people work well together.

This describes the typical "stock," or subscription, company. However, Stratford and Shaw operate as "repertory" companies, hiring a group of actors for one or more seasons, and allocating roles among the members of the company. Repertory companies typically sell tickets for individual plays, while subscription companies sell their series at the beginning of the season, with few single-ticket sales.

Lead times are considerable. In Stratford, for example, plays that open in May are firmly cast by the previous December, and the entire session is planned by March, when rehearsals begin.

THEATRE LONDON

Background   The Grand Opera House was opened in London on September 9, 1901, by Ambrose J. Small, a Toronto theatrical entrepreneur and frustrated producer. It quickly became the showcase of Small's theatrical chain, opening with such attractions as the Russian Symphony Orchestra, and later offering such performers as Barry Fitzgerald, Bela Lugosi, Clifton Webb, Sidney Poitier, and Hume Cronyn. Small sold his theater chain in 1919, deposited a million dollars in his bank, and disappeared. There has been no explanation to this day; however, Small's ghost is said to haunt the Grand.

Famous Players bought the theater in 1924, tore out the second balcony, and converted the theater to a cinema. They sold to The London Little Theatre for a token amount in 1945, and the building housed an amateur community theater until the spring 1971. The theater employed professional business management and a professional artistic director, but the actors were all amateurs. Some of London's leading citizens acted in plays, and some even displayed a high level of competence. The theater was prominent in the social life of the city and attracted one of the largest subscription sales in North America, both as a percentage of available seats and in absolute terms. It also achieved a reputation for a very high level of quality, given that it was essentially an amateur theater. Articles about the theater appeared in such magazines as *Life*.

However, there was some concern in the theater that the level of quality was as high as it was going to get as a company of amateurs and that the community deserved, and was ready to support, a professional theater. Another local organization, the London Symphony, had engaged a conductor with an international reputation, and it was changing from an amateur to a professional orchestra. An association was formed to work toward providing London with a major art gallery. Although strong objections were raised against the proposal for a professional theater (particularly because of the increased financial burden, the risk, and the denial to many of the theater's supporters of an opportunity to participate in their hobby of acting), London Little Theatre changed to Theatre London in 1971 under artistic director Heinar Piller. The progressives were vindicated, as theatergoers in the London area were treated to a decade of artistically and financially successful theater.

Piller was succeeded, at the end of the 1975 season, by William Hutt, who had achieved great success as an actor at Stratford, and was well known to Londoners. He served from 1976 to 1978. Bernard Hopkins arrived in 1979, and was artistic director until May 1983.

The Grand was attractively and authentically renovated at a cost of $5.5 million, reopening in fall 1978, after being closed for a full season. (The company had a reduced season during that time, in small, rented accommodations.) During the renovation, seating capacity was reduced from 1,100 to 845.

Theatre London ran successful stock seasons from 1979 to 1982. The 1981–1982 season was particularly successful, operating at 85 percent of capacity. Eighty percent of its tickets were sold through subscription to some 13,431 subscribers. Financial statements are shown in Exhibits 3 and 4.

THE LONDON ENVIRONMENT

London was founded at the forks of the Thames River in 1793 by Governor Simcoe with the intention of making it the capital of Upper Canada. Instead, it became the cultural and commercial center of southwestern Ontario. Located on three railroad lines and on Highway 401 serving the Quebec–Windsor corridor, London also has a major airport served by two airlines. London is 2 hours away from Detroit and Toronto; however, it is in a major snow belt. London is a major retail center, with the second highest per capita retail capacity in North America. It serves as a trading area for almost a million people, although its own population is only 259,000. (See Exhibit 5.) There are four hotels near the core area and motels in outlying areas. Many interesting restaurants had opened with a great deal of excess capacity; a few restaurants closed or changed hands.

There is little heavy industry in London, but there is a major university, a community college, a teacher's college, and two small church-affiliated colleges. Four major hospitals serve a wide area and provide teaching facilities for the university

EXHIBIT 3 Theatre London, condensed 5-year operating results

Revenue	June 30, 1979	June 30, 1980	June 30, 1981	June 30, 1982	June 30, 1983 (estimate)
Productions					
Ticket sales	$ 551,650	$ 585,938	$ 620,313	$ 664,058	$1,100,000
Sponsored programs	26,000	25,000	26,500	9,000	9,000
Program advertising	17,283	17,270	19,652	24,241	24,000
	594,933	628,208	666,465	697,299	1,133,000
Grants					
Canada Council	145,000	163,000	173,000	185,000	210,000
Ontario Arts Council	145,000	152,000	160,000	170,000	180,000
Wintario	89,254	—	—	—	—
City of London	12,500	—	—	—	—
Cultural Initiative Program	—	—	25,000	—	—
	391,754	315,000	358,000	355,000	390,000
Other					
Operating fund drive	41,222	27,462	182,559	183,188	160,000
Special projects	36,811	36,525	43,881	41,281	65,000
Interest	34,553	50,608	62,128	86,106	80,000
Concessions	33,500	75,073	69,581	62,065	78,000
Theater school	8,720	17,687	19,481	—	—
Box office commissions	3,319	3,721	651	6,142	3,000
Theater rental & misc.	3,170	—	—	4,704	2,000
	161,295	211,076	378,281	383,486	388,000
Total revenue	$1,147,982	$1,154,284	$1,402,946	$1,435,785	$1,911,000
Expenses					
Public relations	179,880	128,502	139,907	177,267	270,000
Administration	91,973	115,798	162,723	167,749	330,000
Production overhead	190,911	237,606	282,270	339,474	350,000
Productions	466,906	414,644	416,440	421,151	780,000
Front of house, box office, and concessions	75,563	123,910	107,617	126,673	140,000
Facility operation	131,445	139,215	152,153	142,061	140,000
Theater school	9,742	20,832	34,804		
Total expenses (see Salaries and Supplies, below)	1,146,420	1,180,507	1,295,914	1,374,375	2,010,000
Excess of revenue over expense	1,562	(26,223)	107,032	61,410	(99,000)
	$1,147,982	$1,154,284	$1,402,946	$1,435,785	$1,911,000
Salaries, fees, and benefits	$ 658,507	$ 754,109	$ 791,954	$ 823,260	$1,000,000[a]
Supplies and expenses	487,913	426,398	503,960	551,115	911,000
	$1,146,420	$1,180,507	$1,295,914	$1,374,375	$1,911,000

[a] In addition, development costs for the establishment of a repertory company in the 1983–1984 season could be incurred which could be largely offset by federal and provincial grants.

EXHIBIT 4 Theatre London, condensed balance sheets

	June 30, 1979	June 30, 1980	June 30, 1981	June 30, 1982
Assets				
Current assets				
Cash and term deposits	$351,010	$372,868	$325,631	$316,939
Accounts receivable	3,908	13,957	35,208	10,916
Inventory	7,463	7,146	6,050	
Prepaid expenses	20,257	32,788	46,938	72,471
	$382,638	$426,759	$413,827	$400,326
Liabilities and Surplus				
Current liabilities				
Bank loan		$ 25,000		
Accounts payable	$ 26,253	24,041	$ 30,112	$ 67,198
Advance ticket sale	280,431	324,524	319,843	302,983
Advance grants	1,060		15,201	14,805
Payable to Theatre London Foundation		4,523		15,340
	307,744	378,088	365,156	400,326
Surplus	74,894	48,671	48,671[a]	
	$382,638	$426,759	$413,827	$400,326

[a] In addition, there was equity of $453,080 from the Wintario Challenge Fund Program in 1981 and $807,289 in 1982. Under the terms of the program, Wintario would match $2 for every eligible contributed dollar raised (during the 3-year period ending June 30, 1983) in excess of 5.9 percent of the current year's operating expenses. All these matching contributions were placed in a separate investment fund for at least 5 years, although interest earned on the fund could be used for current operations.

medical school and dental school. In addition to being a retail center, London is the home of major financial institutions and agribusiness firms as well as a major brewery.

London is also a major cultural center. In addition to Theatre London, London has a professional symphony orchestra and a couple of significant choral groups. The university has an active program of theater and music, and the community is a center for visual artists. There are various commercial art galleries, an art gallery connected with the university, and a major public art gallery located in the city center. There are several museums, including a unique children's museum and a museum of Indian archaeology. The latter two attract visitors from a wide area.

THE GRAND THEATRE COMPANY

In late 1981, a decade after the company had become professional, concern was again raised in the Theatre that the level of quality had stagnated, and the Theatre would have to move in new directions. Bernard Hopkins was a superb actor and a

EXHIBIT 5 Grand Theatre Company, disposable income by census metropolitan area, 1983

	Income rating		Per capita personal disposable income	
	Index	*Rank*	*Dollars*	*Rank*
Toronto	117	6	$12,693	7
Montreal	103	11	11,212	14
Vancouver	118	5	12,793	6
Ottawa-Hull	118	5	12,796	5
Edmonton	126	4	13,668	4
Calgary	132	1	14,324	1
Winnipeg	111	8	11,997	9
Quebec	98	14	10,623	18
Hamilton	112	7	12,114	8
St. Catharines	103	11	11,223	13
Kitchener	101	13	10,974	16
London	106	10	11,462	11
Halifax	101	13	10,923	17
Windsor	107	9	11,602	10
Regina	130	2	14,056	2
Saskatoon	129	3	14,021	3
Oshawa	106	10	11,450	12
Thunder Bay	102	12	11,089	15
Canada	100		10,851	

Note: This list shows all eighteen census metropolitan areas in which the principal city had a population of at least 100,000 in the 1981 Census.

London-centered seven-county market area data

	Population, June 1, 1983 (thousands)	*10-year growth rate*	*Households, June 1, 1983 (thousands)*	*Wage earner average income, 1981*	*Per capita disposable income, 1983*	*Per capita retail sales, 1983*
Seven counties	838.5	5.7%	293.7	$14,522	$10,669	$4,238
Canada	24,886.6	12.0	8,335.0	$15,141	$10,851	$4,153

Source: *Canadian Markets*, 1984, and 1981 income tax returns.

competent artistic director. He had directed a few plays, rather than have to pay for a freelance director, with some success. However, some members of the board believed that he had taken the Theatre as far as he was able, and there was no initiative on either side to extend Hopkins's contract beyond its expiration in May 1983.

A planning committee, under one of the board members, addressed the issue of continuing the growth in quality. They conducted a number of retreats and interviewed experts in professional theater as well as officers of the Canada Council and Ontario Arts Council. During the course of the investigation, they interviewed Robin Phillips.

Phillips had been artistic director at the Stratford Festival and was well known to Barbara Ivey (who served on both the Stratford and Theatre London boards) and to other Theatre London directors. He also had directed, with considerable artistic success, two productions for Theatre London: *The Lady of the Camellias* and *Long Day's Journey Into Night.*

Robin Phillips

Robin Phillips is a highly talented artistic director and a person of incredible charm. (In *all* of the interviews conducted by the casewriter, words such as *charm, charisma,* and *talent* abounded.) Actress Martha Henry said, "Once you've worked with Robin, it's almost impossible to work for anyone else."

He came to Canada from England in 1974 to plan the 1975 Stratford season, although he would not direct any specific plays until 1976. His tenure at Stratford has been described as successful but stormy. When he was contracting to direct a production for the Canadian Opera Company in 1976, he said he would not renew his Stratford contract unless he had more evidence of support for his ambition to make Stratford the focus of Canadian theater, with film and television productions as well as live theater. He received a 5-year contract to run from November 1, 1976; the contract could be terminated with 4 months notice.

There was a series of resignations from, and returns to, Stratford starting in July 1978, until Phillips's departure in 1981. In addition to his Stratford activities, Phillips was involved with theater in Calgary, New York, Toronto's Harbourfront, and Vancouver. He also filmed *The Wars,* a novel by Timothy Findley. It was generally understood that he was seeking a theater in Toronto to serve as a base for his stage, film, and television ambitions. However, none was available.

The Phillips Plan

Robin Phillips had a plan for Theatre London, and he would only come if he had a budget to fulfill his plan and complete artistic autonomy. His plan called for raising Theatre London from eighteenth place in Canadian theater to third and changing its name to "The Grand Theatre Company."

The plan required a budget of $4.5 million, up from $1.9 million. This included $400,000 of capital cost to improve the Grand's facilities. Box office and concessions would provide 73 percent of the budget, 18 percent would come from donations, 5 percent from the Canada Council, and 4 percent from the Ontario Arts Council. Revenue projections were based on playing to 80 percent of capacity; this was considered feasible because Phillips had surpassed that performance at Stratford, and Theatre London had been operating at 85 percent. The Theatre requested a permanent tax exemption from the City of London; the deputy mayor described this request as "cavalier."

Three of the stage productions would be adapted for television and filmed by Primedia Productions of Toronto. This would provide some $100,000 of additional revenue for each production as well as audience exposure.

Robin Phillips strongly favored a repertory company over a subscription policy. He believed, and often stated, that subscriptions denied audiences a choice, and audiences must learn to discriminate. A change had to be made to make the theater different, special, and exciting. A repertory company would provide a company of salaried actors who could not be lured away during the season and who would be attracted by steady employment.

Another advantage of the repertory concept is the flexibility afforded patrons who may choose the dates they see a play and their seat locations. In a subscription series, patrons are restricted to the same seat location on the same night for each performance. In repertory theater, several productions are typically run simultaneously.

The Playbill   Phillips proposed to offer these plays on the main stage (in addition to a children's program in a small, secondary theater):

Godspell by John-Michael Tebelak. A rousing rock musical with audience appeal, especially for younger audiences

The Doctor's Dilemma by George Bernard Shaw. An established, classical hit

Waiting for the Parade by John Murrell. A Canadian play, with an all-female cast, showing what women did while their men were fighting World War II

Timon of Athens by William Shakespeare. A little-performed, little-known Shakespearean play, ignored by Stratford

The Club by Eve Merriam. A musical spoof of men's clubs, with a female cast playing the part of men

Arsenic and Old Lace by Joseph Kesselring. A well-known classic comedy of American theater

The Prisoner of Zenda adapted by Warren Graves. A comedy of political intrigue and romance, set in a mythical Eastern European kingdom

Hamlet by William Shakespeare. One of his best-known plays

Dear Antoine by Jean Anouilh. A comedy by a leading contemporary French playwright

Casting for these plays would not be a problem, as leading actors from Canada, the United States, and England were eager to work with Phillips.

Pricing   Since the plan envisioned a box office yield of $3.2 million, up from the $1.2 million planned for the 1982–1983 season, revenue would have to be increased in two ways. The number of productions would be increased, with nine productions in the season instead of the previous six. There would be a record 399 performances, instead of the 230 performances in the 1982–1983 season. Thus the plan projected an audience of 217,000, compared with the 137,000 planned for the 1982–1983 season. In addition, prices would be increased.

A subscriber in the 1982–1983 season could see five plays for $55 on weekends or $45 on weekdays. This pricing schedule was proposed for the 1983–1984 repertory season:

	Price	
Number of seats	*Weekdays*	*Weekends*
178	$20.00	$22.50
245	$14.50	$15.50
422	$10.50	$12.50

Promotion

Since the Theatre would require an expanded audience from a wider area, the plan envisioned a program of investment spending in major area newspapers: the *Toronto Star* and *Globe and Mail*, the *Kitchener-Waterloo Record*, and the *Detroit Free Press* as well as the *London Free Press*. The advertising would be directed at a first-time audience.

Group sales would be stressed, particularly to schools. Hotel-restaurant-transportation-theater ticket packages were projected. However, data on expenditures was not available.

THE DECISION

The directors were impressed by the charm and reputation of Robin Phillips. The proposal to hire Phillips — and to accept his plan — was supported by board members who had sound business backgrounds and who had worked in theater for some years. They had a comfortable, modern theater with a recently acquired computer to issue tickets. They had a proven record in selling tickets, as did Robin Phillips.

On the other hand, if Phillips were hired, his artistic strengths might not be matched administratively. There was an administrative director (who had been there for only two years) and a chief accountant, but no controller. And Stratford, Canada's leading theater, was less than an hour's drive down the road. Would this be an audience-builder or a competitive threat?

MAGNA INTERNATIONAL, INC.

By mid-1986, annual sales of Magna International, Inc. were projected to top $1.0 billion for the first time. As Canada's largest manufacturer of automotive parts, Magna had just realized one of its corporate objectives of having an average of $100 of its auto parts built into every North American car.

Although company founder Frank Stronach and his management team continuously espoused a "small is beautiful" philosophy, their dreams for Magna were, by no means, small. Stronach stated in 1985 that he was intent on creating "one of the largest corporations in North America," and that he felt Magna could maintain 30 percent annual growth for many years. By 1986, it was also clear that Magna was committed to a strategy of increased internationalization of its operations. These goals clearly raised questions about the appropriateness of Magna's current operating philosophy and organization for the planned growth.

FRANK STRONACH AND MAGNA INTERNATIONAL

In 1985, Magna's flamboyant chairman and chief executive officer, Frank Stronach, was the highest-paid executive in Canada with a salary of $1.85 million. Many felt this was justified given Magna's almost unprecedented 30 percent annual growth in sales and profits over the past 15 years. Exhibit 1 provides statements from Magna's 1985 annual report detailing the company's financial performance.

The company, in its original form, was founded in 1957 by its controlling shareholder, chairman, and CEO Frank Stronach. By 1986 it employed more than 7,500 people in approximately sixty-five Canadian and five American plants and in one additional plant in West Germany. In 1984, 75 percent of sales were to U.S. customers. Magna's primary customers were the various operating divisions of Ford, General Motors, Chrysler, and AMC — the "Big Four" North American auto manufacturers. In fact, 95 percent of their products went into North American cars.

This case was written by Mr. William Webb under the direction of professor Paul W. Beamish, School of Business and Economics, Wilfrid Laurier University, as a basis for classroom discussion. Copyright © 1986 by Paul W. Beamish. Reprinted by permission.

EXHIBIT 1 10-year financial summary

	1985	1984	1983	1982	1981[a]	1980	1979	1978	1977	1976
Operations data										
Sales	$690,400	$493,559	$302,451	$226,534	$232,114	$183,456	$165,738	$128,189	$80,953	$55,010
Income from operations	69,430	57,124	25,473	9,055	12,054	9,249	15,924	12,899	8,185	5,734
Net income[d]	43,191	31,480	14,647	5,265	6,911	5,640	8,455	6,595	4,093	2,786
Extraordinary items						(1,922)	272	795		
Basic earnings per Class A and Class B share[b,c]	$ 2.00	$ 1.93	$ 1.10	$ 0.49	$ 0.64	$ 0.34	$ 0.89	$ 0.80	$ 0.48	$ 0.36
Fully diluted earnings per Class A and Class B share	$ 1.93	$ 1.85	$ 1.07	$ 0.44	$ 0.57	$ 0.33	$ 0.78	$ 0.68	$ 0.47	$ 0.32
Depreciation	24,322	15,044	11,267	9,325	9,188	6,154	4,506	3,349	2,210	1,416
Cash flow from operations	85,974	55,945	32,522	14,604	14,672	12,052	15,275	13,160	7,542	5,171
Dividends declared per Class A and Class B share[b,c]	$ 0.48	$ 0.31	$ 0.13[e]	$ 0.13	$ 0.18	$ 0.18	$ 0.14	$ 0.10	$ 0.06	$ 0.03
Financial position										
Working capital	64,121	79,804	48,291	31,792	30,792	28,223	19,174	15,351	7,412	4,925
Capital expenditures	222,878	110,239	29,806	17,434	21,052	23,630	23,085	16,231	8,584	3,456
Fixed assets (less accumulated depreciation)	357,371	179,817	87,388	70,553	74,074	62,629	47,089	30,269	19,387	8,940
Long-term debt	103,997	96,497	42,159	55,554	56,308	45,830	30,441	19,588	10,238	4,627
Equity relating to Class A and Class B shares	297,935	143,566	81,590	41,071	39,631	33,792	32,086	23,270	15,226	9,646
Equity per Class A and Class B share[b,c]	$ 12.44	$ 8.43	$ 5.59	$ 4.13	$ 3.84	$ 3.35	$ 3.18	$ 2.41	$ 1.68	$ 1.25

Note: *Canadian dollars in thousands except per share figures.*
[a] 1981 and prior figures include sales and income from Aerospace/Defence operations sold effective August 1, 1981.
[b] Adjusted for years prior to 1979 to give effect to the capital reorganization during 1979.
[c] 1983 and prior figures adjusted to give effect to the stock dividend issued June 1983.
[d] Before extraordinary items.
[e] In addition, stockholders received a special stock dividend issued June 1983.

The history of Magna was really the entrepreneurial life story of Frank Stronach, who emigrated to Canada from Austria in 1954. Trained as a tool and die maker, Stronach invested what little savings he had and opened up his own tool and die shop in a rented Toronto garage while still in his midtwenties. Business was good in the first 2 years and Stronach soon employed thirty people. When his foreman told him that he wanted to leave and start his own business, Stronach offered the man part-ownership in the business in order to keep him. The foreman stayed and set up the company's second tool and die shop. This was the first glimmer of what was to be part of Magna's future strategy for corporate growth — decentralization with equity participation by its employees.

Stronach summed up his feelings and reasons behind the philosophy: "If I lose a good person, I'm losing somebody who could be a competitor. I want those people in my camp. That's what business is all about — people management."

By 1969, Stronach owned eight plants that were run autonomously. In order to implement a plan to facilitate employee share ownership, he merged with the publicly traded Magna Electronics Corporation, substituting "International" for the word "Electronics" to reflect the company's broad range of products and greater ambitions.

For the next 15 years, Magna grew almost continuously at an annual rate of 30 percent or more and by 1985 was opening one new factory every 6 to 8 weeks to keep pace with demand. Its product lines had grown to over four thousand different components and assemblies, encompassing parts for nearly every section of the automobile. Exhibit 2 provides a list of product families manufactured by each of Magna's operating groups in 1984. Some products were manufactured to customer specifications while others were designed by Magna's staff and sold as original equipment based on their innovative designs.

THE MAGNA "SUCCESS FORMULA"

Magna consistently performed well in the cyclical auto parts industry whose performance followed the auto industry's traditional 4-year up-and-down cycle. One investment analyst commented that Magna had "the best growth record and highest returns on equity in the business." Appendix A provides a brief analysis of the auto parts industry and shows Magna's financial performance in comparison with three other major auto parts manufacturers.

Many explanations were offered for Magna's unequalled success. In the end, however, it seemed to boil down to the company's ability to manufacture the highest-quality product at the lowest possible cost.

Some observers, including Magna's management and, especially, Frank Stronach, attributed its success to Magna's unique "corporate culture" whose key elements were embodied in the company's "Corporate Constitution" published for the first time in Magna's 1984 annual report. The stated purpose of the Constitution was to "define the rights of employees and investors to participate in the Company's profits and growth and impose discipline on management." Stronach thought that Magna

EXHIBIT 2
Magna product
directory

CMT Group

Seat track mechanisms	Door latches
Window winding regulators	Hood latches
Hand brake assemblies	Trunk latches
Hood hinges	Clutch and brake pedal assemblies
Door hinges	

Decorative Products Group

Front bumper and grille fascia	Windshield mouldings
Rear bumper fascia	Rear window mouldings
Rocker panels	Drain trough mouldings
Wheel house opening mouldings	Exterior window mouldings
Window channels	Tail light bezels
Weather strip channels	Rocker panel mouldings
Headlamp retainers	Body size mouldings
Center hood mouldings	

MACI Group

Cooling fan motors	Relay switches
Heating fan motors	Instrument clusters
Windshield wiper motors	Fuel control devices
Immersible fuel pumps	Electronic tone and voice
Thermostatic air controllers	synthesized alarms
Magnetic capsule switches	Electronic fluid level devices

Magna Manufacturing Group

Aluminum bumper reinforcements	Glove box doors
Shock absorber towers	Seat belt anchors
Rear cross members	Heat shields
Fuel tank straps	Catalytic converters
Sill plates	Thermostat housings
Scuff plates	Water pumps
Alternator fans	Instrument panel supports
Motor mounts	Headrests
Canister support brackets	

Maple Group

Poly V crankshaft pulleys	Compressor pump pulleys
Power steering pulleys	Two speed accessory drive system
Alternator pulleys	Oil strainers
Automatic Poly V belt tensioners	Oil pick-up tubes
Water pump pulleys	Dip-stick tubes

might be the only company in the Western World with a corporate constitution that guaranteed employee rights and imposed discipline on management. Exhibit 3 shows the Magna Corporate Constitution. Appendix B provides some excerpts from the 1985 annual report that demonstrate the Constitution in practice at Magna.

Other critical components of the corporate culture included a commitment to keeping all Magna plants small with a maximum of one hundred employees each, an emphasis on research and development, and rewards for both management and workers through an attractive profit-sharing plan and a range of social benefits from day care for employees' children to a recently opened company-owned conservation and recreation area.

ORGANIZATION AND OPERATING STRUCTURE

Appendix C illustrates and describes Magna's unique operating structure of three levels of responsibility: the operating unit, group management (in charge of an operating group), and executive management.

EXHIBIT 3
Magna's corporate constitution

Board of directors: Magna believes that outside directors provide independent counsel and discipline. A majority of Magna's board of directors will be outsiders.

Employee equity and profit participation: Ten percent of Magna's profit before tax will be allocated to employees. These funds will be used for the purchase of Magna shares in trust for employees and for cash distributions to employees, recognizing both performance and length of service

Shareholder profit participation: Magna will distribute, on average, 20 percent of its annual net profit to its shareholders.

Management profit participation: In order to obtain a long-term contractual commitment from management, the company provides a compensation arrangement which, in addition to a base salary comparable to industry standards, allows for the distribution to corporate management of up to 6 percent of Magna's profit before tax.

Research and technology development: Magna will allocate 7 percent of its profit before tax for research and technology development to ensure the long-term viability of the Company.

Social responsibility: The company will contribute a maximum of 2 percent of its profit before tax to charitable, cultural, educational, and political institutions to support the basic fabric of society.

Minimum profit performance: Management has an obligation to produce a profit. If Magna does not generate a minimum after-tax return of 4 percent on share capital for two consecutive years, class A shareholders, voting as a class, will have the right to elect additional directors.

Major investments: In the event that more than 20 percent of Magna's equity is to be committed to a new unrelated business, class A and class B shareholders will have the right to approve such an investment with each class voting separately.

Constitutional amendments: Any change to Magna's corporate constitution will require the approval of the class A and class B shareholders with each class voting separately.

At the operating unit or individual factory level, maximum employment was kept to no more than one hundred workers because of Stronach's belief that management and employees should maintain close working relationships and that smaller units sparked individual initiative and a degree of entrepreneurialism. Stronach felt that a "family relationship" should exist among coworkers and management, with each person knowing the name of all fellow employees.

"Communication is very important. If you have a few thousand people under one roof, you need a hundred thousand rules. You lose the human touch. You create a faceless kind of management," said Stronach, adding that Magna's environment simply created "a damned good atmosphere to work in!"

Every Magna factory was unique in its own right, with its own product mandate, R&D department, marketing responsibilities, and production and profit objectives established by that unit's management team. Every employee had access to management and, since each earned shares in the company through a profit-sharing plan, they were likely to come forward with assembly-line suggestions to improve quality or cut costs — suggestions that could lead to promotion, more profits to share, and increased equity participation. The small scale of each unit's operations and Magna's emphasis on factory-floor technical skills (promoted by in-house technical education and upgrading programs) resulted in a high degree of flexibility and an ability to adapt quickly to changes in manufacturing operations.

Growth at the operating unit level, as for all levels of Magna, was somewhat "organic" in nature, rather than "planned" in the traditional sense. When a particular unit (factory) could no longer keep pace with demand and was running three shifts of one hundred people on a 24-hour schedule, the unit's general manager would be allowed to build a second factory. If more factories had to be built for a common product line, these might eventually form the basis of a new management group with the former general manager as group vice-president. As this suggests, Magna had a rather unusual and interesting method of delegating responsibility and controls between the executive management, group management, and the operating units. Magna's unit general managers were given 100 percent control, authority, and responsibility for their units, with the requirement that they clearly identify themselves as part of Magna International when communicating with suppliers or customers.

This high degree of decentralization did give rise to a number of trade-offs at the operating unit level. Magna realized higher transportation costs shipping from widely dispersed locations to the automotive assembly plants of the major manufacturers; however, significant quantities were still shipped such that discounts were not completely forgone.

Some diseconomies also arose from the lack of centralized purchasing of raw materials. Each unit dealt with its own suppliers but, frequently, general managers in the same operating group would cooperate to secure volume discounts when available.

Administrative costs were duplicated in some cases since each operating unit had its own personnel, accounting, and other departments, but management felt that, in general, the benefits of decentralization outweighed its costs.

At Magna, financial control was maintained by accountants at each of the Group offices and operating units. Each operating unit was required to submit a business plan for the year outlining the operating and capital budget to Group management. These plans were assessed by the Groups and submitted to corporate executive officers for final approval.

Once approved, the Groups and operating units set out independently in pursuit of their defined business goals. Performance was monitored monthly using uniform financial reports comparing actual operating results to budget and measuring capital spending against plan.

Although organic, growth was not indiscriminate at the factory level and was monitored by group management which worked within the broad corporate policy set by executive management. Executive management consisted of Frank Stronach and a handful of senior executives. Corporate headquarters were housed in a two-story office in a suburban Toronto business park and consisted of a lean, one-hundred-person staff.

Operating units were grouped geographically and by market under one of five group management teams which were destined to divide and form more groups as Magna expanded. Each group was responsible for specific technologies and product lines and had its own marketing, R&D, and planning responsibilities.

On average, each group management nucleus had ten to fifteen factories responsible to it. Magna's strategy was to keep these factories close together geographically, wherever possible, and, as the company grew sufficiently, to develop its own industrial parks.

In 1985, Magna consisted of five management groups: the CMT Group (Creative Mechanical Technologies), the Decorative Products Group, the MACI Group, the Magna Manufacturing Group, and the Maple Group. The products manufactured by each group in 1984 are found in Exhibit 2.

EQUITY PARTICIPATION

Frank Stronach maintained that employees had ''a moral right to some of the profits they help generate. . . . If they get profit, and they put it into the company equity, there's a sort of discipline which helps the employee. We've got some people on machines who've got $30,000 sitting there. That's a lot of money for an average person.''

In keeping with Stronach's belief, Magna had a type of deferred profit-sharing program for its employees to reward productivity and loyalty. Employees were awarded a point for every $1,000 they earned and a point for each year they stayed with the company. The more points they accumulated, the greater their share in the fund. Each year, 7 percent of profits before tax were transferred to an employee equity trust fund. Employees received quarterly statements of how many shares they owned and their value. If an employee left within 2 years, his or her shares reverted to other employees. After the third year with Magna, an employee owned a percentage which increased until the tenth year, when they became the employee property, even if he or she left. In Magna's earlier years, profit sharing was only available to middle management, but was expanded to cover all employees in 1978.

Magna's senior management team of about twenty executives enjoyed a separate profit-participation program for which 6 percent of before-tax profits were set aside. The result was some very generous bonuses in addition to their competitive salaries, but Frank Stronach had no qualms about this, stating that, "good management doesn't come cheap — I don't come cheap." The compensation received by Stronach and four other Magna executives placed them among the fifteen most highly paid managers in Canada in 1985.

Exclusive of the top executive, Magna's approximately 250 managers owned about $12\frac{1}{2}$ percent of the company. The over seven thousand workers held about the same equity position.

Although Magna's workers enjoyed equity participation, their hourly salaries were very low by industry standards — approximately $6 per hour in 1985. Some estimated that Magna, without a single union in any of its plants, therefore had an hourly wage burden about half the size of its unionized competitors — a substantial competitive advantage in an industry where cost control was a key success factor. Stronach maintained that increases in productivity were resulting in rising wages at Magna and that Magna would soon be catching up in terms of hourly wage rates, but low hourly wages and the lack of a union in any of its plants made Magna a favorite target of attacks by the United Auto Workers (UAW).

MAGNA AND THE UAW

Magna seemed to be an impregnable target for union organizers — a fact that some industry followers felt was vital to Magna's success. Stronach, himself, did not appear to harbor anti-union sentiments, stating: "Unions can be part of free enterprise because society needs checks and balances. . . . If you run a lousy ship, you deserve a union."

Regardless of the sincerity of these views, Stronach had the grudging respect of his UAW adversaries. Buzz Hargrove, administrative assistant to Canadian UAW leader Bob White, knew Frank Stronach personally and said, "I didn't agree with his ideology or his philosophy, but I thought he was a well-motivated, decent human being."

In one instance, in 1978, the UAW was granted automatic certification at one of Magna's Toronto plants because of management interference in the organizing drive. However, some union cards were burned; the UAW failed to negotiate a contract and was then voted out by the Magna employees. The negotiations stalled on the single issue of the now mandatory Rand formula (where all employees in the bargaining unit must pay union dues regardless of whether they choose to become union members), but in the UAW's opinion, this issue was irrelevant because Magna had really just chosen to dig in its heels.

Buzz Hargrove said:

Frank Stronach and I had lunch together one day and he told me that their strategy was essentially to find an issue that they knew we would not agree to that would force us to strike the plant in order to try to get an agreement and they would just let the thing sit. They wouldn't try to run the plant, or hire scabs, but to all intents and purposes the plant would remain closed as long as there was a picket line. Whether it took a year, or two, or three, or forever, it didn't matter. They were not going to have a union in their shop.

We have no alternative but to continue . . . and probably even step up . . . our efforts to organize Magna. We can't have a major segment of the automotive parts industry unorganized.

It was possible that the UAW would be aided in subsequent attempts to organize Magna by the company's ongoing strategy to cluster its five management groups and their related plants into industrial campuses. Frank Stronach, in a 1985 interview, admitted that he was concerned by the threat of renewed UAW action because "it's always a concern if someone would interfere with your environment, with your philosophies, with your basic framework." In an interview a year earlier, he had claimed:

I don't believe the UAW would really get out to organize us. They would if they heard complaints, or if the employees were unhappy. . . . We try to provide a better alternative. We say that if we had unions, we would lose individually because everything is then divided into group one, group two, group three. Such groups stop a person from voicing his opinion. This is the danger when one body or one group gets too strong; it's too structured and the individual gets lost. . . . Three or four years ago we had two people in labor relations. Now we have a department with ten people. We employ a labor lawyer, whose function is to make our managers understand that we insist on certain principles and standards. His job is not to squeeze employees but to educate managers.

CORPORATE STRATEGY

Magna had a clear set of corporate objectives and a strategy for achieving them. As Magna's success became well known, its senior executives, expecially Frank Stronach, were increasingly sought out for interviews. Features appeared repeatedly in newspapers and popular magazines, on television, and even in books, which described Magna's objectives and plans for realizing them.

The company's primary objective was to become the most diversified supplier of parts, components, and assemblies to the North American automotive industry and to steadily increase its dollar share of total industry sales from its 1985 level of one percent. Magna intended to accomplish this by increasing its average "penetration level" or the average dollar value of Magna parts that went into every North American automobile.

Over the period 1979 to 1985, Magna's penetration level had risen from $8.95 to $49.00, with a goal of $100 per vehicle by 1988. The company exceeded the $100 goal in the middle of its 1986 fiscal year.

Management consistently referred to a three-pronged strategy that it felt would allow Magna to sustain its remarkable growth and achieve its objectives: (1) continued increases in market share for existing Magna products, (2) introduction of new products and technologies to the marketplace, driven by ongoing in-house research and development and joint ventures with partners who were leaders in product design and manufacturing capabilities, and (3) manufacturing and marketing of modular assemblies using a variety of Magna parts and components. For example, instead of manufacturing cooling fans and radiators independently, Magna intended to market one complete unit which included a fan, radiator, and shrouds and could be bolted directly into a vehicle on an assembly line.

In addition to its diversification strategy of building ever greater numbers of parts and components, Magna simultaneously pursued an ongoing strategy of vertical integration. This was mainly in the form of backward integration, described by many as a key reason for Magna's success as it allowed the company to reduce costs and respond quickly and flexibly to design changes by its customers. Magna integrated vertically by undertaking its own tool and die making — the company's original business — and by developing and applying its in-house expertise in robotics and computer-aided design/computer-aided manufacturing (CAD/CAM) to equip Magna for the so-called factory of the future. There was even speculation that a Magna company, which had designed and built its own robotics system, might market the systems as another product in the future.

Magna's medium-term strategy was to geographically cluster its operating units and their plants into "industrial campuses," each with an infrastructure of company-supported social and recreational services, such as day care, medical, educational, and fitness centers. Each campus would consist of a cluster of ten to twenty small autonomous plants, with the related operating group's office and product development center located on the campus as well. The goal of this concept was to enhance the working environment for Magna employees. Stronach estimated that "50 cents spent on something like day care in our campuses will return $1.50 in increased productivity." Magna's first campus was begun in Newmarket, Ontario, in 1985 with three new plants and associated offices. Land for other campuses was quickly being assembled in anticipation of future growth. An announcement had also been made that Magna would begin construction of another ten to twenty factory industrial campus on a 26-acre parcel of land in Waterloo, Ontario, in 1986.

One strategy for dealing with the company's rapid growth was raised by Jim McAlpine, Magna's executive vice-president and chief financial officer, who suggested in a 1985 interview that Magna intended to spin off at least one of its operating units by selling or distributing shares to the public in 1986. Magna would retain at least 52 percent of the unit's shares, 20 percent would be given to the unit's employees, 5 percent would go to management, and the remainder would probably be distributed to the public through an equity issue or divided plan. Such a strategy would reinforce Magna's corporate philosophy of decentralization. McAlpine added that "a spin-off allows our management teams to continue to grow as managers. We hope it reduces the buildup of bureaucracy." It seemed that Magna

International's main role in the future might be that of a holding company or a birthplace for a number of new companies.

INTERNATIONAL ACTIVITIES

An increasingly important component of Magna's corporate strategy was the recognition of the emphasis on international activity within the automobile industry. By 1985, Magna's international activities, on a number of fronts, had been relatively modest, but had resulted in the development of relationships that management felt would position the company to take advantage of a variety of opportunities. The 1985 annual report stated: "With patience and persistence, we will be able to build successfully upon these relationships and establish Magna as a participant in the key automotive markets of the world."

Magna's international activities before 1986 had consisted primarily of joint ventures with foreign companies where Magna's goal was to acquire new technologies and knowledge of new products and processes. Magna sought joint ventures to build a technology base quickly. Frank Stronach said, "It's too time-consuming to do it on our own. . . . We don't want to reinvent the wheel constantly." Here is a list of some major joint ventures that Magna had been involved in up to 1986. In 1985, Magna was in thirteen active joint ventures.

Joint venture partner	Partner's nationality	Part produced
1. Philips Group	Dutch	Electronic components
2. Veglia SA	French	Instrument clusters for Renault
3. Chausson	French	Aluminum radiators for Renault
4. Webasto GmbH	West German	Sun roofs
5. Willibald Grammer	West German	Foam technology for seats
6. Brown, Boveri et Cie AG	Swiss	Power trains for electric vehicles

Typical joint ventures entered into by Magna were those with two French auto parts suppliers. With Veglia SA, a French producer of dashboard equipment, Magna set up Invotek Instruments of Toronto to manufacture instrument clusters for the Renault Alliance and Encore. In 1984 with Société Anonyme des Usines Chausson, a Renault subsidiary, Magna established Thermag Industries Inc. of Mississauga. The purpose was to produce aluminum radiators for Renaults built in North America by AMC, instead of shipping radiators from France. An $8 million plant was to be built with production to begin in 1986. Magna took a 60 percent interest in the venture, in order to gain access to technology and markets, while Chausson took the minority 40 percent interest and supplied its technology.

In July 1984, Magna signed a joint venture agreement with the Japanese parts manufacturer Niles Buhin Co. At that time Japanese manufacturers were beginning to try to increase their penetration of the lucrative North American market. Simultaneously, Magna began negotiating with four or five other Japanese companies for similar ventures that Frank Stronach felt could bring Magna hundreds of millions of dollars in revenues over the next few years.

Niles Buhin was an electronics components maker. Unlike many Japanese parts suppliers, it did not belong to a particular car-making group, although most of its business was with Nissan and Mitsubishi. At the time, Niles Buhin had annual sales of $150 million, while Magna's sales were $302 million.

Magna was again seeking access to advanced technology, primarily in electronics and light-weight materials, while Niles Buhin saw the venture as a good way to gain entry to a large and growing market far from its domestic bases. They were being encouraged to do so by the large Japanese car makers who wanted the parts makers to follow them to North America; but, because Japanese vehicle production would be insufficient to support them, the Japanese parts manufacturers required access to the big U.S. manufacturers as well. Some planned to try this on their own, but many saw joint ventures such as the one between Magna and Niles Buhin as a better alternative.

Japanese manufacturers were extemely sensitive about labor problems, but Magna's main selling point to the Japanese was its record of good labor relations. Management was of the opinion that the Japanese felt "quite comfortable" with Magna.

According to its 1985 annual report, in seeking additional joint ventures with the Japanese, Magna's primary targets were the Japanese vehicle manufacturers who had, or were planning to locate, production facilities in North America, as well as their suppliers, who were exploring opportunities to do business in North America. Magna's strategy was to demonstrate to the manufacturers that it could provide "world-class" products in terms of quality and value. With Japanese part suppliers, Magna sought to develop forms of cooperation in North America where both parties could contribute and prosper.

By 1985, Magna had licensed one of its products to Japanese parts suppliers for production and sale in Japan and had acquired licenses to manufacture and sell certain Japanese products in North America. The company was also in the midst of establishing a trading company with a Japanese parts supplier to coordinate the supply of certain products manufactured by Magna to one of the Japanese auto makers located in North America.

In 1985, a tooling and production facility had been established in West Germany to supply European OEMs. Contracts had also been signed to supply some North American components to two German automakers.

An agreement was signed late in the year to establish a joint venture in the People's Republic of China to manufacture components for the Chinese auto market.

As fiscal 1986 approached, it was increasingly clear that Magna International was stepping up the pace of its international activities with ambitious hopes for the future of these operations.

MAGNA'S FUTURE PROSPECTS

As fiscal 1986 came to a close, it was becoming increasingly evident that the company Frank Stronach had built up from a rented Toronto garage might be coming to a crossroads in its history. A number of issues required resolution.

It appeared certain that the company's strong growth would continue unabated for at least the next few years. However, one could not help but wonder if Magna's traditional success formula would be adequate to accommodate further phenomenal growth. Would continued growth and the spinning off of new companies make it easier for the UAW to finally unionize some of Magna's factories and what repercussions would such an event have on Magna as a whole?

There had been a trend for the North American auto makers to obtain 100 percent of their components in one place to ensure consistency. Certainly no company in Canada was better positioned than Magna to make the most of that trend. Yet would this trend continue?

Magna's increasing international activities seemed to be the next logical step in the company's uninterrupted growth, but concern existed about how this would fit into Magna's current organizational structure which emphasized geographic clustering and a commonality of product lines among related operating units. Would modifications or exceptions to the Magna formula have to be made to accommodate these relatively new activities which were growing rapidly in relative importance?

Stronach's dynamic, entrepreneurial personality and vision undoubtedly accounted for a considerable measure of Magna's success. How would this role change as Magna continued to grow and Stronach became a smaller part of Magna's operations? One person noted that Stronach had all the pieces in place so that any of his chief executives could manage the company quite well. Yet others asked what effect his retirement might have on the company.

Frank Stronach once called Magna International's Corporate Constitution "perhaps the most important chapter in western industrial society in many years . . . that I believe will have an enormous bearing in the future structure of corporations [and] law making." As the new fiscal year approached, one could not help wondering whether that document was well suited to guide Magna International and other corporations into the 1990s.

REFERENCES

Arnott, Sheila, "What Our Top Executives Are Earning." *Financial Post*, May 1986.
Avery, Nick, and Alison Burkett, "Comparison of the Auto-Parts Market 1981–1984." Wilfrid Laurier University MBA Report, November 27, 1985 (unpublished).
Barnes, Kenneth, and Everett Banning, *Money-Makers! The Secrets of Canada's Most Successful Entrepreneurs*. Toronto: McClelland & Stewart, Ltd., 1985.
"Everybody's Business" (Global Television Program), *Various Video Excerpts re: Magna International, Inc.*

Galt, Virginia, ''Decentralizing, Worker Participation Plans Help Put Magna on the Road to Recovery.'' *Globe and Mail*, July 6, 1981, B1, B5.

Harrison, Douglas, ''Franco-Canadian Economic Bonds Are Increasing.'' *Kitchener-Waterloo Record*, February 17, 1985, B9.

Hart, Matthew, ''Frank As He'll Ever Be.'' *Financial Post Moneywise Magazine*, May 1986, 64–67.

Koch, Henry, ''Magna Spinoffs to Spur Waterloo Growth: Carroll.'' *Kitchener-Waterloo Record*, January 23, 1985, B9.

Lilley, Wayne, ''Small Is Beautiful.'' *Canadian Business*, 57 (6) (1984), 170–71.

''Magna Executive Optimistic About Firm's 1985 Showing.'' *Globe and Mail*, August 3, 1985, B5.

Magna International, Inc., *Annual Report 1984*, 1984.

Magna International, Inc., *Annual Report 1985*, 1985.

''Magna International, Inc.'' *Toronto Stock Exchange Review*, November 1984, 1–4.

Milner, Brian, ''Magna, Japanese Firm Form Joint Venture.'' *Globe and Mail*, July 30, 1984, B1.

Partridge, John, ''Small Is Beautiful to Magna Chief but He Still Aims to Be the Biggest.'' *Globe and Mail*, January 5, 1985, B1, B3.

Waddell, Christopher, ''Magna Chairman Sells Shares but Remains Firmly in the Saddle.'' *Globe and Mail*, December 7, 1984, B1–B2.

Waddell, Christopher, ''Magna Hopes to Be Supplier for GM's Saturn.'' *Globe and Mail*, April 19, 1985, B3.

Walker, Dean, ''The Capitalist's Gospel According to Frank Stronach.'' *Executive*, May 1984, 46–49.

Wilson, Sharon E., ''The Best of Both Worlds: How Large Corporations Can Benefit from Decentralized Manufacturing,'' Wilfrid Laurier University Report, August 1985 (unpublished).

APPENDIX A: MARKET OVERVIEW

The autoparts market can be divided into eight sections. Passenger car, light truck, medium and heavy truck, and off-highway vehicles give the four major sections and each of these can be broken into original equipment (O.E.) and aftermarket. A further subdivision could be made in aftermarket between the original equipment aftermarket and the third-party aftermarket. That subdivision is not considered here.

Most autoparts companies cover more than one segment, so companies can be competitors with some products and not others. Competitors also depend upon whether a company is in the original equipment market or aftermarket. Canadian aftermarket firms concentrate on the Canadian market because of the duty collectible in crossing the Canadian–U.S. border. Original equipment, on the other hand, is duty-free under the autopact, and therefore firms in both Canada and the United States compete for this business.

The business cycles for original equipment and the aftermarket tend to be counter-cyclical. When new vehicle sales are down, the sales of replacement parts tend to be up, thereby giving some protection to firms that are in both market segments. Major companies have the following characteristics:

Budd Canada	Passenger car	O.E. & aftermarket
	Light truck	O.E.
Hayes-Dana	Passenger car	O.E. & aftermarket
	Light truck	O.E. & aftermarket
	Medium and heavy truck	O.E. & aftermarket
	Off-highway vehicles	O.E. & aftermarket
Magna International	Passenger car	O.E. & aftermarket
	Light truck	O.E. & aftermarket
Long Manufacturing	Passenger car	O.E. & aftermarket
	Light truck	O.E. & aftermarket
	Medium and heavy truck	O.E. & aftermarket
	Off-highway vehicles	O.E.

INDUSTRY OVERVIEW FOR 1984

Sales of cars and light trucks again increased by 19 percent. The market for other trucks and off-highway vehicles did not improve.

Statistical process control and just-in-time delivery were taken up by the whole autoparts industry. The new threat to the autoparts industry was the statement from the manufacturers that the supplier base was to be cut 50 percent within 3 years to reduce their overhead in dealing with suppliers as well as to increase control.

BUDD CANADA IN 1984

Budd had a good year in 1984. Sales increased by 36 percent and net profits were $11.2 million compared to 1983's loss of $2.2 million.

This was due to several factors:

General administration expenses were kept under control, resulting in expenses as a percentage of sales of only 8 percent compared with their historical average of about 10 percent.

Cost of goods sold was reduced even lower than the 1980 level (81.2 percent compared with 84.9 percent in 1980). This was the result of fully utilizing the Kitchener plant because of the increased sales, as well as productivity gains made with the recent plant additions.

Budd not only showed a good profit in 1984, it also outperformed the market when we look at the net profits/net sales ratio. Return on investment ratios show it comparing favorable with the industry average.

The working capital management ratios show Budd comparing favorably with other companies. Aggressive management of accounts receivable shows a decrease from days receivable from 78 to 58 days.

Liquidity and solvency ratios show excellent positions.

HAYES-DANA IN 1984

1984 saw Hayes-Dana's sales increase by 31 percent, and profitability increase by 170 percent. The favorable profit picture comes from:

Improving the cost-of-goods-sold percentage by 3.5 percent of sales, resulting in a favorable variance of $11.9 million.

Depreciation expense was not at the 1983 levels, resulting in an additional favorable variance of $2.5 million. This and the increase in investment income were offset by increased operating expenses of a full one percent of sales, resulting in an unfavorable variance of $3.9 million.

Days receivable again continued to increase in a year where all other manufacturers studied managed to reduce their collection period. Inventory turnover improved, but still lagged behind the industry. These working capital items accounted for $24 million of the funds available. As well, plant additions of $9 million and an increase of investment in affiliates used the funds raised from increasing current loans and other liabilities and from increasing long-term debt.

The end-of-the-year inventory at Hayes-Dana was higher than in other companies. Cost of goods sold was improving, but was not at the level Budd had achieved.

The $9 million plant addition in 1984 should improve the operating expense ratio in coming years. It would be reasonable to assume that Hayes-Dana could achieve the 81 percent cost of goods sold level that Budd and others have achieved.

MAGNA IN 1984

Magna's sales increased 63 percent in 1984, and net profits more than doubled. Magna obtained more than its share of the improving market in 1984, when we see the other companies' sales increase somewhere from 30 to 40 percent. The very favorable net profit results can be explained by the management of operating expenses. Operating expenses as a percentage of sales dropped from 85.3 percent to 74.9 percent. This level of operating expense reduction was not achieved by any of the other three companies.

Accounts receivable management was excellent, reducing the days receivable from 68.8 days to 63.9 days, the lowest it had been since 1980. It still remained significantly higher, however, than at the other companies studied.

Inventory management resulted in a slight drop of inventory turns; the result was, however, well within the results obtained by the other companies studied.

Plant expenditures for the year totaled $107 million; this obviously had a good effect on the operating expense reduction already discussed. The plant expansion was funded by an increase in long-term debt of $54 million and a stock offering which raised an additional $35 million.

At year end 1984, Magna was in a favorable liquidity and solvency position relative to the other companies studied.

LONG MANUFACTURING IN 1984

Long's sales increased to $49.5 million, up 39 percent from 1983. Return on equity at 41 percent was the best of the companies studied.

Long was driving down debt. The success was shown by the long-term debt to total assets ratio dropping to the low of the group of companies studied as well as the common stock equity to total assets ratio rising to a more usual level of 26 percent. This was achieved by paying off $6 million of the $7 million long-term debt and an additional $1.1 million of current debt.

The current ratio remained at 1.1 and the quick ratio dropped slightly to 0.5. Accounts receivable were brought down to 35 days and inventory turns rose again, up to 9.3; both were better than the other three companies showed.

APPENDIX B: EXCERPTS FROM 1985 ANNUAL REPORT (CORPORATE CONSTITUTION IN PRACTICE)

Magna's continued growth is based upon our unique corporate culture which allows the Company to make a better product for a better price.

Our culture recognizes that it takes three ingredients to be successful in business, namely: management, employees, and capital. Furthermore it requires that each of these ingredients has a right to share in the profits that it helps to generate. This foremost principle and other operating principles are enshrined in Magna's Corporate Constitution.

We in management continuously search for ways to stimulate employees to achieve greater productivity. In recent years this has been partially accomplished through the introduction of new technology. At Magna we continue to emphasize the human capital as we introduce technology in a manner that does not result in the displacement of employees. We are focusing on productivity improvements through new technology as a means of continuing to upgrade wages for production employees in the years ahead while maintaining our competitive position in the marketplace.

Management's primary responsibility is to demonstrate to employees that we care for their well-being, particularly with regard to wages, environment, safety in the workplace, fairness and equal opportunity for advancement. We are committed to these principles and intend to strengthen further our Human Resources department to make sure that our standards are maintained. A structure like this can only function through total openness. It is an education process. In our view the employees must fully understand the competitive factors facing the company as well as the facts surrounding our financial structure. I like to see employees reading the financial section of the papers in the morning realizing that they are shareholders of Magna. In fact, at this stage, our manufacturing and office employees own more than $30 million of Magna stock.

Members of management are also large shareholders in the Company. The value of their shares amounts to approximately $30 million and accordingly they have an interest in protecting the value of their investments. It is important for a healthy, growing company to have a strong equity base in relation to debt but we are sensitive to the effect of equity dilution on our ability to maintain investor confidence. Accordingly, we try to balance issues of new equity with growth in earnings per share.

Sales growth translates into the need for new production facilities. As a result, Magna's investment in land and buildings continues to increase. Management utilizes Magna's job creation capability to obtain favorable terms when purchasing land. We also seek joint venture partners to assist in the development of those lands. Our objective is to minimize Magna's capital outlay for land so as not to divert capital from our automotive components manufacturing activities.

QUALITY ASSURANCE

Quality is stressed throughout Magna — our success has been built on it — our future depends on it. We continue to train employees at all levels in matters relating to quality including the use of sophisticated measuring devices and statistical process control techniques. As a result of efforts in the area of quality, our operating units received many quality awards from our customers. Magna is dedicated to supplying automotive components and systems which are "world class" in quality and value.

HUMAN RESOURCES

Magna's greatest asset is its motivated work force. We continuously strive to provide a positive, safe and fair environment for all employees.

With this in mind we continue to expand our Human Resources departments at the Group and Corporate offices and sponsor seminars which stress the importance of good communications between management and employees. Wherever possible productivity gains are recognized with improved wages and expenditures to improve the working environment.

During the year we introduced *Magna People*, a bimonthly newsletter about Magna and its people. Simeon Park, which opened officially in June 1984, saw the introduction of many employee-organized functions, both winter and summer. The allocation to our Employee Equity Participation and Profit Sharing Program amounted to $8.3 million in 1985 compared to $6.4 million last year.

OTHER EMPLOYEE PROGRAMS

We provide a number of other programs for our employees including the following:

1. *Simeon Park*: Magna has developed a recreational park on 100 acres of natural countryside just north of Toronto. This park, available to all Magna employees and their families, features a 23-acre lake, sports and recreation facilities including children's playgrounds, tennis and volleyball courts, soccer fields, a baseball diamond, barbecue pits and picnic areas, nature trails, fishing docks and a large swimming pool.

The park is readily accessible to the majority of Magna's employees. During 1985 it was used extensively for company picnics, competitive team sports and casual family outings.

2. *Industrial Campus Concept*: To provide employees with an improved work environment, Magna is developing an industrial campus which will consist of a cluster of ten to twenty small autonomous plants together with the related group office and product development center supported by social and recreational facilities such as day care, a medical office, educational and sporting facilities.

In 1985 three new plants went into production in our first campus being developed in Newmarket, Ontario. A new group administration office and product development center associated with these plants also opened during the year. Two additional plants were under construction at year end. Land for other campuses is being assembled in preparation for our future growth.

3. *Technical Training Center*: Consistent with our commitment to high quality in-house technical strength, Magna opened its first Technical Training Center in the fall of 1984. The school is equipped with modern classroom and shop facilities and the latest in machinery and equipment.

On completion of their training, apprentices will work in a Magna operating unit to complete the requirements for trade qualification.

The purpose of the center is to help fulfill Magna's demand for skilled tool and die makers and other technical trades. These students will also receive training in management practices.

4. *Continuing Education*: Magna encourages all employees continually to improve their skills and education. For this reason, we offer in-house training and education in areas of communication, safety, quality control, microcomputer applications and management skills.

SOCIAL RESPONSIBILITY

Magna believes it has a responsibility to support the basic fabric of society. We fulfill this obligation by giving financial assistance and contributing our time to programs and projects in the areas of health and welfare, youth, the advancement of art and culture, education, and in support of the political process. Examples of the programs we support include:

1. *University Teaching and Research Support*: Magna currently provides financial support to four universities for teaching and research concerning entrepreneurship and fair enterprise.

2. *Student Sponsorship*: Each year Magna sponsors a number of outstanding students to attend the GMI Engineering and Management Institute in Michigan. GMI is a private university offering degrees in engineering and industrial administration.

Sponsorship guarantees students financial support and planned work assignments in Magna plants as well as the offer of a full-time position with Magna upon graduation.

APPENDIX C: OPERATING STRUCTURE

OPERATING UNIT

Each operating unit is directed by a general manager and an assistant general manager who have complete authority and responsibility for the operation of their unit within broad guidelines established by Executive Group Management. These decentralized units generally employ approximately one hundred people, thus giving the management teams close contact with staff and immediate control of all matters affecting personnel, product quality, efficiency, and profitability of the unit.

GROUP MANAGEMENT

The operating units are grouped — geographically and by markets — under the direction of a group management team which is accountable to Executive Management. A group vice-president is responsible for all areas of activity in his group and is supported by marketing, financial, and human resources executives.

Each group has its own sales team which maintains the day-to-day contact with the customers, the group office, and the operating units.

The group financial staff monitors all financial activities including capital spending and operating results. Each group has its own quality control and human resources personnel which review the operating unit's performance and serve as a resource to the units.

Group Management also oversees research and technology development conducted for their group.

EXECUTIVE MANAGEMENT

Executive Management is responsible for establishing policies consistent with the company's philosophy as developed by the board of directors.

Strategic planning is a priority of Executive Management. This involves the

FIGURE 1
Magna operating
structure

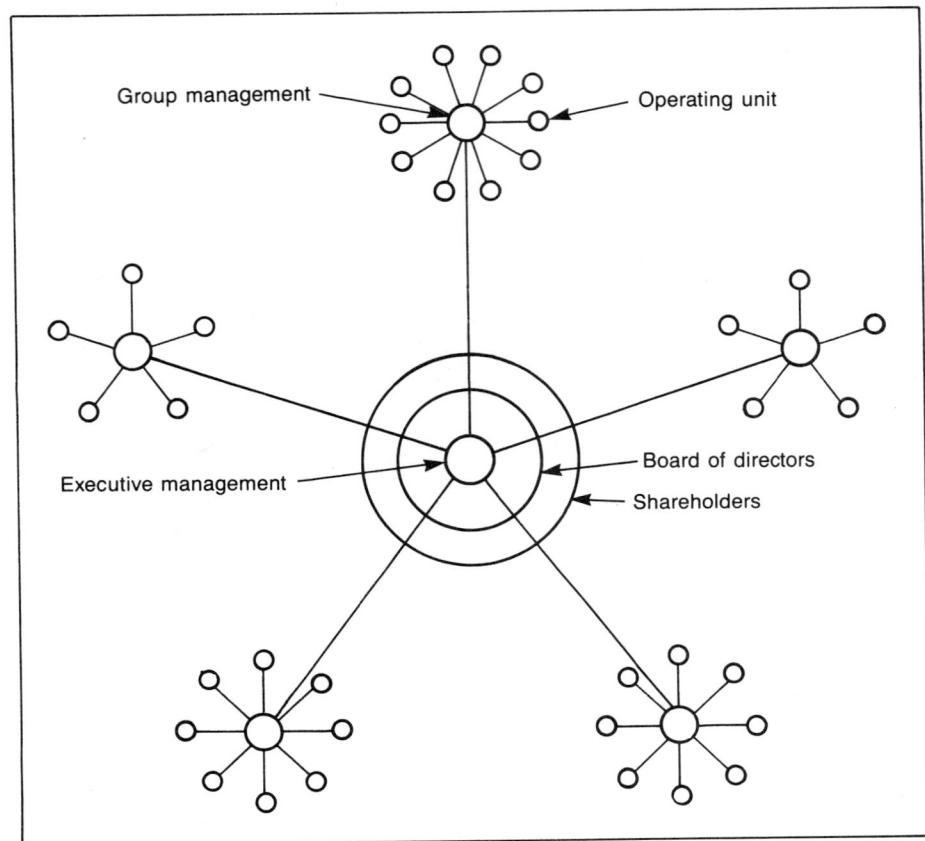

identification of specific products and technologies that Magna must develop in order to meet the challenges of an evolving marketplace. It also includes the establishment of management teams capable of implementing Magna's marketing, quality, human resources, and financial goals and objectives. As part of its responsibilities, Executive Management secures and allocates financial resources and, together with Group Management, monitors the performance of the operating units.

The corporate office serves as a resource to the groups and operating units in the acquisition of capital equipment, raw materials, and services. This system allows the groups and operating units to benefit from Magna's corporate buying power when it is to their advantage. However, responsibility for product quality and delivery rests with each operating unit and, accordingly, the units make purchases from whatever source best meets their individual requirements.

ASHLAND OIL, INC.

EARLY HISTORY

In 1924, Swiss Oil, an oil and gas exploration and production company based in Lexington, Ky., bought a small refinery near Catlettsburg in eastern Kentucky. Twelve years later the refinery was so successful that it merged with Swiss to form Ashland Oil & Refining Company. Since then, Ashland's history has included a significant number of acquisitions. The company grew initially by acquiring refining capacity, pipelines, and crude supply. Acquisitions included Allied Oil Company and Freedom-Valvoline Oil Company. In the 1960s, the company took its first step toward diversification by entering the chemical business. In 1962, it purchased United Carbon Company. This was followed by the acquisition of other chemical-producing companies. These chemical companies and Ashland's petrochemical operations were consolidated in 1967 to form Ashland Chemical Company.

During the 1960s, the company also expanded into highway construction and construction materials supply. In 1975, the construction company, later operated through APAC (Ashland Paving and Construction), was formed to encompass all the company's construction activities.

By the 1970s, Ashland Oil, Inc., as the parent company was called, had grown into a large conglomerate. In 1985, Ashland was the 48th largest industrial corporation in the United States with operations in refining, transporting, and marketing petroleum products; chemicals; coal; oil exploration; highway construction; and engineering services.

EXPLORATION ROLLERCOASTER

During the later 1960s, under Chairman and C.E.O. Orin Atkins, the company diversified heavily into crude oil exploration and production. These activities required

This case was written by John J. Craighead, research assistant, and Robert R. Gardner, associate director of the Maguire Oil and Gas Institute, under the direction of Professor M. Edgar Barrett. It was prepared as a basis for class discussion rather than to illustrate either effective or ineffective handling of an administrative situation. Copyright © 1986 by M. Edgar Barrett. Reprinted by permission.

an initial investment of $43 million between 1966 and 1969. One of these early exploration efforts resulted in eight dry holes in the Santa Barbara channel and an $8 million write-off. Exploration success continued to elude Ashland in the 1970s, when more write-offs were taken for abandoned projects in Alaska, Iran, and the Java Sea. Although it did drill some successful wells, by 1977 the company could supply only 20 percent of the crude oil requirements for its refineries. Citing high exploration costs (Ashland spent almost $900 million on exploration between 1972 and 1978) and lack of results, the company abruptly began selling much of its oil- and gas-producing property in 1978. The company sold its interest in Ashland Oil Canada Limited for $316 million in October 1978. In March and April 1979, the company sold various producing properties and leases in the Rocky Mountains, Southeast, Southwest, Midcontinent and Gulf Coast regions of the United States for $731 million. In the same year, Ashland sold all its interest in North Sea producing properties for $94.5 million. Management decided that the more than $1 billion raised from these property sales would be used for retiring debt, repurchasing stock, paying higher dividends, and making new acquisitions. In addition, funds were used to buy higher-priced crude and to pay an additional $256 million in taxes that resulted from the sale.

Following the property sales, Ashland became even more dependent on foreign sources of crude. Foreign supplies accounted for roughly 70 percent of the firm's crude requirements, most of this coming from OPEC countries. Iran in particular supplied more than 20 percent of Ashland's crude. (Crude supply from Iran was cut off entirely on November 12, 1979, when President Carter suspended imports of Iranian oil following a well-publicized incident in which American citizens in Iran were taken hostage.) Less than 4 percent of Ashland's crude oil requirements in 1980 came from production owned by Ashland.

COMPANY OPERATIONS BY 1985

Refining

In 1985, Ashland was the nation's largest independent refiner of petroleum products. All refining operations were controlled by Ashland Petroleum Company, a subsidiary of Ashland Oil. It operated refineries in Catlettsburg, Ky.; St. Paul Park, Minn.; and Canton, Ohio, with a total daily capacity of 357,000 barrels. Ashland's refineries operated at 83 percent of capacity in 1985, running an average of 297,458 barrels per day (bpd) of crude. (By comparison, the nation as a whole had a refinery utilization of 76.0 percent in 1984.[1]) The company supplied 7.9 percent of this amount with its own crude. (Exhibit 1 shows Ashland's crude oil and gas production.) The main refinery in Catlettsburg, Ky., included a recently completed 40,000 bpd reduced crude conversion complex. This conversion process increased the yield of gasoline, diesel, and jet fuel from heavy and high-sulfur crude or allowed current

---

[1] *National Petroleum News 1985 Factbook*, p. 134.

production levels to be maintained while using 20 percent less light crude.[2] In 1985, refining, wholesale marketing, and transportation of petroleum products amounted to 48 percent of the company earnings.[3]

Marketing

Marketing was also under the control of Ashland Petroleum. The company marketed gasoline through 1,910 outlets located throughout the Midwest and Mid-Atlantic states. The company owned 520 of these outlets, including 347 SuperAmerica convenience stores. The remaining 173 of these Ashland-owned outlets were independently operated, but sold gas under the Ashland name.

SuperAmerica sold one-fourth of all Ashland's gasoline. These convenience stores, or "C-stores," were on a larger scale than most of Ashland's competitors. SuperAmerica stations often had as many as thirty-six pumps. The store operation inside was larger than most convenience stores as well and could be described as a minigrocery store. SuperAmerica stations offered a wide variety of "nongas" merchandise, which accounted for approximately half of the stores' total sales. In addition to food products, the stores carried their own brand of cigarettes and (in some outlets) liquor.[4] Outlets in the Minneapolis-St. Paul area offered fresh-baked goods under the SuperMom's brand name.

Also part of Ashland Petroleum was Valvoline Oil Company. A registered trademark since 1873, Valvoline brand motor oil was the third-largest-selling motor oil in the nation in 1985 (in a motor oil market that Ashland officials considered to be extremely competitive). Valvoline products were sold through 107,000 retail outlets (including SuperAmerica) and in more than ninety-six countries throughout the world.

Exploration and Crude Supply

The subsidiary in charge of exploration and production was Ashland Exploration, Inc. With the sale of most of its producing properties in 1978 and 1979, the company was left with only a fraction of its former production. By 1985, Ashland's domestic producing interests were concentrated in the Appalachian region and the Illinois Basin. New drilling occurred primarily in the Houston region, mostly in southern Louisiana, with offshore drilling planned for the Gulf of Mexico.

All foreign operations were located in Nigeria. Foreign reserves rose to 49.2 million barrels during 1984, up 29.5 million barrels from the previous year.[5] This increase was mostly due to development of the Akam field, offshore Nigeria. The division expected to complete a floating storage facility in early 1986 which would

---

[2] "Ashland Oil Begins Production at Facility for Crude Conversion," *Wall Street Journal,* April 12, 1983, p. 3.

[3] "Remarks by John R. Hall, Chairman and Chief Executive Officer Ashland Oil, Inc. at the Year-end Presentation to Security Analysts," November 6, 1985, p. 13.

[4] "Ashland Believes It Can Pump Out Earnings Despite Uncertainties Concerning Oil Refining," *Wall Street Journal,* February 26, 1985, p. 63.

[5] "Nigerian Exploration Efforts Help Boost Ashland's Proved Reserves," *The Oil Daily,* November 9, 1984, p. A2.

	1985	1984	1983	1982	1981	1980
Crude oil (bpd)						
United States	2,755	2,500	2,700	2,700	2,800	3,100
Foreign	20,781	19,100	14,000	13,900	9,500	9,600
Total crude	23,536	21,600	16,700	16,600	12,300	12,700
Natural gas (mcf/day)						
United States	32,156	29,000	27,000	27,000	28,000	26,000

Note: Figures for fiscal year ending September 30.
Source: Ashland Oil company documents.

allow production to begin from eight development wells at the offshore Adanga field in Nigeria. The company's 5-year production data is shown in Exhibit 1.

Chemicals

Ashland Chemical Company, a wholly owned subsidiary of Ashland Oil, engaged in the manufacture, distribution, and sale of a wide variety of chemical products. It was divided into several specialty divisions.

One of these specialty divisions, Industrial Chemical and Solvents, was the largest distributor of industrial chemicals in the country. It sold its own products, as well as those of many other manufacturers, through seventy-seven distribution centers located throughout North America. The division specialized in supplying mixed truckload and less-then-truckload quantities to the paint, oilfield, automotive, paper, and rubber industries. This flexibility was said to allow them to sell to small, specialized companies that purchased in smaller quantities than large firms.

Ashland manufactured and sold high-purity chemicals to the electronic and high technology industries through its Electronic & Laboratory Specialty Division. These liquid chemicals and gases were used in manufacturing silicon chips. The Petrochemicals Division marketed aromatic hydrocarbons, malic anhydride and other petroleum-based products.

Coal

The company was a major coal producer through Ashland Coal Inc., a 65-percent-owned subsidiary, and Arch Minerals Corporation, in which the company had a 50 percent interest. These firms mined coal in Alabama, Illinois, Kentucky, West Virginia, and Wyoming and sold to electric utilities and industrial users. Combined sales of these operations placed Ashland among the top coal producers in the nation.

Engineering and Construction

Ashland's Engineering and Construction unit was composed of the APAC construction subsidiaries and a group of companies known as the Engineering Services Group, which were acquired in 1981 as part of the purchase of U.S. Filter Corporation.

Ashland's APAC subsidiary manufactured construction material and performed contract construction work. This contract work included paving highways, shopping centers, and parking lots. APAC operated in 13 Sunbelt states, with its administrative offices in Atlanta. The subsidiary owned 131 asphalt plants and 18 quarries.

The Engineering Services Group included several firms that were involved in architectural design, engineering services, and project management. One of these subsidiaries, Holmes and Narver, had designed security systems for the Los Angeles Olympics. Williams Brothers Engineering Company, another firm within the Engineering Services Group, was a leader in the design of oil, gas, and water pipelines and was a leading supplier of pipeline engineering services on the Alaskan North Slope. Projects of other firms included managing airport expansion and manufacturing pollution-control equipment.

STRATEGY DECISIONS, 1980–1983

Diversification into Unrelated Businesses

In addition to retiring debt, repurchasing stock, and paying increased dividends, management targeted a major portion of the cash raised from the 1978–1979 property sales for acquisitions in areas outside Ashland's normal operations. Ashland's 1981 annual report contained the following statement:

> *Since the early 1970s, the climate for U.S. business in general and the petroleum industry in particular has been affected increasingly by events beyond the control of either individual companies or the U.S. government. To survive and prosper in such a volatile environment, companies must be willing to reappraise traditional operations and aggressively explore and develop new business opportunities.*

These words came on the heels of two major acquisitions by Ashland. In the first of these, the firm entered the insurance business on January 1, 1981, with the purchase of the Integon Corporation for $238 million. (Payment was composed of $116 million in cash and $122 million of preferred stock. The excess $88,148,000 of the cost over the fair value of the assets acquired would be amortized over a 40-year period using the straight-line method.) Integon was an insurance holding company based in Winston-Salem, North Carolina. The company's primary business was the sale of life and health insurance; home protection policies; group life, annuity and health policies; and credit life and health policies. Through its subsidiaries, Integon also conducted a multiple line property and casualty insurance business, covering such risks as auto liability, fire, and workers' compensation. Integon Mortgage Guaranty Corporation, another subsidiary, was engaged in the mortgage guaranty business in the southeastern United States. Integon Realty Corporation invested in income-producing projects such as motels and office buildings and provided mortgages in the form of construction loans for new projects. As of August 31, 1981, Integon had a total of $10.6 billion of life insurance in force.

In the second of its major acquisitions, Ashland purchased United States Filter Corporation on January 1, 1981 for $402 million. (Payment was composed of $376 million in cash and $26 million in 13.5 percent notes. Goodwill of $150,532,000 would be amortized over 40 years by the straight-line method.) U.S. Filter was the parent company of a number of foreign and domestic firms whose activities included engineering and project management services for the oil, mining, pipeline, and steam-generation industries; design and manufacture of environmental control systems; production of steel castings for use in pumps, valves, turbines, and compressors for the petroleum, chemical, and power-generation industries; production of specialty chemicals for industry and marine shipping; design and manufacture of industrial process instruments; coal mining; and cement production. In 1980, U.S. Filter earned nearly $28 million on sales of $865 million.[6]

Ashland immediately transferred the specialty chemical division (Drew Chemical) of U.S. Filter to Ashland Chemical. The remaining U.S. Filter units were placed into a new subsidiary called Ashland Technology. The catalyst and clay operations of U.S. Filter were sold for $99 million in late 1981. Ashland Technology was divided into four operating groups: (1) the Engineering Services and Power Generation Group, (2) the Process Instruments Group, (3) the Environmental Systems Group, and (4) the Metal Fabrication and Casting Group.

Ashland officials made the following comments concerning the acquisitions of Integon and U.S. Filter and their position in future strategy:

Ashland's strategy has been to further diversify its asset base, enhance its flexibility to adapt to changes and take advantage of new opportunities as they arise. In 1981, the strategy moved forward dramatically with the two largest acquisitions in Ashland's history. Through U.S. Filter the company has expanded its chemical operations and acquired a very solid base in the fields of engineering services for energy-related projects and environmental control systems for industry. Through Integon, the company has entered the vital and rapidly expanding insurance industry. These new fields promise to enhance Ashland's financial strength and technological and engineering capability while at the same time opening doors for further growth into new areas of business.

Having made these two acquisitions, the company's strategic planning will now be concentrated in the following areas: (1) further strengthening of current operations and divestiture of any operations which do not hold strong prospects for growth, (2) continued reduction in operating costs, (3) further strengthening of the balance sheet, and (4) development of the company's many promising new technologies, such as the RCC process, as sources of income. Continuing diversification efforts will be highly selective and in areas compatible with existing core operations, to stimulate growth as well as new business opportunities. With the addition of Integon and U.S. Filter, we now have strong positions in energy, chemicals, construction, engineering and technology, and insurance. These will be our primary areas for expansion in future years.[7]

Management Changes

In September 1981, Orin Atkins unexpectedly retired as Ashland's chairman and chief executive officer. He was replaced by John R. Hall, a 24-year company veteran and, most recently, vice-chairman.

The exact reasons for Atkins's retirement were not made public at the time.

[6] U.S. Filter Corporation, 1980 Form 10-K, p. F-4.

[7] Ashland Oil, Inc., 1981 Annual Report, pp. 7–8.

Several months later, however, rumors of impropriety involving Atkins began to surface.[8] In 1980, on his personal order, Ashland paid $1,350,000 to a wealthy Libyan middleman, Yehia Omar, in return for his securing a contract with the country of Oman to supply 20,000 barrels of crude a day to Ashland. Soon after, top Ashland officials met to discuss whether this payment was legal. (These concerns were raised because under the 1977 Foreign Corrupt Policies Act, corporate payments to foreign government officials were illegal.) Since Omar had at one time carried an Omani diplomatic passport, it was possible that Ashland, by making these payments, had broken the law. The company's directors commissioned an independent investigation to look into the matter. The findings of this investigation cleared Atkins and Ashland of violating any U.S. law because Omar had not been an Omani official at the time of the payment. However, even though no law had been broken, the report criticized the impropriety of such payments.[9]

In early September 1981, Atkins met privately with several of Ashland's directors. It was reported that, at the meeting, the board voiced strong concerns regarding both Ashland's diversification moves and the nature of the Omani transaction.[10] "An element of the board thought we were doing too many things too fast," recalled F. H. Ross, a director and former Ashland executive.[11] Moreover, the company had just reported a 76 percent drop in profits for the months ending June 30, 1981. In a meeting on September 17, 1981, outside directors sought and received Atkins's resignation.[12]

Changing Economic Situation

The economic conditions that existed by the early 1980s were very different from what Ashland and many other U.S. firms had forecasted. Ashland's 1977 strategic plan had anticipated U.S. energy demand to increase steadily from 38.3 million barrels a day (mmbpd) of oil equivalent in 1978 to 47 mmbpd oil equivalent by 1990. In fact, actual U.S. energy demand was falling by the early 1980s. Real GNP growth was 1.3 percent annually instead of the 3 percent to 4 percent that had been expected. Interest rates were much higher than the company had anticipated. Furthermore, the U.S. economy experienced back-to-back recessions in 1980 and 1981–1982.

World crude prices, which had increased by this time to record levels, forced Ashland to use a greater portion of its cash flow on crude supplies for its refineries. At the same time, U.S. demand for petroleum products was falling. The national recession, high inflation, increased automobile fuel efficiency, and individual conser-

---

[8] "Ashland Oil Chief's Sudden '81 Departure Is Linked by Insiders to an Oman Payment," *Wall Street Journal,* May 16, 1983, p. 4.

[9] "Dubious Deals, Ashland Oil Criticizes Its Payments to Libyan To Get Oman's Crude," *Wall Street Journal,* May 24, 1983, p. 1.

[10] It was reported, for instance, that Ashland lost $2.3 million in a venture designed to produce reusable sausage casings. ("Dubious Deals," op. cit.)

[11] Ibid.

[12] "Ashland Oil Chief's Sudden '81 Departure," op. cit.

vation were all factors that led to a 6.4 percent drop in petroleum product demand in 1980.[13] The spread between crude and product prices had become so narrow that, in some instances, the prices received for petroleum products were less than refiners' crude oil costs.[14]

Alternative Sources of Energy

The economic conditions that existed in the early 1980s led Ashland officials to make investments that would take advantage of the situation. Since low-grade crude was cheaper and more readily available than light crude, the company converted some of its refineries so they could handle lower grades. In 1981, Ashland also began building a new 40,000 bpd refinery in Catlettsburg, Ky., that utilized its RCC process. The project cost was initially estimated at $190 million (though the final cost was $295 million).[15] The company justified the investment based on an estimate that the new refinery would increase pretax earnings by $10 million a month.[16]

With crude oil so expensive and in such short supply during the early 1980s, alternative methods for producing hydrocarbons became more attractive. One process, coal liquefaction, converted coal to liquid hydrocarbons. Ashland participated with the Department of Energy and other companies in building a coal liquefaction pilot plant near its main refinery in Catlettsburg. The company also planned a joint venture to build a commercial-scale liquefaction facility. Under the proposal, Ashland and five or six other companies would each invest $100–150 million in the project. The group would then negotiate guaranteed loans with the federal Synthetic Fuels Corporation. By 1982, Ashland had spent a total of $13 million on both projects.[17]

Hall's Initial Strategy

After John R. Hall took office in late 1981, he outlined a new direction for the company, which included three major strategic goals.[18]

The first goal was to strengthen the core business — refining. He proposed doing this by reducing the cost of raw materials used, namely crude oil. This was to be accomplished by becoming less dependent on foreign suppliers, which, as in the case of Iran, tended to be less reliable and more expensive than domestic sources. Hall also proposed reducing operating costs, mainly by improving refining efficiency. He wanted to put more emphasis on the marketing of Ashland's refined products as a way to strengthen the core business. This would involve increasing sales efforts

---

[13] Ashland Oil, Inc., 1980 Annual Report, p. 11.

[14] Ashland Oil, Inc., 1981 Form 10-K, p. 3.

[15] Ashland Oil, Inc., 1983 Form 10-K, p. 1.

[16] "Ashland Oil Begins Production," op. cit.

[17] "Ashland to Quit Role in Project For Synfuels," *Wall Street Journal*, November 23, 1982, p. 4.

[18] "Ashland Oil: Sequel To The Asset Redeployment Program," presented by John R. Hall at the Seminar for Senior Executives in the Oil & Gas Industry, Vail, Colorado, June 25, 1985.

and improving distribution of finished products. Reducing overhead was the final area in which Hall proposed strengthening the core business.

Hall's second major goal was to strengthen the financial situation of the company. Again Hall outlined several ways to achieve this. First, the company would try to maintain an "A" bond rating with the two major bond-rating services. To do this, it was felt that they would have to reduce the ratio of debt (plus preferred stock) to total capitalization to less than 40 percent. This was to be accomplished by repurchasing preferred stock and reducing long-term debt. Second, Hall wanted to achieve an overall return on equity of 17 percent, a return on assets of 12 percent, and a return on investment of 15 percent. Third, Hall hoped to reduce the dividend payout to 30–40 percent of normalized primary earnings. Fourth, he proposed improving the company's balance sheet by achieving real earnings-per-share growth. Finally, he desired to reduce corporate overhead. This could be accomplished, he asserted, by reducing G&A expenses through layoffs or realigning the corporate organization.

Hall's third major goal was defined under the broad heading of "diversifying profitability." For Ashland, diversification involved reducing dependence on the refining end of the business for earnings and cash flow. Hall stated that effective diversification could be achieved in two ways: (1) through investment in other segments of Ashland that had potential for profitable growth and (2) by acquiring outside businesses in either related or nonrelated fields.[19]

COMPANY DEVELOPMENTS AND DECISIONS

Refinery Closings

In 1980, Ashland operated seven refineries with a total daily capacity of 457,000 bpd. Throughout that year, its refinery system operated below capacity and processed an average of 363,000 bpd. The Findley refinery in Ohio, with a capacity of 21,000 bpd, was closed in the spring of 1981. A little over a year later, operations were suspended at the Buffalo, N.Y., refinery. The company blamed an "unprecedented decline in the demand for petroleum products" and "bleak prospects for a rebound" for this latest closing.[20] A third refinery in Louisville, Ky., closed its doors in April 1983. The company planned to make up the 13,000 bpd that the Louisville refinery had been producing by increasing operations at its main refinery in Catlettsburg, which was operating at 70 percent of capacity.[21]

In April 1985, the company suspended crude oil processing operations at its 7,000-bpd Freedom, Pa., refinery. The facility continued to operate as a product terminal and motor oil blending and packaging plant. The remaining refineries at

[19] Ibid.

[20] "Ashland Oil Unit To Idle Refinery Near Buffalo, N.Y.," *Wall Street Journal*, May 11, 1982, p. 12.

[21] "Ashland Expects Loss In Fiscal 2nd Quarter, Mulls Dividend Cut," *Wall Street Journal*, March 18, 1983, p. 7.

EXHIBIT 2
Ashland Oil refinery capacity and utilization (barrels per stream day)

	1985	1984	1983	1982	1981	1980
Catlettsburg, Ky.	220,000	220,000	195,000	195,000	195,000	220,000
St. Paul, Minn.	69,000	69,000	69,000	69,000	69,000	69,000
Canton, Ohio	68,000	68,000	68,000	68,000	68,000	66,000
Buffalo, N.Y.	—	—	—	—	48,000	48,000
Louisville, Ky.	—	—	—	26,000	26,000	26,000
Findlay, Ohio	—	—	—	—	—	21,000
Freedom, Pa.	—	7000	7000	7000	7000	7000
Total	357,000	364,000	339,000	365,000	413,000	457,000
Crude oil refined (bpd)	297,000	301,813	285,029	312,200	321,499	363,427
Refinery runs/ capacity	83%	83%	84%	86%	78%	80%

Source: Ashland Oil company documents.

Catlettsburg; Canton, Ohio; and St. Paul Park, Minn., were equipped to process a wider variety of crudes, including low-quality crude. (See Exhibit 2.)

Acquisitions   Late in 1982, the company bought the crude oil gathering and transportation system of Scurlock Oil of Houston for $80 million. Scurlock's system, mostly in Texas and Louisiana, included 2,300 miles of oil pipeline (capable of moving 200,000 bpd of crude) as well as 2.5 million barrels of storage capacity. This system gave the company access to a significant amount of domestic crude, kept it in contact with major domestic producers, and allowed it to make offers to purchase the oil it transported. "We believe the acquisition will prove to be one of the most beneficial ever made," said Charles J. Luellen, president of Ashland Petroleum and senior vice-president of Ashland Oil, "because it will substantially increase our supply of secure, economically priced U.S. crude oil."[22] "This was a very positive acquisition," echoed John Dansby, Ashland's vice-president of planning. "It's hard to imagine a single decision that could have had a more decisive impact on the company."[23] Overnight, the Scurlock acquisition had increased Ashland's supply of domestic crude by 60,000 to 80,000 bpd.[24] Scurlock also had the advantage of posting the price it was willing to pay for crude. This allowed Ashland to adjust its purchasing price just like other majors did.

The company also acquired Tresler Oil Company in 1982. Tresler marketed oil products in the Ohio River Valley and operated a river-front petroleum-product

[22] "A Troubled Ashland Banks On Chemicals," *Chemical Week,* June 23, 1982, p. 44.

[23] John Dansby, vice-president strategic planning, Ashland Oil, Inc. (December 3, 1985 interview, Ashland, Ky.).

[24] Ibid.

storage terminal. Ashland officials believed this acquisition would strengthen the company's marketing and distribution network for refined products in the Ohio River market.

Coal

In November 1982, Ashland pulled out of its proposed coal-liquefaction project. The company suspended participation because of uncertainty about crude prices, the massive capital investment necessary to construct the project, exposure to possible cost overruns, and tax law changes that reduced the tax benefits of the project. Ashland officials said costs of the project had been expended as incurred, so the decision would not affect the company financially.[25]

In June 1981, Ashland sold a 25 percent interest in Ashland Coal to Saarbergwerke A.G. of West Germany for $102.5 million in cash. Saarbergwerke was 74 percent owned by the West German government. Proceeds from the sale were used to retire short-term obligations of Ashland Coal. Company officials said the deal provided Ashland Coal with a new export dimension in its overall marketing activity.[26]

The company sold an additional 10 percent of Ashland Coal in June 1982 for $44.3 million to Carboex S.A., a coal supply firm owned by the Spanish government. This reduced Ashland's ownership of the coal subsidiary to 65 percent.[27]

Cost Control and Debt Reduction

In an attempt to promote efficiency and cost control in all operations, Ashland Oil, the parent company, was realigned along the lines of a holding company. A core group, made up of seven top parent-company executives, monitored and reviewed the overall performance of the divisions. However, day-to-day operational decisions were turned over to divisional managers. This management structure was expected to give the divisions something close to the autonomy of separate companies.[28] By taking on their own administrative functions, the divisions were said to avoid a good measure of bureaucracy and to respond faster to market forces.[29] Through this process of realignment, Ashland was able to trim corporate staff by one-third.

Between 1981 and 1985, Ashland reduced debt and capitalized leases by $206 million. This included exchanging $23,167,000 of capital stock for long-term debt in 1983. During the same 5-year period, the company reduced preferred stock by $109 million. In 1985 alone, the company reduced redeemable preferred stock by $54 million and long-term debt and capitalized leases by $41 million. As of September 30, 1985, long-term debt, capitalized leases, and redeemable preferred stock represented 39 percent of total capitalization, compared to 44 percent the year before.

---

[25] "Ashland Drops Breckenridge H-Coal Project," *Oil & Gas Journal,* November 29, 1982, p. 43.

[26] "Ashland Nears Sale of Coal Unit Stake to West Germany," *Wall Street Journal,* May 28, 1981, p. 7.

[27] Ashland Oil, Inc., 1982 Form 10-K, p. 7.

[28] "A Troubled Ashland Banks On Chemicals," op. cit.

[29] Ibid.

EXHIBIT 3
Summary of
earnings per share
and dividends per
share

	1985	1984	1983	1982	1981	1980	1979
Earnings							
From operations and investments	$4.12	$2.13	$2.23	$4.75	$2.22	$6.49	$ 5.31
From divestitures and write-offs		(9.53)		.54		.31	10.24
From extraordinary gain from exchange of common stock for long-term debt			.23				
Total earnings per share	4.12	(7.40)	2.46	5.29	2.22	6.80	15.55
Dividends per share	1.60	1.60	2.20	2.40	2.40	2.20	1.80

Source: Ashland Oil company documents.

(Appendixes B and C provide greater detail on this subject.) Exhibit 3 shows earnings per share and dividends per common share paid by the company.

Integon

To compete in the increasingly competitive deregulated insurance industry, Integon, in 1982, started selling a more flexible universal life policy offering a higher yield to policyholders. During fiscal 1983, the insurance company sold most of its group accident and health business — reportedly because of rising costs of healthcare claims.[30] Exhibit 4 shows Integon's financial results for 1981 through 1984.

For the 6 months ending February 29, 1984, Integon's profits declined 59 percent to $4.9 million (from $7.8 million in the year-earlier period).[31] At Ashland's annual meeting in January 1984, William Seaton, vice-chairman and chief financial officer, said that Integon's income had decreased because of higher losses on property and casualty insurance. Further, he said, volatile interest rates and other available investment opportunities made Integon's ordinary life insurance policies less attractive to consumers.[32] Policyholders continued to surrender ordinary life insurance policies at higher than normal rates.

Ashland Technology

By late 1983, it was becoming clear, as well, that many units within Ashland Technology were not performing up to company expectations.[33] Most of the former U.S. Filter businesses were not market leaders and company officials concluded

[30] Ashland Oil, Inc., 1983 Annual Report, p. 30.

[31] "Ashland Oil Seeks Buyer for Integon, Its Insurance Unit," *Wall Street Journal,* May 22, 1984, p. 10.

[32] Ibid.

[33] "Ashland Oil: Trying to Cope With a Diversification Hangover and a Lingering Scandal," *Business Week,* November 7, 1983, p. 134.

EXHIBIT 4
Summary of Integon financial results (in millions)

	1984	1983	1982	1981
Net income	$9	$13	$14	$8
Life insurance in force	14,332	12,324	9,314	10,600

Source: Ashland Oil company documents.

EXHIBIT 5
Summary of Ashland Technology financial results

	1984	1983	1982	1981[a]
Sales and operating revenue	$677,239	$633,123	$817,727	$588,786
Operating income	21,916	700	22,506	8,798
Funds provided from operations	34,863	18,720	20,100	22,522
Backlog of projects	614,000	527,000	666,000	784,000

Note: Figures in thousands of dollars, for fiscal year ending September 30.
[a] Includes only nine months starting January 1.
Source: Ashland Oil company documents.

that they probably paid too much for U.S. Filter.[34] Segment data for Ashland Technology appears in Exhibit 5.

BACK TO BASICS

Divestiture and Redirection

In September 1984, Ashland announced plans to sell Integon and most of the U.S. Filter units (by now part of Ashland Technology) it had acquired just 4 years earlier.[35] The decision resulted in a one-time charge against after-tax earnings of $271 million in the fourth quarter of 1984. The write-down included the difference between the book value of the units to be divested and the $300 million after-tax proceeds expected to be generated from their sale in fiscal 1985.[36] It also included the write-down of an unprofitable methanol plant in Louisiana. After taking the charge, Ashland showed a net loss of $172 million for the year.

Ashland's 1984 "Letter to the Stockholders" justified the divestment and write-downs as follows:

[34] Ibid.

[35] As part of the divestment, Ashland sold all of Ashland Technology with the exception of the engineering services group, Riley-Beaird (which was part of the metal fabrication and casting group) and the recently acquired Daniel, Munn, Johnson & Mendenhall (an architecture and civil engineering firm).

[36] "Back to the Basics, with a $270 Million Loss," *Chemical Week,* September 26, 1984, p. 9.

After careful study, we decided to reduce the scope of our activities in order to concentrate resources in growth areas which offer the greatest potential return to shareholders. We expect the divestiture to generate approximately $300 million which we plan to use to reduce outstanding preferred stock, retire debt and fund investments in growth businesses. Although the write-offs adversely affected the debt-equity ratio by reducing shareholders' equity, the balance sheet will be strengthened by our planned use of the proceeds. In addition, earnings per share will be improved as outstanding preferred stock is reduced. Despite the impact on 1984 earnings, we believe the divestiture and use of proceeds will be in the long-term best interest of shareholders.[37]

The company continued to pursue two of its three original major goals: strengthening the refining business and improving the balance sheet. However, the third goal, to diversify profitability, was altered. Ashland managers were determined that they would no longer attempt to diversify by acquiring businesses in nonrelated industries. Rather, they would attempt to reduce Ashland's reliance on refining by investing only in related nonrefining businesses. Moreover, Ashland officials planned to divest unprofitable units and concentrate on ones that had proved consistently successful.

In particular, six of Ashland's existing businesses had been identified in late 1983 as growth areas that the firm would actively pursue. Management hoped these areas would provide increased profits as well as diversification away from refining. These areas were: (1) Valvoline Motor Oil, (2) SuperAmerica convenience stores, (3) chemical distribution, (4) specialty chemicals, (5) domestic exploration and production, and (6) engineering services.

In selecting these six areas, Ashland's management had particularly emphasized their firm's competitive position in each of the various businesses. Once these businesses were selected, they were analyzed under varying scenarios in an attempt to gauge their relative contributions to corporate income. In so doing, Ashland officials determined that these six areas might well be sufficient to meet the firm's financial goals.

Valvoline

Company officials believed success for Valvoline could be achieved through innovative marketing and product flexibility. The firm, for example, sponsored auto racing teams, which allowed the Valvoline trademark to be displayed on race cars during such races as the Indianapolis 500. They were also an active sponsor of NCAA basketball games.

The Valvoline division had recently introduced several new products, including FourGard Motor Oil (an oil specifically designed for small, four-cylinder passenger cars) and Turbo V (an oil designed for turbo engine cars).

Management intended to start packaging its Valvoline products in one-quart plastic bottles in 1986, as some other motor oil companies already had. By the summer of 1986, it expected all nine U.S. packaging plants to be able to produce the plastic bottles. Valvoline targeted the do-it-yourself consumer and sold its motor oil mostly through distributors, such as K-Mart, rather than through service stations.

[37] Ashland Oil, Inc., 1984 Annual Report, pp. 2–3.

EXHIBIT 6
U.S. annual share-of-purchases for all motor oil

	1984	1983	1982	1981	1980
Carried out by purchaser	69%	70%	71%	70%	69%
Installed where bought	31	30	29	30	31

Source: *1985 National Petroleum News Factbook.*

EXHIBIT 7
Ashland Petroleum Company financial summary

	1985	1984	1983
Sales and operating revenues	$5,377	5,678	5,700
Operating income			
Refining, wholesale marketing, and transportation	$ 180	40	138
Retail marketing[a]	$ 12	13	4
Valvoline	$ 43	40	39
Other	$ (22)	27	(5)
Total	$ 213[b]	120[b]	176

Note: Figures in millions.
[a] Includes SuperAmerica.
[b] Includes $12 million in income from unusual items in 1985 and $46 million in 1984.
Source: Ashland Oil company documents.

As Exhibit 6 illustrates, do-it-yourself consumers constituted more than two-thirds of the motor oil market.

Valvoline was third in motor oil market share behind Quaker State and Pennzoil. Valvoline management foresaw growth for their product in further market share penetration and expected to be the number two motor oil marketer by 1990.[38]

The Valvoline product line was expanded in September 1985 with the purchase of IG-LO Products Corporation. IG-LO was the nation's largest packager and marketer of refrigerant for automobile air-conditioners. Operating results for Valvoline, included as a part of the entire Ashland Petroleum Company's results, are shown in Exhibit 7.

SuperAmerica

Ashland officials planned to continue the rapid expansion of SuperAmerica by adding fifty new outlets each year. Many of these were planned in Southern Florida, which was outside SuperAmerica's established retail areas of the upper Midwest (where SuperAmerica held a 20 percent share of the retail gasoline market in the Minneapolis-St. Paul area) and the central Ohio Valley.

[38] "1984 Year-End Presentation," by John F. Boehm, vice-president of Ashland Petroleum Co. and president of Valvoline Oil Co., November 7, 1984, p. 14.

EXHIBIT 8
SuperAmerica
financial and
operating data

	1985	1984
Sales and operating revenues	$902	$810
Operating income[a]	$12	$13
Merchandise sales	$241	$212
Number of stores	347	306
Average gallonage per store per month	143,000	142,000

Note: Figures in millions.
[a] Includes other retail operations.
Source: Ashland Oil company documents.

Each new store required an investment of approximately $1 million, including land. Start-up costs were expensed as they were incurred. Each SuperAmerica outlet pumped an average of 143,000 gallons of gas per month. (By comparison, the average U.S. gasoline outlet pumped 66,311 gallons per month in 1984.[39]) Super-America also averaged $700,000 of nongas sales per year per outlet. (The average C-store, meanwhile, had $460,000 of in-store annual sales in 1984.[40]) Whereas most C-stores attracted customers with lower gas prices and then took relatively high margins on food items, Ashland management stressed that SuperAmerica's food and merchandise were priced competitively with lower-margin traditional grocery stores. Operating information for SuperAmerica is shown in Exhibit 8.

Chemical Distribution

Chemical distribution was conducted in part by the Industrial Chemical and Solvents Division. Ashland management intended to increase the number of distribution centers and offer a greater variety of products. The IC&S Division added three new distribution centers in 1985. In addition, Ashland bought General Polymers National in 1983 for $10 million. General Polymers manufactured thermoplastic resins and had distribution centers in Ohio, Illinois, Minnesota, and Texas. During 1985, General Polymers added two distribution centers, in Portland, Ore., and Seattle, bringing the total number of locations to sixteen. The company's goal was to have twenty locations by 1988.[41]

Specialty Chemicals

The specialty chemicals area of Ashland Chemical was seen by management as a means of establishing a niche in the chemical business. This division produced chemicals to fill a specific demand, such as the high-purity chemicals sold to the electronics industry. During 1983 and 1984, Ashland Chemical made several acquisitions and divestitures. The specialty chemical area acquired Scientific Gas Products, which produced and marketed equipment and high-purity gas to the electronics,

[39] *National Petroleum News 1985 Factbook,* p. 116.

[40] Ibid., p. 122.

[41] Ashland Oil, Inc., 1985 Annual Report, p. 17.

EXHIBIT 9
Ashland Chemical
financial data

	1985	1984	1983
Sales and operating revenues	$1,499	$1,501	$1,208
Operating income (loss)			
Chemical Distribution	40	42	36
Specialty Chemicals	28	27	11
Commodity Chemicals	22	3	(20)
Other	(22)	(17)	(26)
Total	68	55	1

Note: Figures in millions.
Source: Ashland Oil company documents.

medical, and industrial laboratory markets. It had facilities in Colorado, California, New Jersey, and Texas.

Two other large acquisitions were made by Ashland Chemical during this time, as well. Goodyear's adhesive manufacturing facilities and technology were acquired in 1984. Goodyear officials claimed to have sold the line because it did not match its business objectives.[42] In October 1985, Ashland agreed to purchase J. T. Baker Chemical Company. Ashland officials said the acquisition would permit them to broaden the line of chemicals the company offered to the electronics, semiconductor, laboratory, and other specialty markets. Baker's worldwide operations had annual sales of $80 million. Data on Specialty Chemicals and Chemical Distribution is shown in Exhibit 9.

Domestic Exploration and Production

Though the company had moved increasingly back into exploration since the massive divestitures of the late 1970s, company officials stressed that their reasons were now entirely different. They claimed no longer to view exploration and production as a means of supplying crude to their refineries (as the major companies did). Instead, said officials, they viewed exploration and production as a source of profits. This time, said Hall and his administration, the company would limit its efforts to projects with high probability of success. In this way, the exploration segment of the firm would function much more like an independent producer.[43] The company's goal for exploration and production was simply to "create value for the shareholder."[44] In effect, said John Dansby, Ashland's vice-president of planning, the company considered exploration and production just another nonrefining segment whose profits would contribute to the diversification plan.

As part of this new effort, Ashland, in 1981, brought in the former chief geologist of Shell Oil Co. to head Ashland Exploration. Until then, E&P operations had been limited to Nigeria, the eastern United States, and the Gulf Coast area. (Only

[42] "Ashland Oil Acquisition," *Wall Street Journal,* February 2, 1984, p. 10.

[43] "Ashland Oil: Sequel To The Asset Redeployment Program," op. cit., p. 25.

[44] John Dansby interview, op. cit.

EXHIBIT 10
Engineering
Services financial
and operating data

	1985	1984	1983
Sales and operating revenue	$396	$336	$287
Operating income	14	7	4
Backlog	345	466	492

Note: Figures in millions.
Source: Ashland Oil company documents.

domestic exploration and production operations, however, were considered to be one of the six so-called growth areas.) Domestic exploratory drilling was carried out in Texas and Louisiana and, by 1985, had resulted mainly in natural gas discoveries. Additions to domestic oil reserves came primarily from developmental drilling in the eastern United States. (See Table 6 in the appendix.)

Engineering Services

The last growth area, engineering services, included the remaining units from the U.S. Filter sell-off and the Los Angeles-based Daniel, Mann, Johnson & Mendenhall (DMJM). DMJM's projects included joint management of the Los Angeles International Airport expansion and design of the Baltimore Metro System.

The combination of DMJM, Holmes & Narver, and Williams Brothers made Ashland one of the leading providers of architectural, engineering, and other technical services. Holmes & Narver ranked sixth in total billings among the top five hundred design firms ranked by *Engineering News-Record*. DMJM placed in the top ten, while Williams Brothers was in the top fifty.[45]

According to company officials, the engineering services group required only limited capital expenditures. All firms within this growth area were heavily reliant on contracts from government entities.[46] Results for engineering services are shown in Exhibit 10.

OVERALL GOALS AND OBJECTIVES

The stated overall objective of Ashland's late 1983 shift in strategy was to reduce the percentage of earnings coming from refining by substantially increasing the earnings from the six growth areas. Exhibit 11 provides data on Ashland's stated 1990 goals regarding relative contribution to earnings. It also provides information on the firm's progress toward these goals.

Management further stated that it would like the firm's nonrefining businesses to be able to support earnings of $5 per share — even if refining should earn nothing.[47]

---

[45] Ashland Oil, Inc., 1984 Annual Report, pp. 27–28.

[46] "Remarks by John R. Hall," op. cit., p. 12.

[47] "Ashland Oil: Sequel To The Asset Redeployment Program," op. cit.

EXHIBIT 11
Ashland's relative
contribution to
earnings

	1983	1985	Proposed 1990
Refining and wholesale marketing	51%	48%	25%
Six growth areas	37	40	60
Other businesses	12	12	15

Source: Ashland Oil company documents.

APPENDIX: ASHLAND OIL, SELECTED FINANCIAL DATA

TABLE 1 Consolidated statements of income

	Years ended September 30		
	1985	*1984*	*1983*
Revenues			
Sales and operating revenues (including excise taxes)	$8,183,733	$8,544,064	$8,108,169
Other	54,206	77,168	91,302
	8,237,939	8,621,232	8,199,471
Costs and expenses			
Cost of sales and operating expenses	6,745,700	7,214,937	6,960,088
Excise taxes on products and merchandise	292,510	291,500	255,870
Selling, general, and administrative expenses	606,808	611,338	564,574
Depreciation, depletion, and amortization (including capitalized leases)	202,174	212,547	192,006
Foreign exploration taxes	38,690	38,887	30,905
	7,885,882	8,369,209	8,003,443
Operating income	352,057	252,023	196,028
Other income (expense)			
Interest income	20,309	19,723	31,821
Interest expense	(67,413)	(80,814)	(78,501)
Equity income	10,421	20,387	27,517
Other — net (including corporate administrative)	(57,014)	(67,446)	(72,807)
Divestitures and asset write-offs	(39,652)	(286,641)	—
Income (loss) before income taxes and extraordinary gain	218,708	(142,768)	104,058
Income taxes	71,986	29,710	7,421
Income (loss) before extraordinary gain	146,722	(172,478)	96,637
Extraordinary gain from exchange of common stock for long-term debt	—	—	6,196
Net income (loss)	$ 146,722	$ (172,478)	$ 102,833
Earnings (loss) per share			
Income (loss) before extraordinary gain	$4.12	$(7.40)	$2.23
Extraordinary gain	—	—	.23
	$4.12	$(7.40)	$2.46
Average common shares and equivalents outstanding	28,227	27,783	27,011

Note: Figures in thousands (except per-share data); years ended September 30.
Source: Ashland Oil, Inc., 1985 Annual Report.

TABLE 2 Consolidated balance sheets

	Years ended September 30	
	1985	*1984*
Assets		
Current assets		
Cash and short-term securities	$ 173,391	$ 132,111
Accounts receivable (less allowances for doubtful accounts of $27,409,000 in 1985 and $29,097,000 in 1984)	923,822	939,831
Construction completed and in progress — at contract prices	70,770	67,176
Refundable income taxes	—	33,837
Inventories	306,607	393,613
Deferred income tax benefits	62,360	59,605
Other current assets	58,782	50,799
	1,595,732	1,676,972
Investments and other assets		
Noncurrent net assets of operations held for sale	157,000	262,217
Investments in and advances to unconsolidated subsidiaries and affiliates	172,492	167,020
Cost in excess of net assets of companies acquired (less accumulated amortization of $4,626,000 in 1985 and $3,176,000 in 1984	50,107	48,190
Advance coal royalties	58,366	55,157
Other noncurrent assets	77,932	80,643
	515,897	613,227
Property, plant, and equipment		
Cost		
Petroleum	1,773,309	1,711,457
Chemical	335,154	305,428
Coal	180,503	185,631
Engineering and construction	379,132	353,325
Exploration	582,194	469,581
Other	8,037	8,089
Corporate	61,269	64,641
	3,319,598	3,098,152
Accumulated depreciation, depletion, and amortization	(1,503,594)	(1,351,410)
	1,816,004	1,746,742
	$3,927,633	$4,036,941
Liabilities and stockholders' equity		
Current liabilities		
Debt due within one year (including short-term notes of $1,200,000 in 1985 and $726,000 in 1984)	$ 30,455	$ 49,644
Trade and other payables	1,314,278	1,423,721
Contract advances and progress billings in excess of costs incurred	34,577	52,566
Income taxes	47,774	89,639
	1,427,084	1,615,570

TABLE 2 (continued)

TABLE 2 (continued)

	Years ended September 30	
	1985	*1984*
Noncurrent liabilities		
Long-term debt (less current portion)	510,467	544,846
Capitalized lease obligations (less current portion)	105,519	113,204
Other long-term liabilities and deferred credits	268,675	225,980
Deferred income taxes	380,240	331,783
Minority interest in consolidated subsidiaries	57,223	56,288
	1,322,124	1,272,101
Redeemable preferred stock (1985 redemption value — $260,305,000)	249,014	303,371
Common stockholders' equity		
Common stock, par value $1.00 per share		
Authorized — 60,000,000 shares		
Issued — 28,672,000 shares in 1985 and 28,264,000 shares in 1984	28,672	28,264
Paid-in capital	229,135	217,979
Retained earnings	690,621	619,373
Deferred translation adjustments	(12,682)	(14,506)
Common shares in treasury — at cost (285,000 shares in 1985 and 252,000 shares in 1984)	(6,335)	(5,211)
	929,411	845,899
Commitments and contingencies	$3,927,633	$4,036,941

Note: Figures in thousands for years ending September 30.
Source: Ashland Oil, Inc., 1985 Annual Report.

TABLE 3 Statements of changes in consolidated financial position

	Years ended September 30		
	1985	*1984*	*1983*
Funds retained from operations			
Income (loss) before extraordinary gain	$ 146,722	$(172,478)	$ 96,637
Expense (income) not affecting funds			
Depreciation, depletion and amortization	209,102	212,547	192,006
Deferred income taxes	53,981	49,894	24,084
Equity income — net of dividends	(4,981)	(16,785)	(21,032)
Divestitures and asset write-offs — net of current income taxes	25,952	291,915	—
Other — net	16,452	12,356	1,547
Funds provided from operations	447,228	377,449	293,242
Decrease (increase) in working capital	(89,541)	(64,405)	(26,799)
Dividends	(74,142)	(76,165)	(94,449)
	303,545	236,879	171,994
Funds provided from (used for) financing			
Issuance of long-term debt and capitalized lease obligations	63,417	59,623	7,827
Issuance of common stock	11,672	9,820	34,593
Repayment of long-term debt and capitalized lease obligations	(123,706)	(57,315)	(91,633)
Purchase, conversion and exchange of capital stock	(56,813)	(36,386)	(9,543)
Increase (decrease) in short-term notes	474	(15,057)	134
	(104,956)	(39,315)	(58,622)
Funds provided from (used for) investment			
Additions to property, plant and equipment	(290,371)	(279,675)	(322,074)
Net assets of companies acquired			
Working capital (excluding cash and short-term securities)	—	(996)	(5,373)
Property, plant and equipment	—	(18,445)	(1,808)
Investments and other assets	—	(42,019)	(2,621)
Noncurrent liabilities	—	2,060	—
Proceeds from sale of operations (including working capital of $44,900,000 in 1985)	87,715	13,923	—
Net book value of property, plant and equipment disposals	23,717	51,970	55,874
Other — net	21,630	41,374	47,408
	(157,309)	(231,808)	(228,594)
Increase (decrease) in cash and short-term securities	$ 41,280	$ (34,244)	$(115,222)
Changes in components of working capital			
Decrease (increase) in current assets			
Accounts receivable	$ (18,010)	$ (13,680)	$ 78,689
Construction completed and in progress	(3,594)	(6,477)	2,644
Refundable income taxes	33,837	(8,366)	(25,471)
Inventories	56,123	(5,133)	(22,619)
Deferred income tax benefits	(10,912)	(43,949)	(4,098)
Other current assets	(9,218)	(7,829)	(2,281)
Increase (decrease) in current liabilities			
Trade and other payables	(84,068)	(24,950)	(17,068)
Contract advances and progress billings	(17,814)	(19,308)	(16,915)
Income taxes	(15,885)	65,287	(19,680)
	$ (69,541)	$ (64,405)	$ (26,799)

Note: Figures in thousands of dollars.
Source: Ashland Oil, Inc. 1985 Annual Report.

TABLE 4 Six-year selected financial information

	1985	1984	1983	1982	1981	1980
Summary of operations						
Revenues						
Sales and operating revenues (including excise taxes)	$8,184	$8,544	$8,108	$9,110	$9,506	$8,366
Other	54	77	91	94	75	64
Costs and expenses						
Cost of sales and operating expenses	(6,745)	(7,215)	(6,960)	(7,837)	(8,453)	(7,278)
Excise taxes on products and merchandise	(293)	(291)	(256)	(245)	(244)	(247)
Selling, general, and administrative expenses	(607)	(611)	(564)	(570)	(564)	(370)
Depreciation, depletion, and amortization	(202)	(213)	(192)	(171)	(153)	(131)
Foreign exploration taxes	(39)	(39)	(31)	(52)	(38)	(40)
Operating income	352	252	196	329	129	364
Other income (expense)						
Interest income	20	20	32	57	100	80
Interest expense	(67)	(81)	(79)	(79)	(98)	(89)
Equity income	11	20	28	13	23	11
Other — net (including corporate administrative)	(57)	(67)	(73)	(108)[a]	(34)[b]	(50)
Divestitures and asset write-offs	(40)	(287)	—	28	—	9
Income (loss) before income taxes and extraordinary gain	219	(143)	104	240	120	325
Income taxes	72	29	7	59	30	120
Income (loss) before extraordinary gain	147	(172)	97	181	90	205
Extraordinary gain from exchange of common stock for long-term debt	—	—	6	—	—	—
Net income (loss)[c]	$ 147	$ (172)	$ 103	$ 181	$ 90	$ 205
Balance sheet information						
Working capital						
Current assets	$1,596	$1,677	$1,630	$1,766	$1,867	$1,862
Current liabilities	(1,427)	(1,616)	(1,551)	(1,614)	(1,662)	(1,355)
	$ 169	$ 61	$ 79	$ 152	$ 205	$ 507
Total assets	$3,928	$4,037	$4,133	$4,210	$4,122	$3,358
Capitalization						
Long-term debt (less current portion)	$ 510	$ 545	$ 528	$ 585	$ 583	$ 462
Capitalized lease obligations (less current portion)	106	113	147	175	187	167
Deferred income taxes	380	332	290	252	206	123
Minority interest in consolidated subsidiaries	57	56	55	56	39	—
Redeemable preferred stock	249	303	344	353	358	245
Common stockholders' equity	929	846	1,085	1,047	972	907
	$2,231	$2,195	$2,449	$2,468	$2,345	$1,904
Cash flow information						
Funds provided from operations	$ 447	$ 377	$ 293	$ 380	$ 248	$ 339
Funds used for						
Additions to property, plant, and equipment	290	280	322	423	281	79
Dividends	74	76	94	99	94	264
Common stock information						
Earnings (loss) per share	$ 4.12	$ (7.40)	$ 2.46	$ 5.29	$ 2.22	$ 6.80
Dividends per share	1.60	1.60	2.20	2.40	2.40	2.20

Note: Data in millions except per-share data.
[a] Includes a loss of $26,000,000 from the write-off of investments in and loans to a foreign company and $22,000,000 in employee retirement, termination, and relocation costs.
[b] Includes a gain of $23,000,000 from prepayment of long-term debt.
[c] Divestitures and asset write-offs did not have a material effect on net income for 1985, but resulted in a net loss of $265,000,000 in 1984 and net income of $16,000,000 in 1982.
Source: Ashland Oil Inc., 1984 and 1985 Annual Reports.

TABLE 5 Five-year information by industry segment

	Years ended September 30				
	1985	1984	1983	1982	1981
Sales and operating revenues					
Petroleum (including excise taxes)	$5,377	$5,678	$5,700	$6,485	$7,044
Chemical	1,499	1,501	1,208	1,197	1,330
Coal	196	197	150	177	175
Engineering and construction	1,217	1,292	1,152	1,330	1,144
Exploration	287	276	226	241	190
Other	1	1	4	41	85
Intersegment sales	(393)	(401)	(332)	(361)	(462)
	$8,184	$8,544	$8,108	$9,110	$9,506
Operating income (loss)					
Petroleum	$ 213	$ 120	$ 176	$ 220	$ (6)
Chemical	68	55	1	28	41
Coal	15	19	—	16	15
Engineering and construction	54	45	2	36	38
Exploration (net of foreign exploration taxes)	5	15	20	39	42
Other	(3)	(2)	(3)	(10)	(1)
	$ 352	$ 252	$ 196	$ 329	$ 129
Identifiable assets					
Petroleum	$1,782	$1,831	$1,885	$1,775	$1,571
Chemical	496	503	423	402	463
Coal	220	226	195	244	209
Engineering and construction	433	503	602	675	672
Exploration	414	364	264	210	129
Other	7	15	8	11	117
Corporate	576	595	756	893	961
	$3,928	$4,037	$4,133	$4,210	$4,122
Funds provided from operations					
Petroleum	$ 242	$ 201	$ 224	$ 233	$ 59
Chemical	63	53	18	44	52
Coal	27	30	12	27	30
Engineering and construction	58	63	34	46	63
Exploration	67	66	49	69	40
Other	1	4	—	5	(2)
Corporate	(11)	(40)	(44)	(44)	6
	$ 447	$ 377	$ 293	$ 380	$ 248
Additions to property, plant, and equipment					
Petroleum	$ 86	$ 87	$ 186	$ 214	$ 118
Chemical	39	22	20	27	35
Coal	7	26	11	43	23
Engineering and construction	30	26	20	26	28
Exploration	120	116	74	92	35
Other	—	—	2	1	4
Corporate	8	3	9	20	38
	$ 290	$ 280	$ 322	$ 423	$ 281

TABLE 5 (continued)

TABLE 5 (continued)

	Years ended September 30				
	1985	1984	1983	1982	1981
Depreciation, depletion, and amortization					
Petroleum	$ 93	$ 92	$ 80	$ 72	$ 64
Chemical	24	23	21	19	16
Coal	11	12	14	17	16
Engineering and construction	27	36	40	38	36
Exploration	47	42	28	13	11
Other	—	—	1	4	4
Corporate	7	8	8	8	6
	$ 209	$ 213	$ 192	$ 171	$ 153

Note: Figures in millions.
Source: Ashland Oil, Inc., 1985 Annual Report.

TABLE 6 Crude oil and natural gas reserves

	1985			1984			1983		
	U.S.	Nigeria	Total	U.S.	Nigeria	Total	U.S.	Nigeria	Total
Crude oil reserves (in millions of barrels)									
Proved developed and undeveloped reserves									
Beginning of year	5.5	49.2	54.7	5.7	19.7	25.4	6.2	11.5	17.7
Revisions of previous estimates	(.1)	2.8	2.7	(.1)	—	(.1)	—	—	—
Extensions and discoveries	.6	4.3	4.9	.8	36.5	37.3	.5	13.3	13.8
Production	(1.0)	(7.6)	(8.6)	(.9)	(7.0)	(7.9)	(1.0)	(5.1)	(6.1)
End of year	5.0	48.7	53.7	5.5	49.2	54.7	5.7	19.7	25.4
Proved developed reserves									
Beginning of year	5.2	34.5	39.7	5.2	19.7	24.9	5.8	11.5	17.3
End of year	4.9	45.5	50.4	5.2	34.5	39.7	5.2	19.7	24.9
Natural gas reserves (in billions of cubic feet)									
Proved developed and undeveloped reserves									
Beginning of year	213.9			206.2			208.5		
Revisions of previous estimates	(4.6)			(.2)			4.6		
Extensions and discoveries	18.7			18.7			2.8		
Production	(11.7)			(10.8)			(9.7)		
End of year	216.3			213.9			206.2		
Proved developed reserves									
Beginning of year	161.6			155.2			151.6		
End of year	166.6			161.6			155.2		

Note: Data for years ended September 30.
Source: Ashland Oil, Inc., 1985 Annual Report.

TABLE 7 Selected operating information

	Years ended September 30				
	1984	*1983*	*1982*	*1981*	*1980*
Net proved developed and undeveloped reserves[a]					
Crude oil (millions of barrels)					
United States	5.5	5.7	6.2	6.3	6.2
Nigeria	49.2	19.7	11.5	10.8	12.7
Natural gas (billions of cubic feet)[b]	213.9	206.2	208.5	216.9	213.3
Net production					
Crude oil (barrels per day)					
United States	2,508	2,677	2,725	2,815	3,141
Foreign					
Nigeria					
Onshore	11,858	14,066	12,079	7,505	6,876
Offshore	7,222	—	—	—	—
Sharjah	—	—	1,761	1,927	2,660
Natural gas (thousands of cubic feet per day)[b]	29,483	26,715	27,360	28,359	26,321
Average sales price					
Crude oil (per barrel)					
United States	$28.84	$29.59	$32.68	$35.04	$32.90
Foreign	29.95	31.74	35.44	37.61	33.70
Natural gas (per thousand cubic feet)[b]	3.59	3.26	2.74	2.26	1.82
Net producing wells					
Crude oil					
United States	1,531	1,516	1,475	1,451	1,487
Foreign	24	16	16	11	13
Natural gas[b]	1,015	902	899	949	896
Net oil and gas acreage (thousands of acres)					
Producing					
United States	514	501	501	495	489
Foreign	174	75	98	98	98
Undeveloped					
United States	337	288	277	269	277
Foreign	—	99	99	99	99
Drilling activities					
Net productive exploratory wells drilled					
United States	20	4	8	7	—
Foreign	3	—	—	—	3
Net dry exploratory wells drilled					
United States	24	18	6	3	1
Foreign	—	3	—	—	—
Net productive development wells drilled					
United States	51	31	60	26	29
Foreign	6	7	5	2	2
Net dry development wells drilled					
United States	8	6	5	1	8
Foreign	1	1	—	—	—

[a] United States crude oil and natural gas reserves are reported net of royalties and interests owned by others. Nigeria crude oil reserves relate to reserves available to Ashland, as producer, under a long-term production-sharing contract with the Nigerian National Petroleum Corporation.
[b] Amounts relate to U.S. operations. Ashland has no material natural gas reserves outside the United States.
Source: Ashland Oil Inc., Financial & Operating Supplement 1984.

148

TABLE 8 Sales, production, and processing data

| Year ended September 30 | Crude oil processed (in barrels) | | Refined products produced (in barrels) | | | | |
	Total for the period	Average per day	Gasoline jet fuel, aromatics, & naphthas	Kerosene & distillates	Heavy fuel oils	Asphalt	Other
1984	110,463,493	301,813	68,993,847	25,415,162	3,880,719	6,222,736	3,108,061
1983	104,035,875	285,029	65,221,538	23,434,424	4,381,274	5,887,099	3,248,995
1982	113,953,033	312,200	66,945,886	28,036,535	7,629,663	5,866,136	2,320,887
1981	117,346,974	321,499	69,708,758	23,780,197	10,705,817	6,647,059	1,497,295
1980	133,014,201	363,427	76,205,915	27,133,078	12,851,355	9,243,840	3,805,802
1979	134,225,778	367,742	71,039,800	31,920,124	11,785,281	10,783,068	4,988,164
1978	128,827,589	352,952	71,898,241	29,153,321	11,839,621	9,829,217	3,763,301
1977	130,752,556	358,226	70,983,767	31,155,164	12,952,142	8,232,363	5,213,858
1976	127,425,451	348,157	69,181,740	31,027,020	12,172,167	7,746,326	5,895,269

Sales (in barrels)

Year ended September 30	Gasoline jet fuel, aromatics, & naphthas	Kerosene & distillates	Heavy fuel oils	Asphalt	Other
1984	79,942,401	29,492,890	13,386,085	7,335,784	7,409,397
1983	73,732,045	25,745,913	22,369,293	6,224,221	7,192,872
1982	75,601,370	29,894,597	28,791,680	7,009,221	6,768,048
1981	76,506,260	27,681,764	40,718,069	7,130,262	7,921,595
1980	82,832,857	29,714,190	52,830,738	9,851,572	6,946,309
1979	85,170,381	34,787,595	53,264,429	11,238,881	9,184,310
1978	82,729,048	35,199,381	48,496,000	10,654,214	8,634,643
1977	82,647,976	35,762,119	52,846,571	9,376,714	8,034,905
1976	80,962,190	34,337,810	47,721,071	8,902,286	8,238,500

Source: Ashland Oil, Inc., 1984 10-K.

TABLE 9 Debenture information

| Debenture | Trustee | Rating | |
		Moody's	Standard & Poor's
4.725% Sinking fund debentures, due 1988	Chemical Bank	A3	BBB+
4.875% Sinking fund debentures, due 1987	Citibank, N.A.	A3	BBB+
6.15% Sinking fund debentures, due 1992	Citibank, N.A.	A3	BBB+
8.00% Guaranteed debentures, due 1987	Citibank, N.A.	—	—
8.20% Sinking fund debentures, due 2002	Citibank, N.A.	A3	BBB+
8.80% Sinking fund debentures, due 2000	Citibank, N.A.	A3	BBB+
4.75% Convertible subordinated debentures, due 1993	Chase Manhattan Bank, N.A.	Baal	BBB
11.10% Subordinated debentures, due 2004	Chase Manhattan Bank, N.A.	Baal	BBB

Source: Ashland Oil, Inc., *Financial & Operating Supplement 1984.*

AMERICAN SKATE CORPORATION

INTRODUCTION

In August 1979, Mr. Alan Adams (general manager of American Skate Corporation) and Mr. C. Herbert Charlton (president of American Skate's Canadian parent, Dominion Skate, and, incidentally, Mr. Adam's father-in-law) were reviewing the $2,000,000 financial package put together during the summer of 1979 for the opening of a roller skate plant in Berlin, New Hampshire. The New Hampshire plant was viewed by both men as a critical element in the Canadian parent's plan for a major United States expansion to take advantage of the tremendous roller skating boom in North America. Nonetheless, Alan Adams and Herb Charlton wanted to reconsider all the relevant aspects of the plan before making a final decision to proceed with the Berlin plant. The proposed package involved a $1,650,000 long-term debt from various U.S. and New Hampshire development groups, a lease-purchase agreement totaling $500,000 for a 44,000-square-foot plant capable of initially adding 20 percent (and, within a year, 200 percent) to Dominion's production capacity. All of the debt issued to the subsidiary American Skate was to be guaranteed by both Dominion Skate, which owned all of American Skate's stock, and by Herb Charlton personally.

"Alan, I don't mind going out on the limb if the deal is a good one," Herb told his son-in-law, "but I want you to help me doublecheck this New Hampshire project in all its aspects. I know I've called the shots pretty much so far, but this will be your baby."

The following paragraphs describe the roller skate industry, the backgrounds of both Dominion and American Skate and their top managements, and the financial package put together during spring and summer of 1979.

This case was prepared by John Barnett, University of New Hampshire, with Jonathan Foster, London School of Economics, for classroom discussion only. It is not intended to illustrate effective or ineffective handling of an administrative situation. © 1984 by J. Barnett. Reprinted by permission.

THE ROLLER SKATING INDUSTRY

Roller skates were first introduced in Holland during the eighteenth century, but consisted of wooden spools strung on a wooden frame, which was in turn nailed onto the bottom of wooden shoes. These skates were difficult to turn, but this problem was overcome by an American inventor, James Leonard Plympton of New York. In 1863 Mr. Plympton put four independent wooden wheels on a shoe, making the skate easier to turn. This original pair of Plympton's skates is now housed in the National Museum of Roller Skating in Lincoln, Nebraska, along with pictures of the first roller skating arena, which Mr. Plympton opened in New York a few years later.

The modern roller skate consists of the boot, a base plate, wheels, ball bearings, and the toe stop. The manufacturing process of a complete roller skate includes the following steps: (1) using sets of dies to cut the various parts of the boot from leather or other boot material; (2) machine stitching the various parts of the boot, including adding "counters" of reinforcing material in the heel and adding eyelets; (3) stitching the boot together around a mold of a foot, called a "last"; (4) buffing or "roughing" the leather so that it will accept glue; (5) using a combination of glue and staples and a series of machine steps to complete the toe and heel; (6) removing the last; (7) attaching the base plate; (8) securing the wheels and toe stops to the base plate; and (9) inspecting and packing.

Very few manufacturers performed all these steps. Many bought the finished boot from others, and attached the base plate, wheels, and toe stop. The manufacturers sold completed skates to sporting goods retailers, distributors, wholesalers, chain stores and roller skating rinks.

The stimulus for growth in the roller skating industry came from skateboard technology. During the skateboard craze in the mid-1970s, wide polyurethane wheels and precision bearings were perfected that allowed for a quiet ride on pavement. Further, the polyurethane wheels were much more absorbent than earlier metal or hard rubber wheels. As the roller skate manufacturers adopted these wheels and bearings in the late 1970s, the roller skate explosion began as skates moved out of rinks and into the streets and parks.

The roller skating industry just prior to the 1978–79 explosion consisted of a few privately held companies of which Dominion Skate was the only fully integrated major manufacturer. *Time* reported that total industry sales were about a million pair of skates per year.[1] The major firms included Roller Derby Skate, Chicago Roller Skate, Dominion Skate, and Sure-Grip International; total dollar sales for the industry were estimated by the casewriters as $25 to $30 million. Roller Derby Skate of Litchfield, Illinois, *Business Week* observed, "dominated U.S. roller skate manufacturing with aggressive pricing of its low-end models."[2]

[1] *Time*, August 6, 1979, p. 66.

[2] *Business Week*, August 27, 1979, p. 120.

The roller skate explosion had North American and international repercussions. Exhibit 1 shows *Business Week*'s estimate of 1979 sales by the U.S. leaders. Keith Parker, the marketing vice-president of Nash Manufacturing, described how his company, a major skateboard manufacturer, converted to roller skates in a 60-day period in the fall of 1978. Producing eight thousand pairs a day by the summer of 1979, Mr. Parker commented:

The key to our success is that we've expanded much quicker than others. But demand has to hold for another year if we're going to make much profit. . . . The skate business is in such an uproar that we could ship a million pairs tomorrow and still have back orders.[4]

New U.S. manufacturers joined the industry, including Nash and Mattel, the $500 million toy manufacturer that invested over $1 million to begin producing roller skates in March 1979. Further, foreign manufacturers expanded into the North American market. Imports rose from $2 million in 1978 to $30 million in 1979, led by Taiwanese imports. Over ninety factories produced skates in Taiwan, and that nation soon had 85 percent of the U.S. imported market.[5]

The top-of-the-line, premium-priced skates continued to be manufactured in the United States. While children's and low-priced skates might retail from $20 to $50, with adult prices averaging $60, the well-regarded competition skates produced by the Dayton-based Snyder Skate Company were selling from $110 to $175 a pair. Snyder reports 1979 sales up 30 percent from 1978.

EXHIBIT 1
Estimated 1979
skate sales

Company	Estimated 1979 sales[a]
Roller Derby Skate (Illinois)	$ 50–60
Nash Manufacturing (Texas)	25
Sure-Grip International/RC Sports (California)	$ 20–25
Chicago Roller Skate (Illinois)	15–20
Mattel (California)	7–10
Total top five U.S. companies	$117–140
Estimated total U.S. sales	$200

[a] In millions of dollars
Source: *Business Week*[3]

[3] *Business Week*, op. cit.

[4] *Business Week*, op. cit.

[5] *Wall Street Journal*, April 6, 1981, p. 25.

Articles on roller skating appeared in almost every major periodical during 1979, including *Changing Times*, *Saturday Evening Post*, *Popular Mechanics*, *People*, *McCall's*, *Redbook*, and *Glamour*. Skates were endorsed by O. J. Simpson and were worn by Linda Ronstadt on a phonograph album cover. The number of roller skating rinks doubled to over six thousand during the 1970–78 period — five hundred new rinks were being added in 1979 — and roller disco became a major leisure activity.

Bill Butler, the "godfather of roller disco," looked forward to the opening in the fall of 1979 of his chic New York nightspot, the Roller Ballroom. Butler, who had skated for thirty-eight of his forty-five years, had a perspective on skating including a "whole philosophy of life" based on the sport. Nonetheless, *Popular Mechanics* commented:

> *New products come on the market so fast nowadays that even the Godfather of Roller Disco has trouble keeping up. Consider, for example, the two cycle, 1.2 h.p. engine that Motoboard International of Sunnyvale, California, suggests you slip on the back of your skate. For $289 you can zip down the highway at 40 m.p.h. with the wind blowing through your hair and your whole life passing before your eyes.*[6]

Sports Illustrated devoted several pages to a guide to buying skates in its October 15, 1979 issue; it specifically recommended Reidell and Oberhamer tops for boots ($40 to $90 retail), Chicago or Sure-Grip for the plates and wheels ($20 to $100 retail), and Snyder as the top of the line, with custom skates as high as $400 a pair. Butler commented that his ideal choice was a plate by Snyder, a Reidell boot, and Krypto wheels.

Positive signs for the roller skating industry included a Gallup Sports Poll in early 1979 showing roller skating fifth in popularity among teenagers, ahead of both tennis and skiing, and following basketball, baseball, swimming, and bowling. Both the Girl Scouts and Boy Scouts gave merit badges for roller skating proficiency.

Fifty percent of the U.S. teenage market would represent about 25 million pairs of skates. The total for North American skaters was estimated at between 30 and 40 million individuals, most of whom skated at rinks where rental skates were available. Chicago Roller Skate was particularly aggressive in skating rink sales.

Many commentators were optimistic. A vice-president of Herman's World of Sporting Goods reported a 400 percent increase in skate sales during the first half of 1979 at its ninety stores, noting that "the only thing that is slowing growth is product availability."[7] Mattel's Louis Miraula stated:

> *The universe of potential skaters is enormous. Because of the new wheel, people discovered roller-skating was an outdoor sport, à la jogging, but a lot more fun. The growth of*

[6] *Popular Mechanics*, vol. 151, June 1979.

[7] *Business Week*, op. cit.

this industry has a fad quality right now, but there is still that hard-core business that is not going to change substantially.[8]

The optimistic manufacturers predicted $400 million in annual skate sales would be achieved by the early 1980s.

Somewhat more cautious views were expressed by Chicago Skate, which had concentrated on rink sales. Said Joseph Sheuelson, Chicago Skate's vice-president of sales: "An idiot could make money in today's market. I'm walking on tiptoe, trying to gauge whether this is just another fad or has several years of life."[9] Roller Derby's national sales manager, Kenneth Neidl, said, "The demand is tremendous, but we don't know exactly where it is going. In many ways, what is happening is as new to us as to anybody, although we're the leader in the business."[10] Dennis Lane, international marketing director for Sure-Grip/RC Sports, was also cautious: "This is an extremely fast-growing industry, paralleling the sustained demand for bicycles that began 10 years ago. Most manufacturers are now living in a fairy-tale world where demand exceeds supply. In such an atmosphere, those that don't keep their heads could get hurt very badly."[11] A more negative view was expressed by financial analyst Harold Vogel: "By its very definition, the 'in thing' gets stale after a while. When everyone who is interested in roller skates has a couple of pairs, that's going to be it." Brunswick Corp., the national sporting goods company, sold its small skate division. A skateboard manufacturer, whose 1979 sales were one-fifth of 1978's, said he couldn't tell if "roller skates might be like skateboards — here today, gone tomorrow."

DOMINION AND AMERICAN SKATE

Dominion Skate's Early Years

Herb Charlton had gone to work for his uncle, owner of Dunn's Skate, Ltd., when he was very young. By the time his uncle died in 1946, Herb, then thirty-two, had substantial experience in all aspects of roller skate manufacture. Not wishing to continue working for his aunt, Herb left Dunn's and began Dominion Skate in the basement of his house in Ontario. Within a few years, Dominion with its three employees overflowed Herb's basement and garage, and it moved into a vacant school a few doors from the house. In 1958 an older plant facility in Mississauga, a short drive from Herb's house, was leased, giving Dominion a 3,000-square-foot, two-story building. Additions were made to this plant in 1962, 1970, and 1972. A second plant was leased 15 miles away in Toronto in 1973, as was an

---

[8] *Business Week*, op. cit.

[9] *Business Week*, op. cit.

[10] *Business Week*, op. cit.

[11] *Business Week*, op. cit.

assembly plant in Mississauga in January 1979. By August 1979, Dominion employed 120 people at three rented locations:

Location	Year opened	Activity	Square feet
Mississauga	1958	Manufacturing, assembly	20,000
Toronto	1973	Manufacturing, assembly	20,000
Mississauga	1979	Assembly	10,000

Each plant had a salaried plant manager who had worked with Herb for some time. Herb Charlton's policy of no layoffs and competitive wages resulted in a hard-working labor force which also had a low turnover rate.

Management

Herb Charlton, sixty-five years old in 1979, is president and chief financial officer of Dominion Skate and president of American Skate. While Herb made all important decisions, he was assisted by his son Paul (age thirty-three, director of plant engineering), his daughter Naomi (age thirty-one, office manager), and his son-in-law, Alan Adams (age thirty-seven, production manager and, more recently, general manager of the American subsidiary, American Skate Corporation).

Like Herb Charlton, Alan had dropped out of school and had held several positions as a factory worker and as a printer's apprentice. In 1958, Alan, then seventeen, went to work for Dominion Skate at the suggestion of Herb's daughter, whom Alan was then dating and subsequently married.

Dominion sold roller skates, ice skates, and children's double-runner bob skates through a distributor to a small group of retail accounts throughout Canada, ice skates helping to offset the seasonality of roller skates. Paul and Alan would occasionally call on these retail accounts; Herb would infrequently show customers around the Ontario plants. Dominion had a reputation for a high-quality, medium-priced skate. Dominion had kept pace with industry technology, and its advertisements referred to its ''space age skates'' with models called ''All American Dream'' and ''Inertia.''

U.S. sales were handled by a marketing firm, King R. Lee and Associates, of Santa Ana, California. King Lee in turn called on ten specialty distributors in the United States. These distributors bought from Lee and from others.

Operations were financed by small working capital loans from local banks, by advances from Herb Charlton, and by trade credit.

Total production capacity was about 285,000 pairs a year. This capacity was based upon one-shift operations. Alan Adams noted that Herb Charlton did not like to have more than one shift.

I guess it was partially due to his wanting to be on top of things. Herb relied on personal inspection rather than formal production control systems. This philosophy of personal control extended to stock ownership as well. I had asked him about my owning some stock, so that I could have some security, but even after twenty-plus years of working for him, I never got any stock.

Financial Results

Exhibits 2, 3, and 4 present balance sheets, income statements, and related financial statistics for the years 1976, 1977, and 1978 and the 6 months ending June 1979.

The Financial Package

Berlin, New Hampshire, was considered as a site for U.S. expansion because a Canadian supplier had recently expanded into New Hampshire and had told Mr. Charlton that he "got a good deal" in New Hampshire. Northern New Hampshire was less than a day's drive from Toronto and less than half a day's drive from Montreal, where Dominion's Canadian distributor was located. Finally, Berlin development groups had actively pursued Dominion once its expansion interests were known.

EXHIBIT 2 Dominion Skate balance sheets

	1979 (June 30)	1978 (December 31)	1977 (December 31)	1976 (December 31)
Assets				
Current assets				
Cash, certificates of deposit	$ 109,100	$ 239,700	$173,800	$ 22,400
Accounts receivable	1,081,300	682,600	464,000	286,300
Net inventory	486,000	461,700	218,300	211,500
Total current assets	$1,676,400	$1,384,000	$856,100	$520,200
Fixed assets — net				
Machinery, equipment	$ 93,100	$ 103,400	$ 78,100	$ 50,400
Vehicles, leasehold improvements	23,400	26,700	13,300	4,400
Total fixed assets	$ 116,500	$ 130,100	$ 91,400	$ 54,800
Other assets				
Goodwill	$ 15,000	$ 15,000	$ 15,000	$ 15,000
Land deposits	211,200	211,200	—	—
Total other assets	$ 226,200	$ 226,200	$ 15,000	$ 15,000
Total assets	$2,019,100	$1,740,300	$962,500	$590,000
Liabilities				
Accounts payable, accruals	$ 636,800	$ 706,100	$497,400	$257,600
Taxes payable	173,700	170,200	38,600	12,200
Bank loan	–0–	50,000	–0–	95,000
Shareholder advances	246,600	219,900	101,200	54,800
Total liabilities	$1,057,100	$1,146,200	$637,200	$419,600
Equity				
Preferred stock	$ 100	$ 100	$ 100	$ 100
Retained earnings	961,900	594,000	325,200	170,300
Total equity	$ 962,000	$ 594,100	$325,300	$170,400
Total liabilities, equity	$2,019,100	$1,740,300	$962,500	$590,000

Note: Figures are in Canadian dollars.

EXHIBIT 3
Dominion Skate
income statement

	Six months ending June 30, 1979	Twelve months ending		
		December 31, 1978	December 31, 1977	December 31, 1976
Sales	$2,655,800	$4,267,100	$3,182,600	$1,518,600
Less: cost of sales	1,581,900	2,540,500	2,099,900	889,200
Gross profit	$1,073,900	$1,725,600	$1,082,700	$ 629,400
Operating expenses				
Administrative payroll, sales commissions	$ 410,500	$ 811,800	$ 649,800	$ 445,800
Supplies, freight	65,500	137,500	69,300	51,300
Advertising	1,100	10,600	3,400	2,400
Insurance	12,200	15,800	9,700	6,800
Professional fees	1,800	2,200	1,200	900
Office expenses	4,500	10,500	6,700	4,600
Repairs	3,300	2,700	2,100	500
Rent	34,300	52,800	42,000	33,800
Telephone, utilities	13,400	20,000	15,400	11,100
Travel	1,300	1,300	500	200
Vehicle	2,400	2,200	4,100	2,800
Miscellaneous[a]	27,500	54,400	30,200	16,400
Depreciation	13,600	34,400	24,800	15,000
Bad debt	12,700	21,500	1,000	(5,300)
Total operating expenses	$ 604,100	$1,177,700	$ 860,200	$ 586,300
Operating profit	$ 469,800	$ 547,900	$ 222,500	$ 43,100
Interest expense	$ 5,900	$ 5,100	$ 9,200	$ 6,800
Taxes	180,500	189,300	58,500	17,400
Total	$ 186,400	$ 194,400	$ 67,700	$ 24,200
Profit after tax	$ 283,400	$ 353,500	$ 154,800	$ 18,900

Note: Figures are in Canadian dollars.
[a] Donations to Baptist Church, 1978, 1979 at annual rate of $22,000. Pensions at annual rate of $11,000 (1978), $15,000 (1979). Balance is discounts.

EXHIBIT 4
Dominion Skate
selected financial
statistics

	1979	1978	1977	1976
Solvency				
Debt/equity	1.1	1.9	2.0	2.5
Times interest earned	47	70	17	3
Liquidity				
Net working capital	$619,300	$237,800	$218,900	$100,600
Current ratio	1.6	1.2	1.3	1.2
Funds management				
Day's sales in receivables	74	58	53	68
Day's cost goods in payables	72	101	87	107
Inventory turnover	3.3	7.5	9.8	
Profitability				
Return on sales	11%	8%	5%	1%
Return on assets	14%	20%	16%	3%
Return on equity	29%	60%	48%	11%

The financial plan put together as of August 1979 included: (1) a working capital loan of $1,150,000 from the U.S. Economic Development Administration (EDA), (2) a loan of $100,000 from a New Hampshire venture capital group, (3) a loan of $400,000 from the Berlin (New Hampshire) Economic Development Council (BEDCO), and (4) a lease purchase agreement with the Berlin Industrial Development and Park Authority (BIDPA).

Berlin, New Hampshire, about 175 miles north of Boston, had a serious unemployment problem among its population of thirteen thousand. The Converse Rubber Company, a manufacturer of athletic shoes, had closed in early 1979, laying off four hundred. The only significant employers in Berlin were the James River Paper Company, employing 1,200 to 1,500, and Bass Shoe, employing 250 to 350. Thus BEDCO and BIDPA were anxiously encouraging American Skate to locate in Berlin. BEDCO, directed by a board of business and labor officials and city government representatives, usually lent $5,000 for every job created by a new employer. BEDCO offered American Skate $400,000 at 6 percent annual interest, due in quarterly installments of $10,000, provided that American match its $400,000 with equity.

BIDPA, the developer/administrator of a small industrial park, had a board of directors similar to BEDCO. BIDPA had already built a 44,000-square-foot building, which was vacant and incurring interest charges. BIDPA offered American a 22-year lease purchase agreement totaling $500,000, with gradually increasing monthly payments. Real estate taxes were waived.

In addition to the Berlin debt, a New Hampshire venture capital group offered a $100,000 loan at prime (then about 12 percent) plus one percent. The state of New Hampshire was of course attractive to Charlton and Adams as it had no personal state income, sales, or use taxes and was replacing inventory and similar taxes with a flat tax on businesses of 8 percent of net profits.

The EDA, a branch of the U.S. Department of Commerce, offered a 10½ percent $1,150,000 loan, payable over 7 years, with gradually increasing monthly payments. Thus, pressure for economic support expressed itself not only from local and state groups, but at the federal level as well.

Equipment for the Berlin plant location was available to American Skate for $130,000 from Tiera Footwear of Dover, New Hampshire, which was in liquidation. Tiera's equipment would be sufficient for U.S. needs.

In trying to determine sales and costs, Herb Charlton and Alan Adams asked King Lee for an estimate of the potential total skate orders from the ten U.S. distributors for all skate manufacturers. This estimate, totaling 586,500 pairs a year, is reproduced in Exhibit 5. Lee was unsure what percentage of these total orders American Skate might expect to receive.

Dominion Skate estimated its own Canadian sales potential as 312,000 pairs a year, as opposed to its production capacity of 286,000 pairs a year. Dominion estimated that the total North American industry sales for all manufacturers would climb from the pre-1979 level of $30 million to over $200 million in the early 1980s, falling to $100 million by 1984.

The Berlin plant would initially produce at an annual level of 65,000 pairs, and within one year could be producing as many as 520,000 pairs on a two-shift basis. Initial employment of one hundred should rise to three hundred in 2 years, if the company's predictions were accurate.

The differential cost of producing a pair of skates as estimated by the company is shown in Exhibit 6. This cost is for an average pair, and it would be equally valid for Ontario and New Hampshire production. New Hampshire administrative salaries would be about $200,000 a year, half of which would be the general manager's salary; other overhead costs might total an additional $100,000.

EXHIBIT 5
Estimated total skate orders by Lee's ten distributors for all skates of all manufacturers

Firm	Annual volume in pairs
Gordon & Smith, San Diego, Calif.	93,500
L. Cohen, Los Angeles, Calif.	20,500
Smoothill, San Rafael, Calif.	65,000
West Coast Cycle, Culver City, Calif.	156,000
Bike Factory, Bellevue, Wash.	31,000
Donel Distributors, Garland, Tex.	31,000
Southeastern Sales, Florence, Ala.	15,500
Tuflex, Ft. Lauderdale, Fla.	78,000
A.W.H. Sales, Evanston, Ill.	65,000
Lubins, Watertown, Mass.	31,000
Total	586,500

EXHIBIT 6
American Skate cost estimates for average pair of skates

Selling Price		$12.95
Materials		
Boot	$2.85	
Plate	.77	
Wheels	1.28	
Bearings	1.04	
Toe stop	.14	
Hardware	.35	
Axle	.20	
Box	.19	
Other	.16	
Total materials		6.98
Labor		.75
Selling commission		1.56
Total		$ 9.29
Gross profit		$ 3.66

Summary

Both Herb Charlton and Alan Adams believed that the financial package available to them at the time could not be modified further. At a meeting to reach a decision on the Berlin plant, the following dialogue occurred:

ADAMS: *In addition to liens on all the equipment, you will have to personally guarantee all these loans. But how can you beat $400,000 at 6 percent and $1,500,000 at 1½ percent below prime?*

CHARLTON: *Alan, I believe in growth. Every two or three years we've leased new space or bought new equipment. That cycle means 1979 is a year for more growth. Still, it will be your project to live with. What do you think?*

MARY KAY COSMETICS, INC.

BACKGROUND OF THE COMPANY

A proliferation of products and a change of patterns that might dazzle a square dance caller have characterized the cosmetics industry in the late 1970s and the 1980s. Witness Eli Lilly's purchase of Elizabeth Arden, Squibb's acquisition of Lanvin-Charles of Ritz, Pfizer's take-over of Coty, Norton Simon's of Max Factor, Colgate-Palmolive's of Helena Rubenstein, not to mention British-American Tobacco's gobbling up Germaine Monteil.

Accompanying the change of corporate identities there has been a distinct shift in management styles as practiced in cosmetics concerns. The ''flair and flamboyance'' of the old school cosmetics moguls — the Revsons, Rubensteins, and Ardens of the industry — has been replaced by a new breed of management types. Charisma has given way to pragmatism. The new styles are diverse, however — as urbane, cool, and international as ITT-trained Revlon's chief executive, the Frenchman Michel Bergerac, or as fundamentalist, *nouveaux riches*, and Texas-grown as Mary Kay Ash, founder and driving force behind Mary Kay Cosmetics, Inc., whose pink Cadillac incentive plan for sales agents and skyrocketing corporate profits have made Mary Kay a legend in the highly competitive American cosmetics business.

In 1963 Mary Kay Ash, a much decorated veteran of in-home sales (Child Psychology Bookshelf, Stanley Home Products, World Gift) founded Mary Kay Cosmetics, Inc., on $5,000 for product formulas, containers, and secondhand office equipment and on the belief that women could be sold on using a proven skin care regimen through an educational approach. Mary Kay Ash's expertise in the area of human motivation and in direct sales combined with son Richard Rogers's wizardry in finance and marketing catapulted the company from its humble Dallas beginnings to a major national cosmetics corporation. Exhibit 1 charts this growth pattern. By August 1976 Mary Kay Cosmetics was listed on the New York Stock Exchange.

Case prepared by Charles L. Hinkle, University of Colorado, and Esther F. Stineman, Yale University. © 1984 Prentice-Hall, Inc. Reprinted by permission.

EXHIBIT 1
Mary Kay growth,
1971–1981

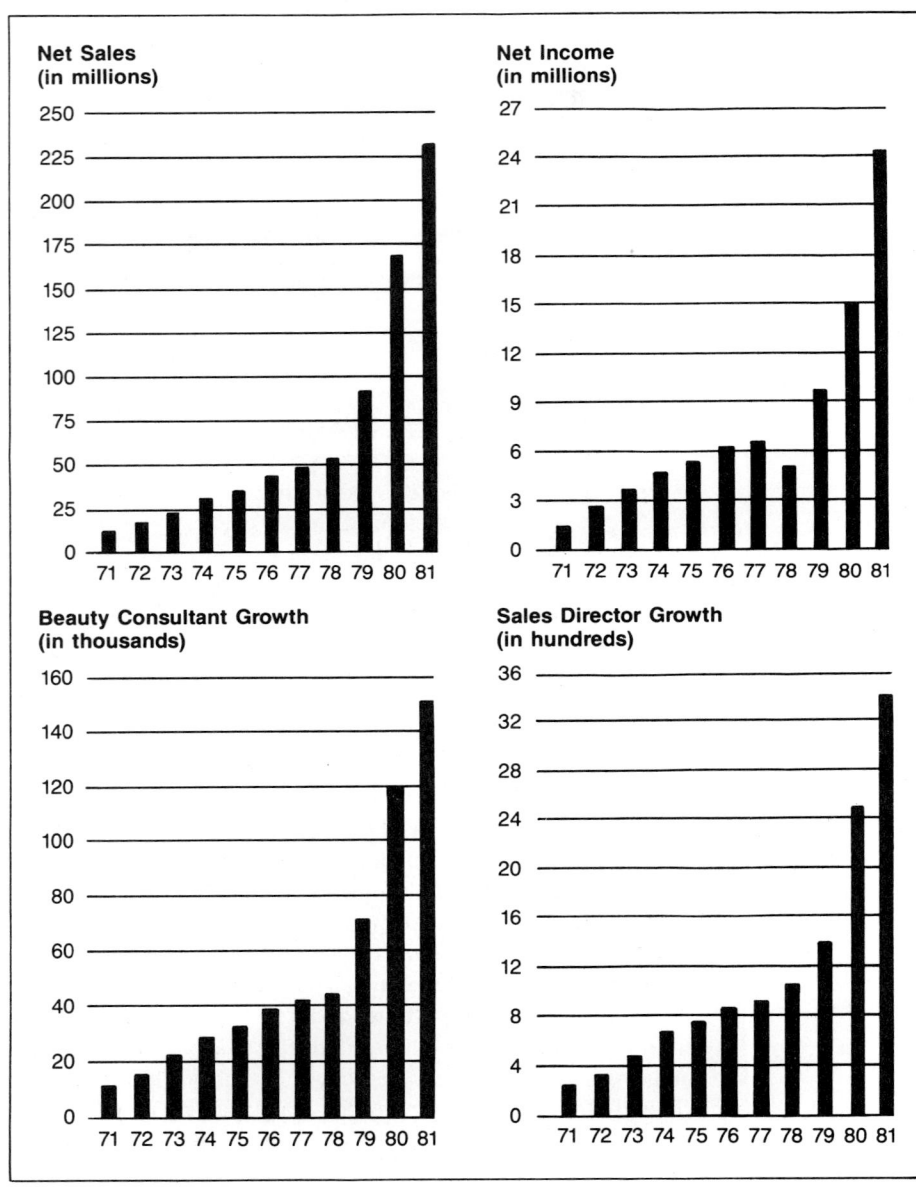

Source: Mary Kay Cosmetics, Inc., *1981 Annual Report*, p. 20.

THE FIVE STEPS TO BEAUTY

MOVEMENT OF APPLICATION

Follow this movement of application when applying Cleansing Cream, Cleanser, Magic Masque, Skin Freshener, Night Cream or Moisturizer:

Always apply with the tips of the fingers. Beginning with the neckline, apply with upward and outward motion. Be sure to use the ring finger when working around the delicate tissue near the eyes. Remember to stroke delicately — don't massage.

1 CLEANSE

All of the Mary Kay cleansing products cleanse the skin deeply, thoroughly and gently, penetrating and loosening impurities and softening the skin.

Cleansing Cream Formula 1 and Formula 2 — Smooth on face and throat. Follow movement of application. Remove with warm, wet facial cloth.

Cleanser Formula 3 — Shake well. Apply thoroughly to face and throat. Lightly pat water on top of cleanser and follow movement of application. Splash skin with warm water and remove remainder with warm, wet facial cloth.

2 STIMULATE

Mary Kay Magic Masque® stimulates circulation, removes impurities and dead surface cells. Also brightens, refines and freshens the skin.

Magic Masque Formula 1 and Formula 2 — After cleansing, smooth on face and throat, avoiding eyes and mouth. Let dry for approximately 10 minutes. Soften and gently remove with warm, wet facial cloth. Apply Skin Freshener and allow to dry naturally. Use Magic Masque twice a week.

3 FRESHEN

Mary Kay Skin Freshener further stimulates circulation, makes pores appear smaller and removes any residue of previous products.

Skin Freshener Formula 1 and Formula 2 — Apply a few drops to clean cotton pad and gently smooth on face and throat. Avoid use in the immediate area of the eye. Allow to dry naturally. Always use Skin Freshener after Magic Masque.

4 LUBRICATE/MOISTURIZE

All of the Mary Kay moisturizing products help to smooth and condition the skin, working as a preventive measure against dryness.

Night Cream Formula 1 — After cleansing and freshening, moisten face and throat with warm water and gently apply a very small amount of Night Cream. Leave overnight.

Night Cream Formula 2 — After cleansing and freshening, gently smooth a small amount of Night Cream over face and throat. Leave overnight.

Moisturizer — After cleansing and freshening, gently smooth a thin film on the dry areas of the face

5 PROTECT

Mary Kay's Day Radiance® provides daytime protection for the skin with a subtle tint of color that covers minor imperfections and gives a smooth, even toned finish to your complexion. Day Radiance is available in perfectly blended shades, ranging in color from the lightest to the darkest skin tones, including white and yellow shades for highlighting and correcting.

Day Radiance Formula 1 — Provides an emollient moisture base and luminous powder finish. Using fingertips, apply a thin film to a moistened face. When using Moisturizer under Day Radiance, do not moisten face

Day Radiance Formula 2 — Water based product that provides a fresh sheen without shine. Shake well. Using fingertips, blend over a dry face with outward sweeping strokes

---

Each morning, cleanse, freshen and protect.
Each evening, cleanse, freshen and lubricate/moisturize.
Twice a week, stimulate.

EXHIBIT 2 The five steps to beauty

Source: Mary Kay, Inc. promotional literature.

Mary Kay Cosmetics consists of "a scientifically formulated line of skin products" that is presented to the user programmatically during home beauty shows with emphasis on Mary Kay's Five Steps to Beauty (Exhibit 2). Over 50 percent of the company's sales are derived from the basic skin care line. Skin, body, and hair care products in addition to cosmetics, toiletries, and fragrances compose the remainder of the relatively small Mary Kay line (Exhibit 3).

The company uses self-employed women billed as Beauty Consultants to introduce the products to customers in the home where customers sample the products and are instructed in their use. This deceptively simple format has resulted in dramatic growth in the company's sales and sales force since the beginning, when Mary Kay Cosmetics had only nine consultants. By 1981 net sales were $235.3 million, and about 150,000 consultants were selling the products (and, one presumes, faithfully using them). Exhibit 4 analyzes the productivity of the Mary Kay sales people. Major distribution centers in the United States assure rapid delivery of the products to the consultants who are able to provide the customers with their products without delay at the beauty show. Thus, there should never be a gap between ordering and receiving the product as there is in Avon's distribution method.

An oft-quoted management truism in the cosmetics industry is Michel Bergerac's conclusion that "every management mistake ends up in inventory." Mary Kay has addressed this concern and has avoided the pitfall through its unique distribution and operations systems. Charged with the task of instantaneously providing each consultant with the inventory she requires at the moment she requires it, Mary Kay has developed five domestic regional distribution centers, located in Atlanta; Chicago; Los Angeles; Piscataway, New Jersey; and the corporate warehouse in Dallas. Dallas is mission control for the company, where the products are manufactured and the orders received. The Marketing Department has instant access via computer to individual and unit sales. Manufacturing uses the data bank at Dallas to control inventory by forecasting and planning products' runs. On the microlevel, directors of sales units are only a toll-free call away from comprehensive information about the performance of their unit or of specific individuals.

EXHIBIT 3
Analysis of sales by products, 1977–1981

	1977	1978	1979	1980	1981
Skin care products for women	48%	50%	49%	52%	49%
Skin care products for men	2	1	1	2	1
Makeup items	21	21	26	22	26
Toiletry items for women	13	12	10	10	10
Toiletry items for men	2	3	2	2	2
Hair care	4	3	2	2	2
Accessories	10	10	10	10	10
Total	100%	100%	100%	100%	100%

Source: Mary Kay, Inc., *1981 Annual Report*, p. 21.

EXHIBIT 4
Mary Kay Cosmetics
sales analysis,
1970–1982E

Year	Sales (000)	Number of beauty consultants and sales directors at year end	Avg. no. of beauty consultants and sales directors	Sales beauty consultant and sales director (productivity)	Year-to-year increases in productivity
1982E	$346,000	190,000	175,000	$1,980.0	3.4%
1981E	242,000	150,000	140,072	1,915.0	9.0
1980	166,938	120,145	94,982	1,757.6	11.5
1979	91,400	69,820	57,989	1,576.2	26.9
1978	53,746	46,158	43,282	1,241.7	0.7
1977	47,856	40,407	38,818	1,232.8	−3.4
1976	44,871	37,229	35,176	1,275.6	13.3
1975	34,947	33,123	31,042	1,125.8	−6.0
1974	30,215	28,961	25,234	1,197.4	1.4
1973	22,199	21,508	18,805	1,180.5	−3.1
1972	17,232	16,103	14,142	1,218.5	1.5
1971	12,367	12,181	10,299	1,200.7	7.2
1970	8,091	8,418	7,224	1,120.0	−6.3
Average annual growth					
1975–1980	36.7%	29.4%	25.1%	9.3%	
1970–1975	34.0	31.5	33.9	0.1	

Source: Mary Kay, Inc. data.

In 1978 Mary Kay Cosmetics formed a sister company in Toronto that has evolved into one of Canada's largest cosmetic enterprises. As of 1971 and 1980, respectively, separate operations were launched in Australia and Argentina. The Argentine Mary Kay undertaking has run into difficulties because of international problems. During May 1982, in the midst of the dispute between Argentina and Britain over the Falkland Islands with sky-high inflation in Argentina, Mary Kay was forced to write off $1.5 million there in a reassessment of the value of the company's marketing unit in Argentina.

MARY KAY ASH'S PERSONAL STORY

Mary Kay Ash's personal story is a rags-to-riches success saga in the great American tradition, and it mirrors the stories of many of the company's beauty consultants. In her autobiography, the best selling *Mary Kay*, ''the success story of America's most dynamic businesswoman,'' published by Harper & Row in 1981, Mary Kay tells of her life. In the company literature, this simple story is told and retold, and the lesson of self-discipline is underscored (Exhibit 5). Mary Kay Ash received the Horatio Alger Award from Dr. Norman Vincent Peale in 1978, and the company refers to Mrs. Ash's story as ''a Horatio Alger Story.''

EXHIBIT 5
Mary Kay — A
Horatio Alger story

A Childhood Filled with Challenge

From a small Texas town to national prominence was not an easy journey. Mary Kay's success can largely be attributed to the discipline and independence she learned in her childhood.

The youngest of four children, she was born in the small town of Hot Wells, Texas, where her parents owned a hotel. When her father's health deteriorated and he became an invalid, the family moved to Houston so Mary Kay's mother could find work.

While her mother worked 14-hour days managing a restaurant, seventeen-year-old Mary Kay stayed home cleaning, cooking, and caring for her father.

Throughout those early years, Mary Kay's mother strongly influenced her daughter by encouraging her to excel in everything she did and told her over and over again, "You can do it." Whether in school or at home, Mary Kay wanted to be the best. Another lasting influence on her life has been her Christian faith. Her sincere convictions enabled her to express her love and affection toward those around her, and her faith has also been the cornerstone of her business success. Her basic philosophies are "God first, family second, career third," and the Golden Rule.

Young Adulthood

After finishing high school, Mary Kay married and had three children. Her husband was soon called away for World War II active duty, leaving Mary Kay with mounting financial problems. She worked as a secretary at a Baptist Church to help support the overwhelming cost of raising three children.

A postwar divorce left Mary Kay the lone support of her young family. With the same determination that brought her through her earlier years, Mary Kay became a dealer for Stanley Home Products, a direct sales party plan company. This job enabled her to earn a living and still spend time with her children.

After three weeks of work and average sales of only $7 worth of products per party, Mary Kay attended a sales convention. She sat in the back row and decided that she would one day be crowned "Queen of Sales." Upon sharing her goal with the president of the company, Frank Stanley Beveredge, he replied, "Somehow, I think you will."

Mary Kay triumphantly won the crown the following year and eventually moved to Dallas where she continued her 13-year career with Stanley Home Products. But this was only the beginning of Mary Kay's rise to success.

Later, upon joining World Gift, a company that sold decorative accessories, she quickly became National Training Director. In 1962, though, she experienced a personal ordeal that threatened her health and her career. She suffered from a rare form of paralysis on one side of her face, but after surgery and several months of hospitalization, she recovered completely.

The Company Begins

Upon her recovery and after her retirement from World Gift, Mary Kay remarried and began to think about starting her own direct sales company. She planned to run the sales division, while her husband acted as administrator. One month prior to the launching of the company, her husband had a heart attack and died. Mary Kay's three children joined their mother in the early days of the new venture. Today, Richard Rogers, her youngest son, is the president of Mary Kay Cosmetics, Inc.

Source: Mary Kay, Inc. promotional literature, 1981.

THE BEAUTY CONSULTANT
AND THE BEAUTY SHOW

The lifeblood of the Mary Kay organization is the beauty consultant and director force who have generated Mary Kay's phenomenal sales and following. Independent beauty consultants, who buy their own sample case and products, are organized into sales units led by a sales director. Mary Kay Ash believes the cash system has assured the health of the company. "At Mary Kay, our consultants and directors pay in advance for their merchandise with a cashier's check or money order — no personal checks."

> *It's impossible for a Consultant to run up a debt with the company. Therefore, we have few accounts receivable. We don't have the expense of collecting bad debts, and we pass the savings on in the form of higher commissions. This way, everyone benefits. Most financial people just marvel at it — it's unheard of for a company of our size.*[1]

Richard Rogers sums up the distribution plan this way: "Each Mary Kay consultant is an independent contractor. They are not employees of the company. Mary Kay serves as a wholesale house — freight in, freight out. The consultant buys directly from the company at wholesale prices and sells at retail prices. The difference is her profit."

Although the beauty consultant is in business for herself — the point is stressed in the corporate literature that "she is not by herself." The director is available as a consultant and teacher to the beauty consultant to help her successfully present the all-important beauty show. An effective director, according to the company, can handle in embryo the problems of poor consultant performance and thus control turnover in the ranks.

Because the beauty consultant is not a cosmetologist, federal and state laws prohibit her from applying cosmetics to the faces of the five or six participants at each show. Rather, her task is to assist each woman who attends the session, usually held at the home of a voluntary hostess, to determine her skin type and to answer questions about the five steps of beauty process. "This is an effective teaching method. We don't sell — we teach!" emphasizes Mary Kay. "Polite persuasion" is the Mary Kay euphemism for selling. The hard sell is avoided, according to the literature.

In its *1981 Annual Report*, Mary Kay Cosmetics, Inc., shared with readers the philosophy of the beauty show.

> *The Beauty Show is our primary marketplace. Its importance cannot be overstated. Here the Consultant has undivided attention as she presents the entire line. She has ample time to give each guest personal attention. The customer learns valuable tips on skin care and grooming and, because she receives her order at the Show, puts the lessons into practice immediately.*

[1] Mary Kay Ash, *Mary Kay* (New York: Harper & Row, 1981), p. 29.

During the course of the two-hour beauty show, the consultant demonstrates, presents, persuades, collects, and delivers. (Exhibit 6 is the price list for Mary Kay products demonstrated in the beauty show.) In addition to the sales activities implicit in the show, a consultant may recruit other consultants and arrange bookings for future shows at the demonstration. The person who agrees to host a show at her home "earns" Mary Kay products. Often if the consultant notes a potential customer's reluctance to purchase because of the cost, she may suggest that the woman earn products by hosting.

To become a consultant, a woman submits a signed beauty consultant agreement with a cashier's check or money order to Mary Kay Cosmetics. The pink beauty showcase is then shipped immediately to her from Dallas. Before she is a full-fledged consultant, a recruit must attend three beauty shows with an experienced consultant, book five beauty shows for her first week's activity, and attend training classes conducted by a director in her area. Because each Mary Kay show provides yet another opportunity to recruit beauty consultants into the company, to book future shows, and to establish reorder business, Mary Kay puts a premium on running a smooth and professional show. Mary Kay consultants are expected to present a well-groomed, Mary Kay–cosmeticized image and to dress in a manner consistent with Mary Kay Ash's personal philosophy of feminine attractiveness.

Mary Kay annual reports feature attractive models representing the consultants on their appointed rounds, dressed in tailored suits, tastefully manicured, coiffured, and made up, usually wearing soft, pastel blouses and Mary Kay jewelry (golden bumblebees and Mary Kay pins are sought-after prizes in the company). The ideal image of the consultant is that of the "dressed-for-success" career woman.

EXHIBIT 6 1982 Mary Kay price list

ITEM	PRICE	✔
Complete Collection (as shown)	$71.00	
Basic Skin Care	39.00	
CLEANSE		
Cleansing Cream Formula 1, 4 oz.	6.50	
Cleansing Cream Formula 2, 4 oz.	6.50	
Cleanser Formula 3, 3.75 oz.	6.50	
STIMULATE		
Magic Masque Formula 1, 3 oz.	7.50	
Magic Masque Formula 2, 3 oz.	7.50	
FRESHEN		
Skin Freshener Formula 1, 5.75 oz.	7.50	
Skin Freshener Formula 2, 5.75 oz.	7.50	
LUBRICATE/MOISTURIZE		
Night Cream Formula 1, 4 oz.	12.00	
Night Cream Formula 2, 4 oz.	12.00	
Moisturizer, 2.8 oz.	12.00	
PROTECT		
Day Radiance Formula 1, .5 oz.	5.50	
Day Radiance Formula 2, 1 oz.	5.50	
☐ Ivory Beige ☐ Toasted Tan		
☐ Light Beige ☐ Cinnamon		
☐ Medium Beige ☐ Chestnut		
☐ Warm Beige ☐ Coffee		
☐ Suntan Beige ☐ White		
☐ Suntan ☐ Yellow		
☐ Honey Tan		
GLAMOUR COLLECTION		
Blush Rouge	4.00	
Eyeliner	5.00	
☐ Black ☐ Brown		

ITEM	PRICE	✔
Eyebrow Pencil	$ 3.00	
☐ Black ☐ Brown ☐ Auburn		
☐ Charcoal ☐ Light Brown ☐ Blonde		
Mascara	5.50	
☐ Black ☐ Brown		
Lip and Eye Palette	14.50	
(Complete with 2 brushes)		
Lip Palette	12.50	
(Complete with lip brush)		
Eye Palette	12.50	
(Complete with eye brush)		
Retractable Lip or Eye Brush	2.00	
Lip or Eye Palette Refill	4.00	
Great Fashion Lip Color Shade		
Selections:		
☐ Pinks ☐ Plums ☐ Russets		
☐ Reds ☐ Corals ☐ Spices		
Great Fashion Eye Shadow Shade		
Selections:		
☐ Blues ☐ Greens		
☐ Browns ☐ Plums		
Blusher	8.50	
☐ Soft Pink/Soft Peach		
☐ Tawny Rose/Tawny Amber		
☐ Cinnamon/Mahogany		
Lip Liner Pencils	6.50	
☐ Raisin/Ripe Cherry		
Lip Gloss	4.50	
SPECIALIZED SKIN CARE		
Moisturizer, 2.8 oz.	12.00	
Facial/Under Makeup Sun Screen, 2.7 oz.	7.00	
Hand Cream, 2.8 oz.	5.50	

ITEM	PRICE	✔
BODY CARE		
Cleansing Gel, 8 oz.	$ 7.00	
Buffing Cream, 6 oz.	7.50	
Moisturizing Lotion, 8 oz.	6.50	
Sun Screening Lotion, 6 oz.	8.50	
BASIC HAIR CARE		
Shampoo for Normal/Dry Hair, 8 oz.	4.50	
Shampoo for Oily Hair, 8 oz.	4.50	
Protein Conditioner, 8 oz.	6.00	
Intense Conditioner, 3 oz.	7.00	
Non-Aerosol Hair Spray, 8 oz.	4.50	
FRAGRANCE BOUTIQUE		
Avenir Spray Cologne, 2 oz.	15.00	
Intrigue Spray Cologne, 1.75 oz.	10.00	
Facets Spray Cologne, 2 oz.	11.00	
Facets Cologne, 1 oz.	6.50	
Angelfire Spray Cologne, 1.75 oz.	12.00	
Exquisite Body Lotion, 8 oz.	6.50	
MEN'S PRODUCTS		
Mr. K Skin Care System	34.50	
Cleanser, 2.7 oz.	4.50	
Mask, 2.6 oz.	6.50	
Toner, 2.6 oz.	4.50	
Moisture Balm, 2.5 oz.	12.00	
Sun Screen, 2.7 oz.	7.00	
Mr. K Cologne, 3.75 oz.	9.50	
Mr. K Lotion, 3.4 oz.	4.50	
ReVeur After Shave Cologne, 3.75 oz.	10.00	

Source: Mary Kay, Inc., price list for beauty consultants.

A career woman should dress in a businesslike manner. Personally, I'm opposed to wearing pants on the job. In fact, that's a company policy at Mary Kay (except in the manufacturing area). After all, we are in the business of helping women look more feminine and beautiful, so we feel very strongly that our Beauty Consultants should dress accordingly. We suggest they always wear dresses to Shows, rather than pants, and we emphasize well-groomed hair and nails. After all, can you imagine a woman with her hair up in curlers, wearing jeans, calling herself a Beauty Consultant — and trying to tell other women what they should be doing to look good? We're really selling femininity, so our dress code has to be ultra-feminine.[2]

MOTIVATION — MARY KAY STYLE

Within the honeycomb of the sales unit — the basic organizational entity in Mary Kay, though it is not included in the company organization chart — the consultant receives weekly sales training and encouragement, sings Mary Kay booster songs, and applauds the successes of others. Personal vignettes are as legitimate in this revival-style gathering as is instruction in specific sales techniques. The professionalization program at Mary Kay also includes regional workshops, Jamborees (conducted by national sales directors), leaders' conferences, and seminars. "The Seminar" is the "multimillion-dollar extravaganza" staged each year at the Dallas Convention Center where thousands of Mary Kay consultants and directors converge for inspiration, entertainment, and education — Mary Kay style. It is in this immense convention forum that Mary Kay leaders are recognized publicly, where they share their own sagas of success with the audience. Here the Cadillacs, mink coats, diamond bumblebees, and other coveted Mary Kay status symbols are meted out to the deserving ones; and here women aspire to these material rewards by goal-setting activities for the coming year. Seminar classes, conducted by successful Mary Kay directors, teach the intricacies of sales technique, bookkeeping, leadership, customer service, and other skills necessary for Mary Kay entrepreneurship. In 1980 the special effects staff for the seminar arranged for the pink Buicks and Cadillacs to "float" phantomlike through mist onstage via a remote control process much to the delight of the assembled. Seminar showmanship has proven effective in creating the Mary Kay myths.

The company believes that tangible symbols of success motivate the Mary Kay women and serve to fuel the belief "that if they work hard enough — if they give of themselves — that they will be successful, personally and professionally." Vacation trips, prizes, contests, photographs of Mary Kay with members of the sales force, and constant praise are among the motivators the company has used with great success. In 1980, 311 sales directors earned more than $30,000; 98 earned more than $50,000. Almost 500 are designated as "Cadillac-status" directors. The highest-paid Mary Kay saleswomen are the national sales directors, a group of

[2] Ibid., p. 10.

more than 39 women who began as consultants. They average more than $150,000 annually. Mary Kay Cosmetics gives a great deal of publicity to these star earners, for example, Helen McVoy who started back in the humbler days of the company and now earns $300,000 a year.

EARNINGS

A consultant is in business for herself and therefore her earnings are determined by her sales at retail. She purchases products from the company at a discount (up to 50 percent) from retail and her gross profit is the difference between her purchase price and the retail selling price that she herself determines.

In 1981 Mary Kay Cosmetics raised prices 16 percent and simultaneously upped the commission thresholds to increase productivity on a sustained basis. If the consultant wants to qualify for a 50 percent discount, she must order $1,000 of products at the suggested retail price. Previously an $800 order qualified her for a 50 percent discount. Selling $800 of merchandise currently entitles her to $360. Price hikes and the revised commission thresholds allow the consultant to increase her earnings if she manages to maintain her customer base. But there is no time to rest on her laurels, because the Mary Kay system is geared toward the sales woman who aggressively builds her business.

While it is relatively easy to become a Mary Kay consultant, the company demands considerably more of those women who wish to qualify as sales directors. The labor of the sales director is sweetened by the possibility of substantially increased financial rewards over the consultant status, however. Like the consultant, the sales director is self-employed. As the resident advisor for her unit, she supplies her people with inspiration, positive suggestions for improving sales performance, and business advice of all kinds. A carefully orchestrated program for the directors and a rigorous screening process that admits only those women who have met stringent performance standards in terms of volume sales and number of recruits assures that the directors will be an experienced, aggressive sales group. In 1982 the company numbered 3,500 directors. The director-in-qualification travels to Dallas (at her own expense, as is the case of travel arrangements for the entire Mary Kay sales force) to receive training in management of a sales unit.

The directors' commissions were revised upward in 1981 along with the consultants'. To receive the pink Cadillac ("those little pink jars mean little pink cars"), the director must maintain a wholesale volume of $12,000 per month. Under the previous commission scheme, the director earned 12 percent if her unit volume topped $6,000. After the revision, her unit needed to "politely persuade" customers to buy from $8,000 to $12,000 to receive 12 percent. Although the director currently gets only 11 percent on unit volume between $5,000 and $8,000, a 13 percent commission is now possible for the director on volume over $12,000. The director must maintain the momentum of her unit if she is to succeed. Simply put, success for consultants spells success for directors, and vice versa.

GROWTH OF THE COMPANY

Inside and outside of Mary Kay, declining recruitment of consultants was expected in the early 1980s, and the 50 percent growth rate experienced up until 1980 was considered unsustainable. Anxiety that the company might reach an early saturation point due to its rapid growth has proved to be groundless, however, with 180,000 consultants projected by December 1982.

Cosmetics, along with beer and cigarettes, have generally been earmarked "recession-proof." Yet cosmetics unit sales in late 1981 and 1982 for Mary Kay and other companies did falter as disposable incomes declined in recessionary environment. During this period Mary Kay Ash's autobiography went on sale. Her promotional tour to major U.S. cities to discuss her life, career, and company on television and radio provided unprecedented visibility for the Mary Kay message and gave recruitment a shot in the arm. The company spent an estimated $450,000 in television and other advertisements during this period (Exhibit 7).

THE MARY KAY PHILOSOPHY

At Mary Kay, attention to the family unit is central to company ideology. Mary Kay Ash often states the formula, "God first, family second, career third." Since most Mary Kay consultants have families, the organization realizes that enlisting family cooperation makes for happier, more successful Mary Kay salespersons. A husband who is unfavorably disposed to his wife's Mary Kay career, "who gets upset when she comes home an hour late from an evening beauty show" may be "disastrous" to the business. So Mary Kay consultants are urged early on to enlist the cooperation of husbands with tact and caring. At the seminar in Dallas each year, husbands participate in workshops led by experienced Mary Kay husbands designed to imbue them with "that Mary Kay enthusiasm" at best or at least to help them handle issues that sometimes arise in a Mary Kay household: ego crises that occur when a wife brings in more income than her spouse, household crises when a woman may not be on hand to perform all the "wifely" functions to which the family has become accustomed, readjustment problems for the family when the wife and mother may be away from home attending Mary Kay functions. To cheer those husbands left at home when wives are in Dallas, training to be directors, letters are dispatched to them from Mary Kay headquarters thanking them for the support they are giving to their wives' careers.

If you are a working woman, getting your husband involved is so important! It's always been my observation that people will support that which they help to create. *When a woman goes to work, she must not only sell her husband on her career, but if she's wise, she'll find ways to get him involved. Once he's involved, she'll get his support. One area where many of our Beauty Consultants have gotten their husbands involved is in the bookkeeping and record-keeping that goes with any business. Many sales-oriented*

"YOU'VE GONE PRETTY FAR FOR A WOMAN." THEY SHOULDN'T HAVE TOLD ME THAT.

"I had been a success in my field for more than 25 years. A promotion to a top executive position was long overdue. Instead, I was passed over again and again. Has that happened to you?

"Well, my response was to create an opportunity that would reward women for what they were really worth!

"My dream was to offer women not only a wonderful new Skin Care Program, but also an opportunity to prove how far we can go."

Today Mary Kay Cosmetics has more than 120,000 Beauty Consultants on three continents and our sales are in the hundreds of millions of dollars!

Now the Mary Kay story is available in a book.

It is a personal business history of a dream that happened when all the skeptics said it would fail.

"If you have ever been told you can't do something,

Yes, there really is a Mary Kay.
Portrait by Francesco Scavullo, June 1981.

my story will prove you can. I urge you to read it right away, and I hope it will open some closed doors and closed minds in your life."

It's available at your local bookstore. Or ask your Beauty Consultant how you can get a copy. If you don't have a Consultant, look in the Yellow Pages under Cosmetics/Retail. Or call toll-free (800) 527-6270.

women don't especially like record keeping, so they welcome their husband's help in this area, and it's been our experience that most husbands enjoy keeping their wives' records.[3]

To assist the woman in rendering to the family the time that is theirs, and to Mary Kay Cosmetics its fair share, Mary Kay Ash advocates good time management. Since she has found that getting up at five in the morning gives her an additional workday each week, she urges consultants and directors to join her Five O'Clock Club: a routine of rising early each morning, using the early hours to dress, apply makeup, do household chores, and prepare to begin Mary Kay business-related activities by 8:30 A.M. The ideal consultant will stop for a half-hour lunch and stay with business until five in the evening. In the best of all possible Mary Kay worlds, a woman will earn enough to allow her to delegate many household duties to a housekeeper, the better to perform her sales duties. Getting organized, however, is key to the success of the woman who cannot afford a housekeeper:

I know many women do manage to wear all those hats, but it can certainly take its toll. In order to be effective in their careers and still be good wives and mothers, they must be organized. As a general rule, I have found that getting organized is one of the biggest problems working women have. And if a woman is trying to wear a great many hats and she isn't organized, she's operating under a tremendous handicap.[4]

A unique feature of the company is the flexibility built in for working mothers. Inherent in the company philosophy is the notion that women working as a team can cover for each other in case of family emergency. The beauty show will go on, but perhaps another consultant will carry on when a woman needs to care for a sick child or spouse, a procedure called "the dovetail system."

The Mary Kay organization becomes an extended family for its sales force, a bountiful maternal figure dispensing prizes of minks, diamonds, and Cadillacs to dutiful daughters. The nonhierarchical family atmosphere of the company promotes high morale, according to Mary Kay and upper-level staffers.

The personal touch — be it serving cookies mixed up by Mary Kay Ash with her own hands at company functions or sending Christmas, birthday, anniversary cards and condolence messages — underscores the familial concept of the organization and builds company loyalty. The allegiance of the sales force to the company, personified in Mary Kay Ash, surfaces in every aspect of the consultant's training. In problem solving, consultants are asked to think what Mary Kay herself "would do in your situation," much as if Mary Kay Ash were an exemplary, albeit absent, mother. Adopting Mary Kay Ash's personal routine as their own in many cases, consultants and directors are attached to Mary Kay by an umbilical cord of personal habit and life-style. Many of the sales force display photographs of Mary Kay in their workspaces at home.

[3] Ibid., p. 72.

[4] Ibid., pp. 169–170.

SKIN CARE PRODUCTS AND MARY KAY

Mary Kay Cosmetics in 1963 had hit upon an idea whose time had come with its introduction of skin care products, now the staple of almost every major cosmetics house. The basic five-step skin care process includes cleansing, stimulating, freshening, moisturizing, and protecting the skin. The company suggests that the basic set not be broken as it is the centerpiece of the Mary Kay concept, that is, to teach people how to care for their skin.

> *The best reason to start a new company is that* there is a need for what you have to offer, *or that you're better than what is being offered. When we began, no cosmetic company was actually teaching skin care. All of them were just selling rouge or lipstick or new eye colors. No company was teaching women how to care for their skin. So we came into a market where there was a real need — and we filled it. Oddly enough, it's still true today that women are not knowledgeable about skin care, despite all the information on television, in magazines, and in newspapers. They buy a product here, there, and everywhere, but they don't have a coordinated program. We fill a void by helping women understand how to take care of their skin. So, if you want to start a successful business, you must offer something different or something better than what is available.*[5]

In what is being called a "cosmetic revolution" by some, major cosmetics firms in the 1980s are taking scientific approaches to beauty. While the promise of cosmetics before the 1980s was one of glamor, the present appeal is made to the customer's consciousness that the scientific result of good skin care is healthy, younger-looking, cleaner skin. Advertising stresses the chemical properties of collagen, linoleic acid, and many more ingredients. Consumers are presumed, in such high-tech ads, to be conscientious about skin care and conversant with its sophisticated vocabulary replete with such terms as *cell renewal*, *exfoliation*, and *hydration*.

This scientific approach began in the 1960s when Dr. Erno Lazlo introduced his pathbreaking line of skin care products to an enthusiastic public. Worship at the altars of Revlon's Eterna 27 and Clinique also began in the 1960s and has continued into the 1980s.

Scientific research in the 1950s set the stage for the cosmetic revolution. Although Mary Kay Cosmetics maintains that the original recipe for its skin preparations emanated from a hide tanner in Texas.

From the 1950s to the 1970s, soluble collagen became available to cosmetic chemists at that time seeking a protein to be used in products to treat dry, flaking, aging skin.[6] Marketing research had demonstrated (and continues to reveal) that approximately 90 percent of American women perceive their most serious skin problem to be dry skin.

---

[5] Ibid., p. 120.

[6] See R. D. Todd and L. I. Biol, "Soluble Collagen: New Protein for Cosmetics," *Drug and Cosmetic Industry*, Vol. 117 (October 1975), pp. 50–52.

According to scientist Bernard Idson of Hoffman-La Roche, when it was understood that it is not oil but water that causes skin to be soft and flexible, cosmetic marketing shifted emphasis from total emolliency to the moisturizing qualities of various products. Idson and other researchers found that a water level of less than 10 percent in an individual's skin results in dried keratin, which causes lowered skin elasticity, a characteristic of sun-damaged, chapped, and aged skin.[7]

With over half its sales in the skin care area, Mary Kay finds itself in the 1980s heavily invested in the fastest-growing product category in cosmetics. Industry analysts project continued growth for skin care products, estimating in optimistic moments the general moisturizer market to number 100 million persons.

PSYCHOGRAPHICS, DEMOGRAPHICS, AND MARY KAY

Psychographic market segmentation stretches beyond the more traditional demographic and socioeconomic descriptors used to predict consumer behavior. Product psychographics are bound up with product promises, price-value perception, and the overall image of the product. Because of this relational posture, psychographic market segmentation is particularly applicable to the behavior of the cosmetics purchaser, who according to an old aphorism, is buying not only a product but hope. In a way, however, proponents of the scientific approach to marketing skin care are placing bets on a consumer's responding to demonstrations of empirical results and moving away from purchasing merely out of *hopes* that the product will deliver.

The past decade has seen a tremendous consumer responsiveness to computerized and education-oriented beauty programs (Clinique) and carefully orchestrated, scientific-based programs to control "age zones" (Charles of Ritz). According to those in the testing area at Ritz, their test methodology for the product Age-Zone Controller used 100 subjects and, according to Eileen Kregan, Director of Consumer Education for Charles of Ritz (1982), "consisted of making silicone skin replicas of the subject's outer eye area on the first, seventh, and fourteenth days of the test. To measure line reduction, light was passed through the positive skin replicas and a transparency was made. Direct measurements were then made of the transparencies to determine what changes occurred in the length and number of age lines over a 14-day period." Advertising for the product will reflect the scientific findings.

Mary Kay relies much more heavily on the educational than on the high-tech approach with its customers. *Quality control* is a term that surfaces more often at Mary Kay than specific scientific terminology and vocabulary. The company envisions customers as interested more in the process of using the product than its specific theoretical underpinnings.

---

[7] See Bernard Idson, "Dry Skin Moisturizing and Emolliency," *Drug and Cosmetic Industry* Vol. 117 (October 1975), pp. 43–45.

The demographic trends as projected by U.S. Census figures indicate that Mary Kay will continue to find an increasing number of women customers in the 25- to 44-year age group, a group Mary Kay has already targeted as one vitally interested in skin care. Projections call for the 63 million persons in the 25- to 44-year age group in 1980 to increase to 80 million in 1990. Although the teenage and early-twenties market is dwindling, this should not be problematic for Mary Kay since its products presently do not get high visibility among this group due to the beauty show method of sales.

Mary Kay Cosmetics sees many positive signals in the 1980 Census data (Exhibit 8). Constructing ''the woman of the '80s,'' the company profiled a woman ''in her mid-30s'':

> Her husband has a good job, but they could use extra income. They have one child.
>
> She has completed some college and would like to return, part-time, for more. She is highly inclined to a job or career — both from economic necessity and from a desire to experience something new and to test her abilities.
>
> The woman of the '80s has a new awareness of political affairs but, at the same time, is keenly aware of improving herself, physically, intellectually and professionally.
>
> She wants to live life on her terms. She is interested in acquiring things and achieving goals, but above these she places experience. She is not content to be a spectator. While she may admire the looks and figure of a fashion model, she would rather be one.
>
> Even though she enjoys her homelife, she seeks to expand her world by finding a part-time job or full-time career. This new world makes her more aware of her appearance. She works hard to stay fit; she is nutrition-conscious; she cares deeply about how she looks — her wardrobe, her skin, and her grooming.
>
> To the ends of feeling and looking good, she has educated herself in the accoutrements

EXHIBIT 8
U.S. population projections by age group (both sexes)

Age group	1970	1975	1980	1985	1990	Compound % increase (decrease)			
						1975 vs. 1970	1980 vs. 1975	1985 vs. 1980	1990 vs. 1985
15–19	19.3	21.0	20.6	18.0	16.8	1.7%	(0.4)%	(2.7)%	(1.4)%
20–24	17.2	19.2	20.9	20.5	18.0	2.3	1.7	(0.5)	(2.6)
25–29	13.7	16.9	18.9	20.6	20.2	4.3	2.3	1.7	(0.4)
30–34	11.6	14.0	17.2	19.3	20.9	3.8	4.2	2.3	1.6
35–39	11.2	11.6	14.0	17.3	19.3	0.6	3.8	4.9	2.2
40–44	12.0	11.2	11.7	14.1	17.3	(1.3)	0.9	3.8	4.1
45–49	12.1	11.8	11.0	11.5	13.9	(0.7)	(1.4)	0.9	3.8
50–54	11.2	12.0	11.7	10.9	11.4	1.4	1.4	(1.4)	0.9
55–59	10.0	10.5	11.4	11.1	10.4	1.0	1.7	(0.5)	(1.3)
60–64	8.7	9.2	9.8	10.6	10.4	1.1	1.3	1.6	(0.4)

Note: Figures in millions.
Source: U.S. Department of Commerce, Bureau of Census, 1970, 1980, Series P-25, *Population Estimates and Projections.*

of fitness and appearance. She is more conscious than her mother's generation about matters of sophistication, taste in clothing and cosmetic fashions.

She eagerly searches for products and services that satisfy her powerful sense of self and her need for self-improvement. She is a customer in the market for what Mary Kay has always offered. And now, more than ever, she is willing to try both our products and our career opportunity.

The inevitable meeting of Mary Kay and the woman of the '80s usually takes place at a Mary Kay beauty show.[8]

As Mary Kay Cosmetics looks to the 1990s, it sees a population in which 60 percent of all women will be working. Women working outside the home have clearly demonstrated that they spend more on cosmetics than do their counterparts in the home. One-third of all households will be composed of single persons, people who have discretionary income to spend on their own needs. Mary Kay sees great opportunities to convert a "middle-aged" population to skin care products. On another level, there will be a large middle-aged working female population from which to recruit the corps of Mary Kay consultants. That the number of women entering the labor force is tapering off (in 1980, 50 percent of the female population between ages 18 and 65 were working) does not appear to be of major concern to the company.

MARY KAY AND
THE FOOD AND DRUG ADMINISTRATION

Inquiries made to the Food and Drug Administration (FDA) regarding the claims made by cosmetics companies for their products is a major escalating problem at the agency, which is receiving less funding than it says it needs to investigate. The FDA sustains the burden of proof in establishing that the claims made by cosmetics companies are misleading to the consumer. Although cosmetics companies, including Mary Kay, express concern about a climate of increased regulation, the FDA complains that "we are not in any position to challenge the cosmetics industry. It is a $12 billion industry being regulated by a handful of people at the FDA."

Until the 1970s, the government took a strong stance with regard to the regulation of cosmetics formulations. Consumer activism across the board in the 1970s resulted in more stringent regulation of the industry. The use of dyes, hexachlorophene, and mercury in cosmetics and toiletries sparked debates and engendered legislation on the appropriate labeling of cosmetics. Major regulatory requirements imposed on manufacturers included

Responsibility for the safety of the cosmetic being marketed

Responsibility for required testing to determine toxicity, irritation, and/or sensitivity to the product

[8] *1980 Annual Report*, p. 5.

Compliance should the FDA insist on further discretionary testing by an FDA-appointed, independent organization to verify the safety of ingredients

Mandatory labeling of cosmetic packages or containers with specific ingredients in order of predominance, although flavor and fragrance need only be indicated by the words ''flavor'' and ''fragrance''

A waiting period of 20 days before the release of the new product after notification of the FDA

Reports of increased regulation hover over the industry, but the fact is, according to the *1982 U.S. Industrial Outlook*, that less than 1 percent of the FDA's budget goes toward regulation of the cosmetics industry. The FDA depends on voluntary programs for the reporting of product formulas and adverse effects, for example, the Cosmetic Ingredient Review (CIR), a screening and warning process to alert the industry to possible harmful effects of cosmetic ingredients.

Mary Kay's reaction to regulation has resulted in expansion of its laboratories, acquisition of capital equipment to support skin science, and development of contacts in the scientific fields of dermatology and skin science. ''Regulatory agencies are responding to increased scientific information, ensuring a more complex environment in the '80s for our entire industry,'' the company reported to stockholders in 1981.

OF TOILETRIES AND COSMETICS

Increasingly the distinction drawn between toiletries and cosmetics is becoming a matter of semantics. Because they are higher priced, cosmetics theoretically are geared to the individual whereas toiletries at a lower unit price are targeted to the mass market. The mode of distribution of cosmetics — through department stores and drugstores on a franchise or semifranchise basis or through direct sales — differs from that of toiletries, which are found in mass marketing outlets. This distinction is beginning to blur as cosmetic houses begin limitedly to place lower-priced lines in grocery stores and discount houses, although it is doubtful that toothpaste will appear in department stores. More utilitarian in nature, toiletries, including shampoos, toothpastes, and deodorants because of their proletarian nature, occupy a more competitive marketing niche, one in which higher promotional advertising expenditures are the rule. Lipsticks, fragrance products, eye makeup, face makeup, and the treatment lines — the mainstays of cosmetics — tend to engender a strong brand-name loyalty if the product delivers, even though it may be less advertised than a toiletry. A satisfied Mary Kay customer, for instance, often will use no other brand of cosmetic, although she may use several brands of toothpaste. Mary Kay and other cosmetic companies are making strong bids to sell toiletries as cosmetics, especially in the hair care line, by marketing a cluster of such products as a hair care program with much the same educational approach found successful for the skin care line (Exhibit 9).

EXHIBIT 9 Total U.S. cosmetic and toiletry trends, 1970–1980

Year	Sales manufacturing prices (millions)	Price increase (decrease)	Real sales (increase)	U.S. female population (millions)	Cosmetic and toiletry sales per woman[a] (mfg. prices)	Real cosmetic use index[b] (per capita)
1980	$3,950	n/a	n/a	113.6	$29.55	1.33
1979	3,653			112.7	27.55	1.36
1978	3,317			111.8	25.18	1.32
1977	3,040			110.9	23.29	1.20
1976	2,816			110.1	21.71	1.25
1975	2,476			109.2	19.27	1.19
1974	2,275			108.5	17.84	1.16
1973	2,110			107.7	16.62	1.15
1972	1,980			106.9	15.74	1.10
1971	1,875			106.0	15.06	1.04
1970	1,735			104.9	14.08	1.00
% Increase (decrease)						
1980–1979	8.1%	10.1%	(2.1)%	0.8%	7.3%	(2.8)%
1979–1978	10.1	6.0	4.1	0.8	9.4	3.4
1978–1977	9.1	4.0	5.1	0.8	8.1	4.1
1977–1976	8.0	4.0	4.0	0.7	7.3	3.3
1976–1975	13.7	7.2	6.5	0.8	12.7	5.5
1975–1974	8.8	4.6	4.2	0.6	8.0	3.4
1974–1973	7.8	6.4	1.4	0.7	7.3	0.9
1973–1972	6.7	0.0	6.7	0.8	5.6	5.6
1972–1971	5.4	(0.8)	6.2	0.9	4.5	5.1
1971–1970	8.1	2.5	5.6	1.0	6.9	4.4
Compound growth						
1980 vs. 1970	9%			1%	8%	3%
1980 vs. 1975	10			1	9	3
1975 vs. 1970	7			1	6	3

Note: From sources believed reliable. Excludes toothpaste and other categories in which Mary Kay does not compete.
[a] Assumes 85% of U.S. cosmetics and toiletry industry sales of products Mary Kay sells are used by women.
[b] Cosmetic and toiletry sales per woman minus price increases, indexed to 1970.

A common property to both cosmetics and toiletries is their appeal to the psyche of the user. No one would argue with the idea that people buy these products with the expectation that they will look and feel better after using them.

Analysts have concluded that one problem in capturing the potentially vast market for men's cosmetics is in breaking down the image that it is normal for a man to buy toiletries but somehow "abnormal" for him to purchase cosmetics. In recent years men appear to have been convinced that colognes are acceptable masculine cosmetic items. Mary Kay and other firms believe that growth in the men's cosmetic market will be slow and will probably begin with a skin care line accompanied by an educational process of some sort.

MARY KAY COSMETICS AND THE FUTURE

Returning to the familial theme at the end of her autobiography, Mary Kay reflects on the possibility of her retirement — if and when she can no longer present the glamorous, ageless public persona that people recognize through photographs such as the one taken by celebrity photographer Francesco Scavullo for the cover of her book. In passing she remarks that her mother's skin, even at age 87 "looked wonderful."

Looking toward the long term, Mary Kay Cosmetics purchased 176 acres of land in Dallas in June 1981 to pursue a major four-year expansion program to encompass production, distribution, and administrative facilities. Construction was set to start in October 1982 on the first of several manufacturing and distribution facilities.

We're also so fortunate to have as president my son, Richard, who has filled in for me on many occasions and won the hearts of our people. He, one day, will not only fill his job as chief executive but mine as well, as motivator of our people.[9]

Appendix A portrays the management team at Mary Kay Cosmetics.

The development strategy to see the company through a lengthier expansion period will call for construction as needed to support sales, to be financed from retained earnings. The leased 300,000-square-foot manufacturing facility allows Mary Kay Cosmetics to support $400 million in sales volume. The $12 million site development project, underway in 1982, was capitalized and also financed by internal cash flow and limited bank borrowing — a conservative fiscal strategy consistent with Mary Kay Ash's personal philosophy of paying cash rather than incurring heavy, long-term debts.

Richard Rogers has publicly set the goal of $500 million in annual sales by 1990, emphasizing that 35 percent of the Mary Kay business is repeat sales to faithful customers. "As we grow, we're bringing our customer base forward," he states. His plan for growth reflects the guarded optimism of industry analysts. They predict that beauty products will rebound in the 1980s as the economy limps toward recovery. Most companies are placing their chips on moisturizing products, although many will continue diversification strategies, for example, Chesebrough-Ponds, a leader in the moisturizing business with Vaseline Intensive Care Lotion, but also a leader in spaghetti sauce, children's clothing, and casual footwear with the Ragu, Health-tex, and G. H. Bass brands. Meanwhile, Avon, Mary Kay's most look-alike competitor, continues to diversify. In 1982 Avon began peddling magazine subscriptions along with its vast cosmetic and costume jewelry lines. In a surprising 1979 move, Avon picked up Tiffany and Company, the preeminent jewelry concern.

[9] Ash, *Mary Kay*, p. 205.

Mary Kay intends to ride the moisturizing and skin care wave. Its Basic Skin Care Program will remain the staple product line. While other cosmetic companies (Avon and Bonne Bell, to name just two) are sponsoring women's running, bowling, and tennis competitions, Mary Kay Cosmetics will channel its energies into support of women working — for Mary Kay. An Avon piece of advertising copy reads, "At Avon, sports, health and beauty go naturally together." Mary Kay, however, will continue to endorse a work and beauty ethic.

Introduced in 1982, the four-step Body Care Program seemed the next logical step for Mary Kay Cosmetics, a continuation of the company's appeal to the 25- to 44-year-old segment. Other major product constellations for the 1980s include Specialized Skin Care products (sun screen and hand cream), the Glamour Collection (cosmetics), and the Beauty Boutique, an array of bath and after-bath products. In keeping with the programmatic presentation pioneered in the Skin Care System, the company has developed a Basic Hair Care System, including shampoos, conditioner, and hair spray. Mary Kay Cosmetics hopes to nurture the presently minuscule market for the Mr. K. line of men's skin care products.

> *I've talked about how important it is for women to look good, but I think men care just as much about their appearance. However, unfortunately, often you'll see a man dressed in beautiful clothes, with good-looking shoes, an expensive briefcase, well-groomed hair, and manicured nails — but whose face could look so much better with a little help! A woman wouldn't look complete without her face made up. So why shouldn't a man do the same thing?*[10]

As the company feels its way through the 1980s, it will accentuate quality control aspects ensured by a vigilant R&D policy. John Beasley, vice president of manufacturing, addressed this major concern in an interview, which appears as Appendix B. Also, see Appendix C, an excerpt from *U.S. Industrial Outlook.*

Because of the style of life that Mary Kay is selling along with the product — that of the independent, well-compensated, career-woman beauty consultant — the company has not been altogether successful in translating the Mary Kay concept into other, non-English–speaking, more patriarchal cultures. Mary Kay Cosmetics internally appears sanguine that "the philosophy of Mary Kay Cosmetics has proven well suited for women everywhere," but this remains a debatable area in places like Japan.

Mary Kay Ash has stated on many occasions that Mary Kay Cosmetics is "in the business of helping women create better self-images so that they will feel better about themselves." Whether she is invoking Ralph Waldo Emerson's "Nothing great was ever achieved without enthusiasm" or leading her devoted consultants and directors in a chorus of "That Mary Kay Enthusiasm," Mary Kay Ash, genius of direct sales motivation, thinks and dreams enthusiasm: "My own dream," she states in her autobiography, "is that Mary Kay Cosmetics will someday become the largest and best skin care company in the world."

[10] Ibid., pp. 130–131.

APPENDIX A: MARY KAY MANAGEMENT TEAM, 1982

Mary Kay Ash, Chairman of the Board

Richard Rogers, President. Co-founder of Mary Kay Cosmetics, Inc. Served as General Manager, Vice President. 1968 "Marketing Man of the Year" Award from North Texas Chapter of the American Marketing Association.

Gerald M. Allen, Vice President, Administration. Responsible for planning, organizing, and directing the delivery of administrative services to the beauty consultant and supervising a staff of sales promotion directors. Supervises company security, communications and word processing, sales administration and compensation programs. B.B.A., Arlington State College.

J. Eugene (Gene) Stubbs, Vice President, Finance, and Treasurer. Responsible for financial planning and accountable for company's financial assets and profitability objectives. Directs the treasury, controllership, and internal audit functions. Also responsible for all financial reporting. M.B.A., University of Texas; C.P.A.; B.B.A., Texas A & M University.

Richard C. Bartlett, Vice President, Marketing. Responsible for planning and implementing marketing strategy including incentive programs, education and development of consultants, special events and meetings, public relations, and market-related research. B.S., University of Florida.

Monty C. Barber, Vice President, Secretary, and General Counsel. Responsible for supervising activities prescribed by law and the company regulations, establishing legal policies, advising and rendering opinions, supervises the public affairs program. As corporate secretary, attends to administrative matters for the board, shareholder relations, consumer relations, and coordinates all contribution requests. J.D., University of Texas; B.B.A., University of Texas.

John Beasley, Group Vice President, Manufacturing. Responsible for planning, organizing, and evaluating all manufacturing decisions. Directs the development of the product line and ensures the quality of the products. B.A., Georgia Tech, Industrial Engineering National Merit Scholarship.

Phil Bostley, Vice President, Operations. Responsible for planning, directing, and coordinating the distribution of all Mary Kay cosmetics and sales aids through regional distribution centers. Also responsible for directing the forecasting of product mix, the maintenance of inventory levels and coordinating the company's data processing group. B.A., Penn State University, math and science.

Myra O. Barker, Ph.D., Vice President, Research and Product Development. Responsible for planning and directing skin technology, process technology, and product development. Directs regulatory and medical affairs and ensures product safety. Ph.D., Tulane University, biochemistry; B.S., University of Texas, chemistry.

Bruce C. Rudy, Ph.D., Vice President, Quality Assurance. Responsible for the procedures that assure the quality of raw materials in the product line. Controls the finished products certifying that they meet cosmetic, FDA and company standards. Plans and directs quality audits of all phases of product development, research, manufacture, and distribution. B.S., E. Stroudsburg State College; M.S., Clemson University; M.B.A., Columbia University; Ph.D., University of Georgia.

Pat Howard, Vice President, Manufacturing Operations. Responsible for manufacturing material control including purchasing, warehousing, production, planning, and international manufacturing. B.S., St. Mary's University; M.S., Texas A & M University.

Jack Dingler, Vice President, Controller. Responsible for all operating financial functions of the company, including expenditure review, to ensure the continuation of the company's sound financial position. B.B.A., University of Texas at Arlington, accounting; C.P.A.

William H. Randall, Director, Marketing Services. Responsible for marketing research, incentive program, visual communications, marketing publications, communications, and creative efforts. M.B.A., Harvard; B.A., Rutgers, economics.

Dean Meadors, Director, Public Relations. Responsible for all public relations activity. M.S., University of Illinois, advertising; B.S., University of Illinois, journalism.

Netta Jackson, Director, Product Service. Responsible for the marketing rationale for product development. Ensures that the company remains competitive in price and positioning. Active in sales force training. B.S.B.A., University of Arkansas, marketing.

Michael C. Lunceford, Director, Public Affairs. Responsible for monitoring of local, state, and federal laws and regulations; community liaison with emphasis on corporate philanthropy. Master's program, Southern Methodist University, business administration; M.S., Southern Methodist University, public administration; B.B.A., East Texas State University, business administration, finance/economics.

APPENDIX B: AN INTERVIEW WITH JOHN BEASLEY

The following is an interview with John Beasley, Vice President, Manufacturing Group for Mary Kay Cosmetics, Inc. Mr. Beasley has been with Mary Kay since September 1975 and is currently responsible for planning, organizing, and evaluating all U.S. and international manufacturing decisions. A major portion of his responsibility is quality assurance. The interview was conducted in May 1982 at Mary Kay's corporate headquarters in Dallas.

Q: How does the quality of Mary Kay products compare with others on the market?

A: We direct our research and development and all our efforts toward producing the finest products we can produce. We know what other companies are producing. We understand all major competitive concepts, formulas, and approaches. But our focus is on producing the best product for the Mary Kay system. You see, we have a different orientation from most cosmetic companies. We can't just produce a product for a particular market segment. Our skin care products are used in a teaching system, so we are systems oriented. Our products work together, they're modular, and there's a synergism between them.

Q: Wasn't Mary Kay a pioneer in teaching skin care?

A: Mary Kay, as a specialist in skin care, has set trends for the only product segment of the market that's really growing. In 1963, we began marketing a five-step program of skin care. In 1976, we started teaching the scientific basis of skin care to and through our beauty consultants who today number over 150,000. Now every major cosmetic company in the country is talking about the scientific basis of skin care.

Q: How did the new Body Care System happen?

A: We've always had products aimed at body skin. The idea evolved from what we had learned about facial skin care. Body skin is different from facial skin, yet there are functional needs that need to be addressed in a complementary way. Body care was a natural extension from the Mary Kay tradition of scientific skin care.

Our Body Care products have been formulated according to the same high standards we use in skin care. We've tested them and used them ourselves. We've come up with a very, very high-quality system for an economical price.

Q: What standards do you use internally for making product decisions?

A: We came up with four factors that have to be included in every decision that is made from every level. Since we are a participative management organization, everybody has to know what the rules are, exactly what is important. The first thing that has to be considered in every decision is quality . . . the impact on product quality. The second is service. Service to the beauty consultant and consumer.

The third thing that everybody has to take into account is the flexibility of the decision. What range does it work in? The fourth is the actual cost of the decision: total cost of capital investment, impact on cost of goods, and cash flow.

We teach all management and some hourly people to use the four criteria. I will not look at any proposal that doesn't address these four things — and the first thing I see has to be quality. Richard Rogers [president of Mary Kay] uses the saying "If it's worth doing, do it right." That is the kind of quality statement that underlines everything we do all day long. That's the way the company was founded.

Q: You mentioned you are a "participative management organization." How does this work at Mary Kay?

A: You cannot get quality by having only one part of your company responsible for quality. The assumption that the better traditional organizations have made is that if you want to get something accomplished, you have to focus on it through a special part of your organization.

Our assumption here is much different. Everybody is in charge of quality. The Research and Development Department is in charge of quality. The Marketing Department is in charge of quality. The Material Control Department is in charge of quality.

The actual "Quality Assurance" function serves as a measuring device. The quality audit measures how well we are matching our stated quality standards. These specifications are set in a type of committee process that starts in research and development and get approved right up through the CEO in final form. From there our job is to expand them backward, through all the maze of processing, all the way back to vendor level. It's very much like the idea behind the Japanese quality circles when you get everybody involved in focusing on quality. For example, in 1976 we gave everybody in the hourly (nonexempt) group an across-the-board pay increase, explaining that we were adding the quality inspection responsibility to their job. We said, "Part of your job is to make sure we always produce Mary Kay quality."

Q: How did they respond to this?

A: Many of them consider quality to be the predominant part of their job. The people in the plant don't simply report a problem; they are actually the ones doing the rejecting. And most of them are very tough. They see things that you and I won't see because they have developed a whole different set of skills out there. We normally produce on only one shift, we hire special people, we evaluate them and reward them. Mary Kay was always, from the very beginning, attracted to people who are quality conscious. If you look around, you see a very consistent type of person in dress and quality standards. When new people come in from other companies, and we've had to do a good bit of recruiting because we've grown so fast, they usually come from companies that were more interested in cost as the first factor. Even top executives don't understand that quality is the first criterion. So we create a whole culture that reinforces our standards.

Q: How many of the products Mary Kay sells are made in your own facilities?

A: We manufacture probably 99 percent of the products in house; and 100 percent is quality inspected here. The same quality standards apply internationally. In general, if they don't pass the same quality standards that we use here in the United States, they don't go to the consumer.

Q: How does your sales force respond to this?

A: The sales force is very, very conscious of the quality aspect. Sometimes there has been some disappointment when we've said, "We're sorry, we can't sell this product because it's not Mary Kay quality." But it's very important to the sales force that they be very proud of the products and systems they teach . . . and sell.

Q: What are your long-term goals for Mary Kay?

A: We want to be the finest teaching-oriented skin care company in the world with sales of $500 million by 1990. That's our corporate objective. It has been stated in our annual report, and everybody around here can quote it.

Q: How do you begin to meet that goal?

A: Research and development is the leading edge. Since 1975, Research and Development has grown from 1 Ph.D. and a technician to a staff of 47. We recruited Dr. Myra Barker to be our vice president of research and development. We go after the top 10 percent of the people in the country who have the skills that we're looking for and personal integrity. They don't come necessarily from the cosmetic industry. Many have come from the drug industry because we see cosmetics, especially skin care products, more like drugs than traditional glamor products.

In addition, the Research and Development Department is in the forefront in developing new technology. We have a group that has been formed to do nothing but research how the skin relates to the rest of the body and how it relates to its environment. A very large part of the research and development budget, for example, is aimed at research all over the world. We're funding a research dermatologist in Wales who is doing research into skin attribute measurement. We have grants in England. When you came in, I was signing a purchase order that goes for a research grant to Southwestern Medical School.

Q: What types of tests are you doing?

A: There are many levels of testing and two major issues: one is safety, one is efficacy. We don't take risks with the consumer. Our products must meet acceptable levels in terms of oral toxicity . . . sensitization . . . irritation. We are having to stretch current technology in establishing some new standards in the industry in the area of comedogenicity, the interaction of the new product, the environment, and the skin-causing comedones (acne).

We screen raw materials at the vendor level. If you get something that's 99 percent pure, it means it's 1 percent impure. In our business we're interested in the 1 percent impure. We made substantial investments in computerized instrumentation so that we can screen raw materials routinely for impurities.

Efficacy testing is also something that is fairly new. Cosmetic products used to be a coverup, but now we're producing skin care products that are functional. We need to measure how a product actually performs, but we're having to develop the technology.

Q: As vice president in charge of manufacturing, how do you challenge your departments?

A: We have no negatives in terms of product quality, number one. We can't afford any big savings in quality. We have to be consistently above the line in terms of the impact on the consumer. Consistently positive! Then what we try to do is to raise that line to the top of the industry. We establish a consistent quality level, and then we figure out how to make that better. That's our drive, our constant challenge. The quality standard has never, ever been stagnant. We always strive to be the best we can be.

APPENDIX C: SUMMARY OF COSMETICS PROSPECTS FOR 1982 AND BEYOND

Moderately priced products are expected to sell best, especially hair, skin, nail, and eye care products.

Fragrances will become more popular, especially among men, in the 1980s.

Source: *1982 U.S. Industrial Outlook.*

Ethnic cosmetic sales are expected to pick up.

Up to 45 percent of males in the population will use cosmetics by 1986.

Sun-screen agents that reportedly protect skin from damaging ultraviolet rays will be added to many skin care products to prevent premature aging, wrinkling, or cancer of the skin.

An estimated 65 percent of all cosmetics are purchased on impulse, although during recessionary periods consumers are most cost conscious.

The industry's principal target group of teenagers and young women is shrinking, although the "baby boom" generation is aging and is likely to spend money for beauty aids.

Among the present 20- to 35-year-old age group, there is a much larger lower-income sector.

Rising costs of raw materials and the high cost of research are the scourge of the cosmetics industry.

New products are essential for greater sales, yet new product introductions lag because of the decrease in research and development.

The skin care market, including moisturizers, sun-care creams, lotions, scrubs and cleansers, collagen and elastin protein rejuvenating agents, is growing and reached $2.5 billion in 1981 because of increased concern among consumers over aging skin, personal cleanliness, and the damaging effects of ultraviolet rays.

Hypoallergenic and fragrance-free products have been demonstrated to be most successful in the skin care market.

The hair preparations market increased to $2.2 billion in 1981 due to consumer interest in healthy looking hair and frequent shampoos by both men and women. Women frequently use cream rinse and hair conditioning products, although an untapped male market exists for such products. Hair spray remains popular with older women.

Industry shipments of cosmetics, toiletries, and fragrances were valued at $9.9 billion in 1981, only a 0.6 percent increase from 1980, as opposed to a 2.6 percent average annual increase from 1972 through 1981.

APPLE COMPUTER, INC. 1986

INTRODUCTION

Apple's CEO, John Sculley, faced product compatibility and market saturation issues in the personal computer industry in 1986, and customer confidence and employee morale issues following the departure of co-founder Steven Jobs, who left Apple to form a competing company. Jobs had led the company during a period of incredible success.

A computer-age version of the American dream became a reality when Apple Computer went public with an initial stock offering of 5 million shares at $22 per share in 1980. Incorporated in 1977, Apple Computer, Inc. designed, developed, produced, marketed, and serviced microcomputer-based personal computers (PC) and related software and peripheral products.

This famous "hacker-in-blue-jeans" computer company took less time to reach the Fortune 500 than any other start-up in the history of the index, and stands a good chance of falling among the one hundred largest U.S. industrial corporations before its tenth birthday in 1990, according to Michael Moritz, author of *The Little Kingdom*.[1]

The following pages describe industry growth, Apple's history, management (including the fall of Jobs), marketing, target markets, competition, operations, technology, research and development, finances, legal issues, and the outlook in 1986.

INDUSTRY GROWTH

With the emergence of the microcomputer, American industry experienced an explosion in technology and business. Consumers were so caught up in the high spirited "keep-up-with-the-Joneses" attitude that many were unsure of their specific needs,

[1]Michael Moritz, *The Little Kingdom: The Private Story of Apple Computer* (New York: W. Morrow, 1984), p. 11.

This case was prepared by Rusty Crews, Cherie Lyon, Russell Neely, and John Williams under the supervision of Professor Sexton Adams, North Texas State University and Adelaide Griffin, Texas Woman's University. © by Sexton Adams. Reprinted by permission.

yet joined the masses. Likewise, computer manufacturers who were springing up on every street corner were not altogether sure of the consumers' specific needs. Before long, the industry was trying to convince the public that the PC was the latest necessity for the household, joining ranks with the likes of the microwave oven. By 1984, the dust had begun to settle and dealers and manufacturers alike found their shelves stocked full of inventory, which in turn led to an industry price slump.[2]

The overzealous nature with which the industry had grown led many entrepreneurs to believe that the market was inexhaustible in size. As a result, the PC market was confused due to the numerous competitors. Businesses over-purchased microcomputers for which they were unsure how to best utilize their capabilities and others purchased machines that were incompatible with other makers', thus inhibiting flexibility and expandability. In addition, many manufacturers specializing in the same area were facing an over-supply of computers and accessories because of the unanticipated low demand level. As a result, a survival-of-the-fittest situation existed and only those manufacturers who could effectively determine the needs of the marketplace and could provide them in time at a suitable price would prevail in this young industry. Market analysts agreed with Apple co-founder Stephen Wozniak who believed the industry's problems to be the sign of a shrinking market.[3]

APPLE'S HISTORY

Apple's origin began long before the famous 1976 graduation of the first Apple computer, designed and built in the garage of Apple's co-founder, Steven P. Jobs. Jobs and Steve Wozniak, Apple's other co-founder, had known each other since junior high school and both graduated from Homestead High School in Santa Clara, California.[4]

Steve Wozniak was first introduced to computers by his father who was employed as an electronic engineer with Lockheed Corporation's Lockheed Missiles and Space Company. Wozniak's father began teaching Steve the workings of computers by helping him design logic circuits when Steve was in the fourth grade and continued to guide him through computer projects to the extent that by the eighth grade, the boy was building an entire computer.

After completing high school, he attended the University of Colorado where he developed an interest in minicomputers. But after just one year in attendance, Wozniak transferred to De Anza College in Cupertino, California where he came close to building what he believed to be the first low-cost hobby computer.

Steve Jobs' experience with college was not as successful as Wozniak's. He

---

[2]Deborah C. Wise, "What's Scaring the Customers Away?" *Business Week,* June 24, 1985, p. 80.

[3]Mike Lewis, "PC Papa Abandons His Baby," *Nations Business,* May 1985, p. 32.

[4]"Building Computers Is As Easy As Apple Pie," *Industry Week,* June 9, 1980, p. 81.

dropped out of school after just one week and spent the next year in India. In 1975, the two were reunited and began meeting in Jobs' garage so as to build a circuit board that could be sold to hobbyists. With surprise as to their board's popularity, Jobs and Wozniak discovered that their board could be sold for twice what it cost them to make. By early 1976, they had obtained an order from one customer for 50 boards. This would be, in retrospect, the Apple I computer.[5]

In March 1976, Jobs and Wozniak formed a partnership, and in June the first of the ordered boards were shipped. Sensing that there was a great demand for their board, the two partners sold a Volkswagen and Wozniak's calculator to raise $1,300 and also obtained $10,000 in grants on credit. The money enabled them to produce 200 boards.

As the new venture continued to grow, the two young entrepreneurs discovered that their paramount problems were money and marketing. These problems were quickly solved by Mike Markkula of Intel Corporation, a semiconductor manufacturer. Markkula became interested in the new circuit board designed by Jobs and Wozniak that would later become the Apple II computer, to which the company would owe a great deal of its success. Convinced of its potential, Markkula invested $91,000 of his own money into the new venture, secured a $250,000 line of credit from Bank of America, and raised $600,000 from venture capitalists.

As Apple grew, more people became involved in the company and contributed to its formation. With this growth evolved the problem of deciding who would assume responsibility for the day-to-day operations. Neither of the two co-founders were interested in the position; therefore, Markkula was selected to be chairman of the board and Mike Scott, a director at National Semiconductor Corporation, was recommended by Markkula to be Apple's first president. With both in agreement, Steve Jobs then assumed the position of vice chairman and Steve Wozniak became vice president, research and development.

Stephen Wozniak left Apple after an airplane accident and a resulting loss of memory for more than a month. "Woz" the wizard, with personal assets over $50 million, signed up for undergraduate computer science courses at Berkeley.

MANAGEMENT

John Sculley (age 46) joined Apple as president and chief executive officer in May 1983. Prior to joining Apple, Mr. Sculley was president and chief executive officer of Pepsi-Cola Company, a manufacturer and distributor of soft drink products, for five years. Pepsi-Cola is a division of PepsiCo, Inc., of which Mr. Sculley was also a senior vice president.

William V. Campbell (age 45) joined Apple as vice president of marketing in June 1983, was appointed executive vice president, sales, in September 1984, and

[5]Ibid., p. 81.

became executive vice president, group executive of U.S. sales and marketing in June 1985. Before joining Apple, Mr. Campbell served as director of marketing for Eastman Kodak, a photographic equipment and supplies manufacturer, from June 1982 to July 1983, and as account director for J. Walter Thompson Advertising from January 1980 to June 1982.

Delbert W. Yocam (age 41) joined Apple in November 1979 as director of materials. In August 1981, he was promoted to vice president and general manager of operations, and in January 1984, was appointed executive vice president and general manager, Apple II Division. In June 1985, Mr. Yocam was named executive vice president, group executive of product operations.

Albert A. Eisenstat (age 55) joined Apple in July 1980 as vice president and general counsel; he has also served as secretary of Apple since September 1980. In November 1985, Mr. Eisenstat was promoted to senior vice president and was elected to the board of directors to fill the vacancy created by the resignation of Steven P. Jobs.

David J. Barram (age 41) joined Apple in April 1985 as vice president of finance and chief financial officer. Prior to his employment with Apple, he was the vice president of finance and administration and chief financial officer of Silicon Graphics, a manufacturer of high-performance engineering workstations, from April 1983 to April 1985. From January 1970 to April 1983, Mr. Barram was controller of the Computer Products Group of Hewlett-Packard, a diversified electronics measurement and computer equipment manufacturer.

Deborah A. Coleman (age 32) joined Apple in November 1981, initially as controller and subsequently as director of operations of the Macintosh Division. Prior to her promotion in November 1985 to vice president of manufacturing, Ms. Coleman had been director of manufacturing from June 1985 to November 1985. Before joining Apple Ms. Coleman served as a financial manager and cost accounting supervisor at Hewlett-Packard.

Jay R. Elliot (age 46) joined Apple as senior human resources manager in May 1982, and became vice president, human resources, in September 1983. Before joining Apple, Mr. Elliot served as personnel manager for Intel Corporation, a semiconductor manufacturer, from August 1980 to May 1982.

Jean-Louis Gassee (age 41) joined Apple in February 1981 as general manager of Seedrin S.A.R.L., a wholly-owned subsidiary of the company. In May 1985, Mr. Gassee became director of marketing for the Macintosh Division in Cupertino, California, and in June 1985, he was named vice president, product development. Prior to joining Apple, Mr. Gassee was president of Exxon Office Systems from July 1979 to February 1981, in Paris, France.

Thomas Marano (age 35) joined Apple as vice president, U.S. sales, in January 1985. Before joining Apple, Mr. Marano served as director of business development for Pepsi-Cola Company from October 1978 to February 1985.

Michael Muller (age 46) joined Apple in September 1979 as president of The Keyboard Company, then a wholly-owned subsidiary of Apple. In April 1982, The

Keyboard Company became Apple's Accessory Products Division, and Mr. Muller was promoted to vice president and general manager of that division. In June 1985, Mr. Muller was appointed vice president in charge of special projects.

Michael Spindler (age 43) joined Apple as European marketing manager in September 1980, was promoted to vice president and general manager, Europe, in January 1984, and was named vice president, international, in February 1985.

Roy H. Weaver, Jr. (age 53) joined Apple in September 1980 as U.S. distribution manager. Beginning in April 1981, he was director of distribution and service operations, and in April 1982, was promoted to general manager of distribution and service. In September 1982, he was appointed vice president and general manager of the Distribution, Service and Support Division; in September 1983, vice president, field operations; and in June 1985, vice president, distribution.

Robert Saltmarsh (age 35) joined Apple as assistant treasurer in November 1982, and was promoted to treasurer in November 1985. Between February 1979 and November 1982, Mr. Saltmarsh worked for Data General, a minicomputer manufacturer, first as European treasury manager and then as corporate treasury manager.[6]

John Sculley

The man Steve Jobs and Apple's board of directors chose to help Apple Computer develop professional management was John Sculley, the mid-forty-year-old president of the Pepsi-Cola Company, the domestic drink subsidiary of PepsiCo, Inc. John Sculley represented the opposite of Jobs who dropped out of college and spent his youth experimenting with electronic gizmos, mystical religions, and fruitarian diets.[7] Sculley was cool, disciplined, and orderly; a character developed through strict eastern boarding schools.

After Sculley earned a bachelor's degree in architecture from Brown University, he then pursued a MBA degree at Wharton School, at the University of Pennsylvania, where he graduated in 1963. "He wasn't a particularly noteworthy academic at school, but people tended to follow him," said his younger brother, David.[8] This quality followed Sculley to Pepsi where, by age 38, he had become president of Pepsi-Co, Inc.'s Pepsi-Cola subsidiary. Sculley's ambition and achievement at such a young age attracted Jobs who realized Apple was in need of headstrong leadership.

To lure Sculley away from a shot at becoming chairman of the $7.5 billion food conglomerate, Jobs promised Sculley a deal which included:

$2 million in salary and bonuses for his first year.

Help with the purchase of a $2 million home in Woodside, California, fourteen miles from Apple headquarters.

[6]Apple Computer, Inc., *Form 10-K For Fiscal Year Ended September 27, 1985* (Cupertino, California: Apple Computer, Inc., [1985]), pp. 33–34.

[7]Deborah C. Wise, "Apple, Part 2: The No-Nonsense Era of John Sculley," *Business Week,* January 27, 1986, p. 96.

[8]Ibid., p. 97.

Options in 350,000 shares of Apple stock.[9]

Upon joining Apple in May 1983, Sculley was faced with a company full of problems. Committed to turn Apple around in the microcomputer industry, Sculley established structure and discipline within Apple, unlike the free and unstructured organization followed by his predecessor. Sculley brought boot-camp drill to Apple, classifying employees as A, B, or C players.[10]

In the fall of 1983, Sculley invented a dismissal program designed by one Apple programmer:

> *They've been telling people they've got two choices. They've got five days to resign or they're going to be put in a job for which they are unqualified, unsuited, and ill-equipped where they'll be allowed to fail and then be fired.[11]*

Less than one year after Sculley joined Apple, only eight of the fourteen senior executives who were present when Sculley joined remained at Apple, and eventually both co-founders departed.

"I am alone at the top now," declared Sculley, referring to the removal of Steve Jobs.[12] Jobs had recruited Sculley to help Apple develop a professional management. Sculley saw it as his mission to teach Apple marketing and to improve its response to retailers and customers.

Sculley began his mission by merging the company's nine highly decentralized divisions, most of which had been responsible for one product line, into an organization structured according to business functions as demonstrated in Exhibit 1.

Transforming Apple became a tougher task than Sculley had first imagined. Under the leadership of Steve Jobs, Apple had acquired a near maniacal focus on products. Jobs talked of creating "insanely great" new computers, and made stars out of product designers. Sculley refocused Apple's direction through the consolidation of Apple's divisions into just three: a sales division for all products, a division for the Apple II family, and a division for Macintosh with Jobs as its general manager.

The Fall of Jobs   "They've cut the heart out of Apple and substituted an artificial one. We'll just have to see how long it pumps," said one Apple insider shocked at the announcement of Steve Jobs' departure from Apple Computer, Inc.[13]

The decline of Steve Jobs began as the personal computer industry was experiencing a slump in demand, and Apple was experiencing disappointing sales in its Macintosh

---

[9]Michael Moritz, p. 319.

[10]Michael Moritz, p. 322.

[11]Michael Moritz, p. 322.

[12]Deborah C. Wise, "Apple, Part 2: The No-Nonsense Era of John Sculley," *Business Week,* January 27, 1986, p. 96.

[13]Bro Uttal, "Behind the Fall of Steve Jobs," *Fortune,* July 28, 1985, p. 20.

EXHIBIT 1 Apple Organizational Structure

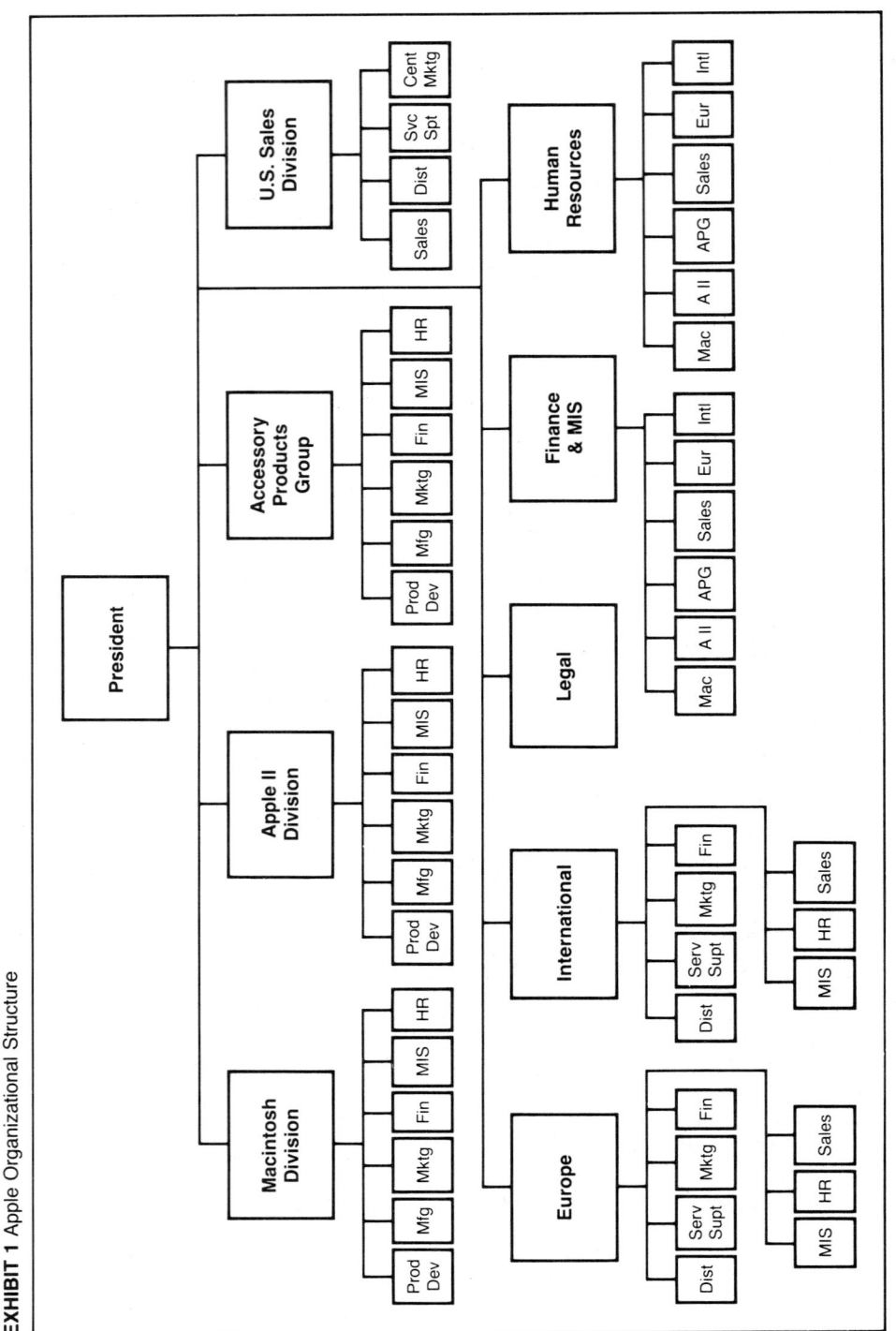

Division, headed by Jobs as its general manager. Urging John Sculley to assert his authority over the company in order for Apple to be spared any additional losses was Arthur Roull, a San Francisco venture capitalist and member of Apple's board of directors. Sculley was reluctant to act as hastily as the board wished, putting off any confrontations with Jobs due to a cautious feeling about radical organizational changes and also out of concern for Jobs' feelings.[14]

"I decided to change my life and come to Apple because of my admiration for Steve and what he had done. Our reorganization was all the more painful because we are such close friends," said the president.[15] Sculley was forced to reorganize Apple and eliminate the company co-founder when he learned that Jobs was plotting to dispose of him.

The Macintosh Division considered itself the company's elite due to the protective environment created by Jobs who publicized the members of the division as superstars. This attention was not to the liking of the Apple II Division whose president was responsible for 65 percent of Apple's total sales. Although the Apple II Division was producing more of the company's sales and profits, the Macintosh Division was receiving all of the perks which included free fruit juice and a masseur on call.[16]

Born out of the belief that new technology should supersede the old, Jobs once referred to the Apple II Division's marketing staff as members of the "dull and boring product division."[17] So protective of the Macintosh Division was Jobs that whenever there was a complaint about the division, Jobs would confront the source on the telephone and, said a Macintosh staff member, "chew the guy out so fast your head would spin."[18]

Falling 50,000 computers short of its plan to sell 150,000 Macintoshes during the Christmas 1984 season, Apple's board began to develop concerns regarding its new product and how it was being perceived by the market as "a cutesy avocado machine for yuppies and their kids," not as a sophisticated and innovative office machine.[19]

On 11 April 1985, at an Apple board meeting, the company's directors urged Sculley to assert himelf as the chief executive officer, but Sculley stated it was difficult to act as CEO when he had to "boss a general manager who happened to be chairman of the board." With that situation in mind, Apple's directors resolved to have Jobs relinquish his position as general manager of the Macintosh Division; however, Jobs would remain as Apple's Chairman. Jobs believed that his removal from the Macintosh Division was a cruel, surprise act.[20]

[14]Ibid., p. 21.

[15]Ibid., p. 21.

[16]Ibid., p. 22.

[17]Ibid., p. 22.

[18]Ibid., p. 22.

[19]Ibid., p. 22.

[20]Ibid., p. 23.

No set schedule for Jobs' abdication was established, an error which lead Jobs to forget the meaning of the board's resolution. In Jobs' mind, the board's decision was a reprieve and not to be taken seriously, but in the minds of Sculley and Apple's other directors, it was a phase-out. This difference in perceptions concerning the removal of Jobs lead to the final eruption within Apple.[21]

Gassee

To strengthen the Macintosh Division, Jean-Louis Gassee, head of Apple France, was recruited as the eventual replacement for Steve Jobs as general manager. Gassee was a strong-willed and talented mathematician who was responsible for turning Apple France into the company's fastest growing and most profitable division.

Sculley's plan was to move Gassee into the Macintosh Division as its marketing director with the intent to move him to the position of general manager at some unspecified date. Gassee, however, insisted upon a written guarantee stating an exact date for his promotion to general manager; a demand viewed as an outrage by Jobs who thought Gassee should earn his way to the position.[22]

Reluctant to relinquish his authority, Jobs began suggesting to his friends at Apple that the company was too small for both Sculley and himself and that the board would have to choose between them. The day after Apple's board announced that Gassee would become the marketing manager for the Macintosh Division, Jobs called together his top aides and asked in a hypothetical vein whether they would support him if forced to make a choice. What Jobs had hoped to be a coup to dispose of Sculley turned out to be the catalyst that set off a company reorganization and his ultimate removal.[23]

During the 24 May 1985 executive committee meeting attended by both Jobs and Sculley, the president of Apple firmly stated that he was the one calling the shots at Apple and the company would undergo a restructuring. As a result of the discussions in the meeting, the committee failed to find a future role for Jobs in the day-to-day operations of Apple. Jobs agreed to take a long vacation and return after the reorganization was complete. In two marathon meetings held on May 29 and 30, Apple was reorganized, structured entirely on a functional basis (as shown in Exhibit 2), with Jobs removed as chairman and left with no direct authority other than a role described as "global visionary."[24]

Final Split

During the 12 September 1985 board meeting, Steve Jobs declared that he wished to proceed with his life and he had a plan to start a new company that would design and produce products that would complement Apple. In order to avoid any more disruption at Apple, he offered to resign as chairman.

Jobs' idea for a business was to design and produce high-tech computers that

[21]Ibid., p. 23.

[22]Ibid., p. 23.

[23]Ibid., p. 23.

[24]Ibid., p. 24.

EXHIBIT 2

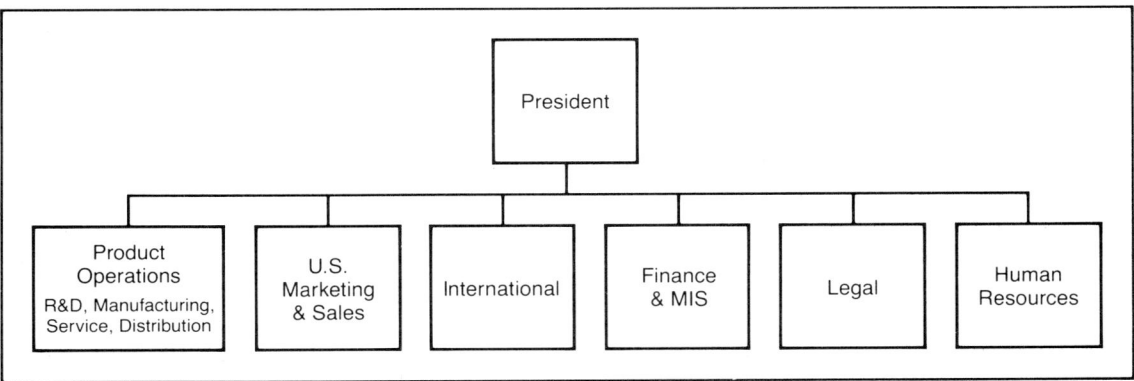

Source: 1985 Apple Annual Report.

could display lifelike simulations of laboratory experiments. The company he envisioned would have modest sales of $50 million annually, because he was not interested in another high-growth firm destined for public status. It would offer the heady environment Jobs had created for the development of Macintosh.

Several board members became alarmed when Jobs alluded to the possibility of hiring Apple personnel for his venture, although he assured them that the employees he might possibly hire would most probably be those who already had plans to leave Apple and that none would be important to the development of Apple products.

The following day, Jobs informed Sculley as to the identity of the five Apple employees he had hired. Sculley became enraged to learn that among the five, three of the employees were those whom Apple could ill afford to lose:

David Lewin.

Head of Apple's marketing to schools and colleges.

Bud Tribble.

Manager of software development for all the company's computers.

George Crow.

Apple's senior engineer for power circuitry.[25]

The board decided to demand the resignation of Jobs and began discussing legal actions to take against him due to his blunder in hiring Apple employees while still chairman.

On 17 September 1985, Jobs sent an elaborate letter of resignation to major newspapers before he submitted a formal resignation to Sculley and the board. In the

[25]Bro Uttal, "The Adventures of Steve Jobs (cont'd)," *Fortune*, October 14, 1985, p. 124.

letter, the "original employee" cast himself as a wronged innocent who held the belief that in a publicity battle he had the advantage because he felt that the "folk hero" always would win. He continued a public fight with his former colleagues through press releases and public interviews.[26]

MARKETING

Product

Apple's product line was basically dependent upon two families of PCs comprised of four machines. The Apple IIc, the "everything-you-need-in-one-box" computer, was a portable version of the Apple II, first introduced in 1977. Although the Apple II was built with an "open architecture," the IIc was provided with a "closed" system because add-on capabilities were not considered to be necessary with a small portable model. The Apple IIe was the other member of this family of PCs with its own line of software and peripherals that would accommodate the IIc machine. The IIe was a 128k memory machine that could be expanded to a capacity of 256k of memory. The Apple II line was very popular in the educational sector and subsequently accounted for nearly 60 percent of Apple's sales and the majority of its profits. In addition to the Apple II line, the Macintosh had its own family. The original Macintosh was a powerful machine that offered 512k of memory. This PC, originally designed with a "closed architecture," was still offered to those consumers who were not interested in expandability or flexibility, yet needed powerful PC processing capabilities. To answer to the needs of those users who were interested in starting out simple or complex and growing into a near minicomputer machine, the Macintosh Plus was introduced in January 1986. Sculley's accommodation to the third-party developers provided users with the ability to "pick and choose among variables instead of having to accommodate absolutes."[27] The new machine, referred to as "Modular Mac," had two megabytes of random-access memory (RAM), double-sided disks, and a read-only memory (ROM) with an operating system that would accommodate hard disks and file servers.[28]

Distribution

While trying to predict which computer would be the product most accepted by the business world, many dealers worried that Apple's management turmoil, as well as the company's subsequent restructuring and dismissal of 1,200 workers in a cost-cutting campaign, would hamper Apple's ability to form a marketing strategy.

Apple's principle method of distribution of its products was through independent retail dealers, national retail accounts, and direct sales; however, Apple's new sales strategy included a larger role for retailers. This followed a long period of strained

[26]Ibid., p. 124.

[27]Jim Forbes and Christine McGeever, "New Products Slated by Apple," *InfoWorld*, July 1, 1985, p. 37.

[28]Ibid., p. 37.

relations between Apple and its independent dealers caused by the direct sales force's erosion of the profit margins of independent retail dealers. ''Apple has been ripping us apart,'' said Billy Ladin, chairman of Computercraft, Inc. ''I recently asked my dealers 'Who's your biggest competition with Apple?' and they said, 'Apple.' ''[29] In marketing to business customers, the company took positive steps to reduce the conflict between dealers and Apple's sales force by reducing the size of its national account sales force and focusing their efforts on specific major corporate customers, thus allowing dealers to sell and support Apple's products to a larger business customer market.

Outside Accessory Dealers

For the Macintosh computer, Apple had worked to strengthen its relations with outside companies that produce and sell accessories, some of which complained they were disregarded by Steve Jobs in his pursuit of Mac's development within the company. Although Mac's innovative built-in software allowed a user to easily enter commands by pointing to symbols on the display, it made it difficult for accessory companies to design a wide range of well tailored accessories for Macintosh as they were able to for the IBM PC.[30]

Mac's unorthodox design could be attributed to Jobs who conceived the computer after he was shut out of the development of the Lisa model which was discontinued in April 1985. It was Jobs' approach in product development to always begin with a clean slate, starting from zero.

After Apple's reorganization under Sculley, the company promised a significant role for outside accessory companies through the adoption of a long overdue open architecture design for Macintosh as well as for all Apple products.

TARGET MARKETS

The Home-User Market

Because the Apple IIe had historically been a success in the educational sector, Apple was excited about its introduction of the extension of the Apple IIc in 1984. The Apple IIc was designed for the home-user market, an estimated market of more than 20 million potential customers with an expected purchasing power amounting to $5.7 million or 6 million units in 1985.[31]

The 1984 Christmas season was a learning experience for most personal computer manufacturers. The market for PCs was believed to be moving away from lower priced computers, such as the Commodore C64, to more expensive and more powerful

---

[29]Michael W. Miller, ''Apple Promises Big Role for Retailers and Producers of Computer Accessories,'' *The Wall Street Journal*, 27 June 1985, p. 8.

[30]Michael W. Miller, ''Apple Is Expected to Revise Marketing As Company's Overhaul Takes Hold,'' *The Wall Street Journal*, 24 June 1985, p. 4.

[31]Geoffrey Lewis, ''Junior Was Too Expensive, Even for IBM,'' *Business Week*, April 1, 1985, p. 35.

machines such as the IBM PCjr and the Apple II. As a result, IBM, Apple, and other PC manufacturers heavily invested in the promotions of their high-end machines, and the 4 percent drop in the home market took a toll on them.[32] Wozniak, whose new venture post-Apple was in the development of microprocessor-based electronic home appliances, had been predicting a "permanent slide in computer sales, particularly for the home." He said, "All people really need is a $30 typewriter and a vacation to Hawaii."[33] According to "Woz," there was "no market for the PCs as helpers with routine household chores like cooking, cleaning, and laundering," and that "PCs will sell at a level a lot lower than people think."[34] Others agreed with the inventor of the first personal computer and said that until small machines were capable of accessorizing television sets, an area the Japanese had been exploring, or until more powerful machines could "drive home appliances that make life's little chores more palatable," PCs would be used predominately for in-home office work.[35]

Apparently, there was much "finger-pointing" going on in the industry as companies were looking at "disappointing sales and stock prices."[36] Timothy Williams, a senior analyst at Future Computing, Inc. research company said, "It's our belief that a lot of uncertainty is from self-inflicted wounds caused by individual manufacturers' optimistic assumptions about their market growth."[37]

"That segment of the market has not experienced growth as fast as we had hoped," said John Pope of IBM's Entry Systems Division.[38] Pope said his company had inventory levels necessary to meet projected demand for the PCjr, because although the company discontinued production of the super-small machine in 1985, it would still "market and fully support" the micro.[39] IBM discovered with the PCjr that the home market favored a machine priced under $1,000. Sales of the PCjr were weak until its price was slashed to $900.[40] However, IBM was unable to continue to sell "junior" due to its price's inability to support its manufacturing cost.

The Educational Market

The educational market and telecommunications industry were open avenues of use for PC owners at home. The educational market was application-intensive, with the use of microcomputers for drill practices in the primary education field and program instruction in the secondary educational field. As this market expanded, parents could

---

[32]Mike Lewis, p. 32.

[33]Kathy Rebello and John Hillkirk, "Apple's Story 'Oldest in Silicon Valley,' " *U.S.A. Today*, June 5, 1985, p. 2B.

[34]Mike Lewis, p. 32.

[35]Ibid., p. 32.

[36]Ibid., p. 32.

[37]Ibid., p. 32.

[38]Ibid., p. 32.

[39]Ibid., p. 32.

[40]Geoffrey Lewis, p. 35.

have purchased computer models that were used in the schools by their children for home use (homework). The telecommunications industry offered an even greater opportunity for home computer application with the vision of machines connected to telephone lines that could be used to gain access to databanks to allow home shopping and banking and to send electronic mail messages to others.[41]

In 1984, the home-user market accounted for 4.8 million computers sold, and the Apple IIe and IIc claimed a 16 percent share of the market.[42] Future Computing, Inc., a Dallas based research firm, predicted the home computer market would grow at an average rate of 26 percent until 1989, as shown in Exhibit 3.[43]

The growth in the educational market for personal computers was considered to be the possible savior of the home PC market due to the belief that those consumers who would be purchasing a personal computer for use in their home would choose the machine used in the schools by their children. Unlike the home PC market, specific need applications had been identified by the educational sector. The Apple IIe had long been a popular tool with which to solve problems. The educational market had the opportunity to influence future sales of PCs with the brand awareness the school exposure provided to the student population. When students were ready to purchase their own PC, manufacturers who had entered the educational market would be positioned as quality producers that had played a role in the education of those students.

The combined enrollment for all U.S. public and private schools was 44,701,367 students in the 1984–85 school-year. In 1985, the entire educational expenditures for instructional materials was an estimated $2,625,527,000 ($2.7 billion) for all U.S. schools (refer to Exhibit 4).[44]

EXHIBIT 3
Home-Computer Market Sales Forecast

Year	Sales Forecast (billions)
1986	$ 7.18
1987	9.05
1988	11.40
1989	14.40

Source: *Mini-Micro Systems*, June 1985, p. 123.

[41]Andrew Pollack, "A Market or Just a Mirage?" *The New York Times*, 21 March 1985, p. D15.

[42]William F. Ablondi and Laura Lundquist, "IBM, Apple Rule Office Market," *Mini-Micro Systems*, June 1985, p. 123.

[43]Ibid., p. 123.

[44]Market Data Retrieval, *1984–1985 Educational Mailing Lists Catalog*, p. 15.

EXHIBIT 4
Number of Public
and Private Schools
in the United States

	Public	Private
Elementary	51,255	16,070
Jr. High	9,841	—
Sr. High	13,874	2,436*
K–12	2,851	4,058
	81,982	23,649

*Jr. and Sr. combined.
Source: *Market Data Retrieval,* 1984–1985, pp. 15–16.

In small schools with an enrollment under 500 students, the principal had the greatest influence and approved procurement.[45] Schools of this size represented 34 percent of all elementaries and junior highs.[46] In larger schools, the principal typically conferred with teachers and specialists. With 72,784 elementary school principals, 39,049 junior high school principals, and 23,286 senior high school principals, the possibilities for infiltration of PC makers into this sector seemed endless. In addition, with the influence teachers have had with the purchase of instructional material and equipment (including microcomputers), the 243,189 public junior high and 384,539 public senior high school teachers furthered the opportunities this target market could provide.[47] Computers most commonly used in this sector are shown in Exhibit 5.

The Business Market

With the introduction of Macintosh in 1984, Apple had begun to focus on the estimated five million small- and medium-sized businesses in the United States as a target market.[48] In companies consisting of 20 or less employees, one in four used PCs in the course of conducting business. In companies comprised of between 20 and 99 employees, 33 percent of those companies used PCs. As the size of the firms increased, so did the frequency of microcomputer use, as 47.1 percent of companies who employed between 100 and 499 people used PCs and an astounding 71.8 percent of companies with 500 to 999 employees used PCs.[49]

Expandability was a key necessity to the business user of a personal computer. A user could take advantage of the numerous third-party manufacturers' add-on hardware and software accessories for additional flexibility. Not only was technology vital, but service, advice, and training rated extremely high on the list of priorities

[45]Ibid., p. 9.

[46]Ibid., pp. 4 and 6.

[47]Ibid., pp. 5–16.

[48]Mike Lewis, p. 32.

[49]"PC Use Skyrockets," *Management Information Systems Week,* June 12, 1985, p. 20.

EXHIBIT 5 Microcomputers in Education

Brand Used	Primary Education (number of schools using)			
	Public	Private	Catholic	Total
Apple	23,107	2,410	2,462	27,979
Radio Shack	6,631	1,011	1,097	8,739
Commodore	6,030	1,242	890	8,162
IBM	420	94	36	550
Brand Used	Secondary Education (number of schools using)			
	Public	Private	Catholic	Total
Apple	14,236	1,204	672	16,112
Radio Shack	7,348	715	532	8,595
Commodore	3,851	563	270	4,684
IBM	694	100	61	855

Source: *Market Data Retrieval,* 1985, p. 17.

a business user made in the purchase of a PC.[50] With the increase in efficiency in the day-to-day performance of their jobs and more effectiveness in decision-making that a microcomputer could offer to today's managers, a PC became a necessity. With an estimated 11 million managers in the United States, there was room for many PC makers with astute awareness, knowledge, and tools to be very profitable.[51]

In 1984, the $6.6 billion spent by businesses for PC represented 2.7 million machines sold. Future Computing, Inc. projected that the average growth rate of the business market for PCs would be 26 percent until 1989.[52]

COMPETITION

''The market for the design, manufacture, sale, and servicing of personal computers and related software and peripheral products is highly competitive. It has been characterized by rapid technological advances in both hardware and software development advances that have substantially increased the capabilities and applications of personal

[50]Deborah C. Wise, p. 80.

[51]Mike Lewis, p. 32.

[52]William F. Ablondi, p. 123.

computers. The principal competitive factors in this market are product quality and reliability, relative price/performance, marketing and distribution capability, service and support, availability of hardware and software accessories, corporate reputation, and ease of use.''[53]

Apple originally positioned itself as the alternative to IBM by adopting the company motto of "the computer for the rest of us." One former company executive said, "Jobs would on occasion respond to marketing suggestions with 'That's IBM talk,' whereas Sculley is far more conscious of what the market demands of PCs and how he thinks they should be sold.''[54] Marketing Vice President William Campbell had been as aware of Apple's failure to accurately recognize the effects of IBM-inism in the business PC market as Sculley—"We will be careful not to pose ourselves in an obvious confrontation with IBM.''[55]

IBM

IBM stated its company goal to be the leader in every market it entered.[56] In August 1981, "Big Blue" introduced its PC, the IBM PC, and set in motion an avalanche of software products. By 1982, the company had claimed an 18.4 percent share of the $2.7 billion office PC market, but was still trailing Apple who led the industry with a 23.3 percent share. By 1983, IBM had taken over with a 30 percent share of the $4.2 billion in sales to which the business market had grown. Not only had the original PC company lost the market share leadership, but Apple found its share had dropped to 12.1 percent. IBM continued to devour the business market at such a rapid pace that by 1984, its share was four times that of Apple's dwindling 11 percent at 41.4 percent of the $6.6 billion office PC market.[57] The industry giant continued to consume the office PC market and by 1985, owned 60 percent, along with a 34 percent share of the entire PC market.[58]

The IBM PC had become the standard in the PC industry. Of the approximately ninety different machines aimed at the business market, sixty claimed to be compatible with the IBM PC.[59] The IBM PC compatible market accounted for $5.5 billion in sales.[60]

---

[53]Apple Computer, Inc., *Form 10-K For Fiscal Year Ended September 27, 1985* (Cupertino, California: Apple Computer, Inc., [1985]), p. 30.

[54]Jim Forbes and Christine McGeever, p. 38.

[55]Ibid., p. 42.

[56]John C. Hart, "IBM: The Next Five Years," *Office Administration and Automation,* April 1985, p. 29.

[57]Rick Dalrymple, "System Integrators Exploit PC Compatibility," *Mini-Micro Systems,* March 1985, p. 147.

[58]Geoffrey Lewis, "The New Computer Wars," *Business Week,* July 15, 1985, p. 96.

[59]"Compaq's Compact," *Business Week,* July 15, 1985, p. 96.

[60]Bob Marich, "Researchers Warn of Computer Glut," *Advertising Age,* July 16, 1984, p. 12.

IBM employed an "open architecture" design that allowed a multitude of hardware accessories vendors to supply add-on features that greatly expanded the market for their PC. The computer was distributed through a combination of computer specialty stores, and by IBM direct sales representatives that also handled IBM mainframe computers. The IBM product line was carried by 80 percent of the computer specialty stores in the United States which accounted for 30 percent of all PC sales to businesses.[61]

IBM's success in the home and educational markets had not been quite the fairy tale of the business sector. The failure of the PCjr (a smaller version of the PC discontinued in 1985) had undermined confidence in IBM which had benefitted from the perception among its customers that the firm would never leave the business and abandon its customers as "computer orphans."

By promoting itself as the leader in the market and emphasizing its dedication to service, IBM priced its products above the market to maintain its quality image (although discounts were offered to retailers for large orders of IBM PCs which allowed dealers to realize a larger margin of profit with every sale of an IBM PC).

IBM selectively distributed its products through computer/business equipment stores and mass merchandisers. A strong belief existed among competitors that they should build product image through the use of a selective distribution strategy which utilized only computer stores. This represented a unique characteristic of IBM in that the product was independently strong so as to allow the PC to obtain greater exposure through the use of nontraditional outlets for business oriented customers.

Compaq

In 1983, Compaq offered its first line of personal computers aimed at the business sector. The young company's revenues were impressive in 1984, at $329 million while it had captured a 16 percent share of the office market with the Deskpro PC.[62] The Deskpro was a microcomputer that could be enhanced for compatability with both the PC XT and the PC AT.

The rapidly advancing firm boasted of the fact that it sold more micros in the IBM PC compatible market than any of its competitors. It was very costly for a retailer to provide shelf space for the estimated sixty microcomputers in this category, so due to Compaq's 100 percent IBM compatibility with all accessories carried for the PC, any retailer could well afford to carry the Compaq line. Through an exclusive distribution to specialty retailers, Compaq had successfully flooded 66 percent of all U.S. computer dealerships.[63]

The "compact" computer company was committed to second place status behind IBM in the business computer market through the use of an imitator strategy. In order to set the company apart, IBM-cloned machines of the highest level of quality

[61]Michael W. Miller, "Apple Promises Big Role for Retailers and Producers of Accessories," *The Wall Street Journal*, 27 June 1985, p. 8.

[62]"Compaq's Compact," *Business Week*, July 15, 1985, p. 92.

[63]Ibid., p. 94.

and technology were produced and priced at a competitive level.[64] Such a strategy was affordable to Compaq due to a two-level distribution system that simply consisted of middlemen and computer business equipment stores.

In order to allow for open comparison between computers, Compaq's desire was to find shelf space in every outlet that carried the IBM line of products — not necessarily a fantasy. Compaq had a very unique relationship with its dealers because of the absence of a competitive sales force. Through the use of incentive programs and exclusive dedication to dealers, it had been able to build one of the strongest company/dealer relationships in existence.

Commodore

Although not quite the "young pup" Compaq was, Commodore's experience in the business market had been launched. With the introduction of the Amiga, the company had joined the mainswing of the personal computer market toward business. Unfortunately, the microcomputer was better suited for the home due to its low price and color graphics. In addition, the native operating system, Amiga DOS, was incompatible with software for other computers.

To further the limitations, the development of application programs very vital to PC office use seemed to have been almost forgotten. Commodore had announced its line of software designed for the Amiga of which most were games, programming languages, and programming tools.

Historically, Commodore had relied on success in the home personal computer market. The C64 was a very popular 64k machine that the consumer could purchase at a very low price of approximately $100 and take home to hook up to the family television set. There was a wide range of game and home application software from which to choose that owners found very appealing. For those who outgrew the C64 and those modern high-tech-student types, a more powerful version, the C128 was introduced for the educational market.

Commodore distributed its low end home computer through an extensive infiltration of mass merchandisers, discount stores, and department stores. The C64 could be found in such popular stores as Sears, K-Mart, and Toys-Я-Us. Plans for the C128 would follow the same strategy and also be priced competitively so as to encourage sales and increase volume. As for the Amiga, Commodore continued to follow an innovative strategy whereby product enhancements were aimed at successful competition against the Macintosh (which used the same microprocessor) and the IBM PC; the Amiga offered to the consumer an accessory that allowed the machine to act as a PC clone.

OPERATIONS

Apple strove to use the most innovative manufacturing tools. The company believed that Japanese dominance in the electronics industry was due in large part to their concentration on maintaining highly innovative factories, whereas the American

[64]Ibid., p. 94.

companies had concentrated their efforts more in the laboratories. Apple's "goal is to be as good in manufacturing technology as the best Japanese electronics companies will be."[65] The long-term goal was to achieve status as "one of the world's lowest cost, highest quality manufacturers."[66] In order to achieve such, Apple built six state-of-the-art facilities worldwide. A plant located in Fremont, California occupied 160,000 square feet and was highly automated. In 1985, the company closed three manufacturing sites as part of the plan to restructure. Although it was an unpopular decision among plant employees, Debbie Coleman, head of worldwide manufacturing, felt it was necessary to keep the company competitive in the midst of the PC slump. A surprisingly young vice president at 32 years of age, the Stanford MBA graduate said, "I had a concise and particular strategy about what I wanted to do. I had to choose which factories to shut down and which were crucial to our success."[67] Her decision was based on which plants had the most flexible machinery. "It was a technical issue. Fremont was supposed to be a single-product factory, but in 1984 and 1985, we changed strategy. To be world-class, it would have to handle multiple production in varying volume."[68] So the Fremont plant became the primary facility for the assembly of the Macintosh and Apple IIc, and the Singapore plant was left with the responsibility for the Apple IIe. To accommodate the European market, Apple IIe and Apple IIc would continue to be assembled at Apple's Cork, Ireland facility. The company also transferred the operations for peripherals at the recently closed Mill Street, Ireland plant to the Cork facility.[69,70] Operations at the Dallas plant (Apple IIc and Apple IIe factory) and the Garden Grove, California plant (peripherals factory) were shut down, leaving the Fremont plant all alone on the home turf.

Coleman's expertise and experience in innovative manufacturing techniques, stemming from her days in production and quality control at Hewlett-Packard, had kept Apple's operations technologically superior. She switched the factories from a "hard" automation process system to one that was "flexible." Coleman said, "A hard system is right for a single product. In the late '70s it was state-of-the-art. We were tooled for high volume, to get process quality up, and get product costs down. I had gone for it, but was wrong. It was right in 1984, but things change. With flexible automation you have robotics with sensors you can reprogram, so you can produce eight to twenty-four products on one line."[71] The Fremont factory could

[65]Apple Computer, Inc., *Annual Report* (Cupertino, California: Apple Computer, Inc., [1984]), p. 8.

[66]Apple Computer, Inc., *Annual Report* (Cupertino, California: Apple Computer, Inc., [1983]), p. 7.

[67]Marty Olmstead, "Apple Polisher," *Savvy,* May 1986, p. 26.

[68]Ibid., p. 27.

[69]David E. Sanger, "Apple Cuts 1,200: Loss Seen," *The New York Times,* 15 June 1985, p. 36.

[70]"Apple Shuts Plants, Drops 1,200 Jobs," *Electronic News,* 17 June 1985, p. 63.

[71]Marty Olmstead, p. 27.

produce 80,000 Macintoshes monthly, although demand was approximately 30,000 per month.[72]

Coleman also switched the plants from the stockpiling of parts and inventory system to a "just-in-time" scheduling system. In an effort to reduce inventory, Apple would build machines to "keep up with demand rather than overshoot it."[73] As a result, inventory decreased from $261 million to $107 million in 1985.

In her efforts to clean up the excessive plant operations, Coleman had to relieve 700 manufacturing employees of their jobs. In total, 1,200 employees were laid off as a result of the clean-up plan in the reorganization at Apple. Coleman said it was the most difficult part for her but that "it was a question of the long-term success of Apple versus these jobs."[74]

TECHNOLOGY

Apple's claim to fame had always been that of the innovative leader in the personal computer industry. It began with Apple and although the company had been over-powered by IBM and found itself competing for the number two position in the market with an abundance of other hardware companies, it prided itself as an original, not a user of "off-the-shelf-tool-technology."[75] This role that the company had assumed had been integral to its ability to differentiate itself from all the companies that had contributed to the explosion in the personal computer market and Apple historically felt the need to remain distinctive.

Apple also incorporated into its philosophy the idea of "user-friendliness." Jobs always stressed the importance of an easy-to-use, yet highly innovative and technologically superior machine. The realization that people who lacked technical knowledge and skill were not so eager to use a machine bogged down with complex procedures came to him long before the IBM PC was born. The incentive to use a computer was that it could simplify the complexity of a task.

Although Apple's drive to remain lead innovator distinguished it from other industry giants, the company had found itself alienated from the business community. Jobs' insistence on a closed architecture had thus far crippled Macintosh's ability to thrive in the business market. Michael Joseph, of Lomega Corporation, said "the good side is that he made computers that were easier for people to use. The bad side is that they were harder for people like me to build parts for."[76] Joseph was referring

[72]Deborah C. Wise, "Can John Sculley Clean Up the Mess at Apple?" *Business Week,* July 29, 1985, p. 70.

[73]Marty Olmstead, p. 26.

[74]Marty Olmstead, p. 26.

[75]Apple Computer, Inc., *Annual Report* (Cupertino, California: Apple Computer, Inc., [1983]), p. 13.

[76]Michael W. Miller, "Apple Is Expected to Revise Marketing As Company's Overhaul Takes Hold," *The Wall Street Journal,* 24 June 1985, p. 4.

to the Macintosh's "unorthodox" design. Because hard disk drives and other peripherals were becoming a necessity for PCs in order to store more data, buyers had turned to IBM and other makers who did provide such hardware in addition to a "wide variety of well tailored accessories."[77] Other competitors had seen the advantages to joining "Big Blue" rather than trying to beat the giant. William H. Bowman of Spinnaker Software Corporation said, "Jobs was totally dedicated to pushing the Macintosh against IBM in the business channel."[78] Jobs felt the Macintosh was a superior machine to the IBM PC and "thought it would be slumming to support the PC," according to Charles Rubin, an Apple software book author.[79] Since the reorganization in 1985, Sculley's job had been to redirect some of the technological energies that had historically driven the company to realistic marketing strategies.

The key to a realistic marketing strategy in Sculley's mind was to be "a more responsive market-driven firm"[80] that would stay in tune with customers', dealers', and third-party software and hardware developers' needs. He firmly believed the Macintosh should be compatible with IBM in order "to achieve the primary goal we set for Macintosh at the beginning of 1985 — significant penetration in the business market."[81] Sculley had developed a "customer-driven" strategy to focus in on two new growing market segments. One was called desktop publishing. It was a "solution to create reports, presentations, proposals, and newsletters of superb quality on a quick turnaround low-cost basis,"[82] that could be used by connecting the Macintosh with LaserWriter. The other opportunity Sculley felt that was prevalent in the business market was communications. By the employment of data communication links between workstations and hosts, and local networking between workstations, information sharing "may launch a rejuvenation of the personal computer industry."[83] Sculley felt that Apple could "be the leader in bringing together a superior human interface with real functionality in an IBM-defined-systems world."[84]

In 1985, sources outside of Apple said the reorganized company would soon announce new product releases which included a Macintosh hard disk drive, file server, ImageWriter II printer, new Apple II disk drives, new 800k Sony drives for Macintosh, and a revised Macintosh disk operating system.[85] Yocam said, "I absolutely believe

[77]Ibid., p. 4.

[78]Ibid., p. 4.

[79]Charles Bermant, "Apple Will Link Mac to IBM Computer World," *PC Magazine*, January 14, 1986, p. 34.

[80]Apple Computer, Inc., *Annual Report* (Cupertino, California: Apple Computer, Inc., [1985]), p. 17.

[81]Ibid., p. 17.

[82]Ibid., p. 17.

[83]Ibid., p. 18.

[84]Ibid., p. 18.

[85]Jim Forbes and Christine McGeever, p. 35.

in open architecture.''[86] With his guidance, it was expected that Apple products would change and users would be able to increase memory as well as the number of peripherals used.

In January 1986, Sculley announced plans for a software link between the Macintosh and IBM mainframes, minis and micros (PCs), and Digital Equipment Corporation's VAX system. Sculley said ''the systems will not penalize the user with slower response time or other limitations and will provide not only terminal emulation or PC-like functions, but also access to completed office systems and distributed data processing functionality.''[87] Bill Krause, president and CEO of 3COM Corporation, said ''Apple recognizes that anyone who wants to exist in the computer market has to support IBM.''[88] He did not think the company made any compromises but was simply ''pragmatic.''[89]

RESEARCH AND DEVELOPMENT

In order to continue the position of the innovative leader in the PC industry, Apple's research and development expenses had averaged 4.5 percent to 6.5 percent of net sales from 1982 to 1985.[90,91] In 1985, the company spent $73 million compared to $71 million in 1984.[92] There was an increase in product development centered around the Macintosh in 1984, and in 1985 several product projects were cancelled due to the reorganization. In spite of the transitionary slowdown in research and development, Apple continued its commitment to a significant research and development budget to support new product development in order to manufacture products of superior design and quality.

FINANCES

After the Christmas slump of 1984, Apple was off to a dismal start in 1985. The company had planned to sell 150,000 Macintoshes over the season, but reached only about two-thirds of its goal. As a result, there was not the same stream of back

[86]Ibid., p. 36.

[87]James A. Martin, ''Apple Push on for More System Links,'' *ComputerWorld*, November 4, 1985, p. 1.

[88]Charles Bermant, p. 35.

[89]Ibid., p. 35.

[90]Apple Computer, Inc., *Annual Report* (Cupertino, California: Apple Computer, Inc., [1985]), p. 28.

[91]Apple Computer, Inc., *Annual Report* (Cupertino, California: Apple Computer, Inc., [1982]), p. 24.

[92]Apple Computer, Inc., *Annual Report* (Cupertino, California: Apple Computer, Inc., [1985]), p. 28.

orders as the 1983 season had produced, and dealers were deep in inventory stock. Sales of Macintoshes declined to 19,000 units monthly for the first quarter. Although Apple earned a record $46 million on sales of $698 million during the Christmas quarter, the figures were due to the strength of Apple II.[93]

The picture became even more bleak as the reorganization rapidly progressed. Eugene G. Glazer, an analyst for Dean Witter Reynolds, Inc., felt that the industry slump was harder for Apple than competitors because of the company's narrow range of products. He predicted that in 1986, Apple would earn $1.55 per share and said, "if there isn't an upturn in the computer market, there's no way they can make these numbers."[94] By the end of the third quarter, Apple's stock had hit a four-year low of $14 compared to a high of $63 in 1983.[95] Even more disillusioning was a $17.2 million loss for the quarter. This was a first for Apple since its incorporation in 1977.[96] The loss was the result of a one-time charge against earnings of $40.3 million due to the reorganization of the company. On the bright side was that Apple had lowered its break-even point considerably from $425 million at the beginning of the year to $350 to $370 million.[97] This had been the direction management had hoped to move in by the layoff of 20 percent of personnel and the closings of three factories in addition to other costs incurred from redundancy under the old structure. Another positive stroke was that Apple's balance sheet was very strong as cash reserves had grown to $254.6 million.[98]

As the year rolled on, Apple's situation improved. Net sales increased 27 percent to approximately $1.9 billion for the year. The gross profit margin remained stable at 42 percent of net sales, albeit the gross profit margin improved to 46 percent during the fourth quarter of 1985.[99] The reduction in facilities and payroll costs and declining semiconductor prices were offset by competitive price pressures and expenses resulting in excess and obsolete inventories. Research and development expenditures increased approximately $1.4 million during 1985, but declined as a percentage of sales.[100] Also Apple began to keep a closer eye on marketing expenditures which decreased as a percentage of net sales from 26 percent to 25 percent.[101] Campbell said such measures as withdrawal from the National Computer Conference would

[93]Bro Uttal, p. 22.

[94]Deborah C. Wise, "Can John Sculley Clean up the Mess at Apple?" *Business Week*, July 29, 1985, p. 71.

[95]Ibid., p. 71.

[96]Andrew Pollack, "Apple Computer Posts a Loss of $17.2 Million," *The New York Times*, 19 July 1985, p. D4.

[97]Ibid., p. 4.

[98]Ibid., p. 4.

[99]Apple Computer, Inc., *Annual Report* (Cupertino, California: Apple Computer Inc., [1985]), p. 27.

[100]Ibid., p. 27.

[101]Ibid., p. 27.

help dramatically since the company typically spent $800,000 per show to participate. A decrease in advertising was the predominate factor in the decline in marketing expenditures.[102] Also over the 1985 fiscal year, interest income decreased due to declining interest rates available on cash and temporary investments.

Coleman's "as-needed" basis for purchases of raw material realized a $97.6 million decrease in inventories.[103] As for Apple's capital structure, the board of directors authorized for issuance five million shares of preferred stock in one or more series.[104] The effective income tax rate of the company had increased from 41 percent in 1984 to 48 percent in 1985.[105] Apple had over 8 million shares in stock option plans, outstanding under various stock option plans, ranging in excise prices from $19 to $59 per share.[106] By the quarter ended September 27, 1985, the company had $337 million in cash and temporary cash investments and no long-term debt.[107]

As time progressed, Apple continued slowly to recover costs since the consolidation of functions within the company. In January 1986, Apple's reported break-even point had been reduced further to $325 million.[108] Although the first quarter of the 1986 fiscal year resulted in a sales decline of 23 percent, the cost-cutting measures that had improved margins to 52 percent of sales and produced higher inventory turnover allowed Apple's profits to grow 23 percent to a record 0.91 cents per share.[109] The company also announced plans to increase research and development expenditures by 50 percent to an estimated $108 million.[110]

The pattern had continued in the same direction for Apple as the firm focused on costs to survive the on-going sales slump. Earnings increased for the quarter ended 28 March 1986, despite the 6 percent decline in sales from $435 million in 1985 to $409 million. Earnings jumped to $32 million compared to $22 million in the second quarter of 1985. Apple's rise in the quarter profit to $1.40 per share generally surprised Wall Street analysts who had been expecting a per-share net of $0.30 to $0.35 cents.[111] The improved financial state of Apple was attributed to the deep cost-cutting measures,

---

[102]Ibid., p. 27.

[103]Ibid., p. 32.

[104]Ibid., p. 32.

[105]Ibid., p. 32.

[106]Ibid., p. 33.

[107]Ibid., p. 29.

[108]Deborah C. Wise, "Apple, Part 2: The No-Nonsense Era of John Sculley," *Business Week,* January 27, 1986, p. 96.

[109]"Apple Net Rose 23% to Record in Its 1st Period," *The Wall Street Journal,* 15 January 1986, p. 4.

[110]"Business Briefs," *The Wall Street Journal,* 30 January 1986, p. 19.

[111]"Apple's Net Tripled in Its 2nd Quarter; Lotus MicroSoft Earnings Rise Sharply," *The Wall Street Journal,* 17 April 1986, p. 5.

improved foreign sales, and higher than average sales of high margin printers, disk drives, and peripherals.

LEGAL ISSUES

Patents and Trademarks

Apple held the rights to patents and copyrights relating to certain aspects of its computer and peripheral systems. In addition, Apple had registered trademarks in the United States and a number of foreign countries for "Apple," the Apple silhouette logo, the Apple color logo, and numerous product trademarks.

Apple had licensed rights for use of the trademark "Macintosh" that extend through May 1983, and were renewable thereafter. Although Apple believed that the ownership of such patents and trademarks was an important factor in its business and that success depended in part on the ownership thereof, Apple relied primarily on the innovative skills, technical competence, and marketing abilities of its personnel.

Litigation

"Apple's called me a thief in public, and that's simply not true," said Steve Jobs responding to a lawsuit filed by his former employer.[112] The lawsuit alleged that Steve Jobs, by virtue of his position in Apple as its chairman, had access to confidential business information relating to Apple's future computer products, strategic business plans, and key personnel, and that he conspired to use such information to form a new company which would hire away Apple employees and compete with Apple.

"Steve is trying to turn this into a trial-by-press, and we're not going to do this," said Albert Eisenstat indicating Apple's displeasure with the numerous comments made by Jobs to the press.[113] Since Jobs still owned approximately 9 percent of Apple's stock, he had the financial means to fight a legal battle with Apple and also start a new venture.

Six class-action lawsuits had been filed against Apple and fourteen of its officers and directors, alleging violations of state and federal securities laws relating primarily to allegations of fraud and inside trading based upon the company's alleged failure to make certain disclosures of material facts during the period from 12 November 1982 to 23 September 1983.

An $11 million lawsuit was filed against Apple by a distributor in Chile charging Apple had improperly terminated the company in Chile as an Apple distributor. Six dealers filed suits against Apple seeking to restrain the company from implementing a prohibition of mail order sales. Apple received a favorable summary judgment, but the case was appealed by the dealers.

Apple believed that the suits filed against them were without merit, and the company continued to litigate vigorously the asserted claims in these actions. In addition,

[112]Deborah C. Wise, "Valley Squalls: Apple Drags Jobs Into Court," *Business Week,* October 7, 1985, p. 35.

[113]Ibid., p. 36.

Apple maintained liability insurance which would help to defray the legal expenses of any unfavorable outcome.

In January 1986, Apple Computer, Inc. reached an out-of-court settlement with its former chairman in which Jobs' new company, Next Inc., was prohibited from marketing its new computer, targeted at the university market, until July 1987. Under the settlement, Apple was given the right to inspect the new computer to determine if it used certain proprietary technology, and Jobs agreed not to use certain other undisclosed technologies. In the settlement, Apple was given the right to inspect the prototype of the new computer for thirty days to determine if any of Apple's proprietary technology was utilized. The thirty-day limit agreement for Apple's inspection of Jobs' computer was regarded by industry experts as a coup for Jobs since disputes of this type often could drag on for several months and disrupt marketing and production plans.[114]

1986 OUTLOOK

As the computer slump continued, many companies were fighting to avoid becoming victims in an inevitable shakeout in the industry. Computer manufacturers were struggling to compete by offering lower prices and cutting production costs so as not to lose much profit margin. The American dollar remained stronger than foreign currency, such as the Japanese yen, and a large trade deficit continued to hamper American industry.

The future was left to tell who would be able to survive in the new PC world of IBM. For the first near-decade, Apple was successful as the personal computer ideal and could afford to thumb its nose at the computer mammoth. Could the company who was responsible for the creation of an industry of the personal computer's proportions thrive under the rule of "King" IBM? With the original "hackers-in-blue-jeans" gone (Jobs and Wozniak), would the image so endearing to Apple computer disappear? And if so, how would the company set itself apart from the rest in an IBM-clone world? Jean Richardson, who headed Apple's marketing communications department for seven years, made this observation, "Can you think of one company that created the brand awareness, the innovation, that Apple did in seven years? There's an incredible amount of positive 'stuff' inside Apple. Apple won't be hurt dramatically by all the changes. The company still has so many dollars working for it that the public will not notice a lot of differences other than a stronger market presence."[115]

[114]Patricia Bellew Gray, "Apple Computer and Jobs Reach Pact Barring Sales of New Machine Until 1987," *The Wall Street Journal*, 20 January 1986, p. 2.

[115]Jim Forbes and Christine McGeever, p. 43.

APPENDIX: APPLE COMPUTER FINANCIAL HIGHLIGHTS

EXHIBIT A-1 Comparative Financial Status, 1981–1985

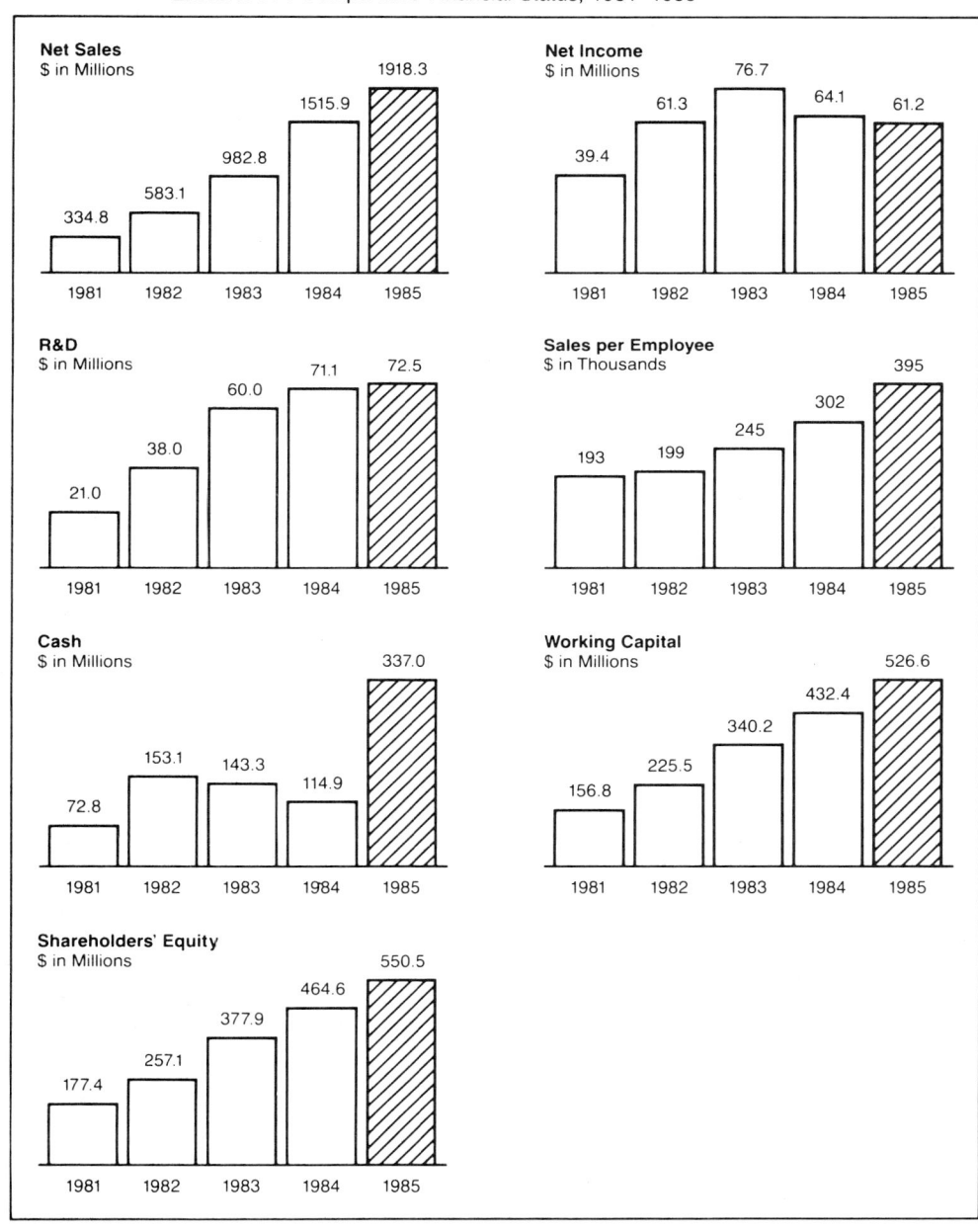

Source: 1985 Annual Report, Apple Computer, Inc.

EXHIBIT A-2 Consolidated Statements of Changes in Financial Position (in thousands)

	Year Ended			Quarter Ended	
	9/27/85	9/27/84	9/27/83	12/27/85	12/28/84
Working capital was provided by:					
Operations:					
Net income	$ 61,223	$ 64,055	$ 76,714	$ 56,925	$46,099
Charges to operations not affecting working capital:					
Depreciation and amortization	41,841	37,963	22,440	13,140	7,550
Deferred income taxes (noncurrent)	21,228	20,453	35,697	23,073	8,322
Total working capital provided by operations	$124,292	$122,471	$134,851	$ 93,138	$61,971
Net book value of property, plant, and equipment retirements	12,744				
Increases in common stock and related tax benefits, net of changes in notes receivable from shareholders	23,652	23,242	44,095	6,070	3,496
Other				3,133	4,393
Total working capital provided	$160,688	$145,713	$178,946	$102,341	$69,860
Working capital was applied to:					
Purchase of property, plant and equipment (net of retirements in 1984 and 1983)	$ 54,064	$ 39,614	$ 52,666	$ 6,510	$15,056
Other	12,351	13,939	11,531	2,180	9,222
Total working capital applied	$ 66,415	$ 53,553	$ 64,197	$ 8,690	$24,278
Increase in working capital	$ 94,273	$ 92,160	$114,749	$ 93,651	$45,582
Increase (decrease) in working capital by component:					
Cash and temporary cash investments	$222,125	$ (28,396)	$ (9,772)		
Accounts receivable	(38,081)	121,818	64,942		
Inventories	(97,668)	122,162	67,089		
Prepaid income taxes	43,624	(1,198)	25,860		
Other current assets	4,514	4,172	9,660		
Accounts payable	34,294	(56,337)	(27,576)		
Accrued compensation and employee benefits	(5,139)	(4,686)	(3,996)		
Income taxes payable	(16,532)	(11,268)	15,307		
Accrued marketing and distribution	(25,296)	(29,087)	(8,976)		
Accrued cost of consolidation of operations	(20,173)				
Other current liabilities	(7,395)	(25,020)	(17,789)		
Increase in working capital	$ 94,273	$ 92,160	$114,749		

Note: figures in thousands.

EXHIBIT A-3 Consolidated Statements of Income

	Year Ended			Quarter Ended			
	9/27/85	*9/27/84*	*9/27/83*	*12/27/85*	*12/28/84*	*12/27/85*	*12/28/84*
Net sales	$1,918,280	$1,515,876	$982,769	$533,890	$698,297	100.0%	100.0%
Costs and expenses:							
Cost of sales	$1,117,864	$ 878,586	$505,765	$262,959	$415,802	49.3	59.6
Research and development	72,526	71,136	60,040	22,400	17,666	4.2	2.5
Marketing and distribution	470,588	392,866	229,961	105,763	144,280	19.8	20.7
General and administrative	110,077	81,840	57,364	28,809	29,511	5.4	4.2
	$1,771,055	$1,424,428	$853,130	$419,931	$607,259	78.7	87.0
Operating income before unusual item	147,225	91,448	129,639	113,959	91,038	21.3	13.0
Unusual income—provision for consolidation of operations	(36,966)						
Interest and other income, net	9,786	17,737	16,483	1,040	(648)	0.2	(0.1)
Income before income taxes	$ 120,045	$ 109,185	$146,122	$114,999	$ 90,390	21.5	12.9
Provision for income taxes	58,822	45,130	69,408	58,074	44,291	10.8	6.3
Net income	$ 61,223	$ 64,055	76,714	$ 56,925	$ 46,099	10.7	6.6
Earnings per common and common equivalent share	$ .99	$ 1.05	$ 1.28	$ .91	$ .75		
Common and common equivalent shares used in the calculations of earnings per share	61,895	60,887	59,867	62,783	61,587		

EXHIBIT A-4 Consolidated Balance Sheets

	12/27/85	9/27/85	9/28/84
Assets			
Current assets:			
Cash and temporary cash investments	$ 441,531	$337,013	$114,888
Accounts receivable, net of allowance for doubtful accounts of $16,209 ($10,831 in 1984)	260,280	220,157	258,238
Inventories	108,839	166,951	264,619
Prepaid income taxes	71,623	70,375	26,751
Other current assets	32,863	27,569	23,055
Total current assets	$ 915,136	$822,065	$687,551

EXHIBIT A-4 (continued)

EXHIBIT A-4 (continued)

	12/27/85	9/27/85	9/28/84
Property, plant and equipment:			
Land and buildings	$ 22,633	$ 23,621	$ 24,892
Machinery and equipment	79,367	78,725	68,099
Office furniture and equipment	39,552	38,551	30,575
Leasehold improvements	38,166	34,738	26,008
	$ 179,718	$175,635	$149,574
Accumulated depreciation and amortization	(92,102)	(85,189)	(73,706)
Net property, plant and equipment	$ 87,616	$ 90,446	$ 75,868
Other assets	$ 19,271	$ 23,666	$ 25,367
	$1,022,023	$936,177	$788,786
Liabilities and Shareholders' Equity			
Current liabilities:			
Accounts payable	$ 61,780	$ 74,744	$109,038
Accrued compensation and employee benefits	33,469	25,595	20,456
Income taxes payable	41,513	27,800	11,268
Accrued marketing and distribution	61,107	75,934	50,638
Accrued cost of consolidation of operations	13,516	20,173	—
Other current liabilities	83,460	71,179	63,784
Total current liabilities	$ 294,845	$295,425	$255,184
Deferred income taxes	$ 113,338	$ 90,265	$ 69,037
Commodities and contingencies			
Shareholders' equity:			
Common stock, no par value, 160,000,000 shares authorized; 61,849,802 shares issued and outstanding in 1985 (60,535,146 shares in 1984)	$ *241,539	$234,625	$208,948
Retained earnings	377,249	320,324	259,101
Accumulated translation adjustment	772	414	(633)
	$ 619,560	$555,363	$467,416
Notes receivable from shareholders	(5,720)	(4,876)	(2,851)
Total shareholders' equity	$ 613,840	$550,487	$464,565
	$1,022,023	$936,177	$788,786

*62,289,458 shares outstanding.
Note: figures in thousands.

HARPER CHEMICAL CORPORATION

The Harper Chemical Corporation (HCC), with 1982 sales of $945 million was a medium-sized producer of industrial chemicals located in Philadelphia, Pennsylvania. Titanium dioxide and caustic soda, which were sold primarily to customers in the paper industry, were Harper's main products. Other large users of Harper's products were companies in the ink, paint, and plastics industries.

In 1977, HCC diversified into the production of a mineral called Dominite. As of the end of 1982, the Dominite operation, administered by HCC's Special Products Department, had accumulated a $7.5 million before-tax loss. In January 1983, Jim Hood, general manager of the Special Products Department, received an unsolicited offer to purchase the complete Dominite operation. HCC's management asked Hood to consider the offer and to recommend what action the company should take. If he recommended selling, he would have to establish and justify a sales price. On the other hand, if he decided not to sell, he would have to make concrete proposals regarding the marketing program for Dominite.

Dominite was a vitreous, white, translucent, siliceous mineral found in deposits on or near the earth's surface. After being mined, the mineral was broken into large blocks, put through a coarse crusher, and then reground into fine grades in another operation. Some further processing was necessary to remove impurities.

The HCC Dominite deposit in Hawley, Pennsylvania, formerly operated by the Hawley Mining Company, was one of the largest deposits of the mineral available and the only deposit in the United States being quarried. Other deposits of unknown quality were located in Pennsylvania, Oregon, Arizona, and in certain parts of Mexico. Harper's management thought it was possible to produce Dominite commercially at these locations.

BASIC USES OF DOMINITE

Ceramic Tile Applications

Dominite had a potentially large use as a replacement for talc in making ceramic wall tiles. It could be used in proportions from 2 percent to 70 percent of the tile body weight depending on the other materials used, the process employed, and the type of tile desired. The strength of the tile could be increased and manufacturing breakage reduced by using Dominite instead of talc. In addition, a Dominite tile had minimal moisture expansion, which lessened the tendency for the glaze to craze (crack) in use. Tiles containing 20 percent or more of Dominite had a low coefficient of thermal expansion which allowed rapid heating and cooling without cracking. Therefore, tiles made with Dominite could be fired in the kiln in less time than talc tiles (½ to 15 hours for Dominite tiles compared to 18 to 40 hours for talc tiles). Tiles made with Dominite could also be fired at lower kiln operating temperatures than talc tiles (1800°F versus 2100°F). For these reasons tile manufacturers using Dominite could effect fuel economies and could increase the firing capacity of their kilns.

Kiln capacity usually determined total capacity in a tile plant, and the cost of the kiln represented up to 25 percent of the total capital cost of the plant. Firing costs, including fuel, labor, and depreciation, typically amounted to 25 percent of the cost of goods sold. The cost of firing a Dominite tile at 1800°F for 15 hours was about one-third of the cost of firing a talc tile at 2100°F for 40 hours. (In 1983, one medium-sized tile company, using about 4 tons of Dominite per day, reported savings of $300 per day in fuel costs alone after shifting from talc to Dominite.)

To convert from using talc to Dominite, however, tile manufacturers had to replace their dies at a substantial cost to allow for the differences in shrinkage factors for talc and Dominite tiles. In some instances they also had to develop new sets of glazes.[1] One large tile manufacturer reported that a new set of dies would cost $1,500,000.

Paint Applications

Dominite could also be used as an extender pigment[2] or a filler in making paints. (The cost of the extender pigment accounted for up to 5 percent of the total manufacturing cost of the paint.) In this application, Dominite competed against talc and

[1]The glaze is the glasslike finish which provides texture and color to one side of a finished tile. The glaze, in liquid form, is sprayed on the unbaked or green tile body just before firing. Each tile body requires a specially formulated glaze so that during firing, the tile and the glaze would grow and contract together. An improperly matched glaze would cause cracks in either the glaze or the tile, or both.

[2]Paint is composed of two elements, the pigment and the vehicle. The pigment accounts for about 65 percent of the unit weight, with the vehicle making up the remaining 35 percent. The pigment is composed of a prime pigment, which gives the color and the hiding power, and the extender pigment, which reduces the unit cost of the pigment, adjusts pigment consistency, and sometimes affects the wearing characteristics of the paint. The vehicle is made up of a nonvolatile part (such as linseed oil), which gives the paint its film-forming characteristics, and a volatile part or solvent (such as turpentine), which controls the paint's consistency and ease of application.

calcium carbonate (whiting), a lower-cost material than talc. Dominite could be used as an extender for house paints and as a white prime pigment; it had high brightness and it produced a paint with superior durability. Dominite had lower oil absorption characteristics than talc, which meant that less of the expensive vehicle was needed. For this reason it was possible to reduce manufacturing costs by 12 to 18 cents per gallon by using Dominite. Dominite was harder than talc and more abrasive; thus, in some cases, it made scratches in mixing equipment.

ACQUIRING OF THE DOMINITE OPERATION

In 1976, HCC executives were interested in diversifying to reduce the company's dependence on the paper industry. They hoped to find opportunities yielding at least a 15 percent return on investment after taxes and utilizing Harper's technical strengths. A consultant, working to find diversification opportunities for HCC, heard about the Hawley Mining Company and was informed that the owners were interested in leasing the property. After a preliminary investigation, the consultant referred the situation to Arnold Fraser, HCC's chief engineer, who was responsible for investigating new product opportunities. Fraser gave Robert Moore, a chemical sales engineer, responsibility for appraising the market potential for Dominite and asked John Moe, a production engineer, to investigate production and capital requirements.

Determining of Market Potential

In late 1976 HCC obtained an eight-month option to lease the Hawley Mining Company property and began investigating Dominite's sales potential. Hawley executives had very little information about potential markets. Moore therefore called on Hawley agents, who were selling a limited volume of the mineral to some manufacturers, to question them about present uses. In addition, people within the HCC organization were able to suggest potential markets, and research studies sponsored by HCC at four universities indicated additional markets.

Moore then sent form mailings to all companies that might be interested in Dominite, describing Dominite's qualities and including an offer to send samples upon request. All inquiries were answered with additional information, samples, and technical data. In many cases Moore made personal visits to companies from which inquiries were received. Meanwhile, visits were made to two companies that had at one time expressed an interest in purchasing the Hawley Mining Company. Executives in these companies provided whatever technical information they had on Dominite, and they gave HCC representatives their estimates of market potential. Finally, Moore studied the total consumption of talc and whiting in paint and ceramics manufacture as one measure of total market potential for Dominite.

In March 1977 Messrs. Moore, Moe, and Fraser reviewed the information collected and, using their best judgment, concluded that Dominite sales could be 55,000 tons a year by January 1980 (see Exhibit 1). (Talc and whiting sales for 1980 to both the paint and ceramic industries were forecast at 1.1 million tons.) They further estimated that 55 percent of Dominite sales could be for ceramic applications with 70 percent

EXHIBIT 1
Estimated Sales of
Dominite, 1977–
1980 (estimates
made in 1977)

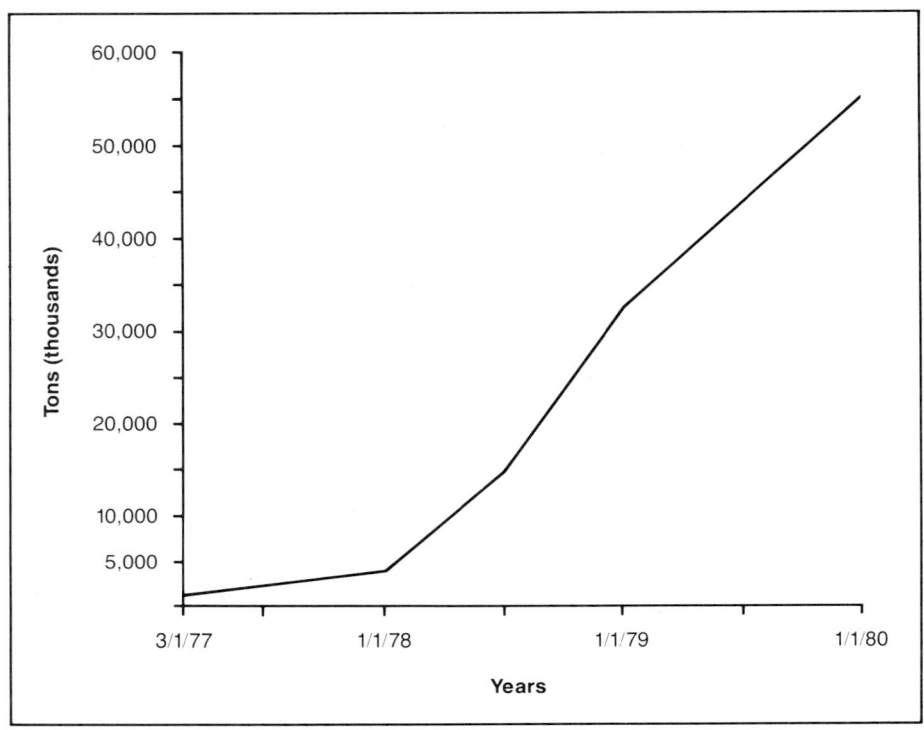

Source: Harper Chemical Corporation company records.

to 85 percent of that amount being sold to wall tile manufacturers.[3] The paint industry[4] was expected to account for 35 percent of Dominite sales and the remaining 10 percent was to come from its use in a wide variety of products such as cement, insulating materials, plastic floor tiles, and certain types of glass.

Determining Production and Capital Requirements

John Moe studied Hawley's production facilities and concluded that the installed equipment was inefficient and required extensive modification. Coarse crushing equipment was needed; Moe thought that a crushing unit having a capacity of 150,000 tons per year should be installed to permit long-run growth in output. Fine grinding

[3]The ceramics industry was rapidly expanding with wall tile manufacturers leading the trend: four large tile companies had 33 percent of the market; 12 medium-sized companies had another 33 percent, and the remaining portion was divided among 30 small companies.

[4]The paint industry was dominated by 10 large multiplant national companies which had 25 percent of industry sales. The remaining 75 percent was sold by some 1,500 smaller companies. The paint industry was growing rapidly and its growth had been aided by extensive new product development.

equipment was available in units of 20,000 tons per year capacity and Moe decided that initially three such units should be installed. Finally, Moe discussed building costs with several companies specializing in mining construction. The construction company selected by Moe submitted an estimate of $5.4 million for plant and equipment having a capacity for 60,000 tons of average-grade[5] Dominite.

The conditions of the lease proposed by Hawley's owners were that the Hawley Mining Company would receive a royalty of 3 percent of net sales on Dominite for as long as HCC used the Hawley site, with a minimum royalty of $15,000 per year for 1976 to 1980, $22,500 per year for 1981 to 1985 and $30,000 each year thereafter.

Estimating Yields and Operating Expenses

John Moe, assisted by the construction company engineers, then estimated manufacturing costs. As a first step, sample drillings of the Hawley deposit were taken; they indicated a yield of 62 percent pure Dominite and a deposit of 15 million tons. Fraser and Moore then estimated that for the long run, sales, research and development, and administrative expenses would average 10 percent of gross sales a percentage figure that approximated HCC's overall rate for these expense categories. High sales, R&D, and administrative expenses were expected, however, in the early years. Therefore, Fraser and Moore budgeted an annual amount of $540,000 (10 percent of gross sales at capacity operation) for these expenses.

Pricing

In setting a price schedule, Moore and Fraser reasoned that Dominite prices should be equal to talc prices, grade for grade (see Exhibit 2). (No price schedule had been established by the Hawley Mining Company.) At these price levels and at projected sales volumes, the Dominite operation would break even in a year and a half and would have a 10 percent after-tax profit in the fifth year. Over a 20-year period, the operation would produce an average after-tax return on investment of 15 percent.

The depletion allowance would increase the cash flow from the Dominite operation. This allowance was set by the federal government at 10 percent of gross Dominite sales or 50 percent of before-tax profits on the Dominite operation, whichever was less, and could be taken only in the year earned.

DOMINITE SALES PROGRAM

In early 1977, the HCC board of directors authorized the leasing of Hawley's Dominite deposit and the construction of a processing plant having 60,000 tons capacity at a cost of $5.4 million.[6] At the same time a Special Products Department was established

---

[5]Dominite was to be produced in seven grades, with each grade requiring a different length of time to process. The average grade referred to is the grade with the median processing time.

[6]This plant was completed in the summer of 1978. While it was under construction, the decision was made to reduce its planned capacity from 60,000 tons to 40,000 tons because sales had not materialized as forecasted. Total construction costs were then $4.5 million.

EXHIBIT 2
Dominite List
Prices, December
1982

Grade	Per Ton in Bags*
GP-1: General-purpose grade	$ 55.35
CG-1: Coarse ceramic grade	67.65
CG-2: Medium ceramic grade	72.00
CG-3: Medium paint grade or fine ceramic grade	78.00
PG-1: Medium fiber grind	84.45
PG-2: Fine fiber grind	101.25
PG-3: Fine paint grade or extra-fine ceramic grade	108.90

*All prices F.O.B., Hawley, Pennsylvania. Bulk shipments, $7.50 per ton less. Rail carload minimum, 60,000 lbs. Truckload minimum, 30,000 lbs. Terms: 1% 25th or 10th. Net 30 days.
Source: Harper Chemical Corporation company records.

in the company to administer the Dominite program. Jim Hood, who had been in charge of sales for one of HCC's product lines, was made general manager of this department and John Moore was named sales manager.

Two special salespeople were hired and assigned to work under Moore, one to cover ceramic industry customers and the other to work in the paint industry. In 1977, Moore also initiated a modest advertising program to promote Dominite through trade journal advertising and appropriate trade shows.

In 1979, two more ceramics sales engineers were added to the Special Products Department. These three ceramic engineers then called directly on potential customers; all salespeople were paid on a straight salary basis.

In contrast to the approach taken in the ceramics industry, Moore decided to reach paint manufacturers largely through sales agents. Harper was already selling certain industrial chemicals to the paint industry and the large accounts were handled personally by HCC's vice president of sales. A small sales force, working through and with eight sales agents, contacted the great majority of customers. These same sales agents were used to reach a wide number of potential Dominite customers in the paint industry. The Dominite paint salespeople worked with these agents and at the same time called directly on a few large paint manufacturers.

When the Special Products Department added a second new product called Superfine to its line in 1979, this product was also assigned to the paint salespeople. Superfine had a wide range of potential applications,[7] one of which was in the manufacturing of paint. Superfine was produced abroad and distributed in the United

---

[7]Superfine was an extremely fine, airborne silica used as a thickening and/or thixatropic agent, a dry lubricant, an anticaking agent, an antislip agent, a suspension agent in paint, and as a low-temperature thermal insulator. It was also used in reinforcing butyl rubber and certain plastics.

States only by HCC. Anticipating that Superfine would be a very profitable product with a high potential sales volume, the Special Products Department then hired four more paint salespeople in 1979 to 1980, to bring the total number to five. These five salespeople were instructed to spend 75 percent of their time on Superfine and 25 percent on Dominite.

TECHNICAL RESEARCH PROGRAM

Dominite sales engineers were aided in their work with potential customers in the paint and ceramic industries by HCC's research laboratory. Salespeople issued requests on the laboratory to undertake technical work on the uses of Dominite and on particular customer problems. The HCC laboratory charged this work to the Special Products Department on the basis of hours worked plus overhead.

For some time the laboratory had conducted research on the use of titanium dioxide in paint. It had good research facilities and skilled personnel in this area. The HCC laboratory's work was well known in the paint industry. Its reputation proved to be a valuable asset in gaining acceptance among paint manufacturers for its technical findings.

The laboratory had done no initial research in ceramics; at that time, research on the use of Dominite in ceramic products was contracted out to two universities. In a short time, however, both new facilities and skilled technicians were added to the HCC laboratory to carry out ceramics research. As of 1980, the laboratory had established a reputation for having ceramics research facilities nearly equal to those of the four largest tile companies.

Once in 1981, Hood arranged to rent a tile plant, owned by Northern Artware, to conduct research on ceramics manufacturing methods. Northern Artware was in weak financial condition. At a cost of $135,000 plus the cost of the time of laboratory technicians, HCC representatives experimented for six months with processing refinements for using Dominite in tiles and in improving Northern's tile quality. The success of this work was evidenced by the fact that in 1982, Northern Artware was the largest user of Dominite.

Appendices A, B, and C each describe the work of a Dominite sales engineer with a single account over a period of time. These appendices were prepared by taking excerpts from the reports of calls which salespeople submitted after each visit with a customer.

OPERATING RESULTS OF THE DOMINITE PROGRAM

Between 1978 and 1982, annual sales of Dominite grew only to 8,700 tons, falling far short of the expectations of HCC executives. In each year, high operating expenses combined with low sales volume to produce a deficit (see Exhibit 3). Hood believed that the failure to achieve projected sales was mainly due to underestimating the

EXHIBIT 3 Income Statement for the Dominite Operation

	1978	1979	1980	1981	1982
Sales*	$ 62,400	$ 117,000	$ 284,700	$ 530,400	$ 678,600
Total plant costs**	621,000	1,105,200	1,200,300	1,381,500	1,212,900
R&D costs***	60,600	276,600	647,400	638,300	391,200
Sales expense#	57,600	150,000	249,000	339,000	339,000
Administrative expense##	60,000	90,000	90,000	120,000	120,000
Total costs	799,200	1,621,800	2,186,700	2,473,800	2,063,100
Gross profit (loss)	$(736,800)	$(1,504,600)	$(1,902,000)	$(1,943,400)	$(1,384,500)
Tax (46%)	338,928	692,208	874,920	893,964	636,870
Net profit (loss)	(397,872)	(812,592)	(1,027,080)	(1,049,436)	(747,630)

*Average price — $78 per ton.
**Approximately 65% of these costs were fixed in 1982. Fixed costs in this year included $387,000 for depreciation.
***In 1978, 25% of these costs were spent on ceramics research and 75% on paint research. In each year, 1979–82, about 45% went for ceramics research, 45% for paint research, and 10% for research on miscellaneous applications for Dominite.
#In 1978 half of the sales expense was charged to ceramic industry sales and half to sales to paint manufacturers. In 1979 and 1980 sales expense was divided 60% for ceramics and 40% for paint industry sales. In 1981 and 1982 the split was 70% for ceramics sales and 30% for paint sales. The figures do not include sales expense charged to the Superfine operation.
##Administrative expense charged to the Dominite operation. Equal amounts were charged to Superfine sales.

requirements for market development. While a number of potentially large users had been experimenting for long periods of time with Dominite, no large ceramic company had included Dominite in its production operations, and the big paint companies had not yet used Dominite in any of the best-selling paint lines. In 1983, the major users of Dominite were generally smaller companies, but by far the largest potential market was still with the large manufacturers. Any one of the big four tile companies could have used 30,000 to 40,000 tons of Dominite a year, and a large paint company could use 4,000 tons a year in a single popular line of paints. It may be noted that some managers, especially ones in large tile companies, had expressed reluctance to use a material for which there was only a single source of supply.

As of 1982 there were 26 Dominite customers in the ceramic industry and 16 of these companies were tile manufacturers. The largest Dominite account, Northern Artware, took 800 tons of this mineral in 1982. In all, ceramics manufacturers purchased 5,200 tons of Dominite in 1982 (see Exhibit 4).

Approximately 60 paint companies purchased a total of about 2,000 tons of Dominite in 1982. Of the total amount sold to paint manufacturers, about 60 percent was sold directly by Dominite salespeople and 40 percent went through sales agents.

About 1,500 tons of Dominite were sold for miscellaneous applications in 1982. These applications included usage in fiberglass products, structural clay products, glaze for sanitary ware, sealers (or mastics) for automobiles, and plaster.

Manufacturing expenses in 1982 were 14 percent higher than originally estimated. One reason was that labor rates had increased more than expected. In addition, the yield of pure Dominite was only 50 percent instead of the estimated 62 percent. Because of the lower yield, costs of transportation, processing, and inspection were higher per ton of pure Dominite than had been originally calculated.

Sales and administrative expenses were near original estimates. It was anticipated that such expenses would continue to be accurately controlled and no major increase in sales expense was anticipated with any increase in sales volume up to 60,000 tons. The Special Products Department administrative expenses were charged equally to Superfine and Dominite and these expenses were not expected to change in the near future.

Research and development expenses had been far greater than were expected. Because Dominite had found uses that were at first unfamiliar to the Special Products

EXHIBIT 4 Sales of Dominite (tons), 1978–1983

	Ceramics	Paint	Miscellaneous	Total
1978	—	—	—	800
1979	700	400	400	1,500
1980	1,600	1,000	1,050	3,650
1981	3,400	1,800	1,600	6,800
1982	5,200	2,000	1,500	8,700
1983 (6 months)	3,300	1,400	1,100	5,800

Department management, original estimates of research expenses had been largely conjectural. Only limited control had been exercised over the type and amount of research conducted and Dominite sales engineers had had considerable freedom in initiating laboratory research work on Dominite applications. By 1982, however, it was believed that major R&D projects had been completed and Hood anticipated that research expenditures would decline in the future.

In addition to the factors cited above, two other factors contributed to the annual deficits. First, since a profit was not earned in any year, it had not been possible to take the depletion allowance. Second, the average price per ton of Dominite sold was lower than had been anticipated. The coarser and cheaper grades were more popular and as a result average receipts per ton were $78 instead of an expected $93. It may be noted that the prices of Dominite had remained constant since 1977. Talc prices, however, were increased in 1978, 1980, and 1982 with the resulting price differential on comparable grades of talc and Dominite ranging from $6 to $10.50 per ton.

Superfine sales had grown rapidly as expected. In 1982 sales of Superfine had been 1.1 million pounds or $2,250,000. Superfine sales volume was forecasted for 1.7 million pounds in 1983, 2.3 million pounds in 1984, and 3.2 million pounds in 1988.

SALE OF THE DOMINITE OPERATION

In January 1983 Diane North, vice president and director of a medium-sized tile company, met with Jim Hood to discuss the use of Dominite by her company. North said that new small companies making wall tile were bypassing traditional channels of distribution and selling directly to retail outlets and tile contractors at low prices. North stated that her company could not continue to meet this competition with its present raw materials and processes, and she was looking for ways to reduce costs.

North then mentioned that her laboratory had developed a Dominite tile that would enable her company to reduce production costs considerably and to become one of the nation's leading tile manufacturers. She asked if HCC executives would be willing to sell Dominite to her company exclusively; she said that unless such an arrangement could be made, her company would not use Dominite. Hood answered that he could not limit the sale of Dominite to any single customer.

In a subsequent meeting, North asked Hood whether HCC executives would sell the Dominite business to her company. The following excerpts are from Hood's memorandum describing his discussion with North about selling the Dominite operation:

> She [Diane North] is not interested in a short-term preferred position, but wants a very long-term arrangement. To achieve this, she stated that their board of directors is willing to consider purchasing our Dominite operation. I told Diane our Dominite operation was not for sale, but our mind was not closed on selling it if a mutually satisfactory price could

be established. I also stated that our present price would be much higher than any price we might have considered a year ago because of our sales progress, and that in all probability the operation would not be available for purchase after another year or so.

Diane made a flat statement that unless they control the distribution of Dominite for the wall tile industry, her company will not become a Dominite user. I told Diane I would work out a few alternate plans by which she might obtain her goal, and our company would not receive less than we believe we will gain by our present course.

It could well be that she was just trying to determine whether we might be feeling desperate about our Dominite situation and would sell out cheaply. On the other hand, I have great respect for Diane's integrity and find it difficult to believe that she would change a position she had outlined so adamantly.

Incidentally, I told North I had not given any thought to selling our Dominite operation, but as a rough benchmark, the value would be not less than $6 or $9 million and probably not more than $30 million.

COURSES OF ACTION

Jim Hood had to recommend a course of action regarding the sale of the Dominite operation. If Harper was to continue to produce Dominite, Hood had to present plans for making the operation profitable. On the other hand, if Hood recommended selling, he would have to establish a sales price. To help him arrive at a decision, he forecasted sales for the 1983 to 1995 period (Exhibit 5). In June 1983, Mr. Hood set forth his recommendations in the following memo to the HCC executive vice president:

Recommendations Concerning the Sale of the Dominite Operation

It is two months since I met with Diane North and promised to give her our answer on her proposal for an "exclusive" on Dominite in wall tile or, alternatively, our price for the entire operation.

In view of our present wall tile customers, we can hardly give North an exclusive

EXHIBIT 5
1983 Estimates of Future Dominite Sales, 1983–1987, 1995

Year	Tons
1983	15,000
1984	22,000
1985	30,000
1986	45,000
1987	60,000
1995	100,000

Source: Harper Chemical Corporation company records.

in this field. Even if we did, the balance of our sales would be to small, scattered users in other industries with resultant high costs of sales.

The alternative — selling the whole operation — must therefore be considered. The financial facets of such a sale have been studied by the assistant treasurer, Bill Williams, using sales and cost forecasts supplied by me.

Briefly, Bill calculates that if sales reach 60,000 tons before 1987 (cash earnings then $975,000), and we compare this to an opportunity to invest cash now at a return of 10 percent or more, we should accept any offer above $4,750,000. If we can earn 15 percent on new investments, we could sell for $2,250,000 if our loss were deductible from ordinary income.

Bill points out that since our period of significant loss on Dominite is behind us, and our knowledge of the operation is quite complete, we should consider only relatively "solid" investments as alternatives. This type of investment usually has a lower rate of return, so he suggests a 10 percent rate as more realistic, and therefore concludes $4,750,000 as a reasonable value.

If after 1987 we forecast continued but slower sales growth to 100,000 annual tons by 1995 maintaining that level until at least 2012, a higher value is indicated.

For this calculation, Bill uses a 15 percent discount rate because of the greater uncertainty of these future costs and profits. He concludes then that our sales price should be $6,300,000 (a 10 percent discount rate raises this to $12,450,000).

There are others in a better position than me to make this financial decision, but I would like to point out some of the less tangible but important considerations beyond the strictly financial question. I feel that the Dominite operation should not be looked at as a separate entity, but as one part of the company's diversification program.

Because Dominite was the first venture for which we set up a distinctly independent production-sales group, this product has been loaded with the extra cost inherent in developing a new kind of business. The Superfine operation has benefited by inheriting a large part of the necessary organization, and the experience derived from Dominite. Eliminating the Dominite business would not effect a proportionate savings in the costs of administration, sales service, or research and development work. It would also mean the loss of a very skilled and able group of ceramic engineers, with the consequent loss of future mineral opportunities for Harper.

If we continue to operate the Dominite business, our cash loss on plant, sales, research and development and administration will amount to $120,000 this year, on estimated gross sales of $1,170,000. In 1984 we predict little or no loss; however, we will have to have $90,000 for plant investment, and $45,000 for inventory increase.

My recommendation is that we continue our Dominite business unless:

1. North's company will pay $6,000,000 for the operation; or
2. Harper has a place to invest $4,750,000 promptly with good assurance of a 10 percent return.

APPENDIX A: THE SAUNDERS PAINT COMPANY

The Saunders Paint Company (SPC) was one of the largest and most profitable paint companies in the country. Saunders operated eight manufacturing plants in the United States and owned a subsidiary with two plants in Canada. The company produced a full line of industrial and consumer paints and protective coatings, and it was an innovator of new and improved paints. Its three best-selling lines were well regarded by the public and Harper engineers calculated that SPC could use 4,000 tons of Dominite annually in any one of these lines.

Each SPC plant was operated semi-independently of the other plants. The best-selling paint lines were manufactured from standard formulas at each plant. Each plant, however, also produced paints for local demand. A central research laboratory was maintained in Buffalo, New York, and a central technical service laboratory was located in Detroit, Michigan. The central laboratories developed new paint formulas, tested raw materials for acceptability, and assisted plant laboratories with local problems. No raw materials could be used in any best-selling line until the product was tested and evaluated at the central lab. Moreover, when local plant labs were formulating new paints they generally used only those products approved by the central laboratory.

The following account was taken from certain call reports submitted by Harper paint sales engineers. It covers only those parts of the sales program which were directed at the research facilities in Buffalo, the technical group in Detroit, and the Canadian laboratory in Hamilton, Ontario. HCC salespeople periodically visited plants in their territories but the major sales effort was directed at these three central laboratories.

April 15, 1980 (Detroit). The purpose of this meeting was to discuss Dominite in PVA (polyvinyl acetate). Apparently, they had tried PG-3 [a fine-grade Dominite] in several colored PVA paints where flocculations had taken place. Dominite did not prevent flocculation in this case. They were quite interested in our results and will test Dominite thoroughly in PVA.

May 25, 1980 (Detroit). They were quite impressed by our PVA corrosion panels. Following conversation about the mechanism of this corrosion a few sample tests were made right on their conference table. House paint is now being produced with Dominite for tests. Discussions were also held with people in charge of automobile paints, polyesters, and sealing compounds — Dominite applications were discussed.

June 20, 1980 (Detroit). They spoke again of the PVA masonry paint. Detroit is now running experimental batches; apparently they have had some trouble with shiners on lapping in, but the stability features of Dominite in PVA are highly rated.

July 7, 1980 (Buffalo). I am sending three samples of SPC emulsion paints recommended for application to metal. They were quite concerned that we should keep our findings in the strictest confidence. The lab technicians feel that SPC has the jump on industrial emulsion coatings and would like to keep it. They said that the samples probably do not have the rust-inhibiting effects that may be obtained with Dominite, but they will be very interested in our opinion of them. They also thought that Dominite would definitely find a place in their formulations and asked for samples of CG-3 [a medium-grade Dominite] and PG- 3.

December 8, 1980 (Detroit). Dominite has been approved for use in a PVA finish, probably a primer or stucco finish. They also informed us that Southern's talc paint employees went out on strike yesterday. They felt this would be an inducement to utilize Dominite where it had previously been tested.

During 1981 and 1982, Dominite was used in small quantities in styrene butadiene paint and was still on the approved list of materials for PVA paints. Testing on Dominite was continued but no important results were reported by either the central or local labs.

November 18, 1982 (Buffalo). They reported that they were limited, at present, to using Dominite in their styrene butadiene paint at the Pittsburgh plant because Dominite's advantages are not outweighed there by its costs. On December 13, the emulsion department will have a sales meeting presentation on the tint-retention advantages obtained by using Dominite in masonry paint. They feel that the use of Dominite in PVA should increase steadily. They ordered their first ton of CG-3 today.

December 27, 1982 (Detroit). They decided not to use Dominite in the aluminum coating. Their reasoning was that they were unable, after exhaustive testing, to suspend Dominite in the system as well as they could another extender. They are still very interested in Dominite and would appreciate any information we have covering superior suspending methods.

January 10, 1983 (Detroit). Dominite is being used more extensively in PVA formulations. Their caulking progress has been at a standstill but they will start evaluating PG-2 in caulking next week.

April 28, 1983 (Detroit). They did laboratory work on GLOSS (masonry paint) about a year ago. Serious dispersing troubles arose with CG-3, and grinding time has been lengthened from 45 minutes per batch to two hours. Some batches have been reground three times and this has not made Dominite popular with the production people. If we can solve these problems GLOSS will be manufactured at five more plants.

May 5, 1983 (Detroit). We worked on the mixing problem but our suggestion apparently developed the same problems. They said they would consider their own production problems from now on and would keep us informed on their progress wherever possible.

The Canadian subsidiary of SPC manufactured and distributed a medium-sized line of paints in Canada. A research laboratory was located in Hamilton, Ontario, and Harper salespeople spent considerable time in Hamilton working with the Saunders' technicians. (All of the following excerpts are from call reports made on the Hamilton, Ontario, location.)

March 30, 1980. This group is finally giving Dominite serious consideration in flat alkyds. The lab is devoting full time to reformulating this paint line; I think the primary motive is cost. Secondary purposes might be to improve polishing and reduce sheen. They said that RM [raw materials] costs had been $4.71 to $5.01 per gallon and that they were shooting at $3.81. They were pretty well convinced that the latter price was impossible with any kind of quality, and thus a compromise of about $4.26 would be about the best they could do.

May 18, 1980. They are formulating Dominite in their PVA and spreading the news throughout the United States that Dominite's buffering action is a valuable asset in PVA. A 10-gallon batch of industrial primer containing PG-3 has been submitted for customer approval.

January 4, 1981. The final report on the flat alkyd tests (containing Dominite) will soon be submitted to the technical director and the sales manager. They expect the first production to be sold through the Hamilton line in about three months without any difficulty.

November 17, 1982. One of the lab engineers spent some time at a number of test fences where he saw exposure series containing Dominite as the extender. He was not too impressed with the tint retention qualities compared to a calcium carbonate formulation. He noticed something interesting, however, and he would like to see the test panels that we have exposed in Mississippi and around Philadelphia.

November 22, 1982. According to engineers, when costing was done on formulating exterior whites using Dominite, in a majority of cases a savings of only 3 cents per gallon was realized. The chief engineer plans to make a trip to Saunders (Detroit) in mid-December, where he hopes to check on results obtained there by using Dominite as an extender. I think he's afraid of going off on a tangent by displaying too much interest in Dominite, or risking the substitution of Dominite in some of their formulations, until he has had the OK from Detroit. I believe that he is also most anxious to see what results he obtains on his own test fences.

January 17, 1983. The sales department turned down the PVA paints that the lab had been working on for some time. They had included Dominite in the PVA formulation. If sales decided to market a PVA paint, we would be asked to supply the Dominite. A large fiberboard manufacturer recently came to the lab for a one-coat sealer that could be applied in-house. A PVA sealer was made using Dominite; if it is acceptable, it could mean carload or truckload volume. The chief engineer made no report following his visit to Detroit; this might indicate his renewed interest in Dominite.

February 4, 1983. The chief engineer said that they now had a series of tests using eight or ten extender pigments, with Dominite among them, on test fences. In addition, they have exposed R&D formulations to meet the Canadian government specifications. They think final results will not be out for three years; in the interim, however, if certain panels seem to be superior to others, they will then apply these formulations to test houses.

April 8, 1983. They had good news for us today. The field tests on higher concentration PVA had been approved, and as soon as they use up their overstock, they propose formulating up to a concentration of 45 percent Dominite. They will be purchasing in 60-drum lots. They will be closing down for vacation during early July and during that time the chief engineer may visit Philadelphia to see our test fence and test house.

APPENDIX B: DOVER TILE COMPANY

The Dover Tile Company of Dover, Ohio, one of the four largest U.S. ceramic wall tile producers, was known for its high-quality tile and was considered by many within the industry as a leader in promoting new production methods. Its laboratory was one of the best in the industry and its recommendations were important factors in many company management decisions. Jim Hood, of HCC, was anxious to shift Dover to Dominite for two reasons: Dover could use more than 25,000 tons of Dominite per year, and such a shift would be an influencing factor on the rest of the industry.

Ralph Tillman, the Harper ceramic sales engineer for the Midwest, started calling on Dover in 1978. The calls were made at the laboratory where Tillman worked with Bruce Daly, director of research; John Davis, the tile body engineer; and George Ledder and Jerry Faber, the engineers in charge of glaze research. Excerpts from some of Tillman's call reports follow:

September 23, 1978. John Davis is interested in Dominite and is a good man to have on our side. I got the impression that Dover was not sold on the supply of the product, and thus I have not pushed it too much. Davis could be developed by constant calling. Dover has experimented with Dominite in tile glazes but is not too happy about it.

January 27, 1979. Davis has taken an interest in Dominite, as was shown by the fact that he voluntarily chose my table at the Ceramic Association's dinner the previous Wednesday evening. I have been tipped off to make sure Sam Pearlman, the production manager, knows about me and Dominite. Davis thinks he might try Dominite in a tile body with 40 percent talc.

February 23, 1979. I told Davis about our work with Triangle Tile [medium-sized tile manufacturer], and he told me he was already following it closely. He said that the boys from Triangle were going to Hawley. I think it might be wise to invite Davis to visit the mine on his trip to Philadelphia next summer. He has a son in Philadelphia and will visit him on his vacation.

April 2, 1979. Davis is looking forward to the trip to Hawley this summer; he was pleased with our invitation. He did not discuss the tile work, except that he was following reports from the East. They had tried Dominite as a replacement for talc, but they had encountered severe warping. He said they would continue to work with Dominite in the lab.

June 24, 1979. For the first time, Davis had me back in his lab for a long chat about tile. *Important:* John is running Dominite in a production trial in the next 30 days. It will replace dolomite and pyrophyllite to see if it will give a better pressing body. If it works out well, Dominite could be 10 percent to 15 percent of the Dover tile body.

July 30, 1979. Davis said they are again using Dominite in tile glazes. The body work is still going on and he hopes to be completed by mid-August. He is looking forward to the Philadelphia visit and he wants to see Hawley.

In August 1979 Mr. and Mrs. Davis and Mr. and Mrs. Hood went to Hawley and spent a day at the plant. David Marshall, the executive vice president of HCC, wrote to the Dover president, William Rogers, and set out the Harper philosophy of being a supplier of raw materials. Marshall said that Dominite was being produced as a long-term proposition and that Harper had a reputation for being a reliable producer of products. Marshall mentioned the company's investment in Dominite facilities, the large size of the deposit, and the long history of Harper's fine labor relations.

Tillman increased his sales efforts with Dover during the summer of 1979. Dover continued with their comprehensive testing of Dominite and Tillman continued suggesting new procedures and providing technical assistance. Dover personnel preferred to do their own laboratory work and they did not often discuss their detailed technical findings.

September 15, 1979. Davis did not talk enthusiastically about his results using 11 percent Dominite in their regular body; he was rather noncommittal. I believe that even if they are convinced of Dominite's merits, it may take them time to get it into production.

November 11, 1979. The purchasing agent today showed a little more interest in Dominite, citing the fact that talc was going up in price. Davis was noncommital, as usual, but he did say that he was taking another look at the use of Dominite as a replacement for talc rather than for dolomite. Bruce Daly said that he had watched the Triangle operations with interest, and while he was confident that Dominite had a place in Dover's body, he said he felt it would be a long-term proposition.

December 6, 1979. I had hoped to spend two hours going over tile samples and reports with Davis but was in and out in 20 minutes. He is extremely busy, but he does not want to lose out on any information we may have on Dominite bodies.

January 24, 1980. Daly is definitely a booster for Dominite, and if he is kept abreast of things, he could easily swing management to our side, whatever progress is made in Davis' department.

March 24, 1980. Davis has done very little work on Dominite since my last visit, but he is still experimenting and the work looks promising. Daly and I had a long chat; Dover is now repeating some of their previous tests.

During the summer of 1980, Bruce Daly visited the Harper laboratories and commented on the ceramic projects on which HCC was working. The testing program at Dover was still operating but Tillman was unable to establish what progress was being made. Tillman continued to visit Dover periodically, even though his calls were far from successful.

October 11, 1980. Davis is still noncommittal but he is doing some work; results are not too encouraging. Daly verified the rumor that Dover is planning expansion. They will build a plant in Alabama with facilities to produce 6 million square feet of tile a year. George Ledder said it would be a big job to convert all of Dover to a new body and new process, but he has been thinking of our fast fire.* It appears that we are making progress with Dover. Since they think in terms of firing a tile twice in their production process, it may be necessary to work with them on this basis.

December 23, 1980. Progress is slow, but now that Pearlman can be brought into the discussions, once in a while, along with his assistant, we may be able to get some action out of Davis.

January 21, 1981. Ledder has not done anything yet on glazes; that is still in the future. As soon as the news gets around that Premium and Trenton [small tile manufacturers] are on 70 percent to 30 percent, I think we will get some action out of Dover.

February 23, 1981. Davis is working on a new body. Dover has tried a 2 percent mix and is going to try a 3 percent mix. Dover makes 150 batches a day. At 3 percent, this means 45 *tons* per month. We are getting more attention at Dover these days; I will keep after them.

March 4, 1981. A visit finally coincided with Rogers' presence at the office, and he and I spent an hour going over all phases of Dominite, Harper, one source of supply, new tile producers, and present users of Dominite.

March 30, 1981. Davis mixed a 1,700-pound batch and pressed it yesterday. He is interested in seeing how good 70 percent to 30 percent is. While he feels Dominite is a good tile material, he said Dover will use it only after he recommends it. I feel better about the situation at Dover each time I call. Even at 10 percent, they would use 20–25 cars of Dominite per month.

April 24, 1981. Spent a social visit today with Pearlman. It was an informal chat about plays, baseball, cameras, grandchildren. Later, I visited with Davis and he said Dover's

---

*Fast fire is a process where the tile and glaze are fired together. The standard process for Dover had been to fire the body once, apply the glaze, and then fire the tile a second time.

regular body was not strong enough to suit him; cracking in trim tile was another big problem. The lab has compounded and tried what they feel is a very successful body using 17 percent Dominite, so Davis ordered a production run. This was completed and the results were very good; even Davis was enthusiastic. Another production trial has been ordered by Davis. They were taking a lot of time on this project and it was gratifying to see their interest.

May 9, 1981. The second production run was completed and the average manufacturing breakage was cut from 22 percent to 2 percent. Some tiles were glazed with their most troublesome glaze, and losses were cut from a normal 20 percent to 100 percent down to 4 percent with Dominite; another run was ordered.

June 25, 1981. Davis said the tests still look encouraging; he hoped to have something by July 1. He also invited me down to his river cottage for the Fourth, and I'll take him up on that.

July 2, 1981. Dover is very close to starting commercial production of Dominite tile. Their problem has been occasional unexplained cracking, particularly on the edge of trim pieces; this may be solved by changes in die design.

July 30, 1981. Davis gave me 200 bisque tiles and 40 green tiles for testing. They have been shipped to the lab. Nothing definite on the 17 percent body; according to Davis, the results have been good and then only so-so.

Throughout the remainder of 1981, Davis and Daly informed Tillman that work on Dominite was continuing, but that nothing was definite. Furthermore, the laboratory personnel were reluctant to discuss their problems with Tillman. During late 1981, the demand for Dover's tile slackened. Production was decreased and some personnel were laid off.

February 15, 1982. Davis was still working on the Dominite body, but he had little to say, except that progress was being made. A recent ruling makes it difficult to get a trip through the plant. Neither Davis nor Pearlman would OK a trip through for me.

February 25, 1982. Production is down quite a bit and the boys have been cautioned about discussing the situation.

March 23, 1982. Jerry Faber said that work was progressing satisfactorily. He said that unquestionably Dover would switch to the Dominite body immediately if the die problem wasn't such a big item.

May 3, 1982. William Rogers was pleased to hear that David Marshall (executive vice president of HCC) plans to visit him. From what I heard at the lab, the 25 percent body is all ready to go; all they need now is decisions from top management to spend money for dies and start the changeover. Marshall's visit could well expedite some action from upstairs.

Marshall visited the Dover headquarters in early June. During the visit, Rogers said that Dover generally did not use a material with a single source of supply. Rogers further stated that this policy was one reason why his company was not using Dominite. Marshall, in turn, presented Harper's outstanding record of reliability as a supplier but Rogers was not moved from his viewpoint. This visit in general was very cordial, but no contract was signed.

June 17, 1982. Trials are continuing and the project looks good; Rogers is following the progress of this project very closely. Business is picking up at Dover and some of their old help is being called back.

September 28, 1982. Daly indicated that some of the younger people were trying to rush things with Dominite, but he said that thousands of dollars were being spent to make sure that the product was sound, and that Dover would not find itself in difficulty after production began.

In November 1982, Tillman reported that Rogers might be more interested in Dominite if a ready three-month supply was stored near Dover's plant. Hood consulted with Harper's construction engineers and it was determined that sufficient storage facilities could be built for $75,000. Hood then told Tillman to sound out Rogers to see what sort of purchasing arrangements would be made in return for a building. Rogers would not commit himself to any firm agreement, however, and the warehouse proposal was then dropped.

During October, November, and December, various production problems required the undivided attention of all the laboratory personnel. Research and testing on all projects, including Dominite applications, was stopped. It was not until January 1983 that the laboratory was able to resume work on the Dominite project. Tillman, in turn, resumed his visits to Dover.

February 15, 1983. Joe Price is now in charge of the engineers. I feel for the first time that someone in Dover is "on the ball." We should make some rapid progress once Joe starts studying the results. Future calls to the plant should be pretty much confined to Price.

March 27, 1983. Calls here becoming involved and sometimes the visits are completely discouraging and frustrating. This week was one of those times. "No work is being done on Dominite. Still busy with production problems, and don't forget it would take $1,500,000 to change dies if Dover ever switched to Dominite." Joe Price said, "Very busy, all tied up with meetings. Yes, I know you want to sell some Dominite. I see your point, and I think you are right. I am going to Europe next month — busy, busy, busy." There is still a *big* selling job to do here.

APPENDIX C: LANCASTER ARTWARE COMPANY

The Lancaster Artware Company of Lancaster, Ohio, was an established producer of kitchen pottery, lamps, artware, and special ceramic products. Stephen Klein was president of the family-owned corporation and his son, Harvey, and his son-in-law, Charlie Scott, were the ceramic engineers. Competition within the pottery industry was increasing partly due to foreign imports, and in 1981 Steve Klein decided to produce ceramic wall tiles in an effort to increase Lancaster's profitability.

Ralph Tillman, the Harper ceramic sales engineer for the Midwest, started calling on Lancaster in early 1981. The following accounts of the sales of Dominite to the Lancaster Artware Company were taken from the call reports submitted by Tillman.

April 13, 1981. Harvey Klein has resigned his position with Triangle Tile and will go into tile production with his father and his brother-in-law, converting their artware plant at Lancaster, Ohio to tile production by July 15. Scott said they have two presses, have done very little work, and are interested in Dominite's possibilities. Harvey is sold on Dominite; as long as he is at Lancaster, this account is a definite possibility.

June 15, 1981. Harvey and Charlie showed me the plant and said they hope to be in production on regular tile within two months. They are interested in Dominite, and might use up to 70 percent to 30 percent body if their lab work is satisfactory. They propose to run our body and glazes against talc-pyrophyllite type during June. I arranged to send them a one-ton sample of Dominite.

July 23, 1981. Steve Klein told me the presses were in, but other equipment had been delayed and it would be several weeks before they could run production trials. He will keep me advised, and I will plan to visit them at the time they run their first trials.

August 3, 1981. Harvey Klein reported some progress in their lab work, but production will not get under way before August 15. Charlie Scott has glazed some 70 percent to 30 percent body and fired several trials in a small production kiln to cone 03 [refers to heat conditions in the kiln] in 12 hours. Various glazes are being tried with a variety of results; most of them are not too good. I plan to spend a day there within the next two weeks.

On August 9, Jim Hood wrote to Tillman saying: In view of the fact that they (Lancaster) are in the early stages of Dominite trials and could use a lot of guidance now, we question if a day is enough, or whether this is not the time to give Lancaster some continued attention.

August 20, 1981. We ran a series of 70 percent to 30 percent bodies with various clays and talc bodies. We made about 50 tiles on each trial. The Kleins liked 70 percent to 30 percent because it presses well; they could not make it laminate, whereas they had a lot of lamination with talc-type bodies. Next step is to run longer batches through the production unit; this will take place about September 1. In the meantime Charlie is going along with his color work.

October 15, 1981. Nothing has been run in production yet. The kiln is being fired now and some trials should be coming out this coming Monday. I suggested to Charlie that he raise the clay content in the 349 type of glaze, as well as the 3286/3470 type. He will have experimental runs completed by the week of October 22nd, and I will to go out then.

October 22, 1981. Steve Klein told me they have definitely decided to go ahead on the 70 percent to 30 percent body for their production. They are still working on their glazes and feel that some are entirely satisfactory. They will appreciate any help we can give them.

The Kleins began using Dominite; at the same time, they continued to test through January 1982. Wall tile test samples were sent by Lancaster to the HCC ceramic laboratory where they were tested; suggestions were made for modifications in the Lancaster manufacturing process. The Kleins utilized most of the lab's recommendations, as well as Ralph Tillman's suggestions.

February 2, 1982. Harvey Klein reported that they are in production, making about 2,500 square feet per day. No particular problems, except for some spotty concave warpage.

February 18, 1982. They are producing about 3,200 square feet per day, and still experimenting. Satisfied with their progress to date. Are selling "kiln-run grade." Have 12 colors in their line. I saw no signs of breakage or lamination and they claim they get none. Their biggest problems are excessive concave warpage and low-fired modulus of rupture. They are not worried about their sales or quality because they feel they have good product and can produce it cheaply. Since they developed their body and glaze with very little help from Harper, they prefer to keep the composition to themselves. This should be OK with us. We will sell 30 to 50 tons of Dominite per month if their tile sells.

Tillman continued to visit Lancaster during early 1982 and the Kleins were receptive to many of his suggestions. The Lancaster tile production was continued without serious problems, and the other Lancaster ceramic lines were being favorably received in the market. Testing of Dominite continued and periodic tile samples were shipped to the HCC laboratory for evaluation.

June 3, 1982. I discussed the results of the recent lab tests with Harvey and Charlie. They agree the strength is low, but they are not worried because it sells. Harvey claims that they can make strong tile in the lab but it loses strength in production. I suggested he make up a 55 percent to 15 percent body in the lab for a comparison test. He promised to do this and will have the tile ready for me on my next visit out here.

June 17, 1982. Lancaster is producing 2,500 feet per day and it is picking up. Their inspection is good. The kiln is loaded to 50 percent capacity and does a good job with no cracking, no lamination, no crawling, no shade variation, and no size difficulty. They have just 22 people involved in the operation, and the kiln is firing at 03 to 02 in 15 hours. This is a very nice operation; from what I could see of the tile being made, it is stronger than the tile made three months ago.

As the production process at Lancaster became established, Tillman made fewer and fewer visits. The Kleins continued to conduct minor experiments with Dominite, however, and occasionally they sent tile samples to the HCC lab for evaluation. Tillman continued to assist in the experimentation program when he visited Lancaster, but his main purpose was to keep the home office current on Lancaster's sales progress and plans.

December 18, 1982. The body composition is now 35 to 25 to 10 to 30 with Dominite being the 35 percent. They make about 3,000 feet per day and sales are improving slowly each month. No further bodywork testing is contemplated. They are now making 20 colors. I had them send the lab a set of colors for further reference.

April 21, 1982. Sales continue to climb, and Steve is thinking about expanding to a 2-million-square-feet-per-year capacity. He will probably add floor tile to his line.

CELESTIAL SEASONINGS, INC.

STATEMENT OF PHILOSOPHY

Celestial Seasonings is a consumer packaged goods company committed to marketing internally manufactured, health-oriented, high-quality products to the consumer and sold via health food and mass market outlets. Our job is to serve consumers by filling voids in the marketplace with quality products that consumers want. Our mission is to solve major health problems according to our corporate definition. Our objective: a healthy, nourished, disease-free, exercised public.

Under the name Celestial Seasonings, the product line and style of magic is set for the future. We sell high-quality products with the most beautiful packaging possible. Each package is sprinkled with bits of wisdom and is designed to give consumers an added bonus . . . Lighthearted Philosophy.

For stockholders our objective is a minimum sales growth of 27 percent compounded annually with a minimum of 27 percent growth in earnings. Celestial offers shareholders the opportunity to reap financial reward while getting people healthy.

For our employees, our objective is to build a strong and stable company with dynamic opportunity for upward mobility through loyalty, pursuit of excellence, hard work, and quality. This company is dedicated to mutual reward systems based on the achievement of worthwhile and aggressive goals. We remain loyal to the continual search and practice of advanced management systems that build working bridges between exempt and nonexempt employees, believing that a united, fully utilized work force can accomplish far-reaching objectives with work satisfaction and mutual reward for all. Our philosophy encourages creative, productive, possibility thinking throughout the organization.

In summary, the foundation of Celestial Seasonings is based on serving health needs through good products and expressed in a beautiful form. Our profit will increase 100-fold by dedicating our total efforts to these ends, which in turn will make this world a better place for our children and our children's children.[1]

[1] Source: Corporate files.

Case prepared by Charles L. Hinkle, University of Colorado, and Esther F. Stineman, Yale University. © 1984 by Prentice-Hall, Inc. Reprinted by permission.

BOULDER, COLORADO, 1982

Boulder, Colorado, is a sleepy but fashionable town located north of Denver on the Front Range of the Rocky Mountains. During the early 1970s, hippies trudged through its streets lugging worn backpacks and sleeping bags, many of them living from hand to mouth supporting themselves by panhandling or selling "dope" to university students around The Hill area of town. Today, Boulder presents a more affluent face to visitors. The hippies have either left town or have cashed in their patched jeans for snappier, more socially acceptable though casual attire — Chemise La Coste shirts and L. L. Bean chinos, for example. Many have joined the ranks of the young professionals and zip around the town in foreign-made cars, said to be better than domestic models for mountain driving.

Jogging and bicycling are popular Boulder pastimes. Former marathon Olympic star Frank Shorter is now a local businessman selling chic running shorts and shoes in his own shop on the Mall, which marks the center of town. Most of the youthful, health-conscious people in town are glad not to have a ragtag population marring their peaceful local scenes of outdoor cafés and trendy businesses done up in natural cedar or red brick façades. Casualness seems to be a fetish.

CELESTIAL SEASONINGS BACKGROUND

In this idyllic setting Mr. Mo Siegel, president and co-founder of Celestial Seasonings, Inc., reigns over his herb tea kingdom, an empire that includes among its all-natural products such innovative no-caffeine offerings as Red Zinger, Mandarin Orange Spice, and Cinnamon Rose herb teas, graphically tricked out in flamboyant fantasy packaging (see Exhibit 1). Celestial competes in its own small market, the $75-million-a-year herb tea share of all tea sales, with other counterculturally costumed competitors — Select, San Francisco Herbs, Lipton, and the rest. The purchaser of Siegel's tantalizingly titled teas buys not only a beverage to sustain body but messages from such unlikely and diverse sources as Abraham Lincoln and Sophia Loren to sustain the soul. "Please write, we like to respond. We are interested in your suggestions, ideas, queries, quotations, and short essays for use on the packages," invites a box-top bit of prose. Mo Siegel, himself an inveterate collector of quotations, includes pithy morsels of wit and wisdom in business correspondence. Under the cable and Telex information on a recent Siegel letter, the reader is treated to some Goethe: "Whatever liberates our spirit without giving us self-control is disastrous."

Mr. Siegel sits at mission control site between a portrait of Lincoln on one wall and the Iced Delight bear on the other. He has little reason to meditate on disasters these days with his closely held Celestial Seasonings now dominating the domestic herbal tea market with annual earnings of more than $1 million. Sales to foreign markets have leapt to 6 percent of Celestial's total current annual sales. Still a dwarf in the overall $825 million black tea market, Celestial at $23 million a year

EXHIBIT 1
Description of selected products

CELESTIAL SEASONINGS

AMERICA'S #1 SELLING HERB TEA

SLEEPYTIME®: Our No. 1 Selling Herb Tea — The perfect before bedtime drink. A great non-caffeinated tea with chamomile, spearmint leaves and lemon grass with seven other herbs. Helps you relax and wind down from a hectic day. Designed to round off the day's rough edges. Its sweet flowered flavor can be enjoyed by young and old.

MANDARIN ORANGE SPICE: One of our most popular teas. The delicious flavor of imported natural mandarin oranges makes this tea drinkable any time of day. We captured a tangy citrus flavor with just the right spice bouquet by combining orange peels, hibiscus flowers, rosehips, blackberry leaves and a touch of sweet cloves, a flavor you will also enjoy iced.

CINNAMON ROSE™: A bright, refreshing tea that combines the sweet explosion of imported cinnamon with the naturally round flavors of rosehips, orange peels, blackberry leaves and sweet cloves. A uniquely flavored herbal blend that is excellent both hot or cold.

COUNTRY APPLE™: The luscious apple flavor unfolds with every sip. The aroma of Country Apple Herb Tea will take you back to breezy afternoons in a country orchard. Truly an apple adventure, combining rosehips and hibiscus flowers for a bit of tartness, chamomile and chicory for smoothness and body, plus cinnamon and nutmeg for just the right touch of spice.

ALMOND SUNSET™: Our newest tea, a romantic blend of herbs with the soothing natural flavor of almonds. A delicate blend of rich roasted carob, barley and chicory root; spiced with cinnamon, sunny orange peel and a hint of anise seed. A taste for almond lovers of all ages.

RED ZINGER®: A Celestial tradition, imitated often but never equalled. The deep ruby red color, the tangy citrus flavor, the powerful bolt of flavor. All these combine to make Red Zinger a unique herbal soft drink enjoyed by young and old alike. Red Zinger is an indescribable brew that can only be appreciated by tasting it.

Soothing teas for a nervous world.

in sales has stunned the big tea marketers by making steady inroads into major supermarket chains, gourmet and health stores, and into foreign markets during the late 1970s and early 1980s.

Tea giants such as Thomas J. Lipton, until as recently as 1980, tended to discount Celestial's entrepreneurs as amateurs playing flower-child games in a tough marketplace. Now Lipton and others look at Celestial, a company that has experienced a high growth rate, as a feisty wunderkind to emulate and contend with. Lipton in 1982 began marketing herb teas packaged in rainbow colors at prices close to Celestial's — about 5½ cents a bag, although Lipton packaged its herbals in packs of 16, while Celestial preferred the 24-teabag format.

The compelling Mr. Siegel was the subject of wide-ranging publicity.[2] He popped up regularly on television programs such as "Merv Griffin" and "Donahue," and business magazines took turns publishing a colorful sketch of the president who was given to quotable remarks as he ruminated aloud. "We have an obligation to make the shelves astonishing! to keep magic alive," he said when asked about Celestial Seasonings' devotion to creative packaging. "We must continue to create beautiful, outstanding-quality packaging with truthful writings." Later he told the casewriters upon entering the elegant Celestial board room, "We want Louvre quality in our artwork," and "If Walt Disney could do it better, we aren't interested" (Exhibit 2).

Some of the press that Siegel received suggested that the success realized for Celestial "just sort of happened." In fact, Mo Siegel is a very ambitious person, addicted to reading management books, Drucker one of his favorites. "I like big rather than small," he admitted to us with a gleam in his eye. Then he explained how he recruited outside of Celestial to professionalize management, hiring a regional manager from Lipton and a plant manager from General Mills. Along the way he recruited a vice president of PepsiCo for his marketing team and brought in a chief engineer from Pepperidge Farm. Celestial's head tea brand manager was recruited from Quaker Oats, another from Vaseline Intensive Care, and still another from Samsonite. Clearly, Siegel sought marketing expertise for the company from proven training camps. He followed marketing stories of large companies as if they were detective novels: "Tylenol is bright," and "Johnson & Johnson is as good as P and G." And his strategy was pragmatic: "We don't have the time or the money to test in the same way as Quaker."

His objectives for the company were specific and hardhitting. In 1981, which was "the first year for our real-live-moving-growing marketing department," Siegel decided that any product line not reaching $10 million in sales in five years should be discontinued. Other objectives included the achievement of a 30 percent increase

---

[2] See Eric Morgenthaler, "From Hippies to $16 Million a Year, *The Wall Street Journal*, May 6, 1981; "What's Brewing at Celestial," *Money*, January 1981; Margaret Thoren, "It Wasn't the Bankers' Cup of Tea. . .," *The Christian Science Monitor*, April 21, 1981; and Barth David Schwartz, "How to Make a Million Doing Your Own Thing," *Fortune*, June 4, 1979, among others.

EXHIBIT 2
Celestial Season-
ings graphics

of tea sales in standard units; a broadening of grocery volume from 35 percent to 55 percent on at least four items; and the expansion of tea section placements from 15 percent to 30 percent on Sleepytime, Mandarin Orange Spice, Cinnamon Rose, Country Apple, Iced Delight, Red Zinger, Almond Sunset, Emperor's Choice, Peppermint, and the variety-pack four flavors.

Siegel believed that Celestial should continue expanding trial tastings among nonusers and increase the frequency of consumption among users from one to two cups each day. Since Colorado was Celestial's most active market area, Siegel's 1981 goals stated that the company needed "to determine upside volume potential outside of Colorado." Finally, and perhaps most important since Siegel claimed he was not interested in being a "food company" but was interested in preventive health care, Celestial targeted an improvement in its position in health food stores through a carefully orchestrated shelf management program in 1981 and 1982.

Siegel is not particularly modest about what he thinks are Celestial's most successful characteristics. At the top of the list he counts the distinctive and unique aspects of Celestial, including quality, packaging, products, names, and writings. In the "tricky herb industry," because of the adverse publicity about herbs and regulatory difficulties, he believes that he has accomplished no small feat in achieving the "highest quality standards in the herb industry." Because health products, not food, is the area in which he is interested, Siegel believes Celestial's success to be inextricably tied to its provision of a "real alternative to other caffeinated hot beverages." That the company has embraced a "wide variety of flavors and product concepts" he believes is all to the good. The lead products in Celestial have a strong consumer positioning and best of all — from Mo Siegel's perspective of the health-focused "corporateur" as he terms himself — Celestial's products remain all natural and health oriented. Exhibit 3 summarizes Celestial's strengths, weaknesses, and strategies for the 1980s as seen by top management.

Not that everything is coming up rosehips, however. Celestial has experienced its share of problems. A brief and abortive romance with a product called Salad Snacks failed to meet quality control standards. Juice products, despite great corporate hopes, could not make a go of it.

Observed Siegel:

The caution is that we deal with limited resources, both people and finances, and we cannot effectively execute against multiple priorities especially when the objectives are not compatible with our central corporate mission. The key is maximum sales effectiveness. An example of the dilution of resources was the introduction of BreakAway during the major drive for Iced Delight — no one's fault — and penetrating a new channel of distribution — placing Salad Snacks in produce departments — without adequate development of our basic business. Launching VITA during the key prewinter sales drive on Herb Tea would have been a similar mistake.

Mo Siegel hardly underestimates the importance of marketing. One of his trump suits has been a strategy of strong and consistent marketing to the health foods market segment. As markets drift away from hot caffeinated products, there Celestial

EXHIBIT 3
Strengths, weaknesses, and strategies of Celestial Seasonings

Strengths

Growth via health consciousness
Strong consumer loyalty
Financial stability and excellent gross margins
Distinctive packaging
Readily acceptable flavor varieties
Significantly higher brand awareness than the competition
Professional management
Vertical integration: from raw product to finished teabag

Weaknesses

Extensive product line
Premium product line
No line pricing
24-teabag count
Compressed timetables

Strategies for the 1980s. Continue to take the leadership position in

Unique packaging
Inventing blended herb teas
Offering the largest selection of blended teas
Offering special packs
Ability to sample
Offering the best quality herb teas
Marketing solution teas, for example, Sleepytime

will be. The sweet dream of high coffee prices has always kept spirits high at the tea factory, and the strong growth of health food stores has been a trend that fueled the Celestial team's marketing enthusiasm. With increasing professionalization of the team, however, no one is naïve enough to think that people can rest on their tea leaves and achieve continuing growth. Rather, the annual building of new distribution channels is seen as a perennial strategic topic as are plans to develop a wider product mix (Exhibit 4). Always Celestial is striving to improve its professional approach to sales and marketing.

MARKETERS AND MARKETING AT CELESTIAL

Keith Brenner, a pleasant, self-assured Canadian — some might say slightly arrogant — became vice president of marketing at Celestial in 1980. Before that, marketing at Celestial had been strictly an in-house, family affair. Brenner, who owned his own beverage manufacturing company in Canada, met Mo Siegel at a food show. He worked with Celestial first as a consultant, assisting the company in its attempt to enter the natural beverage market, an effort that flopped. Although Brenner

EXHIBIT 4 Advertising for a new (1982) product

Delicious to the core.

Before you decide on your favorite Celestial Seasonings Herb Tea, try this one.

Country Apple Herb Tea is a delicious blend of apples, rosehips and cinnamon enhanced by hibiscus flowers and chamomile, with absolutely no caffeine.

The flavor of Country Apple unfolds with each sip, as the aroma of orchards takes you back to breezy afternoons in the country and all your fondest memories.

Try our new Country Apple Herb Tea. Then pick your Celestial favorite.

hoped to work in general management, he was asked by Siegel to head the marketing function of the organization. He has not put aside his preference to get into general management where he could be involved in finance and production as well as marketing.

Besides his stint as a beverage manufacturer Brenner acquired an impressive set of credentials from his work with Pepsi Cola in Canada and with General Foods. Like Siegel, he attained success early. At 32 he was a vice president and general manager for Pepsi Cola, globetrotting for a three-year period to Pepsi operations in South Africa and the Philippines as well as serving in Canada. He cited as his major reason for joining Siegel and Celestial "the opportunity to impact a healthy growing concern instead of attempting to climb the ladder in a vast corporation."

Both Brenner and Siegel believe in the Celestial mystique: "Our goal is to manufacture only healthful, nutritional products — nothing artificial." At Brenner's urging, Celestial planned to abandon its sole caffeine product, Morning Thunder: "Since Celestial Seasonings' customers are a segment based upon their penchant for natural food products, a clean bill of health with customers will be strengthened by severing ties with caffeine."

As for his marketing efforts, Brenner terms Celestial "an alternative kind of company which has achieved success without hammering people with incessant advertising. We tell a simple story in a colorful way, only the truth, not embellished with a lot of hoopla."

Brenner professes a belief that "Celestial's success was a major reason why Lipton decided to enter the herb tea market. Instead of thinking that such competition works to Celestial's detriment, we credit the Lipton move to raising overall public awareness of products such as ours. In fact, the Lipton competition creates a bigger market for everyone." Brenner is sanguine about growth possibilities for Celestial even though teas was a low-growth category, according to the marketing vice president, 1 percent annual growth, the same as the population growth rate:

> Any extra we get has to come out of somebody else's business, but there is a trend by large stores to stock more nutritional foods . . . health foods and the like . . . which is good for us. This will help us reach our target of 25 percent annual growth, compounded, but only through 1985, I believe, with our present product line. This means that to continue meeting our objective we must develop new ideas — beyond herbal teas.

Brenner's overall strategy for growth in 1982 was succinct:

> First, we widen our grocery distribution base with tea section placement. This has been difficult, but it gets easier as we get stronger. Second, we go after consumer awareness and trial through the use of Sunday supplement coupons, trial packages, and displays. Last, we move more strongly into the iced tea market, which is three times larger than that for hot tea.

Regarding trips into the marketplace, Brenner has confessed, "I do get into the field occasionally, but not enough." Like Siegel, he is emphatic that one distribution channel cannot be sacrificed to another. "We had 100 percent distribution in the health food outlets, so we moved into the supermarkets. But we are not neglecting our health food outlets."

LIFE AT THE TEA FACTORY

The music of James Taylor wafted through the tea factory on a typical day in 1982 as Italian-made machinery moved the teas 24 hours a day on a computerized schedule. This new equipment made it possible to pack the major Celestial blends into horizontal boxes, found by market testing to lure the purchaser more effectively than vertical packages. Employees in production appeared to be blissfully engaged in their tasks. The cafeteria awaited them at some point in their shift, with a meal of natural foods — soup, salad, granola cookies, and a selection from the company's herb tea line. Mo Siegel, who frequently dresses in shorts and a sports shirt for the office, and rides his bicycle to work, stresses quality of the workplace.

If it is possible to tell something about a person or an organization by surveying the reading material that is strewn about, perhaps the following survey of books and magazines in the Celestial Seasonings' employee waiting room offers some insights: Pierre Teilhard de Chardin's *Man's Place in Nature*; M. Scott Myer's *Every Employee a Manager: More Meaningful Work Through Job Enrichment*; works by Drucker and Toffler; and copies of the periodicals *New Health*, *New Age*, *Prevention*, *Runner*, *New West*, *Runner's World*, and *Processed Prepared Foods*.

In one section of the main plant, Marelynn W. Zipser, Ph.D., a food technologist and the mother of Mandarin Orange Spice, Cinnamon Rose, Iced Delight, and BreakAway, presides over herbs and test tubes in a pristine but cheery testing laboratory. As manager of new product development, Zipser reports directly to Brenner. "I take the concept and turn it into reality," she explained. Among her research and development tasks, Dr. Zipser conducts taste panels — mainly among women's groups and employees — to test the latest reactions to Celestial's expanding product lines. Quality and taste of the tea are as important to Celestial as other major points of difference with their competition: packaging style and graphics, the number of teabags per box, premium pricing, and channels of distribution. Thus, Celestial taste tests against Select, Alvita, Golden Harvest, Health Valley, Traditionals, San Francisco Herbs, Worthington, Horizon, and other regional and local brands in the health food market as well as Bigelow, Lipton, and Magic Mountain in the grocery market.

Systematic product development grew out of Mo Siegel's demands for specific types of products that he and Brenner instructed Zipser and her group to conjure up in the laboratory. "Conservative planning plus optimistic action plus intelligent work equals success" is a favorite Siegel maxim, which seems eminently practicable in the laboratory part of the tea factory.

HISTORY OF CELESTIAL

In the beginning were the herbs. Siegel, his wife Peggy, and sidekick Wyck Hay pioneered the operation by gathering Colorado mountain herbs with other friends "for fun" and selling them to local health food stores. These were the early days of health food awareness of the late 1960s and early 1970s, and Siegel and Hay's philosophy then was to provide a pleasant living for themselves and a congenial group of Boulder comrades by selling a product that was good for people. "One of the things we found in Europe is that people who live to 100 drink a lot of herb tea and eat herbs continually," Siegel states.

The company's appellation, derived from the fanciful nickname of a female friend who participated in the early days of Celestial's movement into what some have termed "cosmic capitalism," suggests the tone and tempo of those early times. Celestial began as a relatively tranquil cottage business in which Siegel, Peggy, and friends patiently stuffed the heady concoctions of orange peel, wild cherry bark, rosehips, hibiscus flowers, lemon grass, and peppermint into hand-sewn, hand-stamped muslin bags with solicitous instructions to buyers as to the particulars of brewing and steeping, along with a reminder to them that a bit of honey would enhance flavor. This early, successful blend, entitled Red Zinger, propelled Celestial out of the cottage and into a corporate setting. In 1982 Celestial required six buildings to house its manufacturing, warehousing of herbs and spices from 35 countries, and other functions.

From the outset, Celestial espoused causes and amplified these from its boxes — reminding customers about a foundation needing support to protect vanishing species of flowers, sometimes warning about world hunger, and promoting save the whales or other conservational causes. Celestial saw itself as having an instructive, positivistic mission, perhaps as important as its more pedestrian, grocery-focused one. "Happiness is the only thing we can give without having" and other messages of its kind became inherent aspects of Celestial's packaging concepts. But such aphorisms were more to Celestial than a way of selling tea. Siegel's enterprise was a mission (see Appendix for a brief biography).

With lots of help from his friends, Siegel organized a corporate structure based on communitarian concerns and centered on quality-of-life issues: concern with providing employees enough time for family and leisure, flexitime, pleasant working conditions, and many more. As the alternative to business that they were, the merry band was not quite able to do away with a hierarchical structure, and they developed a seven-person board of directors, most of them major stockholders, to hold down the fort. Living was easy then with only a few blends in their tea portfolio, and only 50 or so stockholders in the entire corporation.

MOVING INTO THE 1980s

Red Zinger was ultimately joined by some 40 other herbals, including a new tea in 1982, Almond Sunset: "a wonderfully romantic blend of herbs with the soothing natural flavor of almonds. A delicate blend of lovely things like rich roasted carob, barley and chickory root; spiced with cinnamon, sunny orange peel and a hint of anise seed. . . . Almond Sunset will remind you of holiday cookies baking in the oven of a farmhouse kitchen." Introduction of new products was carefully considered; Celestial's marketing and advertising budget was expected to be $5 million in 1982.

Seeking to market Celestial more aggressively, Siegel recognized the "be big or bust" paradigm that has ruled decision making at the larger beverage companies and the expansion imperative that was its corollary. New products, including body care preparations and vitamins, loom large in Siegel's mind as he looks toward

EXHIBIT 5
Annual changes in
dollar sales, fiscal
1973–1982

Fiscal year	Dollar sales	
	Amount	Increase
1973	$ 70	—
1974	293	+320%
1975	1,316	+350
1976	2,930	+125
1977	5,636	+ 92
1978	8,887	+ 58
1979	10,524	+ 18
1980	11,557	+ 10
1981	16,662	+ 44
1982	23,327	+ 40

Note: Net sales in thousands of dollars.
Source: Celestial Seasonings records.

product expansion and toward a goal of 27 percent compounded annual growth (Exhibit 5) with anticipated sales of $50 million by the mid-1980s.

As time went on Celestial people gave less attention to the fun-and-games enterprises of more carefree years, for instance, the world-famous Red Zinger bicycle races, a promotional activity the company sponsored from 1975 to 1980 because "Mo Siegel is into bikes." The races underscored a long-time Siegel belief that if more people rode bikes as their only transportation, the world would be a better place. "Celestial Seasonings is dedicated to improving the quality of life on this planet, having a major concern in environmental life," he wrote in literature promoting the Red Zinger Bicycle Classic. In 1980, however, it became an issue of bicycle races or teas for Celestial, just as it became an issue of hiring executives with sophisticated managerial expertise versus possible corporate extinction. Case in point: in the summer of 1980 the company came close to being swallowed by General Mills due to one disgruntled, major stockholder's wish to rid himself of $1 million worth of Celestial's stock. Siegel saved the day by borrowing money to purchase the stock himself.

In hiring heavyweight marketing types like Keith Brenner to draft a new marketing strategy, the main component being to move the herbal teas out of the less trafficked, specialty sections of grocery stores into the mainline beverage sections, Mo Siegel underscored his ambition to be big rather than small. Siegel and Brenner shared a perception that "the 35- to 50-year-old market remains to be captured if Celestial is to be truly successful." See Exhibit 6 for estimated herbal tea market shares from 1978 to 1980.

There were significant changes in Celestial's corporate culture once new management began to join the firm. Several members of the original cadre left the company presumably because of the new style of life at the tea factory. Although Siegel continued promoting quality of work life, his corporateurial mind was on priority

EXHIBIT 6
Market share (in $),
estimated U.S.
herbal tea market

	1978	**1979**	**1980**
Celestial Seasonings	38%	33%	30%
Magic Mountain	5	12	11
Lipton	—	—	8
Bigelow	—	4	8
G.N.C.	4	4	4
Other	53	47	39

Source: Company records.

markets for Celestial and criteria for selecting such markets. He reread his Drucker and listened to his cassette tape course on strategic planning. And he repeated to himself a six-word formula: "Concentrate on preventive health care foods." If such foods were curative in nature, so much the better.

A LOOK TO THE FUTURE

To keep the team spirit alive, Mo Siegel retreats frequently with his top staff members to discuss possible new directions for Celestial Seasonings. "We must operate in a basically unfriendly environment as retailers become more self-assured as to their position in relation to manufacturers." In the periodic strategic planning sessions in scenic and secluded Colorado resort areas, top managers at Celestial concentrate in 2½-hour segments on such tough-to-analyze questions as, What business are we in? What business should we be in? What is our company philosophy? Is our philosophy changing and if so in what ways? Who are our customers and how are

EXHIBIT 7
Organizational
structure

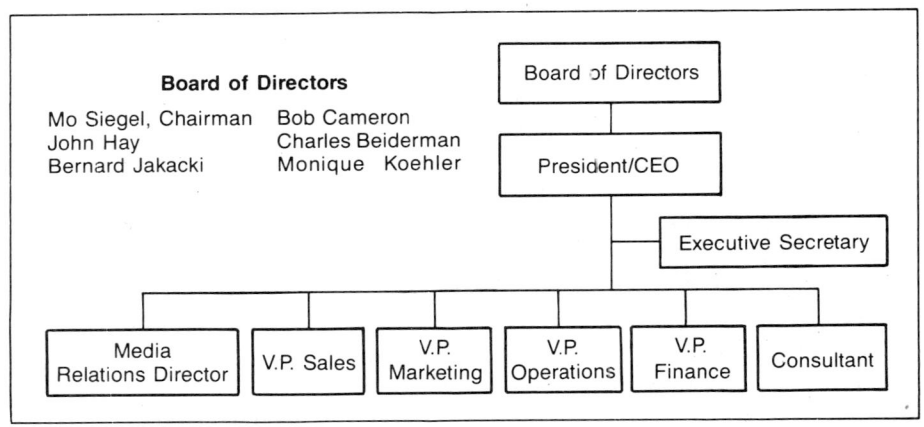

segments changing? What are Celestial's strengths and weaknesses? What threats and opportunities face us over the next several years? Is caffeine compatible with Celestial? What are our criteria for business development ?

Underlying the retreats' agendas was Siegel's own ambition for the company: "To be a billion dollars in sales at the turn of the century."

Exhibit 7 depicts Celestial Seasonings' organizational structure; Exhibit 8, from Celestial's press kit, summarizes some of Mo's reflections for successful living.

EXHIBIT 8

Mo's ideas for successful living

On Successful Living

Ideas: The best ideas are the ones that fill a need. If people want to make money, start with an idea that fills a need for someone else. Do something useful!

Goals: I'm a believer in goal-setting. If you know what you want, it's pretty hard to lose.

Failures: I've had plenty. You've got to learn to accept them. You're going to fail sometimes. Don't be afraid of it.

Hard work: Be persistent. Work hard, but use your intelligence.

Hiring: Never hire anyone else unless they're smarter than you are in the area in which they're going to be working for you.

Marketing: What does the public think of it? Is it good for other people?

Believing: You could do something you don't believe in, but it really takes the fun out of it. I've had some hard times along the way, and if I didn't believe in the product, I would have sold the company a long time ago.

Health: People are tired of paying doctors, and they want to stay healthy. I see people around the country getting more interested in prevention.

Incentives: If we want the labor force to work well, why not let them own part of it?

Labor: Create a condition in which the work force feels better about their lives. What is good for labor should be good for management and vice versa.

Faith: There is only one place to have faith and that is in God. The disappointments that are hardest to bear are those that never come. Faith in an active life is a positive attitude.

Mo's Steps to Successful Living

1. Do something worthwhile for someone else.
2. Have faith, maintain a positive attitude.
3. Learn the art of setting goals, what you want.
4. It isn't enough to work hard, you must work SMART!
5. Do not be afraid to fail.
6. Don't take yourself too seriously.
7. Stay healthy.
8. Believe in and be dedicated to quality.
9. Do not be afraid to take a risk.
10. Family love and support maintain stability and help you keep priorities in perspective.

Source: Company's 1982 press kit.

APPENDIX: MR. SIEGEL'S RÉSUMÉ AND MISSION

CELESTIAL SEASONINGS ®

Cable: CELESEAS BLDR
TWX: 910-940-3448

1780 55th Street
Boulder, Colorado 80301 U.S.A.
(303) 449-3779

MO SIEGEL
630 Spruce Street
Boulder, Colorado 80302
-(303) 447-9599

Business Address: 1780 - 55th Street
Boulder, Colorado   80301
(303) 449-3779

EDUCATIONAL HISTORY

1967
and on-going   Attended parochial schools; attended numerous
college courses; completed numerous professional
CEO and executive seminars and courses.

On-going   Independent Study - I am a devoted and perpetual
student of the health sciences, business management,
religion, philosophy, and government. I am
currently engaged in authoring a series of programs
for political reform in the United States which
began with the publication of the essay "Fire in
the American People".

1979   Travel Study - I sponsored a three-week, 5,000
mile study-tour of health and nutrition through
the Soviet Union with special focus on "The Garden
of the Centenarians" in the Trans-Caucasian
Republic of Azerbaijan and Georgia, home of the
"long dwellers."

1980   Travel Study - I completed a three week interior
study tour of China, involving the study of food
production and Chinese herbal science.

      Other travels include North America, Central
America, South America, Europe, Middle East,
and Asia.

EMPLOYMENT HISTORY

1968 to
1970   Owner, health food store; first mate, commercial
fishing vessel, Key West, Fla.; harmonica playing
sandwich board advertiser; carrot juicer salesman.

1970 to
present

Founder, President and Chairman of the Board,
Celestial Seasonings Herb Tea Company, Boulder
Colorado.

My responsibilities at Celestial Seasonings
include planning, organizing and directing the
over-all growth and development of the company;
providing executive management to the divisions
of Operations, Marketing, Sales, Human Resources,
and Finance.

My principal goals have been to ensure the
achievement of all corporate objectives and
the fulfillment of all responsibilities to
employees, shareholders, and customers by
directing all executive decisions affecting
the current and long-range operations of the
company.

PERSPECTIVE ON CELESTIAL SEASONINGS

In 1971 Celestial Seasonings sold a grand
total of 10,000 hand-sewn tea bags, containing
hand-picked Rocky Mountain herbs, to a small
group of health food stores.

Celestial now imports herbs from 35 countries
for use in blends which are milled at the
Boulder plant at a rate of over 4 million
pounds per year . . .

In 1982 Celestial will manufacture and serve
700 million tea bags and the fiscal year sales
will exceed twenty-five million dollars . . .

Celestial Seasonings Herb Teas are available
in more than 35,000 retail outlets throughout
the world including 60% of all U.S. supermarkets
and foreign distribution in Canada, Australia,
New Zealand, and Great Britain.

PROFESSIONAL ACCOMPLISHMENTS

Founder of America's finest International Class
stage bicycle race; formerly the Red Zinger Bicycle
Classic, now the Coors Classic.

Podium Speaker at the Democratic National Convention
1980; served on the Rules Committee of the Democratic
National Party, 1980.

Keynote Speaker for numerous professional, religious,
and civic organizational activities.

Guest appearances on ABC-TV's "Success, It Can Be Yours, PM Magazine, Donahue, Donahue on Today, HBO's "Money Matters", Merv Griffin, Mike Douglas, Dinah Shore, Sandy Freeman, USam, 700 Club, Cable Health Network.

Featured in People Magazine, Sports Illustrated, Wall Street Journal, Fortune Magazine, Money Magazine, BusinessWeek Magazine, New York Times, Los Angeles Times, San Francisco Chronicle, Boston Globe, Chicago Sun-Times, Christian Science Monitor, Washington Post, Denver Post, Rocky Mountain News, Seattle Times, Minneapolis Tribune, In-Flight Magazines, US Magazine, San Jose Mercury News, Seattle Post Intelligencer.

CHARACTER SKETCHES

Abiding concern...The health and fitness of the American people. Political reform.

Personal Heroes...Jesus, Abraham Lincoln, Walt Disney, Thomas J. Watson (founder of IBM), Dr. Kenneth Cooper (founder of the Aerobics Institute), Eddie Merckx (six-time Tour de France champion).

Quote..."I want Celestial Seasonings to enter the 21st century as one of America's leading corporations."

Favorite tea bag homily..."Angels can fly because they take themselves lightly."

Quote..."Where we go in the hereafter, depends on what we go after here."

Dream...of the day when the typical American employee enjoys the dignity and the equity he has earned and deserves.

Hoped for epitaph..."Mo Siegel was a good father."

Explanation of insatiable appetite for social and business advance...Because I don't believe that when St. Peter asks me, "Mo, what have you done with your life?", that it will be sufficient to reply, "Well, I cornered the herb tea market."

Quote..."I want to help change the course of American business, I want to help make all forms of Art more available to the American People, and I want to get the word out on health and fitness."

POLAROID AND SOUTH AFRICA: THE MANAGEMENT OF SURPRISE

During 1970 and 1971, Robert Palmer, director of community relations for the Polaroid Corporation, was a witness to and participant in a series of escalating events centering around Polaroid's activities in South Africa. This case presents those events as they occurred and as they were perceived by Polaroid's senior management.

A group of senior managers was assigned the initial responsibility of (1) analyzing and responding to these events on a day-to-day basis and (2) determining the longer-term strategic position of the company. These senior managers in 1971 principally included Robert Palmer, Thomas Wyman (vice-president, sales), and Peter Wensberg (vice-president, advertising), oftentimes working with other Polaroid executives. For the purposes of case narrative, events that happened to this Polaroid group will be described as if they happened to Robert Palmer. In reality, they may have happened to others in the group, although they were immediately brought to Mr. Palmer's attention.

Before these events are described as they happened, background data on the Polaroid Corporation is presented.

COMPANY BACKGROUND

Polaroid Corporation's founder, Edwin H. Land, was, in 1970, chairman of the board, president, director of research, and principal (30 percent) stockholder. Just as the Polaroid Corporation was totally built around Edwin Land, Land was totally involved in the process of "sensing a significant human need in our field and delivering the final product. . . . We're not here to make profits. We're here to make innovation."

Case prepared by John Barnett, University of New Hampshire, with Robert Palmer, University of Massachusetts. © 1985 by John Barnett. This case has been prepared for classroom discussion purposes only and is not intended to illustrate either effective or ineffective handling of an administrative situation. Reprinted by permission.

In 1928, Land left his studies at Harvard to work on reducing light glare by diffusion through the polarization of light. Nine years later he had perfected this polarization and started the Polaroid Corporation in Boston to sell polarizers to the automobile industry. When this tactic failed, Land built up the business of Polaroid nonglare sunglasses, which was a success.

During World War II, Land began developing a system of instant photography; the first Polaroid Land camera was introduced in the marketplace in November 1947. Between 1947 and 1970, instant photography product offerings expanded to include color, automatic exposure, and low-price models.

Land wrote to Polaroid employees in August 1970:

This is no ordinary company that we have built together. . . . It is the proud pioneer that set out to teach the world how people should work together . . . Polaroid is on its way to lead the world — perhaps even to save it — by this interplay between science, technology, and real people.

EXHIBIT 1
Financial statements for Polaroid and domestic subsidiaries, 1969–1970 (in thousands of dollars)

	1970	1969
Net assets		
Current assets		
Cash	$ 6,118	$ 8,478
Marketable securities	195,363	200,682
Receivables, less allowance of $670 ($675 in 1969)	103,987	100,203
Inventories	39,899	47,595
Prepaid expenses	2,781	1,453
Total current assets	$348,148	$358,411
Current liabilities		
Payables and accruals	31,291	44,044
Federal and state income taxes	15,824	16,503
Total current liabilities	47,115	60,547
Working capital	301,033	297,864
Property, plant, and equipment, at cost		
Land	2,742	2,577
Buildings	69,064	56,124
Machinery and equipment	112,360	97,484
Construction in progress	63,192	32,082
	247,358	188,267
Less accumulated depreciation	74,909	63,197
Net property, plant, and equipment	$172,449	$125,070
Other assets		
Investments in and advances to unconsolidated foreign subsidiaries, at cost	1,163	959
Patents and trademarks (at nominal value of $1)	—	—
Total net assets	$474,645	$423,893

EXHIBIT 1
(continued)

	1970	1969
Ownership of net assets		
Capital and retained earnings		
Common stock, $1 par value, authorized 36,000,000 shares, issued: 1970 — 32,831,950 shares; 1969 — 32,838,200 shares	$ 32,832	$ 32,828
Additional paid-in capital	119,843	119,725
Retained earnings	321,970	271,340
Total ownership of net assets	$474,645	$423,893
Income		
Net sales and royalty income	$426,534	$454,582
Other income, principally interest and dividends	17,751	11,027
Total net sales and other income	444,285	465,609
Cost of sales	207,266	222,451
Selling, research, engineering, distribution, and administrative expenses	123,445	112,226
Total costs	330,711	334,677
Earnings before taxes	113,574	130,932
Federal and state income taxes	52,438	67,811
Net earnings	61,136	63,121
Retained earnings at beginning of year	271,340	218,631
	332,476	281,752
Less cash dividends paid	10,506	10,412
Retained earnings at end of year	$321,970	$271,340

Note: Figures in thousands of dollars.

Sales in 1970 were $426,500,000 for Polaroid and its domestic subsidiaries and $88,800,000 for its 100-percent-owned unconsolidated foreign subsidiaries. Net earnings were $61,100,000. Polaroid had marketing subsidiaries in thirteen countries and manufacturing subsidiaries in Scotland and the Netherlands. The company held 1,100 American patents, most of them (955) in the field of instant photography. Financial data is contained in Exhibit 1.

CORPORATE CITIZENSHIP

Polaroid was described by the *Boston Globe* (November 1, 1970) as:

> *An enlightened company that takes pride in its national reputation for humanism. . . .*
>   *Its program in black hiring is a matter of record and far ahead of most companies in the nation.*
>   *About 9 percent of the company's employees are black . . . of the 2,383 hired (in 1969), 523, or 22 percent were black.*

Also in 1969 30 percent of the company's black employees completed company courses. Additionally, there is Inner City, a wholly owned Polaroid subsidiary in Roxbury which opened in 1968 to help unemployed and underemployed people develop work records to help them get and hold permanent jobs in industry.

Inner City had 125 graduates by 1970, of whom 82 percent remained in their permanent positions.

The 1970 annual report described Polaroid's participation in more than one hundred urban problem projects in 1970 and detailed its efforts in pollution control.

October 7, 1970   Robert Palmer, out of town on a business trip, was called by his office in Cambridge on October 6, 1970, with the message that two black Polaroid employees, Kenneth Williams and Caroline Hunter, were to hold a protest the next day at corporate headquarters. Palmer thought: "No problem. Williams has been protesting regularly" and did not ask what the protest was about, an omission he was to regret. In a few days Williams and Hunter became the Polaroid Revolutionary Workers Movement.

Caroline Hunter was a laboratory technician at Polaroid. She graduated from Xavier University in New Orleans in 1968, majoring in chemistry.

Williams began employment at Polaroid as a janitor in 1965 and was shifted to a quality control function that involved his taking pictures with Polaroid film. He was thought of as a capable photographer, and a brochure of his Polaroid photographs was distributed with the 1968 Polaroid annual report. Eventually, questions about control of his photographic assignments led to his being reassigned to community relations activities.

The sun-filled midday afternoon of October 7, 1970 witnessed Williams, public address system in hand, yelling in street language about Polaroid's enslavement of black South Africans. The invited press frantically recorded the event for the evening television news and morning newspapers, reporting that "hundreds protest Polaroid's racist South African oppression." The "hundreds" consisted of Hunter and Williams, the press, and hundreds of Polaroid employees who were enjoying the demonstration and eating brown bag lunches in the warm afternoon air.

Exhibit 2 shows the population of South Africa, estimates from *South Africa: Official Yearbook of the Republic of South Africa*. According to the same official publication, in 1969–1971, the national life expectancy for males was 59.3 for Asians, 51.2 for blacks, 48.8 for coloureds, and 64.5 for whites. Blacks are not citizens and do not vote. Whites are divided approximately 60 percent Afrikaner, 40 percent English.

Confronted essentially with integration or segregation, since 1948 the South African electorate has chosen the latter, known as *apartheid* or "separateness." Social segregation between whites and blacks means that separate facilities are provided for the different racial groups, intermarriage is prohibited, separate residential areas

EXHIBIT 2 South Africa population estimates

Year	Total		Asians		Blacks		Coloureds (mixed)		Whites	
	Total	% Incr.	Total	% Incr.	Total	% Incr.	Total	% Incr.	Total	% Incr.
1951	12,671,000		367,000		8,560,000		1,103,000		2,642,000	
1960	15,994,000	2.5	447,000	3.0	10,928,000	2.3	1,509,000	2.7	3,080,000	1.7
1970	21,794,000	3.3	630,000	2.9	15,340,000	3.4	2,051,000	3.1	3,773,000	2.1

are demarcated, population registration on a racial basis is compulsory, and urban blacks are being resettled in their traditional tribal areas.[1]

Compulsory population registration means one thing for whites and another for blacks. Instead of the simple, driver's-license-type card for whites, blacks carry a multiple-page book with an identification photograph, police records of the passbook holder and all relatives, plus rules as to where the holder is allowed to live, work, and to be.

Week One

The Polaroid Revolutionary Workers Movement's (PRWM) demands were three: (1) get out of South Africa, (2) state the company position on apartheid, and (3) turn over all South African profits to black liberation groups in South Africa.

That evening and all that week the lights burned late at Polaroid headquarters. The discussion encompassed (1) the discrepancy between the PRWM charges and Polaroid's corporate citizenship efforts, (2) outrage at the personal abuse of Dr. Land, and (3) methods to contain what the Polaroid executives in their now emotional state felt was "the enemy," the PRWM.

In trying to decide what to do, some asked, "What happens if we do nothing and say nothing?" The answer was that the interest of the press is finite, and General Motors and/or other corporations will be next.

Others said, "Let's find out what, if anything, we're doing in South Africa." And Dr. Land quietly said, "Well, the issues have been raised, we've got to deal with them in the open and honestly."

The morning after the protest, Robert Palmer issued a statement that the company condemned apartheid, that Polaroid would not negotiate in the streets, and that the company would determine its business interests, if any, in South Africa and report its findings.

That day and evening everyone at corporate headquarters was involved in determining what if anything Polaroid was doing in South Africa. No one knew. The company

---

[1] This prohibition on interracial marriage ended in June 1985.

policy was to set up subsidiary distributorships in all countries in which Polaroid had approximately a million dollars in sales, but there was no such subsidiary in South Africa. Marketing executives said there was no involvement in South Africa and "don't worry about it." Nevertheless, a marketing representative was sent on a plane to South Africa "to find out what we're doing" and to report back on any potential problems. Meanwhile, top executives from Polaroid had to accept staff responses ranging from "we're not sure" to the question "are we there?"

Two days later the marketing representative reported that "There was no problem. We aren't really in South Africa at all, since we have no direct sales and only sell our products through an independent distributor there."

Polaroid had no investment whatsoever in this distributor, Frank and Hirsch. Accordingly, Robert Palmer issued a second press release stating that Polaroid had no involvement, although an independent wholesale distributor handled Polaroid cameras and sunglasses.

In early October 1970, all eight thousand Polaroid employees received an internal "memorandum of legal matters" from Polaroid's legal department stating:

> *Polaroid has not sold its I.D. equipment to the government of South Africa for use in the apartheid program. . . . All sales of the I.D.-2 system to the South African distributor have been carefully traced to verify the use of which our equipment has been put. . . . [Our distributor] is unique in South Africa in its adoption of full equal employment practices for blacks.*

This incorrect and inaccurate memo was fuel to the smoldering fire of the Polaroid Revolutionary Workers Movement.

For example, Polaroid's assertion that Frank and Hirsch stood "unique in South Africa" for "full equal employment practices for blacks" assumed a wage policy illegal under South African law.

Helmut Hirsch commented to *The Star* (Johannesburg) on November 21, 1970: "I do not know where they could have obtained such a statement. We are governed by the laws of the country. Would they allow the existence of such a policy? It is not possible."

More importantly, Polaroid's equipment was being used in the passbook program. Any black who paid a slightly higher passbook fee was photographed using Polaroid equipment and received the passbook immediately. About 10 percent of the blacks chose the Polaroid photograph alternative.

Williams and the PRWM then issued a denunciation of Polaroid's "cover-up" and asserted that Polaroid equipment was being used in the oppressive passbook system. The passbook was an integral part of apartheid. The details of the passbook system were generally unknown to most Polaroid executives.

By this time, as the first week drew to a close, Polaroid felt it was in a "lose-lose" situation. Land announced that there was to be a formal review and that a committee should be established to examine the situation. Consensus, not executive action, was to be the desired outcome of the process.

In response to an announcement in the Polaroid internal newsletter, fifteen employees indicated their interest in serving on a committee to review the South Africa–Polaroid connection. The committee held its first meeting on October 28, 1970. Dr. Land told the members that other companies and the world were watching Polaroid.

The Trip

The ad hoc Polaroid committee reviewing Polaroid's connection to South Africa included blacks and whites, males and females, and many levels within the company ranging from corporate vice-president to hourly worker. It decided to send a four-person delegation (two blacks, two whites) to South Africa. This delegation was to report its findings and recommendations to the committee of fifteen.

The idea for the South Africa trip became a fully supported and desired event after one black hourly Polaroid worker told the other committee members, who were asking him what should be done: "Look: For two hundred years you've told me what I've needed and never asked me. Now you're asking me to do the same thing for those blacks, and I won't. We should go ask them."

Polaroid delegations actually made a number of trips ranging from several to ten days each to South Africa. For purposes of this case, no distinction will be made between events occurring on one or another trip. The perceptions and impressions of the delegations are given next. It will be necessary to identify some individuals only in general terms, as the delegation met unofficially, often in somewhat clandestine situations, with individuals whose identity will not be revealed. Bob Palmer commented on the mood of the delegation of four as they prepared to leave for South Africa:

> The group was apprehensive and had a lot of uncertainty about the trip, even though privately three of the four were leaning toward withdrawal of any Polaroid activities and/or products, with only one person undecided as to the best course of action. We were anxious about the glare of the klieg lights and the scrutiny of the media. We were also alarmed at the visa-issuing procedures within the South African embassy, which led to the impression that the embassy knew the names of the four delegates shortly after they were selected by the committee of fifteen at Polaroid's headquarters in Cambridge.
>
> This alarm continued after we landed in South Africa. Each day it became clearer that our "guides" had observing/reporting responsibilities as well as tourism duties within South Africa.
>
> The other immediate impression we got was of the scale of life, even during our first 24 hours of perfunctory meetings, chiefly with Helmut Hirsch, the director of our independent distributor, Frank and Hirsch. Helmut, who was a Jewish refugee from Hitler's Germany, lived, as did the majority of whites, in a style we think of as reserved for Hollywood — pools, polo fields, and multiple servants and bedrooms.

During the trip, the delegation never met officially with any representative of the South African government, although they made known their willingness to do so. They did meet with (1) a non-Afrikaner white observer of the Afrikaner phenomenon, (2) an Afrikaner business leader and other business leaders, (3) a banned black in the antiapartheid movement, and (4) Helmut Hirsch and employees (both black and white) of the distributorship. They also received, in both South Africa and the United States, letters from American businessmen, church leaders, and Polaroid shareholders.

Comments of a White, Non-Afrikaner

The historical roots of the Afrikaner and the Afrikaner version of Calvinism are as critical to your understanding of the Afrikaner or Boer as is the legend of the cowboy and the Hollywood version of John Wayne and Burt Reynolds to an understanding of the American trucker.

First, the Afrikaners, descendants of the Dutch settlers who came to South Africa in 1652, determined to be masters of their own fate and left the now English-dominated Capetown and coastal cities during the Great Trek beginning in 1836. They suffered massacre by the Zulus and, later, continued domination by the expansionary British, led by Cecil Rhodes.

One tactic protected the Afrikaner on the Trek, the laager *or circle of wagons. The worst thing an Afrikaner could do would be to leave the circle.*

Second, the Calvinism of the South Africa Dutch Reformed Church stresses Calvin's notion of an "elect," along with fundamentalism. Thus, in the Afrikaner view, the Afrikaner is God's elite who has a constant, unchanging, and comprehensive guide to life in the Bible. Any turning away from the Afrikaner way, any hint of compromise or negotiation, would be not only leaving the circle of wagons unguarded and unprotected, but would be turning away from God. How can the Right compromise with the Wrong? The Volk, *the Afrikaner people, cannot do wrong and cannot compromise the right.*

Finally, the Afrikaners, although defeated by the English in the Boer War of 1899–1902, regained political control of the Union of South Africa because of their larger numbers, organization, and shared belief in their own destiny to rule South Africa. Immediately after World War II, during which time the Afrikaner sympathized with Germany, the Afrikaner's power, through the parliamentary control of the Boer Nationalist Party, was totally solidified.

The British, though with overwhelming control of industry, particularly mining, were nonetheless politically ineffectual against the Afrikaner, who, though only a supervisor in the English mine — or, more likely, a shopkeeper — was nevertheless politically all powerful.

The all-powerful Afrikaner thus implemented apartheid, the complete separation of the races, especially between 1948 and 1954. The swart gevaar *or black menace was pushed away, as the Afrikaner tried to resettle blacks onto "homelands" in much the same way as you Yanks tried to force the redman onto reservations. About 15 percent of the land is now assigned to the blacks, 75 percent of the population.*

The Afrikaner, by the way, feels that Americans should be sympathetic to apartheid, since it is not all that different from your own segregation policies of a few years ago.

In any event, the Afrikaner sees himself pushing back the blacks just as he did during the Great Trek. The economic motive is just as strong, since the Afrikaner is caught beneath the economic, but not political, dominance of the English. The Afrikaner must protect himself from being replaced by the obviously less-expensive black laborer. Thus the Afrikaner has created a larger bureaucracy and military structure where he can be employed. The Afrikaner has also ensured himself of supervisory positions by laws prohibiting blacks from any supervisory work or training.

Blacks' education is limited, but exists since the whites — English and Afrikaner alike — need the cheap labor and minimal literacy. Total separation of races is economically impossible, but only black males can come into the working areas, and only with the passbook. They return to their families in the ''homelands'' perhaps one month a year.

The black's mobility is totally restricted by means of the passbook, which says what areas, if any, the holder is allowed in, at what hours, and so on, and contains details of all arrests of the holder or of the holder's relatives.

''Waar's jou' pass', jong?'' ''Where's your pass, boy?'' This phrase is the phrase of the control system, and results in 160,000 to 175,000 arrests per year, or about one black every three minutes on the average.

Modern apartheid is based on fear. This fear is substantiated by some black leaders' belief that real change will only occur when minority exploitation is replaced by majority rule.

Comments of an Afrikaner Businessman

America must protect itself. You will be under increasing pressure from Japanese and other competition. You cannot afford to antagonize host country governments. You cannot afford to withdraw from a tremendous market, for your competition will just take your place.

And, on the humanitarian side, the blacks will only suffer by any anti–South Africa acts. Under apartheid we are trying to raise all living standards. Who knows what will happen 50 years from now when everyone here enjoys higher standards of living. But it will take time. You must remember that in your history you exterminated the indigenous populace. We are trying to raise them up, along with the Boer and all in South Africa.

Most assuredly, growth will lead to social change. As Anglo-American's Oppenheimer — by the way, an opposition Progressive Party member — often says, ''Economic growth won't destroy apartheid, but will create the social, cultural, political, and industrial pressures for making changes.'' And this change will be evolutionary, not revolutionary.

Comments of a Black Actively Resisting Apartheid

If apartheid continues, we said in the 1950s, the situation will escalate to disastrous consequences. There is no alternative to the Freedom Charter of 1955, endorsing a nonracial democratic society.

Today we say disinvestment and withdrawal will not bring escalation. Escalation is taking place now, and disinvestment will end it in the longer term by bringing matters to a head. By not withdrawing, you justify the present system and you support apartheid.

The slave will not suffer. The slave will sacrifice.

Comments of Helmut Hirsch. In discussing the possibility of Polaroid trying to make a contribution toward more equality, or less inequality, such as black training programs within the Frank and Hirsch distributorship, Mr. Hirsch said: "If you want to do it, please issue me an order and then I can justify my action by saying, 'Polaroid made me do it.' I have over one hundred products that I distribute, but Polaroid is important to me. It means 15 percent of my business."

GENERAL SUMMARY OF BLACK VIEWS

The group met with about 120 blacks. There were three things generally consistent at each of those 120 meetings.

First, as to location, no black would speak freely and openly if any other person were present, including a family member such as a brother or sister. The only free discussions were held walking through the open streets with the black and the Polaroid employee talking rapidly in low voices.

Second, the blacks assured Polaroid that "revolution is our decision, not yours."

Finally, there was general agreement that the company could make some advances for blacks in South Africa working within Frank & Hirsch. Wage disparities could be decreased between blacks and whites, and blacks could be trained for positions of more responsibility. A black department could be created so that it could have a black supervisor. (It was illegal for blacks to supervise whites.) Medical help could be made available within the company. Further, direct grants might be made to black education programs.

Two Zulu Chiefs   The late Zulu chief Albert Lutuli said: "The economic boycott of South Africa will entail undoubted hardship for Africans. We do not doubt that. But if it is a method which shortens the day of blood, the suffering to us will be a price we are willing to pay."

The current Zulu chief Gatsha Buthelezi argued that:

> *Those who advocate trade sanctions and economic withdrawal to help my people and punish the whites in South Africa may be killing us with kindness. What we need is not disengagement, but full foreign participation in South Africa's overall economic development to create more jobs, higher wages, and better training opportunities. I am no apologist for apartheid, but a realist who knows that a job may make the difference between living and starving for many black families in South Africa.*

Outside Experts   Bob Palmer wrote about his experience with outside advice during this fact-finding period:

> *While there seems to be almost no interest on the part of employees, I can't believe the number of calls from outside people. I've heard from every possible viewpoint, all conflicting and all assuring me that they are objective experts.*
>
> *The largest group of calls are from banned, black South Africans who urge total withdrawal. Clearly the downfall of the present government is the only way they can ever go back to their native land.*
>
> *Others urge withdrawal "as the only moral thing to do," but can't explain the morality of Polaroid condemning a foreign government's policy.*
>
> *All these "experts" have convinced me that I don't as yet have enough information to understand what this is really about.*

Excerpts from comments by two "experts" follow.

"Expert One"

Can you be in South Africa and still have a soul? Does a company have a soul? Can a company have a moral obligation?

Ultimately, the question will be answered based upon your conclusion about the role of a non–South African company. Can such an outside company help to create real progress, or is the outside company a partner, albeit an unwilling partner, in a system that fosters apartheid? Is doing nothing actually siding with the status quo? Is external investment a significant factor in the maintenance of apartheid?

"Expert Two"

You have to be very careful about the facts. For example, some quote public opinion surveys among the blacks, but don't tell you that it is illegal in South Africa under security laws for anyone to publicly advocate divestment or disinvestment.

But we know some facts. These include economic facts such as:

1. Total foreign investment is dominated by Britain, which accounts for 60 percent of South African foreign investment. Twenty-five percent of South Africa's top one hundred companies are British. Britain dominates the mining industry, and invests 10 percent of its overseas investments in South Africa.

2. American companies control numerically few, but strategically significant, industries, including automobiles and trucks (about 50 percent American-controlled, now converting to a 65 percent local-products government regulation), energy (oil), and computers.

3. About half of Fortune's 500 companies have South African offices, and others are involved through licenses and distributors. On the average, South Africa represents one percent (sales) and more than one percent in profits.

4. Between 1946 and 1955, average annual foreign investment was £70,000,000, and between 1956 and 1969, £71,500,000. Overseas capital, 23 percent of total capital investment in the post–World War II period, is now about 11 percent. South African gross domestic product is about £7,000,000,000, currently increasing at about 9 percent per year.

5. The white-to-black wage ratio in 1966 in mining was 17.6 to 1, in manufacturing 5.1 to 1. In 1971 the ratio was 20.3 in mining and 5.7 in manufacturing.

6. Poverty datum line (PDL) figures from the University of Port Elizabeth are R90.00 for a family of six in Johannesburg, with a minimum effective level (MEL) of PDL + 50 percent. Polaroid's distributor's average salaries are R84 for blacks. Frank and Hirsch's minimum wage in Soweto, the South African township outside of Johannesburg where the distributorship was located, was below the Soweto PDL. Frank and Hirsch employs 155 Africans and their sunglass manufacturing subsidiary another 14.

7. American companies employ 100,000 nonwhites. Polaroid's Tom Wyman described the company's acts as "a teaspoon in the ocean."

8. South Africa has 50 percent of the world's known gold; 75 percent of platinum, chrome and vanadium; 20 percent of industrial diamonds; 78 percent of all manganese; and 18 percent of the Western World's uranium.

The Church Church leaders were unanimous in urging withdrawal on moral grounds. During the fall and winter Bob Palmer received many phone calls and letters urging withdrawal.

The Church Ecumenical Committee which visited South Africa in 1971 stated:

Most of us believe that American corporations should totally disengage from southern Africa; that the presence of American corporations in which we are shareholders undergirds the system of racism, colonialism, and apartheid which prevails in southern Africa. . . . Even progressive employment on the part of American companies will not bring the basic changes in society that we support because of our Christian commitment to freedom, justice, and self-determination.

In a conversation with one church leader, Bob Palmer was informed that the churchman would be leading a delegation to the April 1971 stockholders meeting. The churchman requested that Bob send him all information relating to Polaroid's history and investments in South Africa. Bob replied:

We are an $800 million institution that has been in South Africa since 1938. You are a $2 billion institution, the Anglican church, that has been in South Africa for centuries. Would you please send me information about your history and investments in South Africa, and maybe we can learn something from each other.

The churchman hung up.

EXHIBIT 3
PRWM circular

UNWANTED

EDWIN LAND, Pres. & Chair., Polaroid Corp.

Crimes: Complicity in apartheid (the South African racist system which means murder, starvation, and imprisonment of blacks); complicity in grand larceny — the theft of South Africa from its people; espionage; unfair labor practices.

Polaroid's ID-2 system, which produces instant identification cards with photographs, is used in the manufacture of pass books which must be carried by South African blacks. The pass books are a key tool of control for the white minority in South Africa: with the pass book system the blacks may be kept from entering the 87% of all South African land reserved for whites, prevented from holding any kind of meetings, and hounded into submission.

Land has not only ignored the demands of the Polaroid Workers Revolutionary Movement that Polaroid disengage from doing business in South Africa, but has fired PWRM leaders.

Land is not a gangster limited to one branch of crime. As the head of the Intelligence Committee of the Foreign Intelligence Advisory Board under Kennedy, Land is credited with developing the cameras for the CIA's U-2 spy planes.

THIS MAN HAS BEEN CHOSEN ONE OF BOSTON'S TEN LEAST WANTED MEN. THESE ANNOUNCEMENTS WILL BE PUBLISHED AND THE LIST EXPANDED AND REVISED FROM TIME TO TIME IN A CONTINUING EFFORT TO WARN PEOPLE AGAINST THE DANGEROUS CRIMINALS IN OUR MIDST.

**Other
Comments**

As part of fact-finding, Bob Palmer reviewed comments from American business. The commentary from American business was mixed. Some firms were noncommital. Most asked how to handle black employee pressure. A few were highly critical of Polaroid's meddling in "a high-stake poker game with ten-cent chips."

Bob also reviewed material being distributed by the PRWM. (See Exhibits 3 and 4.)

Ken Williams had resigned from Polaroid, spilling a red substance on the desk of the Polaroid receptionist at corporate headquarters and announcing "I will no longer accept blood money." Caroline Hunter was warned several times about issuing proboycott statements; she was finally dismissed in early 1971. Williams and Hunter were later to testify before a United Nations subcommittee about South Africa and foreign business investment.

EXHIBIT 4
PRWM press release

Polaroid Workers Revolutionary Movement

November 2, 1970

Brothers and Sisters:

The Polaroid Revolutionary Workers Movement is a group of black workers in Cambridge, Massachusetts, who have come together to act and protest against the sale of Polaroid products in South Africa.

We see the South African apartheid system as the symbol of the many "inhumanities" in the United States. We cannot begin to deal with racism in Polaroid or in the U.S. until Polaroid and the U.S. cease to uphold and support apartheid. Black people in South Africa are enslaved and dehumanized in order to insure the security of apartheid and the capitalists' margin of profit. The United States and its corporate society have made explicit its intentions of profits at any human expense.

We demand that we no longer be used as tools to enslave our brothers and to insure corporate profits.

On October 8, the Movement presented Polaroid Corp. with the following demands:

1. That Polaroid announce a policy of complete disengagement from South Africa. We believe that all American companies doing business there reinforce that racist system.
2. That Polaroid announce its position on apartheid publically, in the U.S. and South Africa.
3. That Polaroid contribute profits earned in South Africa to the recognized African liberation movements.

Polaroid has refused to meet with the PRWM or recognize the demands.

On October 27, the PRWM called for a worldwide boycott of Polaroid products by all right-on thinking people until Polaroid discontinues all sales in South Africa. We are building a coalition of right-on thinking people to press the demands that Polaroid and all American business discontinue support of the South African racist government.

IMMEDIATE ACTION AND YOUR SUPPORT IS NECESSARY. POWER TO THE PEOPLE.

THE DECISION

It was now time to make a recommendation. What should Polaroid do about the PRWM and Polaroid's activities in South Africa? How should the decision be announced and implemented? What reaction might Polaroid expect? What reaction might the committee expect from Polaroid? Bob Palmer thought: "The facts are easy to discern. It's the truth that is elusive."

THE AMERICAN EXPRESS COMPANY

American Express company executives, meeting in their new fifty-one-story headquarters in the financial district of lower Manhattan, look to the future with a certain optimism. As the chairman and CEO, James D. Robinson, III, put it, "We are extremely active in two of the world's greatest growth industries: financial services and tourism."[1] A trusted name since 1850, AMEXCO looks to the second half of the eighties and into the nineties with a corporate philosophy and values anchored in entrepreneurship, quality, integrity, and service. A brief history of the company appears in Appendix A.

Flushed with the apparent success of its major acquisitions, AMEXCO's total assets had tripled from 1982 to nearly $62 billion by the end of 1984. This international financial supermarket (Exhibit 1) employs 77,000 people in more than 2,000 offices spread throughout 131 countries. Much of its incredible growth has occurred in only 3 years, "faster than expected because of profound changes in insurance, banking and securities wrought by the interplay of higher interest rates, technology and deregulation."[2]

During this period of expansion, AMEXCO revenues doubled to almost $13 billion with net income increasing from $466 million to $610 million (Exhibit 2). Through 1982 AMEXCO enjoyed its thirty-fifth consecutive year of increased earnings. This ended in 1983 with an 11 percent decrease in net income primarily attributed to problems at Fireman's Fund. By the end of 1984, AMEXCO showed respectable growth in net income of 18 percent.

The competition has a very healthy respect for the strength of AMEXCO. Dee Hock, former managing director and CEO of VISA International, commenting on

---

[1] "American Express: Financial Powerhouse," *Dun's Business Month*, December 1983, p. 39.

[2] Arlene Hershman, "The Supercompanies Emerge," *Dun's Business Month*, April 1983, p. 44.

© William D. Wilsted. Financial and organizational data are taken from *American Express Company 1984 Annual Report* unless otherwise noted. Reprinted by permission.

EXHIBIT 1 The American Express Company (December 1984)

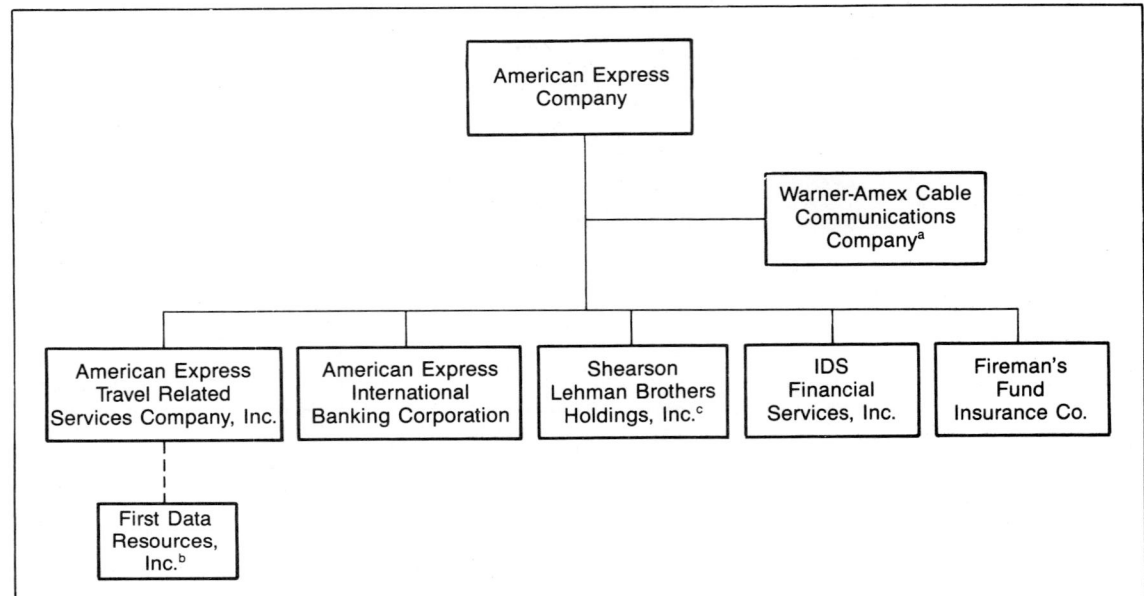

Source: Constructed from information contained in American Express Company 1984 Annual Report.
^a AMEXCO owns 50 percent.
^b TRS owns 75 percent of capital stock of the largest third-party data processor of debit and credit cards in the United States.
^c Includes fourteen major subsidiaries of which Shearson Lehman Brothers, Inc. is the principal.

combat with AMEXCO, said:

> *They [AMEX] are rough, tough, smart competitors with tons of money. There is very little they will not do to achieve their objectives. The advantage of American Express is that James Robinson can say, "To the left, march" and they do. I couldn't think of doing that. Each of our institutions [members] is totally independent.*[3]

George Ball, president and CEO of Prudential-Bache Securities Inc., was quoted in April 1984 as saying, "Four years ago [AMEX] was a plastic card company, but with the addition of Lehman, AMEX is a fully fleshed-out financial services confederation of the type that will be dominant in tomorrow's marketplace."[4] Herbert E. Goodfriend, an analyst with Prudential-Bache, calls American Express "unquestionably the premier company in the financial services industry."[5]

The financial services supermarket is considered to operate in one or more of five major businesses. They include banking, credit cards, insurance, real estate,

[3] Leonard A. Schlesinger, Robert G. Eccles, John J. Gararro, *Managing Behavior in Organizations* (New York: McGraw-Hill, 1983), p. 479.

[4] "The Golden Plan of American Express," *Business Week,* April 30, 1984, p. 118.

[5] "American Express: Financial Powerhouse," p. 38.

EXHIBIT 2 Consolidated summary of selected financial data

	1984	1983	1982	1981	1980
Operating results					
Revenues	$12,895	$ 9,770	$ 8,093	$ 7,291	$ 6,426
Percent increase in revenues	*32%*	*21%*	*11%*	*13%*	*26%*
Expenses	12,159	9,253	7,339	6,586	5,830
Income taxes	126	2	173	181	130
Net income	610	515	581	524	466
Percent increase (decrease) in net income	*18%*	*(11)%*	*11%*	*12%*	*23%*
Assets and liabilities					
Time deposits	$ 5,470	$ 4,071	$ 2,127	$ 1,784	$ 1,120
Investment securities					
Carried at cost	13,449	12,766	7,163	6,446	6,026
Carried at lower of aggregate cost or					
market	315	211	81	148	166
Carried at market	8,566	1,709	948	917	1,235
Accounts receivable and accrued interest,					
net	14,802	11,497	9,204	8,191	6,825
Loans and discounts, net	7,089	6,642	4,379	3,929	3,811
Total assets	61,848	43,981	28,311	25,252	22,731
Customers' deposits and credit balances	13,262	12,511	6,810	6,218	5,818
Travelers checks outstanding	2,454	2,362	2,177	2,468	2,542
Insurance and annuity reserves	8,831	7,667	4,323	4,110	3,856
Long-term debt	3,839	2,643	1,798	1,293	1,293
Shareholders' equity	4,607	4,043	3,039	2,661	2,430
Common share statistics					
Net income per share	$ 2.79	$ 2.53	$ 3.02	$ 2.79	$ 2.59
Cash dividends declared per share	$ 1.28	$ 1.26	$ 1.125	$ 1.025	$ 1.00
Average number of shares outstanding	217	203	192	188	180
Shares outstanding at year-end	217	213	191	188	185
Number of shareholders of record	*51,211*	*45,753*	*36,580*	*36,611*	*34,735*
Other statistics					
Number of employees at year-end					
United States	*59,420*	*53,740*	*48,533*	*43,315*	*39,475*
Outside United States	*17,027*	*16,716*	*15,472*	*14,994*	*15,556*
Total	*76,447*	*70,456*	*64,005*	*58,309*	*55,031*
Number of offices at year-end					
American Express offices worldwide	*1,472*	*1,356*	*1,160*	*1,066*	*1,046*
Representative offices	*810*	*797*	*760*	*782*	*782*
Total	*2,282*	*2,153*	*1,920*	*1,848*	*1,828*

Note: Data in millions, except per share amounts and where italicized.
Note: Operating results for the year ended December 31, 1983 do not include the effect of the acquisition of Investors Diversified Services, Inc., accounted for as a purchase as of December 31, 1983. Where applicable, amounts and percentages for 1984 include the effect of the acquisition of Lehman Brothers Kuhn Loeb Holding Co., Inc., accounted for as a purchase as of May 11, 1984.
Source: American Express Co. 1984 Annual Report.

EXHIBIT 3 The six financial-services leaders

	Banking	Credit cards	Insurance	Real estate	Securities
American Express Co. Assets: $30 billion Revenue: $8.1 billion Net income: $581 million	—	(1)	(2)	(3)	(1)
BankAmerica Corp. Assets: $122.5 billion Revenue: $4 billion Net income: $451 million	(1)	(1)	(3)	(1)	(2)
Citicorp Assets: $130 billion Revenue: $5.2 billion Net income: $723 million	(1)	(1)	(3)	(1)	—
Merrill Lynch & Co. Assets: $20.7 billion Revenue: $5 billion Net income: $309 million	—	(3)	(2)	(2)	(1)
Prudential Insurance Co. of America Assets: $76.5 billion Revenue: $18.5 billion Net income: $2.13 billion	—	(3)	(1)	(2)	(1)
Sears, Roebuck & Co. Assets: $36 billion Revenue: $30 billion Net income: $861 million	(2)	(1)	(2)	(2)	(1)

(1) = Major factor in this industry.
(2) = Medium-sized factor in this industry.
(3) = Small factor in this industry.
Source: "The Supercompanies Emerge," *Dun's Business Month*, April 1983, p. 44.

and securities. AMEXCO is looking for ways to enter the domestic U.S. banking business; Citicorp wants to enter the securities business. Sears, Roebuck, and Co. and Bank America are both involved in all five major businesses. Prudential-Bache and Merrill Lynch, the other two principal financial supermarkets, like AMEXCO, lack domestic banking operations.[6] AMEXCO currently outstrips all the others in the travel-related services industry. Exhibit 3 shows six companies that have major positions in a number of critical financial-services businesses (at end of 1982).

According to a 1984 survey conducted by the *American Banker,* people rate American Express products and services higher than those of any other top financial

[6] "The Supercompanies Emerge," p. 45.

services firm in the United States. The same survey indicates that the American Express name is best known among consumers.[7]

AMEXCO'S MAJOR COMPANIES

Assembled under the American Express corporate roof are five major companies. They include American Express Travel Related Services Company, Inc. (TRS), American Express International Banking Corporation (AEIBC), Shearson Lehman Brothers, Inc. (SLAX), IDS Financial Services Inc. (IDS), and Fireman's Fund Insurance Companies (FF). Additionally, AMEXCO owns 50 percent of Warner AMEX Cable Communications. Appendix B presents 1982–1984 financial data by service category. Appendix C presents 1983–1984 financial data by subsidiary. Following is a discussion of each of these companies.

American Express Travel Related Services Company

Perhaps the oldest name in travel is TRS, the flagship organization of AMEXCO. The company was founded in 1850 and became a separate company under the AMEXCO banner in 1983. Annual growth in revenues exceeded 18 percent from 1982 to 1984. TRS is in the process of modernizing and is emerging as the most customer-responsive travel and credit card service company in the world with great profit potential.

TRS has grown and developed a great deal since its early days as a small package and funds freight company. Currently, TRS is best known for its worldwide network of travel offices, charge card, and traveler's cheques (without which you do not leave home). In addition, TRS offers direct mail merchandise services, publishing (*Travel and Leisure* and *Food and Wine*), and data processing services. TRS is also moving into communications, providing AMEX card members access to MCI. This is primarily a billing service providing MCI long-distance dialing through what AMEXCO calls "Expressphone."

In 1985, TRS launched "Project Hometown America" which raises money for local communities by contributions from American Express Card purchases, AMEX traveler's cheques, purchases of travel packages, and new card applications. TRS continues to utilize extensive advertising which, among other things, features tie-ins with major hotels, resorts, car-rental companies, and Eastern and United Airlines.

TRS operates 1,200 offices in more than 131 countries. Overseas travel has been popular due to the strength of the American dollar and TRS has capitalized on this opportunity. In 1984 and early 1985, TRS acquired new travel companies in Pittsburgh, Denver, and thirty-eight locations in the United Kingdom.

While the proliferation of plastic money and automatic teller machines (ATM) have eaten into the traveler's cheque market, AMEXCO still sold $15.1 billion in 1984, an increase of 9.1 percent over 1983. The average outstanding traveler's

---

[7] *American Express Company 1985 Annual Report*, p. 4.

cheque's volume in 1983 was $2.6 billion, up 8.3 percent. It is on these outstanding cheques, or "float," that TRS makes its profit, which in 1982 was $76 million before taxes. In 1962 the traveler's cheque float accounted for 80 percent of AMEXCO's total income. Twenty years later, it was responsible for only 11 percent of the total income. (Credit cards accounted for 24 percent of income; Fireman's Fund, 36 percent; and Shearson, 18 percent in 1982.) It is the lessons learned from managing the traveler's cheque float that make AMEXCO's management of cash balances anywhere within the corporation masterful.[8]

By the end of 1984 there were more than 20 million American Express Cards in force throughout the world, an increase of 17 percent over 1983. Credit card charge volume grew 24 percent to $47.6 billion during the same time. One out of every four cardholders lives overseas and the card is issued in twenty-eight currencies. In 1984, 125 mainland Chinese establishments accepted the card compared to 14 in 1983.

In August 1984, the platinum card ($250 fee, by invitation only) was offered in addition to the green card (offered since 1958) and the gold card (first offered in 1981). In 1984, AMEXCO added major retailers such as the May Company and the J. C. Penney Company as establishments that accept the American Express Card. TRS also acquired Health Carecard, Inc., a company whose product combines medical record keeping with payment capabilities.

The American Express Card differs from other plastic cards in distinct ways. It must be paid in full monthly (unless special arrangements have been made in advance) and the annual fee is more than other cards. (In 1985 the green card fee increased by 30 percent to $45.) These facts, coupled with economies of scale in billing and extensive experience in managing moving cash balances, make the American Express Card unique and highly profitable.

Another segment of TRS is direct marketing. When American Express began in 1974 to include product inserts in its 5 million monthly bills, it did not envision a merchandise services division of $185 million in sales just 10 years later. The growth of TRS's direct mail business is largely the result of its sophisticated use of customer segmentation based on the exact purpose for which each cardholder uses the card. Particular product mailings are targeted with precision to those customer groups with the greatest potential buying interest in that product. The merchandise services division has six target customer segments:

The frequent traveler, to whom it sells products and services to make business and travel more enjoyable

The upscale male consumer, to whom it sells state-of-the-art electronics for home entertainment and personal productivity

The upscale female consumer, to whom it sells products related to home design and household invention

[8] Priscilla S. Meyer, "Cheques and Balances," *Forbes,* March 14, 1983, p. 50.

Business executives of small- to medium-sized companies, to whom it sells products for the office that will increase chances for success

Portions of each of the above, to whom it offers new products on a test basis

Portions of each of the first four groups, to whom it offers various services, including magazine subscriptions at discounted prices[9]

A key to the merchandise services division's success is its strategy of offering exclusive merchandise. Whenever possible, TRS strives to be the sole source of the merchandise it offers. More than 90 percent of the noncatalog merchandise offered is exclusive. TRS seeks manufacturers who will modify certain aspects of a product just for AMEXCO. As a result, TRS sold 18,000 IBM electric typewriters in 1983 and 42,000 Gucci watches in 1982 and 1983.[10]

The strengths that TRS has identified as its basis for its marketing approach are:

The prestige attached to owning an American Express card

The excellent customer service provided by AMEXCO

A vast, affluent cardmember customer base (over 11 million in the United States)

AMEXCO's orientation toward business

AMEXCO's adeptness at packaging goods and services

A very strong overall quality image

Strong information processing skills[11]

The goals of the merchandise services division are: to continue to use the strong name recognition of American Express to generate sales to new customers; to provide the best service available in direct merchandising, with new, quality products tailored to the customers' needs; and to go outside the AMEXCO cardmember base to allow customers to pay for merchandise by Visa, MasterCard, or other credit cards.[12]

In publishing, TRS saw new highs in both ad pages and revenues in 1984. With almost a million paid subscribers, *Travel and Leisure* saw an increase of 23 percent in advertising revenues over 1983. *Food and Wine,* with 600,000 paid subscribers, saw an 18 percent increase in advertising revenues over 1983.

Since 1984, TRS has owned 75 percent of the capital stock of First Data Resources, Inc. This data processing company is the largest third-party processor of debit and credit cards in the United States. It is this acquisition that gives AMEXCO its economies of scale in processing transactions.

[9] Larry Jaffee, "AMEX Targets Mailings Precisely to List Segments," *Direct Marketing,* May 1984, p. 78.

[10] Ibid., p. 79.

[11] Ibid., p. 78.

[12] Ibid., p. 86.

Historically TRS has exhibited a great deal of support for the arts. From 1979 through 1984 TRS sponsored fifty projects, in one hundred cities, over five continents, to bring the arts closer to the people (at a cost of $20 million in 1984).[13] In AMEXCO's opinion, it has been worth the investment. AMEXCO has gained recognition within these communities and increased opportunities to attract potential customers and financial institutions. The "Project Hometown America" mentioned earlier is an extension of AMEXCO's charitable, goodwill efforts, while it offers potential tax advantages.

American Express International Banking Corporation

Growing out of a need to provide the travel-hungry American tourist financial services abroad after World War I, AEIBC was founded in 1919 as the American Express Company, Incorporated. In 1968, the name was changed to American Express International Banking Corporation.

By 1980 AMEXCO was itching to get rid of its overseas bank, AEIBC. The bank, under the direction of Richard Bliss, had been attempting to establish itself as a big investment banking concern in London. In 1981 Robert F. Smith, formerly AMEXCO's treasurer, took over as vice-chairman of the bank. Smith quickly changed the direction of the bank by slashing its operating costs and paring down its attempt to offer every service imaginable. The bank began to focus on trade finance and private banking for wealthy individual clients. AEIBC evolved into a deal-making organization with trade-related transactions involving export credit guarantees from Western governments.

The big improvement in AEIBC performance through 1983 was clearly a result of sheer cost-cutting. Total operating expenses fell from 63 percent of net financial revenue in 1981 to 52 percent in 1983. Also figuring prominently in the improvement was the acquisition of the Trade Development Bank (TDB) in Switzerland in March 1983. At $800 million in shareholders' equity, the combined bank has more than twice the equity of the old AEIBC. That, in turn, reduced AEIBC's Latin American debt from four times equity to a more manageable, yet still concerning, two times equity.[14]

To acquire the TDB, AMEXCO paid more than 50 percent over the book value of TDB stock. Many believe that AMEXCO paid the premium price to obtain the services of Edmond J. Safra, Lebanese-born banking genius and owner of TDB.[15] Safra needed U.S. government approval to become CEO of AEIBC (a condition of sale). Although the sale was made in January 1983, Safra did not set foot in AMEXCO's corporate offices in New York throughout the year. While waiting for U.S. approval, AMEXCO top executives visited and called Safra frequently (he has controlling interest in other U.S. banks) at his TDB office in Geneva to get

---

[13] Susan Bloom, "Beauty and the Bottom Line," *Business Quarterly*, Fall 1984, p. 86.

[14] "AMEX's Bank: A Wallflower Suddenly Blossoms," *Business Week*, January 9, 1984, p. 101.

[15] Gwen Kinkead, "The Mystery Man American Express Is Banking On," *Fortune*, December 12, 1983, p. 142.

the benefit of his advice and banking instincts.[16] Safra continued running TDB and in 1984 was elected to AMEXCO's board of directors.

As a result of these moves, the AEIBC was a welcome member of the AMEXCO family in early 1984. The former wallflower is a highly profitable bank with $13 billion in assets.[17] The AMEXCO hierarchy sees a great potential for marketing Shearson/American Express Inc. services through the AEIBC. 1984 was a year of record profits for AEIBC, even though it was a year that will be remembered as one of the most difficult in international banking. Net income in 1984 increased 15 percent to a record $156 million after a 126 percent increase to $136 million from 1982 to 1983.

Today, with 82 offices in 39 countries, AEIBC includes international private banking, trade financing operations, correspondent banking (more than 2,000 active correspondent bank relationships worldwide), treasury and foreign exchange services, equipment financing (American Express Leasing Corporation), and military banking for the U.S. Armed Forces overseas.

Citicorp has been a pioneer among the major financial supermarkets in pushing for changes in the law that would permit it, a leader in domestic banking, into the insurance field.[18] Citicorp has made inroads in this regard in South Dakota. If Citicorp is successful on a national basis, the door would be open for AMEXCO, if they so choose, to move into the domestic banking industry either as a separate AMEXCO company or as a division of AEIBC.

Fireman's Fund Insurance Company

Since 1863, when it was founded in San Francisco, Fireman's Fund Insurance Company has grown to be a leading provider of insurance protection for individuals, groups, businesses, and institutions, offering a broad range of property, liability, life, accident, and health insurance. Acquired by AMEXCO in 1968, FF products are offered through more than 10,000 independent agents and brokers throughout the United States.

In 1979 and 1980 the property and casualty industry experienced serious trouble due to price-cutting on many types of policies. In 1981, under the leadership of Fireman's Fund CEO Myron Dubain, FF cut a deal with the Insurance Company of North America to swap certain casualty policies. The swap allowed both companies to discount the loss reserves required on their newly acquired policies, without disclosing a change in accounting practices on their financial statements or to their respective boards of directors. This accounting sleight-of-hand increased FF's reported pretax profits by $66 million in 1981–1982, but resulted in a negative cash flow due to an additional $30 million tax bill[19] (Exhibit 4).

In 1982, Edwin F. Cutler became FF's CEO with guidance from AMEXCO to

---

[16] Ibid.

[17] "AMEX's Bank: A Wallflower Suddenly Blossoms," p. 101.

[18] Carol J. Loomis, "Fire in the Belly at American Express," *Fortune*, November 28, 1983, p. 87.

[19] Carol J. Loomis, "How Fireman's Fund Stoked Its Profits," *Fortune*, November 28, 1983, pp. 99–104.

EXHIBIT 4
Fireman's Fund net income

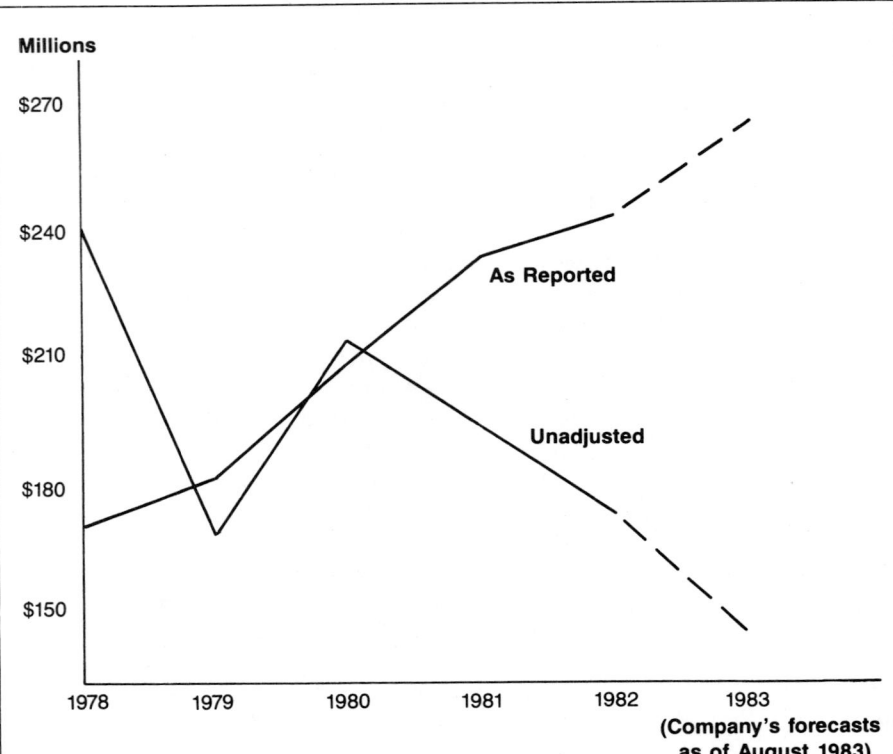

The dollar gap between "reported net income" and "unadjusted net income" at Fireman's Fund in the 1978-83 period was recapped in an August 1983 memo from Edwin F. Cutler, then chairman of the American Express subsidiary, to his boss, James D. Robinson III, chairman of the parent. Unadjusted profits were those earned on the subsidiary's basic insurance business, which as time went on felt increasing cyclical pressure. But "special items" added to or subtracted from those profits allowed Fireman's Fund to report figures that showed the smooth uptrend American Express loves to see. Cutler's memo forecast a further gain for reported profits in 1983. But a subsequent spike in claim costs and a $230-million addition to reserves blitzed 1983 profits. Reported net income for 1983 was $30 million; unadjusted net income was not announced.

Source: "The Earnings Magic at American Express," *Fortune,* June 25, 1984, p. 58.

further increase profits. From January to September 1983, FF dropped its premium prices and generated a 13 percent increase in written premiums while the insurance industry average was only about 4 percent.[20]

In the third quarter of 1983, a sharp rise in claims forced FF to add $10 million

[20] Carol J. Loomis, "How Fireman's Fund Singed American Express," *Fortune,* January 9, 1984, p. 80.

to its loss reserves, which resulted in a fourth-quarter after-tax net loss of $10 million.[21]

A *Fortune* article in November 1983 exposed the paper profits of 1981–1982 and seriously undermined the credibility of FF's and AMEXCO's financial statements.[22]

In December 1983 Cutler was removed as CEO and replaced by acquisition and financial wizard Sanford Weill, an executive with no prior insurance experience. FF simultaneously announced a reduction in its work force of 14,000 by more than 10 percent through retirement and attrition in an effort to reduce costs.

In December 1983, AMEXCO's board of directors added $230 million to FF's loss reserves which contributed to a drop in AMEXCO earnings from $700 million to $520 million for 1983. A public announcement by AMEXCO on December 12, 1983 regarding FF's financial problems caused a single-day drop in AMEXCO stock from $32 to $29 per share.[23] FF's performance, or lack thereof, was the principal reason why AMEXCO had its first downturn in earnings in 36 years.

In the first quarter of 1984, Sandy Weill cut 1,200 employees from the payroll, estimating a $40–50 million annual saving. Weill announced a three-step strategy to become the low-cost producer in the industry: lay-offs and cost cutting, combined with increased efficiencies in decision making due to more autonomy at lower levels; top management compensation tied to performance; and a revamping of FF's data processing system.[24]

The first quarter of 1984 saw a modest $10 million profit, but in the second quarter 1985 FF reported a quarterly loss of $71.7 million on revenues of $1 billion. Once again AMEXCO felt compelled to add $187 million to FF's loss reserves.[25]

By July 1985, Sandy Weill was replaced as CEO of Fireman's Fund by John J. Byrne, former CEO at Government Employees Insurance Company.[26] In December 1985, FF changed executive vice-presidents, with James Ridling, formerly of Crum and Foster, replacing Donald McComber. As the year closed, AMEXCO owned 41 percent of FF.[27]

Shearson Lehman/ American Express

Synergy — the art of making one plus one equal three — was the underlying impetus behind the broad concept of creating financial supermarkets, which, in turn, led to the stampede of acquisitions of large brokerage firms by giant outsiders in 1981. As part of the stampede, AMEXCO acquired the prestigious Wall Street brokerage

---

[21] Ibid.

[22] Loomis, ''How Fireman's Fund Stoked Its Profits,'' pp. 99–104.

[23] Loomis, ''How Fireman's Fund Singed American Express,'' p. 80.

[24] Mary Row, ''Can Sandy Weill Turn Fireman's Fund Around,'' *Institutional Investor*, May 1984, pp. 110–112.

[25] Carol J. Loomis, ''The Earnings Magic at American Express,'' *Fortune*, June 25, 1984, p. 60.

[26] ''A New Chief for Fireman's Fund,'' *Business Week*, August 5, 1985, p. 38.

[27] ''Who's News,'' *Wall Street Journal*, December 19, 1985, p. 14.

firm Shearson at a price of approximately $1 billion. The merger was, to some degree, a response to the Prudential-Bache merger. Sandy Weill, Shearson's CEO at the time, did not want to risk being left behind by the entry of the largest U.S. insurer into the securities business. The merger between AMEXCO and Shearson was brought about by the two firms' belief that the barriers of tradition and regulation separating banking, brokerage, and insurance would eventually evaporate.[28]

In 1984 Shearson, under the leadership of their new CEO, Peter Cohen, purchased the 134-year-old investment bank of Lehman Brothers Kuhn-Loeb. This acquisition provided AMEXCO with additional strength in investment banking and fixed-income trading. As a result, SLAX wields this investment banking strength with a broad-based, soundly capitalized trading capacity and a global distribution network with over 5,000 professional financial consultants in 354 offices located in forty-four states and fifteen countries. Through these consultants, SLAX offers stocks, bonds, options, futures, commercial paper, certificates of deposit, insurance, and tax-advantaged investments as well as investment banking, pension and investment management, real estate, and mortgage banking services.

Mergers such as this have had the effect of moving retail brokers closer to becoming financial consultants, although the SLAX brokers can now refer their clients with specific problems to the specialists who may reside in one of their sister companies and who also fall under the AMEXCO umbrella. This is due in large part to AMEXCO's purchase of such firms as Balcor (the nation's largest real estate syndicator) and Investors Diversified Services and Ayco (both well-known financial planning firms).[29]

Among the mergers' by-products, none seems to have benefited the brokers more than the reputation of AMEXCO. SLAX staff members acknowledge an overnight surge in client confidence. "Once Shearson teamed up with American Express, we got the credibility we needed."[30] Other beneficial side effects include the infusion of capital by AMEXCO (which has enabled many of the brokers to obtain desktop computers, which improves their service to the client); the ability to attend workshops on specific products and selling skills; and stepped-up advertising campaigns to enhance their visibility.

The effect of these advantages can be seen in the year-end summary of activities for SLAX for 1984. The company managed over 300 underwritings in U.S. and international markets. The corporate finance division represented clients in more than 70 completed mergers, acquisitions, and divestitures with an aggregate transaction value of over $12 billion. The public finance division managed tax-exempt financings of $28 billion for state and local governments in 1984. Shearson also

---

[28] Anthony Bianco, "How A Financial Supermarket Was Born," *Business Week,* December 23, 1985, p. 10.

[29] Andrew Marton, "What Have the Megamergers Meant for Brokers," *Institutional Investor,* March 1984, pp. 147–150.

[30] Ibid., p. 148.

recognized a 135 percent rise in revenues in the fixed-income sector and an 8.4 percent increase in revenues from the sale of tax-advantaged investments.

However, there have been certain drawbacks to the merger. The presence of AMEXCO has diminished the informal atmosphere that previously existed at Shearson. "A certain impersonality has emerged, it is no longer the closely knit firm it once was."[31] The bureaucratic system of the conglomerate is also frustrating to the Shearson staffers: "It takes six weeks to get some requests through."[32] Along with the abundance of products has come an abundance of paperwork. Equally as frustrating is the fact that the parent company, as of March 1984, had not yet released the names of its 9 million green-card holders to the brokerage firm. This single source of potential clients could easily double or triple Shearson's client base.[33]

Despite these drawbacks, it is the consensus of the brokerage community that the full effects of the mergers will not be felt for some time. They are convinced that these mergers will give rise to a new breed of broker, one able to deal with a larger client base by supplying a wider range of financial services.

IDS Financial Services, Inc.

IDS Financial Services, Inc. (IDS) was established in 1894 to help people and businesses manage money and achieve their financial goals. Through its sales force of more than 4,400 representatives, IDS offers sound financial plans and the products and services to fulfill those plans. Among its offerings are investment certificates, mutual funds, life insurance, annuities, unit investment trusts, IRAs, limited partnerships, and management and fiduciary services for pension and employee benefit plans. IDS has traditionally concentrated on the lower end of the investing public (incomes in the $25,000–$75,000 range).

IDS was acquired by AMEXCO in January 1984 as part of its multibrand approach to providing financial services.[34] In addition to adding the American Express name to the IDS banner, this merger has also resulted in more training opportunities for the IDS sales force and a continual flow of new and upgraded products. With AMEXCO's support, IDS has launched its most aggressive advertising campaign ever in an attempt to provide the company with further exposure.

Investors were apparently not impressed by AMEXCO's purchase of IDS. In fact, AMEXCO's stock plummeted from $45 to $28 in the year after the announcement of the merger. This was a much greater drop than that of the stock market averages during the same period. However, at the end of 1985, AMEXCO's stock was up to approximately $52.

[31] Ibid.

[32] Ibid.

[33] Ibid.

[34] "The Golden Plan of American Express," p. 119.

Warner Amex (W-A)

In the late seventies, "gripped with doubts about its competitive position in checks and cards,"[35] AMEXCO sought acquisitions in the communications arena. After trying to buy the McGraw-Hill publishing company and looking at others in the field, AMEXCO settled on 50 percent of Warner-AMEX, a cable TV company that has grown to be the sixth largest cable operator in the United States.

W-A owns 104 cable television systems in twenty-one states serving 1.2 million subscribers, but has done poorly with big-city franchises. In its first 5 years of co-ownership, AMEXCO has contributed more than $300 million to W-A's operations.[36] In 1983, AMEXCO's share of operating losses was close to $40 million. In 1984, Drew Lewis, W-A CEO, reduced pretax losses to $94 million with net losses falling from $99 million to $25 million. Looking to 1985 and beyond, W-A owns almost two-thirds of MTV Network which also includes the VH-1 and the Nickleodeon Children's channels. W-A also owns 19 percent of the Showtime Movie channel.

The Cable Company Policy Act of 1984 provided for rate deregulation after 2 years, which will allow cable operators to function in a more competitive market, which may contribute to greater economic stability in the industry. In 1984 W-A sold cable systems in Pittsburgh, Chicago, St. Louis, and twenty smaller locales as well as its regional sports programming service and its security division. Contract modifications in its urban franchises in Milwaukee, New York City, and Dallas were also a part of the cost-containment strategy launched in 1984.

According to Drew Lewis:

> This year [1984] marked a turning point for Warner-Amex. The foundation for the future is now in place and Warner-Amex is moving forward toward its goal of profitability. The cable industry is entering an era of realism and its future is bright. Warner-Amex is well positioned for a key role in that future.[37]

THE FINANCIAL SUPERMARKETS

Deregulation has given rise to many investment alternatives. Americans spent $200 billion in 1982 for financial services with an estimated margin of 25 percent.[38] These facts, coupled with tax breaks for IRAs and capital gains, stimulate demand and encourage supplies of financial services to enter the market. A major barrier to expansion into the financial supermarket category has been the legal restrictions on combining banking operations with insurance or investment banking, or interstate branching by security brokers with investment banking.

As the supermarkets emerge, there is competition to become the low-cost financial service provider. ATMs and 800 telephone numbers make personal banking more efficient and easier for most types of financial transactions. Technology with its

[35] Loomis, "Fire In the Belly At American Express," p. 88.

[36] Ibid.

[37] *American Express Company 1984 Annual Report,* p. 47.

[38] Hershman, "The Supercompanies Emerge," p. 44.

inherent efficiencies makes pursuit of a low-cost strategy more feasible. Other ways to pursue a low-cost strategy include the use of service representatives (rather than more expensive account executives) to handle walk-in low-margin investment clients, selling to individuals at the workplace (corporate benefit programs), and vertical integration.[39]

The supercompanies plan to go after the middle-income families earning $20,000 to $50,000 a year. The company that can profitably serve the middle-income investor is going to make a potload of money, as this market group contains the most people. Further strategies will be to have a broad and diversified base of revenues to overcome the large cycles of financial services. Furthermore, geographic diversification will be necessary to cover costs and enjoy the economies of scale of mass marketing. One method of mass marketing is the national ad campaigns that have just begun. These mass marketing strategies will be aimed at reaching as many people as possible and trying to gain national recognition for each company as a full-service financial provider. Banks have the inside track here as cash and checks are the centerpiece of financial transactions.[40]

AMEXCO considers itself to be in the financial and travel-related service industries. While each of its corporate companies is a separate profit center, AMEXCO attempts to capitalize on its corporate synergy by using multiple distribution channels that target select market segments with strong brand-name products and services. Cross marketing, another synergy of the financial supermarket, allows an AEIBC customer in West Germany, for example, to buy securities or real estate in the United States through SLAX.

In terms of vertical-integration economies, AMEXCO owns Balcor, a firm that puts together and manages real estate syndications which can then be sold through SLAX account executives to potential investors. Another economy of scale is its low-cost, high-speed data processing capability (First Data Resources, Inc.) on which AMEXCO spends $300–400 million annually for hardware and software improvements. A clear goal is for AMEXCO to be the low-cost processor of financial transactions.[41]

As a financial supermarket, AMEXCO competes on many levels within international, national, and regional markets. In the industry, AMEXCO competes with the other financial supermarkets on a corporate basis. This competition includes Sears Roebuck, Prudential-Bache, Bank America Corporation, Citicorp, and Merrill Lynch. To a lesser degree, AMEXCO competes with potential financial supermarkets such as Travelers, Transamerica, Aetna, and Security Pacific Bank. On a regional basis, AMEXCO competes with growing financial empires such as First Interstate Bancorp.

Looking at the leaders (AMEXCO, Sears, Prudential, and Merrill Lynch), it is clear that all are spending money as never before in efforts to revamp their business

---

[39] Ibid., p. 49.

[40] Ibid., pp. 44–50.

[41] Ibid., p. 50.

identities. The strategy for these firms is twofold: first, to make consumers comfortable with once unheard-of combinations of merchandise the supermarkets now offer (e.g., risky tax shelters and riskless life insurance or, in Sears' case, stocks and socks) and, second, to distinguish each firm from its competitors.[42]

Achieving the first goal (one-stop shopping) will take time. A recent sampling survey revealed that most respondents did not see many benefits in one-stop financial shopping. The survey results indicated that younger adults are more receptive to the idea than older ones.[43]

In terms of differentiation, Merrill Lynch ("to be all things to some people") has said frankly that it is after affluent households with incomes over $50,000.[44] This involves courting young professionals, who may not have big incomes now, but seem likely to at some point in the future. Sears is capitalizing on its image of trustworthiness and is using a celebrity spokesman, Hal Holbrook, to convey that image in TV advertising ($3.1 million in first-quarter 1984).[45]

American Express is trying to cover all the bases. The company offers its credit card in three versions — green, gold, and the ultraexclusive platinum card — with the intent to intercept investors at three levels of wealth.

IDS Brokerage firm has always concentrated on the lower end of the investing public (incomes in the $25,000–$35,000 range). For the middle and upper range, there is Shearson. And then for the corporate client, Shearson has the investment banking firm of Lehman Brothers.[46]

American Express ads reflect its multibrand approach. There is intentionally no similarity between IDS ads and those for Shearson Lehman. It is too early to judge the effectiveness of the IDS ("IDS doesn't cater to get-rich-quick schemes") or the Shearson ads ("for the serious investor").[47]

Prudential's advertising is aimed at households with annual incomes of at least $50,000.[48]

THE OUTLOOK

Synergy was touted as the motivation behind the rash of acquisitions and mergers among the financial giants in the early 1980s, but, halfway through the decade,

---

[42] Geoffry Colvin, "Would You Buy Stocks Where You Buy Socks?" *Fortune,* July 9, 1984, p. 50.

[43] Ibid., p. 130.

[44] Ibid.

[45] Ibid., p. 133.

[46] Ibid., p. 131.

[47] Ibid., p. 133.

[48] Ibid., p. 131.

analysts claim that "when it comes to the financial supermarkets' synergy, one plus one well might end up equaling one."[49]

The torrid pace of AMEX's diversification drive is, however, straining its ability to control its far-flung operations. "Their management team has been assembled mostly by purchase," says Walter B. Wriston, CEO of Citicorp. "I don't think there's any question that if a team has played together for 10 years, you have a better chance on Saturday afternoon than the all-star team that was assembled that morning."[50]

Sanford Wiell, who brought Shearson into the AMEXCO family in 1981 and started to turn FF around in 1984, left AMEXCO in 1985. The leadership position at FF has been anything but stable with five CEOs in 6 years. Lewis Gerstner, Jr., CEO of the TRS, is rumored to be unhappy with decisions being made at New York corporate headquarters.[51] Weill's protégé, Peter Cohen, CEO at Shearson Lehman at thirty-six, may not sit well with some of AMEXCO's older executives. If AMEXCO has a major weakness, it may be in senior management, which is often accused of buying its talent rather than grooming it, notwithstanding the fact that such notables as Henry Kissinger and Edward Safra have recently been added to the AMEXCO board of directors. Could the problems at Fireman's Fund mean the beginning of the end of AMEXCO's involvement in insurance? Down to only 41 percent ownership, AMEXCO could be looking to cut bait altogether if and when the price is right.

Warner-Amex has yet to see black ink. How long will AMEXCO dabble in the communications/entertainment industries without a winner?

Visa, MasterCard, and others (including possibly Sears' new entry, Discover) pose a challenge to the AMEX card's dominance. They have erased all vestiges of complacency at TRS.[52]

IDS margins have been considered thin and visibly low. An announcement in December 1985 indicated that AMEXCO was pumping $65 million to expand IDS's business lines, giving IDS capital of more than $900 million.[53] In the same announcement, AMEXCO added $175 million to AEICB, which apparently is now a successful member of the AMEXCO family.

Will AMEXCO, regulations permitting, expand into domestic banking? Will AMEXCO's success in direct marketing take it into retail sales to compete with Sears through acquisition of a retailer such as J. C. Penney or Montgomery Ward? Can AMEXCO make greater use of First Data Resources to further cut internal costs or sell data processing services at a profit?

Are there economies to be gained, as well as synergistic effects, by placing IDS under SLAX management? Would such a move reduce internal competition for

[49] Bianco, "How a Financial Supermarket Was Born," p. 10.

[50] "The Golden Plan at American Express," p. 118.

[51] Ibid., p. 120.

[52] "The Golden Plan of American Express," p. 119.

[53] "Business Briefs," *Wall Street Journal*, December 20, 1985, p. 8.

investors in AMEXCO's three-tiered investment strategy (Lehman — wealthy corporate, Shearson — middle income, IDS — small investor)? Or, conversely, is this too broad a front on which to attack?

APPENDIX A: HISTORY OF GROWTH OF AMEXCO

1850: American Express evolves from the merging of three small freight companies for delivery of small packages and funds by rail and horseback. American Express agents are expected to foil the efforts of masked bandits.

1891: The first traveler's checks are introduced by American Express.

1900: American Express opens the first overseas travel office in Paris.

1919: The American Express Company, Incorporated (known as the "Inc Company") is formed to provide financial services for post–World War I American travelers.

1958: The famous green travel and entertainment charge card is introduced.

1968: The international banking operation known as the Inc Company changes its name to the American Express International Banking Corporation (AEIBC).

American Express acquires the Fireman's Fund Insurance Company.

1981: Shearson investment firm is added to the growing AMEXCO financial empire.

1983: AMEXCO buys the Geneva-based Trade Development Bank and joins it to AEIBC.

AMEXCO formally establishes the American Express Travel Related Services Company, Inc., as one of the five major entities of AMEXCO.

IDS Financial Services, Inc. (a leader in financial planning) joins the AMEXCO corporate family.

1984: Shearson/American Express acquires Lehman Brothers, Kuhn, Loeb Holding Co. Inc. to join the AMEXCO financial conglomerate as Shearson Lehman Brothers, Inc.

APPENDIX B: FINANCIAL PERFORMANCE BY SERVICE CATEGORY

The company is principally in the business of providing travel related services, international banking services, investment services, investors diversified financial services and insurance services throughout the world. Travel Related Services principally consists of the American Express Card and Travelers Cheque operations. The results of the company's 50 percent interest in Warner Amex are included in "Other and Corporate." The following tables present certain information regarding these industry segments at December 31, 1984, 1983 and 1982 and for the years then ended (millions).

TABLE 1 1984 data

	Travel Related Services	International Banking Services	Investment Services	IDS Financial Services	Insurance Services	Other and corporate	Adjustments and eliminations	Consolidated
Revenues	$ 3,620	$ 1,548	$ 2,280	$1,576	$4,025	$ 82	$ (236)	$12,895
Pretax income (loss) before general corporate expenses	$ 625	$ 193	$ 168	$ 95	$ (114)	$ 16	$ (18)	$ 965
General corporate expenses	—	—	—	—	—	(229)	—	(229)
Pretax income (loss)	$ 625	$ 193	$ 168	$ 95	$ (114)	$ (213)	$ (18)	$ 736
Net income	$ 387	$ 156	$ 103	$ 62	$ 43	$ (125)	$ (16)	$ 610
Assets	$12,542	$13,768	$22,735	$6,411	$7,735	$1,239	$(2,582)	$61,848

Insurance services comprises the following:

	Property-Liability				Life and other	Total insurance services
	Commercial lines	Personal lines	Investment income	Total		
Revenues	$ 2,017	$ 817	$ 429	$3,263	$ 762	$ 4,025
Pretax income (loss)	$ (558)	$ (40)	$ 404	$ (194)	$ 80	$ (114)

TABLE 2 1983 data

	Travel Related Services	International Banking Services	Investment Services	IDS Financial Services	Insurance Services	Other and corporate	Adjustments and eliminations	Consolidated
Revenues	$ 2,889	$ 1,437	$ 1,826	—	$3,784	$ (6)	$ (160)	$ 9,770
Pretax income (loss) before general corporate expenses	$ 445	$ 183	$ 326	—	$ (242)	$ (17)	$ (10)	$ 685
General corporate expenses	—	—	—	—	—	(168)	—	(168)
Pretax income (loss)	$ 445	$ 183	$ 326	—	$ (242)	$ (185)	$ (10)	$ 517
Net income	$ 301	$ 136	$ 175	—	$ 30	$ (117)	$ (10)	$ 515
Assets	$10,226	$13,287	$ 9,060	$5,410	$7,057	$1,095	$(2,154)	$43,981

Insurance services comprises the following:

	Property-Liability				Life and other	Total insurance services
	Commercial lines	Personal lines	Investment income	Total		
Revenues	$ 1,925	$ 783	$ 437	$3,145	$ 639	$ 3,784
Pretax income (loss)	$ (609)	$ (95)	$ 452	$ (252)	$ 10	$ (242)

TABLE 3 1982 data

	Travel Related Services	International Banking Services	Investment Services	Insurance Services	Other and corporate	Adjustments and eliminations	Consolidated
Revenues	$ 2,516	$ 1,025	$ 1,318	$3,356	$ 14	$ (136)	$ 8,093
Pretax income before general corporate expenses	$ 363	$ 101	$ 228	$ 220	$ (5)	—	$ 907
General corporate expenses	—	—	—	—	(153)	—	(153)
Pretax income	$ 363	$ 101	$ 228	$ 220	$ (158)	—	$ 754
Net income	$ 247	$ 60	$ 124	$ 244	$ (94)	—	$ 581
Assets	$ 8,445	$ 7,681	$ 6,351	$6,513	$ 784	$(1,463)	$28,311

Insurance services comprises the following:

	Property-Liability				Life and other	Total insurance services
	Commercial lines	Personal lines	Investment income	Total		
Revenues	$ 1,947	$ 640	$ 348	$2,935	$ 421	$ 3,356
Pretax income (loss)	$ (95)	$ (22)	$ 328	$ 211	$ 9	$ 220

APPENDIX C: AMERICAN EXPRESS AT-A-GLANCE

This appendix contains excerpts from the American Express 1984 Annual Report, wherein American Express explains its different activities, with accompanying data.

1. American Express: Top Rated by Independent Study. American Express products and services hold the confidence of millions of people. They look to American Express brand names for better ways to make, use and protect their money. In a survey in 1984, the *American Banker* found that people rate American Express products and services higher than those of any other top financial services firm in the United States.

	Who consumers know (%)[1]
American Express	75
Prudential Insurance	72
Bank of America	70
Merrill Lynch	66
Beneficial Finance	55
Sears Roebuck	54
Citicorp	53
Chas. Schwab	21

2. Travel Related Services. Travel Related Services began the American Express tradition of reliable service in 1850 by moving freight. Today, it moves people and their buying power around the world. People know the quality of the American Express Card, Travelers Cheque and Travel Services.

(Millions, except percentages)	*1984*	*1983*	*Percent increase*
Revenues	$ 3,620	$ 2,889	25%
Net income	$ 387	$ 301	29
Card charge volume	$47,638	$38,356	24
Travelers Cheque sales	$15,116	$13,862	9
Total assets	$12,542	$10,226	23
Average Travelers Cheques outstanding	$ 2,634	$ 2,437	8
Cards in force	20.2	17.3	17
Return on average shareholder's equity	25.3%	24.1%	

[1] Multiple responses permitted. Adapted from the *American Banker*.

3. International Banking Services. At American Express International Banking Corporation, the accent is on "international." The Bank helped American Express expand internationally following World War I. Today, 82 offices in 39 countries offer export financing, private banking and other select services.

(Millions, except percentages)	1984	1983	Percent increase (decrease)
Net income from International Banking Services	$ 156	$ 136	15%
Loans and discounts	$ 6,272	$ 6,290	—
Reserve for loan losses	$ 165	$ 162	2
Total assets of American Express International Banking Corporation	$13,875	$13,309	4
Customers' deposits and credit balances	$10,517	$10,328	2
Shareholder's equity of American Express International Banking Corporation	$ 897	$ 819	10
Primary capital to average assets	7.64%	7.05%	
Return on average assets	1.15%	1.04%	
Return on average shareholder's equity	17.81%	17.67%	

4. Investment Services. Shearson Lehman Brothers Inc. evolved from strategic acquisitions — most recently, Lehman Brothers. Today, Shearson Lehman melds this investment banking franchise with strong trading and distribution capabilities.[2]

(Millions)	1984	1983	Percent increase (decrease)
Revenues	$ 2,280	$ 1,826	25%
Pretax income	$ 168	$ 326	(49)
Net income	$ 103	$ 175	(41)
Total assets	$22,735	$ 9,060	151
Total capital, including subordinated debt, of Shearson Lehman Brothers Inc.	$ 1,896	$ 1,057	79
Assets managed and/or administered	$64,939	$47,144	38

5. IDS Financial Services. IDS Financial Services Inc. and its subsidiaries have earned people's trust, through outstanding financial advice and services, since 1894.

[2] Note: Investment Services 1984 amounts include the effect of the acquisition of Lehman Brothers Kuhn Loeb Holding Co., Inc., accounted for as a purchase as of May 11, 1984.

The 4,400 representatives of IDS provide financial plans and products that stand the test of time.[3]

(Millions)	1984	1983	Percent increase (decrease)
Revenues	$ 1,576	$ —	—
Pretax income	$ 95	$ —	—
Net income	$ 62	$ —	—
Individual life insurance in force	$13,818	$11,424	21%
Assets owned and/or managed:			
Assets managed for institutions	$ 3,080	$ 3,650	(16)
Assets owned and managed for individuals:			
Owned assets	$ 6,411	$ 5,410	19
Managed assets	$ 9,812	$ 9,162	7

6. Insurance Services. Fireman's Fund Insurance Companies was born in San Francisco in 1863 to provide protection against the frequent fires that ravaged the city. Today, Fireman's Fund is an industry leader in developing new products and new approaches to marketing.

(Millions, except percentages)	1984	1983	Percent increase
Fireman's Fund Insurance Companies			
Revenues	$ 4,025	$ 3,784	6%
Net income	$ 43	$ 30	42
Total assets	$ 7,735	$ 7,057	10
Shareholder's equity	$ 1,485	$ 1,304	14
Return on average shareholder's equity	3.1%	2.2%	
Property-Liability Companies			
Premiums written	$ 2,834	$ 2,781	2
Underwriting ratio	121.1%	126.0%	
Loss and loss expense ratio	86.4%	86.5%	
Expense ratio	32.2%	36.6%	
Policyholder dividend ratio	2.5%	2.9%	
Life Companies			
Premiums written	$ 655	$ 539	21
Life insurance in force	$23,133	$15,493	49

[3] Note: The acquisition of IDS Financial Services was accounted for as a purchase effective December 31, 1983. Therefore, revenues, pretax income and net income for 1983 are not presented.

NUCOR CORPORATION

It's the closest thing to a perfect company in the steel industry.

Daniel Roling, analyst for Merrill Lynch

With earnings growth over the past decade averaging better than 23 percent per year, Nucor prospered in the steel industry while giant companies barely survived. Few "high-tech" companies could match Nucor's record. But in 1986, Nucor was moving into an era where the easy pickings were over. One securities analyst believed that Nucor would not be able to find alluring new opportunities, stating: "Their rapid growth of the last 10 years is simply not repeatable."

BACKGROUND

Nuclear Corporation

Nuclear Corporation of America was formed by a merger of Nuclear Consultants, Inc., and parts of REO Motors in 1955. Between 1955 and 1964 various managements tried (unsuccessfully) by way of acquisitions and divestitures to make a profit. One of the acquisitions was Vulcraft, a steel joist manufacturer. By 1965 Nuclear Corporation was losing $2 million on sales of $22 million. A new group got control of the company in 1965 and installed Vulcraft general manager Ken Iverson (who headed the only profitable division) as president. "I got the job by default," Iverson said.

Entry into Steel Industry

Iverson decided that Vulcraft — a manufacturer of steel joists for buildings — ought to make its own steel. His goal was to match the prices of imported steel: "We had some vision that if we were successful, we could expand and create another business by selling steel in the general marketplace." In 1968 Nucor built its first steel mill in Darlington, South Carolina. By 1985 Nucor operated four steel mills, six joist plants, two cold finishing plants, three steel deck plants, and a grinding ball plant throughout the south, southwest, and west. About 65 percent of Nucor's

Prepared by Professors Charles I. Stubbart and Dean Schroeder, the University of Massachusetts-Amherst. © 1986 by Stubbart and Schroeder. Reprinted by permission.

steel was sold in open markets, while 35 percent went to Vulcraft and other Nucor products. Until the recession of 1982–83 sales and earnings grew at an astonishing clip. Even during the recession Nucor managed to eke out a profit while other integrated steel companies lost billions.

STEEL INDUSTRY CONDITIONS, 1985

Industry Participants

Companies competing in the U.S. steel industry in 1985 were of several distinct types: integrated U.S. companies, foreign manufacturers, minimills, and specialty steel producers. The large integrated domestic companies (e.g., U.S. Steel) got their start at the turn of the century. Integrated companies held about 45 to 55 percent of the market. Specialty steel producers manufactured relatively low volumes

EXHIBIT 1
U.S. raw steel production, finished steel shipments, and steel imports, 1956–1984

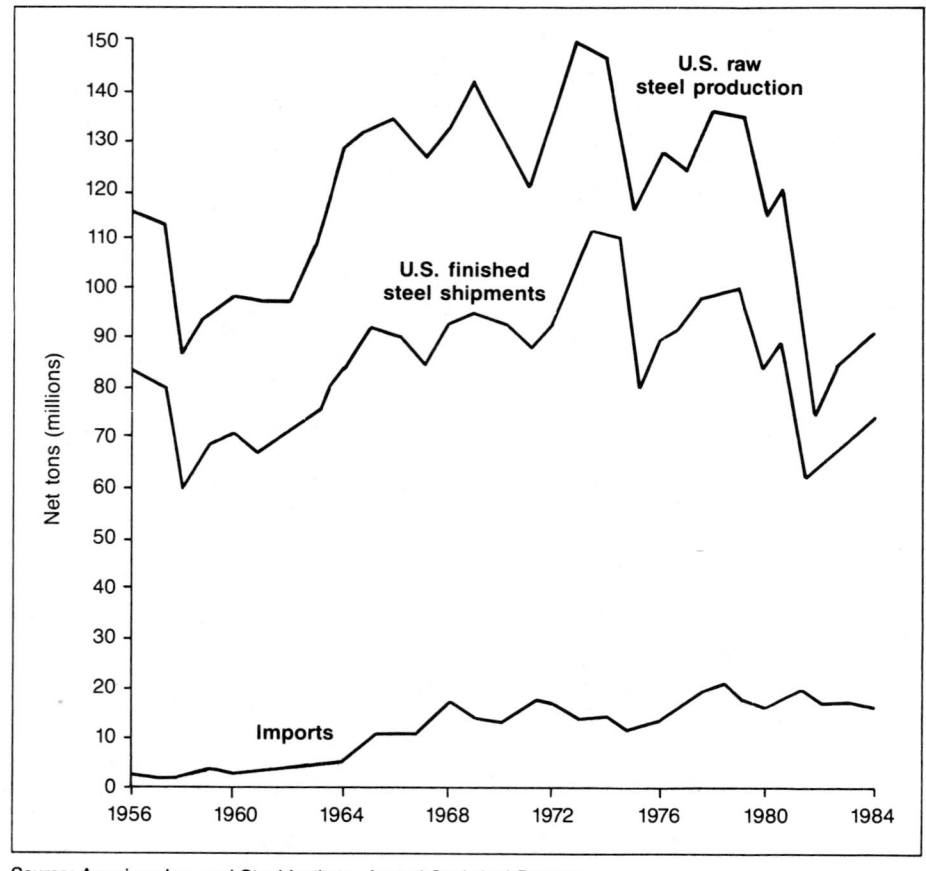

Source: American Iron and Steel Institute, *Annual Statistical Reports.*

of steel with varying degrees of hardness, purity, and strength. Imports of steel into the United States accounted for about 20 to 25 percent of domestic sales. (Imports probably held a larger share, taking into account the steel in imported automobiles and other products.) Minimills, which transformed scrap metal into steel using electric furnaces, had a market share of about 20 to 25 percent of the domestic market.

Recent History   Since the early 1960s the integrated steel industry had suffered a painful decline. The stagnation of the early 1960s gave way to faster growth (and rising imports) in the late 1960s. During 1965–74 steel demand was strong, and industry officials expected major growth after 1974. But they were wrong. Steel production in the United States had fallen from its 1974 level, and many analysts believed that the 1974 levels would never be reached again (Exhibit 1). Much of this decline was traceable to the long-term trends toward smaller, lighter cars; the inroads of competing materials (such as aluminum and plastics); a shift in emphasis away from smokestack industries to service industries; and greater use of imported steel in U.S. products.

Between 1960 and 1985 foreign competitors and domestic minimills invested heavily in building all-new facilities with the latest technology. Major integrated companies invested in older, more familiar technologies to try to spruce up existing plants and correct gross inefficiencies. Facing weak demand, having less efficient facilities, and with the U.S. dollar appreciating in value, the biggest domestic integrated companies suffered huge losses in the late 1970s and early 1980s (Exhibits 2 and 3).

EXHIBIT 2

Production capacity of largest U.S. integrated steel companies, 1984

Firm	Raw steel capacity
1. U.S. Steel	26.2
2. LTV	19.1
3. Bethlehem	18.0
4. Inland	9.4
5. Armco	6.8
6. National	5.6
7. Wheeling-Pittsburgh	4.5
8. Weirton	4.0
9. Ford Motor Co. (Rouge Steel)	3.6
10. McLouth	2.0
11. CF&I	2.0 (partially closed)
12. Interlake	1.4
13. Sharon	1.0
14. California	2.1 (closed)
Total	105.7

Note: Figures in millions of tons per year.
Source: Company reports; Oppenheimer & Co., Metal Bulletin, *Iron and Steel Works of the World,* 8th edition.

EXHIBIT 3 U.S. domestic steel industry, 1972–1984

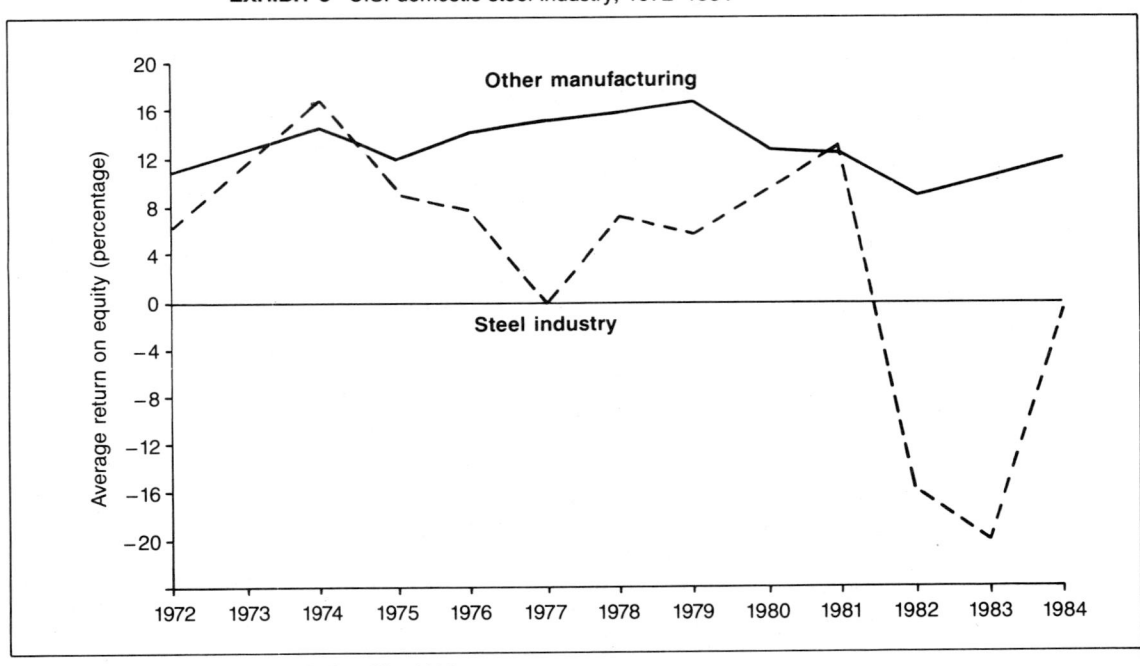

Source: *Forbes*, May 1986.

Other problems also contributed to the rapid slide. The steelworkers union was able to negotiate large wage increases in 1968 and 1971, and union work rules hampered steel company efforts to increase productivity in their plants. Only in 1983 did the steelworkers union reluctantly agree to wage concessions and work rule modifications under the pressure of plant closings.

Investments

Expecting major increases in demand for 1975–85, integrated companies made large investments in ore mines and iron pelletizing facilities. An important share of their investment dollars went into meeting environmental regulations. Integrated companies' financial calculations persuaded them to stick with modifications of existing plants instead of building new "greenfield" (environmentally proper) plants. As a result, not one all-new integrated steel plant had been built for over 20 years in the United States. Given the high cost of capital, the complex environmental constraints, weak demand, and intense foreign/domestic competition, it was unlikely that any new integrated plants would be built in the United States in the foreseeable future.

Imports and Protection

The steel strike of 1959 provided the first opportunity for foreign steel firms to make inroads into the U.S. market. By the 1980s — despite several attempts to limit imports via voluntary restraints and trigger pricing (a minimum pricing rule) —

the integrated companies found themselves with 140 million tons of excess capacity, much of it in old inefficient plants. They had no choice but to face the music and close many plants and sell unproductive assets — a protracted and painful process for the companies, the steelworkers, and many local communities. Within one four-year period steelmakers wrote off $4.4 billion in assets and took $7 billion in losses. Steel companies, steelworkers, and endangered communities struggled mightily to persuade a Reagan administration and the Congress to limit steel imports. A reluctant Reagan administration agreed to negotiate "voluntary" restraints in 1985. Even so, to the integrated companies, the "rust bowl" communities, and to over 200,000 permanently laid off steelworkers, it seemed that too little had been done too late.

Foreign steel imports in 1985 accounted for about 25 percent of the U.S. market in spite of the Reagan administration's negotiating bilateral voluntary restraints with foreign governments. These restraint agreements aimed at limiting imports to about 21 percent of the market. Sentiment was growing in Congress to stem the tidal wave of foreign imports in the face of a $130 billion trade deficit during 1985. Ken Iverson, Nucor's CEO, steadfastly argued against protecting the domestic steel industry:

> We've had this "temporary" relief for a long time. We had a voluntary quota system in the early 1970s. We had trigger prices in the late 1970s. And what happened during these periods? As soon as prices began to rise so that steel companies would begin to be profitable, they stopped modernizing. It's only under intense competitive pressure — both internally from minimills and externally from the Japanese and the Koreans — that the big steel companies have been forced to modernize. . . . In 1980 the industry still had rolling mills dating from the Civil War. . . . Out of all this turmoil will come a lot of things which are beneficial: more of an orientation toward technology, greater productivity, certainly a lot of changes in management structure.

Future Prospects

Speculating about 1986, steel producers expected another year like 1985: declining tonnage, stable prices, slightly declining import shares, and overall profitability near zero for the industry. Their forecasts hinged on a GNP growth of approximately 3 percent. Industry analysts foresaw that a reduction in imports (traced to the falling value of the U.S. dollar) would offset an expected decline in steel consumption. Demand for steel in machinery, railroad equipment, farm equipment, and other capital items was falling. Analysts were also uncertain about the 1986 demand for autos. Some estimates placed 1986 domestic steel shipments in the range of 70 to 75 million tons (not counting imports). The prospect of labor negotiations beginning in the second half of 1986 represented a major uncertainty for steel producers and customers.

But there was a bright side too. Steel companies entered the year determined to extract concessions from the United Steelworkers Union. Companies had eliminated most of their grossly inefficient facilities. Prices were edging up. Capacity utilization approached 70 percent, compared to a low of 48 percent in 1982 (Exhibit 4). A weakening dollar made imports less attractive.

EXHIBIT 4
U.S. steelmaking capacity utilization, 1975–1985

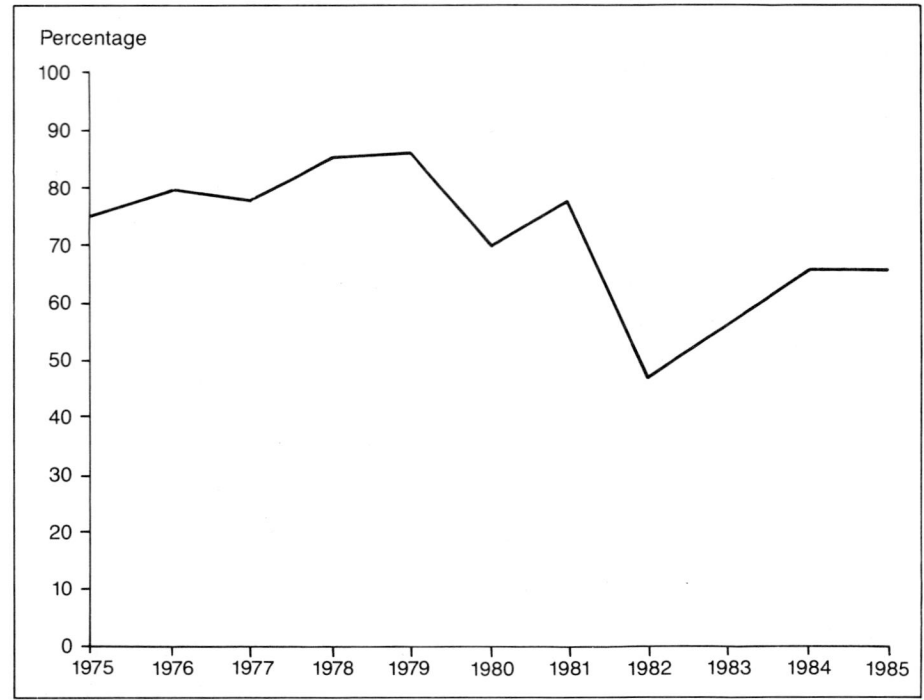

Source: AISI statistics.

Analysts estimated that worldwide demand had stabilized. From 1979 to 1985 steel output in the industrial nations dropped precipitously from 442 million tons to 331 million tons. Capacity had been cut back 28 million tons in Europe, 23 million tons in the United States, and 17 million tons in Japan. One U.S. steel producer predicted that an additional 20 million tons in U.S. capacity would have to go. Exhibit 5 offers some industry projections for steel. A steel executive summed up a grim situation and his skepticism about a future that U.S. steel companies felt helpless about: "You light a candle at every altar."

STEEL MINIMILLS: AN INDUSTRY WITHIN AN INDUSTRY

Nucor is best known for its steel minimill business. Nucor operated four steel minimills in South Carolina, Nebraska, Texas, and Utah, with a total capacity of about 2 million tons. That made Nucor the eighth largest steel company in the United States.

The United States had about 50 minimills. As U.S. Steel, Bethlehem, Republic,

EXHIBIT 5
Steel industry
projections

	1980	1985	1990	2000
Import share of U.S. market (percent)	17.0	24.0	28.0	32.0
Domestic shipments (millions of tons)	83.9	76.0	73.1	71.4– 78.2
Imports (millions of tons)	17.2	24.0	28.4	33.6– 36.8
Total shipments (millions of tons)	86.7	77.0	74.1	72.4– 79.2
Minimill shipments (millions of tons)	12.0	14.4	20.5	29.0
Minimill capacity (millions of tons)	16.0	22.0	27.0	35.0
Minimill productivity (work hours per ton)	4.0	2.8	2.2	1.5
Integrated shipments (millions of tons)	74.7	62.6	53.6	43.4– 50.2
Integrated raw steel production (millions of tons)	102.3	82.3	67.8	49.9– 57.7
Integrated capacity (millions of tons)	138.4	108.3	80.0	55.4– 64.1
Integrated productivity (work hours per ton)	9.5	7.2	6.0	4.5
Capacity utilization rate (percent)	75.3	76.0	85.0	90.0
Total employment (in thousands)	401.6	247.9	195.0	129.6–141.7

Source: Barnett, *Minimills*.

National, and LTV surrendered market share and lost billions, new entrants into the domestic market such as North Star, Nucor, Co-Steel, Florida Steel, and others prospered — and even displaced imports. Contrary to typical relationships between scale and efficiency, minimills manufactured high-quality steel inexpensively, with plants of 200,000 to 1 million tons of annual electric-furnace capacity; integrated plants producing 2 million to 10 million tons using open-hearth and basic oxygen furnace equipment were the high-cost producers.

Technology

The electric-furnace technology of minimills was first developed by Northwestern Steel and Wire in the 1930s. Exhibit 6 shows a comparison of the two processes, integrated versus minimill; the comparative simplicity of minimills is apparent. First, minimills use electric arc furnaces compared to integrated plants that use open-hearth (about 10 percent) or basic oxygen furnaces (about 90 percent). They simply charge scrap into an electric arc furnace to produce molten steel, then continuously cast the molten metal into semifinish shapes. Continuous casters eliminated reheating and increased the yield from molten metal to finished product. Unlike integrated mills, minimills were expressly designed for rebuilding and technical updating. Many integrated plants used obsolete ingot-casting technologies.

EXHIBIT 6
Comparative steel
production

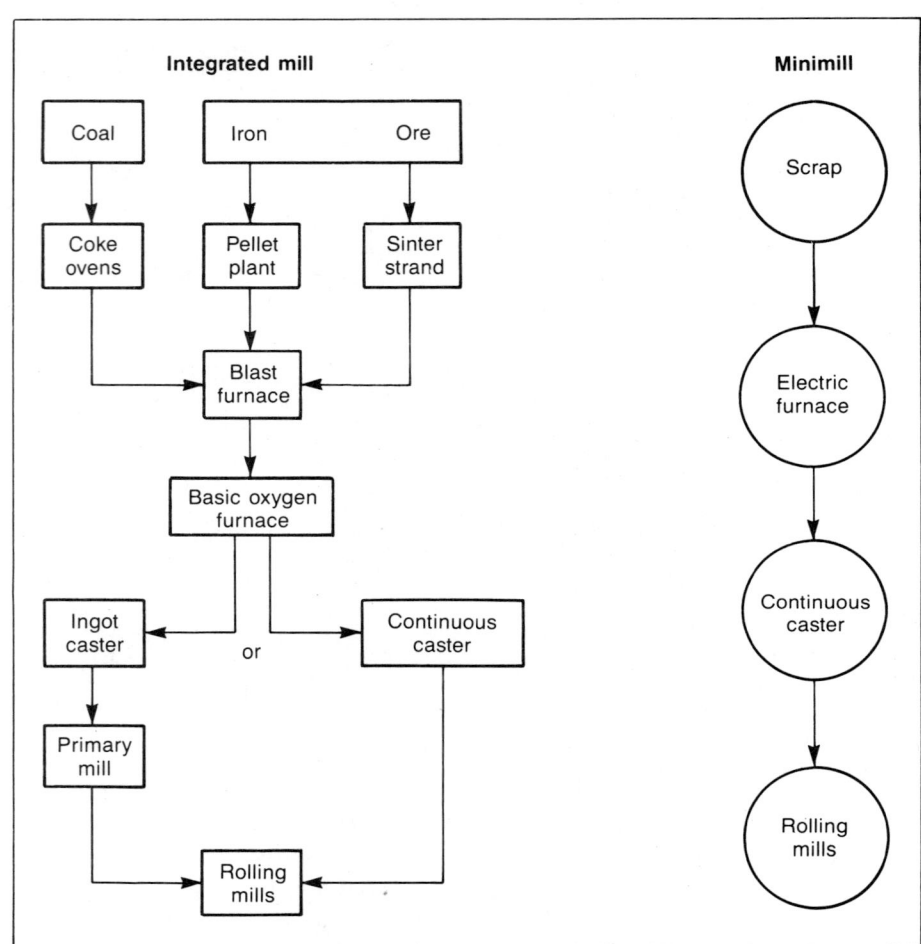

**Product
Specialization**

Early on, minimills fashioned small specialized steel products like reinforcing rods
for use in concrete work, rather than making huge beams, slabs, or sheets. Product
specialization increased their efficiency. Steel slabs were still predominantly the
private preserve of the integrated companies. But, as time passed, minimill companies
expanded their product lines. Exhibit 7 compares minimill product lines to integrated
mill product lines. Nucor in 1985 produced cold-finished bars and was devoting a
major innovative effort to the challenge of adapting minimill technology to sheet
steel production. If Nucor could perfect this new technology, the company would
be able to challenge integrated companies on their "home ground," the flat-rolled
steel used in automobiles, appliances, and roofing.

EXHIBIT 7
Product categories
of integrated mills
and minimills

Integrated products	Minimill production?
Slabs	
Hot rolled sheets	No
Cold rolled sheets	No
Coated sheets	No
Plates	Yes
Welded pipe and tube	Limited
Blooms and Billets	
Wire rods	Yes
Bars	Yes
Reinforcing bars	Yes
Small structural shapes	Yes
Large structural shapes	Limited
Rails	No
Seamless tube	Yes
Axles	No

Location

Only by the 1960s did minimills become a force within the industry. Their strategy was to utilize only electric furnaces and to locate their plants in regions near customer markets and scrap supplies but more distant from integrated plants (steel being expensive to ship). During the 1970s minimills grew explosively, capturing significant market shares (Exhibit 8).

Input Costs

Scrap steel was the principal raw material input for minimill production. While the cost of iron ore had constantly risen (as rich high-quality sources in the United States ran out), scrap remained plentiful. Over the last 10 years scrap prices had declined relative to iron ore prices.

Workforce Flexibility

Another important advantage of minimills was their workforce flexibility. Most minimills employed nonunion workers. Union attempts to organize minimills had met with little success. Although nonunion minimill wages were not always lower than union wages, their worker productivity was always much higher, primarily because of the flexibility and latitude management had in organizing work. Without union work rule restrictions, management could introduce labor-saving technology and link earnings to productivity.

Productivity

Electric furnace technology, workforce flexibility, and constant efforts to operate facilities more efficiently added up to a significant cost advantage (that translated into a price advantage) for minimills. The advantage in 1985 was about $100 per ton ($375 for integrated firms versus $275 for minimills). Much of the advantage stemmed from the fact that output per worker at minimills ran about double the

EXHIBIT 8   U.S. steel production by process, 1975–1985

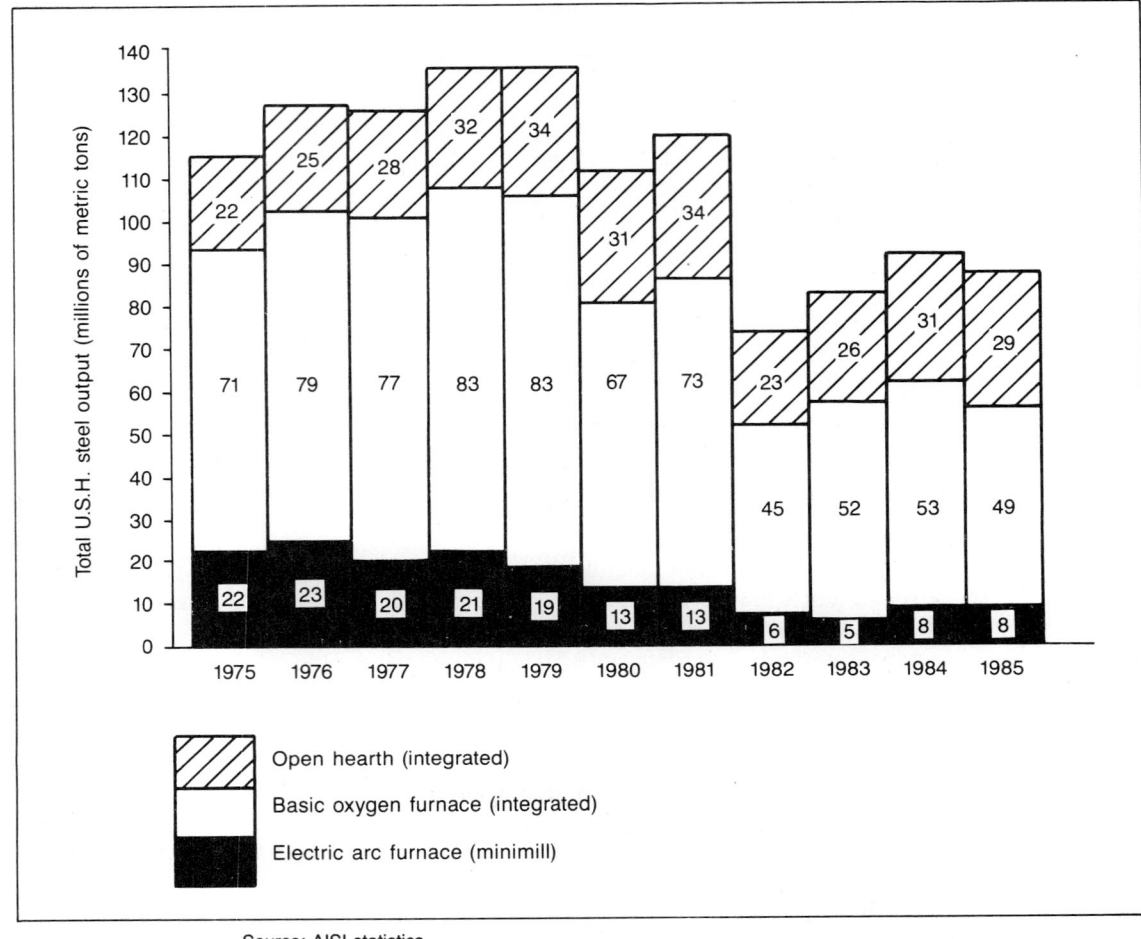

Source: AISI statistics.

350 tons per employee at integrated companies. Because minimill wages were comparable (some lower but not much) to workers' earnings in the unionized plants of bigger, integrated producers, minimills had about half the labor costs per ton of integrated companies.

Developmental Sequence

Minimills did not win their market niche overnight. Some minimills failed. While minimills had advantages in low-cost labor and low-cost scrap, they faced scale disadvantages and began with an untested technology and no customer base. The initial market penetration successes came in low-grade steel products. Then, as they learned and made operating improvements, they moved gradually and selectively to challenge integrated mills and imports in an ever-broadening array of products

EXHIBIT 9
Leading U.S.
minimill companies

Firm	Number of plants	Capacity (tons)	Products
Nucor	4	2,100,000	Bars, small structurals
North Star	4	2,050,000	Bars, rods, small structurals
Northwestern	1	1,800,000	Bars, rods, small and large structurals
Co-Steel	2	1,750,000	Bars, rods, small and large structurals
Florida Steel	5	1,560,000	Bars, small structurals

Note: The minimill segment consisted of 50 firms and 65 plants. Of total minimill production, 55 percent came from plants with less than 600,000 tons of annual capacity.

but always where their relative cost position was strongest. The largest, and generally most successful, minimill companies in 1985 are shown in Exhibit 9.

Intensified Competition

Contrary to popular impressions about imported steel, minimills' production accounted for more of the displacement of integrated companies' share than had imports. The relationship between the minimills and the integrated companies resembled a successful guerrilla war. In 1985, however, the competitive scene was changing. Having used their lower costs to force integrated companies and imports out of many markets, minimills were beginning to compete against each other. An official at an integrated company noted: "Minimills have passed the stage of taking tonnage from integrated producers. We are concentrating on more sophisticated products where they can't compete. Let them have the inefficient productions." Iverson observed: "We are now head to head against much tougher competition. It was no contest when we were up against the integrated companies. Now we are facing minimills who have the same scrap prices, the same electrical costs, and who use the same technologies."

Minimills coveted the bigger market for flat-rolled steel where profit margins were higher. But they were shut out of this segment by technological limitations. In terms of technological capabilities, productivity, workforce practices, and expanding products, Nucor was viewed as the leader among minimill producers.

VULCRAFT: THE OTHER HALF OF NUCOR

Ken Iverson said:

Most people think of us as a steel company, but we are a lot more than a steel company. The business is really composed of two different factors. One is manufacturing steel and the other is steel products. We like it if in an average year each factor contributes about 50 percent of our sales and 50 percent of our earnings. It is important for the company in the long run that we keep this balance. If one of them began to dominate the company it would cause problems we wouldn't like to see.

Products

Vulcraft was the nation's largest producer of steel joists and joist girders. Steel joists and girders served as support systems in industrial buildings, shopping centers, warehouses, high-rise buildings, and to a lesser extent in small office buildings, apartments, and single-family dwellings. Vulcraft had six joist plants, four deck plants, and three cold finish plants. Steel deck was used for floor and roof systems. In 1985 Vulcraft produced 471,000 tons of joists and girders and 169,000 tons of steel deck (Exhibit 10).

Manufacturing Process

Joists were manufactured on assembly lines. The steel moved on rolling conveyors from station to station. Teams of workers at each station cut and bent the steel to shape, welded joists together and drilled holes in them, and painted the completed product.

EXHIBIT 10
Nucor's steel joist and steel production and sales, 1975–1985

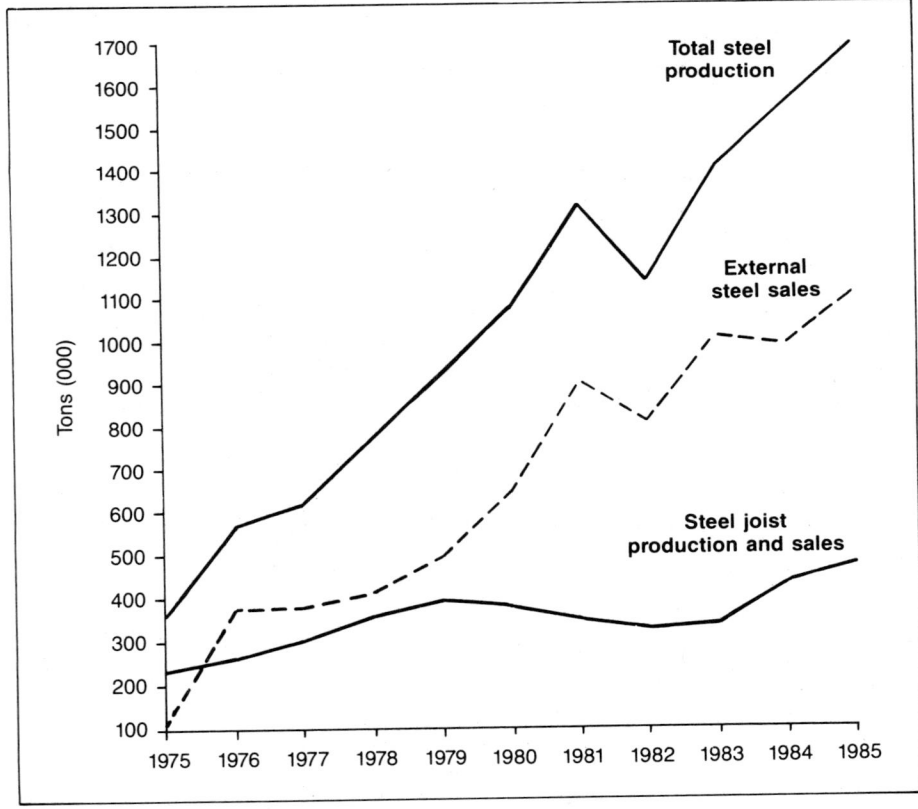

Competition
Many competitors participated in the joist segment, and a large number and variety of customers bought joists. Competition centered around timely delivery and price. Joist manufacturing was not capital intensive like basic steel-making, but was more of an engineering business. Vulcraft bid on a very high percentage of all new buildings which needed joists. Sophisticated computer software was used to design the joists needed on a job and to develop bid estimates. Success also depended on marketing and advertising. Vulcraft had a 40 percent national market share in joists in 1985, making it the largest joist manufacturer in the United States. In 1985 Vulcraft manufactured joists for about 15,000 buildings. Vulcraft management pursued a strategy of being the low-cost supplier of joists.

Organization
Each Vulcraft plant was managed by a general manager who reported directly to Dave Aycock, president of Nucor. Each Vulcraft general manager had spent many years in the joist business. In general, the Vulcraft division's relationships with corporate headquarters paralleled those of the steel division.

OTHER NUCOR BUSINESSES

In addition to steel and joists, Nucor operated three cold finish plants which produced steel bars used in shafting and machining precision parts; a plant which produced grinding balls used by the mining industry; and a research chemicals unit which produced rare earth oxides, metals, and salts. Exhibit 11 shows Nucor's sales by business.

KEN IVERSON AND THE NUCOR CULTURE

Iverson had consciously modeled Nucor on certain bedrock values: productivity, simplicity, thrift, and innovation.

Productivity
Iverson liked to contrast Nucor with integrated companies. He recounted a field trip he took to an integrated steel plant when he was a student at Purdue: "This was the late afternoon. We were touring through the plant, and we actually had to step over workers who were sleeping there. I decided right then that I didn't ever want to work for a big steel plant." The average Nucor worker produced 700 to 800 tons of steel per year versus 350 tons per employee at integrated companies; total labor costs at Nucor averaged less than half that at integrated producers. At the production level people were arranged into groups of 25 to 35 people. Each group had a production standard to meet and a steep bonus schedule for exceeding its standard. Nucor production workers could earn $30,000 or more in a good year. Producing steel and joists entailed hard, hot, dirty, and occasionally dangerous

EXHIBIT 11
Nucor's steel deck
and cold finished
steel sales,
1977–1985

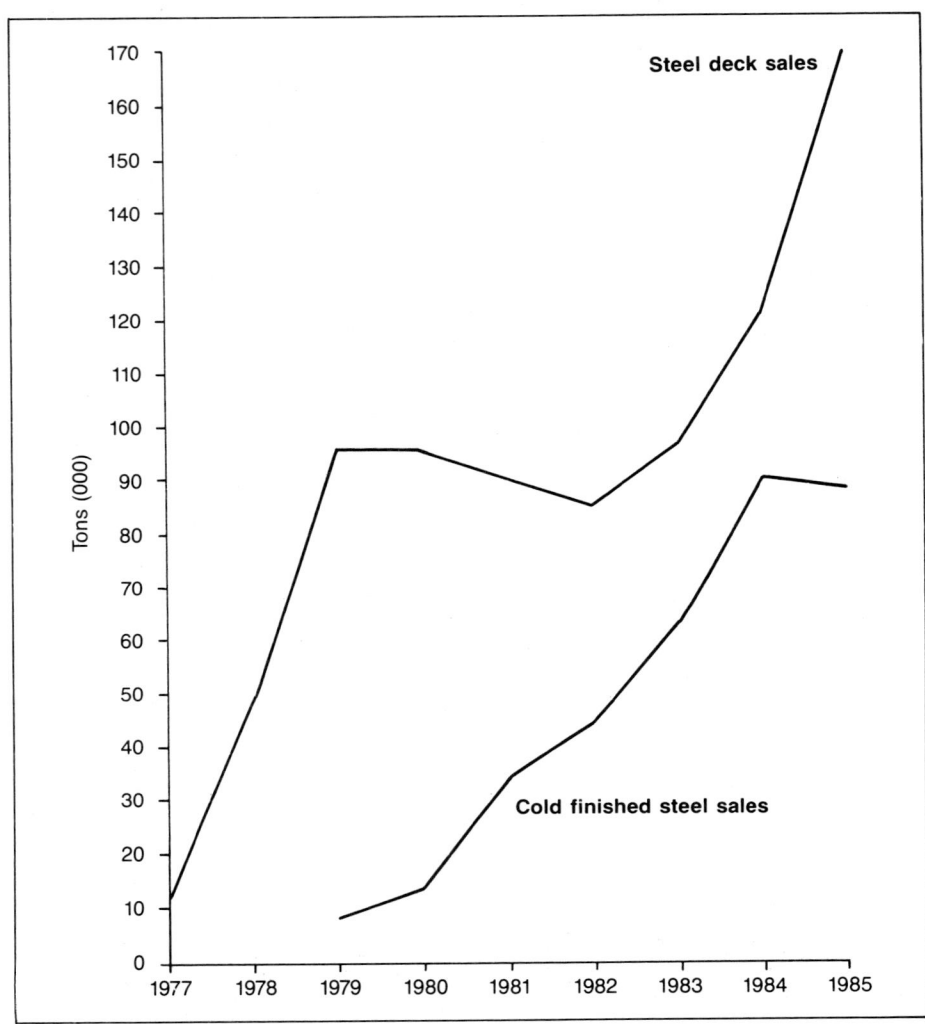

jobs. Performance at all levels of the company was rigidly tied to efficiency and profitability criteria.

Simplicity and Thrift

Iverson and other managers at Nucor had developed practices and symbols which conveyed simplicity. One of their notable achievements was a streamlined organizational structure. Only four levels separated the official hierarchy: workers, department managers, division managers, corporate. Iverson said:

> *You can tell a lot about a company by looking at its organizational charts. . . . If you see a lot of staff, you can bet that it is not a very efficient organization. . . . Secondly,*

*don't have assistants. We do not have that title and prohibit it in our company. . . .
And one of the most important things is to restrict as much as possible the number of
management layers. . . . It is probably the most important single factor in business.*

Iverson's pioneering approach in steel was beginning to be copied by the bigger
companies:

*I spent two days as a lecturer at a business school not long ago. One of the students
heard me talk about getting rid of management layers. He spoke up and said that when
he visited U.S. Steel's new pipe mill near Birmingham, Alabama, the thing they were
most proud of wasn't the technology but that they had only 4 management layers instead
of the usual 10.*

When we asked Sam Siegel about Nucor's organization, he handed us copies
of *Parkinson's Law,* a book that he keeps in ample supply for inquisitive visitors.
Parkinson's Law describes how work always expands to fit the number of workers
assigned to it.

Nucor's spartan values were most evident at its corporate headquarters. Instead
of having a handsome, expensive showcase building sited on landscaped grounds,
Nucor rented a few thousand square feet of the fourth floor of a nondescript office
building with an insurance company's name on it. The only clue that Nucor was
there was its name (listed in ordinary size letters) in the building directory. The
office decor was spartan, simple and functional. Only 16 people worked in the
headquarters — no financial analysts, no engineering staff, no marketing staff, no
research staff. The company assiduously avoided the normal paraphernalia of bureaucracy. No one had a formal job description. The company had no written mission
statement, no strategic plan, and no MBO system. There was little paperwork,
few regular reports, and fewer meetings. Iverson commented on his staff and how
it functioned:

*They are all very sharp people. We don't centralize anything. We have a financial vice
president, a president, a manager of personnel, a planner, internal auditing, and accounting. . . . With such a small staff there are opportunities you miss and things you don't
do well because you don't have time . . . but the advantages so far outweigh the disadvantages. . . . We focus on what can really benefit the business. . . . We don't have job
descriptions, we just kind of divide up the work.*

Innovation

Nucor was a leading innovator among steel minimills and the joist business as
well. Plant designs, organizational structure, incentives, and workforce allocations
synchronized with cultural pressure for constant innovative advancements. Iverson
projected that minimills could eventually capture as much as 35 to 40 percent of
the steel business if they succeeded in developing technological advances which
enabled them to produce a wider variety of steel products very economically. The
breakthroughs hinged on revamping continuous casting technology. Currently, a

minimill couldn't produce certain shapes. Iverson thought the key to unlock the door was the "thin-slab caster":

We are trying to develop a thin slab. Then we could produce plate and other flatrolled products. Right now the thinnest slab that can be produced is 6 inches thick. If we can get down to 1½ inches with the thin slab caster, then we can map out the growth for another 10 years. We could build those all over the country. We're trying to develop this new technology in our Darlington mill. The investment will probably run $10 to $20 million. Now, if we could do it, the new mills would probably cost about $150 million.

Many analysts doubted that such a breakthrough was really in the offing, but Iverson believed it would come within three years and was monitoring seven experimental programs.

Ken Iverson: Public Figure

Nucor's success had made Iverson a public figure. He had been interviewed by newspapers, magazines, radio, and TV; he spoke to industry groups and business schools; and he had been called to testify before Congress. He explained why he was willing to devote his time to these extracurricular activities:

Generally, our policy is to stay as far away as we can from government . . . except that I felt so strongly about protectionism that I thought I should make my views known — especially because our view is so different from the other steel mills. . . . Talking to investors is an important part of the company's relationship with the marketplace . . . the company gets a direct benefit and it makes good sense. . . . I do some talks at business schools just from the standpoint that I get pleasure out of that. . . . We do occasionally hire MBAs, but we haven't had such success with them.

Iverson had a casual, informal, and unaffected style. His office was neither large nor furnished with expensive decorations. For lunch he took visitors across the street to a delicatessen — their "executive dining room" — for a quick sandwich. Nucor had no executive parking spaces, no executive restrooms, no company cars. Everyone, including Iverson, flew coach class. When Iverson went to New York he rode the subway instead of taking a limousine or taxi. Other Nucor managers followed Iverson's example, shunning ostentation, luxury, and status symbols common among other successful companies.

Managers at Nucor described Iverson's management style:

Ken is straightforward. If he says something you can pretty well count on it. He sets the tone and the direction and everybody pitches in. That's the way he acts and approaches things — directly.

Ken is one of the greatest leaders the steel industry has ever had.

Ken is liberal with people and conservative with money.

ORGANIZATION

Organization Structure

Following Iverson's "lean management" philosophy, only four levels of management separated Iverson from the hourly employees. At corporate headquarters they joked that with four promotions, a janitor could become CEO! Exhibit 12 depicts Nucor's organization chart. Below the corporate level the company was organized into divisions. These divisions roughly corresponded to plant locations.

Recently, under the pressure of the growing size of the company and Iverson's busy public role, the jobs of president and CEO were separated. By trying to be "everything to everyone," Iverson was spreading himself a little thin. Dave Aycock was promoted from a plant manager's job to president, responsible for day-to-day operations of Nucor; Aycock talked about his new role:

I worked at Vulcraft when it was acquired by Nucor in 1955. . . . I've been in this new job for about a year. . . . It's very exciting. . . . If I had actually known roughly half

EXHIBIT 12
Nucor's organization structure

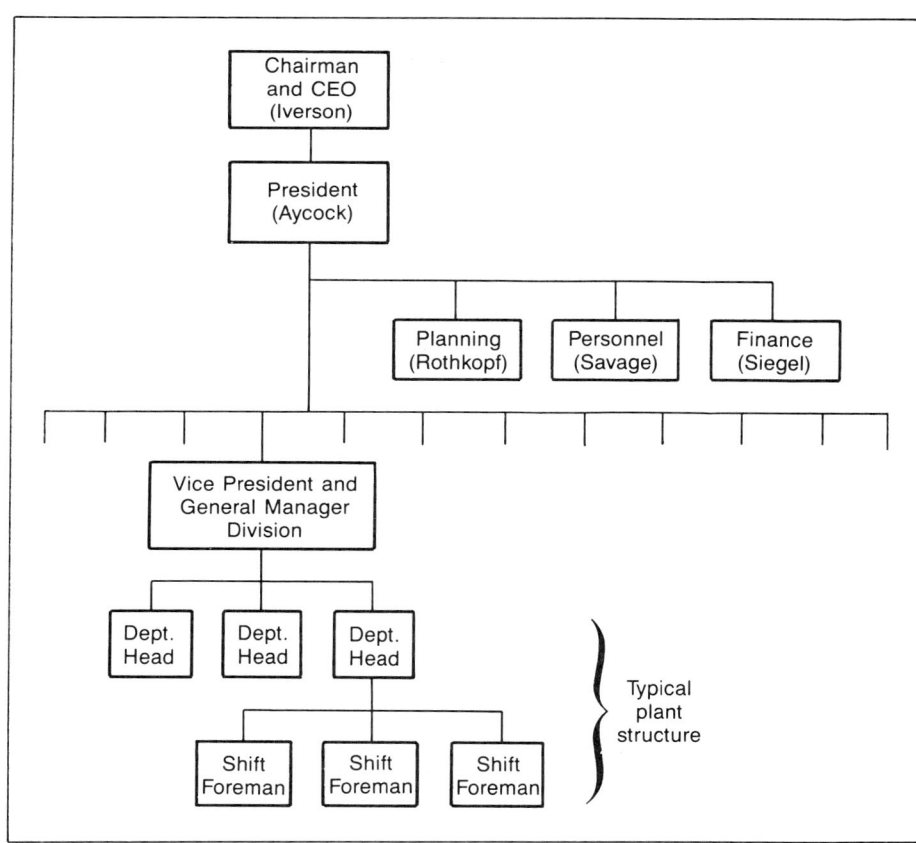

Note: Nucor has four steel mills (divisions), six joist plants, three cold finished steel plants, a grinding ball plant, and a research chemicals division — each is headed by a vice president and general manager.

of what I thought I knew, I would probably have been more valuable. . . . Most of my time has been spent learning the personalities, the reactions, and philosophies of the operating personnel. . . . Many of them were glad to see the change because they thought Ken was overworked.

Division Management

Because Nucor had no headquarters staff and because of top management's great confidence in operating personnel, division managers played a key role in decision making. Iverson said of the division managers:

They are all vice presidents, and they are behind our success. He's at that division. He's responsible for that division. They make the policies of this company. Most of them have been with Nucor at least 10 years. But his pay is based on how this company does — not on how well his division does — it's the group concept again.

Corporate- Division Interaction

Contact between divisions and corporate headquarters was limited to a report of production volume, costs, sales, and margin — the "Monthly Operations Analysis." Each month every division received the "smiling face" report, comparing all the divisions across about a dozen categories of efficiency and performance. One division manager described how Iverson delegated and supervised:

Mr. Iverson's style of management is to allow the manager all the latitude in the world. His involvement with managers is quite limited. As we have grown, he no longer has the time to visit with division managers more than once or twice a year. . . . In a way I feel like I run my own company because I don't get marching orders from Mr. Iverson. He lets you run the division the way you see fit, and the only way he will step in is if he sees something he doesn't like, particularly bad profits, high costs, or whatever. But in the four years I've worked with him I don't recall a single instance where he issued an instruction to me to do something differently.

The casewriters asked a division manager how the corporate officers would handle a division which wasn't performing as it should:

I imagine he (Aycock) would call first and come out later, but it would be appropriate to the situation. Ken and Dave are great psychologists. Right now, for instance, the steel business is showing very poor return on assets, but I don't feel any pressure on me because the market is not there. I do feel pressure to keep my costs down, and that is appropriate. If something went wrong Dave would know.

How does Nucor respond to problems in management performance?

We had a situation where we were concerned about the performance of a particular employee . . . a department manager. Ken, Dave, and I sat down with the general manager to let him know where we were coming from. So now the ball is in his court. We will offer support and help that the general manager wants. Later I spent a long evening with the general manager and the department manager. Now the department manager understands the corporate concern. Ken will allow the general manager to resolve this issue. To do otherwise would take the trust out of the system. . . . We are not going to just call someone in and say "We're not satisfied. You're gone." . . . But, eventually, the string may run out. Ken will terminate people. He takes a long time to do it. I respect that. Ken would rather give people too much time than too little.

Important issues merited a phone call or perhaps a visit from a corporate officer. A division manager told the casewriters that he talked to headquarters about once a week. Divisions made their own decisions about hiring, purchasing, processes, and equipment. There was no formal limit on a division manager's spending authority. Sales policy and personnel policy were set at corporate level. Divisions didn't produce a plan, but: "People in this company have real firm ideas about what is going on and what will be happening . . . mostly by word of mouth."

Relationships between the divisions were close. They shared ideas and information, and sold each other significant amounts of product.

Decision Making Division managers met formally in a group with corporate management three times a year at the "Roundtable." Sessions began at 7 A.M. and ended at 8 P.M. At these meetings, budgets, capital expenditures, and changes in wages or benefits were agreed on, and department managers were reviewed. Iverson waited for a consensus to emerge about an alternative before going ahead with a decision. He did not impose decisions. Corporate officers described Nucor's decision making processes:

Over a long period of time, decisions in this company have been made at the lowest level that they can — subject to staying within the philosophy of the company. We get a lot of work done without too many managers. Ken has the business courage to stay out of the small things. It takes a lot of courage for general managers to resist the temptation to control every event.

I can walk into Ken's office anytime and talk about anything I want to talk about. Agree or disagree with anything he has done. I don't agree with every decision that is made. I have the right to disagree. Sometimes I disagree strongly. Ken hears me out. Ken listens to other people. He does not feel that he is always right. Sometimes he will change his mind.

I remember when I first started to work for Nucor and I was sitting down with Ken Iverson. He told me, "John, you are going to make at least three mistakes with this company in the first few years that you are with us. Each one of these mistakes will cost us $50,000. I want you to be aggressive, and I want you to make decisions. One word of caution. We don't mind you making the mistakes, but please don't make them all in one year."

Ken defers a decision when the executives are strongly divided to give people a chance to consider it more. Ken is a superb negotiator. He might look at the various positions and say "I have a compromise," and lay that out. Many times he can see a compromise that everyone is comfortable with.

FINANCIAL POSITION

The theme of simplicity also extended to financial matters. Sam Siegel, Nucor's vice president of finance, did not use a computer. He told the casewriters:

> *When you make too many calculations they get in the way of business. Each of the divisions uses computers for many purposes, including financial analysis. You could make an economic case for centralizing some of that here at corporate headquarters. We could save money and create all kinds of information, but then we would have to hire more people to study that information.*

Investments

No financial analysts worked at corporate headquarters. Nucor did not use sophisticated models of discounted cash flow or complicated formulas to govern capital expenditures, preferring an eclectic capital investment policy. Iverson commented: ''Priority? No. We don't even do that with capital expenditures. Sometimes we'll say . . . we won't put up any buildings this year. . . . But in recent years we've been able to fund anything we felt we needed. We don't do it by priorities.'' Responding to a query about whether the company used an internal hurdle rate of return, Iverson said:

> *We look at it from the standpoint of whether it's replacement and if it's modernization, what the payback period is, or if it is a new facility. In many cases the payback on a new steel mill is longer than you would like, but you can't afford not to do it. I think maybe that is where other manufacturing companies go wrong — where they have these rigid ideas about investments. If you don't put some of these investments in, after four or five years you are behind. . . . You can't afford to fall behind, even if you don't get the payback. That's why the integrated steel companies didn't put in continuous casters, because they couldn't get the payback they wanted. . . . Now they have got to do it. . . . From an economics point of view they didn't do anything wrong, they didn't make a mistake.*

Financial Reporting

Each division had a controller who reported directly to the division manager and indirectly to Siegel. Siegel saw the role of his controllers as being broad: ''Controllers who merely do financial work are not doing a good job. A controller should become involved with key plant operations . . . should learn the whole operation.'' Siegel spent only about one half of his time on strictly financial matters, contributing the other half toward ''problems, issues, and projects'' of importance to the company.

Financial Condition

According to Siegel, the company was in good financial condition except for having too much invested in short-term assets (Exhibits 13 and 14). Wall Street analysts had speculated about what Nucor might decide to do with its excess short-term assets.

EXHIBIT 13 Financial review, 1980–1985

	1980	1981	1982	1983	1984	1985
Net sales	$482,420,363	$544,820,621	$486,018,162	$542,531,431	$660,259,922	$758,495,374
Costs and expenses						
Cost of products sold	369,415,571	456,210,289	408,606,641	461,727,688	539,731,252	600,797,865
Marketing and administrative expenses	38,164,559	33,524,820	31,720,315	33,998,054	45,939,311	59,079,802
Interest expense (income)	(1,219,965)	10,256,546	7,899,110	(748,619)	(3,959,092)	(7,560,645)
	406,360,165	499,991,655	448,226,128	494,967,123	581,711,471	652,317,022
Earnings before taxes	76,060,198	44,828,966	37,792,034	47,564,308	78,548,451	106,178,352
Federal income taxes	31,000,000	10,100,000	15,600,000	19,700,000	34,000,000	47,700,000
Net earnings	$ 45,060,198	$ 34,728,966	$ 22,192,034	$ 27,864,308	$ 44,548,451	$ 58,478,352
Net earnings per share	$3.31	$2.51	$1.59	$1.98	$3.16	$4.11
Dividends declared per share	$.22	$.24	$.26	$.30	$.36	$.40
Percentage of earnings to sales	9.3%	6.4%	4.6%	5.1%	6.7%	7.7%
Return on average equity	29.0%	17.8%	10.0%	11.4%	16.0%	17.8%
Return on average assets	16.9%	10.3%	5.9%	7.0%	9.8%	11.2%
Capital expenditures	$ 62,440,354	$101,519,282	$ 14,788,707	$ 19,617,147	$ 26,074,653	$ 29,066,398
Depreciation	13,296,218	21,599,951	26,286,671	27,109,582	28,899,421	31,105,788
Sales per employee	150,756	155,663	133,156	148,639	176,069	197,011
Current assets	$115,365,727	$131,382,292	$132,542,648	$193,889,162	$253,453,373	$334,769,147
Current liabilities	66,493,445	73,032,313	66,102,706	88,486,795	100,533,684	121,255,828
Working capital	$ 48,872,282	$ 58,349,979	$ 66,439,942	$105,402,367	$152,919,689	$213,513,319
Property, plant and equipment	$173,074,273	$252,616,074	$239,071,390	$231,304,817	$228,102,790	$225,274,674
Total assets	$291,221,867	$384,782,127	$371,632,941	$425,567,052	$482,188,465	$560,311,188
Long-term debt	$ 39,605,169	$ 83,754,231	$ 48,229,615	$ 45,731,000	$ 43,232,384	$ 40,233,769
Percentage of debt to capital	18.2%	28.3%	17.2%	15.0%	12.6%	10.1%
Stockholders' equity	$177,603,690	$212,376,020	$232,281,057	$258,129,694	$299,602,834	$357,502,028
Per share	$12.96	$15.25	$16.60	$18.32	$21.16	$24.97
Shares outstanding	13,699,994	13,927,014	13,991,882	14,090,181	14,161,079	14,315,005
Stockholders	22,000	22,000	22,000	21,000	22,000	22,000
Employees	3,300	3,700	3,600	3,700	3,800	3,900

	1983	1984	1985
Funds provided			
Operations			
Net earnings	$27,864,308	$44,548,451	$58,478,352
Depreciation of plant and equipment	27,109,582	28,899,421	31,105,788
Deferred federal income taxes	8,200,000	5,600,000	2,500,000
Total funds provided by operations	63,173,890	79,047,872	92,084,140
Disposition of plant and equipment	274,138	377,259	788,726
Decrease in other assets	—	—	364,935
Issuance of common stock	2,201,183	2,006,460	5,387,182
Total funds provided	$65,649,211	$81,431,591	$98,624,983
Funds applied			
Purchase of property, plant and equipment	$19,617,147	$26,074,653	$29,066,398
Increase in other assets	354,170	259,229	—
Reduction in long-term debt	2,498,615	2,498,616	2,998,615
Cash dividends	4,216,854	5,081,771	5,697,290
Acquisition of treasury stock	—	—	269,050
Increase in working capital	38,962,425	47,517,322	60,593,630
Total funds applied	$65,649,211	$81,431,591	$98,624,983
Analysis of change in working capital			
Increase (decrease) in current assets			
Cash	$ (4,283,370)	$ (3,521,115)	$ 5,164,839
Short-term investments	38,445,234	37,177,195	67,269,144
Accounts receivable	16,424,874	7,297,872	1,982,204
Contracts in process	8,402,160	1,404,012	2,015,481
Inventories	7,723,168	17,242,200	4,844,503
Other current assets	(366,052)	(35,953)	39,603
Net increase (decrease)	61,346,514	59,564,211	81,315,774
Increase (decrease) in current liabilities			
Long-term debt due within one year	799,000	—	—
Accounts payable	14,186,217	(4,443,835)	2,781,762
Federal income taxes	2,278,813	8,891,286	3,892,269
Accrued expenses and other current liabilities	5,120,059	7,599,438	14,048,113
Net increase (decrease)	22,384,089	12,046,889	20,722,144
Increase in working capital	$38,962,425	$47,517,322	$60,593,630

HUMAN RESOURCES

Besides being known for its stunning success in joists and steel, Nucor was also known for its remarkable human resources practices. The casewriters visited a Vulcraft plant and talked with a department manager who had worked at Vulcraft for 16 years about what made Nucor different:

Our plants are located strategically. The company puts them in rural areas, where we can find a good supply of quality labor — people who believe in hard work. We have beaten back three unionizing campaigns in the last 10 years. These employees are very loyal. In fact, we had to hire a guard to protect the union organizers from some of our workers. We see about 3 percent turnover and very little absenteeism. They are proud of working with us. It's fun when they come to you and ask for work.

Why did Nucor do so well with employees?

Most companies want to take their profits out of their employees. We treat employees right. They are the ones who make the profits. Other companies aren't willing to offer what is needed to allow people to work. They can't see the dollar down the road for the nickel in their hand. Nucor's people make it strong.

Nucor's incentive systems had been a subject of much discussion and comment. *Fortune* estimated in 1981 that Nucor's workers earned an average of $5,000 more than union steelworkers. Moreover, Nucor workers were the highest paid manufacturing, blue-collar workforce in the United States.

Casewriter: But doesn't that prove the point — that American steelworkers earning $30,000 per year have priced the industry out of business?

Iverson: They earn every bit of it! Sure, it's generous. . . . There's a reason for it. It's hot, hard, dirty, dangerous, skilled work. We have melters who earn more than $40,000, and I'm glad they earn it. It's not what a person earned in an absolute sense, it's what he earns in relation to what he produces that matters.

The incentive system at Nucor had several key elements. John Savage, manager of personnel services, explained the company's personnel philosophy:

Our employee relations philosophy has four primary components. . . . Management's first and foremost obligation to employees is to provide them the opportunity to earn according to their productivity. . . . Next, we are obligated to manage the company in such a way that employees can feel that if they are doing their job properly, they will have a job tomorrow. . . . Third, employees must believe that they are treated fairly. . . . Lastly, employees must have an avenue of appeal if they believe they are being treated unfairly, to Mr. Iverson himself if necessary.

Everyone at Nucor participated in incentive plans. These incentives took several different forms depending on the type of work involved.

Production Incentives

Production groups of 25 to 30 employees were grouped around clearly measurable production tasks. About 3,000 Nucor employees made joists and steel under production incentives based on historical time standards. If, for example, a group produced a joist in 50 percent less than standard time, they got a 50 percent bonus. Bonuses were paid at the end of the following week. When equipment sat idle, no bonus accrued. If an employee was absent for a day, he or she lost a week's bonus — a difference amounting to as much as $7 per hour. Although workers often earned wages far above averages for manufacturing, the system was very tough:

*If you work real hard and you get performance, the payment is there next week. . . .
You worked like a dog and here is the money. . . . There are lots of people who don't
like to work that hard, and they don't last for long. We have had groups get so mad at
a guy who wasn't carrying his weight that they chased him around a joist plant with a
piece of angle iron and were gonna kill him. . . . Don't get the idea that we're paternalistic.
If you are late even five minutes you lose your bonus for the day. If you are late by
more than 30 minutes because of sickness or anything else, you lose your bonus for the
week. We do grant four "forgiveness" days a year. We have a melter, Phil Johnson,
down in Darlington. One day a worker arrived at the plant and said that Phil had been
in an auto accident and was sitting by his car on Route 52 holding his head. The foreman
asked, "Why didn't you stop to help him?" The guy said, "And lose my bonus?"*

Many Nucor workers earned between $30,000 and $40,000 per year. Nucor's monetary incentives made the company attractive to jobseekers (see Exhibit 14). Iverson told a story about hiring new workers:

*We needed a couple new employees for Darlington, so we put out a sign and put a
small ad in the local paper. The ads told people to show up Saturday morning at the
employment office at the plant. When Saturday rolled around, the first person to arrive
at the personnel office was greeted by 1,200 anxious jobseekers. There were so many of
them that the size of the crowd began to interfere with access into and out of the plant.
So the plant manager called the state police to send some officers over to control the
crowd. But, the sergeant at the state police barracks told the plant manager that he
couldn't spare any officers. You see, he was short-handed himself because three of his
officers were at the plant applying for jobs!*

Managerial Compensation

Department managers received a bonus based on a percentage of their division's contribution to corporate earnings. In an operating division such bonuses could run as high as 50 percent of a person's base pay. In the corporate office the bonus could reach 30 percent of base pay. Employees such as accountants, secretaries, clerks, and others who didn't work in production got a bonus based on either their division's profit contribution or corporate return on assets.

Senior officers had no employment contracts or pension plan. More than half of their compensation was based on company earnings. Their base salaries were set at about 70 percent of market rates for similar jobs. Ten percent of pretax earnings were set aside and allocated to senior officers according to their base salary. The base level was tied to a 12 percent return on shareholder's equity. Half the bonus was paid in cash, and half was deferred in the form of Nucor stock. In a profitable year officers could earn as much as 190 percent of their base salary as bonus and 115 percent on top of that in stock.

Other Compensation Incentives

Nucor also operated a profit sharing trust. The plan called for 10 percent of pretax earnings to be assigned to profit sharing each year. Of that amount, 20 percent was paid to employees in the following year, and the remainder was held to fund the worker retirement program. Vesting in the trust was 20 percent after one year and 10 percent each following year. The arrangement had the effect of making the retirement income of Nucor employees depend on the company's success. Additionally, Nucor paid 10 percent of whatever amount an employee was willing to invest in Nucor stock, gave employees five shares of stock for each five years of employment, and occasionally paid extraordinary bonuses.

Lastly, Nucor ran a scholarship program for children of full-time employees. In 1985 over 300 children were enrolled in universities, colleges, and vocational schools. Since the program's inception over 900 students had participated. One family had educated eight children on Nucor's plan.

No Layoffs

Nucor had never laid off or fired an employee for lack of work. Iverson explained how the company handled the need to make production cutbacks:

When we have a difficult period, we don't lay anybody off. . . . We operate the plants four days a week or even three days. We call it our "share the pain program." . . . The bonus system remains in place, but it's based on four days' production instead of five. The production workers' compensation drops about 25 percent, the department managers' drops 35 to 40 percent, and the division managers' can drop as much as 60 to 80 percent. Nobody complains. They understand. And they still push to get that bonus on the days they work.

The Downside

Nucor's flat structure and steep incentives also had certain negative side effects. First, the incentive system was strictly oriented toward the short term. If a general manager was thinking about a major capital investment project, he was also thinking about reducing his short-term income. Iverson described how the ups and downs of the incentive plans affected officers: "If the company can hit about 24 percent return on equity, the officers' salary can reach 300 percent of the base amount. It maxed out in 1979 and 1980. In 1980 and 1981 total officers' compensation dropped way off. In 1980 I earned about $400,000, but in 1981 I earned $108,000. So officers have to watch their lifestyle!" Iverson's 1981 pay made him, according to *Fortune*, the lowest paid CEO in the *Fortune 500* industrial ranking. Iverson commented that it was "Something I was really a little proud of."

Second, promotions came very slowly. Many managers had occupied their current jobs for a very long time. Additionally, Nucor experienced problems in developing the skills of its first-line supervisors.

Many other companies studied Nucor's compensation plans. The casewriters asked John Savage about the visits other companies made to study Nucor's system:

Many companies visit us. We had managers and union people from General Motors' Saturn project come in and spend a couple of days. They were oriented toward a bureaucratic style. . . . You could tell it from their questions. I was more impressed with the union people than with the management people. The union people wanted to talk dirty, nitty-gritty issues. But the management people thought it was too simple, they didn't think it would work. Maybe their business is too complex for our system. . . . We never hear from these visitors after they leave. . . . I believe it would take five to seven years of working at this system before you could detect a measurable change.

High wages and employment stability got Nucor listed in the book *The 100 Best Companies to Work for in America*. A division manager summed up the Nucor human relations philosophy this way: "It's amazing what people can do if you let them. Nucor gives people responsibility and then stands behind them." The appendix presents selected excerpts from interviews with hourly employees about their jobs at Nucor.

STRATEGIC PLANNING

Nucor followed no written strategic plan, had no written objectives (except those stated in the incentive programs), and had no mission statement. Divisions promulgated no strategic plans. We asked Sam Siegel about long range strategic planning. He confided: "You can't predict the future. . . . No matter how great you may think your decisions are, the future is unknown. You don't know what will happen. . . . Nucor concentrates on the here-and-now. We do make five-year projections, and they are good for about three months. Five to ten years out is philosophy." We also asked Bob Rothkopf (planning director) about planning at Nucor:

> I work on the strategic plan with Ken twice a year. It's formulated out of the projects we are looking at. He and I talk about the direction we feel the company is going. . . . The elements of the most recent plan are that we take the basic level of the company today and project it out for five years. We look at net sales, net income, under different likely scenarios. In this last plan I looked at the potential effects of a mild recession in 1986. . . . We add new products or projects to that baseline.

Rothkopf had responsibility for generating most of the information he used in his forecasts. He often used consultants or other companies to get the information he needed. None of the other senior executives or division managers got deeply involved in this planning process.

Nucor didn't rely on its strategic planning system to make strategic decisions. Rothkopf described how strategic decisions were reached:

> Projects come from all over. Some come from our general managers, or from our suppliers, our customers . . . or come walking in the door here. Iverson is like a magnet for ideas, because of who he is and what Nucor is. . . . We evaluate each project on its own, as it comes up. As each opportunity arises, we go in and investigate it. Some investigations are short; we throw out quite a few of them. We don't make any systematic search for these ideas.

Rothkopf compared Nucor's planning to formal strategic planning done by other companies:

> I think there might be some advantages for us to do that sort of thing. However, our business has been pretty simple. Our businesses are all related and easy to keep track of. When a big decision comes up we discuss it. That's easy because of the simple structure of the company. . . . Planning has disadvantages . . . time-consuming . . . expensive . . . hard to get the information for it . . . tends to get bureaucratic.

Although Nucor had no formal planning system, important strategic decisions loomed on the company horizon. Exhibit 15 provides information on Nucor's strategic options.

EXHIBIT 15
Nucor's strategic options

Strategic considerations	Option 1: Build a seamless tube mill	Option 2: Get into pre-engineered buildings
Market	About $2.5 billion Oilfield equipment companies Commodity Mature, competitive, low growth Integrated companies sell here	$350 million Small growth Numerous competitors, all sizes Regional, fragmented Not a commodity
Investment	$150–180 million	$5–7 million plant generates $15–20 million sales in four years. Want about 20 percent market share in five to six years
Time period needed	About two years	8–12 months
Fit to present activities	Could sell some product to joist division Increase efficiency	Already manufacturing parts for such buildings
Revenues/profits	Sales $240–270 million 20–25 percent profit before taxes	About same as present earning power
Support among executives	Some active support Analyses in process	Joist division favors it Corporate execs divided
Skills and resources	Know market Have most skills, others not too hard to learn	Selling to whole new market Manufacturing skills help
Downside risk	Risky, uncertain market	New market to understand Can do gradually Not very risky

Strategic considerations	Option 3: Build bar minimill	Option 4: Acquire bar minimills
Market	Same as current	Same as current
Investment	$50–75 million for a 250,000 ton mill	A six to seven year old, 175,000 ton mill costs $50 million to build Earns $10–15/ton before tax ±1989, 1987 earliest
Time period needed	18 months	
Fit to present activities	Perfect fit	Obvious, yes

EXHIBIT 15
(continued)

EXHIBIT 15
(continued)

Revenues/profits	$65–75 million sales. Lose money years one and two. Over long term make $5–10 million before taxes.	$45 million sales, earns ±$1 million Under Nucor, such a mill can see sales of $60 million, earn ±$5 million
Support among executives	Quite a bit	Unknown
Skills and resources	In place, no problems	OK, in place
Downside risk	No growth in market. Must take business from entrenched competitors	Anti-trust? Company culture might not fit; exposure to union problems

Strategic considerations	Option 5: Innovative flat-rolled minimill	Option 6: Build bolt plant
Market	25–30 million tons Stable, a commodity Integrated mills dominant	$800 million Mature, stable Commodity dominated by four companies
Investment	$125–175 million for 400,000, to 600,000 ton mill	$25 million/plant
Time period needed	Could build four plants in 5–10 years	
Fit to present activities	Extends product range Sales to joist division Keeps steel/joist "balance"	Steel currently produced goes into product
Revenues/profits	Must project 25 percent profit before tax to justify Lower cost $100/ton?	$28–32 million sales per plant
Support among executives	High company support; spending $10 million to develop process at Darlington	Agreed to build one plant
Skills and resources	Don't know marketing of flat-rolled products Must learn flat-rolling of steel	Need marketing skills
Downside risk	Must invest $10–15 million in any case Hard to invest new technology Competitors leap-frog with new processes Estimate 50–75 percent chance it will work	If foreign steel is barred in United States, bolts get "dumped" here International prices of bolts unstable

EXHIBIT 15
(continued)

Strategic considerations	Option 7: Increase dividends ($.10/share now)	Option 8: Purchase Nucor stock for treasury
Market	Stockholder reaction uncertain Number of shares × increase	14,000,000 shares at $45 currently Number of shares × price
Time period needed	Anytime	One to two years
Fit to present activities	Change in philosophy	Underlines management confidence
Revenues/profits	N/A	Sell shares for profit? Enrich remaining stockholders?
Support among executives	Iverson thinking about it	At the right price/earnings ratio
Skills and resources	N/A	N/A
Downside risk	If earnings slip, could pressure ability to invest	Price of stock could decline

Strategic considerations	Option 9: Diversification outside steel products or joists
Market	Faster growing markets open
Investment	Nucor has $100–150 million Could borrow more
Time period needed	One to two years
Fit to present activities	Depends on business
Revenues/profits	Greater profitability?
Support among executives	Very little
Skills and resources	Nucor understands heavy manufacturing Nucor has skills in streamlined management Employee-relations philosophy
Downside risk	Company has to learn new things? Might require different organizational set-up

NUCOR'S FUTURE: WHAT NEXT?

In spite of Nucor's remarkable successes, Iverson stated a modest, cautious view of the company's capabilities:

We are not great marketers or financial manipulators. . . . We do two things well. We build plants economically and we run them efficiently. We stick to those two things. . . . Basically, that's all we do. We are getting better at marketing, but I wouldn't say we are strong marketers . . . that is not the base of the company. . . . We're certainly not financial manipulators. We recognized a long time ago how important it was for us to hold down overhead and management layers.

Iverson talked about the future of Nucor:

The company's position is much different than it was in past years. In the 60s we nearly went bankrupt. It was a miniconglomerate, so I got rid of half the company. We started all over again. We built steel mills. From the late 60s to the 80s our constraints were financial. We decided that we wanted debt to be less than 30 percent of capital. That restricted the number of mills we could finance. But then in the 1980s things changed. Our restraints are not financial now. We no longer see the opportunities in minimills which we saw in the 60s and 70s. So, what direction should the company go? We have about $120 million in cash and short-term securities.

Since we don't see much opportunity for building additional minimills, we have been looking at various alternatives . . . merger or acquisition, internal growth . . . buying back our own stock . . . and other things. It goes forward by project. We looked at buying another steel company that had problems. Dave visited their plant. Bob (the planner) did some projections on what it would cost us to put that mill in shape. We also have an outside consultant working on it. That is what we have done so far (Iverson points to a report). . . . We are looking at the bolt business too. About 95 percent of bolts used in the United States are made outside of the United States. We are studying whether we should spend $25 million to build a plant. . . . Maybe we ought to buy our own stock. It reduces the number of shares and increases the per share earnings. I feel comfortable with that with the price/earnings ratio we are at.

Was he worried about a takeover?

I really don't expect someone to try to take us over. We have a staggered board. So if someone tries to do it they will have to wait for quite a while to control enough directors. We have other provisions in the bylaws which would make a takeover difficult. Besides, we're in a lousy business — steel.

What about an acquisition by Nucor?

We have some problems with going that route. We don't have any experience with acquisitions, all our growth has been internally generated. The second thing, we would never acquire outside our business, which is the manufacture of steel and steel products. We might be able to go into some nonferrous metals. But if we went into, say, textiles or something else like that . . . it's not . . . If stockholders want to invest in those businesses, let them do it themselves. Conglomeration is a lot of nonsense.

Iverson mentioned additional opportunities:

We are thinking about a seamless tube mill. That business seems to meet many of our requirements. Also, the Vulcraft people believe that we could easily enter the business of pre-engineered buildings. Although that is a new market for us, it's not very risky and it is a logical extension of the joist business.

We are also talking to the Japanese about a joint venture to produce large and medium structural steel shapes. That's a 6-million-ton market worth about $2 billion per year. It's cyclical because it's tied to the construction industry. Imports have about 32 percent of that. We might invest $200 million. We know this market but we lack some technology which the Japanese can supply. We would be 51 percent partners and run the plant.

For fifteen years, Nucor had made the right decisions. The company successfully managed the difficult balancing act of combining outstanding profitability with keeping its workforce loyal, alert, and innovative. Nucor had developed a unique corporate culture and grown rapidly. Now, the material bases for that culture and those successes were changing. The wide open opportunities in minimills had been used up. The company was getting much larger. Ken Iverson wondered where Nucor's future lay. In acquiring other minimills? Bolt plants? Repurchasing stock? Developing new technology? Diversifying? Tube mills? Pre-engineered buildings? In addition to the question of which businesses to pursue, he wondered how future growth and change would affect, and be affected by, Nucor's distinctive competence and its unique corporate culture.

REFERENCES

"Ken Iverson, Man of Steel," *Inc.*, April 1984.

Ken Iverson's speeches.

"Minimills Incentives Give Steelmaker an Edge," *Journal of Commerce*, June 3, 1982.

"Minimills, Maxiprofits," *Time*, January 24, 1983.

Nucor, Frank C. Barnes, 1984.

"Nucor Chief Executive Adds Chairman's Title," *New York Times*, June 18, 1984.

"Nucor Profits from Innovation," *Los Angeles Times*, March 6, 1984.

"Pilgrims Profits at Nucor," *Fortune*, April 6, 1981.

"Steel Man," *Inc.*, April 1986.

"Steel Minimills," *Scientific American*, May 1984.

"Steel Minimills Prosper Despite Industry Woes," *Washington Post*, August 9, 1983.

"The Going Gets Tough at the Nucor Minimill," *New York Times*, August 4, 1983.

The 100 Best Companies to Work for in America, 1984.

JIM

Jim is 32 years old, did not finish school, and has worked at Vulcraft for 10 years. He works at a job that requires heavy lifting. Last year he earned about $38,500.

> *This is hard physical work. Getting used to it is tough, too. After I started working as a spliceman my upper body was sore for about a month. . . . Before I came to work here I worked as a farmer and cut timber. . . . I got this job through a friend who was already working here. . . . I reckon I was very nervous when I started here, but people showed me how to work. . . . The bonuses and the benefits are mighty good here . . . and I have never been laid off. . . . I enjoy this work. . . . This company is good to you. They might let employees go if they had problems, but first they'd give him a chance to straighten out. . . . In 1981 things were slow and we only worked three or four days a week. Sometimes we would spend a day doing maintenance, painting, sweeping. . . and there wasn't no incentive. I was glad I was working. . . . I was against the union.*

KERRY

Kerry is 31 years old, married, and expecting a child. He has worked on the production line for about three years.

> *I was laid off from my last job after working there five years. I went without work for three months. I got this job through a friend. My brother works as a supervisor for Nucor in Texas. . . . This is good, hard work. You get dirty, too hot in the summer and too cold in the winter. They should air-condition the entire plant (laughs). On this joist line we have to work fast. Right now I'm working 8½ hours a day, six days a week. . . . I get good pay and benefits. Vulcraft is one of the better companies in Florence (South Carolina). . . . Everyone does not always get along, but we work as a team. Our supervisor has his off days. . . . I want to get ahead in life, but I don't see openings for promotion here. Most of the foremen have had their jobs for a long time, and most people are senior to me in line. . . . This place is very efficient. If I see a way to improve the work, I tell somebody. They will listen to you.*

OTHER COMMENTS FROM HOURLY WORKERS

> *I am running all day long. It gets hot and you get tired. My wife doesn't like it because sometimes I come home and fall asleep right away.*

> *When something goes down, people ask how they can help. Nobody sits around. Every minute you are down it's like dollars out of your pocket. So everybody really hustles.*

FEDERAL EXPRESS CORPORATION

Federal Express proved the virtue of persistence with the right product in a growing market. In 1985 the company held a $1.2 billion share of the $3 billion overnight delivery industry which it had originally created. Most, if not all, of the credit went to the founder, chairman, and chief executive officer of Memphis-based Federal Express, Frederick W. Smith.[1] He had taken an idea originally developed in a college term paper, for which he was awarded a ''C,'' and gone on to change the way America does business. In the process he added a new cliché to the language, ''when it absolutely, positively has to be there overnight.''[2]

In 1985 Fred Smith reviewed the history of the company and its current mix of products and services. Mr. Smith especially focused his attention on its new electronic mail service, ZapMail. The following paragraphs describe the company and the express delivery industry, including Federal Express's principal competitors.

INDUSTRY

Within the aerospace and air transport industry, Federal Express became a leader in only a few short years.[3] While its main competitors had been around for two decades, satisfied with the traditional air freight forwarding market share they occupied, Federal took the market by storm and ''changed the rules of the game.''[4]

Federal Express laid claim to being the founder of the small-package/document express market. This sector experienced phenomenal growth in the late 1970s and early 1980s, constantly expanding into areas of new services and extended service areas.

Markets for all classes of cargo movement grew in 1984, from heavyweight to documents and letters. Those firms involved in cargo movement included all-cargo

This case was prepared by R. J. Balhorn, Beverly Bowen, Jane Shouse, Steve Spencer, and Carey Spriggs under the supervision of Professor Sexton Adams, North Texas State University, and Professor Adelaide Griffin, Texas Woman's University. Reprinted by permission.

air carriers, traditional air freight forwarders, passenger airlines, ground transportation companies, and air couriers. Although air freight movement in general experienced a profitable year in 1984, the small-package express shipping sector continued its 5-year annual growth rate of 20 percent.[5]

Competitors directly involved in the small-package/document express market included Federal Express, Emery Air Freight, Purolator, UPS, and the United States Postal Service. Through 1983 and 1984, price and service innovations abounded as participants struggled to gain a competitive edge.[6] This sector of the air cargo industry was characterized by price wars, constant cost-cutting strategies, and innovative marketing plans. Most competitors felt an urgency to earmark large capital investments for future expansion in order to keep in the running for the growing market.[7]

Regulatory authority for participants in this industry was under the Federal Aviation Act of 1958, the Civil Aeronautics Board (CAB), and the Federal Aviation Administration (FAA). When the CAB was in existence, its authority related to the economic aspects of air transportation. The FAA's regulatory authority, however, related primarily to the safety aspects of air transportation, including aircraft standards and maintenance. Ground transportation services were exempt from regulation by the Interstate Commerce Commission, but because of the use of radio and communication equipment in ground and air units, Federal Express operations were subject to regulation by the Federal Communications Act of 1934. Finally, Federal Express, as of May 1984, was in compliance with all regulations of the Environmental Protection Agency with regard to smoke emissions.[8]

HISTORY

Fred Smith obtained his revolutionary idea for his firm — an air cargo firm that specialized in door-to-door overnight delivery, using its own planes — in the 1960s while majoring in economics and political science at Yale. He had a close acquaintance with aviation: he'd earned a pilot's license at age fifteen and pursued his flying hobby while a student at Yale. During this same period, such companies as IBM and Xerox were already flying material out of airports not far from Yale's Connecticut campus.[9]

Smith spelled it all out in an overdue economics paper. To cut cost and time, packages from all over the country would be flown to a central point, there to be sorted, redistributed, and flown out again to their destinations. The flying would be late at night when air lanes were comparatively empty. Airports used would be in sizeable cities; trucks would carry packages to their final destinations, whether in those cities or in smaller communities. Equipment and documents from anywhere in the United States could be delivered anywhere else in the United States the next day.[10]

Smith was thinking not only of parts and contracts, but also of canceled checks. His concept, he thought, could be sold to the Federal Reserve to cut down on the float, the period between receipt of a check and collection of funds. A general commercial delivery system could be built on that basis. When the time came to create his company years later, his ambition to serve the Federal Reserve and his desire for an impressive name with a broad geographic connotation led him to the name "Federal Express." The Fed turned down his contract bid, but it now has its own check-delivery system, which Smith said was patterned after his operations.[11]

After college, Smith served two tours of duty in Vietnam, first as a platoon leader and then as a reconnaissance pilot. Upon returning home, he decided to give his air express idea a try. Starting with $4 million which he had inherited, he chose Memphis as a home base. A company study showed that Memphis was near the center of business shipping in the continental United States, and it was only closed an average of 10 hours per year due to adverse weather conditions. The airport offered long runways, a large abandoned ramp, and a pair of inexpensive World War II hangars.[12]

Of course, $4 million was not much for starting a company that needed an entire fleet of planes. Smith had to have more funds. He went to New York and Chicago and brought Wall Streeters to Memphis. His knowledge of the air freight field impressed investors, and at the end of the year he had managed to raise a whopping $72 million in loans and equity investment.

Then Federal Express, which had been marking time operating a charter service, got down to its present business. It began transporting packages of under 70 pounds in April 1973, serving thirteen airports. The first night's package total was eighteen. Volume picked up rapidly, and service was extended. Federal Express was an overnight success, but not for long. OPEC's inflation of fuel prices sent costs up faster than revenues were growing, and by mid-1974, the company was losing more than $1 million per month.[13]

Smith went back to his disappointed investors for more money to keep the company growing until revenues could catch up with expenses. Bankruptcy was a real possibility. After being turned down many times, Smith was able to raise $11 million, enough to get Federal Express over the hump. Federal Express, which lost $27 million in its first 2 years, went $3.6 million into the black in 1976 on $75 million in revenues. It has remained on the upswing ever since.[14]

Federal's short-term goals included increased surface productivity, telecommunications, and international expansion. Federal Express also considered the tempting possibility of going into the passenger business. All of Federal's big jets were easily convertible between freight container pallets and passenger seats, and the utilization of these jets averaged only 4.7 hours out of every 24. Nevertheless, the return on investment from carrying passengers would have been far below that from carrying small packages, and the chance of planes being delayed and out of position for the nightly race to deliver packages on schedule was too great. "Nothing," said Smith, "can be allowed to impair our primary business."[15]

MANAGEMENT/PERSONNEL

Fred Smith — Entrepreneur

Fred Smith was a man of integrity whose charisma enabled him to motivate investors and employees to believe in his dream. His drive was mainly attributed to the scars that he carried from his military service — feelings so strong that Smith himself stated that Federal Express was a creature of Vietnam, and he would not have had the same perspective if not for his experiences there.[16]

As a true entrepreneur, Smith never threw in the towel. When the Arab oil embargo in 1974 forced fuel costs sky high, Smith ran to investors, courting them for more money. When outdated CAB regulations made it impossible for Federal to expand into the larger aircraft which it needed, Smith went to Washington and lobbied for deregulation of the airlines. When the Postal Service relaxed its regulations against private delivery of extremely urgent mail, Smith jumped at the opportunity and began testing the overnight letter service.[17]

Smith did all this with style. To win support from prominent Capitol Hill figures, he wined and dined them. To win the confidence of investors, he was always prepared with thorough market and economic analyses to support his ideas.[18] Unfortunately, by the late 1970s, Federal Express had grown too large for the wheeler-dealer, entrepreneurial approach to running an organization. But Smith believed that some principles remained the same between managing a $1.2 billion operation and a $1.2 million operation:

> One of the biggest principles is that you've got to take action. Most large organizations reach a static point. They cannot take any action, because there are all types of barriers to doing so. There are institutionalized barriers that weren't there when the company was considerably smaller. What changes is your knowledge and your appreciation of how to deal with those institutional barriers, to eliminate them or use them to your advantage. . . . There are myriad number of changes that have to take place in the management style for the company to continue growing.[19]

Corporate Giants

Smith's colleagues had the same "fighter pilot attitude" toward Federal Express. They were all former pilots and entrepreneurs. Although most thought his idea very strange, each one had the "right stuff" needed to make Federal Express fly.[20] From day one, the comradery and loyalty exhibited by employees of Federal Express was strong, strong enough to hold Federal together and transform it from an "entrepreneurial crusade" (us against them) to a respected corporate strength. (See Exhibit 1 for organizational chart.)

The year 1979, however, brought much change to Federal's ranks. President Art Bass, one of the initial crusaders, decided to leave and, like a wave, took five vice-presidents with him, all but one of whom had been with Federal from the start. The reason for their departure was shocking to some but easily understood by Smith. Federal had matured, and Bass and his colleagues felt they lacked the ability to adapt their entrepreneurial perspectives to managing a mature operation. Smith replaced his elite few with managers who were more comfortable with the traditional corporate organization, but he maintained associations with Bass and

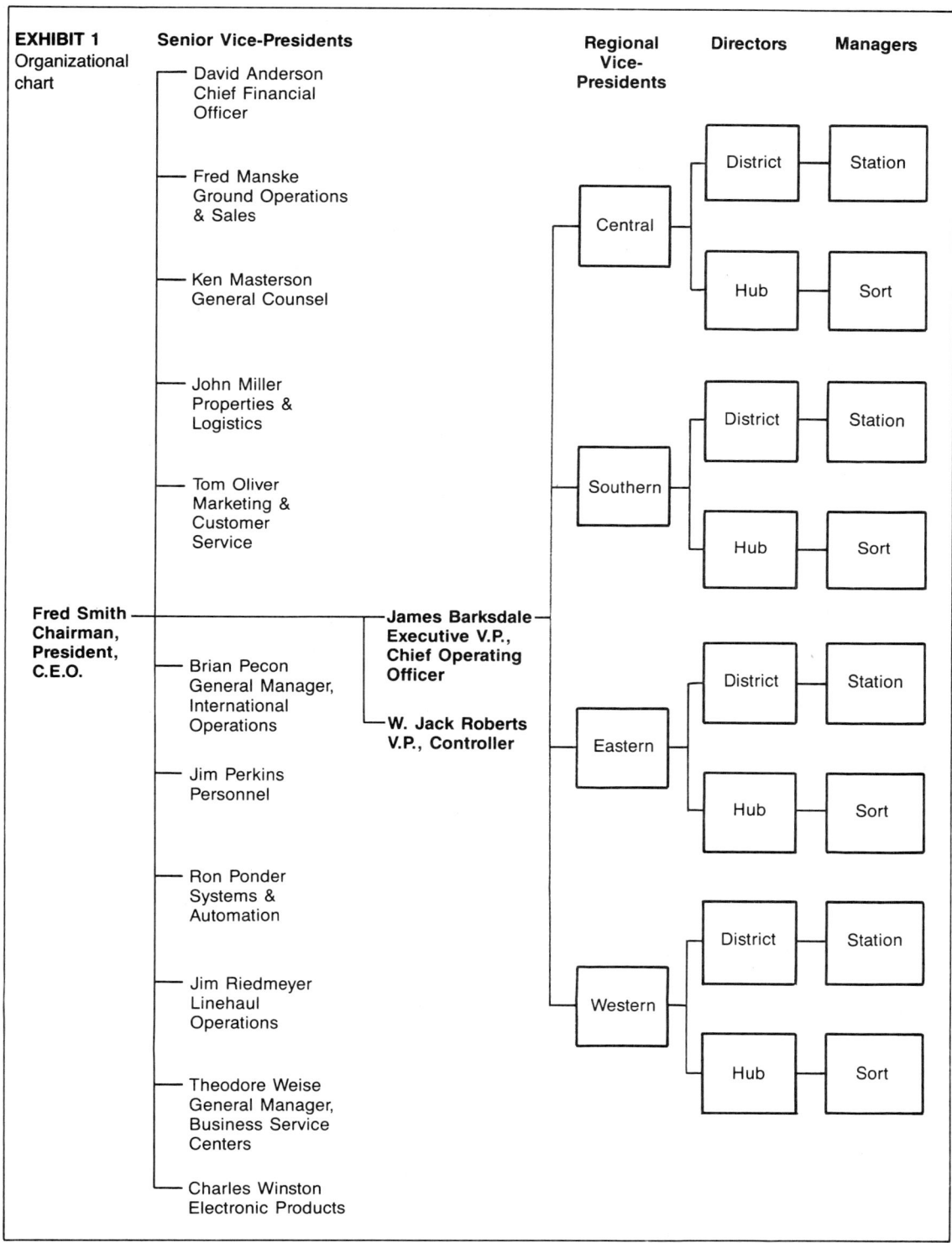

EXHIBIT 1
Organizational chart

Senior Vice-Presidents

David Anderson
Chief Financial Officer

Fred Manske
Ground Operations & Sales

Ken Masterson
General Counsel

John Miller
Properties & Logistics

Tom Oliver
Marketing & Customer Service

**Fred Smith
Chairman, President, C.E.O.**

Brian Pecon
General Manager, International Operations

Jim Perkins
Personnel

Ron Ponder
Systems & Automation

Jim Riedmeyer
Linehaul Operations

Theodore Weise
General Manager, Business Service Centers

Charles Winston
Electronic Products

**James Barksdale
Executive V.P., Chief Operating Officer**

**W. Jack Roberts
V.P., Controller**

Regional Vice-Presidents

Central

Southern

Eastern

Western

Directors

District

Hub

District

Hub

District

Hub

District

Hub

Managers

Station

Sort

Station

Sort

Station

Sort

Station

Sort

Source: Federal Express 1984 Annual Report. J. C. Camillus, "Federal Express Corporation," in W. F. Glueck and L. R. Jauch, eds., *Business Policy and Strategic Management* (New York: McGraw-Hill, 1984).

333

the others in a think-tank type of arrangement.[21] Their only responsibility, as far as Smith was concerned, was to think about the future of Federal.

The key executives in 1985 included:

James L. Barksdale, executive vice-president and chief operating officer. Jim Barksdale joined the company in February 1979 as senior vice-president–data systems. He was appointed executive vice-president and chief operating officer in May 1983. From 1973 until his employment by the company, he had held various positions with Cook Industries, Inc., including corporate vice-president. He served as president of ISD, Inc., a data processing subsidiary, the assets of which were purchased by Cook in 1978, and president of its subsidiary, Cook, Treadwell & Harry, Inc., a general insurance agency and brokerage firm.

David C. Anderson, senior vice-president and chief financial officer. Dave Anderson joined the company in 1976 as vice-president–controller. He was named vice president–treasurer in 1979, senior vice-president and treasurer in 1980, and senior vice-president and chief financial officer in September 1983. For more than 4 years prior to joining Federal Express, he was employed in various accounting and financial positions at Trans World Airlines, including director of general accounting and director of cost and disbursement accounting.

Fred A. Manske, Jr., senior vice-president–ground operations and sales. Fred Manske joined Federal Express in April 1978 as vice-president of the central region. From 1968 to 1978, he was employed by Eastern Airlines in various management positions including manager of airport services, manager of reservations, director of training, and executive assistant to the president. He assumed his present position in September 1980.

Kenneth R. Masterson, senior vice-president and general counsel. Ken Masterson was a partner in the Memphis law firm of Thomason, Crawford and Hendrix prior to his appointment as vice president–legal in January 1980. Ken was elected senior vice-president and general counsel in 1981.

Thomas R. Oliver, senior vice-president–electronic products. Tom Oliver joined Federal Express in 1978 as vice-president–marketing and was elected senior vice-president–marketing and customer service in 1980. In August 1985, he moved into his present position which is responsible for leading the ZapMail product into the profit column for the company. For more than 5 years prior to joining the company, Tom was a senior vice-president and director of Thomas Cook, Inc., a retail and wholesale travel company.

James A. Perkins, senior vice-president and chief personnel officer. Jim Perkins joined the company in 1974 and was employed in various training and personnel capacities before being elected senior vice-president in 1979.

Ron J. Ponder, senior vice-president–information systems. Ron Ponder joined the company in 1977 as director of operations research. He was named vice president–advanced projects in 1980, vice-president–systems design in 1982, and senior vice-president in June 1983.

James R. Riedmeyer, senior vice-president–linehaul operations. Jim Riedmeyer joined the company in 1974 as senior vice-president–maintenance and engineering and then was appointed senior vice-president–linehaul operations in 1983.

Theodore L. Weise, senior vice-president–central support services. Ted Weise joined the company during its formative stages in Little Rock in 1972. He came from General Dynamics Corp., where he was a flight test engineer on the F-111 series fighter/bomber aircraft. He became a vice-president–special projects and advanced planning in 1977 and became vice-president of operations planning in 1978. He was named senior vice-president of that division in 1979. In March 1985, he assumed his present position.

W. Jack Roberts, vice-president and controller. Jack Roberts joined Federal Express in 1977. He served as manager of general accounting and director of accounting until his appointment as vice-president and controller in June 1979.

Federal's Backbone

Dedication to professional, faultless service enabled Federal to "get it there overnight." From the beginning Federal was a people organization. With an employee force of over 24,000, management felt a strong responsibility to provide an array of training programs to support the image it wanted to portray.[22] For example, training for the ZapMail service when it was first introduced included courses for over 18,000 employees.[23] In addition to a thorough training program, Federal boasted of an active file of 45,000 applicants for positions ranging from pilot to courier and made the claim that this was an indication of the attractiveness of company policy and benefits.[24] One generous benefit offered by Federal was paying the tuition in full for college students working at the hub in Memphis.

These policies further supported Federal's commitment to maintaining the image of professionalism and stability.

When the company hired an employee, it was viewed as a long-term investment. To minimize the necessity to furlough any employee, Federal utilized the scheduling of part-time employees which permitted operations to expand or contract according to traffic levels.[25] Smith, though, was exceedingly canny about labor. By employing part-time college students who would come and go as their education progressed, Federal set up a buffer between its operations and the entrance of unions to the hub.[26] This approach also allowed Federal to keep its labor costs low, lower than any other company in the industry.[27]

Recruiting

Because of Federal's reputation of being a leader in the industry, it was never difficult to find qualified people to uphold that image. Unfortunately, the old tactics used to fill Federal's ranks did not work when it came time for Federal to staff its ZapMail operation in 1984. The ZapMail operation required high-tech professionals who could go out to a client and sell them on the new, revolutionary service, but the ads Federal was running were not attracting this type of candidate. Federal had to target advertising to a new, young professional crowd who were looking for career opportunities on the leading edge of technology.[28]

Hundreds of qualified candidates were recruited, all because Federal targeted its advertising to a specific audience. But not only did Federal change its recruiting approach, it also restructured its compensation plan for the ZapMail sales force. ZapMail salespeople received lower base salaries with commissions based solely on the number of machines installed in offices. Federal's management felt that this would help make ZapMail grow at a faster rate.[29]

OPERATIONS

Federal Express provided an overnight door-to-door express delivery service for high-priority packages and documents. In essence, two industries were merged together to accomplish this: aviation and pickup/delivery trucking service. Federal Express services were available Monday through Saturday between 145 airports in the United States, Canada, Puerto Rico, Europe, and Asia. Approximately 90 percent of the U.S. population was serviced through an intricate ground/air network, Smith's brainchild, the hub-and-spoke system.

Hub and Spoke　The service operation that made Federal Express unique in its field was its central sorting facility located in Memphis. The key factor was that every package and letter transmitted by Federal passed through the center in Memphis, where it was sorted and dispatched to the points of delivery across the country and world.

The operations at the hub had been fine-tuned for maximum efficiency. The central sorting process occurred in the middle of the night under "time bomb" pressure.[30] An executive gazing out over the bustling hub said, "If they decide to sit down for an hour, we're dead."[31] All during the day packages had been collected in sorting facilities and local offices in three hundred cities. Once transported to the local airports, the packages were flown to Memphis, where all planes arrived about midnight. The planes were directly unloaded into a giant warehouse of elaborate conveyor belts where they were frantically sorted and loaded back into the planes headed for their intended destinations. By 3 A.M. the planes were ready to depart for sorting facilities located at the local airports, where couriers would then transport packages to local offices and then on to the receiver — and all of this happened overnight!

Contact with couriers was maintained through the use of digitally assisted dispatch systems (DADS). The system was installed in over 70 percent of Federal's vehicles and enabled the company to leave dispatch information in couriers' vans even when unoccupied. In late 1984, hand-held DADS units were introduced to help eliminate duplicated routes, retraced steps, and other inefficiencies.[32] This prototype microprocessor maintained constant data and voice contact between the courier and dispatcher even if the courier was on the upper floor of an office building, as foot couriers often were.

COSMOS, Federal Express's computer network for dispatch entry and tracking, used a satellite and telephone network to locate a customer's shipment at any time as it passed through six electronic gates during transit. Each parcel was bar-coded so that movement could be monitored and recorded every step of the journey. Thus, the whereabouts of a package, not just the paperwork, could be recalled at an instant.[33]

Facilities

Federal Express leased its facilities at the hub from the Memphis-Shelby County Airport Authority. These facilities consisted of a central sorting facility, aircraft hangars, flight training and fuel facilities, warehouse space, and a portion of the administrative offices.[34] Off-airport facilities in Memphis, also leased, consisted of Federal Express headquarters, PartsBank operations, and other administrative offices.[35]

City station operations were located in three hundred cities throughout the United States, Canada, Puerto Rico, Europe, and the Far East. These stations were leased for 5- to 10-year periods. In 1984, a station and service center expansion program was begun which included the construction of Business Service Centers and the installation of unstaffed Overnight Delivery Counters to supplement the city stations and to provide improved access to services in high-density areas.[36]

Equipment and Vehicles

Federal operated almost ten thousand delivery vehicles with approximately two thousand of these leased. Other vehicles owned by Federal mainly included ground-support equipment, cargo loaders, transports, and aircraft tugs.[37] As of July 31, 1984, Federal owned fifty-eight aircraft and an inventory of spare engines and parts for each type. The company was committed to purchase eleven additional aircraft to be delivered in 1985 through 1987.[38] Deposits and payments made according to these agreements were:

$ 98,700,000 in the remainder of 1985
$169,800,000 in the remainder of 1986
$105,800,000 in the remainder of 1987

PRODUCT LINES

On a domestic level, Federal Express offered three basic services, Priority One, ZapMail, and Standard Air, a one- to two-day package and document delivery service. Additionally, Federal provided special handling for dangerous goods and restricted articles, an air cargo charter service, and an inventory parts shipment service. Through the use of expanded direct service and exclusive agents, Federal Express could also deliver documents and custom-cleared packages internationally to areas in Canada, Puerto Rico, Western Europe, the Far East, and Australia.[39]

Priority One

Priority One, an overnight door-to-door delivery of business goods, absolutely, positively guaranteed a 10:30 A.M. next-morning delivery. In either the sender's packaging or that of Federal Express, time-sensitive letters, boxes, and tubes up to

150 pounds in weight, 62 inches in length, or 120 inches in length and girth combined could be shipped to almost any location in the contiguous states.[40] Couriers were utilized for pickup and delivery or customers could bring packages and documents to self-service centers or Federal Express Business Service Centers. Permitting face-to-face customer contact, these staffed, storefront facilities were located in high-traffic, high-density areas. Over three hundred of the centers were planned to be in place by the end of fiscal 1985.[41]

Rates for overnight letters were $11 if delivered to a drop-off location by the sender and $14 if picked up by a courier. Courier-Pak boxes and tubes were subject to a 5-pound or $34 minimum charge, while Courier-Pak envelopes were priced at a 2-pound or $25 minimum. Schedules indicating price per pound then applied for parcels over the minimum weight. Discounts of up to 40 percent were offered to qualified shippers.[42]

Standard Air

Standard Air gave the same array of service features offered under Priority One, only packages were scheduled for delivery no later than the second business day after pickup. At approximately one-half the Priority One rates, Standard Air was promoted as, "when it has to be there, but doesn't have to be there overnight."[43] Many packages arrived the next business day, making this one- to two-day service an economical alternative for time-pressured shippers.

Charter/ PartsBank

Beyond delivering packages, Federal offered two unique services to serve the larger distribution needs of American business. The first, Air Cargo Charter, allowed the charter of McDonnell DC-10s, Boeing 727s, or Dassault Falcons on either a one-time or contractual basis. Subject to availability, aircraft could be chartered 24 hours a day, 7 days a week. The second, PartsBank, arose from the need for the speedy handling of critical inventories. Combining a parts warehouse system with an overnight airline, PartsBank allowed companies to place time-sensitive inventory such as computer parts, medical supplies, and electronic components in Federal's Memphis PartsBank warehouse. A toll-free telephone call to PartsBank could have the item shipped immediately.[44]

ZapMail

Zapmail was conceived approximately 7 years before its 1984 introduction as an answer to electronic mail. (See Exhibits 2, 3, and 4.) It evolved into a major product because of indications of strong demand.[45] Users called requesting the service, and within an hour a courier arrived to pick up the document. The courier then delivered the document to the nearest input station where the document was inserted into a scanner, digitized, and sent over the Federal Express network to the receiving station. There it was printed and delivered to the recipient by courier. Total elapsed time from initial call to delivery time was 2 hours. If the sender took the document himself to a manned Federal Express facility, ZapMail delivery was accomplished in one hour. In contrast to electronic mail, ZapMail was an electronically transmitted document rather than just a message. As a result, charts, contracts, invoices, and artwork could be reproduced into high-resolution copies.

EXHIBIT 2
ZapMail press release

For Immediate Release

Federal Express Corporation has launched the major phase of its ZapMail electronic transmission service, installing ZapMail equipment in customers' offices. It is the first single-source paper communications system that reaches almost everybody in America with the best quality, most convenient, and most economical facsimile service ever seen.

Installation of the specially designed equipment not only enables customers to establish intracompany networks, but also to avail themselves of the entire Federal Express ZapMail network, putting them within hours of the majority of the nation's business population.

Cost to customers for a "ZapMailer" on their premises is minimal. There are neither equipment leasing fees nor telephone bills because the units are directly linked to Federal Express's own communications network. Charges are based solely on a per-page basis (subject to a minimum charge), with discounts available based on length of time of service agreements and quantities of terminals installed. (See attached price list.)

The ZapMailer scans, sends, and prints high-quality copies of documents on plain bond paper. The documents are reproduced at either another ZapMail unit in the recipient company or at a Federal Express office with delivery by a courier to the recipient. The document is transmitted over Federal Express's own vast, packet-switched network which is already handling more than 40,000 pages a day of the highest-quality facsimile ever available. ZapMail has eight times more resolution per square inch than standard Group 3 facsimile, the highest industry standard up to this point.

Federal Express markets and services ZapMail equipment through its own sales and service network.

The ZapMail unit can also be used as a local convenience copier.

Federal Express views the ZapMailer as a natural replacement for facsimile systems and telex terminals and as a complement for its overnight document delivery services.

–30–

Source: Federal Express Corporation.

Original documents would either be forwarded to the recipient or returned to the sender by 10:30 A.M. the next business day.[46]

ZapMail charges were $25 for the first twenty pages and $1 per page after twenty pages. If sent from a Service Center, the cost was reduced by $5.[47] For a leasing fee of approximately $200 per month, a frequent user could have a ZapMail terminal placed in his office with no installation or maintenance fees.[48]

Although much had been staked on the success of ZapMail, initial results had been disappointing. Several marketing and operational problems had hindered the initial launch of the project, but optimism remained high for the long term.

From an operational standpoint, there had at first been a delay, later resolved, in the installation of dedicated long-distance lines by AT&T. More recently, in the second stage of the project, that of placing on-premise terminals (ZapMailers) with volume users, a one-month delay resulted from awaiting installation of the software required for simultaneous transmission of documents to multiple destinations. Thus the targeted goal of three thousand ZapMailers in place by the end of May 1985

EXHIBIT 3
ZapMailer pricing,
February 1985

Term	Minimum	Quantity	Page price	Delivery charge
1 year	$200	1–9 units	.95	$10.00
2 years	$200	1–9 units	.90	$10.00
3 years	$200	1–9 units	.85	$10.00
1 year	$125	10–50 units	.90	$10.00
		51–100 units	.85	$10.00
		101+ units	.80	$10.00
2 years	$100	10–50 units	.85	$10.00
		51–100 units	.80	$10.00
		101+ units	.75	$10.00
3 years	$ 75	10–50 units	.80	$10.00
		51–100 units	.75	$10.00
		101+ units	.70	$10.00

Local copy charge is 25¢ per page.
Transmissions, local copies, and delivery/pickup services apply to attaining monthly minimums.
No drop-off or hold-at-location charges.

1. All orders must be installed within 12 months of order date to guarantee quantity pricing.
2. On a quarterly basis, subject to item # 1, Federal Express will extend additional discounts to customers that have moved into a higher discount range based on the combination of open orders and installations the customer has achieved on a rolling year-to-date basis.
3. For billing purposes, these discounts will be applied to all customer installations 30 days after the close of the quarter.
4. This price list is part of your service agreement.
5. Above monthly minimum charge is applicable for Dial-Up circuit only.
6. Prices are subject to change prior to actual order.

Source: Federal Express Corporation.

was in doubt. As of the end of January 1985, over seven hundred orders for the machines had been placed.[49]

On the marketing front, management noted it had been perhaps overly optmistic in relying on its market research indicating a pent-up need for the new service. ZapMail shipments were averaging about 3,200 per day, far below the 20,090 to 30,000 needed to reach the initial projected breakeven level 12 to 18 months after start-up.[50] It had become clear that the marketing approach that had been effective for small packages was not working in the same-day market. Part of the problem rested in consumer education. As with its overnight express service, Federal needed to get potential customers to understand exactly what was being offered and how

EXHIBIT 4
ZapMailer service
agreement/pricing
summary

Term	Number of terminals	Monthly rental per terminal	Transmitted price per page	Copier price per page
1 Year	1	$525	.25	.10
1 Year	2–15	$500	.25	.10
1 Year	16+	$475	.25	.10

Additionally

1. Pickup/delivery charge of $10 will apply to documents picked up or delivered by Federal Express that are billed to your ZapMailer account.
2. Drop-off or hold-at-location charge of $5 will apply to documents dropped off or held for pickup at Federal Express locations that are billed to your ZapMailer account.
3. All orders must be installed within 4 months of order date to guarantee quantity pricing.
4. Prices are subject to change prior to actual order.
5. Move charges: within the same building — $250.
   to another building — $250 plus freight.
6. The above pricing is applicable to domestic services only.

Source: Federal Express Corporation.

to use it. The company had overestimated the ease with which its customer base could be educated about the benefits of ZapMail and set about rectifying the problem.

Stressing how the new service should be used as a part of the business routine rather than merely in emergencies, Federal began pumping an additional $10 million into its planned advertising budget.[51] Anticipating difficulty in convincing prospects of the necessity for on-premise ZapMailers, Federal equipped its sales force with preprogrammed Radio Shack calculators. These were to be utilized in running a comparison of the prospect's current communications systems cost (based on estimated activity levels) with that of a comparable ZapMailer system.[52] Federal targeted the following industries as having the highest potential, at least initially, for ZapMailer installations:

Legal

Accounting

Consulting

Retail

Insurance

Banking

Manufacturing

Advertising

Commercial and financial printing

Government[53]

In spite of its initial difficulties, ZapMail was highly regarded by analysts in the investment community who felt it would become an unqualified success once the glitches involved with any new product were resolved. Further, Federal's management indicated that possible future enhancements to ZapMailers might include the ability to communicate with word processors and personal computers.[54] Speculation was that Federal intended to be a major player in the office of the future through the use of ZapMailers. By connecting word processors and personal computers to the ZapMail network, Federal could leverage its ability to capture office document traffic once the software was developed to do so.

Executive Vice-President and Chief Operating Officer Jim Barksdale described the evolution of ZapMail at a press conference on January 31, 1985:

> *About 3 years ago . . . we had a series of meetings in which we looked toward the future, trying to picture the business world of the late 1980s, the 1990s, and the twenty-first century. Would Federal Express, we asked ourselves, continue its meteoric growth as the needs of the commercial world changed? Those were months of soul-searching.*
>
> *As we looked out over the next several years, we saw a threat to what had become such a comfortable leadership position: the increasing reliance on computer technology in every facet of business, and the world becoming gradually wired together electronically.*
>
> *In the face of these fundamental, sweeping changes, we knew we had to make major adjustments in our corporate strategy or see our leadership position gradually erode. While we could have taken the safe course and continued with business as usual, that would have been counter to everything we have come to symbolize in our brief but exciting corporate history.*
>
> *We decided to take an aggressive approach. . . . What people really wanted when they used Federal Express was delivery as soon as possible. They settled for overnight because that was the best thing going. . . .*
>
> *We quickly established a few ground rules for what a Federal Express same-day service would have to include. We knew it would have to be of the highest quality since Federal Express built its reputation on a first-class service. We didn't want to enter this market with a "me-too" product. We also knew it would have to build on the essential strengths that Federal Express had already established: a vast telecommunications network, the largest fleet of vehicles and aircraft in the transportation industry, and a proven record of marketing expertise. More than that, the final product would have to capitalize on our most important resource, the army of highly motivated Federal Express employees that covered this continent with friendly smiles and helpful attitudes every working day.*
>
> *The final result of this effort in rethinking our corporate strategy is now well known . . . Zapmail. Zapmail builds solidly on our strong foundation; it plays to our strengths. It prepares us for entry into the next century by turning back the hand of the delivery clock once again.*

International Operations

Federal Express also delivered Courier-Pak envelopes and packages up to 70 pounds to many international locations. Because of distance and time differences in the areas served, time of day of delivery varied. For those areas they did not serve, Federal Express offered a Worldwide Referral Service to arrange delivery to additional locations.[55]

In an effort to expand outside North America, in fiscal 1984, Federal acquired Gelco Express International, a worldwide, on-board courier service with offices in London, Amsterdam, Paris, Brussels, Hong Kong, Tokyo, and Singapore. In 1985, the Gelco operation was to be absorbed into the system with the Federal Express name and identity.[56]

At home, Federal was preparing for international service by opening an international customer service department with multilingual representatives. An added effort by Federal was made to give special attention to customs and cultures of the international markets.[57] But critics abroad said that running a domestic service in the United States was entirely different from operating an international one because it required a different expertise, and a common market approach could not be taken. Competition was growing in the international market as well as the U.S. market, so analysts felt that Federal could have problems promoting itself in Europe with only the experience of a small European courier to depend on for guidance.[58]

MARKETING/ADVERTISING

The image of Federal Express was one of an innovator. Smith and his colleagues had created a demand for small-package express delivery and then cleverly set out to satisfy that demand. Smith, in analyzing Federal Express, stated that Federal was selling time and that people who save time in their daily routines and functions are more effective.[59] Once the message was heard, the public immediately altered their perspective from ''get it there as soon as possible'' to ''get it there overnight.''

Smith spared nothing to get the message across. Federal Express needed dramatic advertising to reach an indifferent world that needed to know about Federal Express.[60] Tom Oliver, senior vice-president of marketing and customer service, said, ''At the outset the advertising was oriented toward explaining the network system . . . focusing on the difference in Federal's system from their competitors''; however, people could not understand how this strange combination of airplanes, hubs, and couriers could keep the boss from yelling.[61] The public just wanted to trust that Federal would do what it claimed to do, no matter how they did it.

After much effort, Federal did get the message across and won award after award for clever spots. In recalling the ''motor-mouth'' businessman, the pitch was ''Federal Express. When it absolutely, positively has to be there overnight''; a man was uprooting a phone booth as the announcer said, ''Federal Express is so easy to use, all you have to do is pick up the phone.'' It was easy to appreciate the humor, and that was what Oliver wanted.[62]

But not everyone felt that Federal's humorous ads were of benefit to the company objective. Competitors and advertisers alike felt that Federal ads often offended the little guy, and, although attention-getters, the ads left no message as to what Federal really offered.[63] Unaffected by criticisms hurled at its campaigns, Federal believed that another factor, price, was not as important as dramatizing the problem people have getting fast, sure, easy delivery. Cost of delivery was important to people only after they were sure it was going to get to the destination when they wanted it to.[64]

Federal's marketing plan for ZapMail also came under fire by industry analysts. The original ZapMail marketing plan was ill conceived: no one really understood what ZapMail was.[65] But, with the newly recruited sales force for ZapMail and new leasing plans as an alternative to purchase of the machines, analysts still believed that ZapMail would evolve into a necessary tool for business activities.

COMPETITION

Federal Express Corporation was a major competitor in the time-sensitive package-delivery or courier industry. It faced stiff competition from such firms as Purolator Courier Corporation, Emery Air Freight Corporation, United Parcel Service, and the U.S. Postal Service.

Purolator Courier Corporation

Purolator said its packages were "overnight not overpriced," and the company mandated that each package be delivered the next business day or on some other time-sensitive schedule. Most packages weighed less than 5 pounds, and each was picked up and delivered door-to-door, either on call or on a scheduled basis.[66]

The company in 1984 had two major products that were designed to make its door-to-door courier services easier and more economical. Customers could send 2 ounches (up to ten pages) of important documents anywhere in the continental United States at a very low price with the PuroLetter. The PuroPak could handle as much as 2 pounds of documents for delivery across town or across the country, and the customer was automatically billed at the lowest applicable rate. Very low rates applied up to 300 miles or between certain pairs of cities, and a competitive rate was applied for longer distances. A related product, PuroPak Box, offered a very low rate for one- to 6-pound shipments.[67]

Purolator operated an air network with its central hub located in Columbus, Ohio, to enable the movement of shipments over longer distances for next-day delivery. However, major volume constraints and operating inefficiencies were being experienced at the Columbus facility. To alleviate this problem and in anticipation of future growth needs, Purolator had a continuing program to upgrade terminal facilities. A major new air hub facility was under construction in Indianapolis, Indiana, and upon its completion in 1986 would have a capacity of 125,000 packages per night.[68]

Purolator Courier, Ltd., the company's Canadian subsidiary, offered courier services to over six thousand cities and towns in the ten provinces of Canada. Partly because of sluggish growth in the Canadian economy, operating results of this subsidiary had been mediocre. Management had concentrated on improving operating efficiency and modestly expanding its terminal facilities.[69]

The management of Purolator Courier Corporation saw the company as "the most economical national supplier of overnight package delivery." Purolator planned to aggressively exploit this position by capitalizing on its large fleet of airplanes and ground-delivery vehicles, all supported by an aggressive advertising campaign. As the U.S. and Canadian economies continued to improve, management expected Purolator to continue its record growth.[70] For a comparison of Purolator, Federal Express, and their competitors, see Exhibits 5 and 6.[71]

Emery Air Freight

Emery was one of the largest domestic air cargo carriers and was a major competitor in the international field as well. The company maintained 165 offices, 53 of which were outside the United States in twenty-seven different countries and territories. In another forty-two countries, agents acted on the company's behalf.[72]

Emery could provide overnight door-to-door delivery of any size, any weight package or shipment to over 56,000 cities and towns in North America. The company also had 24- to 72-hour door-to-door service to various cities around the world. Emery offered a variety of overnight delivery services including, Same Day, A.M., P.M., Day 2, and the 5-ounce Emery Urgent Letter.[73]

According to management, Emery's goal was to have "the lowest-cost, highest-quality, worldwide transportation system." In order to achieve this goal, Emery had spent large sums for expansion of existing facilities and the modernization of existing aircraft as well as the acquisition of new aircraft. In addition, the company had made major capital investments in state-of-the-art technology to foster its future business growth. For example, a $20 million expansion of its "superhub" terminal facility in Dayton, Ohio, was begun in March 1984 and was completed at year's end. This expansion increased the company's handling capacity to almost 2 million

EXHIBIT 5
Sales revenues of Federal Express and selected competitors, 1983

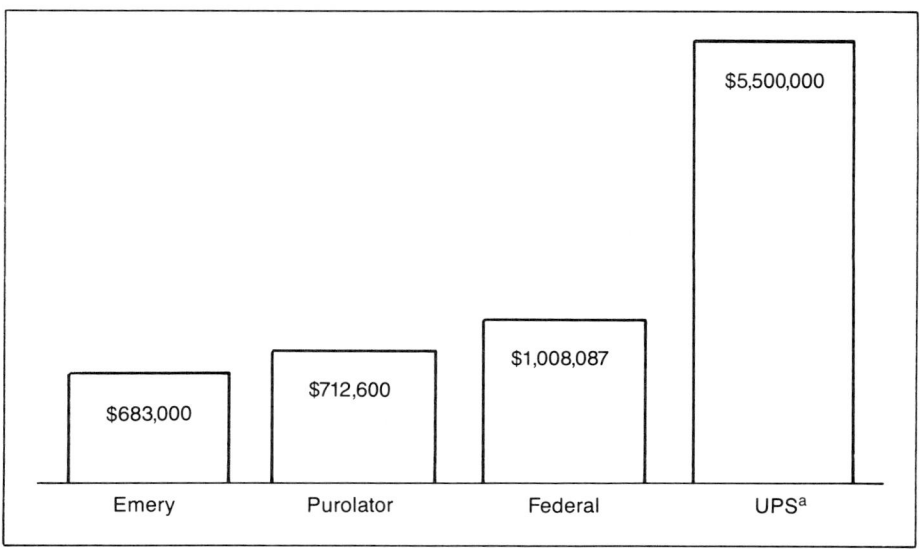

Note: Figures are in thousands of dollars.
[a] Estimated sales revenue as no actual figure is available.

EXHIBIT 6
In-service aircraft and vehicles: Federal Express and selected competitors, 1983

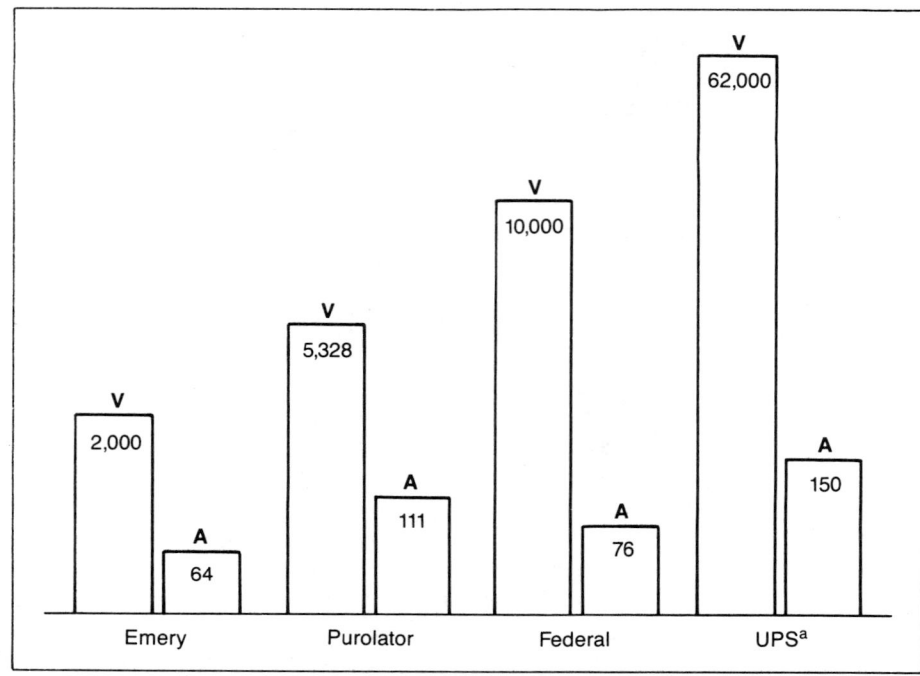

Note: V = Number of revenue-producing vehicles in service.
     A = Number of aircraft in service.
[a] U.P.S. also makes extensive use of commercial airlines to ship its parcels.

pounds per night, up from 1.7 million pounds. A major capital improvement at the Dayton facility in 1983 was the installation of an automated envelope-sorting system capable of handling 10,000 Emery Urgent letters or envelopes per hour.[74]

Emery had maintained a special "heavyweight" niche in the package delivery business. Its unique ability to deliver heavy air cargo the next day gave the company a competitive edge during the recent economic recovery. Approximately 45 percent of the company's 70-pound traffic had a next-morning delivery requirement. This ability was particularly useful to large customers that often required cargo transportation services for shipments of any size, weight, or shape. This heavyweight service was restricted to customers who purchased over $1 million of air cargo transportation services per year.[75]

Emery suffered a sharp drop in earnings per share in 1982 but had made a strong recovery in 1983 and 1984. Historically, Emery had shown consistent growth in earnings per share, and dividends had been paid without interruption since 1952.[76]

United Parcel Service

United Parcel Service was a giant in package delivery with its only competitor in terms of volume being the U.S. Postal Service. No other company could match its basic claim that it could deliver a package in 2 days anywhere in the continental

United States if the customer was willing to pay the price. UPS had long had a reputation for dependability, productivity, and efficiency which was admired by customers and envied by competitors.

Building upon the success of its basic business, UPS late in 1982 entered the overnight package delivery market. Any UPS customer currently served by daily pickups could make use of this overnight delivery service. Rates were usually 50 percent lower than those charged by Federal Express.[77]

UPS occupied a very strong position in the transportation industry. It was the largest single private shipper on most railroads, owned a large fleet of airplanes, and also shipped packages on other airlines. In addition, it owned a huge fleet of delivery trucks. (See Exhibit 6.) Its drivers were unionized and called on some 600,000 offices, factories, and stores each day.[78]

Financially, UPS was solid, with earnings that had more than quadrupled from $76.1 million in 1978 to $331.9 million in 1982. During this same period, revenues doubled, going from $2.8 billion in 1978 to $5.2 billion in 1982. Very few companies in any industry could match this earnings and productivity record.[79]

U.S. Postal Service

The U.S. Postal Service had been a competitor in the overnight package delivery business for a number of years. With its Express Mail next-day service, the postal service could ship packages weighing up to 70 pounds and guarantee delivery to the addressee the next day. To make use of this service, customers simply took their packages and letters to the Express Mail window at the post office. Shipments were delivered to the addressee by 3:00 P.M. the following day. The addressee also had the option of picking up the package personally as early as 10:00 A.M. of the next business day. All shipments were guaranteed to arrive on time, and if they did not, the customer could obtain a full refund. According to Postal Service statistics, 95 percent of all shipments did arrive on time.[80]

The U.S. Postal Service also offered package pickup from the customer's place of business, but only on a planned, regularly scheduled basis. A single, flat charge was made per pickup, regardless of the number of packages or letters the customer might be sending.

The Express Mail Service could ship packages and letters to almost any major metropolitan area in the United States. Express Mail Service was also available on an international basis, serving major cities in the United Kingdom, Australia, Brazil, Japan, Belgium, France, and the Netherlands, as well as Hong Kong.[81]

FINANCIAL

Federal Express was not a financial success overnight. It took 4 years and $70 million in venture capital before their first profitable period in late 1975. The company nearly went bankrupt several times during that 4-year drought because the venture capital market was in a profound depression of its own.

In 1975, new capital was $10 million (versus $3 billion in 1983), and the initial

EXHIBIT 7
Consolidated
financial highlights
for years ended
May 31

	1984	1983	1982
Operating results			
Express service revenues	$1,436,305	$1,008,087	$803,915
Operating income	165,208	150,737	119,466
Income before income taxes	152,260	150,216	131,080
Net income	115,430	88,933	78,385
Earnings per share	$2.52	$2.03	$1.85
Average shares outstanding	45,448	43,316	41,788
Stock price range	$27.75–$48.50	$21.13–$43.00	$21.07–$35.63
Financial position			
Working capital	$ 72,226	$ 89,878	$ 79,669
Property and equipment, net	1,112,639	596,392	457,572
Long-term debt	435,158	247,424	223,856
Common stockholders' investment	717,721	503,794	350,319
Other operating data			
Average daily package volume	263,385	166,428	125,881
Average pounds per package	5.5	5.8	6.5
Average revenue per pound	$3.80	$4.02	$3.81
Aircraft fleet at end of year:			
McDonnell DC-10-10s	6	6	4
McDonnell DC-10-30s	4	0	0
Boeing 727-100s	35	38	31
Boeing 727-200s	12	0	0
Dassault Falcons[a]	0	32	32
Average number of full-time			
equivalent employees during year	18,368	12,507	10,092

Note: Figures in millions of dollars, except per share and other data.
[a] As of May 31, 1984, the company removed its Dassault Falcons from scheduled operations. Ten of the aircraft had been disposed of at that date, and, as of July 31, 1984, twelve were under contract for sale. The company is evaluating plans for the ultimate disposition of the remaining fleet.

offering in 1974–1975 raised only $32 million (against $5.5 billion in 1984). Federal Express was constantly asking banks, corporations, and venture capitalists for new loans and equity participations. Ultimately, the company survived as over a dozen equity groups participated in three major rounds of financing. In his desperate search for money, Smith had to give up virtually all his equity in his company. (He eventually recaptured a substantial portion in later refinancings.)

Throughout the bad times, however, Smith earned the undying loyalty of those who worked for him. "He was a fantastic motivator of people," said Charles Tucker Morse, the company's first general counsel. "I have not worked since in a situation so intense and so free of politics."[82]

Financial results for fiscal 1984 were gratifying, despite the considerable expense incurred to improve existing service and to introduce a new electronic document transmission product. Revenues increased by 42 percent to $1.4 billion. Net income totaled $115 million or $2.52 per share, gains of 30 percent and 24 percent, respectively, over $89 million or $2.03 per share in fiscal 1983. (See Exhibits 7 and 8.)[83]

Other extraordinary expenses during 1984 were incurred to expand the network geographically and to add Business Service Centers in high-density, downtown areas. Also, increasing customer use of volume discounts and the relatively rapid growth of the lower-priced Overnight Letter and Standard Air Services resulted in a decline in the yield, or average revenue, per package. This trend exceeded the impressive decrease in operating costs per package achieved during the fiscal year.

Management expected the trend in declining yields to reverse because of three policy changes the company made during fiscal 1984 which produced higher than average yields. The first change was increasing the per package weight limit from 70 to 150 pounds. The second change was introducing a Saturday pick-up for Monday morning delivery service. The third and most important change was charging by the pound rather than the package for multiple-package shipments. Management hoped the third policy change would enable the company to enter the high-revenue, air freight market for the first time.[84]

EXHIBIT 8
Consolidated statement of income

	1982	1983	1984
Express service revenues	$803,915	$1,008,087	$1,436,305
Operating expenses			
Salaries and employee benefits	320,345	419,644	622,675
Depreciation and amortization	56,353	77,421	111,956
Fuel and oil	69,282	71,262	93,520
Equipment and facilities rental	46,116	59,115	89,775
Maintenance and repairs	38,795	44,083	59,482
Advertising	25,302	34,558	39,345
Other	128,256	151,267	254,344
Total	684,449	857,350	1,271,097
Operating income	119,466	150,737	165,208
Other income (expenses)			
Interest expense	(15,933)	(23,451)	(36,350)
Interest capitalized	2,852	5,831	11,851
Interest income	11,994	9,679	13,166
Gain on aircraft sales	7,318	4,224	2,463
Other	5,383	3,196	(4,078)
Total	11,614	(521)	(12,948)
Income before income taxes	131,080	150,216	152,260
Provision for income taxes	52,695	61,283	36,830
Net income	$78,385	$88,933	$115,430
Earnings per share	$1.85	$2.03	$2.52
Average shares outstanding	41,788	43,316	45,488

Note: Figures in thousands of dollars.

EXHIBIT 9
Consolidated
balance sheet for
fiscal year ended
May 31

	1983	1984
Assets		
Cash	$ 204	$ 2,190
Short-term investments	105,233	35,500
Net receivables	124,841	207,256
Inventories	16,203	39,725
Prepayments, etc.	18,690	43,465
Total current assets	$ 265,171	$ 328,136
Property, plant, and equipment	817,650	1,427,281
Accumulated depreciation and amortization	(221,258)	(314,642)
Net property, plant, and equipment	596,392	1,112,639
Construction funds in escrow	47,839	32,168
Equipment deposits and other	82,315	52,862
Total assets	$ 991,717	$1,525,805
Liabilities and equity		
Current debt maturity	$ 12,171	$ 22,001
Notes payable	15,912	0
Accounts payable	59,047	129,960
Accrued liabilities	88,163	103,949
Total current liabilities	$ 175,293	$ 255,910
Long-term debt	247,424	435,158
Deferred income tax	59,094	112,439
Total liabilities	$ 481,811	$ 803,507
Preferred stock	6,112	4,577
Common stock	2,197	4,639
Paid-in-surplus	222,782	321,768
Retained earnings	278,815	391,314
Total equity	$ 509,906	$ 722,298
Total liabilities and equity	$ 991,717	$1,525,805

Note: Figures in thousands of dollars.

Federal Express had a fiscal 1984 current ratio of 1.28:1 which declined from 1.5:1 in fiscal 1983. One of the reasons for this decline was the 1984 implementation of ZapMail. The company had been relatively conservative with its financial policies in order to maintain large credit agreements with banks and other lenders. They had not paid any dividends on common stock throughout their incorporated history and maintained minimum levels of working capital and certain financial ratios. Their stock price showed consistent growth and split three times since the company went public in 1978. As of May 31, 1984, there were 46,386,287 shares of common stock. The 1983 and 1984 balance sheets are compared in Exhibit 9.[85]

The company was determined to grow and expand service geographically, as evidenced by the large increases in capital expenditures during the 3 years prior to 1985. (See Exhibit 10.) The bulk of these expenditures were for additional aircraft plus additions and improvements to ZapMail equipment. The source of these capital

EXHIBIT 10
Capital expenditures

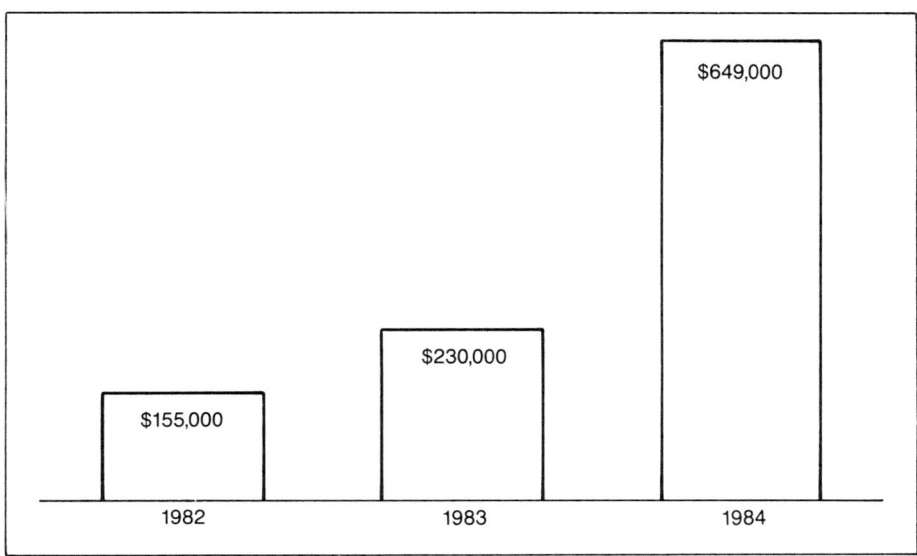

$649,000

$230,000

$155,000

1982   1983   1984

Note: Figures in thousands of dollars.

funds had been internally generated money, proceeds from loan agreements, tax-exempt bond issues, and equity offerings. Their commitment to growth had a significant effect on the company's cash and working capital, which, as of May 31, 1984, had suffered declines of 64 percent and 20 percent, respectively, from the previous year.

LEGAL

Federal's only threat for liability due to litigation involved their ZapMail product. Federal was sued in November 1984 by Zap Legislative Courier Service of Albany, New York, for alleged trademark infringement over the use of the name ZapMail. A judge ruled the company could seek unspecified monetary and punitive damages from Federal Express. As of May 1985, a trial date had not been set.[86]

OUTLOOK

Industry
Andrew B. Kim, a stock analyst for F. Eberstadt & Co., Inc., predicted that from a stock market standpoint, investors perceived that the profit margin squeeze would intensify as downward pressures on prices increased, especially if a downturn in the economy materialized. Kim also felt that the rapid increase in demand for the services of the air express and freight industry had been partly due to price reduction,

but on the other hand, felt that investors were asking why the companies were all cutting prices when demand was so strong.[87]

With respect to customers, large frequent shippers had become relatively more sensitive to pricing than before. But service quality was still the dominant variable for both frequent and infrequent shippers. Federal Express's 400,000-customer base at that time included many infrequent shippers.[88]

The industry's rapid consolidation process had invited temporary pricing instability resulting more from the service mix change than actual price cutting. Once their product lines were broadened, it was expected that future pricing would be essentially dictated by the differential in the cost structure of six or seven major participants. The barrier to entry was expected to grow higher, not only in terms of capital requirements, but also service capability in the full range of markets being served. These markets included 4-hour courier service, extended delivery, short-haul trucking, and international forwarding.

Federal Express

Looking at product differentiation, Fred Smith was worried about the start-up difficulties of Federal Express's electronic mail service. He blamed these on the painfully slow process of educating the users, even among the sophisticated customers.[89]

However, the possibility still remained that predicted demand for ZapMail did not actually exist. Start-up losses already dramatically exceeded projections, and volume was significantly below expectations. Considering the enormous capital investment involved in the project, Federal was determined to make ZapMail a success and was placing a large stake of the company's future on the service. Viewing the enormity of the challenge and the complexity of the logistical problems, historical experience suggested that such a revolutionary new service would need both time and effective marketing to generate volume.

ZapMail and Federal Express Services

Fred Smith discussed ZapMail at length in a January 31, 1985, press conference:

With the ZapMail product, we have begun an odyssey which I think will do nothing less than change the way people do business forever. . . .

A recurring theme over the last several years has been heard from our customers who ship documents. They have told us unequivocally and clearly that they want a system to move exact copies over long distances on an instantaneous basis. Since its inception, the ZapMail project has been aimed towards the point in time when we could begin offering our customers machines for their offices which would let them achieve this type of instantaneous communication. Our development of a pickup and delivery service with ZapMail in July was a deliberate step to establish Federal Express's credentials in the same-day document transmission business. To date we have been disappointed with the rate of growth of this particular service.

I believe one of the reasons our initial ZapMail Service has not grown at the rate we expected is that our marketing message was not specified enough about the service. . . . We modified our approach in November and succeeded in increasing our volume growth substantially. We will be increasing these efforts even further in February.

I must also point out, however, that the level of user satisfaction among those who have tried ZapMail has been exceedingly high, and these customers have told us they are very interested in achieving even faster and easier-to-use same-day transmission capabilities. . . .

I personally believe there is another message coming through loud and clear from our customers. And that is, if anything, we have underestimated the rapidity with which this demand for same-day transmission services is accelerating. . . .

What an entrepreneurial company like Federal Express must continue to do is to listen to its customers and make changes accordingly. This ability to recognize the signals

EXHIBIT 11 Quarterly product line statistics

	1984				1985		
	First quarter (June–Aug.)	Second quarter (Sept.–Nov.)	Third quarter (Dec.–Feb.)	Fourth quarter (Mar.–May)	First quarter (June–Aug.)	Second quarter (Sept.–Nov.)	Third quarter (Dec.–Feb.)
Total packages (thousands)							
Priority One and Courier-Pak	8,469	9,093	9,828	10,689	11,295	12,319	13,180
Standard Air	1,921	2,448	3,089	3,678	4,092	4,487	4,990
Overnight letter	3,126	3,919	4,993	6,173	6,832	7,522	8,513
ZapMail	—	—	—	—	28	112	168
Total	13,516	15,460	17,910	20,540	22,247	24,440	26,851
Yields							
Priority One and Courier-Pak	$28.58	$28.64	$28.08	$27.40	$27.05	$26.96	$25.98
Standard Air	14.49	14.25	13.56	13.30	13.09	13.97	13.23
Overnight letter	10.77	10.66	10.58	10.52	10.44	10.91	11.02
ZapMail	—	—	—	—	26.12	30.50	25.19
Composite[a]	22.46	21.81	20.70	19.80	19.38	19.65	18.86
Percentage of revenues							
Priority One and Courier-Pak	78.7%	76.4%	73.5%	70.9%	69.6%	68.5%	66.7%
Standard Air	9.1	10.2	11.2	11.8	12.2	12.9	12.8
Overnight letter	11.0	12.3	14.1	15.7	16.2	16.9	18.3
ZapMail	—	—	—	—	.2	.7	.8
Other	1.2	1.1	1.2	1.6	1.8	1.0	1.4
	100.0%	100.0%	100.0%	100.0%	100.0%	100.0%	100.0%
Operating weekdays	65	63	63	65	65	63	62
Pounds/package	5.6	5.7	5.5	5.4	5.5	5.8	5.5
Revenue/pound	$ 4.02	$ 3.80	$ 3.78	$ 3.66	$ 3.50	$ 3.40	$ 3.43
[a] Composite yields excluding ZapMail	$22.46	$21.81	$20.70	$19.80	$19.36	$19.60	$18.82
Composite costs excluding ZapMail	19.56	18.90	18.37	17.60	17.30	17.50	17.08
ZapMail revenues (thousands)					$90	$3,400	$4,110
ZapMail operating costs (thousands)					$30,000	$33,000	$35,500

being sent by the marketplace and then respond to them is what entrepreneurship is all about. We are listening to what our customers are telling us about ZapMail and we are responding to them with modifications that we feel will make ZapMail easier to use, more competitive, and more in line with what our customers most need and want for communicating intracompany and intercompany.

I would like to emphasize Federal Express's commitment to ZapMail. We believe this market is huge. No one can name the clear market leader for same-day document transmission services because there is no clear leader. We intend to attain an unequivocal leadership position in this market and then to build on that lead.

ZapMail was becoming increasingly important to Federal Express, and might reach $175,000,000 in investment (or about 7.5 percent of total assets) in a year. In preparation for Mr. Smith's review of company services, product line statistics for the most recent quarters had been collected. These statistics are summarized in Exhibit 11.

Fred Smith pondered the future of ZapMail:

How do you start a whole new communications system like this, where you need a machine at both ends? It's like the early telephone system. The most remarkable salesperson in history was the first telephone salesman. You had this fantastic instrument to talk to people, but unless everyone else had one, it wasn't worth much.[90]

REFERENCES

1. Linden, Eugene, "Frederick W. Smith of Federal Express: He Didn't Get There Over Night," *Inc.*, April 1984, p. 89.
2. Ibid.
3. Standard & Poors *Industry Surveys*, December 6, 1984, p. A36.
4. Colvin, Geoffrey, "Federal Express Dives into Air Mail," *Fortune*, June 15, 1981, pp. 106–8.
5. *Industry Surveys*, p. A36.
6. Ibid.
7. Ibid.
8. *Federal Express 10K*, May 31, 1984.
9. Altman, Henry, "A Business Visionary Who Really Delivered," *Nation's Business*, November 1981, p. 50.
10. Ibid.
11. Ibid.
12. Colvin, "Federal Express Dives," p. 107.
13. Altman, "Business," p. 54.
14. Ibid.
15. *Business Week*, "Federal Express Rides the Small Package Boom," March 31, 1980, p. 111.
16. "Creativity with Bill Moyers: Fred Smith and the Federal Express," *PBS Video*, 1981.
17. "The Memphis Connection," *Marketing & Media Decisions*, May 1982, p. 62.

18. Ibid., p. 63.

19. Hafner, Katie, "Fred Smith: The Entrepreneur Redux," *Inc.*, June 1984, p. 40.

20. Ibid.

21. Colvin, "Federal Express Dives," p. 107.

22. *Federal Express 1984 Annual Report*, p. 13.

23. Ibid.

24. *Federal Express 1982 Annual Report*, p. 14.

25. Ibid.

26. Colvin, "Federal Express Dives," p. 107.

27. Ibid., p. 108.

28. Stoops, Rick, "How Federal Express Recruited for a New High-Tech Image," *Personnel Journal*, August 1984, p. 16.

29. "Federal Express Readdresses ZapMail," *Sales and Marketing Management*, March 11, 1985, p. 26.

30. Ibid.

31. Colvin, "Federal Express Dives," p. 107.

32. Ibid., pp. 6, 7.

33. Ibid., p. 9.

34. *Federal Express 10K*, May 31, 1984, p. 9.

35. Ibid., p. 10.

36. Ibid., p. 10.

37. Ibid., p. 9.

38. Ibid., p. 10.

39. *Federal Express Corporation 1984 Annual Report*, p. 1.

40. *Federal Express Service Guide*, October 1, 1984, p. 19.

41. *Federal Express 1984 Annual Report*, p. 10.

42. *Service Guide*, p. 19.

43. Ibid., p. 23.

44. Ibid., p. 27.

45. *Air Freight Progress Report*, Morgan Stanley Investment Research, New York, January 21, 1985, p. 1.

46. *Service Guide*, p. 17.

47. *Air Freight Progress Report*, p. 1.

48. *Research*, *Federal Express*, Morgan Keegan & Company, Inc., November 28, 1983, p. 4.

49. *Air Freight*, January 21, 1985, p. 1.

50. Ibid.

51. Ibid.

52. *Research*, *Federal Express*, Morgan Keegan & Company, Inc., February 14, 1985, p. 4.

53. Ibid.

54. Ibid., pp. 3, 4.

55. *Service Guide*, p. 162.

56. *Federal Express 1984 Annual Report*, pp. 14, 15.

57. Ibid., p. 14.

58. Milmo, Sean, "British Air Couriers Welcome U.S. Entrant," *Business Marketing*, April 1984, p. 9.

59. Ibid.

60. Ibid.
61. "The Memphis Connection," p. 62.
62. Ibid., p. 128.
63. Seiden, Hank, "The Delivery Doesn't Fly," *Advertising Age*, October 31, 1983, p. M66.
64. "The Memphis Connection," p. 62.
65. "Federal Express Readdresses ZapMail," p. 26.
66. Ibid.
67. *Purolator Courier Corporation 1982 Annual Report*, Introduction.
68. *Standard & Poors N.Y.S.E. Stock Reports*, 1984, p. 1885.
69. *Purolator Courier Corporation 1982 Annual Report*, p. 10.
70. Ibid., p. 8.
71. *Standard & Poors N.Y.S.E. Stock Reports*, p. 1885.
72. Ibid., p. 827.
73. *Emery Air Freight 1983 Annual Report*, Introduction.
74. Ibid., p. 3.
75. Ibid., p. 13.
76. *Standard & Poors N.Y.S.E. Stock Reports*, p. 827.
77. "Behind the UPS Mystique: Puritanism and Productivity," *Business Week*, June 6, 1983, p. 66.
78. Ibid.
79. Ibid.
80. "Express Mail Next Day Service," *U.S. Postal Service Pamphlet Notice # 43*, July 1977, p. 2.
81. Ibid., p. 6.
82. Linden, p. 89.
83. *Federal Express 1984 Annual Report*.
84. Ibid.
85. *Standard & Poors Industry Report*, 1984, p. 2551.
86. *Wall Street Journal*, December 28, 1984, p. 33.
87. "Research Notes," F. Eberstadt & Co., Inc., May 3, 1984.
88. Ibid., p. 2.
89. Ibid.
90. "Federal Express's Fred Smith," *Inc.*, October 1986, p. 42.

NEW HAMPSHIRE BALL BEARINGS, INC.

Theodore Kanell, president of New Hampshire Ball Bearings, sat at his desk early one July morning in 1984, studying the terms of the proposed acquisition of New Hampshire Ball Bearings (NHBB) by Minebea Co. Ltd., the Japanese electronics, controls, bearings, and machinery conglomerate. Ted thought: "It's easy to see black and white through hindsight, but there are only shades of gray in the thick of the battle."

The following paragraphs describe (1) the product and production of ball bearings; (2) the founding of NHBB by Arthur Daniels; (3) changes in the ball bearing industry, including competition in the 1970s; (4) the strategic acts of NHBB in response to these trends; (5) Minebea, the suitor; and (6) the current status of the company as Mr. Kanell considers the Minebea offer and his strategic alternatives.

THE PRODUCT

Uses

Bearings reduce friction by converting sliding friction (linear motion) to rolling friction (rotary motion). A ball bearing is a bearing that provides rolling contact and consists of hardened steel balls that roll between two hardened steel rings.

Early societies using round stone wheels to move larger stones and objects sooner or later discovered that the stone wheel rolling around an axle could be better controlled and could be made easier to operate if small sticks were placed between the axle and the bore of the wheel. Antifriction bearings were invented. The ball bearing is the most widely used antifriction bearing, although there are also needle roller bearings, tapered roller bearings, and cylindrical and spherical roller bearings.

The ball bearing has two rings, one within the other, separated by balls. A retainer may be used to hold the ball bearings in place. Ball bearings come in all sizes. The smaller bearings are referred to as precision and as miniature by convention. Miniature bearings include all ball bearings with outside diameters less than 9 millimeters (.3543 inches). Instrument or precision ball bearings are those with outer diameters

EXHIBIT 1
Sample end uses
of bearings

ABEC *quality* standard	Possible use
Miniature bearings (9 mm)	
1	Fishing equipment, pneumatic tools
3	Copiers, computer peripherals
5	Dental equipment, floppy disc drives
7	Flight recorders, circuit production equipment
9	Aircraft gyroscopes
Precision bearings (9–30 mm)	
1	Hand-held tools, flow meters
3	Photo typesetters, check-sorting systems
5	Aircraft fuel controls
7	Missile gyroscopes
9	Military aircraft gyroscopes

of 9 to 30 millimeters (.3543 to 1.1811 inches) and of ring tolerances of fifty-millionths of an inch and ball sphericity or roundness of three-millionths of an inch.

Ball bearing manufacturers recognize the Annular Bearings Engineers Committee (ABEC) quality standards. The higher the ABEC number (1 to 9), the greater the quality. These standards are primarily dimensional tolerances, although higher standards also may include dynamic characteristics such as torque and vibration limitations. The ABEC Committee is a subcommittee of the Anti-Friction Bearing Manufacturers Association (AFBMA), the industry association for ball bearing manufacturers.

Sample end uses of miniature bearings (9 millimeters of outside diameter) and precision bearings (9 to 30 millimeters outside diameters) are described in Exhibit 1.

Production

The production of the inner and outer rings and the balls that comprise the ball bearing (see Exhibit 2) can be summarized as follows (page 359):

EXHIBIT 2
Ball bearing

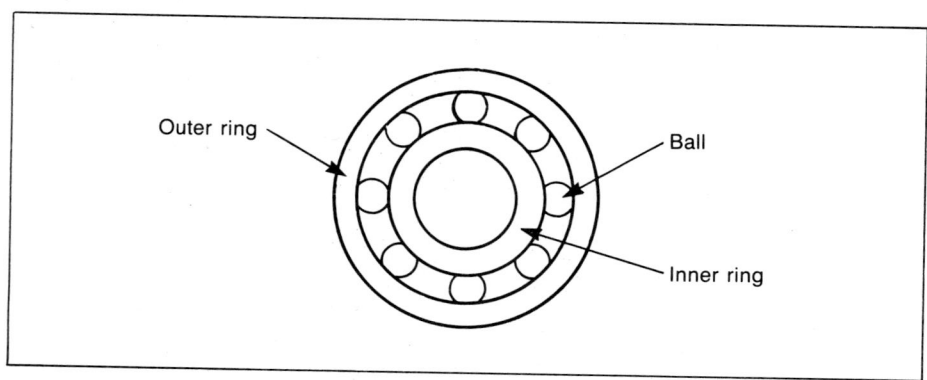

Inner and Outer Rings

1. *Cutting and boring*: Rods of stainless steel (or other material such as chrome steel or aluminum called for by the application) are cut to their approximate outside diameter and bored to their approximate inside diameter on automatic screw machines. Steel at this point is "soft" and can be notched with a file.

2. *Heat treatment*: For added strength with a resulting increased ability to be machined to fine tolerances, rings are placed in high-heat furnaces. This heat tempering makes the steel hard.

3. *Tumbling*: Rings are "tumbled" in vibrating machines with a mixture of abrasives of varying hardness and size depending on the desired finish. Tumbling removes surface imperfections and polishes.

4. *Grinding*: The outer and inner rings may have one or more tracks or races ground into their surface to accommodate the balls and/or have their inside and outside diameters sized further. Grinders can be set to produce varying levels of diameter tolerances. One ring may be processed on one or several grinders. Grinding or finishing the surfaces may be done with grinding wheels, burrs, or points. Grinding may be rough grinding (primarily concentrated on width and making the faces of the ring parallel), centerless grinding to make the outside diameter square with the face, or bore grinding to make the bore round and with the same center as the outside ring.

5. *Honing*: Rings are given a final smoothing and polishing in honing machines.

6. *Inspection*: Throughout each of the five previous steps, operators select a sample of each batch to test for ring dimensions and other characteristics.

Balls

1. *Cutting*: Wire of varying materials and widths is cut (slugged) or pressed with dies (headed) to produce the object that will become a sphere.

2. *Heat treatment*: The rough spheres may be treated in furnaces, depending on the desired characteristics.

3. *Grinding and polishing*: The cut metal is made increasingly spherical by various grinding, tumbling, and polishing steps, including simultaneous grinding of more than one surface at one time.

4. *Inspection*: The balls are sampled at each production step.

Retainers. Retainers are generally punched out of thin strips of steel by punch presses.

Assembly. The finished bearing is assembled by applying pressure to the partially positioned bearing (thus "snapping" it together), by insertion of the balls through openings or chutes in the outer rings, and by other means.

Assembly may take place in NHBB's "white room," a dustfree environment for high precision and for specified-characteristics bearings.

EXHIBIT 3
Ball bearing parts

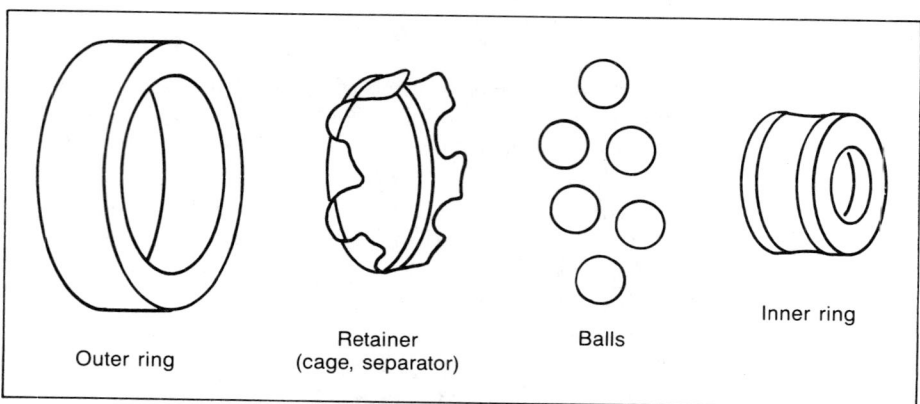

Outer ring · Retainer (cage, separator) · Balls · Inner ring

Final Inspection and Shipping. The documentation that accompanies the order shipped to the customer may include inspection certificates and even documentation as to steel source and other product characteristics.

The parts of the ball bearing are shown in Exhibit 3.

ARTHUR DANIELS, FOUNDER OF NHBB

Arthur Daniels was born in California on October 1, 1908. Both of his parents and three of his grandparents were teachers. Daniels commented to an interviewer in 1968 that one of his grandmothers was the first white child born in Oregon, though "her playmates were Indian children who ate worms and similar things."

After dropping out of school to go to sea for a semester as a janitor/machinists' helper, Daniels entered the United States Naval Academy, graduating in 1931. Following graduation, Mr. Daniels was married to Dolores DePierrefeau, and spent 4 years aboard Admiral Leahy's flagship, the *USS Raleigh*. He then transferred to the Navy Reserves. Daniels received a master's degree in engineering from Harvard and joined the mechanical engineering faculty at Dartmouth College.

In 1939 Daniels invested $5,000 in the Split Ballbearing Company, which was being run by Winslow Pierce, who had patented a split ball bearing in 1921. The split bearing meant that the two "half-moon" segments of the bearing could be pulled apart, meaning that a failed bearing could be much more easily replaced, greatly reducing downtime for bearing failures.

Although barely afloat financially, Split Ballbearing had a resource in the tiny (one-sixteenth of an inch in diameter) miniature ball bearing capability Pierce had developed. Although Pierce, the engineering press, and the occasional engineers and researchers who wrote to Pierce or visited him in Lebanon, New Hampshire, were not particularly excited about the miniature bearing capability, Daniels was intrigued. Daniels convinced Pierce to start a separate division of Split Ballbearing, called Miniature Precision Bearings. Daniels became Miniature Precision Bearing's (MPB) part-time manager, while continuing on Dartmouth's faculty.

In the summer of 1939 MPB received an order for a dozen quarter-inch bearings from Carl Norden, who was developing a new bomb sight. This Norden order resulted in the first commercial manufacture of miniature ball bearings for the one-room, two employee company. The next months saw the Norden bomb sight orders coming in on the stationery of Sperry Gyroscope, and Split Ballbearing's MPB division began a war-related climb to profits and success.

Arthur Daniels returned to active duty after Pearl Harbor, serving 5 years. He commanded a destroyer escort in the Pacific and ended his war career against the Japanese in the Pacific on the staff of Admiral Nimitz at Pearl Harbor. After the war, Daniels decided to stick with ball bearings rather than return to Dartmouth. A disagreement between Daniels, Pierce, and Daniels's wartime "replacement," Horace Gilbert, led Daniels to found NHBB in an abandoned feed store and warehouse in Peterborough, New Hampshire, in 1946.

Some five years later Mr. Daniels described NHBB's first facility: "The warehouse was full of rats, naturally. We installed a cat, but it couldn't stand the loneliness of weekends and moved over to The Diner." It took 5½ years for NHBB to produce one million bearings but only 5 months in the spring and summer of 1953 to produce the second million. As the company grew, it was a pioneer in employee relations, offering a profit-sharing plan to its workers. By 1957 the company employed over four hundred persons.

One aspect of Mr. Daniels's personality was his sense of humor. His letter to stockholders in an early annual report ended with a sentence: "The whippoorwills have returned after an absence of about ten years, offering no explanation." A letter to stockholders and employees noted that "we'll be needing sales engineers, automatic machinists, machinists, mechanical technicians . . . any sex. . . . Come on up, we'll use you good. . . . We haven't laid off a toolmaker or die maker in 20 years. Did fire one, for punching a foreman in the nose."

The *Peterborough Transcript* (June 20, 1968) described these whimsical departures as "a sign of his dislike for the prosaic, of his feeling for the mystery, the beneficence and the enhancement of nature, and his innate conviction that it is not worthwhile to go round the world to count the cats in Zanzibar."

CHANGES IN THE DOMESTIC BALL BEARING INDUSTRY

The three major American companies were founded around World War II. Barden, founded in 1939, concentrated on the more difficult, high-technology applications. MPB (1942) concentrated on the higher ABEC ratings. NHBB (1946) produced the high volume ABEC 1 and 3 ratings.

After the Korean War, divisions of larger firms such as General Motors, Textron, and TRW, entered the precision and miniature bearings industry not only because of their base in larger bearings, but also because the technology for mass production of instrument precision bearings was now available through advances in grinding machine technology.

Defense and military orders and commercial jet aircraft were significant determinants of demand during this period, while increasing Japanese and other foreign competition were an important factor in the supply of ball bearings.

Appendix A presents further details of this period and of the domestic industry's attempt to get governmental protection against imports.

COMPETITION IN THE 1970s

The trends in foreign competition during the 1970s and a summary of the major players in the industry follow.

Imports and NHBB

Foreign producers included Japan's Nippon Miniature Bearing (NMB) of the Minebea group, four other Japanese companies (Koyo Seiko, NTN, NSK, and Nachi), Germany's FAG (producing bearings in Canada), RMB of Switzerland, and SKF (producing in several European countries).

Exhibit 4 shows the U.S. market for 6 post-Vietnam years. Japan represented 27 percent of the imported miniature units and 45 percent of the imported precision units in 1983, Singapore 49 percent of miniature and 37 percent of precision, and Switzerland 10 percent of miniature and 1 percent of precision in 1983. Japan's 27 percent of the 1983 miniature units was 26 percent of miniature 1983 dollar sales, Singapore's 49 percent was 41 percent of sales, and Switzerland's 10 percent was 15 percent of sales. Imports (62 percent of miniature and 65 percent of precision bearing consumption in 1983) had grown from 30 percent and 49 percent in 1973.

The Competing Companies

Barden. Barden specialized in precision grade bearings used in sophisticated aircraft and missile guidance systems and ultraprecise machine tool applications. Barden represented NMB's ABEC 1 and 3 miniature and precision bearings beginning in 1968, but this Barden-NMB agreement was terminated in 1973. Barden sold a West German manufacturer's line to replace the NMB products.

MPB. MPB expanded its miniature and precision bearings capacity at the same rate as NHBB, but concentrated on the higher ABEC grades. MPB manufactured only a limited number of high-volume ABEC 1 and 3 grades.

MPB entered into an agreement with NMB of Japan in September 1960 for joint distribution. This agreement was terminated in January 1964. Industry observers commented:

> *NMB learned a lot of technology from MPB. MPB believed it had NMB's assurance that the latter would stay out of the stainless steel bearings and would only produce chrome. Subsequent events proved that it did not have that assurance. NMB, having learned heat-treating concepts from MPB, turned to Barden for retainer technology.*

EXHIBIT 4 U.S. market data

Year	Consumption	Imports	Imports as % of consumption	Domestic production	NHBB production	NHBB % of U.S. consumption
Miniature (0–9 mm)						
1973	7.9	2.4	30.4%	6.0	2.8	35.4%
1975	7.0	2.3	32.9	5.3	2.4	34.3
1977	9.3	2.8	30.1	7.2	3.0	32.3
1979	11.5	4.1	35.7	8.0	3.6	31.3
1981	13.2	7.3	55.3	6.5	2.7	20.5
1983	14.3	8.9	62.2	5.8	3.0	21.0
Precision (9–30 mm)						
1973	108.0	53.0	49.1	56.0	4.1	3.8
1975	77.0	41.0	53.2	41.0	4.3	5.6
1977	107.0	58.0	54.2	54.0	7.4	6.9
1979	131.0	78.0	59.5	58.0	12.2	9.3
1981	121.0	80.0	66.1	45.0	12.5	10.3
1983	134.7	87.1	64.7	50.7	14.7	10.9

Note: Data in millions of units.
Source: NHBB records.

NHBB. In the late 1960s and early 1970s NHBB specialized in the high-volume, low–ABEC-class bearings. In policies it continued to follow, NHBB produced to order with only a limited inventory. Two-thirds of NHBB's manufacturing lots average 2,000 pieces with more than one-half less than 1,000 pieces. Lot sizes became smaller after the early (screw machine, heat-treating) manufacturing steps due to customized product characteristics. During this period, computer industry and military demands for higher ABEC classes were limited, although they would become most important in the 1980s. For example, in 6 to 20 millimeters, computer peripherals were expected to account for 85 percent of domestic demand for low-ABEC classes in the second half of the 1980s. Thus technological advances (such as computers and, later, videocassette recorders) continued to produce swings in demand. NHBB dealt with customers through an internal sales group with an engineering or "problem-solving" approach.

General Motors, Textron, and TRW. In 1956–1957 the Bryant Division of the Excello Corporation introduced their new series of state-of-the-art bore and race grinders. This equipment was a tremendous assistance to the industry and enabled the miniature manufacturers to significantly increase their output of small-diameter hardened and ground parts. At the same time, the machines made it easier for domestic and overseas manufacturers to move down into the miniature and instrument bearing business.

When New Departure-Hyatt Division of General Motors, Fafnir Bearing Division of Textron Corporation, and TRW Bearings Division of TRW Corporation moved into the miniature bearings market between 1956 and 1970, they were volume producers of ABEC 1 and 3 grade along with other larger size and volume series. They also manufactured these series in ABEC 5 grades on a smaller scale. Their interest in the miniature series was brought about by the increased use of miniature bearings by the military in analog computers for fire-control systems, navigation and bombing systems, and engine and flight-control units. The market decline over the 1961–1965 and 1967–1972 periods saw these manufacturers withdraw from the miniature market in order to concentrate on the more profitable volume side of their business along with their larger bearings (such as bearings for aircraft engines and precision machine tools) which carried very high unit value.

NMB. Minebea was established July 1951 as the first Japanese firm specializing in miniature bearings. NMB's managing director, Mr. Takama Takahashi, visited the United States in the fall of 1959 to explore U.S. market prospects. He also inspected MPB's facilities, and a year later MPB and NMB entered into a joint distribution effort, which lasted 3 years. In 1965 NMB entered into a technical assistance agreement with Société Nouvelle de Fabrications Aeronautiques and later into an agreement with Barden. By the late 1960s, NMB produced 70 percent of the Japanese miniature bearings exported. About 75 percent of NMB's production was exported.

NSK, Nachi, Koyo, and NTN. As bearing requirements expanded internationally because of the office automation industry and domestically within Japan because of the videocassette recorder industry, four additional major Japanese producers of larger ball bearings moved into the miniature and precision bearing marketplace. These were NSK (Japan's largest rolling-element bearing manufacturer), Nachi Fukikoshi (which was particularly strong in the precision disc drives, appliance, and automotive markets), Koyo Seiko, and NTN (Japan's second largest rolling-element bearing producer). In 1970 NTN entered into a technical agreement with Fafnir to learn the technology of quality aircraft bearings. By 1981 NTN had 60 percent of the Japanese aircraft bearing market, and it announced its intention to market aircraft bearings in Europe and America and to diversify into ultraprecision bearings. Many Japanese firms began adding subsidiary factories in Singapore and, later, Thailand, during the late 1970s and early 1980s.

FAG. FAG is Germany's largest domestic manufacturer of bearings. Their plant in Canada produces miniature and instrument bearings for sale in Canada and the United States. Production of precision instrument bearings started in 1954.

RMB. RMB of Bienne, Switzerland has been manufacturing miniature and instrument bearings since 1932. The company supplies a quality product in all precision grades throughout the world marketplace. RMB was the first producer of miniature bearings, and there are exciting stories of bearings smuggled out of Switzerland during World War II in diplomatic pouches that eventually reached the Allied war effort through Portugal.

SKF. SKF is the world's largest producer of ball bearings. Its ADR division in France started a significant push into the U.S. market in the early 1980s, aided in part by the low value of the franc relative to the dollar.

SKF Industries transferred the manufacture of 0- to 30-mm OD bearings to Europe in the midseventies and sold off much of their equipment to NHBB, where the machines were rebuilt and tooled according to NHBB methods. This gave NHBB a significant increase in capacity at the time of a major boom in the computer peripheral/office automation industry during the 1975–1980 period.

SKF had been operating in the United States under terms of a consent decree with the U.S. Department of Justice limiting imports. SKF sold its Reed Division in Chatsworth, California, to NMB and Reed's equipment to NHBB. After the consent decree was lifted in the 1980s, SKF began to rationalize production worldwide.

Exhibit 5 summarizes imports into the United States in 1979 and 1983.

NHBB IN THE 1970s

In March 1971 Mr. Daniels reorganized the managerial group to include an enlarged "strategy board" whose stated objective was to determine "where are we and

EXHIBIT 5
Selected data on imports

Year	Country	Units	Dollars	Dollars/unit	Percentage Units	Percentage Dollars
Under 9 mm						
1979	Canada	62	126	2.03	1%	4%
	Japan	1547	1097	.71	37	35
	Singapore	1877	1173	.62	46	38
	Switzerland	676	730	1.08	16	23
	Total	4162	3126	.75	100	100
1983	Canada	114	215	1.89	2	3
	Japan	2270	2013	.89	31	31
	Singapore	4143	3191	.77	56	49
	Switzerland	827	1134	1.37	11	17
	Total	7354	6553	.89	100	100
9–30 mm						
1979	Canada	1611	1551	.96	3	4
	Japan	45,191	31,309	.69	76	74
	Singapore	10,984	7413	.67	19	18
	Switzerland	1466	1965	1.34	2	4
	Total	59,252	42,238	.71	100	100
1983	Canada	1573	1743	1.11	2	4
	Japan	38,838	24,543	.63	53	57
	Singapore	31,716	15,935	.50	44	37
	Switzerland	803	814	1.01	1	2
	Total	72,930	43,035	.59	100	100

Note: Data in thousands.
Source: NHBB records.

where the hell do we go from here?'' The board included a half-dozen company officers "and of course Mr. Daniels." Mr. Daniel's announcement of March 25 concluded: "We will meet at noon sharp to avoid phone calls, etc., for lunch where we can have enough privacy, on call from me or any member. There will be no booze until we reach the point of just shooting the breeze." A letter to all employees the next day continued:

A lot of people here, and I get it outside too, seem to think that since I have made Cherwin president and kicked myself upstairs to chairman, I have retired. . . . As I told Cherwin and Kanell [executive vice-president] at the time, we are all going to keep doing what we've been doing, and by God, I'm still the boss, and don't you forget it.

In January 1972 Mr. Takama Takahashi, president of Nippon Miniature Bearings, visited Peterborough, having expressed an interest in talking to NHBB principals.

Although state and national flags of visitors were customarily flown from the flagstaffs outside NHBB headquarters, no Japanese flag was visible. A company official noted that "Chairman Daniels had originally stated that in any event this foreign flag would not be flown." Following the visit, Mr. Daniels posted an announcement to employees: "Japanese visitors given a quick censored plant tour to show them our horse power. I think they got the message."

President Kanell   Theodore Kanell was elected president of NHBB in March 1979. Mr. Kanell had joined NHBB in 1957 as a sales engineer whose job was to open a California sales office. He had previously been with General Electric and Bendix after serving in World War II and receiving a B.S. in mechanical engineering from the University of Connecticut. During Ted Kanell's first two weeks of NHBB employment, Mr. Daniels had traveled to California to meet with his new employee. Two anecdotes from this first meeting of an association that was to become mentor-protégé provide insight into these personalities.

Mr. Daniels and Mr. Kanell took four clients to lunch in Los Angeles. Ted Kanell, with $15 in his billfold, first tried unsuccessfully to cash a personal check, having been told to "take care of the bill" by Mr. Daniels. Returning to the table with the $36 lunch bill, the NHBB team was further chagrinned to find that Mr. Daniels only had $10. The client paid for the lunch and announced loudly to the client staff as the lunch group returned to the client offices: "Quick, give these boys an order so that they will have enough money to get home to New Hampshire."

At the conclusion of the 2-week visit, Mr. Daniels asked Ted Kanell to take him to the train station for a ride to San Francisco. Ted had never been to the Los Angeles train station, having always used airplanes for any distance traveling, but he thought he knew where the station was in downtown Los Angeles, and he did not want to seem lost or inexperienced in his new sales territory. After several moments of fast turns, peering up streets, and assuring his boss that there was no problem, Ted parked in front of a large building and walked quickly up the steps with Mr. Daniels and his baggage, as train time was rapidly approaching. Once up the marble steps, Ted realized they were in the lobby of the Los Angeles branch of the United States Post Office. Mr. Daniels looked at Ted, and asked, "Should I go parcel post or first class?"

Anecdotes and stories such as these circulated through the company and strengthened the image of Mr. Daniels with his employees. A particular favorite in Peterborough was the response of Mr. Daniels to the critical comments by a brash, aggressive New York financial whiz about Mr. Daniel's "style of seat-of-the-pants management." "Well, at least I've been sitting in these pants for a sufficiently long period," replied Mr. Daniels.

Mr. Kanell became sales manager in 1962, vice-president for sales and a director in 1968, and executive vice-president in 1970, prior to becoming president. He received an M.B.A. from Boston University in 1974.

Post-Vietnam Strategies

MPB: Diversification. MPB's history was summarized for the casewriter by Bill Scranton, MPB's president during the period of Japanese competition. MPB joined with NHBB in attempts to get the government to act, and MPB made several attempts to diversify. In 1976 MPB was acquired by Wheelabrator-Frye. Mr. Scranton's comments are contained in Appendix B.

NHBB: Product Expansion, Automation, Engineering Service. Faced with no change in prices of low-grade miniature bearings from 1968 to 1978, NHBB tried to broaden its product line to include spherical bearings, rod ends, specially designed bearings, and bearing subassemblies to "turn a $6 sale into a $30 or $40 sale." Plant capacity was expanded 72 percent from 1976 to 1981, and a sales target of $110 to $120 million for 1985 was established in 1976.

Looking back in October 1982, Mr. Kanell told *Forbes* (October 11, 1982, page 60) that because of the Vietnam buildup:

> *There was a heavy burden placed on small military suppliers like ourselves. It used to be that we would ship 4 to 6 weeks after getting an order. Well, during Vietnam our lead time went to 35 to 40 weeks. . . . It was at that time that the Japanese . . . came in and said, "We can deliver those products off the shelf overnight. Moreover, our price will be 30 percent less than you currently pay." . . . When things in Vietnam subsided, we looked around and found that Japan had cornered about 40 percent of the market . . . virtually overnight. That was 1971, the only time this company took a loss. . . . We couldn't withdraw. This was the only business we had.*

Plants automated, computer-assisted design and manufacturing were used, and $8,000 worth of ball bearings per employee produced in 1971 grew to $42,000 in 1981.

Further, NHBB moved into the technical precision-engineering bearing market. Sales engineering staff was doubled. Mr. Kanell noted: "We had the reputation for being the high-volume, low-cost producer. . . . We were good if you wanted a Chevrolet, but if you wanted a Rolls-Royce, you went elsewhere."

Production

NHBB had three plant locations: (1) Peterborough; (2) Jaffrey (a few miles from Peterborough), where primary balls were produced; and (3) Laconia, which produced bearings other than ball bearings, such as torque tube, rod end, and sperical bearings. Exhibit 6 shows the original cost, cost of additions, and estimated current replacement cost for these facilities exclusive of land cost.

In 1984 the Peterborough facility operated at about 78 percent of capacity, with three-fourths of its business coming from custom modifications of its catalogued bearings. In the same year Jaffrey operated at 71 percent of capacity, with 90 percent of its production being standard, catalogued items and only 10 percent custom items. Laconia operated at 70 percent capacity, primarily producing spherical bearings. An automated ball bearing factory has been opened in Laconia specifically to respond to Japanese low prices, but NHBB closed this plant several years later.

EXHIBIT 6
Facility costs

Plant	Date opened	Original cost	Additions	Total cost	Replacement cost
Peterborough	1956	$ 660,000	$3,840,000	$4,500,000	$13,630,000
Jaffrey	1976	380,000	620,000	1,000,000	1,520,000
Laconia	1968	910,000	2,440,000	3,350,000	5,930,000
Total		1,950,000	6,900,000	8,850,000	21,080,000

Peterborough and Jaffrey unit production (in thousands) is summarized in the following table (source: NHBB records).

	1979 units	%	1981 units	%	1983 units	%
ABEC 1	1,690	10.3	1,515	10.0	1,835	10.3
ABEC 3	12,300	74.6	11,050	71.9	13,365	74.7
ABEC 5	1,455	8.8	1,630	10.6	1,570	8.8
ABEC 7	1,045	6.3	1,170	7.6	1,125	6.2
ABEC 9	9	0.0	5	0.0	5	0.0
Total 0–30 mm	16,490	100.0	15,370	100.0	17,900	100.0

Production of the higher ABEC grades is more likely to be customized. The production lot size is about equally distributed among under one thousand pieces, between one and two thousand, and over two thousand pieces. NHBB's unit and dollar sales for selected ABEC classes appear in Exhibit 7.

Sales

Too much concentration on ABEC grades and sizes can be misleading, since any one customer and any one end use is likely to involve a mixture of sizes and ABEC grades. The computer disc drive, the fishing reel, and the missile gyroscope may well use larger and smaller bearings of varying ABEC quality. Another way to look at sales is to look at NHBB's top ten customers. Exhibit 8 summarizes the units shipped and dollar sales of NHBB in 1979 and 1984. Exhibit 9 reflects shifts in demand.

Economies of Scale

New Hampshire Ball Bearing estimated the consequences of economies of scale in order to measure such things as (1) the benefit of spreading fixed costs over higher volumes, (2) the potential percent reduction in costs that would be necessary to justify investments in capital equipment costing $100,000 per installation, and (3) the relationship between labor and materials direct costs. That company estimate is shown in Exhibit 10. The direct cost of this production is summarized in Exhibit 11.

EXHIBIT 7
NHBB sales by
ABEC class

Year	Sales		Average price
	Units	Dollars	
Miniature ABEC 1			
1979	4,687,000	2,900,000	$0.62
1983	1,778,000	2,359,000	$1.33
Change 1979–83	−62%	−19%	+115%
Miniature ABEC 3			
1979	7,507,000	6,218,000	$0.83
1983	9,020,000	10,513,000	$1.17
Change 1979–83	+20%	+69%	+41%
Miniature ABEC 5			
1979	1,172,000	2,156,000	$1.84
1983	1,162,000	3,577,000	$3.08
Change 1979–83	−1%	+66%	+67%
Miniature ABEC 7			
1979	536,000	1,582,000	$2.95
1983	507,000	1,895,000	$3.74
Change 1979–83	−5%	+20%	+27%
Precision ABEC 1			
1979	855,000	1,145,000	$1.34
1983	843,000	2,285,000	$2.71
Change 1979–83	−1%	+100%	+102%
Precision ABEC 3			
1979	1,318,000	1,484,000	$1.13
1983	2,613,000	3,777,000	$1.45
Change 1979–83	+98%	+155%	+28%
Total under 9 mm, ABEC 1, 3, 5 and 7			
1979	13,902,000	12,856,000	$0.92
1983	12,467,000	18,344,000	$1.47
Total 9–30 mm, ABEC 1 and 3			
1979	2,173,000	2,629,000	$1.21
1983	3,456,000	6,062,000	$1.75

Note: Totals do not equal total sales because of customized and other bearing sales.
Source: NHBB records.

Exhibits 12, 13, 14, and 15 present selected financial and operating data, including balance sheets and income statements for 1980 through 1984, employee, and per share data. An organization chart as of April 1984 appears in Exhibit 16.

MINEBEA THE SUITOR

Mr. Daniels's health was fading at age seventy-three. His stock ownership of 18 percent, plus another 5 percent under his control, led to rumors of a takeover. Mr. Kanell said "We are courted almost constantly."

EXHIBIT 8 Sales by top ten customers

Dollar sales rank			Unit sales		Dollar sales		Price per unit	
1979	1984	**Principal end use**	1979	1984	1979	1984	1979	1984
1	2	Aircraft engine fuel controls	260,000	130,000	$1,407,000	$1,765,000	$ .41	$13.58
2	a	Disc drives, pointers	1,360,000	a	1,185,000	a	.87	a
3	3	Pumps, valves for aircraft engines	95,000	80,000	835,000	1,735,000	8.79	21.69
4	6	Repair and maintenance by government agency	350,000	280,000	795,000	1,315,000	2.27	4.70
5	10	Fishing tackle	450,000	475,000	620,000	930,000	1.38	1.96
6	15	Precision blowers, fans for motors	820,000	520,000	570,000	570,000	.70	1.10
7	11	EEC distributor	255,000	75,000	565,000	845,000	2.22	11.27
8	20	Radar (and computer '79 only)	70,000	70,000	515,000	395,000	7.36	5.64
9	19	Precision motors	440,000	330,000	470,000	420,000	1.07	1.27
10	12	Distributor	250,000	480,000	385,000	780,000	1.54	1.63

[a] Market segment showed little activity in 1984 because of the decline in the computer industry.

EXHIBIT 9
New additions to the top ten customers in 1984

	Sales		
1984 rank in dollar sales	Units	Dollars	Price per unit
1. Disc drives (Singapore)	2,450,000	$1,940,000	$ .79
4. Disc drives (U.S.)	1,000,000	1,450,000	1.45
5. Disc drives (U.S.)	1,400,000	1,380,000	.99
7. Aircraft engines[a]	15,000	1,310,000	87.33
8. Stepping motors for disc drives, printers	1,365,000	1,305,000	.96
9. Blower, fans, and coolers for motors[b]	1,410,000	1,130,000	.80

[a] New customer to NHBB.
[b] 1979 orders 395,000 units, $370,000.
Source: Company records.

EXHIBIT 10
NHBB estimate of
economies of scale

	Production volume in units					
	50	400	1,600	2,000	3,200	25,600
Per unit time in hours						
Set-up at 40 hours total	.800	.100	.025	.025	.013	.002
Run time[a]	.100	.072	.059	.057	.053	.038
Scrap[b]	.014	.003	.001	.001	.000	.000
Time allowed in hours	.914	.175	.085	.078	.066	.040
Cost per unit						
Labor[c]						
Set up	$ 6.40	$ .80	$ .20	$ .16	$ .11	$ .02
Run	.80	.58	.47	.46	.42	.30
Scrap	.11	.03	.01	.01	.00	.00
Total labor	$ 7.31	$1.41	$0.68	$0.63	$0.53	$0.32
Material[d]	.25	.21	.19	.19	.18	.16
Factory[e]	25.60	4.94	2.39	2.20	1.86	1.14
General administration cost[f]	9.04	1.80	.91	.84	.72	.45
Total cost/unit	$34.89	$6.95	$3.49	$3.23	$2.76	$1.75

[a] Based upon a rate of 500 per hour adjusted for 0.9 learning curve as quantity doubles.
[b] At 14% of run time adjusted for 0.95 material improvement.
[c] At $8/hr.
[d] Adjusted for 0.95 material improvement rate.
[e] 350% of total labor.
[f] At 35% of factory and material cost.

EXHIBIT 11
Direct costs and
economies of scale

	Production volume in units					
	50	400	1,600	2,000	3,200	25,600
Variable cost per unit by component						
Running time	$ .80	$ .58	$.47	$.46	$.42	$.30
Setup	6.40	.80	.20	.16	.11	.02
Scrap	.11	.03	.01	.01	.00	.00
Materials	.25	.21	.19	.19	.18	.16
Total direct cost	$7.56	$1.62	$.87	$.82	$.71	$.48
Cost of component as % of direct cost						
Running	10.6	35.8	54.0	56.1	59.2	62.5
Setup	84.7	49.4	23.0	19.5	15.5	4.2
Scrap	1.4	1.8	1.2	1.2	0.0	0.0
Materials	3.3	13.0	21.8	23.2	25.3	33.3
Total	100.0%	100.0%	100.0%	100.0%	100.0%	100.0%

EXHIBIT 12
Statements of
financial position,
years ending
June 30

	1984	1983	1982	1981	1980
Assets					
Cash	$ 1,400	$ 9,100	$ 4,700	$ 8,100	$ 700
Accounts receivable	9,200	7,500	8,700	8,700	8,500
Prepaid expenses	800	400	500	500	500
Inventories	14,600	13,200	13,500	13,200	11,500
Total current assets	$26,000	$30,200	$27,400	$30,500	$21,200
Land and buildings	9,100	8,600	8,700	7,900	6,800
Machinery and equipment	29,500	26,300	24,900	22,400	20,300
Less depreciation	(21,500)	(19,000)	(17,200)	(15,400)	(14,000)
Other assets	2,700	600	800	800	700
Total assets	$45,800	$46,600	$44,600	$46,200	$35,000
Liabilities					
Current liabilities	$ 6,000	$ 5,800	$ 7,200	$ 8,000	$ 5,100
Long-term debt	5,000	5,500	5,700	10,800	10,700
Other liabilities	1,300	1,100	800	400	500
Total liabilities	$12,300	$12,400	$13,700	$19,200	$16,300
Common stock	11,400	11,500	10,900	10,400[b]	5,000
Retained income	24,800	22,700	20,000	16,600	13,800
Less treasury stock[a]	(2,700)				(100)
Total equity	$33,500	$34,200	$30,900	$27,000	$18,700
Total liabilities, equity	$45,800	$46,600	$44,600	$46,200	$35,000

Note: Figures in thousands of dollars.
[a] 97,200 shares were purchased in the open market during fiscal 1984 in order to clear the market of a large block of shares being offered by the estate of Mr. Daniels.
[b] Two-for-one stock split in December 1980.

EXHIBIT 13
Statement of
operations

	Years ending June 30				
	1984	*1983*	*1982*	*1981*	*1980*
Net sales	$59,000	$55,200	$60,700	$53,900	$44,400
Cost of goods sold[a]	$38,000	$33,300	$35,700	$32,500	$27,800
Engineering	2,700	2,300	2,100	1,700	1,300
Selling, general, administration[a]	11,000	10,500	11,200	9,000	7,000
Interest	600	600	600	1,200	1,200
Profit sharing	1,300	1,800	2,700	2,300	1,600
Other (net)	(700)	(800)	(500)	(100)	
Income before tax	$ 6,100	$ 7,500	$ 8,900	$ 7,300	$ 5,500
Taxes	2,700	3,400	4,200	3,400	2,500
Net income	$ 3,400	$ 4,100	$ 4,700	$ 3,900	$ 3,000
[a] Depreciation expense	2,400	2,300	2,100	2,000	1,800

Note: Figures in thousands of dollars.

EXHIBIT 14
Employee data

	1984	1982	1980	1979	1969
Total employed	1,494	1,454	1,510	1,396	1,150
Men	NA	800	815	720	521
Women	NA	654	695	676	629
Average service (years)	8	7	6	6	6
Number over 20 years	143	166	141	142	4
Over 10 years	451	436	405	412	352
Over 5 years	799	701	672	747	449
Less than 5 years	101	151	292	95	345

Note: NA = not available.

EXHIBIT 15 Selected data per share, years ending June 30

	1984	1983	1982	1981	1980
Quarterly price range in American Stock Exchange					
Qtr. 1 (July–Sept.)	40–44⅛	23¼–30	21–28	12⅞–19⅜	10½–12⅜
Qtr. 2 (Oct.–Dec.)	40⅜–44¾	28⅞–33¾	22⅞–32	17¼–29¼	8⅞–11½
Qtr. 3 (Jan.–March)	34½–46½	31½–43⅞	23¾–31¾	21⅜–33¼	9⅝–14¼
Qtr. 4 (Apr.–June)	25½–35⅞	41⅛–48	25½–29	24–32⅜	10⅞–13¾
Shareholders	1,116	1,203	1,387	1,419	NA
Shares outstanding (average)	1,658,000	1,666,000	1,652,000	1,483,000	1,372,000
Earnings per share	2.05	2.44	2.85	2.65	2.19
Dividends	.80	.80	.80	.76	.55
Book value per share	21.20	20.54	18.65	16.51	13.52

Note: NA = not available.

At an AFBMA meeting in 1983, Ted Kanell was talking to Mr. Takama Takahashi, the former president of Nippon Miniature Bearing who had visited Peterborough in 1972, and who was now chief executive officer of Minebea of Tokyo, the conglomerate parent of Nippon Miniature Bearing. After a few moments of cocktail-party conversation, Mr. Takahashi asked Mr. Kanell, "Have you ever thought about how strong our two companies would be together?"

Although before his death in 1982 (the year before this Takahashi-Kanell meeting), Mr. Daniels had emphatically told Mr. Kanell never to bring up the subject of any kind of cooperative effort with the Japanese, Mr. Kanell felt he was responsible

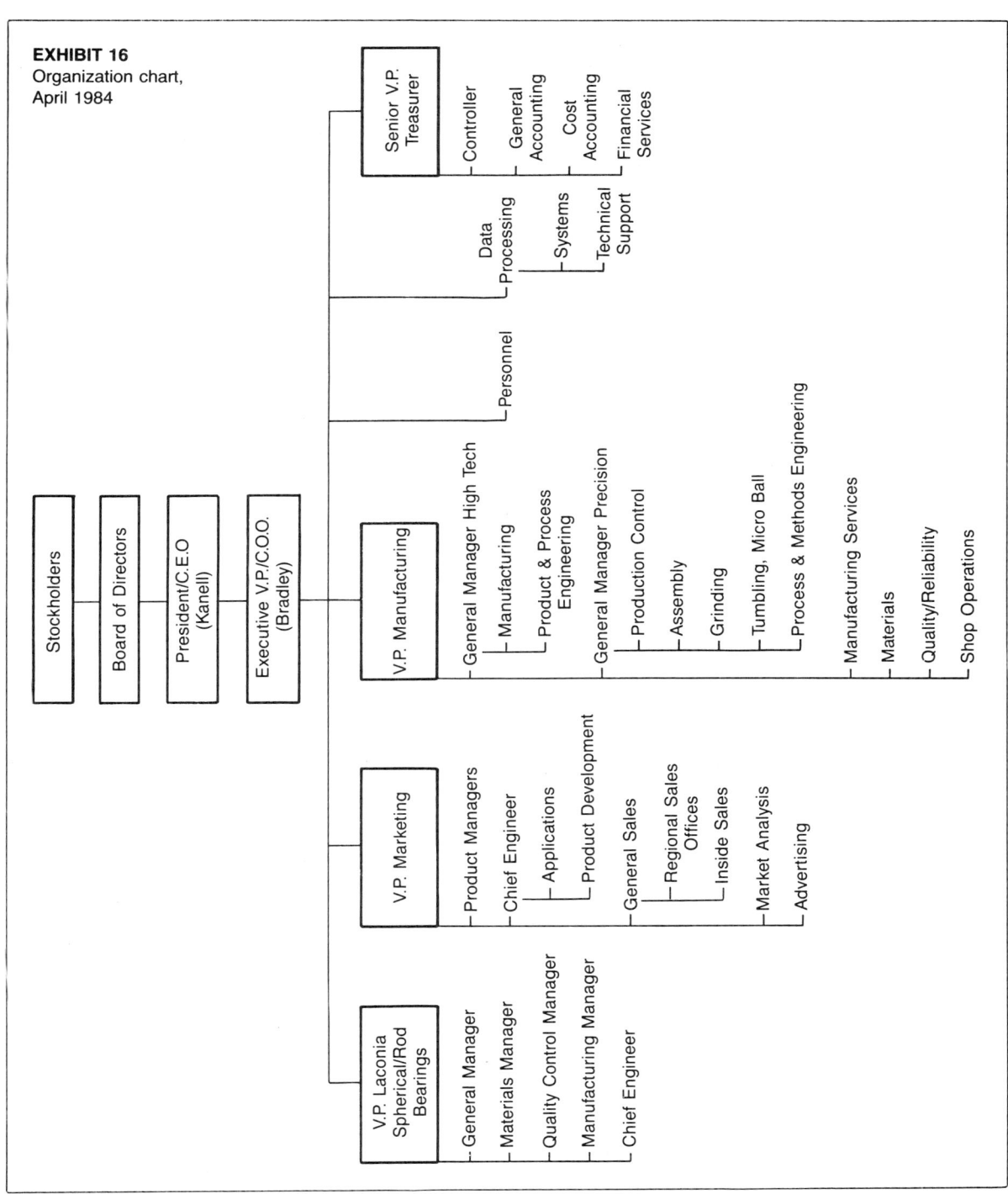

EXHIBIT 16
Organization chart,
April 1984

Source: Company records.

for NHBB's employees, customers, and stockholders. He decided to pursue the topic further with Mr. Takahashi.

Minebea Co. Ltd. had net sales of $403,000,000 and $481,000,000 for the fiscal years ending September 30, 1982 and 1983, respectively. It was estimating 1984 sales at between $580,000,000 and $620,000,000. Total assets were over $1,140,000,000 and annual capital expenditures averaged over $75,000,000. In 1983 the company became Japan's third largest loudspeaker producer by acquiring an audio components subsidary of Sony Corporation. Minebea expanded its small precision motors and computer key boards through U.S. acquisitions in 1983 and early 1984. It was a major participant in the founding in May 1984 of NMB Semiconductor Co., Ltd. Principally, however, Minebea was the world's leading supplier of small bearings. Thailand was an increasingly important production base for Minebea.

Minebea's overseas activities included 36 plants and 66 sales offices throughout the world. The company employed over 3,500 employees in Singapore and expected to have twice that many in Thailand when its plant expansion there was completed in 1985.

Now in July 1984 Minebea's offer was on the table. This offer included:

$65 per share in cash

A commitment to invest $50 million to modernize NHBB's two plants

Assurance that NHBB would be the head of the new firm and would assume responsibility for managing Nippon Miniature Bearings' plant in California

Ted Kanell knew the feelings of his deceased friend and mentor, NHBB's founder. These feelings were well known to Ted's "boss," the board of directors. (The directors of the company in 1984, as described in the 1984 10-K Annual Report, are listed in Appendix C.)

Mr. Kanell also knew that some employees would be most opposed to the merger. The Antitrust Division of the Department of Justice might also oppose the merger because some small portions of the product market might be 60 percent controlled by the merged firms. "It would depend on how you define the relevant market," Mr. Kanell thought. "Also there could be some problem from the Defense Department." Mr. Kanell knew a decision was required, since Minebea was making an offer that could not be sweetened further. "This is the science of management," Ted thought, "judging shades of gray."

Still fresh and vibrant in Ted Kanell's memory was his last meeting with Mr. Daniels. Only minutes before his death, Mr. Daniels had said goodbye to his protégé of a quarter of a century with these words: "Take care of my company, take care of my employees, and, most of all, keep my company independent."

APPENDIX A: THE BALL BEARING INDUSTRY PRE-1970s

MPB/Pierce-Daniels began in 1939, Barden Corporation in 1942, and NHBB in 1946.

Barden Corporation was formed by the Barth family of Connecticut and Carl Norden, the bomb sight developer. Barden was active in the gyroscope, military, and precision machine tool industries and, later on, in the high-speed turbine industry. Barden was the first bearing producer to make batches of specified tolerances, as opposed to the industry practice of sorting output into varying tolerance categories or standards. An industry observer noted that "the job no one else can do, Barden does." Leaving these "high tech" applications to Barden, NHBB and MPB produced less "esoteric" miniature and precision ball bearings. Generally, MPB concentrated on the higher ABEC ratings, while NHBB was strongest in volume ABEC 1 and 3 ratings.

The three significant changes in the ball bearing industry were (1) the swings in volume and profits produced by defense orders and by technology, (2) the introduction of mass production techniques, and (3) foreign competition.

Defense and Military Orders

Volume dropped off after World War II but increased with the Korean War buildup (1950–1954). The reduced demand of the post–Korean War period led to excess capacity and a domestic price war. Competitive pressure and price cuts eased during the late 1950s.

Technology played a part in the easing of competitive pressure, as the jet aircraft industry expanded substantially. A jet plane such as the 707 might contain ten thousand miniature bearings. What technology gave to the ball bearing industry it could also take away. Shortly the strategy of smaller and smaller bearings ran into a dead end as transistors were introduced. Eventually transistors converted many bearing applications, or mechanical processes, into transistor or electronic applications. For example, the number of miniature bearings in a 707 might be reduced to two or three thousand instead of ten thousand.

During the 1960s domestic shipments increased to record levels, as competitive pressures decreased during the Vietnam buildup, most notably between 1964 and 1966. Domestic production decreased from these peak Vietnam levels during the end of the 1960s. Exhibit A-1 summarizes the sales and income for the three major miniature and precision manufacturers from 1956 to 1968.

Mass Production Techniques

A second industry fact was the competitive pressure caused by the entry of such firms as General Motors (New Departure Division), Textron (Fafnir Division), and TRW (MRC Division) due to the opportunities presented by the defense buildup and, more importantly, the possibilities of mass production.

From the beginning of World War II and throughout most of the 1950s, miniature and instrument precision ball bearings required highly skilled labor with continuous

EXHIBIT A-1 Sales and net income

	Barden			MPB			NHBB		
	Sales	Net income	Percentage	Sales	Net income	Percentage	Sales	Net income	Percentage
1956	$ 7.7	.7	9.1	$ 2.0	.2	10.0	$ 2.0	.1	5.0
1957	10.2	1.1	10.8	3.9	.2	5.1	3.1	.3	9.7
1958	8.6	.7	8.1	5.5	.3	5.5	3.4	.2	5.9
1959	12.1	1.3	10.7	6.8	.4	5.9	4.9	.4	8.2
1960	14.9	1.1	7.4	10.2	.8	7.8	7.1	.6	8.5
1961	14.6	1.0	6.8	10.4	.5	4.8	8.3	.7	8.4
1962	15.5	.9	5.8	9.8	.2	2.0	7.2	.5	6.9
1963	16.3	.9	5.5	10.5	.3	2.9	6.8	.4	5.9
1964	15.4	.9	5.8	9.7	.2	2.1	6.0	.2	3.3
1965	21.9	1.9	8.7	11.1	.4	3.6	7.0	.4	5.7
1966	26.9	2.9	10.8	14.1	.7	5.0	12.1	1.2	9.9
1967	30.0	2.7	9.0	19.5	1.6	8.2	17.1	2.1	12.3
1968	27.7	1.4	5.1	20.0	1.2	6.0	14.2	1.0	7.0
Index 1956 = 100	360	200		1000	600		710	1000	

Note: Figures in millions of dollars. Barden's fiscal year ends on October 31, MPB's on March 31, and NHBB's on June 30.

and close supervision of the entire manufacturing process. True mass production and automation became possible in the late 1950s with the important step of the development of the Bryant internal grinder model C, which allowed for close tolerances of internal grinding. Bryant subsequently introduced precise yet high-volume production machines for miniature as well as instrument precision bearings. A subsidiary of the Cincinnati Milling Machine Company produced a similar internal grinder for miniature and instrument bearings (the Heald machine) and a microcentric grinder for external grinding. Flange grinders, external ball race grinders, and honing machines to further eliminate roughness after the grinding process completed the mechanical advances allowing automation in ball bearing production. One worker with minimum training could adjust a group of machines to operate more or less automatically. NHBB's 1963 Annual Report noted that "automation . . . made good progress, notably in the development of machines with which one person now does the work formerly done by eight or ten." Many of the improvements in machine capabilities were produced by collective efforts of the bearing manufacturers.

General Motors and others, attracted by automation and mass production possibilities, entered the miniature and precision bearing industry. Thus, the three principal U.S. manufacturers of miniature and precision bearings from World War II to 1984 — Barden Corporation, MPB, and NHBB — were joined by other domestic companies including (1) the New Departure — Hyatt Division of General Motors, (2) the Fafnir Bearing Division of Textron, and (3) the MRC Bearings Division of TRW.

Foreign Competition

The principal imports of miniature and precision ball bearings came from Europe, Canada, and, increasingly, from Japan. The industry's reaction to increased competition included turning to Washington.

The Trade Expansion Act of 1962 contained a provision (Section 232) whose purpose was "safeguarding national security." Section 232 provides that the director of the Office of Emergency Preparedness must recommend, and the president must take, action necessary to control imports "so that such imports will not so threaten to impair the national security."

Under the leadership of Mr. Daniels and others, the domestic industry trade association, the Anti-Friction Bearing Manufacturers Association (AFBMA), filed an application for an investigation with the Office of Emergency Preparedness in October 1964, concluding that "reliance upon imports for supplies of . . . miniature bearings and instrument bearings, so essential to the national defense, clearly poses a menacing threat to the national security." Two years later, after supplementary filings were submitted by both the AFBMA and by the Japanese bearing industry association, the AFBMA withdrew its application for investigation because of inadequate import data.

In January 1969 the AFBMA again submitted an application for investigation under Section 232. This 1969 *AFBMA Application for Investigation* included the following:

1. An analysis showing production, exports to the United States, and percentage of production exported the United States by Nippon Miniature Bearing Co., Ltd. (founded in 1951 in Tokyo) and data showing Nippon's investment in fixed assets to be $4,600,000 U.S. in 1967 with planned 1968 additions of $4,200,000.

Nippon Miniature Bearings (millions of units)

Year	Production	Exports to U.S.	Production exported to U.S.
1965	3.3	.7	22%
1966	4.8	1.9	39
1967	7.4	5.1	70
1968	10.7	7.5	70

2. Data on Swiss (primarily RMB Roulements Miniatures, S.A.) and Nippon Miniature Bearings imports and domestic shipments.

Shipments (in millions of units)

Year	U.S. domestic shipments	Swiss exports to U.S.	Nippon exports to U.S.	Swiss and Nippon exports as a % of U.S. shipments
1965	13.7	2.7	.7	25
1966	20.4	2.7	1.9	23
1967	18.9	2.6	5.1	41
1968	14.5	2.3	7.5	68

3. A reminder that the U.S. government had officially recognized the strategic importance of ball bearings by banning a sale of forty-five Bryant grinders to Russia.

4. The conclusion that 65 percent to 75 percent of all U.S. consumption of miniature and instrument bearings are defense end-uses.

5. The conclusion that foreign producers had become the dominant force in the nondefense market as the domestic industry responded to urgent defense orders.

6. A request for an investigation of this "threat to national security."

The reply of the Japan industry group filed in April 1969 *(Reply of the Japan Bearing Industrial Association to the Application for Investigation)* argues in return that

1. Industry sales and profit fluctuations are caused by military procurement, not by imports.

2. Domestic capacity has been expanding even if domestic companies have been diversifying.

3. Future defense needs can be met by relatively easily accomplished domestic expansion. Thus imports from Japan do not now, and will not in the future, threaten the productive ability of the domestic bearing industry essential to national security. The Japanese reply closes with the observation that "We probably will never again experience a conventional war of global scale such as World War II where the United States was cut off from most foreign sources of supply. In any foreseeable situation other than a worldwide nuclear war, the United States could import defense-essential items from friendly nations to supplement domestic sources."

In support of the AFBMA application, Mr. Daniels and his aide Theodore Kanell traveled extensively between Washington and Peterborough, submitting additional data include Exhibits A-2 and A-3 concerning lost business and price comparisons. MPB also participated extensively in the AFBMA application effort. Barden, however, was then involved with NMB, the Japanese manufacturer. Barden, which was withdrawing from the miniature bearing market, exchanged technology with the Japanese in exchange for an ownership position in NMB and a distribution arrangement whereby Barden distributed NMB products. This agreement was terminated after a few years.

NHBB continued to suffer earnings decline: 1968 earnings of $975,000 ($1.42 per share) fell to $149,000 ($0.22 per share) in 1969. Company officers kept up a weekly activity schedule in Washington and talked to Congressional representatives, personnel in the Office of Emergency Preparedness, and Treasury officials in their push for some kind of protection, whether it be embargoes, mandatory quotas, voluntary quotas, or tariffs. Assistant Secretary of Commerce Kenneth Davis came to Peterborough in December 1969 and noted that it is a "black and white situation whether or not an industry is important to defense, and I don't think there is much question that miniature and precision bearings are important." Davis further noted that Japan was expected to have a $1.5 billion trade surplus with the United States

EXHIBIT A-2

NHBB lost business report

Customer	End product	1966	1967
A	Motor manufacturings	$245,000	$ 600
B	Potentiometers	171,000	1,100
C	Counters	121,000	7,200
D	Motors & pots	291,000	12,400
E	Pots	164,000	0
F	Gear heads	94,000	7,600
G	Synchros & servo machinery	237,000	5,100
H	Test equipment	91,000	1,107
I	Pots	89,000	450
J	Computers	176,000	4,100
K	Gear heads	461,000	9,700
L	Clutches	62,000	450
M	Guidance & fire control systems	290,000	13,000
N	Motors	176,000	11,000
O	Motors & gear heads	144,000	7,200
P	Motors	114,000	0
Q	Atomic energy	40,000	2,100

Note: Exhibit shows business lost to Japanese imports by showing NHBB's sales to a few customers selected at random by NHBB.
Source: Company records.

that year and that General Motors, Federal-Mogul, and MRC-TRW had dropped out of the bearing industry.

The AFBMA was especially encouraged by a decision (albeit after many months) by the Deputy Defense Secretary David Packard in April 1971 to order that all military purchases of ball bearings with an outside diameter of 30 millimeters or less "must be procured from domestic or Canadian sources to the maximum extent practicable." At this point the AFBMA petition had been pending 26 months.

Nonetheless, in May 1971 the Office of Emergency Preparedness issued a report which, while conceding that imports were hurting the domestic bearings industry, declined to recommend any import limits. OEP Director George Lincoln stressed that the Pentagon had recently taken specific action to "preserve the mobilization base for production of bearings." Lincoln concluded that, since OEP legislation restricted the OEP to consider the national security impact only, the current "deterioration can be ascribed in some part to imports, but I consider that it has been related more directly to a sharp decline in demand."

EXHIBIT A-3 Price comparison, selected domestic versus Japanese prices on balls

General-Purpose Bearing Steel

| | Grade 10 | | | Grade 25 | | |
Size	Japanese price	Domestic price	Price index[a]	Japanese price	Domestic price	Price index[a]
1/16	.98	4.63	21	.88	3.09	28
3/32	.93	3.15	30	.83	2.02	41
1/8	.78	3.38	23	.68	2.55	27
5/32	1.12	3.77	30	1.02	2.71	38
3/16	1.54	4.21	37	1.44	3.01	48

Corrosion-Resistant Steel

| | Grade 10 | | | Grade 25 | | |
Size	Japanese price	Domestic price	Price index[a]	Japanese price	Domestic price	Price index[a]
1/32	1.55	10.75	14	—	—	—
3/64	1.70	10.48	16	—	—	—
1/16	1.76	9.18	19	1.60	8.34	19
5/64	1.64	10.23	16	—	—	—
3/32	—	—	—	1.60	7.45	21
1/8	2.18	7.00	31	2.14	5.85	37
5/32	—	—	—	3.65	7.15	51

Note: Prices in dollars per thousand balls.
[a] Price index = Japanese price as a percentage of domestic price.
Source: NHBB records.

APPENDIX B: COMMENTS OF WILLIAM M. SCRANTON

Bill Scranton, former president of MPB, talked to the casewriter about the evolution of MPB's strategy. Mr. Scranton had joined MPB in 1950, after graduating from Princeton with a degree in mechanical engineering and Harvard Business School, plus completing military service and 6 years at Pratt & Whitney Aircraft. His comments make up the rest of this appendix.

I was newly married when I worked for Pratt & Whitney as a production foreman on the night shift. After 3 years of night shift work, I started talking to the guys at the top about a transfer. They were not totally sympathetic to me as the youngest foreman in the company, so I started looking around for a job. I had seriously considered on two previous occasions working with a small company, and I decided to go with my third chance, which I got through Harvard's placement service. The job was as production manager for Horace Gilbert at MPB. I thought I had better take the risk.

During World War II, Bud Daniels had brought in his brother-in-law, Horace Gilbert (their wives were sisters) to take his place as the operating and administration part of MPB, since the founder, Mr. Pierce, was a technical, nonmanagerial person.

After the war, Daniels and Pierce disagreed over production strategy. Pierce, who had invented the split ball bearing, had made the first miniature bearings with what was essentially watch-making technology. Daniels wanted to bring in screw machines and grinders and pursue automated production, while Pierce had become committed to the production process as opposed to the product.

Daniels left MPB and started NHBB, and, although Horace Gilbert tried to stay out of the Daniels-Pierce dispute, there was bad blood between the two brothers-in-law, aggravated by a disagreement as to whether Daniels left agreeing to stay out of the miniature ball bearing field or whether he agreed not to use Pierce's production process but was free to develop his own process.

In 1950, NHBB had the lead based upon the conventional screw machine-grinder full mechanized production system developed for miniature bearings by Daniels and Dick Cherwin. But the Korean War period was a great one to join a bearing company, because demand really was strong. Gilbert needed administrative help and I took on whatever needed doing. Everything was going straight up. MPB added people and started a night shift and we were badly back-ordered. Even elevator operators, hearing my name when I called on customers, would say, ''Boy, are they looking for you!''

After the Korean War, the bad blood intensified as NHBB tried to drive MPB under by way of a price war. We all traveled with cost-volume estimates and charts, and the price cutting was extensive. There were moments when things were very tough for MPB, but we survived and caught up to NHBB's automated production lead.

Two things ended this bitter price war. One was New Departure's entry into the miniature and precision bearing business. Big companies in a market that is a sellers' market don't engage in price wars. So, a system of price leadership or administered prices evolved, aided by the other thing that made the price war end — the explosion in demand caused by the technological pull of the aircraft industry. We came into the period of major aircraft construction — the 707, DC-8, and the F101. We had lots of demand and a price umbrella, and everyone published their price lists, and things calmed down. We expanded based on forecast. We didn't know it, but we could have sold all we could make.

During this prosperous period, others entered the industry. Barden dropped down in size range into miniature bearings, and Fafnir and other larger companies started producing miniature and precision bearings. The price discipline broke, in part because of the new entrants and in part because of the swing in technology. There were no more large aircraft programs and, most importantly, the emphasis on mechanical miniaturization ended as electronics technology advanced. You miniaturize things electronically, so the mechanical technology need dropped off, the analogs were replaced by digital computers, and the days of boom demand were over.

The next big change in MPB and the industry was the Japanese competition. As executive vice-president — I did not become president until 1962 when Horace Gilbert's outside interests made it appropriate that he should become board chairman and I became president — I met Mr. Takahashi of Nippon Miniature Bearings (NMB) in 1959. Mr. Takahashi briefly toured our plant, and we began a series of negotiations with NMB.

We had earlier explored joint efforts with France's SFNA (Société Française Nationale Aeronautical) and we bought from NMB some chrome steel bearings — a small part of the market — and tried to sell them in the U.S. and in Europe, while talking about a more comprehensive arrangement. As the offers and counteroffers went back and forth, it became clear that our objectives — to have majority interest in any joint venture into which we put any technological knowledge — was not compatible with Takahashi's objective of control of the American market. Mr. Takahashi kept asking, "Don't you know how powerful our two companies could be together?" But, it wasn't possible, given each company's objective.

We broke off negotiations, and NMB finally entered into a technology agreement with Barden, which agreement gave Barden a minority interest in NMB. This agreement lasted a few years and was terminated. Barden did sell its interest back to NMB at a profit. Nonetheless, this Barden-NMB effort was a problem to the rest of us in the industry who were requesting federal assistance to limit imports in order to maintain a ball bearing industrial capacity for defense purposes.

Assessing Japanese competition during this period of predatory Japanese pricing we decided we had three courses of action: (1) to join them, (2) to turn to the government, and (3) to find a basis to compete.

We knew we couldn't join them on our terms, having already tried that option.

The government appeals took a long, long time. We eventually made a valuable convert in our congressman, Jim Cleveland, but it was a lengthy process with him and much more so with the Defense people. The process was humorous at the same time, because there I would be with representatives from our fierce competitor NHBB, each of us trying to stress the economics of the situation as plainly as possible while, at the same time, both concentrating on not revealing any costs to each other, while also straining to hear any cost data from our competitor.

Finding a basis to compete was the most difficult. Dick Cherwin, Bud Daniels, and others at NHBB talked about rolling the Japanese back into the sea. NHBB built a plant in Laconia, New Hampshire, to produce low-ABEC miniatures.

But we didn't think anyone could "roll the Japanese back into the sea," because NMB wasn't interested in short-term costs, but rather in long-term market share. We could cut back on products, but where would that leave us?

Further compounding the problem was the stock market. We were a glamor industry in the fifties, but multiples slid in the sixties and collapsed in the seventies. We couldn't raise equity without diluting earnings, and we didn't have a high multiple for acquisitions.

We made acquisitions and tried to diversify, while NHBB was trying to fine-tune. We misjudged some of our efforts to enter other markets. We opened a gyrooptic plant, which had to be closed — just as NHBB had to close their Laconia plant as the Japanese wouldn't "roll back."

We investigated an assembly plant in Mexico, having developed direct sales to the Common Market through a Holland assembly plant. We added a specialty chemical line and other diversifications, but we were sacrificing profits through these new product efforts.

A new power base was developing on the board, and Horace Gilbert's death and the sale of his stock by the estate, along with our diversification problems, meant that I lost the initiative. A banker became chairman and C.E.O., and I became chief operating officer, and the acquisition offers came in, some solicited by our banker-chairman. Although the executive team was supposed to have golden parachutes, only the pilot did, when we were sold to Wheelabrator-Frye in 1976. I left the company, but I understand Wheelabrator-Frye—which subsequently merged with Signal, and which was in turn acquired by Allied — was able to succeed at MPB by narrowing the product line and investing in equipment. It also kept and promoted the middle managers who knew the business.

Looking at MPB and the ball bearing industry from the perspective of national policies, one significant fact is the need for a large industrial market base to compete effectively. You don't have Japanese products made with other than Japanese components, if the latter exist. So when the union-pushed labor costs got high enough in critical U.S. industries such as automobiles and steel, Japan — with its U.S.-supported and -aided postwar industrial reconstruction — built an industrial base which had a snowball effect on components and related industries because they use Japanese components — bearings for example. Japan builds up its domestic demand, tools up for volume, and then eventually exports with a long-term, market-share view. Japan's efforts have been aggressive and across the board. Japanese companies, the offshore companies they control, and the limited local assembly facilities they have to go through to satisfy local requirements are part of a relentless cycle. Our experience in ball bearings is being mirrored in microchips today.

This leads to a second fact. The financial community measured us with standards that did not allow investing at the expense of current earnings whether in inventory or in future profits through capital and diversification expenditures. Since MPB was not a closely controlled ball bearing company like Timken, we had to respond to the financial community's return-on-investment and current-profit yardsticks. We all skimped on the plants, and the plants became obsolete. Conglomerates, also following national financial measuring sticks, began buying up the specialty companies, put in control systems, and brought in management that focused on profits, so the specialty divisions eventually did less well and were dumped.

These two facts were the things that killed the ball bearing industry. Except for a few specialty areas, the domestic industry is all but dead. You may never see it come back.

APPENDIX C: DIRECTORS

Nicholas Babich, fifty-four, a director since May 1984, is president, chief executive officer, and a director of Hitchiner Manufacturing Co., Inc. (investment castings and machine components manufacturing), a position he has held since November 1981.

Robert H. Bradley, fifty, a director since October 1982, is executive vice-president of the company, a position he has held since November 1981. Prior thereto, he was vice-president from April 1979. Mr. Bradley is the beneficial owner of 8,640 shares.

Theodore T. Daniels, forty-five, is a researcher and consultant in social communications and a lecturer at the University of Pennsylvania, a position he has held since September 1978. Mr. Daniels is the brother-in-law of Ernest V. Klein. He is the beneficial owner of 18,580 shares.

Michael Kaminsky, Jr., fifty-seven, a director since October 1974, is a consultant (manufacturing), a position he has held since August 1983. Prior thereto, he was vice-president of Fenwal Incorporated (manufacturer of temperature and explosion controls), a division of Kidde, Inc., from April 1982. From July 1981, Mr. Kaminsky was with A.D.E., Inc. (noncontact automatic gaging and measuring products manufacturing) as vice-president, operations. He is chairman of the Executive Compensation Committee, a member of the Audit Committee, and the beneficial owner of 3,300 shares.

Theodore Kanell, sixty-one, a director since July 1968, is president of the company, a position he has held since March 1979. He is a member of the Pension Fund Committee and the beneficial owner of 17,366 shares.

Ernest V. Klein, fifty-one, a director since January 1977, is a brother-in-law of Theodore T. Daniels and is a partner in the law firm of Gaston Snow and Ely Bartlett (general counsel for the company), a position he has held in this and a predecessor firm since October 1966. Mr. Klein is chairman of the Audit Committee, a member of the Executive Compensation Committee, and the beneficial owner of 207,808 shares (approximately 13 percent), which includes 202,368 shares of five trusts for which he is trustee or cotrustee and shares voting and investment power. Not included in Mr. Klein's shares are 9,300 shares owned beneficially by Mrs. Klein, to which Mr. Klein disclaims any beneficial ownership.

Frederick P. Koallick, sixty, a director since September 1971, is senior vice-president (since April 1980) and treasurer (since May 1955) of the company, having served as a vice-president from May 1971 to April 1980. Mr. Koallick is a member of the Pension Fund Committee and the beneficial owner of 11,634 shares.

Henry H. Meyer, Jr., sixty-three, a director since March 1977, is vice-president of Eaton & Howard, Vance Sanders Inc. (investment counsel), a position he has held in this and a predecessor firm since June 1968. He is chairman of the Pension Fund Committee, a member of the Executive Compensation Committee, and the beneficial owner of 7,100 shares, which include 2,400 shares of two trusts for which he is cotrustee and shares voting and investment power. Not included in Mr. Meyer's shares are 2,500 shares for which Mrs. Meyer is a cotrustee and to which Mr. Meyer disclaims any beneficial ownership.

David F. Putnam, seventy, a director since October 1979, is chairman emeritus of Markem Corporation (identification and decoration machinery manufacturing), a position he assumed in May 1979. Mr. Putnam was chairman of Markem Corporation from July 1973 to May 1979 and is currently a director of that company. He is a member of the Audit and Executive Compensation Committees and the beneficial owner of 1,800 shares.

SPECIALTY PRODUCTS DIVISION—
CONTINENTAL PACKAGING COMPANY

STRATEGY IMPLEMENTATION
AT SPECIALTY PRODUCTS, 1984–1985

Continental Packaging Company's Product Line and Customers

Continental Packaging Company (CPC) was founded almost 150 years ago. After a long and successful history, Continental Packaging Company was acquired by BMF International in 1967. CPC's products include a wide variety of paper packaging materials and office products. CPC was organized into three businesses based upon types of customers. Of the three business units, Distribution Division concentrated its efforts on several thousand distributors of office and stationery products. Retail Division sold directly to certain large retail outlets. Specialty Products had a very narrowly focused business — a few very large accounts which required slightly customized products in large batches. Specialty Products was considerably smaller in sales dollars than its sister units — hence its name. Specialty Products had to take care not to intrude upon Distribution Division or Retail Division territory and customers.

In recent years, CPC had experienced some performance problems. Its leadership position eroded in some markets. Exhibit 1 shows the strategic capability profile of CPC. Some of CPC's strengths included its superior distribution channels, ability to manage financial affairs, availability of financial resources (being a division of BMF International), and its market share in college and commercial markets. On the other hand, CPC's executives believed that the company was relatively weak in product development, costs were too high, and CPC's profitability lagged behind competitors'.

The 1984 Strategic Planning Effort

When Neil Greene was appointed president of CPC in 1982, the division faced serious difficulties. Because CPC's business depends upon a derived demand, and because CPC customers are very sensitive to general economic conditions, CPC suffered during the 1981–1982 recession. Some executives felt that, prior to Greene's

Case prepared by Charles Stubbart, University of Massachusetts, © 1986. Reprinted by permission.

EXHIBIT 1
Continental
Packaging
Company's
strategic
capability
profile

	Strength rating (+3 to −3)[a]	Importance rating (0 to +3)[b]
Marketing		
Market share		
Retail Division	+1	+2
Distributor Division	+3	+2
Specialty Products Division	0	+1
Product line	+1	+2
Recognition by market	+1	+2
Market research	+2	+1
Awareness customer needs	−1	+3
Advertising	−1	+2
Sales force	−1	+3
Distribution	+2	+3
Product management	−1	+3
Product design	0	+2
Product development		
New products design	0	+2
Rate of new products introduction	−2	+1
Product development,		
Facilities and personnel	+1	+1
Manufacturing		
Costs	−2	+3
Manufacturing costs	−2	+3
Production control	+3	+2
Flexibility	0	+1
Adequate facilities	−1	+2
Cost of materials	−1	+1
Reliability of supplies	+1	+1
Capacity	0	+2
Financial		
Financial abilities	+1	+2
Management information systems	+2	+1
Financial resources	0	+2
Human resources		
Personnel policies	0	+1
Union relations	+2	+2
Turnover	+2	+1
Skill and commitment		
of work force	+1	+2
Corporate management		
Profitability	−1	+3
Senior management	−1	+3
Planning	−2	+2
Control	+1	+1
Coordination and communications	+1	+2
Organizational structure	−1	+1
Climate	−1	+2

EXHIBIT 1 (continued)

EXHIBIT 1 (continued)

Principal opportunities and threats — 1984

Opportunities
Expand market share in fast-growing wholesale segment
Expand market share in fast-growing info-processing market
Cost reduction
Develop human resources
Expand Specialty Products segment

Threats
Not positioned for new products
Changing wholesaler strategies
Undermotivated, uninspired work force
Specialty Products diverts resources better used elsewhere
Unresponsive to customer needs
Change in competitor's strategies
Commodity orientation of customers

[a] +3 to −3, where +3 is very strong, −3 very weak in comparison to competitors.
[b] 0 to 3, where 3 is very important.

arrival, the division had been (perhaps unconsciously) ''milked.'' Greene concluded that many long-standing problems had progressed to a dangerous stage, that the business was unfocused, and that some type of genuine strategic planning was long overdue. Strategic planning attempts during earlier years created plans that were never adequately implemented. Executives' sentiments generally converged with Greene's thinking — something big was needed — a turnaround.

During summer of 1984, using the guidance of a consultant, fifteen top executives of CPC gathered frequently to initiate strategic planning. No fewer than 6 entire working days were spent off-site, and several series of 3 half-day, on-site sessions were held. Top executives spent hundreds of hours doing planning. Some of the planning activities included strategic capability profiles, environmental analysis, customer profiles, competitor profiles, product analysis, critical success factors, scenario generation, setting objectives, and action plans.

Initially, some executives felt skeptical about the value of this planning exercise, and some participants were reluctant to divulge everything they knew.

Comments by Executives About the 1984 Strategic Planning

During fall of 1984 (after that first year's planning sessions had concluded) CPC executives characterized the planning done that summer:

The first thing I wondered was, "How honest do they really want us to get?"

I knew it would be successful because I've seen strategic planning done elsewhere.

Greene initiated it, but he stayed in the background. He wanted to know what we thought. Greene makes me nervous when he does this.

I learned an incredible amount about our business.

When Greene came in, he realized we needed some direction. This was his way of getting it.

We did planning before, but that planning never really amounted to much. Distractions were pouring over the walls. The plans never got implemented. Those plans didn't have actions specified. These do. For example, the old plan said "de-emphasize a certain business," but nothing happened. The new plan says "stop doing a certain business by Tuesday" and it gets stopped.

It was a good idea to go off-site.

The plan gives us a common language.

The plan suits Greene's style perfectly. He is a man who wants thorough preparations and no loose ends. Greene says, "Do it right, do it once, do it now."

Given the history of the company and the style of Greene's predecessor, this is a hard religion for us to practice. But we are making strides.

Greene inherited some good programs.

When we did planning before Greene arrived, the same problems and issues came up. But the management situation couldn't resolve conflicts so nothing much was done. Fortunately, Greene doesn't have to face that.

Brother, I'm not sure we can do the things the plan calls for.

I'm not sure we understand what we're doing.

Implementing the plans is forcing some painful issues.

Planning is worthwhile. Changed our direction.

The good recent results we've had don't really come from the plan.

The plan identified goals. Easy. Now we're down to the level of people, systems, dollars, information. It's getting harder.

Greene was quite a shock to the CPC system. He's very different from his predecessor, MacDonald. Greene is aloof and reserved, MacDonald was gregarious. Greene is circumspect, while MacDonald was a "straight-ahead" fellow. Greene understands marketing and strategy, MacDonald was an operations man. . . . Strategic planning served as a way for us to get to know Greene, and vice versa.

The strategic plan stated several ambitious financial and product objectives for CPC:

$20 million after-tax profit by 1987
Increase sales 12–15 percent per year
Increase productivity 15 percent by 1987
An 8 percent return on sales after tax

Actions plans included:

Prune the product line
Reorganization
Improved service
Install an MBO system

A renewed emphasis was placed on concentrating CPC efforts on critical challenges to the firm.

MEET PAUL GOODMAN

Paul Goodman works as the operations manager for CPC. He is in his midthirties. Paul has a wife and two children. He is a jogger and an exsmoker. Paul graduated from Lowell Tech. with a bachelor of science degree in industrial management in 1971. His first job was with American Optical Company, where he held positions in distribution, warehousing, engineering, and production control. Paul came to CPC in 1977. He moved from production control manager to bindery plant manager. In 1981 corrugated products were added to his responsibilities. In July 1984 he was appointed operations manager for CPC.

His office is located in a hundred-year-old manufacturing facility beside a canal, near several sets of railroad tracks. The plant sits in an old, somewhat run-down, New England manufacturing center of intermediate size. CPC headquarters sits in a modern glass building located about 10 minutes away.

A consistent management style and philosophy shape his interactions with coworkers. Paul always notices and deals with the interpersonal elements of situations — the intentional and unintentional impacts of words and events. He demonstrates particularly good skills for giving feedback or direction in sticky situations, such as performance appraisals or when failures occur. But his style also accommodates open expressions of anger or enthusiasm. Paul constantly seeks to find the positive elements in a situation and work with them — what he calls "problem-tunities." Paul likes numbers. On the other hand, he does not have extraordinary faith in what he refers to as "bean-counting," although he usually seems to know exactly how many beans there are.

Paul is strongly committed to his marriage and his family. He will sometimes put aside work demands in favor of pressing family concerns. He worries that the work demands placed upon a company executive might erode the quality of family life. Paul leaves the plant at quitting time, usually taking some work home in his briefcase.

In the late summer and early fall of 1984 Paul Goodman was a very busy man. He had just received his promotion. At the same time, he attended an executive M.B.A. program at a well-known nearby university. Besides all that, he was a member of the strategic planning group which was meeting regularly to deal with the future strategy of CPC.

Among Paul's numerous new responsibilities in fall of 1984 was the general management of Specialty Products. Paul remarked that he found this new responsibility for Specialty Products ironic because as a factory executive, "I used to be against this business!" He explained that the special requirements and operations of Specialty Products diverted plant personnel from more important operations supporting the other two units — Distribution Division and Retail Division.

Actually, Paul welcomed the chance to take responsibility for a profit center, realizing that his upward mobility would be limited if he did not broaden his experience from manufacturing operations to include marketing, finance, and so on.

Exhibit 2 depicts CPC organization in fall 1984. Under this organization, Specialty Products reported to the manufacturing vice-president. CPC executives explained that they could not afford a traditional product-line divisional setup because of the extra costs required.

EXHIBIT 2 Continental Packaging Company's organization structure

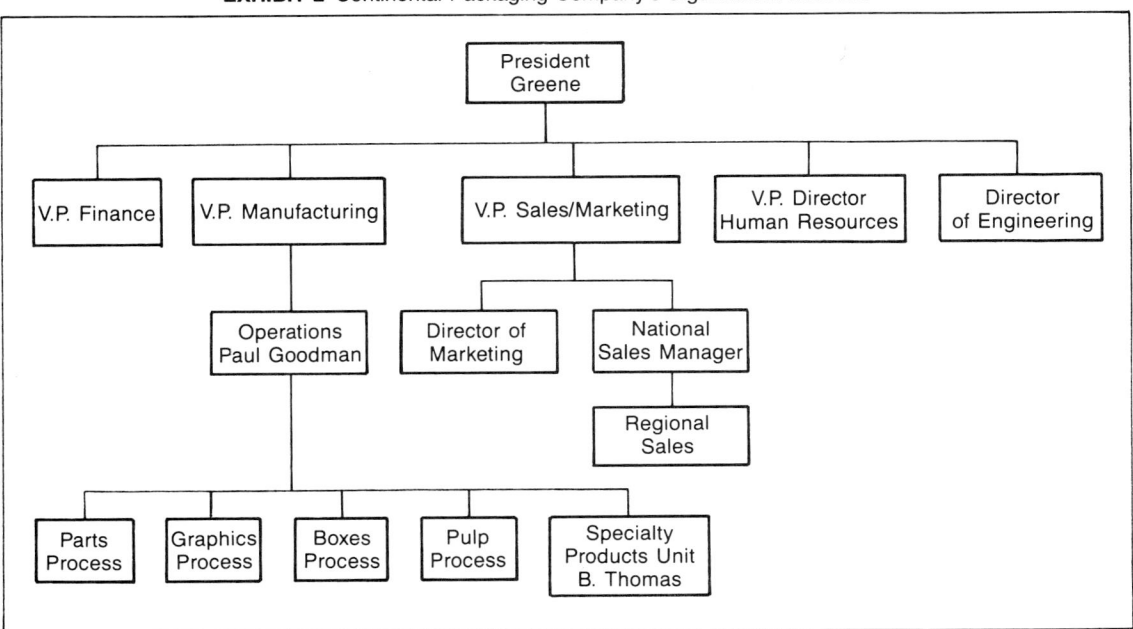

In the past, Specialty Products had never been considered an important part of CPC. In fact, during the 1984 strategic planning sessions, executives among the planning group seriously considered whether Specialty Products ought to be divested or, more likely, simply disbanded. Many executives argued that Specialty Products was a distraction and that margins would never reach satisfactory levels. CPC nearly abandoned Specialty Products. At times, however, Specialty Products looked good. When Retail Division and Distribution Division lagged, causing excess capacity in the plant to hurt profits, Specialty Products was the mechanism for soaking up that excess capacity. However, when business was good for Retail Division and Distribution Division, Specialty Products faded into a distinctly secondary role. Paul called this phenomenon "the light-switch business." Ultimately, Specialty Products survived this scrutiny — but only as a means for soaking up unused capacity — not as a genuine opportunity area. In fact, Specialty Products' mission expressly ruled out additional investment for Specialty Products except under extraordinary circumstances.

Exhibits 3 and 4 show financial data for the BMF International and the CPC. Although Specialty Products was expected to lose money in 1984, certain ambiguities remained. First, executives at Specialty Products argued that they received allocations for too much division overhead. Second, analysts could not calculate precisely how much assets were committed to Specialty Products. The reason for this confusion was that all three business units shared the same products (to a degree) and the same intermingled manufacturing equipment and processes in the plant.

SPECIALTY PRODUCTS
FALL 1984–SUMMER 1985

Bob Thomas manages the Specialty Products unit. He has been working for Continental about 20 years. Prior to managing Specialty Products, Bob held positions in manufacturing, customer service, and sales. Bob is a friendly, open person, with a smile always ready. People at CPC comment that Bob knows the products particularly well and that he loves new ideas. Occasionally, Bob has been criticized for what some people call his tendency to charge off in too many directions at once. Bob counters, "You've got to take advantage of your opportunities when you get them, not necessarily when you are ready for them."

Specialty Products concentrates its efforts in New England. The customer base includes mainly very large divisions of Fortune 500 companies with a need for customized packaging products. Special decorated boxes constitute the principal product. Specialty Products' mission is stated in the 1984 strategic plan:

Specialty Products is specifically authorized to pursue any customer who offers the potential for large orders of custom merchandise for resale. Specialty Products will be addressed as a growth business with the particular intent to use excess capacity. New business will be at 20 percent margin or better. Major capital investment to support this market will

EXHIBIT 3
BMF International's recent performance

	1980	1981	1982	1983	Projected 1984
Net sales ($000)	$899,188	$910,965	$968,491	$990,122	$1,130,000
Earnings as a percent of sales	5.6	4.7	5.3	3.6	4.5
Return on equity	17.9%	14.7%	16.5%	10.8%	15.1%

EXHIBIT 4 Operating performance and projections for Continental Packaging Company

	1980	1981	1982	1983	Projected 1984	Projected 1985	Projected 1986	Projected 1987
Sales	$131,682	$152,524	$151,846	$175,883	$185,477	$190,816	$220,245	$237,861
Gross profit from sales	43,191	51,400	47,831	59,624	61,763	66,976	80,389	87,532
General and administrative expenses	29,628	35,843	37,354	46,608	47,111	49,039	53,960	55,897
Selling expenses	29,628	35,843	37,354	46,608	47,111	49,039	53,960	55,897
Depreciation	3,400	3,400	2,500	5,300	3,820	4,120	4,400	4,400
Capital expenditures	8,200	9,600	5,000	2,500	2,800	6,000	6,000	6,000
Net earnings	8,296	9,304	7,896	7,563	8,160	9,350	12,554	15,461

Note: Figures in thousands of dollars.

not be made, except in unusual circumstances and after very careful examination and justification.

Recently, Specialty Products had suffered several serious reverses:

Customers, shocked by the economic contraction and high interest rates, began managing their inventories more tightly to help their cash flow.

Although Specialty Products produced custom products, customers remained sensitive to prices. Specialty Products' standard costs rose 13 percent in the most recent year in spite of continued efforts (such as installing a class-A MRP system) to drive down labor and materials costs.

Several serious quality problems upset sales efforts.

Sales force morale hit an all-time low. Without clear objectives, having little training, and believing themselves ''second-class citizens'' compared to salespeople in other divisions, the Specialty Products' sales effort floundered.

On the other hand, Thomas believed that Specialty Products could produce the best-made products on the market, that his in-house customer service constituted an important advantage, and that CPC's vertical integration and skillful inventory planning formed an advantage. The key problem was, according to Thomas: "How can I increase sales, increase market share, and increase margins in the face of high costs and no investment?"

Specialty Products encountered a large number and variety of competitors. Many of these companies offered only a very narrow product line from a single type of material or in just a few types of construction, choosing to compete in local or regional markets. Thus, Specialty Products faced different competitors for nearly every account. These accounts ordinarily divided their purchases among two, three, or four suppliers, preferring not to rely on a single supplier. Most supply relationships in the industry last a long time. Although binders with this type of packaging did not constitute a significant cost for most customers, nevertheless, mistakes, problems, and shortages in supply could severely disrupt a customer's operations — imposing large costs.

Specialty Products' affiliation with CPC provided an advantage insofar as customers believed that they could rely on CPC's distribution efficiency and financial health. But the image of "bigness" also carried a cost. Customers regarded Specialty Products (and CPC) as "stodgy," not dynamic. Worse, some customers (with justification) doubted CPC's long-term commitment to their particular market.

In fall of 1984, Goodman and Thomas tried to define Specialty Products' competitive situation. They called in a consultant to help them with strategic planning. Here are excerpts of an initial discussion:

Bob: As you know, Paul, Specialty Products is only a small part of the CPC pie. First, you've got Distribution Division serving the wholesalers, the contract stationers, and dealers. That's $140 million. Then there's Retail Division which takes care of another large market. Another $50 million there. Also, there was Chain, which was about $15 million — but CPC decided as a result of the 1984 planning to get out of that business. Finally, here we are at Specialty Products. We take our business from large, corporate accounts. We only take very large orders, at least $500,000 each, and we provide semicustomized products.

Paul: We get the low-margin business.

Bob: That's it.

Paul: What do we have going for us?

Bob: Well, CPC is one of the biggest, oldest, and most respected firms in the industry. The customers say that CPC can provide fast service plus a broad line of products, and we have distribution everywhere. Also, in the past, anyway, our quality has been superior in areas such as packaging, shipping, and products themselves.

Paul: But we've got high costs, right?

Bob: Yes, and that's a constant problem. Our customers will sometimes pay a little extra for quality, service, and so forth, but not much more.

Paul: That's why we've always been forced into price-cutting, and that's why margins are never good for Specialty Products.

Bob: Exactly. The sales force, whose compensation is tied to sales volume, can't resist the temptation to cut prices and promise the world. The sales force is coming off a very bad year. No bonuses. They are very demoralized.

Paul: So the problem is, how do you differentiate and innovate in a traditional, high-cost business?

Bob: Right.

Paul: According to the objectives for Specialty Products contained in the 1984 strategic plan, we need 20 percent margins and 4 percent return-after-taxes while increasing business from $8.2 million to $10.9 million.

Bob: A mighty tall order. Plus, you've got to consider that CPC won't make any capital expenditures for Specialty Products.

Paul: How do we define this market? Where do we start?

Bob: Well, one problem is that nobody keeps organized data about our business. All we have to go on are rumors, our experience, etc. We presently serve a number of very large accounts. These people always use multiple sources. For most of these accounts we are number 1 or number 2.

Paul: We've been losing ground with some of these accounts, right?

Bob: That's right. We've lost our relative share with some accounts, such as Western. Others, like Macintosh, have even displaced us to a lower slot. Most of these defeats have been caused by quality problems. There was that green gunk on some binders that we shipped to Phillips. There was that mistaken color for Becker. Altogether we've got twelve big accounts. Our competitors for this business are basically small, poorly financed outfits who serve very limited geographic areas or who go for a product niche.

Paul: We're going for customized business on basically standard products.

Bob: Yes. But I've got an idea for a four-color printing process that we could work on. For this, we would go to all kinds of corporations who publish boxes holding product information, for example. We can provide a colorful, splashy product that other suppliers can't touch. CPC even has the printing capability for this. I've already talked to advertisers about this idea.

THE COURSE OF EVENTS

This section contains a brief synopsis of important events involving implementation of CPC's plans for Specialty Products between summer of 1984 and fall of 1985.

Late Summer 1984

In July, CPC presented its strategic plan to BMF International. Executives at the parent company examined financial relationships. How much profit will CPC contribute? How much investment will be needed? They seemed to view Greene's planning efforts as slightly eccentric — "Greene's thing." Nevertheless, Greene found that the plan provided good justifications for his requests. The parent company accepted the goals outlined in the CPC plan.

The overall 1984 CPC strategic planning had finished. Executives began implementing action plans.

Serious quality problems continued to plague Specialty Products. For example, there was the infamous case of the green gunk on a product. Extensive investigation revealed that the green gunk originated in a chemical reaction brought about by exposing plated metals to moisture. Another emergency rocked the unit when a large customer received a shipment of boxes with discolored covers.

October 1984   Goodman and Thomas remained uncertain about plans to submit for their upcoming planning review meeting. They suspected that Greene harbored ideas about what Specialty Products' plans ought to entail. But Greene would not reveal his ideas. What did Greene want? Goodman took advantage of occasions when Greene was present to initiate informal discussions with Greene. The closest Greene came to evaluating Goodman's trial balloons during these asides was to remark cryptically: "You are teetering on the edge of acceptable."

Goodman and Thomas were having trouble answering basic strategy questions about Specialty Products: What was their market position? How did customers view Specialty Products/CPC? How could Goodman and Thomas discern whether a particular plan would be acceptable to Greene before having to present that plan? The most troublesome question was: "How can Specialty Products differentiate itself?" Goodman jokingly referred to one possible strategy, "We can ship you high-cost products better than anyone."

Goodman made informal contacts with quality control, accounting, marketing, and finance. How would other departments of CPC react to potential Specialty Products plans?

Thomas approached advertising agencies with his idea about a new product — the four-color lithographed cover for boxes. He claimed that nobody else had anything like it. He felt sure that CPC would manufacture this technically difficult product.

Specialty Products was experiencing paperwork snafus in October. Other departments found it hard and/or annoying to deal with the special routines needed for Specialty Products shipments, customer service, and accounting.

Goodman and Thomas tried to outline a planning document for Specialty Products. They wondered about major uncertainties. What should they include? What sequence should they follow for presenting topics? How much quantitative data? What promises are they willing to make? What kind of plan did Greene want?

Parts of that discussion follow:

Bob: Well, I've got an idea of what the plan should contain. Here it is. [shows Goodman some notes] I'd say we have 20 percent of the publisher's business. High costs hurt us. The market size is probably $400 million. Maybe the market is called "custom decorated products."

Paul: We need more information about competitors in there.

Bob: OK. I'll put in Benson, Coral, and Great Lakes.

Paul: You're kidding. Benson is in there?

Bob: Sure, they're in there. They do Washington Products.

Paul: Well, suppose the segment is $60 million, and we should say we have 10–20 percent.

Bob: I'd say $75 million.

Paul [figuring on a pad]: Let's call it 15 percent. Do we have 80 percent of our business in publishers? What do you call Honeywell? Western is different?

Bob: Call it the corporate segment.

Paul: Who else is a big competitor for the corporate business?

Bob: Nickelstone.

Paul: I never heard of Nickelstone.

Paul: Can we classify these competitors? Who is the toughest?

Bob: Probably Denton, then Creighton.

Paul: How do these competitors see us?

Bob: We're General Motors. We're an ocean liner and they are rowboats. Our size worries them. When we sneeze, they catch cold.

Paul: Let's hope we are not the *Titanic!*

Paul [reaching into his filing cabinet]: I think we should take another look at the CPC plan to get more ideas.

Bob: You know, what worries me most is that our excess capacity is in the traditional boxes. That area is not growing. That is not the best place to look for new business. I've got ideas for new materials, special printing, exciting new constructions. There are your growth areas. I personally feel we should go more for your growth areas.

Paul: We don't have the capacity. That's not our mission.

Bob: What does Greene want to see in this plan? He's a marketing man.

Paul: I'm not sure. He plays it pretty close to the vest. He'll make changes. If there are problems, he'll see them.

Bob: I feel as if we're in a defensive position.

Paul: Yeah, the squeaky wheel at CPC.

Bob: I hope the plan isn't set in concrete. Costs are the major issue.

Goodman began attacking Specialty Products' quality problems. Goodman revamped procedures for shipping Specialty Products' items, adding a final, extra quality-control inspection. He conducted meetings with manufacturing and shipping personnel in the plant to impress upon them that Specialty Products could not afford any more quality slip-ups.

The Executive Committee (CPC's senior executives) met on October 15 to examine budgets based on functional and business unit plans derived from CPC's strategic plan. After hearing the Specialty Products plan (detailed in Exhibit 5), Greene concluded: "Sounds like the same old stuff to me. You wanted support. I'm giving it [in reference to an approval for a new job position for Specialty Products]. Now go out and get some growth."

The executive committee raised the 1985 Specialty Products sales target to $14 million from Goodman's proposal of $13 million. After the meeting, in an aside,

EXHIBIT 5
Outline of Specialty Products' strategic plan, October 15, 1983

1. *Charter/Mission*
   Growth business . . . unused production capacity . . . large corporate customers . . . custom products . . . no investment except unusual circumstances
2. *Situation*
   Concentrate in Northeast
   Few customers, mostly large divisions of Fortune 500 firms
   Binder products
   "Good" market share
3. *Problems*
   Economy hurt customers
   High costs, heavy overhead allocations
   Quality problems
   Demoralized salesforce
   Long lead-time on new product
   Regional approach limits sales
   Paperwork confusion
4. *Strengths*
   Good service due to MRP and specialized customer service
   Part of a Fortune 500 company
   Excess capacity?
   Broad line in collateral products
   Excellent distribution system
   Good product engineering
5. *Product Strategy*
   Use excess capacity
   New products
6. *Projections*

	1984	1985	1986	1987
Sales (millions)	10.0	11.3	13.5	16.5
Percent increase	0	13	20	22
Margin percent	20	23	22	21.5

Marketing Vice-President McCracken confided to Goodman, "What you have is OK, but it needs a spark." Goodman considered that meeting "a base hit, not a home run."

Here are some comments about Specialty Products from top executives after hearing Specialty Products' plans explained by Goodman.

Joe Parker, vice-president of manufacturing:

In the past, CPC has never taken Specialty Products seriously. Now that is changed. The plan Goodman and Thomas are proposing is good. Our competitors are vulnerable. Perhaps the plan is even too modest. Goodman and Thomas are too conservative. . . . Sounds like the same old stuff to me. . . . They do have organizational problems at Specialty Products, especially in the area of sales force training. Unit needs strong direction. You can achieve more sales and higher margins with better sales effort. Sure, it's unusual for a business unit to report to manufacturing, but we can't afford high-priced organizational structures. I'm thrilled about the prospects for Specialty Products. I like a challenge. In 6 or 8 months we'll know.

Frank Holden, vice-president of finance:

Specialty Products is only 5 percent of CPC's business. Some people think it could be more. I'm not sure. You could call me a borderline believer. In 1984 we missed all our targets for Specialty Products. Specialty Products has a low margin, and it's declining . . . quality problems. Specialty Products isn't even as good as it looks, because allocations of costs are dubious. It reminds me of a business we had at another company where I worked. People kept asking, "When will we crack this big market?" We never did. Getting more business and more margin will be tough. We need to see good progress in 1985. A critical year.

Dick McCracken, vice-president of marketing:

The Goodman-Thomas plan needs more work. Right now there is a widening gap between the plans and slipping results. Maybe they are now bottoming out. Specialty Products has to grow like hell. Bigger steps. Run fast. New organizational setup is real good. They need the sales manager position. . . . Problems with the customer service department. The four-color idea is interesting. Thomas knows the factory and he knows the products. Unless we come up with something new, we can't get the margins. Nasty quality problems must be solved. I think Specialty Products can meet the objectives; we just don't know all the steps yet. Plans aren't finished. We need to pin our hopes to attainable things . . . solid steps, no panaceas. Thomas shouldn't conclude that everything is okay now that they have a sales manager. My role is to help them with their marketing.

Phil Townsend, vice-president of human resources:

I don't really know much about the Specialty Products plan, except in those respects which involve personnel. My experience has been that you can't consider national accounts a real market. Customers want a broad-based supplier for these products. I don't think you can be a specialty supplier of particular products over the long run. . . . I would only intervene in their planning if they were screwing up.

Neil Greene, president:

I'm supporting Specialty Products because I think they have a market there.

November 1984   At Goodman's initiative, Specialty Products reorganized. (See Exhibit 6.) Thomas returned to an inside office (next to Goodman) from working in the field. Discussion began concerning prospects for a sales manager position. New positions were, at that time, very hard to get approved. Greene promised Goodman that the position would receive approval.

    Goodman and Thomas met with their Specialty Products sales force to explain the thrust of strategic planning and the recent changes in Specialty Products' organization. Thomas was particularly enthusiastic during the sessions. A salesman remarked,

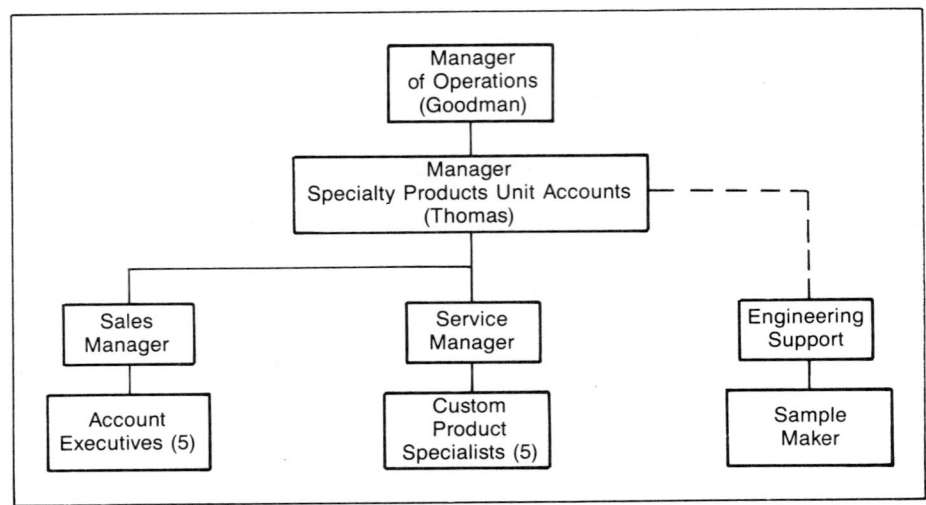

"For the first time, we have a direction." Goodman and Thomas concluded that morale had improved.

Goodman intervened to smooth ruffled feathers in disputes between Thomas and Callahan. Customer Service found Specialty Products' demands increasingly difficult to satisfy. Callahan did not like working for Thomas. Emotions ran high as Goodman spent hours with the two of them, seeking resolutions for their problems. After an extended meeting of Goodman, Thomas, and Callahan, the issue seemed ironed out.

"The spirit is here," commented Goodman. "It was a big move to get Thomas inside, instead of on the road."

Improved quality-control procedures were now firmly in place.

Goodman began working with flow charts, trying to translate the strategy he had presented to the Executive Committee into specifics. He said, "We need to know who is going to do what." He began to draft a written plan, which he said he would give to Greene. The consultant helped Goodman write the plan. Greene had not asked for a written plan.

December 1984 Goodman confided to the consultant, "I wish we were moving faster." Sales and profit figures revealed that Specialty Products fell far short of its 1984 budget requirements. (See Exhibit 7.) Goodman and Thomas could feel the psychological pressure-level rising. Specialty Products' shortcomings became a topic of frequent, sometimes bitter comment. At the December profit and loss meeting Greene commented, "Either we are going to grow this business [Specialty Products] or we are going to shut it down." Goodman and Thomas worried. Goodman remarked that the excitement had left him sleepless at night once or twice.

Discussions and feedback between Thomas and a higher-up outside the official

EXHIBIT 7
1984 actual
performance versus
budget, Specialty
Products

	1984 Budget	1984 Actual
Revenues		
Net sales	$12,309	$ 9,600
Direct costs	9,594	7,815
Gross margin	2,715	1,785
As percent of net sales	22.1%	18.6%
Variances (see Note)	374	794
Gross profit	2,341	991
As percent of net sales	19.0%	10.3%
Operating expenses		
Selling	663	666
Warehousing	1,047	850
Transportation	85	68
Total operating expense	1,795	1,584
As percent of net sales	14.6%	16.5%
Contribution	546	(593)
As percent of net sales	4.4%	(6.1)%
Overhead expenses		
Research and engineering	215	204
General and administrative	511	345
Corporate overhead	129	126
Total overhead	855	675
As percent of net sales	7.0%	7.0%
Earnings before tax	$ (309)	$(1,268)

Note: Figures in thousands of dollars. Continental Packaging Company computed "direct costs" at a standard, then figured in any variance from standard costs as an expense.

chain of command confused Thomas and annoyed Goodman. Angry words were exchanged between Goodman and one of his superiors.

Marketing Vice-President McCracken continued to make supportive asides to Goodman. McCracken commented that he was pleased by changes in Specialty Products.

The Thomas/Callahan dispute continued to simmer.

January 1985
The Specialty Products plan, revamped to reflect changes mandated by November's budget meeting, was formally presented to Greene. At that meeting, Goodman used transparencies to convey their plans. (See Exhibit 8.) Basically, the revised plan entailed: pushing three new product variations, continuing to investigate the new four-color process, solving quality problems, increasing penetration into existing accounts, and reorganizing. Sales volume growth targets were upped from original 12–22 percent yearly to 25 percent yearly. The Executive Committee agreed that more work on the Specialty Products plan was needed. Some executives remained

EXHIBIT 8
Specialty Products'
strategic plan

> **Tasks Needing Attention**
>
> I. Organization
>   Improved sales training
>   Clear up problems with Customer Service
> II. Quality
>   Enhance work-in-process audits
>   Continue workshops on quality
> III. Market
>   Document market strategy
>   Review pricing policy, increase prices? (Paul Goodman said no)
>   Introduce four-color process
> IV. Issues
>   Problems with capacity allocations

skeptical. Greene decided that the latest month for Specialty Products was "semi-solid."

End-of-the-year work overwhelmed planning. Planning projects were all put on a back burner. Goodman's other operating responsibilities dominated his time.

CPC executives and salesmen attended their annual sales meeting in Florida. At an awards banquet (where Specialty Products received no awards) Goodman commented to Greene, "Next year we are going to win all the prizes." Greene responded, "I'd love to worry about that."

February 1985

Goodman and Thomas met with their sales force for 3 days. They discovered that the sales force was "loaded with useful competitive information." The sales force evidently appreciated the attention.

Greene remarked to Goodman (after 2 months of improving sales volume), "It's no longer a question of whether Specialty Products will succeed. It is a question of when." Goodman was pleased with the recent sales volume increases, but he still worried that the key to a successful strategy was somehow missing. He also worried that his margins were not high enough. (See Exhibit 9.)

According to Goodman, Thomas was beginning to lose sight of their strategic trajectory. Goodman constantly coaxed Thomas away from tempting new products and from under operating details. Goodman told Thomas to concentrate on the strategic aspects of the situation.

March 1985

Thomas now had his sights set on the VHS/video market, an exciting, rapidly growing business. According to Thomas, Specialty Products could manufacture and print the product packaging for video tapes. "The computer revolution will replace paper. It's so exciting! But not if you sell traditional products. If you sell traditional products, it stinks," he explained.

Specialty Products margins hovered around 16 percent. Goodman complained, "This is not good enough." A senior consultant observed that CPC remained wedded

EXHIBIT 9
1984 monthly gross margins for Specialty Products

Month	Actual margin	Budgeted margin
January	17.7	25.1
February	21.2	24.7
March	22.5	26.3
April	17.9	26.0
May	21.9	25.3
June	21.0	27.1
July	22.0	25.6
August	18.0	24.4
September	20.4	26.6
October	20.4	25.9
November	21.0	24.7
December	26.1	25.1

to sales performance rather than profitability. Improving sales volume for Specialty Products seemed to relieve some pressure from top management.

Goodman was now convinced that Specialty Products needed more business from its present customers rather than new customers. "We need to make them addicts." Until then he had been uncertain whether the strategy should concentrate on getting more business from old customers or finding new customers. Thomas was not happy with Goodman's conclusion. Thomas favored finding new products and new customers.

Goodman mentioned a recent visit of two important customers of Specialty Products, who confided that, with the improvement in Specialty Products' quality that they had experienced (and the resulting increased reliability of Specialty Products), they would give Specialty Products a greater proportion of their business.

Goodman learned about a letter from Greene to another unit, advising that unit: "You ought to copy the activities of Specialty Products. It's gaining credibility."

Goodman reflected: "Greene has given us everything we've asked for so far. He's letting us do it our way. If we don't produce, we have no rock to hide behind."

Specialty Products' new quality-control system detected a big quality problem, saving an important shipment. Goodman and Thomas were ecstatic and elated.

Problems between the Customer Service department and Specialty Products reached another boiling point. Thomas and Callahan argued vehemently. Goodman intervened.

Goodman was now working on competitive analyses. He still was not quite sure where Specialty Products had a competitive advantage or could develop one. "What is CPC? What is Specialty Products? What the hell are we? How can we make customers want us?" Paul wondered.

Martha (administrative assistant to Goodman) was busy learning to use their microcomputer. Martha's analysis of the margin shortfall helped Goodman and Thomas to stave off pressure from their superiors (and a consultant) advocating price hikes. The microcomputer provided forecasts of margins, based on different pricing structures, various mixtures of accounts, and various volumes of sales. Everyone was impressed with the new technology.

Goodman wondered if he could find a way to use MRP to achieve a competitive advantage. (MRP is an inventory management system which strives to limit work-in-process and other inventories to levels adequate to maximum efficiency. About 5,000 firms use MRP in some form.) CPC claimed that it was among the 5 percent of "best" users. Goodman had been a major force behind the installation of MRP at CPC.

April 1985

Goodman concluded that Specialty Products could double its business through its existing accounts. "Do what you've got right. Get more of what you've got," he reasoned.

At a meeting of CPC's Executive Committee (Excom), Goodman presented Specialty Products' latest financial results and ideas. (See Exhibit 10.) Specialty Products'

EXHIBIT 10
Specialty Products' actual performance versus budget 1985

	1985 Budget	Projected 1985 actual*
Revenues		
Net sales	$10,000	$12,000
Direct costs	8,581	10,189
Gross margin	2,401	2,185
As percent of net sales	21.9%	17.7%
Variances	204	85
Gross profit	2,197	2,100
As percent of net sales	20.0%	17.0%
Operating expenses		
Selling	635	639
Warehousing	992	1,115
Transportation	88	136
Total operating expense	1,715	1,890
As percent of net sales	15.6%	15.3%
Contribution	482	210
As percent of net sales	4.4%	1.7%
Overhead expenses		
Research and engineering	210	272
General and administrative	489	516
Corporate overhead	112	113
Total overhead	811	901
As percent of net sales	7.4%	7.3%
Earnings before tax	$ (329)	$ (482)

Note: Figures in thousands of dollars.
* Based on 9 months of 1985.

continuing failure to meet margin requirements was noted by Vice-President of Finance Frank Holden. However, Greene encouraged Goodman, saying, "If you can do what you say you can do, you'll be doing fine." Some Excom members expressed concern about Thomas's performance. Goodman's reaction to the meeting was: "We're in better shape than we were. We've bought some time."

Specialty Products' tight quality-control procedures were now apparently creating more than its share of scrap and waste, thus raising costs. Goodman was concerned.

May 1985

Goodman received his personal performance appraisal covering his prior year. Goodman's appraisal of his appraisal was: "There is nothing specifically relating to Specialty Products."

Using the microcomputer to carry out "what if" scenarios regarding prices and margins, the unit forecasted 19.5 percent margin for 1985.

The 1985 strategic planning sessions began. CPC executives spent one day at a pleasant mountain resort. Topics included reviewing the 1984 plan, critiquing the 1984 planning process, stating expectations for 1985's planning process, and compiling competitor profiles. Goodman was uncertain about what should go into his 1985 plan. He observed: "No new issues seem to be coming up at the sessions. People seem to have the attitude, 'We've agreed upon what should be done. Let's get on with it.' " Sessions seemed too heavily focused on marketing issues. Greene admonished executives about "backsliding, not thinking strategically."

The surge in CPC sales during the prior 4 months now threatened maximum capacity for some types of products — especially those of Specialty Products. (See Exhibit 11.) Thomas and Goodman were increasingly worried that they would get

EXHIBIT 11
Work center capacity analysis, 1984

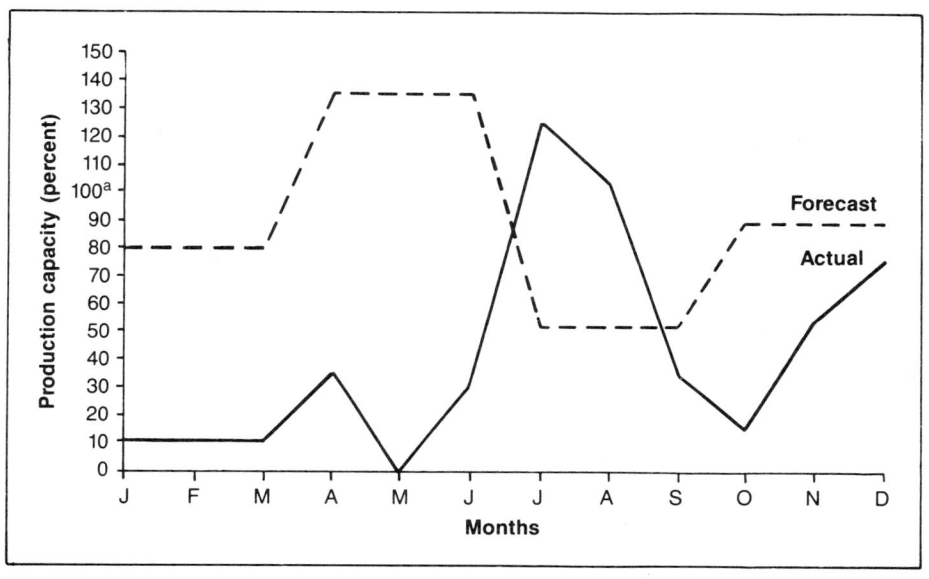

[a] 100 percent capacity means two shifts and average downtime for maintenance and breakdowns.

the "short end of the stick." The situation reminded Goodman of the "light-switch" history of Specialty Products. Goodman complained: "They're taking my capacity while asking me to grow."

An important Specialty Products customer visited the plant. According to Goodman, "They say we are outstanding. They love us." He believed that this feedback was a sign that the new strategy was working.

Goodman and a consultant worked on a written plan to encapsulate Specialty Products' strategy. While Greene had never asked for a formal, written plan, Goodman thought the plan should be written down. (See Appendix.)

Goodman invited several customers to send some of their operations personnel to Specialty Products. He offered seminars on MRP systems for them. He reasoned that Specialty Products' customers struggled under heavy pressure from their parent companies to reduce costs. If Specialty Products could persuade them to use MRP, not only would the customers feel grateful, but, more importantly, the resulting tight connection between Specialty Products' systems and customer systems would constitute a switching cost for these customers.

Although Specialty Products' mission only specified "to use excess capacity," Goodman began to consider making a capital expenditures request of $1 million for 1985. "I think we can get it," he concluded.

CPC's engineering department responds slowly to requests about product design for Specialty Products items. "They don't think we're a high-priority business. Almost all their attention is given to Retail Division and Distribution Division," observed Goodman.

June 1985

CPC executives gathered at a nearby resort for 3 more days of strategic planning. For the first time (according to Goodman), Greene discussed his objectives and expectations. Some executives said that Greene should have made his expectations clear in the beginning. Other issues were discussed:

Goodman wanted to change Specialty Products' mission to remove the "no investment criterion," but his proposal was rejected.

Some executives complained about "staff infection."

Numerous human resources difficulties had cropped up in connection with efforts to implement plans.

Goodman stated: "We have done a good job of planning, the planning is important, but enough is enough. It's time to make it all happen."

Thomas and Goodman found themselves under heavy workload pressure. "I can't afford time to hiccough," commented Bob Thomas.

Specialty Products growing sales, combined with good growth in sister divisions' sales, maintained heavy pressure on capacity. "We have diesel acceleration and disc brakes at CPC," joked Goodman.

Goodman met with Thomas to discuss Thomas's performance appraisal. Among the comments which various senior executives had written were:

The next 12 months are crucial to Specialty Products and Bob Thomas.

It's evident that BT's efforts should be directed toward general management and marketing.

Does Specialty Products really require the additional staffing that Thomas has requested?

Preliminary work on CPC's 1986 budget began.

July 1985   Goodman speculated about the sales-volume resurgence of Specialty Products.

> *Partly the MRP. Partly the conquest of quality problems. Our customers are doing good business, so we do good business. Where would Specialty Products be without the economic recovery? Even without the recovery, we would have done okay, maybe not as well. If the economy took another nosedive, our growth would suffer, but our base would stick. No declines from here on.*

Thomas continued to talk about getting into the computer software packaging business in a bigger way. "I want to go into software packaging!" At the time, Specialty Products had a few software accounts to whom only binders were sold. Bob noted that several expanded avenues seemed open:

Specialty Products could manufacture and print materials for manuals and discs. BMF International's software development division could even provide the program product.

Specialty Products could manufacture and sell to printers.

Specialty Products could sell directly to computer firms.

Specialty Products could manufacture cases for software systems. (Specialty Products already has some accounts of this type.)

Goodman observed that this printing/packaging proposal did not fit within the Specialty Products mission. He told Thomas that it was a distraction. Thomas, unmoved by Goodman's objections, promoted the idea to Greene.

More strategic planning meetings were held. Goodman ordered T-shirts for the participants which read "S.O.B." (strategically operated businesses). Goodman, reflecting on the latest conferences, mused, "I think the fun overshadowed the planning." Goodman noticed quite a bit of "plugging one's own turf." At one point, Goodman came under some group pressure about Specialty Products during an open session, but Greene himself choked off the debate, saying: "Sure, we've got problems, but they are not strategic." Goodman said with a hint of disappointment in his voice: "Most people here still don't understand Specialty Products, and Specialty Products doesn't get much attention at these meetings. It's 99 percent everything else."

The formal Specialty Products plan remained in Goodman's desk drawer.

FALL 1985 PROBLEMS AND PROSPECTS

In early fall 1985, Thomas was preparing to meet with Greene to discuss the Specialty Products 1986 plan. At the same meeting, Thomas hoped to present his idea for software packaging to Greene. He believed that Specialty Products could double its 1985 business in 3 or 4 years, but only if new product opportunities such as software publishing were aggressively pursued. (On the other hand, Goodman felt that the same goals could be reached without the publishing software move.) In arguing for the software publishing alternative, Thomas would make the following main points:

A market is there.

There are many competitors in this business, but none who can do it all.

EXHIBIT 12
Sales performance versus budget of Continental Packaging Company's three principal business segments

1985	Sales (in 000s)	Percent sales above (+) below (−) budget	Actual margin	Budgeted margin
Distributor Division				
January	$ 8,387	+3	42.6	42.3
February	10,805	−8	42.4	42.1
March	13,003	−18	41.5	41.4
April	14,227	+1	35.9	39.1
May	9,652	−12	40.3	41.4
June	12,032	−11	39.5	41.8
July	8,753	+14	41.2	42.6
August	10,082	−5	40.9	41.8
September	12,199	+9	39.8	42.2
Retail Division				
January	$ 1,696	+0	28.9	34.5
February	1,628	+5	31.3	36.9
March	1,616	−2	25.7	36.4
April	1,694	−15	36.4	36.4
May	2,159	−4	31.6	35.3
June	4,000	+21	30.2	32.7
July	8,210	+3	32.5	32.5
August	4,968	−27	27.3	32.3
September	3,189	−4	31.8	34.3
Specialty Products				
January	$ 600	+20	18.1	24.6
February	703	+23	16.4	23.5
March	1,018	+4	15.5	23.7
April	873	+52	16.1	24.3
May	1,005	−34	22.3	24.0
June	1,208	−27	18.0	18.1
July	1,050	+22	16.0	17.5
August	750	+25	12.8	17.4
September	1,566	+18	17.4	18.6

EXHIBIT 13
Selected details of Thomas's software packaging proposal

This proposal involves a complete packaging operation. Specialty Products would provide printed materials, vinyl jackets, disks (from sister division of BMF International), indexing, color printing decoration, warehousing, and distribution.

Why Software Packaging?
  Fast-growing segment
  Market potential $150–$200 by 1986
  Large volume customers
  Quality image important
  Distribution important
  Fits Specialty Products' plans

Strengths of Specialty Products:
  Have full-line of products
  Warehousing
  National distribution network
  Class "A" MRP system
  Brand recognition high
  Excess capacity
  Competitors can't do *packaging*
  (Low vertical integration)

Threats:
  More competition
  Volatile market
  Credit problems of customers?

Market strategy:
  A one-step shopping center for software
  publishers with sales ≥ $5 million.

Market requires:
  Quality product
  Dependable service
  Creativity
  Competitive prices
  Prompt service

Weaknesses:
  Lack of product engineering support
  Sales and service depts. lack product
  knowledge
  High costs
  Some elements strain capacity

Forecast ($000)

	Total sales (with no new marketing personnel)		Proposals	
			Add software specialists	Add new sales person
			Additional sales	Additional sales
1986	$ 500		$1,000	$ 800
1987	700		2,250	950
1988	1,200		3,800	1,750

		1985	1986	1987
Total Software		2,300	4,900	8,560

CPC can make the product, including printing and decorating.

Price is important.

On-time delivery is important.

Specialty Products can sell "CPC" image.

As Neil Greene sat in his office at the executive office building awaiting Bob Thomas's arrival, he reflected upon the year's events and the future of the Specialty Products unit. Noting the difficulties Specialty Products experienced in reaching its margins, he wondered if their strategic plans were enough to reach those ambitious goals. His attention fell upon the latest projections for Specialty Products' 1985 performance (Exhibit 12). He knew that others serving on the Executive Committee still doubted Specialty Products' long-term potential. Was Specialty Products really worth the trouble? He wondered whether he should approve Thomas's software packaging idea (Exhibit 13). Looking ahead to the annual capital budgeting process, he wondered whether a request for $1 million in investment for Specialty Products ought to be granted. Was strategic planning taking hold at CPC? Greene had a lot on his mind as his secretary announced Bob Thomas's arrival. Bob Thomas walked in, carrying details of his plans and projections (Exhibit 14).

EXHIBIT 14

Selected information from Thomas's presentation of Specialty Products' strategic plan to Greene, October 11, 1985

Strengths

Outstanding service
Commitment to market
Financial strength
Vertical integration
Specialized sales force
High level of quality assurance
Using MRP system to "tie" customers

Threats

Price cutting by competitors
Increasing industry capacity
High interest rates
Don't know competitors in software

Weaknesses

Poor engineering support/product development
High prices
"Red tape" of company systems
Limited capacity
Shortage of skilled production personnel for some key areas
Seasonal capacity problem brought on by sharing facilities with other company units
Outdated equipment

1985 Market Strategy

Increase market share
Establish position in software publishing
Develop auditing, consulting, professional education markets
MRP, service, quality as main competitive weapons

	Projections		
	1986	*1987*	*1988*
Sales (millions)	18.5	22.5	26.6
Margin (dollar)	3.3	4.2	5.3
Margin (percent)	18	19	20

APPENDIX: SELECTED PARTS OF SPECIALTY PRODUCTS' WRITTEN PLAN, APRIL 1985

MEMO TO: Neil Greene

FROM: Bob Thomas

SUBJECT: Strategy

Introduction

For years Specialty Products has drifted. The aim of the present management of Specialty Products is to give purpose and direction to this business. This plan outlines the way we think this can be done.

Critical Issue

How can we transform a business with relatively high costs, a history of quality problems, and a near-commodity product into a strong leadership position in satisfying customer needs?

Specialty Products' Mission

Specialty Products focuses on customers having a potential for large orders of custom products using standard construction. Principal market segments presently include accountants and we plan to extend this market to high-tech industries and advertising agencies (as a conduit to new customers). While Specialty Products is seen as a growth business, the growth is limited by available capacity.

Objectives

Penetration of existing accounts (specifics)

Margin (specifics)

Sales (specifics)

New products (specifics)

Reputation (specifics)

Quality (specifics)

Personnel (specifics)

Target Markets

Present main markets
   Others
New markets
   High tech/computer
   Advertising agencies
   Others

Competitive Advantage

In order to achieve the ambitious objectives outlined above, Specialty Products must create a competitive advantage. We believe that this competitive advantage can be secured by combining some advantages Specialty Products has with some of our "hidden assets."

The advantages we plan on using are ones which create added value for customers of Specialty Products. The overall logic is to be better and different in ways that are not traditional in this business and which cannot be easily copied by our rivals.

Quality

We expect to achieve a level of quality that cannot be matched by smaller competitors. This is attainable through manufacturing, engineering.

Service

Because of our size, sophistication, and experience we can be a leader in service.

MRP

We will use the MRP system to lower our costs, to help our customers lower their inventories, and as a promotional technique.

Innovation

(Several new products mentioned)

Action Plans

We have already made a number of strides in the right direction, but much remains to be done. Here is our report of progress and our work-in-progress. (This part of the plan gave details of actions accomplished and actions remaining.)

Forecasts

The steps we have taken and those we plan to take should result in financial performance as follows:

Forecast for Specialty Products

	1984 actual	1985	1986
Sales	9,600,000	14,200,000	18,000,000
Margin percent	18.0	20.2	21.0

Conclusion

Being a high-cost competitor places a constraint on strategy. Because of our position, we need to find ways to add value to our offerings that steer us away from price competition. It is our judgment that the combinations of quality, service, reliability . . . can support the higher prices *and* higher volume we need in order to attain the objectives which have been set.

THE LINCOLN ELECTRIC COMPANY, 1985

INTRODUCTION

The Lincoln Electric Company is the world's largest manufacturer of welding machines and electrodes. Lincoln employs 2400 workers in two U.S. factories near Cleveland and approximately 600 in three factories located in other countries. This does not include the field sales force of more than 200 persons. It has been estimated that Lincoln's market share (for arc-welding equipment and supplies) is more than 40 percent.

The Lincoln incentive management plan has been well known for many years. Many college management texts make reference to the Lincoln plan as a model for achieving high worker productivity. Certainly, Lincoln has been a successful company according to the usual measures of success.

James F. Lincoln died in 1965 and there was some concern, even among employees, that the Lincoln system would fall into disarray, that profits would decline, and that year-end bonuses might be discontinued. Quite the contrary, twenty years after Lincoln's death, the company appears stronger than ever. Each year, except the recession years 1982 and 1983, has seen higher profits and bonuses. Employee morale and productivity remain high. Employee turnover is almost nonexistent except for retirements. Lincoln's market share is stable. Consistently high dividends continue on Lincoln's stock.

A HISTORICAL SKETCH

In 1895, after being ''frozen out'' of the depression-ravaged Elliott-Lincoln Company, a maker of Lincoln-designed electric motors, John C. Lincoln took out his second patent and began to manufacture his improved motor. He opened his new business,

The research and written case information were presented at a Case Research Symposium and were evaluated by the North American Case Research Association's Editorial Board. This case was prepared by Arthur D. Sharplin of McNeese University, Lake Charles, LA, as a basis for class discussion. © 1985 by Arthur D. Sharplin. Reprinted by permission.

unincorporated, with $200 he had earned redesigning a motor for young Herbert Henry Dow, who later founded the Dow Chemical Company.

Started during an economic depression and cursed by a major fire after only one year in business, Lincoln's company grew, but hardly prospered, through its first quarter century. In 1906, John C. Lincoln incorporated his company and moved from his one-room, fourth-floor factory to a new three-story building he erected in east Cleveland. In his new factory, he expanded his work force to 30 and sales grew to over $50,000 a year. John Lincoln preferred being an engineer and inventor rather than a manager, though, and it was to be left to another Lincoln to manage the company through its years of success.

In 1907, after a bout with typhoid fever forced him from Ohio State University in his senior year, James F. Lincoln, John's younger brother, joined the fledgling company. In 1914 he became the active head of the firm, with the titles of general manager and vice president. John Lincoln, while he remained president of the company for some years, became more involved in other business ventures and in his work as an inventor.

One of James Lincoln's early actions as head of the firm was to ask the employees to elect representatives to a committee which would advise him on company operations. The Advisory Board has met with the chief executive officer twice monthly since that time. This was only the first of a series of innovative personnel policies which have, over the years, distinguished Lincoln Electric from its contemporaries.

The first year the Advisory Board was in existence, working hours were reduced from 55 per week, then standard, to 50 hours a week. In 1915, the company gave each employee a paid-up life insurance policy. A welding school, which continues today, was begun in 1917. In 1918, an employee bonus plan was attempted. It was not continued, but the idea was to resurface and become the backbone of the Lincoln Management System.

The Lincoln Electric Employees' Association was formed in 1919 to provide health benefits and social activities. This organization continues today and has assumed several additional functions over the years. In 1923, a piecework pay system was in effect, employees got two-week paid vacations each year, and wages were adjusted for changes in the Consumer Price Index. Approximately 30 percent of Lincoln's stock was set aside for key employees in 1914 when James F. Lincoln became general manager and a stock purchase plan for all employees was begun in 1925.

The board of directors voted to start a suggestion system in 1929. The program is still in effect, but cash awards, a part of the early program, were discontinued several years ago. Now, suggestions are rewarded by additional "points," which affect year-end bonuses.

The legendary Lincoln bonus plan was proposed by the Advisory Board and accepted on a trial basis by James Lincoln in 1934. The first annual bonus amounted to about 25 percent of wages. There has been a bonus every year since then. The bonus plan has been a cornerstone of the Lincoln Management System and recent bonuses have approximated annual wages.

By 1944, Lincoln employees enjoyed a pension plan, a policy of promotion from within, and continuous employment. Base pay rates were determined by formal job evaluation and a merit rating system was in effect.

In the prologue of James F. Lincoln's last book, Charles G. Herbruck writes regarding the foregoing personnel innovations,

> *They were not to buy good behavior. They were not efforts to increase profits. They were not antidotes to labor difficulties. They did not constitute a "do-gooder" program. They were expressions of mutual respect for each person's importance to the job to be done. All of these reflect the leadership of James Lincoln, under whom they were nurtured and propagated* (Lincoln, 1961, p. 11).

By the start of World War II, Lincoln Electric was the world's largest manufacturer of arc-welding products. Sales of about $4,000,000 in 1934 had grown to $24,000,000 by 1941. Productivity per employee more than doubled during the same period.

During the war, Lincoln Electric prospered as never before. Despite challenges to Lincoln's profitability by the Navy's Price Review Board and to the tax deductibility of employee bonuses by the Internal Revenue Service, the company increased its profits and paid huge bonuses.

Certainly since 1935 and probably for several years before that, Lincoln productivity has been well above the average for similar companies. Lincoln claims levels of productivity more than twice those for other manufacturers from 1945 onward. Information available from outside sources tends to support these claims.

COMPANY PHILOSOPHY

James F. Lincoln was the son of a Congregational minister, and Christian principles were at the center of his business philosophy. The confidence that he had in the efficacy of Christ's teachings is illustrated by the following remark taken from one of his books:

> *The Christian ethic should control our acts. If it did control our acts, the savings in cost of distribution would be tremendous. Advertising would be a contact of the expert consultant with the customer, in order to give the customer the best product available when all of the customer's needs are considered. Competition then would be in improving the quality of products and increasing efficiency in producing and distributing them; not in deception, as is now too customary. Pricing would reflect efficiency of production; it would not be a selling dodge that the customer may well be sorry he accepted. It would be proper for all concerned and rewarding for the ability used in producing the product.*[1]

There is no indication that Lincoln attempted to evangelize his employees or customers — or the general public for that matter. The current board chairman, Mr.

---

[1] James F. Lincoln, *A New Approach to Industrial Economics* (New York: The Devin Adair Co., 1961), p. 64.

Irrgang, and the president, Mr. Willis, do not even mention the Christian gospel in their recent speeches and interviews. The company motto, "The actual is limited, the possible is immense," is prominently displayed, but there is no display of religious slogans, and there is no company chapel.

Attitude Toward the Customer

James Lincoln saw the customer's needs as the *raison d'être* for every company. "When any company has achieved success so that it is attractive as an investment," he wrote, "all money usually needed for expansion is supplied by the customer in retained earnings. It is obvious that the customer's interests, not the stockholder's, should come first."[2] In 1947 he said, "Care should be taken . . . not to rivet attention on profit. Between 'How much do I get?' and 'How do I make this better, cheaper, more useful?' the difference is fundamental and decisive."[3] Mr. Willis still ranks the customer as Lincoln's most important constituency. This is reflected in Lincoln's policy to "at all times price on the basis of cost and at all times keep pressure on our cost. . . ."[4] Lincoln's goal, often stated, is "to build a better and better product at a lower and lower price."[5] "It is obvious," James Lincoln said, "that the customer's interests should be the first goal of industry."[6]

LINCOLN'S BUSINESS

Arc-welding has been the standard joining method in the shipbuilding industry for decades. It is the predominant way of joining steel in the construction industry. Most industrial plants have their own welding shops for maintenance and construction. Manufacturers of tractors and all kinds of heavy equipment use arc-welding extensively in the manufacturing process. Many hobbyists have their own welding machines and use them for making metal items such as patio furniture and barbeque pits. The popularity of welded sculpture as an art form is growing.

While advances in welding technology have been frequent, arc-welding products, in the main, have hardly changed except for Lincoln's Innershield process. This process, utilizing a self-shielded, flux cored electrode, has established new cost saving opportunities for construction and equipment fabrication. The most popular Lincoln electrode, the Fleetweld 5P, has been virtually the same since the 1930s. The most popular engine-driven welder in the world, the Lincoln SA-200, has

---

[2] Ibid., p. 119.

[3] "You Can't Tell What a Man Can Do — Until He Has the Chance," *Reader's Digest,* January 1947, p. 94.

[4] George E. Willis's letter to author of 7 September 1978.

[5] Lincoln, 1961, p. 47.

[6] Ibid., p. 117.

been a gray-colored assembly including a four-cylinder continental "Red Seal" engine and a 200 ampere direct-current generator with two current-control knobs for at least three decades. A 1980 model SA-200 even weighs almost the same as the 1950 model, and it certainly is little changed in appearance.

Lincoln and its competitors now market a wide range of general purpose and specialty electrodes for welding mild steel, aluminum, cast iron, and stainless and special steels. Most of these electrodes are designed to meet the standards of the American Welding Society, a trade association. They are thus essentially the same as to size and composition from one manufacturer to another. Every electrode manufacturer has a limited number of unique products, but these typically constitute only a small percentage of total sales.

Lincoln's research and development expenditures have recently been less than one and one-half percent of sales. There is evidence that others spend several times as much as a percentage of sales.

Lincoln's share of the arc-welding products market appears to have been about 40 percent for many years, and the welding products market has grown somewhat faster than the level of industry in general. The market is highly price-competitive, with variations in prices of standard products normally amounting to only a percent or two. Lincoln's products are sold directly by its engineering-oriented sales force and indirectly through its distributor organization. Advertising expenditures amount to less than one-fourth of one percent of sales, one-third as much as a major Lincoln competitor with whom the casewriter checked.

The other major welding process, flame-welding, has not been competitive with arc-welding since the 1930s. However, plasma-arc-welding, a relatively new process which uses a conducting stream of super heated gas (plasma) to confine the welding current to a small area, has made some inroads, especially in metal tubing manufacturing, in recent years. Major advances in technology which will produce an alternative superior to arc-welding within the next decade or so appear unlikely. Also, it seems likely that changes in the machines and techniques used in arc-welding will be evolutionary rather than revolutionary.

Products   The company is primarily engaged in the manufacture and sale of arc-welding products — electric welding machines and metal electrodes. Lincoln also produces electric motors ranging from one-half horsepower to 200 horsepower. Motors constitute about eight to ten percent of total sales.

The electric welding machines, some consisting of a transformer or motor and generator arrangement powered by commercial electricity and others consisting of an internal combustion engine and generator, are designed to produce from 30 to 1000 amperes of electrical power. This electrical current is used to melt a consumable metal electrode with the molten metal being transferred in a super hot spray to the metal joint being welded. Very high temperatures and hot sparks are produced, and operators usually must wear special eye and face protection and leather gloves, often along with leather aprons and sleeves.

Welding electrodes are of two basic types: (1) Coated "stick" electrodes, usually fourteen inches long and smaller than a pencil in diameter, which are held in a special insulated holder by the operator, who must manipulate the electrode in order to maintain a proper arc-width and pattern of deposition of the metal being transferred. Stick electrodes are packaged in six- to fifty-pound boxes. (2) Coiled wire, ranging in diameter from 0.035″ to 0.219″, which is designed to be fed continuously to the welding arc through a "gun" held by the operator or positioned by automatic positioning equipment. The wire is packaged in coils, reels, and drums weighing from fourteen to 1000 pounds.

MANUFACTURING OPERATIONS

Plant Locations

The main plant is in Euclid, Ohio, a suburb on Cleveland's east side. The layout of this plant is shown in Exhibit 1. There are no warehouses. Materials flow from the half-mile long dock on the north side of the plant through the production lines to a very limited storage and loading area on the south side. Materials used on each work station are stored as close as possible to the work station. The administration offices, near the center of the factory, are entirely functional. Not even the president's office is carpeted. A corridor below the main level provides access to the factory floor from the main entrance near the center of the plant. A new plant, just opened in Mentor, Ohio, houses some of the electrode production operations, which were moved from the main plant.

Manufacturing Processes

The electrode manufacturing process is highly capital intensive. Metal rods purchased from steel producers are drawn or extruded down to smaller diameters, cut to length and coated with pressed-powder "flux" for stick electrodes or plated with copper (for conductivity) and spun into coils or spools for wire. Some of Lincoln's wire, called "Inner-shield," is hollow and filled with a material similar to that used to coat stick electrodes. Lincoln is highly secretive about its electrode production processes, and the casewriter was not given access to the details of those processes.

Welding machines and electric motors are made on a series of assembly lines. Gasoline and diesel engines are purchased partially assembled but practically all other components are made from basic industrial products, e.g., steel bars and sheets and bar copper conductor wire, in the Lincoln factory.

Individual components, such as gasoline tanks for engine-driven welders and steel shafts for motors and generators, are made by numerous small "factories within a factory." The shaft for a certain generator, for example, is made from a raw steel bar by one operator who uses five large machines, all running continuously. A saw cuts the bar to length, a digital lathe machines different sections to varying diameters, a special milling machine cuts a slot for a keyway, and so forth, until a finished shaft is produced. The operator moves the shafts from machine to machine and makes necessary adjustments.

EXHIBIT 1   Factory layout

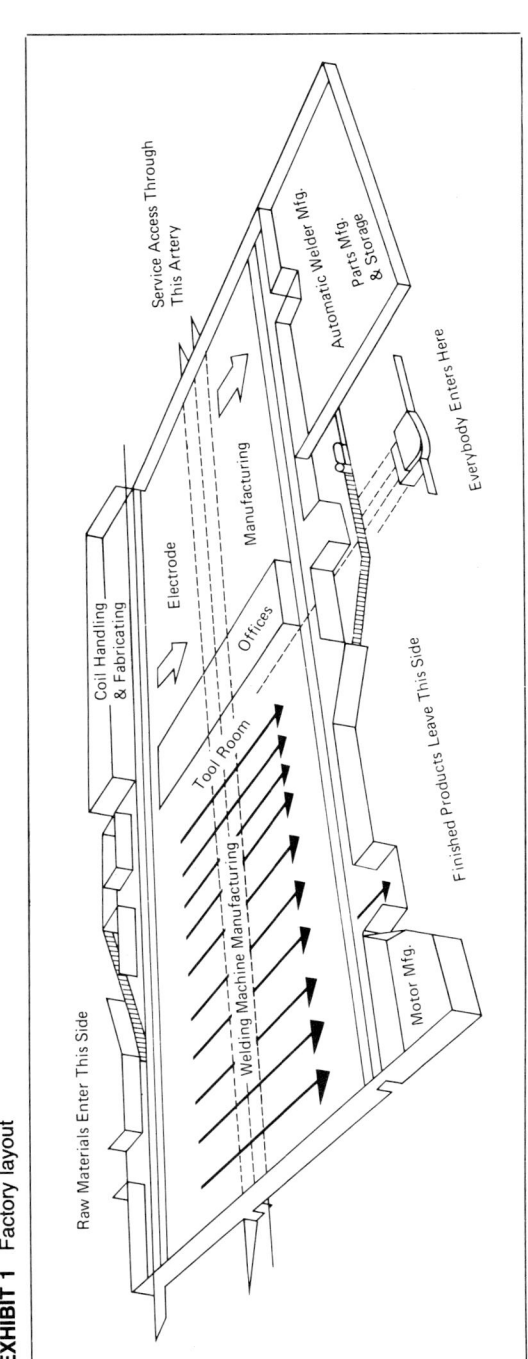

Another operator punches, shapes and paints sheetmetal cowling parts. One assembles steel liminations onto a rotor shaft, then winds, insulates and tests the rotors. Finished components are moved by crane operators to the nearby assembly lines.

Worker Performance and Attitudes

Exceptional worker performance at Lincoln is a matter of record. The typical Lincoln employee earns about twice as much as other factory workers in the Cleveland area. Yet the labor cost per sales dollar at Lincoln, currently 23.5 cents, is well below industry averages.

Sales per Lincoln factory employee currently exceed $157,000. An observer at the factory quickly sees why this figure is so high. Each worker is proceeding busily and thoughtfully about his task. There is no idle chatter. Most workers take no coffee breaks. Many operate several machines and make a substantial component unaided. The supervisors, some with as many as 100 subordinates, are busy with planning and recordkeeping duties and hardly glance at the people they supervise. The manufacturing procedures appear efficient — no unnecessary steps, no wasted motions, no wasted materials. Finished components move smoothly to subsequent work stations.

Worker turnover at Lincoln is practically nonexistent except for retirements and departures by new employees. The appendix includes summaries of interviews with Lincoln employees.

ORGANIZATION STRUCTURE

Lincoln has never had a formal organization chart.[7] The object of this policy is to insure maximum flexibilty. An open door policy is practiced throughout the company, and personnel are encouraged to take problems to the persons most capable of resolving them.

Perhaps because of the quality and enthusiasm of the Lincoln workforce, routine supervision is almost nonexistent. A typical production foreman, for example, supervises as many as 100 workers, a span-of-control which does not allow more than infrequent worker-supervisor interaction. Position titles and traditional flows of authority do imply something of an organizational structure, however. For example, the vice-president, sales, and the vice-president, electrode division, report to the president, as do various staff assistants such as the personnel director and the director of purchasing. Using such implied relationships, it has been determined that production workers have two or, at most, three levels of supervision between themselves and the president.

---

[7]Once, Harvard Business School researchers prepared an organization chart reflecting the below-mentioned implied relationships. The chart became available within the Lincoln organization, and present Lincoln management feels that it had a disruptive effect. Therefore, the casewriter was asked not to include any kind of organizational chart in this report.

PERSONNEL POLICIES

Recruitment and Selection

Every job opening at Lincoln is advertised internally on company bulletin boards and any employee can apply for any job so advertised. External hiring is done only for entry level positions. Selection for these jobs is done on the basis of personal interviews — there is no aptitude or psychological testing. Not even a high school diploma is required except for engineering and sales positions, which are filled by graduate engineers. A committee consisting of vice presidents and superintendents interviews candidates initially cleared by the personnel department. Final selection is made by the supervisor who has a job opening. Out of over 3500 applicants interviewed by the personnel department during a recent period fewer than 300 were hired.

Job Security

In 1958 Lincoln formalized its lifetime employment policy, which had already been in effect for many years. There have been no layoffs at Lincoln since World War II. Since 1958, every Lincoln worker with over one year's longevity has been guaranteed at least 30 hours per week, 49 weeks per year.

The policy has never been so severely tested as during the 1981–83 recession. As a manufacturer of capital goods, Lincoln's business is highly cyclical. In previous recessions Lincoln has been able to avoid major sales declines. However, sales plummeted 32 percent in 1982 and another 16 percent the next year. Few companies could withstand such a sales decline and remain profitable. Yet, Lincoln not only earned profits, but no employee was laid off and the usual year-end incentive bonuses were paid. To weather the storm, Lincoln cut most of the nonsalaried workers back to 30 hours a week for varying periods of time. Many employees were reassigned, and the total work force was slightly reduced through normal attrition and restricted hiring. Many employees grumbled at their unexpected misfortune, probably to the surprise and dismay of some Lincoln managers. However, a modest sales resurgence in 1984 and 1985 seemed to portend brighter days.

Performance Evaluations

Each supervisor formally evaluates his subordinates twice a year using the cards shown in Exhibit 2. The employee performance criteria, "quality," "dependability," "ideas and cooperation," and "output," are considered to be independent of each other. Marks on the cards are converted to numerical scores which are forced to average 100 for each evaluating supervisor. Individual merit rating scores normally range from 80 to 110. Any score over 110 requires a special letter to top management. These scores (over 110) are not considered in computing the required 100 point average for each evaluating supervisor. Suggestions for improvements often result in recommendations for exceptionally high performance scores. Supervisors discuss individual performance marks with the employees concerned. Each warranty claim on a Lincoln product is traced to the individual employee whose work caused the defect. The employee's performance score may be reduced by one point, or the worker may be required to repay the cost of servicing the warranty claim by working without pay.

EXHIBIT 2
Performance
appraisal cards

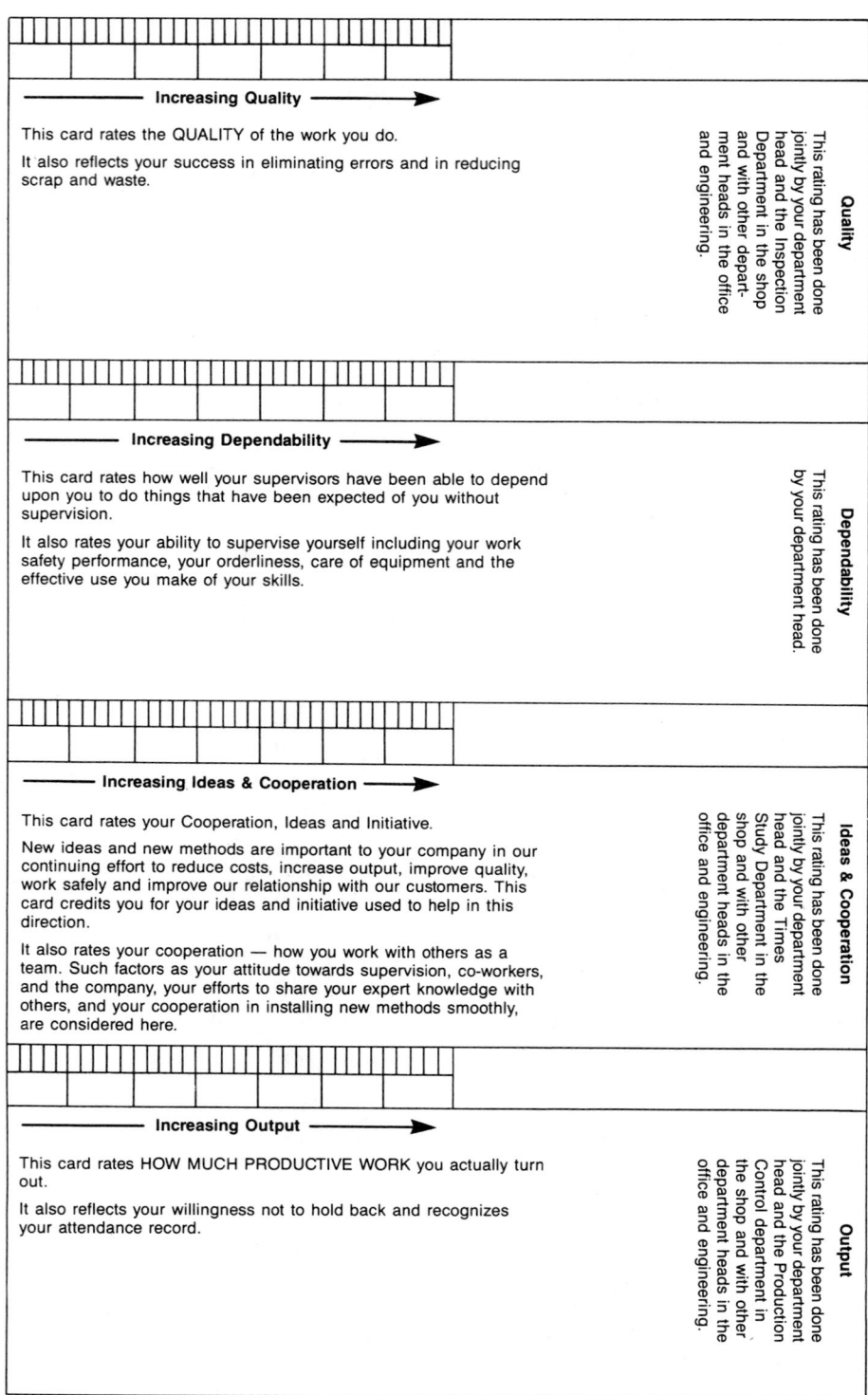

Quality

This rating has been done jointly by your department head and the Inspection Department in the shop and with other department heads in the office and engineering.

Increasing Quality ➞

This card rates the QUALITY of the work you do.

It also reflects your success in eliminating errors and in reducing scrap and waste.

Dependability

This rating has been done by your department head.

Increasing Dependability ➞

This card rates how well your supervisors have been able to depend upon you to do things that have been expected of you without supervision.

It also rates your ability to supervise yourself including your work safety performance, your orderliness, care of equipment and the effective use you make of your skills.

Ideas & Cooperation

This rating has been done jointly by your department head and the Times Study Department in the shop and with other department heads in the office and engineering.

Increasing Ideas & Cooperation ➞

This card rates your Cooperation, Ideas and Initiative.

New ideas and new methods are important to your company in our continuing effort to reduce costs, increase output, improve quality, work safely and improve our relationship with our customers. This card credits you for your ideas and initiative used to help in this direction.

It also rates your cooperation — how you work with others as a team. Such factors as your attitude towards supervision, co-workers, and the company, your efforts to share your expert knowledge with others, and your cooperation in installing new methods smoothly, are considered here.

Output

This rating has been done jointly by your department head and the Production Control department in the shop and with other department heads in the office and engineering.

Increasing Output ➞

This card rates HOW MUCH PRODUCTIVE WORK you actually turn out.

It also reflects your willingness not to hold back and recognizes your attendance record.

424

Compensation   Basic wage levels for jobs at Lincoln are determined by a wage survey of similar jobs in the Cleveland area. These rates are adjusted quarterly in accordance with changes in the Cleveland Area Consumer Price Index. Insofar as possible, base wage rates are translated into piece rates. Practically all production workers and many others — for example, some forklift operators — are paid by piece rate. Once established, piece rates are never changed unless a substantive change in the way a job is done results from a source other than the worker doing the job. In December of each year, a portion of annual profits is distributed to employees as bonuses. Incentive bonuses since 1934 have averaged about the same as annual wages and somewhat more than after-tax profits. The average bonus for 1981 was $20,759. Bonuses averaged $13,998 and $8,557, respectively, for the recession years 1982 to 1983. Individual bonuses are proportional to merit-rating scores. For example, assume the amount set aside for bonuses is 80 percent of total wages paid to eligible employees. A person whose performance score is 95 will receive a bonus of 76 percent (0.80 $\times$ 0.95) of annual wages.

Vacations   The company is shut down for two weeks in August and two weeks during the Christmas season. Vacations are taken during these periods. For employees with over 25 years of service, a fifth week of vacation may be taken at a time acceptable to superiors.

Work Assignment   Management has authority to transfer workers and to switch between overtime and short time as required. Supervisors have undisputed authority to assign specific parts to individual workmen, who may have their own preferences due to variations in piece rates.

During the 1982–1983 recession, 50 factory workers volunteered to join sales teams and fanned out across the country to sell a new Lincoln welder designed for automobile body shops and small machine shops. The result—$10 million in sales and a hot new product.

Employee Participation in Decision Making   When a manager speaks of participative management, he usually thinks of a relaxed, nonauthoritarian atmosphere. This is not the case at Lincoln. Formal authority is quite strong. "We're very authoritarian around here," says Mr. Willis. James F. Lincoln placed a good deal of stress on protecting management's authority. "Management in all successful departments of industry must have complete power," he said, ". . . Management is the coach who must be obeyed. The men, however, are the players who alone can win the game."[8] Despite this attitude, there are several ways in which employees participate in management at Lincoln.

---

[8]Lincoln, *Incentive Management* (Cleveland, OH: The Lincoln Electric Company, 1951), p. 228.

Richard Sabo, manager of public relations, relates job-enlargement to participation. "The most important participative technique that we use is giving more responsibility to employees." Mr. Sabo says, "We give a high school graduate more responsibility than other companies give their foremen." Lincoln puts limits on the degree of participation which is allowed, however. In Mr. Sabo's words,

When you use "participation," put quotes around it. Because we believe that each person should participate only in those decisions he is most knowledgeable about. I don't think production employees should control the decisions of Bill Irrgang. They don't know as much as he does about the decisions he is involved in.

The Advisory Board, elected by the workers, meets with the chairman and the president every two weeks to discuss ways of improving operations. This board has been in existence since 1914 and has contributed to many innovations. The incentive bonuses, for example, were first recommended by this committee. Every Lincoln employee has access to Advisory Board members, and answers to all Advisory Board suggestions are promised by the following meeting. Both Mr. Irrgang and Mr. Willis are quick to point out, though, that the Advisory Board only recommends actions. "They do not have direct authority," Mr. Irrgang says, "and when they bring up something that management thinks is not to the benefit of the company, it will be rejected."[9]

A suggestion program was instituted in 1929. At first, employees were awarded one-half of the first year's savings attributable to their suggestions. Now, however, the value of suggestions is reflected in performance evaluation scores, which determine individual incentive bonus amounts.

Training and Education

Production workers are given a short period of on-the-job training and then placed on a piecework pay system. Lincoln does not pay for off-site education. The idea behind this latter policy is that everyone cannot take advantage of such a program, and it is unfair to expend company funds for an advantage to which there is unequal access. Recruits for sales jobs, already college graduates, are given on-the-job training in the plant followed by a period of work and training at one of the regional sales offices.

Fringe Benefits and Executive Perquisites

A medical plan and a company-paid retirement program have been in effect for many years. A plant cafeteria, operated on a break even basis, serves meals at aout sixty percent of usual costs. An employee association, to which the company does not contribute, provides disability insurance and social and athletic activities. An employee stock ownership program, instituted in about 1925, has resulted in employee ownership of about fifty percent of Lincoln's stock. Under this program, each employee with more than one year of service may purchase stock in the corporation. The price of these shares is established at book value. Stock purchased through this plan may be held by employees only and must be offered back to the company

[9]Incentive Management in Action, *Assembly Engineering,* March 1967, p.18.

upon termination of employment. Dividends and voting rights are the same as for stock which is owned outside the plan. Approximately 75 percent of the employees own Lincoln stock.

As to executive perquisites, there are none — crowded, austere offices, no executive washrooms or lunchrooms, and no reserved parking spaces. Even the company president pays for his own meals and eats in the cafeteria.

FINANCIAL POLICIES

James F. Lincoln felt strongly that financing for company growth should come from within the company — through initial cash investment by the founders, through retention of earnings, and through stock purchases by those who work in the business. He saw the following advantages of this approach:[10]

1. Ownership of stock by employees strengthens team spirit. "If they are mutually anxious to make it succeed, the future of the company is bright."
2. Ownership of stock provides individual incentive because employees feel that they will benefit from company profitability.
3. "Ownership is educational." Owners-employees "will know how profits are made and lost; how success is won and lost. . . . There are few socialists in the list of stockholders of the nation's industries."
4. "Capital available from within controls expansion." Unwarranted expansion will not occur, Lincoln believed, under his financing plan.
5. "The greatest advantage would be the development of the individual worker. Under the incentive of ownership, he would become a greater man."
6. "Stock ownership is one of the steps that can be taken that will make the worker feel that there is less of a gulf between him and the boss. . . . Stock ownership will help the worker to recognize his responsibility in the game and the importance of victory."

Lincoln Electric Company uses a minimum of debt in its capital structure. There is no borrowing at all, with the debt being limited to current payables. Even the new $20 million plant in Mentor, Ohio, was financed totally from earnings.

The unusual pricing policy at Lincoln is succinctly stated by President Willis: "at all times price on the basis of cost and at all times keep pressure on our cost." This policy resulted in Lincoln's price for the most popular welding electrode then in use going from 16 cents a pound in 1929 to 4.7 cents in 1938. More recently, the SA-200 Welder, Lincoln's largest selling portable machine, decreased in price from 1958 through 1965. According to Dr. C. Jackson Grayson of the American Productivity Center in Houston, Texas, Lincoln's prices in general have increased only one-fifth as fast as the Consumer Price Index from 1934 to about 1970. This has resulted in a welding products market in which Lincoln is the undisputed

---

[10]Lincoln, 1961, pp. 220–228.

price leader for the products it manufactures. Not even the major Japanese manufacturers, such as Nippon Steel for welding electrodes and Asaka Transformer for welding machines, have been able to penetrate this market.

Huge cash balances are accumulated each year preparatory to paying the year-end bonuses. The bonuses totaled $32,718,000 for 1984. This money is invested in short-term U.S. government securities and bank certificates of deposit until needed. Financial statements are shown in Exhibits 3 and 4. Exhibit 5 shows how Lincoln's revenue has been distributed.

HOW WELL DOES LINCOLN SERVE ITS PUBLIC?

Lincoln Electric differs from most other companies in the importance it assigns to each of the groups it serves. Mr. Willis identifies these groups, in the order of priority Lincoln ascribes to them, as (1) customers, (2) employees, and (3) stockholders.

Certainly Lincoln customers have fared well over the years. Lincoln prices for welding machines and welding electrodes are acknowledged to be the lowest in the marketplace. Lincoln quality has consistently been so high that Lincoln "Fleetweld" electrodes and Lincoln SA-200 welders have been the standard in the pipeline and refinery construction industry, where price is hardly a criterion, for decades. The cost of field failures for Lincoln products was an amazing four one-hundredths of one percent in 1979. A Lincoln distributor in Monroe, Louisiana, says that he has sold several hundred of the popular AC-225 welders, and, though the machine is warranted for one year, he has never handled a warranty claim.

Perhaps best-served of all Lincoln constituencies have been the employees. Not the least of their benefits, of course, are the year-end bonuses, which effectively double an already average compensation level. The foregoing description of the personnel program and the comments in the Appendix further illustrate the desirability of a Lincoln job.

While stockholders were relegated to an inferior status by James F. Lincoln, they have done very well indeed. Recent dividends have exceeded $7 a share and earnings per share have exceeded $20. In January 1980, the price of restricted stock committed by Lincoln to employees was $117 a share. By February 4, 1983, the stated value, at which Lincoln will repurchase the stock if tendered, was $166. A check with the New York office of Merrill, Lynch, Pierce, Fenner and Smith on February 4, 1983 revealed an estimated price on Lincoln stock of $240 a share, with none being offered for sale. Technically, this price applies only to the unrestricted stock owned by the Lincoln family, a few other major holders, and employees who have purchased it on the open market, but it gives some idea of the value of Lincoln stock in general. The risk associated with Lincoln stock, a major determinant of stock value, is minimal because of the absence of debt in Lincoln's capital structure, because of an extremely stable earnings record, and because of Lincoln's practice of purchasing the restricted stock whenever employees offer it for sale.

EXHIBIT 3 Summary of balance sheet information, 1980–1984

	1980	1981	1982	1983	1984
Assets					
Cash	$ 1,307	$ 3,603	$ 1,318	$ 1,774	$ 3,580
Bonds and CDs	46,503	62,671	72,485	77,872	57,212
Notes and accounts receivable	42,424	41,521	26,239	31,114	34,469
Inventories (LIFO basis)	35,533	45,541	38,157	30,773	37,433
Deferred taxes and prepaid expenses	2,749	3,658	4,635	4,704	5,095
Total current assets	$128,516	$156,994	$142,834	$146,237	$137,789
Other assets	$ 19,723	$ 21,424	$ 22,116	$ 21,421	$ 20,216
Investment in foreign divisions	4,695	4,695	7,696	8,696	8,696
	$ 24,418	$ 26,119	$ 29,812	$ 30,117	$ 28,912
Property, plant, equipment					
Land	$ 913	$ 928	$ 925	$ 925	$ 926
Buildings (net)	22,982	24,696	23,330	22,378	20,860
Machinery and equipment (net)	25,339	27,104	26,949	27,146	28,106
	$ 49,234	$ 52,728	$ 51,204	$ 50,449	$ 49,892
Total Assets	$202,168	$235,841	$223,850	$226,803	$216,593
Liabilities and Shareholders' Equity					
Accounts payable	$ 15,608	$ 14,868	$ 11,936	$ 16,228	$ 15,233
Accrued wages	1,504	4,940	3,633	3,224	4,358
Taxes payable	5,622	14,755	5,233	6,675	4,203
Dividends payable	5,800	7,070	6,957	6,675	6,207
Total current liabilities	$ 28,534	$ 41,633	$ 27,759	$ 32,802	$ 30,001
Other long-term debt	$ 3,807	$ 4,557	$ 5,870	$ 7,805	$ 10,313
Shareholders' equity					
Common stock	$ 276	$ 272	$ 268	$ 257	$ 239
Additional paid-in capital	2,641	501	1,862	0	0
Retained earnings	166,910	188,878	188,392	186,318	176,569
Foreign currency adjustment			(301)	(379)	(529)
	$169,827	$189,651	$190,221	$186,196	$176,279
Total Liabilities and Shareholders' Equity	$202,168	$235,841	$223,850	$226,803	$216,593

Note: figures in thousands of dollars.

A CONCLUDING COMMENT

It is easy to believe that the reason for Lincoln's success is the excellent attitude of Lincoln employees and their willingness to work harder, faster, and more intelligently than other industrial workers. However, Mr. Richard Sabo, manager of publicity

EXHIBIT 4 Summary of income statement information, 1980–1984

	1980	1981	1982	1983	1984
Revenue					
Net sales	$387,374	$450,387	$310,862	$263,129	$321,759
Other income	13,817	18,454	18,049	13,387	11,814
	401,191	468,841	328,911	276,516	333,573
Costs and expenses					
Cost of products sold	260,671	293,332	212,674	179,851	222,985
Selling, general, and administrative expenses	37,753	42,656	37,128	36,348	40,164
Year-end incentive bonus	43,249	55,718	36,870	21,914	32,718
Payroll taxes related to bonus	1,251	1,544	1,847	1,186	1,874
Pension expense	6,810	6,874	5,888	5,151	5,139
Interest on tax assessments	0	0	0	1,946	99
	349,734	400,124	294,407	246,396	302,979
Income					
Income before income taxes	51,457	68,717	34,504	30,120	30,594
Federal income tax	20,300	27,400	13,227	14,246	12,429
State and local income taxes	3,072	3,885	2,497	(989)	1,423
	23,372	31,285	15,724	13,257	13,852
Net income	$ 28,085	$ 37,432	$ 18,780	$ 16,863	$ 16,742
Employees eligible for bonus	2,637	2,684	2,634	2,561	2,469

Note: figures in thousands of dollars

and educational services at Lincoln, suggests that appropriate credit be given to Lincoln executives, whom he credits with carrying out the following policies:

1. Management has limited research, development and manufacturing to a standard product line designed to meet the major needs of the welding industry.
2. New products must be reviewed by manufacturing and all production costs verified before being approved by management.
3. Purchasing is challenged to not only procure materials at the lowest cost, but also to work closely with engineering and manufacturing to assure that the latest innovations are implemented.
4. Manufacturing supervision and all personnel are held accountable for reduction of scrap, energy conservation, and maintenance of product quality.
5. Production control, material handling, and methods engineering are closely supervised by top management.
6. Material and finished goods inventory control, accurate cost accounting and attention to sales cost, credit, and other financial areas have constantly reduced overhead and led to excellent profitability.

EXHIBIT 5 How Lincoln's Revenue Dollar Was Disbursed, 1974–1983

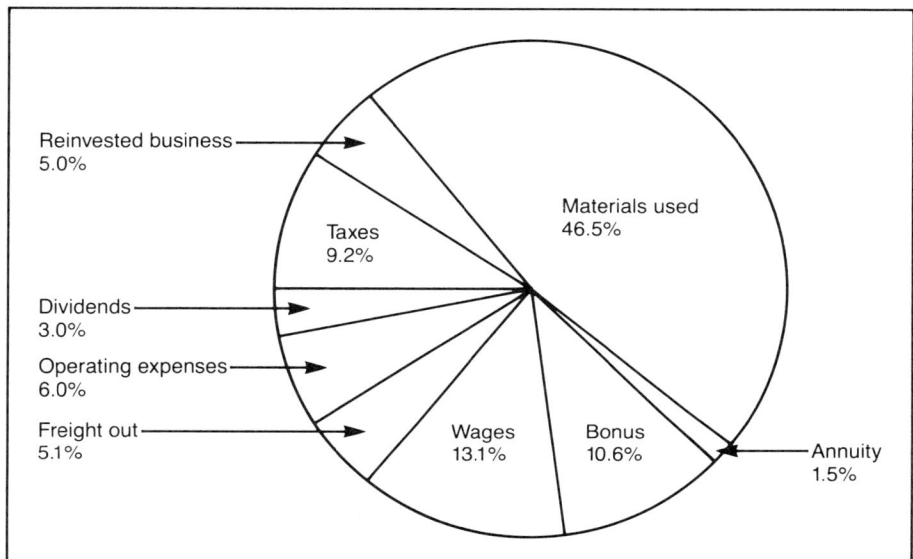

7. Management has made cost reduction a way of life at Lincoln, and definite programs are established in many areas, including traffic and shipping, where tremendous savings can result.
8. Management has established a sales department that is technically trained to reduce customer welding costs. This sales technique and other real customer services have eliminated nonessential frills and resulted in long-term benefits to all concerned.
9. Management has encouraged education, technical publishing, and long range programs that have resulted in industry growth, thereby assuring market potential for the Lincoln Electric Company.

Sabo writes, ''It is in a very real sense a personal and group experience in faith — a belief that together we can achieve results which alone would not be possible. It is not a perfect system and it is not 'easy.' It requires tremendous dedication and hard work. However, it does work and the results are worth the effort.''

APPENDIX: EMPLOYEE INTERVIEWS

Typical questions and answers from interviews with Lincoln employees are presented below. In order to maintain each employee's personal privacy, the names used for the interviewees are fictitious.

PART I

Interview with Betty Stewart, a 52-year-old high school graduate who had been with Lincoln thirteen years and who was working as a cost accounting clerk at the time of the interview.

Q: What jobs have you held here besides the one you have now?

A: I worked in payroll for a while, and then this job came open and I took it.

Q: How much money did you make last year, including your bonus?

A: I would say roughly around $20,000, but I was off for back surgery for a while.

Q: You weren't paid while you were off for back surgery?

A: No.

Q: Did the Employees Association help out?

A: Yes. The company doesn't furnish that, though. We pay $6 a month into the Employees Association. I think my check from them was $105.00 a week.

Q: How was your performance rating last year?

A: It was around 100 points, but I lost some points for attendance with my back problem.

Q: How did you get your job at Lincoln?

A: I was bored silly where I was working, and I had heard that Lincoln kept their people busy. So I applied and got the job the next day.

Q: Do you think you make more money than similar workers in Cleveland?

A: I know I do.

Q: What have you done with your money?

A: We have purchased a better home. Also, my son is going to the University of Chicago, which costs $10,000 a year. I buy the Lincoln stock which is offered each year, and I have a little bit of gold.

Q: Have you ever visited with any of the senior executives, like Mr. Willis or Mr. Irrgang?

A: I have known Mr. Willis for a long time.

Q: Does he call you by name?

A: Yes. In fact he was very instrumental in my going to the doctor that I am going to with my back. He knows the director of the clinic.

Q: Do you know Mr. Irrgang?

A: I know him to speak to him, and he always speaks, always. But I have known Mr. Willis for a good many years. When I did Plant Two accounting I did not understand how the plant operated. Of course you are not allowed in Plant Two, because that's the Electrode Division. I told my boss about the problem one day and the next thing I knew Mr. Willis came by and said, "Come on, Betty, we're going to Plant Two." He spent an hour and a half showing me the plant.

Q: Do you think Lincoln employees produce more than those in other companies?

A: I think with the incentive program the way that it is, if you want to work and achieve, then you will do it. If you don't want to work and achieve, you will not do it no matter where you are. Just because you are merit rated and have a bonus, if you really don't want to work hard, then you're not going to. You will accept your ninety points or ninety-two or eighty-five because, even with that, you make more money than people on the outside.

Q: Do you think Lincoln employees will ever join a union?

A: I don't know why they would.

Q: What is the most important advantage of working for Lincoln Electric?

A: You have an incentive, and you can push and get something for pushing. That's not true in a lot of companies.

Q: So you say that money is a very major advantage?

A: Money is a major advantage, but it's not just the money. It's the fact that having the incentive, you do wish to work a little harder. I'm sure that there are a lot of men here who, if they worked some other place, would not work as hard as they do here. Not that they are overworked — I don't mean that — but I'm sure they wouldn't push.

Q: Is there anything that you would like to add?

A: I do like working here. I am better off being pushed mentally. In another company if you pushed too hard you would feel a little bit of pressure, and someone might say, "Hey, slow down; don't try so hard." But here you are encouraged, not discouraged.

PART II

Interview with Ed Sanderson, 23-year-old high school graduate who had been with Lincoln four years and who was a machine operator in the Electrode Division at the time of the interview.

Q: How did you happen to get this job?

A: My wife was pregnant, and I was making three bucks an hour and one day I came here and applied. That was it. I kept calling to let them know I was still interested.

Q: Roughly what were your earnings last year including your bonus?

A: $37,000.00

Q: What have you done with your money since you have been here?

A: Well, we've lived pretty well and we bought a condominium.

Q: Have you paid for the condominium?

A: No, but I could.

Q: Have you bought your Lincoln stock this year?

A: No, I haven't bought any Lincoln stock yet.

Q: Do you get the feeling that the executives here are pretty well thought of?

A: I think they are. To get where they are today, they had to really work.

Q: Wouldn't that be true anywhere?

A: I think more so here because seniority really doesn't mean anything. If you work with a guy who has twenty years here, and you have two months and you're doing a better job, you will get advanced before he will.

Q: Are you paid on a piece rate basis?

A: My gang does. There are nine of us who make the bare electrode, and the whole group gets paid based on how much electrode we make.

Q: Do you think you work harder than workers in other factories in the Cleveland area?

A: Yes, I would say I probably work harder.

Q: Do you think it hurts anybody?

A: No, a little hard work never hurts anybody.

Q: If you could choose, do you think you would be as happy earning a little less money and being able to slow down a little?

A: No, it doesn't bother me. If it bothered me, I wouldn't do it.

Q: What would you say is the biggest disadvantage of working at Lincoln, as opposed to working somewhere else?

A: Probably having to work shift work.

Q: Why do you think Lincoln employees produce more than workers in other plants?

A: That's the way the company is set up. The more you put out, the more you're going to make.

Q: Do you think it's the piece rate and bonus together?

A: I don't think people would work here if they didn't know that they would be rewarded at the end of the year.

Q: Do you think Lincoln employees will ever join a union?

A: No.

Q: What are the major advantages of working for Lincoln?

A: Money.

Q: Are there any other advantages?

A: Yes, we don't have a union shop. I don't think I could work in a union shop.

Q: Do you think you are a career man with Lincoln at this time?

A: Yes.

PART III

Interview with Roger Lewis, 23-year-old Purdue graduate in mechanical engineering who had been in the Lincoln sales program for fifteen months and who was working in the Cleveland sales office at the time of the interview.

Q: How did you get your job at Lincoln?

A: I saw that Lincoln was interviewing on campus at Purdue, and I went by. I later came to Cleveland for a plant tour and was offered a job.

Q: Do you know any of the senior executives? Would they know you by name?

A: Yes, I know all of them — Mr. Irrgang, Mr. Willis, Mr. Manross.

Q: Do you think Lincoln salesmen work harder than those in other companies?

A: Yes. I don't think there are many salesmen for other companies who are putting in fifty to sixty-hour weeks. Everybody here works harder. You can go out in the plant, or you can go upstairs, and there's nobody sitting around.

Q: Do you see any real disadvantage of working at Lincoln?

A: I don't know if it's a disadvantage but Lincoln is a spartan company, a very thrifty company. I like that. The sales offices are functional, not fancy.

Q: Why do you think Lincoln employees have such high productivity?

A: Piecework has a lot to do with it. Lincoln is smaller than many plants, too; you can stand in one place and see the materials come in one side and the product go out the other. You feel a part of the company. The chance to get ahead is important, too. They have a strict policy of promoting from within, so you know you have a chance. I think in a lot of other places you may not get as fair a shake as you do here. The sales offices are on a smaller scale, too. I like that. I tell someone that we have two people in the Baltimore office, and they say, "You've got to be kidding." It's smaller and more personal. Pay is the most important thing. I have heard that this is the highest paying factory in the world.

PART IV

Interview with Jimmy Roberts, a 47-year-old high school graduate, who had been with Lincoln 17 years and who was working as a multiple-drill press operator at the time of the interview.

Q: What jobs have you had at Lincoln?

A: I started out cleaning the men's locker room in 1963. After about a year I got a job in the flux department, where we make the coating for welding rods. I worked there for seven or eight years and then got my present job.

Q: Do you make one particular part?

A: No, there are a variety of parts I make — at least twenty-five.

Q: Each one has a different piece rate attached to it?

A: Yes.

Q: Are some piece rates better than others?

A: Yes.

Q: How do you determine which ones you are going to do?

A: You don't. Your supervisor assigns them.

Q: How much money did you make last year?

A: $47,000.

Q: Have you ever received any kind of award or citation?

A: No.

Q: Was your rating ever over 110?

A: Yes. For the past five years, probably, I made over 110 points.

Q: Is there any attempt to let others know . . . ?

A: The kind of points I get? No.

Q: Do you know what they are making?

A: No. There are some who might not be too happy with their points and they might make it known. The majority, though, do not make it a point of telling other employees.

Q: Would you be just as happy earning a little less money and working a little slower?

A: I don't think I would — not at this point. I have done piecework all these years, and the fast pace doesn't really bother me.

Q: Why do you think Lincoln productivity is so high?

A: The incentive thing — the bonus distribution. I think that would be the main reason. The pay check you get every two weeks is important too.

Q: Do you think Lincoln employees would ever join a union?

A: I don't think so. I have never heard anyone mention it.

Q: What is the most important advantage of working here?

A: Amount of money you make. I don't think I could make this type of money anywhere else, especially with only a high school education.

Q: As a black person, do you feel that Lincoln discriminates in any way against blacks?

A: No. I don't think any more so than any other job. Naturally, there is a certain amount of discrimination, regardless of where you are.

PART V

Interview with Joe Trahan, 58-year-old high school graduate who had been with Lincoln 39 years and who was employed as a working supervisor in the tool room at the time of the interview.

Q: Roughly what was your pay last year?

A: Over $50,000; salary, bonus, stock dividends.

Q: How much was your bonus?

A: About $23,000.

Q: Have you ever gotten a special award of any kind?

A: Not really.

Q: What have you done with your money?

A: My house is paid for — and my two cars. I also have some bonds and the Lincoln stock.

Q: What do you think of the executives at Lincoln?

A: They're really top notch.

Q: What is the major disadvantage of working at Lincoln Electric?

A: I don't know of any disadvantage at all.

Q: Do you think you produce more than most people in similar jobs with other companies?

A: I do believe that.

Q: Why is that? Why do you believe that?

A: We are on the incentive system. Everything we do, we try to improve to make a better product with a minimum of outlay. We try to improve the bonus.

Q: Would you be just as happy making a little less money and not working quite so hard?

A: I don't think so.

Q: You know that Lincoln productivity is higher than that at most other plants. Why is that?

A: Money.

Q: Do you think Lincoln employees would ever join a union?

A: I don't think they would ever consider it.

Q: What is the most important advantage of working at Lincoln?

A: Compensation.

Q: Tell me something about Mr. James Lincoln, who died in 1965.

A: You are talking about Jimmy Sr. He always strolled through the shop in his shirt sleeves. Big fellow. Always looked distinguished. Gray hair. Friendly sort of guy. I was a member of the advisory board one year. He was there each time.

Q: Did he strike you as really caring?

A: I think he always cared for people.

Q: Did you get any sensation of a religious nature from him?

A: No, not really.

Q: And religion is not part of the program now?

A: No.

Q: Do you think Mr. Lincoln was a very intelligent man, or was he just a nice guy?

A: I would say he was pretty well educated. A great talker — always right off the top of his head. He knew what he was talking about all the time.

Q: When were bonuses for beneficial suggestions done away with?

A: About fifteen years ago.

Q: Did that hurt very much?

A: I don't think so, because suggestions are still rewarded through the merit rating system.

Q: Is there anything you would like to add?

A: It's a good place to work. The union kind of ties other places down. At other places, electricians only do electrical work, carpenters only do carpenter work. At Lincoln Electric we all pitch in and do whatever needs to be done.

Q: So a major advantage is not having a union?

A: That's right.

THE ALCOHOLIC BEVERAGE INDUSTRY

This case describes the alcoholic beverage industry in North America. Coverage include: (1) production techniques for distilled spirits, (2) production economics, (3) distribution, (4) consumption, (5) market segments, (6) antialcohol campaigns, (7) distillers, (8) the production of beer, (9) the brewers, (10) wine markets and production, (11) the wine companies, and (12) an overview of the cases.

PRODUCTION TECHNIQUES FOR DISTILLED SPIRITS

At the simplest level, all distilled spirits are produced through the distilling process that capitalizes on alcohol's property of boiling at lower temperatures than water. Alcohol is produced by fermentation. The natural sugar, found in a vast range of vegetable products which includes almost every type of grain and fruit, is converted into alcohol by the action of yeasts. These yeasts break down the sugar in the fermentation process which produces alcohol. Occasionally, starch is used to produce alcohol. A starch is cooked in a mash that is converted to sugar.

Alcohol can be continuously purified to neutralize all the flavors and aromas of the original fruits or grains. These neutral spirits can be sold as soon as they are produced and can be mixed with soft drinks or juices.

Other alcoholic beverages are produced either by retaining the taste of the original grains (as, for example, bourbon, which has a base continuously distilled from either corn or rye) or by mixing additives (as in gin, flavored with juniper berries). Molasses is the base for rum, as grapes are the foundation for wine. These spirits are then aged in oak casks or barrels for varying periods of time. Blends are produced, as the name indicates, by blending natural spirits with neutralized spirits.

The alcohol contained in beverages is expressed as a percentage (e.g., sake, the Japanese rice wine, is 16 percent alcohol), or, in the United States, as proof,

Case prepared by John Barnett, University of New Hampshire. Copyright © 1987. Reprinted by permission.

determined by doubling the alcohol percentage. Thus, 100-proof whiskey is 50 percent alcohol; 80-proof is 40 percent alcohol.

PRODUCTION ECONOMICS

The production differences between "brown" straight and blended whiskies and "white" neutral spirits have obvious economic impact. These include:

raw materials costs
continuous (neutralized) versus batch ("brown goods") processing
aging, including both container (oak barrel) costs and inventory carrying charges (both interest and evaporation)

DISTRIBUTION

Distribution by the government is the norm in Canada (via provincial liquor boards) and in seventeen states in the United States. These "control" states have state monopolies on retail distribution.

The distillers or importers deal with either the control-state retailer or independent retailers through a network of wholesalers. These wholesalers are the "push-through" distribution system which is of increasing importance with advertising restrictions, including the prohibition of radio or television advertising of spirits.

Regional tastes are strong. New York is a big consumer of scotch, and California of tequila. Per capita consumption in Washington, D.C., is five times that of West Virginia. Bourbon is popular in the South and Canadian whisky in the North. (Note: Canadian and Scotch is *whisky* without an "e"; its plural is *whiskies*. Irish or American is *whiskey* with a plural of *whiskeys*.)

CONSUMPTION

International consumption of distilled spirits is shown in Exhibit 1. Exhibit 2 shows total U.S. consumption and the change in market share of various whiskeys and nonwhiskeys from 1955 to 1982. The drinking trends in the United States are shown in Exhibit 3.

Two strong trends in distilled spirits are mixability and lightness. Distilled spirits have been mixed with soft drinks (e.g., rum and coke) and fruit juices (e.g., Harvey Wallbangers). The fastest-growing segment of all alcoholic beverages in the 1980s was wine and fruit juice mixes or "wine coolers." The trend toward lightness was led by Scotch and Canadian whiskies in the 1960s. During the 1980s many consumers switched to light beer and wine.

EXHIBIT 1
Per capita consumption by country, 1982

	Consumption of 750 ml 80-proof bottles
East Germany	15.8
Canada	11.3
Russia	11.0
United States	9.7
West Germany	8.3
Sweden	8.1
Italy	6.3
Britain	5.3
Australia	4.0
Argentina	3.0

Source: *The Economist,* December 22, 1984.

EXHIBIT 2
U.S. consumption

	Millions of gallons consumed			Market share		
Whiskeys	*1955*	*1964*	*1982*	*1955*	*1964*	*1982*
Blends	82	75	—[a]	40%	26%	—[a]
Straight[a]	46	70	98	23	24	22
Scotch	12	28	45	6	10	10
Canadian	9	17	54	5	6	12
Bonded[b]	13	8	—[a]	6	3	—[a]
Total whiskeys	162	198	197	80%	69%	44%
Nonwhiskeys						
Gin	21	31	41	10%	11%	9%
Vodka	7	28	98	4	10	22
Rum	3	6	31	1	2	7
Brandy	5	9	22	2	3	5
Other	7	15	58	3	5	13
Total nonwhiskeys	43	89	250	20%	31%	56%
Total distilled spirits	205	287	447	100%	100%	100%

[a] Straight whiskey is one that is not blended, such as bourbon. Straight whiskey is natural, i.e., it has not been neutralized and it contains no neutral spirits. 1982 figures for straight include blends and bonded.
[b] Bonded whiskeys are straight whiskeys that are "sealed" and "bonded" to indicate that they are 100-U.S.-proof (50 percent alcohol) as opposed to the normal 86-proof in the United States and 70-proof in Canada.
Source: Heublein, Inc., Harvard Business School 373–103, *The Economist,* December 22, 1984.

EXHIBIT 3
U.S. per capita
consumption

Beverage	1968		1978		1985	
	Gallons	Market share	Gallons	Market share	Gallons	Market share
Beer	17.3	86.1%	23.1	84.9%	23.8	85.3%
Wine	1.1	5.5	2.1	7.7	2.4	8.6
Distilled spirits	1.7	8.4	2.0	7.4	1.7	6.1
Total	20.1	100.0%	27.2	100.0%	27.9	100.0%

Source: "Beverage Industry," *Advertising Age*, February 16, 1987, p. S-1.

One distiller, Seagram, possibly assuming that "lightness" meant "low alcohol," launched an advertising campaign of "equivalency" in 1985, "showing that four 1-oz. jiggers of 80-proof spirits contain no more alcohol than four 10-oz. glasses of beer or four 3-oz. glasses of wine" (*Business Week,* March 22, 1985, p. 229).

Nicholas Furlotte wrote on new styles and new tastes in drinking in *Advertising Age* (February 16, 1987):

> A top executive . . . wanted to know [if] I think the martini . . . would make a comeback. . . . There is no such thing as a comeback in the alcoholic beverage industry. . . . Once a brand has gone into decline it has never been successfully revived. . . . Once a category has gone into serious decline, it has never been brought back. . . .
>
> We are embarking on a new era of alcoholic beverage products and markets. . . .
>
> Because taste preferences are evolutionary rather than cyclical, each generation claims a certain type of drink as its own. There was a time when the drink was bourbon. Later it was vodka, then white wine, and now, perhaps, bottled water.
>
> But, of all the demographic groups influencing the alcoholic beverage industry today, none is having a greater effect than the generation brought up on the sweet, fizzy taste of soda pop.

Mr. Furlotte then cited the efforts of Joseph E. Seagram & Sons with its spirits-based cooler line, James Beam's Zzzingers and Schnapps-based cooler, Heublein's Tropic Freezer ("a sort of cherry slush for adults"), Schiefflin's Petite Liqueur (a wine-based cordial), and Kobrand's Alize (a passion fruit and cognac mix). "These and future new drinks may do for prepared cocktails what Lean Cuisine has done for TV dinners."

Furlotte also suggested that (1) cooler sales will now be a battle for market share and profitability, as enormous growth gains are over ("By 2000, coolers will be about as important as Boone's Farm is today") as consumers tire of the product, (2) the over-fifty age group will be more and more important, (3) the high-priced premium segments will continue their growth, (4) marketing programs, especially discounts and coupons, will cut into brand loyalty, (5) comparative brand advertising will increase, (6) imported beers will grow, and (7) U.S. wine tastes will become more sophisticated, but "the U.S. will never be a wine-drinking country."

Mr. Furlotte concluded: "In 20 years, the last of the serious martini drinkers will have vanished from the face of the earth and the drink will never be heard of again."

Patricia Winters, writing in the same special report edition of *Advertising Age*, described a whole new trend in the alcoholic beverage industry that resulted "when you mix cayenne pepper, a bottle of vodka, and a yuppie." Absolut Peppar, Stolichnaya's Zubrowka (vodka flavored with buffalo grass), Chef Paul Prudhomme's Cajun martini, Stolichnaya's pepper-flavored Pertsovka "Pepper Stoli, The Hot Vodka," and Stolichnaya Okhotnichya and Limonnaya are illustrations of this trend. Jack Shea of Heublein, marketer of Smirnoff, noted in *Advertising Age* (op. cit.) that Heublein was "not going to risk the reputation of the world's No. 1 vodka on a fad."

MARKET SEGMENTS

Price and perceived quality are factors distinguishing a premium market from the bottom-of-the-market commodity products. Seagram's Crown Royal (Canadian) and Chivas Regal (Scotch) are good examples of premium spirits, as is Heublein's Smirnoff (which leaves you breathless).

What contributes to a differentiated or quality product? The quality of materials, the aging process, and the blender's art are certainly a few of the critical factors for premium beverages. Shifting consumer tastes and product promotion help determine market success.

ANTIALCOHOL CAMPAIGNS

Environmentalists are concerned about the litter aspects of alcoholic beverages, especially beer cans. Various states are trying bottle deposits, packaging taxes, and other antilitter projects.

More importantly, the abuse of alcoholic beverages is being attacked through specific drunk-driving citizens' action and advertising campaigns. Mothers Against Drunk Driving (MADD) is especially vocal. Many states are enacting not only stiff drunk-driving laws, but also host-liability laws.

The Center for Science in the Public Interest (CSPI), a consumer-advocacy group in Washington, D.C., began a series of campaigns to restrict or eliminate alcohol advertising in the 1980s. CSPI wants product warnings on beverages and in any allowed advertising, increased excise taxes on alcohol, and elimination of alcohol company sponsorship of concerts and campus parties.

The critics of alcohol point to the 98,000 deaths related to alcohol in 1985 versus 3,600 deaths in the same period related to cocaine, heroin, and other drugs.

A spokesperson for the National Council on Alcoholism commented that it is "certainly in the alcohol industry's interest to keep [the current] debate focused on drug abuse" (*Christian Science Monitor*, September 24, 1986). A drug and alcohol abuse counselor concluded: "If alcohol were suddenly to be discovered today, it would probably be classed as a [Drug Enforcement Agency] Schedule Two drug along with cocaine and some of the barbituates" (ibid).

Bill Coors, Chairman of the Adolph Coors Company, spoke about the most critical issue facing Coors and the brewing industry:

Abuse of our product! Alcoholism! We can't change people's life-styles by advertising. Alcohol is a way of managing stress, just like overeating. The American Medical Association says alcoholism is a disease. How can they be so naive as to treat the product as though it is the problem?[1]

Carl Jung's letter to the founder of Alcoholics Anonymous, Bill W., presents an interesting view of the alcoholic's experience:

[The alcoholic's] craving for alcohol was the equivalent on a low level of the spiritual thirst of our being for wholeness . . . Alcohol in Latin is spiritus, *and you use the same word for the highest religious experience as well as for the most depraving poison. The helpful formula, therefore, is:* spiritus contra spiritum.

THE COMPANIES

The five largest distillers in North America in 1964 were Seagrams Distillers Corporation (with liquor sales of $720 million in 1964), Hiram Walker ($500 million), National Distillers ($430 million), Schenley ($390 million), and Heublein ($120 million).

Seagram came to the United States in 1933 as Prohibition ended. It was the American arm of the Samuel Bronfman Canadian firm formed by the 1928 merger of Bronfman's Distillers Corporation with Joseph E. Seagram and Sons, Ltd., of Ontario. Hiram Walker of Massachusetts founded the Canadian distiller of the same name in 1858 and introduced Canadian whisky to the United States in the last half of the nineteenth century. National Distillers was formed in the 1920s out of the Midwest-U.S.-based whiskey trust. Organized in Illinois in 1887, this pooling and control device was officially known in its early years as the Distillers' Cattle Feeders' Trust. Schenley was formed in 1920 by Lewis Rosenstiel, who purchased a medicinal distillery, the Schenley Products Company, based upon his belief that the Eighteenth Amendment (Prohibition) passed that year would not last. Heublein was established in 1875 by Gilbert and Louis Heublein as an importer of foods and beverages. In

---

[1] C. L. Hinkle and E. F. Stinemann, "Adolph Coors Company," *Cases in Marketing Management* (Englewood Cliffs, NJ: Prentice-Hall, 1984), p. 445.

EXHIBIT 4
U.S. leading brands

1983 rank	Millions of cases sold		
	1983	*1978*	*1968*
1. Bacardi	7.7	6.1	2.1
2. Smirnoff	5.7	6.2	3.2
3. Seagram's Seven Crown	4.9	6.2	7.9
4. Canadian Mist	3.4	2.3	—
5. Jim Beam	3.2	2.8	2.5
6. Seagram's V.O.	3.1	3.9	3.5

Source: *The Economist*, December 22, 1984.

1892 the Heublein brothers produced prepared cocktails. They incorporated themselves as G. F. Heublein & Bro. in 1899.

Seagram's V.O., a Canadian whiskey, had been the number one brand in the United States since the end of Prohibition. Hiram Walker was also active in the Canadian whiskey market in the United States with its Canadian Club brand, while Heublein had the most limited product line, with one product, Smirnoff vodka, accounting for about half of its liquor sales.

Seagram's Seven Crown was surpassed as the number one brand in the United States by Smirnoff and, subsequently, also by Bacardi rum in the early 1980s. Exhibit 4 summarizes U.S. sales of the leading brands.

The Canadian market is naturally smaller than the U.S. market. For example, two of the top U.S. brands in 1978, Bacardi and Smirnoff (which together sold 12,300,000 cases in the United States) sold 2,000,000 cases in Canada in the same year. Seagram's V.O. sold 3,900,000 cases in the United States in 1978 and 500,000 in Canada.

The strategies of the largest distillers often were based upon a combination of premium products and a strong distribution system. Medium-sized distillers such as James Beam might specialize in straight bourbon products, while some distillers might concentrate on one brand, lower-priced goods, or private labeling for the big liquor retailers.

With static or declining demand, liquor distillers turned to new products that are appealing in themselves (such as Bailey's Irish Cream) or are mixable (rum). General Wines' 1982 product, Dr. McGillicuddy's Mentholmint Schnapps, built on the growth pattern of peppermint schnapps.

By 1984 Seagram had the third (Seven Crown), eighth (V.O.), and tenth (Seagram's Gin) best-selling U.S. brands. Hiram Walker (Hiram Walker Resources) had the eleventh (Canadian Club) leading brand. National had the sixth (Windsor Supreme) and the thirteenth (Gibley's Gin). Schenley, now a part of Rapid-American, had the fifteenth brand, Dewar's, while Heublein, now part of R. J. Reynolds, held the second (Smirnoff) and the ninth (Popov) best-selling U.S. brands.

The number one brand in 1984 was Bacardi. Fourth was Canadian Mist, and seventh was Jack Daniel's, both part of Brown-Forman, who specialized in "brown goods," also producing Early Times and Southern Comfort. Fifth came Jim Beam, distilled by the Beam division of American Brands.

Brown-Forman is frequently cited as an example of a successful "niche" strategy, resulting in industry-leading margins through the concentration on leading brands. On the other hand, Seagram and Hiram Walker are examples of diversifying businesses. Hiram Walker Resources consists of Hiram Walker Gooderham & Wort's (distilling), Home Oil (natural resources), and Consumers' Gas (a Toronto gas utility). Seagram in the 1980s exchanged ownership in oil and gas for ownership in Du Pont.

Heublein's success at making deals, such as acquiring manufacturing rights to the profitable A-1 steak sauce during World War I and acquiring the rights to Smirnoff vodka during World War II, stayed with the firm in the early 1960s, as it acquired Arrow Liquors and Vintage (Lancers) wines. Two bad acquisitions were made in the late 1960s, however, as Heublein mistakenly assumed it could successfully market Hamm's beer and mistakenly assumed Kentucky Fried Chicken was a growth industry. Heublein took a $20 million write-off, after learning that marketing of low-margin beer (Hamm) with no brand loyalty was not the same as marketing the high-margin, prestigious Smirnoff. Heublein eventually was acquired by R. J. Reynolds, the tobacco company.

National Distillers' brands were doing well due to aggressive pricing and advertising. National had reduced its Old Crow bourbon prices and had started advertising Windsor Supreme-versus-V.O. taste tests. National introduced its DeKuyper's Peachtree Schnapps in October 1984; during 1985 it sold over 1.5 million cases and was the 24th largest U.S. brand. 1985 sales are shown in Exhibit 5.

EXHIBIT 5
U.S. sales by brand, 1985

Rank				Millions of 9-liter cases	
1985	1984	**Brand**	**Company**	1985	*% change 1984–1985*
1	1	Bacardi	Bacardi	8.5	+0.5%
2	2	Smirnoff	Heublein-Reynolds	7.7	+0.1
3	3	Seven Crown	Seagram	5.1	−4.8
4	4	Canadian Mist	Brown-Forman	4.3	+3.1
5	5	Jim Beam	Beam-American Brands	4.1	+1.5
6	9	Popov	Heublein-Reynolds	4.0	+4.9
7	6	Windsor Supreme	National	3.8	—
8	7	Jack Daniel's	Brown Forman	3.6	−1.4
9	8	V.O.	Seagram	3.6	+0.6
10	10	Seagram Gin	Seagram	3.2	—

Source: John C. Maxwell, Jr., "The Liquor Industry in 1985." New York: Furman, Selz, Mager, Dietz & Birney.

Industry analysts, noting the overall drop in wine, beer, and liquor industry growth rates, concluded that many large companies would be milking the cash cows that were the liquor operations. As (1) life-styles move to white liquor and fruit juice or even totally away from alcoholic beverages, (2) advertising and labeling regulations increase (such as New York City's sign, "WARNING: Drinking alcoholic beverages during pregnancy can cause birth defects"), and (3) governments use alcoholic beverages as sources of increased excise taxes to close budget deficits, companies are expected to cut advertising and to prune brands within their liquor operation.

In 1985 analysts commented on Heublein's success with Popov, as well as National's wonder product, Peachtree Schnapps, which hit 1.5 million cases in one year. Peachtree schnapps had 50 percent of the schnapps market and was included in such new drink promotions as the "Fuzzy Navel," a combination of orange juice and Peachtree Schnapps.

Other new products in the mid-1980s were (1) alcohol in a can, as in Jim Beam ZZZingers, bourbon and soda in a can, (2) "digestives" based on European after-dinner drinks, and (3) sparkling liqueur, such as Schiefflin's Petite Liqueur, a combination of cognac and sparkling wine.

In 1985, imported liqueurs, imported brandy, imported rum, and imported vodka were the only distilled spirits showing any growth rates over 1984. Bonded and straight whiskeys were down 4.1 percent, blended whiskeys down 6.3 percent, Canadian down 0.3 percent, Scotch down 4.0 percent, domestic vodka down 1.4 percent, and domestic gin down 4.0 percent.

THE BREWING INDUSTRY

Beer Production Process

The brewing process for beer begins with a mash produced by grinding malted barley (malt). Hops and other aroma and taste determinants are added. Next, yeast is added, which ferments. Fermentation may take a week or less, and aging varies from a few days to a few months. Finally, beer is filtered, carbonated, and packaged.

The brewing industry ferments using a top-fermentation yeast to produce ale or a bottom-fermentation yeast to produce lager beer. Specialty brewing products include stout (heavier and darker than ale) and bock beer (dark brown in color because roasted malt is used).

The Brewers

The history of the brewing industry since World War II has been a history of increasing competition and concentration. The over 400 firms in 1945 shrunk to 250 in the mid-1950s, 150 in the mid-1960s, and 50 in the mid-1970s. The top ten brewers in the United States controlled 40 percent of the market in 1950, 50 percent in 1960, and 60 percent in 1965. The top twenty-five brewers had a market share of 60 percent in 1950 and 85 percent in 1965. By the mid-1970s the top four breweries' share of 20 percent in 1950 had become 60 percent.

In the mid-1960s the leading national breweries (Anheuser-Busch, Schlitz, and Pabst) competed with expanding regional breweries (Falstaff, Carling, and Hamm) and strong local breweries (National in Baltimore, Schmidt's in Philadelphia, Coors in Denver, Olympia in Washington State, Dixie in New Orleans, and Schaefer, Rheingold, and Ballantine in New York).

Industry analysts argue that there is little brand loyalty among beer drinkers. Advertising is an important part of strategy and is often tied to sports sponsorships.

Competition, especially in advertising, and industry concentration through expanding markets and acquisitions intensified in the 1970s. Industry observers attribute this intensification to Philip Morris's acquisition of Miller Brewing Company. Recognizing the significant economies of scale in the brewing industry, especially in marketing, Philip Morris applied their aggressive marketing strategies to Miller. Eventually, the other national brewers responded by increasing their marketing efforts. Exhibit 6 depicts the trend in advertising dollars per barrel among the industry leaders.

Analysts of the beer industry in the mid-1980s predicted (1) a stable cost environment, with slight but absorbable packaging and raw materials cost increases, (2) limited potential for volume improvement with domestic volume flat and a slight imported volume increase, (3) decreased capacity (1985 closings by Pabst, Stroh, and Miller reduced industry capacity by 20 million barrels or 10 percent), and (4) increased national competition as each national company sees the others as sources or opportunities for increasing the company's market shares, which should impact negatively on regional brewers. Anheuser-Busch and Coors were particularly cited as national brewers with expected strong market share gains. Anheuser moved toward its 40 percent market share objective by the end of the 1980s, and Coors grew in California, Florida, Texas, and New England, the last its primary 1985 expansion area. Coors' light beer experienced strong market growth recently, supported by aggressive marketing.

Ernest Nordtvedt described the effects of the intense marketing efforts of the large national brewers, such as Anheuser Busch and Miller, on a local brewery in his working paper "Dixie Brewing Company, Inc." (North American Case Research Association, 1986 annual meeting). Dixie was the "local beer" of New Orleans. Dixie was founded in 1907 and survived Prohibition by making ice cream, soft drinks, and "near beer." In 1969 Dixie had a market share of 29 percent and was the leading brand in New Orleans, selling 240,000 barrels of beer a year. By 1975 Dixie was producing 190,000 barrels of beer and its market share was 17 percent. By 1984 Dixie's production was under 100,000 barrels, as Dixie, like other regional brewers, suffered the consequences of both the intense advertising campaigns and increased price competition being waged by the national brewers. Dixie was at insolvency's door when it was sold to a beer distributor who was interested in private-label beer production. Selected financial data for Dixie follow:

	1984	1980	1976
Sales	$7,300,000	$11,800,000	$9,800,000
Operating profit	(600,000)	300,000	(200,000)
Total assets	2,700,000	4,300,000	3,200,000
Shareholders' equity	($1,800,000)	$ 2,700,000	$2,800,000

EXHIBIT 6 Top brewers' advertising, 1964–1979

	1964					1974					1977					1979			
	Barrels sold (000,000)	Rank	Advertising			Barrels sold (000,000)	Rank	Advertising			Barrels sold (000,000)	Rank	Advertising			Barrels sold (000,000)	Rank	Advertising	
			Million $	Per barrel				Million $	Per barrel				Million $	Per barrel				Million $	Per barrel
Anheuser-Busch	10	1	$33	$3.30		34	1	$12	$0.35		37	1	$45	$1.22		46	1	$87	$1.89
Schlitz	8	2	$34	$4.25		23	2	$18	$0.78		22	3	$40	$1.82		17	3	$49	$2.87
Pabst	7	3	$16	$2.29		14	3	$ 8	$0.57		16	4	$11	$0.69		15	4	$18	$1.22
Falstaff	6	4	$15	$2.50		—	—	—	—		—	—	—	—		—	—	—	—
Carling	5	5	$16	$3.20		—	—	—	—		—	—	—	—		—	—	—	—
Coors	—	—	—	—		12	4	$ 1	$0.08		13	5	$ 4	$0.31		13	5	$15	$1.16
Miller	—	—	—	—		9	5	$12	$1.33		24	2	$42	$1.75		36	2	$76	$2.10

Source: Advertising in *Leading National Advertisers*; barrel sales in *Advertising Age*, for selected years.

National brewers suffered as much as local brewers such as Dixie. Pabst, for example, was the first U.S. brewer with plants coast to coast, and was once the largest brewer in America. By 1980 a battle began that saw Irwin (Irv the liquidator) Jacobs trying to buy Pabst, Pabst pursuing Schlitz, Schmidt's and Heileman pursuing Pabst, and Heileman finally gaining control of Pabst after Pabst obtained Olympia and Lone Star. Heileman took Olympia, Lone Star, and the important breweries, and sold the empty shell of Pabst to Paul Kalmanovitz, an owner of once popular regional beers such as Ballantine, Lucky Lager, Jax and Pearl. Pabst Blue Ribbon sales fell from 13 million barrels in 1978 to 6 million in 1984.

The beer industry had seen, by 1985, the disappearance of major 1980 competitors as well as the elimination of regional brewers such as Dixie. Olympia, Pabst, and Schlitz were all part of larger brewers. Anheuser-Busch, which had a market share of 28 percent in 1980, had responded aggressively, if belatedly, to the Miller threat. Miller, for its part, had reached a 21 percent market share in 1985, down slightly from its 22 percent peak. Stroh, a 4 percent market share in 1980, had acquired Schlitz and a 13 percent market share by 1985. Some formerly successful brands seemed to be following a liquidation strategy.

Coors, Budweiser, and Miller were expected to continue their national strategies based upon national consumer identification similar to the soft drink industry. These national brewers, however, were faced with competition outside the industry — white wine, wine coolers, diet drinks, and fruit juices as substitutes for beer. These substitute products, the antialcohol social action programs, and the current health-and-exercise life-style all led to a sober forecast for the brewing industry.

Miller revamped its national strategy in the face of its declining sales of Miller's High Life (23.3 million barrels in 1979 — second to Budweiser's 31.4 million — versus 20.3 million in 1982 and 14.1 million in 1984). Miller changed advertising agencies and themes — from Backer & Speilvogel's "Welcome to Miller Time" to J. Walter Thompson's "Made the American Way" — and introduced a packaged draft beer (Miller Genuine Draft — "Look guys, no keg") to capitalize on continued market research that indicated consumers preferred draft beer. Although Coors is also a draft beer, a Miller spokesperson noted that Coors had not promoted that attribute, and consumers did not think of Coors as a draft beer (*Advertising Age,* February 16, 1987, p. 59).

Coors has risen from twelfth to fourth place among the nation's brewers in the second half of the 1960s, but slipped to fifth place in 1975 and sixth in 1982. William (chairman and CEO) and Joseph (president and COO) Coors wrote in their 1981 Annual Report that "we intend to move Coors back into the number one position in our sales territory." Joseph Coors' son Peter, division president, commented:

> *Miller changed the ball game by applying cigarette marketing concepts, and Anheuser responded with a vengeance. We were late fighting back.*
>
> *Coors was perceived as America's fine light beer. Then Miller's Lite came out. In 1978 we hit with Coors Light, a move that saved our bacon.*"[2]

[2] Hinkle and Stineman, op. cit., p. 438.

Peter Coors noted further that "our products were so popular we didn't have to put much effort into marketing." Coors' increased advertising efforts follow:[3]

Year	Amount
1977	$15,500,000
1978	$33,500,000
1979	$46,400,000
1980	$66,800,000
1981	$84,500,000
1982 (estimated)	$80,000,000

Anheuser-Busch has consistently followed a production economies strategy by means of large volume. Adolphus Busch, the son-in-law of Eberhard Anheuser, who financed the original St. Louis brewery, pioneered the pasteurization of beer and developed a national beer market using a fleet of refrigerated freight cars put into service in 1877. August A. Busch III was the fifth Busch to occupy the position when he was made CEO of Anheuser-Busch in 1975.

The brewing industry's increased concentration through internal expansion — as opposed to acquisition — was mirrored by the growth of Anheuser-Busch (A-B). A-B and Miller might share 70 percent of the market by 1990. Having sufficient resources to battle the marketing strategy of Phillip Morris (Miller), A-B uses its resources to underwrite major advertising campaigns and to put several products into the market segments where Miller was successful. For example, A-B waited four years, but then it introduced Bud Light, Natural Light and Michelob Light to battle Miller's Lite. A-B's strategy was to place two products in each category on each side of Miller's products. Budweiser and Busch, for example, compete with Miller High Life.

Since the mid-1980s, A-B's market share continued to increase, while Miller's premium brands, High Life and Lowenbrau, were declining. Industry analysts declared A-B the winner in the war for market share.

As these national firms compete, industry analysts underline Coors' and Anheuser's gross profit advantage over competition. Marc Cohen, writing in "The Brewing Industry" for Sanford C. Bernstein & Co., New York (March 1986), estimated gross profit per barrel by brewer for 1985 as follows:

Coors	$24.35
Anheuser-Busch	23.45
Miller	19.30
Heileman	13.55
Average	$21.25

Operating profit per barrel was estimated by Goldman Sachs research for 1983 as $10.50 for Anheuser-Busch, $6.06 for Miller Brewing, $10.47 for Coors, $1.08 for Pabst, $5.94 for Heileman, and $7.96 for the industry on the average. For

[3] Hinkle and Stineman, op. cit., p. 443.

1980 these same data were Anheuser-Busch, $5.73; Miller, $3.88; Schlitz/Stroh, $2.01; Coors, $6.29; Pabst, $1.42; Heileman, $4.78; and the average industry, $4.56.[4]

Exhibit 7 summarizes Bernstein's estimates of the total U.S. market by segments; Exhibit 8, shipments and shares of U.S. brewers; Exhibit 9, volume and share of premium; Exhibit 10, volume and share of light; and Exhibit 11, volume and share of popular-priced beers. Imported beer brands are covered in Exhibit 12.

Brewer capacity and number of breweries was estimated by Goldman Sachs research department for 1983 as follows:[5]

Company	1983 capacity (millions of barrels)	Number of breweries
Anheuser-Busch	66.0	11
Miller Brewing	44.0	6
Stroh	29.0	7
Pabst Brewing	14.0	4
Adolph Coors	15.0	1
Heileman	26.0	11
Others	27.9	38
Total	220.9	78

EXHIBIT 7
Brewing industry barrelage and market segmentation

	1980	1984
Barrelage (millions of barrels)		
Imports	4.6	7.2
Superpremiums	10.1	8.8
Premium	96.0	83.2
Light	23.5	36.0
Popular	40.8	43.2
Malt liquor	5.2	5.7
All others	1.0	1.1
Market share		
Imports	2.5%	3.9%
Superpremiums	5.6	4.8
Premium	53.0	44.9
Light	13.0	19.4
Popular	22.5	23.3
Malt liquor	2.8	3.1
All others	0.6	0.6
Total	100.0%	100.0%

Source: R. S. Weinberg and Associates, The Beer Institute, and Bernstein estimates.

[4] A. A. Thompson, Jr. and A. J. Strickland III, *Strategic Management* (Plano, TX: Business Publications, 1987), p. 519.

[5] Thompson and Strickland, op. cit., p. 497.

EXHIBIT 8
Shipments and
market share of U.S.
brewers

	1980	1984
Shipments (millions of barrels)		
Anheuser-Busch	50.2	64.0
Miller	37.3	37.5
Stroh	6.2	23.9
Heileman	13.3	16.8
Coors	13.8	13.2
Other	60.5	29.8
Total	181.2	185.2
Market share		
Anheuser-Busch	27.7%	34.6%
Miller	20.6	20.3
Stroh	3.4	12.9
Heileman	7.3	9.1
Coors	7.6	7.1
Other	33.4	16.1
Total	100.0%	100.0%

Source: *Beer Marketers Insights*, corporate reports, and Bernstein estimates.

Modern Brewery Age Blue Book for 1978 had estimated 1978 capacity in millions of barrels for the top five brewers as Anheuser-Busch, 44.3; Miller, 28.0; Schlitz, 32.0; Pabst, 19.0; and Coors, 15.0.

THE WINE INDUSTRY

Wine Markets and Production

The wine market may be segmented into (1) cocktail and dessert wines, such as sherries or ports, which are heavy and sweet with a high alcohol percentage (14–20 percent); (2) sparkling wines such as champagne or "pop" wines, which are given "bubbles" by putting carbon dioxide into a second fermentation process; and (3) table wines with 10–14 percent alcohol content. The higher-quality table wines use grape varietals such as burgundy, cabernet sauvignon, or pinot chardonnay.

The production economics vary according to grape costs and marketing, with production costs being relatively constant except in very low or very high quality wines. Exhibit 13 breaks down production and marketing costs for high-quality, low-volume imported wine and an above-average-quality, high-volume U.S. domestic wine.

Wine Companies

Gallo was not only the dominant U.S. producer, but was also the world's largest by the 1980s. Gallo's 50 million cases of volume early in the 1980s clearly outweighed

EXHIBIT 9
Brewing industry
segmentation for
regular premium
beers

	1980	1984
Volume by brand (millions of barrels)		
Budweiser	34.6	44.5
Miller High Life	23.1	13.9
Coors Premium	11.3	8.5
Stroh	5.6	5.3
Old Style	3.9	4.1
Others	17.5	6.9
Total	96.0	83.2
Share by brand		
Budweiser	36.0%	53.5%
Miller High Life	24.1	16.7
Coors Premium	11.7	10.2
Stroh	5.8	6.4
Old Style	4.1	4.9
Others	18.3	8.3
Total	100.0%	100.0%
Share by company		
Anheuser-Busch	36.0%	53.5%
Miller	24.1	16.7
Coors	11.7	10.2
Heileman	6.3	7.6
Stroh	5.8	6.4
Others	16.1	5.6
Total	100.0%	100.0%

Source: *Beer Marketers Insights,* R. S. Weinberg and Associates, corporate reports, and Bernstein estimates.

the other U.S. national wine companies, such as Heublein (23 million), Seagram (20 million), and Coca-Cola's Wine Spectrum (9 million). Many foreign wine producers ranging from high-quality to the "fun" wines (Riunite, with 9 million cases) entered the U.S. market in anticipation of the time when the average U.S. consumption would move from its 1980 amount of about 8 liters to California's 17 liters or, eventually, to Germany's 25 liters.

The cost structure of the U.S. wine companies varied significantly with strategy. A fully integrated company (one with in-house grapes and glass manufacturing) with modern production facilities — such as Gallo — was estimated by an industry observer to have a pretax return on sales of 15–20 percent. A lower-quality grape and minimal production costs of a Riunite might mean a 25 percent pretax return on sales, even considering marketing costs. On the other hand, a full-line national wine company that lacked vertical integration might be faced with low returns on

EXHIBIT 10
Brewing industry
segmentation for
light beers

	1980	1984
Volume by brand (millions of barrels)		
Lite	13.0	17.9
Coors Light	2.5	4.6
Bud Light	—	4.3
Michelob Light	2.2	2.4
Old Milwaukee Light	0.1	1.5
Natural Light	2.2	1.1
Others	3.5	4.3
Total	23.5	36.0
Share by brand		
Lite	55.3%	49.7%
Coors Light	10.6	12.6
Bud Light	0.0	11.8
Michelob Light	9.1	6.7
Old Milwaukee Light	0.6	4.2
Natural Light	9.4	3.1
Others	14.9	11.9
Total	100.0%	100.0%
Share by company		
Miller	55.3%	49.7%
Anheuser-Busch	18.6	21.5
Coors	10.6	12.6
Stroh	2.1	6.7
Heileman	2.1	2.9
Others	11.3	6.5
Total	100.0%	100.0%

Source: *Beer Marketers Insights*, R. S. Weinberg and Associates, corporate reports, and Bernstein estimates.

sales (3 percent) for its generic table wines, which are often half or even more of its business.

Industry analysts, for example, noted the difference between Paul Masson's table wine margin of less than 5 percent versus Gallo's 25–30 percent profit margin. Paul Masson's champagnes and sparkling wines equaled Gallo's overall margins, but they were only 10 percent of Masson's sales. Wine prices for generic table wines could not get too high because of Gallo's dominance, which was especially noticeable in supermarkets.

Heublein, the number two U.S. producer, had Inglenook, Italian Swiss Colony, Petrie, and other brands in its United Vintners wine subsidiary. United Vintners'

EXHIBIT 11
Brewing industry
segmentation of
popular-priced
beers

	1980	1984
Volume by brand (millions of barrels)		
Old Milwaukee	4.6	7.0
Busch	2.9	5.1
Schaefer	2.8	4.0
Milwaukee's Best	—	2.4
Pabst Blue Ribbon	9.6	5.4
Carling	1.0	1.8
Meister Brau	—	1.7
Others	19.9	15.8
Total	40.8	43.2
Share by brand		
Old Milwaukee	11.3%	16.2%
Busch	7.2	11.8
Schaefer	6.7	9.3
Milwaukee's Best	—	5.6
Pabst Blue Ribbon	23.5	12.5
Carling	2.5	4.2
Meister Brau	—	3.9
Others	48.8	36.6
Total	100.0%	100.0%
Share by company		
Stroh	0.5%	32.1%
Anheuser-Busch	7.2	11.8
Heileman	11.4	15.0
Miller	—	9.5
Others	80.9	31.6
Total	100.0%	100.0%

Source: *Beer Marketers Insights*, R. S. Weinberg and Associates, corporate reports, and Bernstein estimates.

numerous brands and ten separate production facilities resulted in a lack of economies
of scale.

The Taylor California Cellar's brands within Coca-Cola's Wine Spectrum were
especially aggressive advertisers. The beverage industry publication, *Impact,* estimated that Taylor California Cellars spent $1.72 per case on advertising ($8 million
in total) versus $1.64 for Paul Masson ($12 million in total) or $0.50 for Gallo
($22 million in total).

Major wine companies selling in the United States include Almaden, Brown
Forman, Coca-Cola's Taylor, Gallo, Riunite, Seagram's Paul Masson, and United
Vintners.

EXHIBIT 12
Imported beer sales and shares

Brand	Rank 1984	Rank 1980	Millions of barrels 1984	Millions of barrels 1980	Market share 1984	Market share 1980
Heineken	1	1	2.4	1.7	33.1%	37.8%
Molson	2	2	1.0	1.0	13.4	22.4
Beck's	3	3	0.6	0.2	9.0	5.1
Moosehead	4	6	0.5	0.2	6.5	4.0
Labatt's	5	5	0.3	0.2	4.5	4.9
St. Pauli Girl	6	7	0.3	0.1	3.7	1.7
Dos Equis	7	4	0.2	0.2	2.4	4.9
Carling O'Keefe	8	—	0.2	—	2.2	—
Amstel Light	9	8	0.1	0.1	1.8	0.3
Corona Extra	10	—	0.1	—	1.7	—
Total			5.7	3.7	78.3	81.4

Source: John C. Maxwell, Jr., "Annual Brewing Survey." New York: Furman, Selz, Mager, Dietz & Birney, November 8, 1985.

Almaden produced only about one-fifth of its wine, purchasing grapes crushed by or wines produced by others. Almaden's creativity was evidenced by its packaging, as it introduced the 1.5-liter jug wine in the 1970s and supplied at least half the boxed wine sold in the United States during the 1980s.

Brown-Forman Distillers built from an extended relationship with Korbel Champagne and duplicated its premium image (Jack Daniel's Tennessee Whiskey, Old Bushmills' Irish Whiskey, and Martel cognacs) in its wines. It acquired distribution

EXHIBIT 13
Estimated cost breakdown

	U.S. domestic premium[a]	High-quality French import
Grapes	55%	25%
Production	20%	45%
Advertising	5%	15%
Selling	10%	5%
Other marketing, including excise taxes	10%	10%
Retail price per bottle (1980)	$2.40	$6.50

[a] Such as Gallo, Masson, or Taylor.

rights to Bolla and Cella wines in 1968, Noilly Prat vermouth in 1971, and a 25-year extension of its Korbel rights in 1978. It also acquired a 40 percent interest in Bolla in 1972. Brown-Forman's premium market image is supported, then, in wine with an importation and distribution strategy.

Taylor Wines were carrying Coca-Cola's marketing strategy into quality wines. Taylor initially concentrated in the early 1980s in marketing, advertising, and distribution, innovating with comparison taste tests and aggressive couponing.

Gallo's profitability (estimated at about 10 percent return on sales and assets in the early 1980s, with both sales and assets estimated at approximately $500,000,000) was due to its economies of scale. Gallo was dominant in its production, marketing, and distribution. Production economies including crushing, bottling costs (which were perhaps one-half of its competitors' due to its speed of production), storage (Gallo had four large production facilities, which transferred technology from plant to plant), and grape costs. Its distribution economies were volume-related, as Gallo often achieved supermarket turnover double its closest competitors'. Gallo's lower-priced wine was Carlo Rossi, and it also produced dessert and sparkling wines. Gallo's market share was estimated at one-fourth nationally and over one-third in supermarkets.

Riunite's "fun" wine obviously filled a market need, as it increased by 50 percent in the 1970s based on its sweet wine that introduced non–wine drinkers to wine. Riunite was the largest Italian producer, so that its lower labor cost and concentrated (U.S. only) marketing allowed it to compete favorably with U.S. wines.

Seagram's majority of wine sales came from Paul Masson, a premium wine that competed with Gallo and the increasingly strong Taylor. Seagram also marketed imported (Barton & Gustier, Mumm) and high-quality, low-volume varietals.

United Vintners, Heublein's wine division, had a large number of brands which worked against economies of scale. An industry observer thought the company would be a successful competitor if it could upgrade its Colony label to the premium category.

Exhibit 14 suggests a way of analyzing wine products in terms of price per bottle and marketing effort per bottle.

By the early 1980s U.S. wine distribution was essentially (92 percent) handled by individual wholesalers. Three-quarters of those wholesalers also handled spirits. An industry observer noted that Gallo distributed 60 percent of its product through supermarkets versus 40 percent for Seagram's Paul Masson. Seagram was 5 percent higher than Gallo in liquor chains (25 percent versus 20 percent) and liquor stores (20 percent vs. 15 percent), and 10 percent higher in on-premise outlets such as restaurants.

Other U.S. domestic wineries may utilize independent, high-quality strategies or else private labels or subcontracting excess capacity. Franzia, for example, provides a significant part of Taylor's grape supply, Taylor having none of its own grapes. Taylor California Cellars wine was bottled at Franzia's bottling facility in the late 1970s and early 1980s.

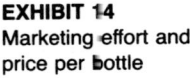

EXHIBIT 14
Marketing effort and
price per bottle

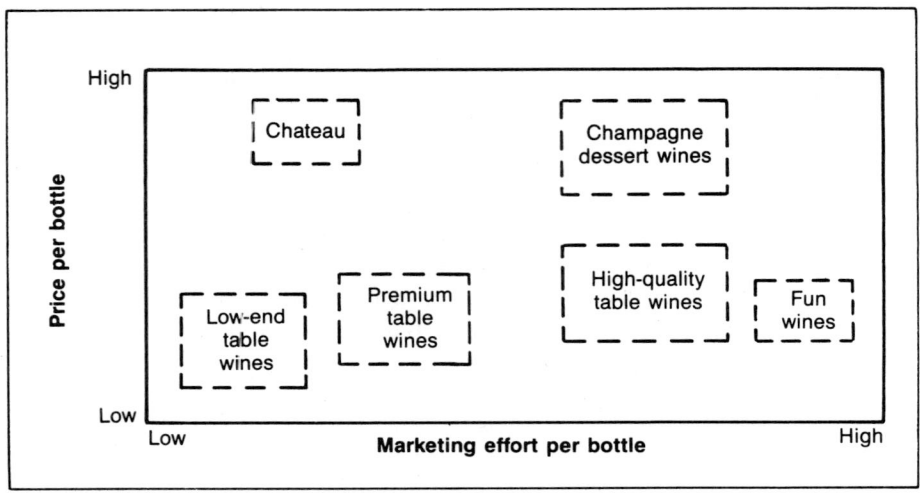

Coca-Cola Inc., acquired Taylor Wines in 1977 and stirred up the wine industry just as Miller had done to the brewing industry by introducing market segmentation strategies. Coca-Cola used couponing, aggressive supermarket distribution, and comparative taste tests to promote a national wine line, Taylor California Cellars. This line consisted of four generic wines — burgundy, chablis, rhine, and rose — bottled by Franzia Brothers.

By 1981 the liquor industry leader, Seagram, was studying the wine business. In a report on her strategic planning for Seagram's wine efforts, Mary Cunningham concluded that Seagram's major competitors, Gallo, Taylor, and Banfi-Riunite, have greater economies of scale, lower costs, and more market focus than Seagram's Paul Masson and related brands. Ms. Cunningham urged constructing an East Coast facility to use transportation costs against Gallo and Taylor. This proposed facility would use frozen-concentrate technology and overseas grape sources to make "fun" and "light" wines.

The Cunningham report also predicted that the 1980 base of 200 million cases of wine a year — Gallo, 51; Heublein (United Vintner, Inglenook, Swiss Colony), 23; Seagram, 20; National Distillers (Almaden), 14; Taylor Wine Spectrum, 9; and Riunite, 9 — would increase by 410 million if the United States matched German consumption levels and by 225 million if the United States reached California levels. Normal growth would result in an increase of 140 million by the mid-1980s.

Seagram had a world-wide wine asset investment of $600 million, with $150 million in Paul Masson. Ms. Cunningham suggested a long-term additional Masson investment of about $450 million.

In 1983, however, Coca-Cola decided to unload their wine business, and Edgar

Bronfman, Seagram chairman, purchased Coke's wine business for $200 million. While many warned that Taylor and Masson were competing brands, Edgar argued that "by acquiring the Wine Spectrum we could have a short cut to profitability simply by economies of scale." The profitability short-cut apparently didn't work; Seagram sold Taylor plus Paul Masson for less than it paid for Taylor.

Edgar Jr., Seagram's heir apparent, meanwhile revised the "moderation" advertising begun by his grandfather and began a national equivalency campaign — 1 ¼ ounces of 80-proof whisky being the same as a 12-ounce can of beer and a 5-ounce glass of wine.

Observers commented that Seagram had not been successful in introducing new products into the U.S. market. For example, the introduction of Canadian vodka as an "imported" vodka was a failure, and the long-term prospects seemed better for Seagram's 20 percent interest in DuPont rather than in the slow growth "brown goods" business. Although Edgar Bronfman asserted that "you can get just as drunk drinking cheap stuff as expensive stuff," half of Seagram's beverage profits came from five brands — Chivas Regal, Crown Royal, 7 Crown, V.O., and Seagram's Gin — in the 1980s.

Wine industry analysts not only had to deal with mergers and changing strategies, but with new-product complexities. The central new-product question in the mid-1980s was the wine cooler. Do wine coolers compete with wine? With beer? With soft drinks?

Sutter Home Winery started a new-product trend when it sought a solution to its oversupply of zinfandel grapes. In 1979 Sutter introduced a few thousand cases of white zinfandel, which it increased to 25,000 cases in 1980. Blush wines — fruity, light pink wines offering the white wine drinker more choice and flavor — were off and booming. Sutter made 1.5 million cases of white zinfandel in 1985 and aimed at 2.25 million in 1987. By the mid-1980s over 100 wineries made blush wine.

ALCOHOLIC BEVERAGE INDUSTRY CASES

The Ontario Wine Industry. The heavily regulated Ontario wineries are becoming increasingly concentrated. While the powerful grape growers resist conversion to higher-quality grapes, the trends in consumer tastes seem to mandate some major product upgrading by the Ontario companies.

Inniskillin. A new, very small Ontario winery formed in 1974 to make high-quality wine is contemplating significant expansion in 1978.

Joseph Schlitz. By the end of 1980 Schlitz, once the number one brewer in the United States, had slipped to fourth place behind Anheuser-Busch, Miller, and Pabst. Plant expansion in the mid-1970s was straining resources at a time when Miller, backed by Philip Morris, was greatly intensifying competition in an already highly competitive industry. Further, Schlitz changed its formula and technology, with a resulting taste change in the mid-1970s. This taste change lost the company many Schlitz fans.

Finally, Schlitz faces a stockholder-management conflict, aggravated by the fact that the majority of stockholders are members of the family that owned and led the Schlitz Company for over one hundred years.

The Adolph Coors Company. Coors has pursued a single product strategy, producing Coors at a single brewery using Rocky Mountain spring water and natural ingredients. This family-run organization asks itself in 1983 if it can continue to be a regional brewer.

THE ONTARIO WINE INDUSTRY

Winemaking began in Canada in 1636. The first vintners were Jesuit missionaries who made sacramental wine (it is said) from native grapes growing along the St. Lawrence River. The first commercial enterprise of record, however, was Clair House, established near Toronto in 1811 by Corporal Johann Schiller. The oldest continuing winery was founded by George Barnes in Toronto in 1873.

The cultivation of domestic grapes was developed in Southern Ontario coincident with the opening of the commercial wineries. By the turn of the century over 4,000 acres were in production and by 1916 Canada had ten wine companies. After the first World War, production and the number of companies grew at an even faster rate, swept along by the contrary political currents of the prohibition movement. Due to pressure from grape growers, wine escaped the clutches of the Ontario Temperance Act and became the only alcoholic beverage legally sold in Ontario. By 1926 there were forty-five companies and by 1927, fifty-seven.

As the only legal supplier of alcohol in Ontario with a large, if illegal, export market in the United States, the industry had to struggle hard to meet demand. With considerable effort and by adding formaldehyde, coal tar, and dyes to provide flavor, body, and color to the wines, some companies managed to "stretch" a ton of grapes from a normal yield of 700 l of wine to as much as 2,700 l.

Unfortunately, what the government gave, it could also take away. In 1927 the Ontario Temperance Act was repealed. The Liquor Control Board of Ontario (LCBO) was set up to control the sale of alcohol. The LCBO established quality standards for wine and tested to ensure that they were met. By 1930 there were only about twenty-seven Ontario wine companies and by 1943 only eight remained. Between 1927 and 1973 no new wineries were licenced in Ontario.

THE CANADIAN AND ONTARIO WINE MARKET

Between 1964 and 1976 per capita wine consumption in Canada increased spectacularly at an 11 percent compounded rate. This growth was paralleled in other historically

Case prepared by Joseph N. Fry with Christopher J. Bart and Paul W. Beamish. © The University of Western Ontario. Reprinted by permission.

EXHIBIT 1

Consumption of
wine in liters per
capita in selected
countries

	1964	1976	Compound growth rate
France	124.0	101.30	(1.6%)
Italy	106.0	99.70	(0.5)
Portugal	83.0	97.80	1.3
Spain	65.0	71.00	0.7
Switzerland	41.0	43.50	0.5
Hungary	31.0	34.00	0.7
West Germany	13.0	23.60	5.1
Czechoslovakia	4.0	16.50	12.5
Belgium	8.0	15.70	5.7
U.S.S.R.	4.0	13.40	10.6
Denmark	3.0	12.53	12.6
The Netherlands	3.0	11.34	11.7
Australia	6.0	11.20	5.3
Sweden	4.0	8.47	6.4
Canada	2.0	7.00	11.0
United States	4.0	6.64	4.3
United Kingdom	2.0	5.64	9.0

Source: GATT statistics.

low-use countries such as Czechoslovakia, Denmark, and the Netherlands (Exhibit 1). In contrast, per capita consumption in the traditionally "heavy-consumption" countries, such as France, Italy, Portugal, and Spain, exhibited the marginal growth pattern of a mature commodity.

In terms of growth, wine consumption in Canada also outpaced consumption of other alcoholic beverage categories. The Canadian annual growth rates for wine, spirits, and beer in the 1964–1976 period were 11, 3, and less than 1 percent, respectively, on a per capita basis.

The increasing popularity of wine in Canada was attributed to a number of forces including increased affluence and sophistication, lower drinking ages, and persuasive marketing programs. Regardless of their particular influences on overall consumption, these same forces also fundamentally changed the wine-type preferences in the market.

Traditionally, Canadians favored the high-alcohol, fortified dessert, or appetizer wines — those with 14–20 percent alcohol and particularly those that cost less than $2.50 for a 750 ml bottle. As one industry wag put it some time ago, "Canadians make their wine purchases on the basis of the biggest bang for the buck." More recently, however, reflecting the impact of the not necessarily consistent phenomena of increased sophistication and mass merchandising, there has been a pronounced shift in consumption to the low-alcohol table and sparkling wines. (See Exhibit 2.)

EXHIBIT 2
Trends in con-
sumption of wine
in Canada

	12 months ended March 31					
	1972	*1973*	*1974*	*1975*	*1976*	*1977*
Not exceeding 14% alcohol by volume	51,400	64,400	70,300	78,200	86,700	101,600
% of total	49.7%	56.5%	60.2%	63.7%	65.6%	70.8%
14–20% alcohol by volume	52,100	49,600	46,500	44,500	45,400	42,000
% of total	50.3%	43.5%	39.8%	36.3%	34.4%	29.2%
Totals	103,500	114,000	116,800	122,700	132,100	143,600

Note: Measures in thousands of liters.
Source: Wine Council of Canada (originally calculated in imperial gallons).

Domestic Versus Import Supply

Coincident with growing consumption and shifting tastes, the share of the Canadian market held by domestic producers declined steadily, and by 1977 imports had captured over half the market. (See Exhibit 3.)

The Ontario Market

Trends in the Ontario market paralleled the national experience. Table wines increased dramatically in popularity (Exhibit 4). Imports steadily increased their share, and, of particular importance to Ontario producers, Ontario wine production, as a share of national wine production, dropped from 76 percent in 1967 to 62 percent in 1974.

The shift in market preference to table wines caught the Ontario wine industry unprepared. They were poorly armed in reputation, skills, grape supply, or flexibility of structure to do battle with imports.

Traditionally, Ontario wines were made from the native northeastern American labrusca grape — grapes hardy enough to survive the Canadian winter, but possessing a distinctively sharp "foxy" taste. This taste could be disguised in fortified wines

EXHIBIT 3
Wine sold in Canada

	12 months ended March 31					
	1972	*1973*	*1974*	*1975*	*1976*	*1977*
Canadian-produced wine sales	67,700	72,200	71,200	69,300	69,300	69,900
% share	65.4%	63.3%	61.0%	56.5%	52.5%	48.7%
Foreign wine sales	35,800	41,800	45,700	53,400	62,700	73,800
% share	34.6%	36.7%	39.0%	43.5%	47.5%	51.3%
Totals	103,500	114,000	116,900	122,700	132,000	143,700

Note: Measures in thousands of liters.
Source: Canadian Wine Institute Report (originally calculated in imperial gallons).

EXHIBIT 4
Wine consumption
in Ontario in (000)
liters by type and
origin

Class	1972–1973	1973–1974	1974–1975	1975–1976	1976–1977
Ports, sherries, and other dessert wines	12,400	12,400	12,000	11,900	11,700
% Canadian	69	66	61	58	56
Full sparkling, champagne, etc.	1,300	1,900	1,400	1,600	1,900
% Canadian	69	77	61	56	55
Table wines					
Crackling	2,500	2,100	2,000	2,000	2,400
% Canadian	67	56	51	47	45
Rosé	3,200	3,300	3,600	3,700	3,900
% Canadian	49	43	39	39	41
Red	6,700	7,500	8,900	10,700	12,800
% Canadian	39	38	34	33	34
White	4,300	4,800	5,400	7,100	9,600
% Canadian	41	38	33	28	27
Total table	16,700	17,800	19,900	23,600	28,600
% Canadian	46	41	37	34	33
7% Sparkling	2,300	2,900	3,500	4,200	4,700
% Canadian	100	100	100	100	100
Cider	400	500	700	1,000	900
% Canadian	91	90	87	89	84
Grand total	33,100	35,400	37,500	42,200	47,900
% Canadian	60	57	53	49	47

Note: Percentages are percentage of class by volume by year. Quantities were originally estimated in imperial gallons.

or ameliorated sparkling wines but made the labrusca grape quite unsuitable for the production of table wine. While market tastes centered on fortified wines, no serious problem was apparent. As tastes changed, however, the industry shifted very slowly to using a series of hybrid grapes (a cross between the European vitis vinifera grape and the vitis riparia or vitis rupestris) suitable for quality table wines. The hybrids, in fact, did not become available in commercial quantities until the mid-1970s.

By the mid-1970s, imports dominated the Ontario table wine market, particularly in the medium- and premium-priced segments (Exhibit 5). Canadian table wines, regardless of origin, were confined to the low-price segment and had, through years of marked indifference or uncertainty, acquired a less than impeccable reputation.

This phenomenon raised the question of whether the rising market share of imported wines was the result of a perceived higher quality or whether consumers simply associated higher quality with higher price. U.S. studies found that price and perceived quality were closely correlated. Despite this correlation, low-priced imported table

EXHIBIT 5

Wine consumption in Ontario by price and origin as a percentage of total market by wine type, 1976–1977

	Low price (less than $2.50)		Medium price ($2.50 to $4.00)		Premium price (greater than $4.00)		Total %
	C	I	C	I	C	I	
Table wines							
Red	33.6	20.9	—	36.3	—	9.2	100.0
White	26.2	9.3	—	57.3	—	7.2	100.0
Rosé	41.6	1.7	—	56.5	—	0.1	100.0

Low-price segment
— Less than $2.50/750 ml
— Less than $3.33/l (1,000 ml)
Medium-price segment
— $2.50–$4.00 for 750 ml
— $3.33–$5.33 for 1,000 ml
C — Canadian.
I — Imported.

High-price segment
— Greater than $4.00/750 ml
— Greater than $5.33/l

Source: LCBO price list, LCBO statistics.

wines were consumed at a high enough rate in Ontario to indicate that European table wines were perceived as innately superior to the domestic products.

The problem for Ontario wineries was even more complex, however, for they were forced, by regulation, to use Ontario-grown grapes almost exclusively and the new hybrids were widely regarded as the highest-priced in the world.

For example, wineries in British Columbia could import bulk wine for bottling from California for as little as 22 cents per liter before transportation costs. The same product, made either in British Columbia or Ontario from locally grown grapes, was estimated to cost between 80 and 85 cents per liter; 50 cents per liter for the raw grape juice alone and 30–35 cents per liter for processing. In addition, wine was conventionally shipped by rail. The cost of rail transportation from Kelowna, British Columbia, to Toronto, Ontario, was approximately 12.5 cents per 750 ml bottle. Consequently, the ability of Ontario wineries to compete in terms of cost and, in some instances, quality with other Canadian wine manufacturers (who could import substantial quantities of grape juices or concentrates) deteriorated.

Over the years, provincial liquor control boards had developed ways of offering preferential treatment (for example, in price and display) to locally produced wines. In 1978 Ontario provincial table wines and champagne were subject to a 47 percent markup from the producer's selling price, while "out-of-province" wines and imported wines were marked up 105 percent and 123 percent, respectively. Other provinces had their own but similar schemes as shown in Exhibit 6. A small annual drop in sales of Ontario wines to other provinces was experienced after 1972, partly as a result of this form of provincial protectionism.

EXHIBIT 6

Selected provincial liquor commission markups for 1977

Ontario	
Ontario table wines and champagne	37%
Ontario fortified, dessert, and 7% sparkling	60
All out-of-province wines	95
Imported wines	117
Quebec	
All Quebec-made wines	85
All out-of-province wines	95
No information on imported wines	
British Columbia	
B.C. table, sparkling, and crackling wines and champagne	45
B.C. fortified and dessert wines	78
All other Canadian wines and imported table, sparkling, and crackling wines and champagne	100
Imported fortified and dessert wines (uncertain)	113–122
New Brunswick	
Canadian and imported dessert wines	132
Canadian and imported table wines and sparkling wines	105

Note: Ontario markups increased in 1978.
Source: Canadian Wine Institute.

Wine Types and the Wine Drinker

In Ontario the wine market was conventionally segmented into three major classes: (1) appetizers and desserts, (2) table wines, and (3) crackling and sparkling wines. The first category represented heavy and sweet wines, such as ports and sherries, with a high alcohol content (14 percent to 20 percent by volume). They required aging for at least 3 years. Table wines, the second class, included reds, whites, and rosés, usually with 10 percent to 14 percent alcohol content by volume. Some crackling and full-strength sparkling wines were also grouped into this category. The third classification differentiated between crackling and sparkling wines on the basis of effervescence. This bubbly effect was caused by introducing carbon dioxide during a secondary fermentation process. Also included in this third group were the 14 percent alcohol champagnes and the 7 percent alcohol "pop wines" such as Baby Duck and Baby Bear. Consumers believed these 7 percent alcohol wines resembled "soda pop" — hence the name "pop wines."

Exhibit 7 presents a forecast, prepared by the LCBO, of wine consumption by class through 1984.

The wine consumer in the mid-1970s, ignored for some time, became the subject of a number of market studies sponsored by such groups as the Canadian Wine Institute[1] and the Ontario Wine Council.[2] These studies found that:

[1] Canadian Wine Institute, "A History" (August 1977) and "Statistical Tables and Wine Information Materials" (August 1977).

[2] Currie Lehman Ltd., "Report to the Wine Council of Ontario" (1976).

1. Growth of the total wine consumption was related to growth of the total adult population, but more particularly, growth in per capita consumption was highly related to growth in disposable income.

2. Wine tended to be used as a substitute for beer, but as a complement for spirits and was more income-sensitive (in demand) than either.

3. Wine was a lightly used beverage. Only 40 percent of Ontario adults had used wine as compared to 52 percent who used beer, 69 percent who used liquor, and 75 percent who used soft drinks. Even among wine users, consumption was low, averaging 3 ounces per week compared to corresponding figures of 70 ounces of beer and 7 ounces of liquor.

4. Wine consumption was associated with particular occasions — while entertaining guests, during the evening meal, or during the Christmas/New Year season.

5. Age, education, and sex all influenced wine consumption. As with soft drinks and beer, per capita consumption was highest in the eighteen- to twenty-four-year-old age group. The high-school educated accounted for 55 percent of the adult population and 65 percent of wine consumption. There was a distinct preference for table wines among the university educated. Women preferred sparkling, rosé, and white wine; men, red table wine. Finally, although female consumption of wine was less than that of men, a higher proportion of women drank wine.

6. Among all users, European imports were preferred to domestic wines. University educated users were far more likely to try new wines, with 60 percent of this

EXHIBIT 7 LCBO forecasts of Ontario wine market in (000) liters

	1977	1978	1979	1980	1981	1982	1983	1984
Total wine	46,400	51,100	56,200	60,700	65,500	70,800	75,700	81,000
% Growth		10.0	10.0	8.0	8.0	8.0	7.0	7.0
Adult population (M)	5,300	5,500	5,600	5,700	5,800	5,900	6,000	6,100
% Growth		3.8	1.8	1.8	1.8	1.7	1.7	1.7
Per capita consumption	8.8	9.3	10.0	10.6	11.3	12.0	12.6	13.3
% Growth		5.7	7.5	6.0	6.6	6.2	5.0	5.6
Total table	26,500	30,600	35,100	39,400	43,900	48,800	53,800	59,100
% Growth		15.5	14.7	12.3	11.4	11.2	10.2	10.0
Total full sparkling and crackling	3,900	4,100	4,200	4,200	4,100	4,000	4,000	3,900
% Growth		5.1	2.4	0.0	(2.4)	(2.4)	0.0	(2.5)
Total 7% sparkling	4,800	5,300	5,600	5,900	6,200	6,500	6,800	7,200
% Growth		10.4	5.7	5.4	5.1	5.0	4.6	5.9
Total sherry and port	7,100	6,700	6,400	6,300	6,100	6,100	6,100	6,100
% Growth		(5.6)	(4.5)	(1.2)	(3.2)	0.0	0.0	0.0
Remainder	4,100	4,500	4,800	5,000	5,200	5,300	5,100	4,800
% Growth		10.0	6.7	4.2	4.0	2.0	(3.8)	(5.9)

Note: LCBO shipments only.
Source: Currie Lehman Report (Originally calculated in imperial gallons)

group having tried Ontario varietals.[3] A majority of university educated users who had tried Ontario varietals, however, did not continue to use them. In contrast, while only 31 percent of high-school and primary-school educated users had tried Ontario varietals, they usually continued to use them. Their preference for them appeared to be rooted in the fact that these wines were either "Canadian," low-priced, or both.

7. Users tended to switch from sweet to dry wine as they gained experience. Entry patterns into wine consumption shifted through time. In the 1950s the novice began with dessert wines, in the 1960s with sparkling wines, and in the 1970s with sparkling, dessert, and low-priced table wines.

8. The table wine market appeared to be going through a complete "Europeanization cycle" with vintaging (i.e., designating the year in which the grapes were grown) and varietal labeling (i.e., designating the type of grapes used in the production of wine such as Marechal Foch, Pinot Chardonnay, and Chelois) becoming increasingly popular.

A recurring fact of market studies relating to alcoholic beverages is that individuals tend to understate their consumption. Point 3 indicates total wine consumption in Ontario at only about one-fifth the true consumption figure.

INDUSTRY STRUCTURE

In Ontario and the rest of Canada, the participants in the wine industry could be classified into four distinct sectors: the provincial regulatory bodies, the retail outlets, the grape growers, and the wine companies. The activities and interrelationships of the sectors were quite complex. A capsule summary is available in Exhibit 8.

The Regulatory Agencies

The aims of relevant government policy in Ontario were to control the use of alcohol for health reasons, to generate revenue, to ensure a satisfactory distribution of products in order to meet consumer demand, to provide enjoyment, and to encourage commercial enterprise within the province.

To accomplish these objectives there were three agencies designed to regulate the production and distribution of alcoholic beverages. These were the Ontario Grape Growers' Marketing Board (OGGMB), the Liquor Control Board of Ontario (LCBO), and the Liquor Licensing Board of Ontario (LLBO).

The OGGMB was created by the Ontario Farm Products Marketing Board to represent all Ontario grape growers in their dealings with grape processors — wineries and the grape jam and juice manufacturers. In 1978, twenty members, elected by the registered grape growers at their annual meeting, comprised the OGGMB. The OGGMB's principal power rested in its authority to license both the grape growers and the processors, thereby regulating supply.

[3] A varietal is a wine made from at least 80 percent of one type of grape, e.g., Chelois or Marechal Foch.

EXHIBIT 8 Industry structure

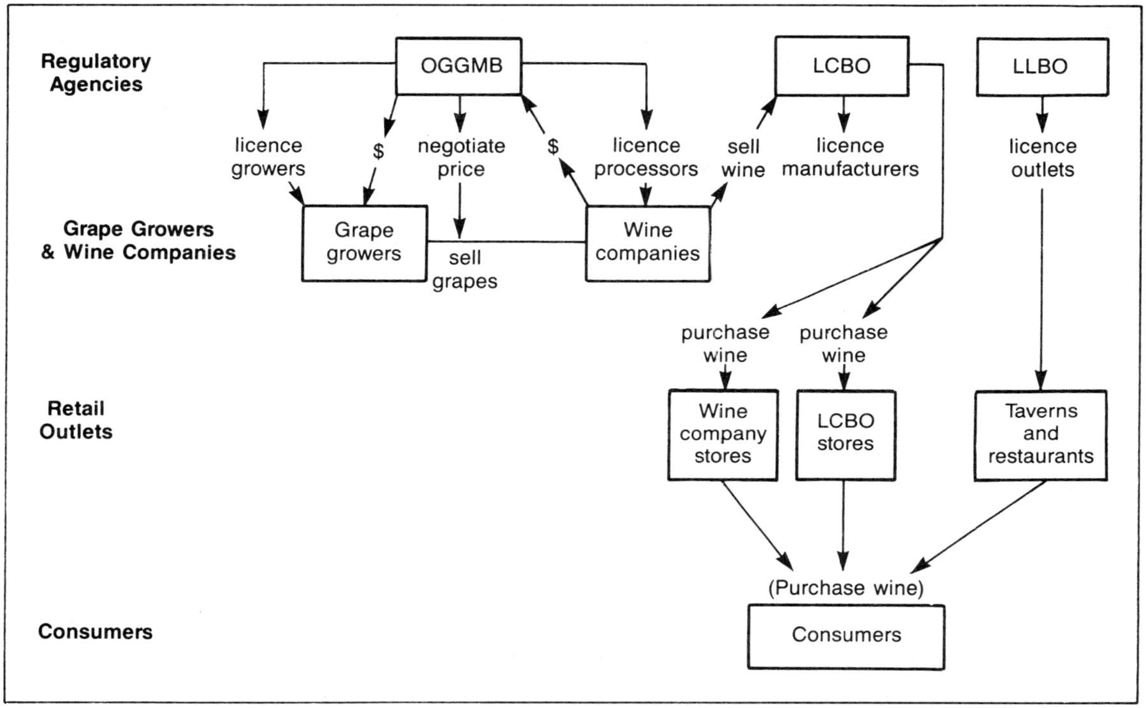

Unlike other provincial marketing boards, this agency did not, as a rule, take physical possession or ownership of the grapes grown by its members. The growers dealt directly with the wineries when purchasing or selling grapes. The OGGMB, however, negotiated the price structure for all Ontario grapes and acted as a collection clearing house. As a result of its functions, this agency provided stability to the marketplace and to the price of grapes.

The LCBO was the provincial government agency responsible for controlling the distribution of all alcoholic beverages in Ontario through its own LCBO retail stores as well as the wine companies' outlets. All wineries, both domestic and foreign, had to apply to the LCBO to have their products listed for sale in Ontario. Canadian and imported listings in Ontario as of early 1977 are summarized in Exhibit 9. This agency regulated the production of wine by licencing manufacturers and by setting standards for hygiene and the amount of sugar and chemicals that could be added. The LCBO limited the amount of wine that could be made from one ton of grapes (i.e., the stretch) to 1,140 l.

For restaurants and taverns wishing to sell spirits, wine, and beer to their patrons, it was necessary to obtain a permit or licence from the third regulatory agency in Ontario — the LLBO.

EXHIBIT 9 Canadian and imported listings

Canadian	Andres			Brights			Jordan			Chateau-Gai		
	Jul. 76	Apr. 77	Nov. 77	Jul. 76	Apr. 77	Nov. 77	Jul. 76	Apr. 77	Nov. 77	Jul. 76	Apr. 77	Nov. 77
Dry White	1.85	1.45	1.75	2.15	1.80	1.90	1.95	1.60	1.85	2.20	1.80	1.95
Marechal Foch[a] red	2.40	1.95	2.20	2.70	2.20	2.20	2.95	2.45	2.25	2.85	2.00	2.25
de Chaunac[a] red	2.40	1.95	2.35	2.50	2.00	2.00	—	—	—	—	1.85	2.00
Still rosé	1.70	1.40	1.60	1.90	1.50	1.60	1.85	1.50	1.85	1.90	1.50	1.80
Champagne	4.55	3.85	4.95	4.95	4.20	4.95	4.95	4.20	5.00	4.85	4.00	4.95
Sparkling	3.40	2.80	2.95	4.15	3.40	3.40	—	—	—	3.70	3.00	3.30
7%	2.45	2.40	2.50	2.35	2.30	2.50	2.35	2.30	2.50	2.45	2.65	2.50

Imported	Jul. 1976	Apr. 1977	Nov. 1977
Lion d'Or	2.56	2.71	2.75
Prix Blanc	2.60	2.50	3.43
Selection (Kressman) White	2.38	2.30	2.49
Colli Albani White	2.15	1.97	1.97
Jaszberenyi Rizling	1.97	2.08	1.97
Mommessin Export Red	3.00	3.25	3.35
Selection (Kressman) Red	2.45	2.38	2.71
Valpolicella (Bosca)	2.65	2.65	2.65
Yago	2.55	2.65	2.50
Szekszardi Red	1.97	1.97	1.97

Note: Many of the imported brands are sold in volumes ranging from 25 to 35 ounces. All prices shown have been calculated (where necessary) for 26 ounce (750 ml) equivalents.
[a] The price of Inniskillin's Marechal Foch was $2.90 in April 1977 and $3.30 in November 1977. De Chaunac was $2.70 in April 1977 and $2.90 in November.
Sources: Ontario Liquor Store Price Lists #50 (July 1976) #51 (April 1977) and #52 (November 1977).

Retail Outlets

As a result of this government structure, wine could be purchased only in LCBO retail outlets, individual wine company stores licensed by the LCBO, and restaurants or taverns licensed by the LLBO.

Approximately 80 percent of consumer purchases were made at the 560 LCBO stores with 47 percent of these purchases in the self-serve outlets. In comparison, only about 10 percent of consumer purchases were made in restaurants and taverns. These latter outlets tended to promote imported wines since they offered a better gross margin to the restaurant owners.

Although there were fifty-two winery-operated outlets located on site at the wineries and in major population centers, their sales as a percentage of total wine sales declined from 31.9 percent in 1972 to 19.3 percent in 1977. There was little enthusiasm within the industry for increasing the number of these outlets, since they tended not to be profitable.

Distribution through food stores represented an area of potential growth for the wineries. Existing legislation limited this to wine company–operated boutiques; Jordans had opened five of these in Towers department stores and Brights was actively considering supermarket outlets. Quebec had recently permitted general distribution of wine through food stores with dramatic effects on sales. And in the United States there were examples of a doubling of per capita wine consumption after the extension of distribution to food stores. Such a change in policy in Ontario, however, was a complicated political decision (and economic decision too because of LCBO revenues). There was some sentiment in this direction, but few observers predicted early action.

The Grape Growers

In Europe, the farmers who grew the grapes were involved in making wine directly or through a local cooperative. In Ontario, the growing of grapes and the production of wine were performed by two separate groups, the growers and the wineries. In Ontario, in 1977, there were some 836 grape growers, concentrated in the Niagara belt region of southwestern Ontario. Production levels of Ontario-grown grapes used by Canadian wineries, by grape type, are shown in Exhibit 10. There were several other uses for Ontario-grown grapes. Besides those grapes used by other

EXHIBIT 10
Ontario grape production used by Canadian wineries

Year	Labrusca		Hybrids & viniferas		Total tons
	Tons	%	Tons	%	
1972	32,233	81.2	7,468	18.8	39,701
1973	38,222	82.7	7,980	17.3	46,202
1974	32,444	70.2	13,786	29.8	46,230
1975	31,312	67.8	14,871	32.2	46,183
1976	27,280	62.4	16,447	37.6	43,727

Source: Ontario Wine Council.

processors, there were fresh market sales and exports. In some years there was a surplus of Ontario-grown grapes.

The average yield was estimated to be 5 tons per acre of the hybrids, 4 tons of the labrusca, and 3 tons of the vinifera. These yields, of course, were subject to considerable fluctuation depending upon the type of grape grown, seasonal conditions, and grower care.

In the midst of a shift from labrusca to varietals, the growers, according to the OGGMB, lost money in grape production. A 1976 study estimated this loss to be $56 per acre in 1975 and $149 per acre in 1976 — both years in which there was a surplus of the labrusca types. Another study by a private winery, of a 100-acre farm, implied, however, that losses, if any, were due to dependence on the labrusca types. The study claimed that, despite greater care and higher costs, hybrid and vinifera varieties were capable of yielding substantial profits per acre. Unfortunately, the report did not include charges for growers' wages nor did it consider the return on investment in vines and land. Land costs alone were considered high, ranging between $5,000 and $7,000 per acre for a producing farm, and $3,000 for raw land in the Niagara Peninsula.

Under some pressure for years, the grape growers developed a close relationship with the government, particularly through the medium of the OGGMB. Through time, the growers were never reticent to use their political ties to the extent they could to serve their purpose.

The Wine Companies

By 1977 only nine of the thirty-one Canadian wine manufacturing facilities were located in Ontario because of a movement during the 1960s to locate their plants near to markets rather than to sources of grapes. One reason for this relocation lay in the preferential treatment given to local wineries by the various provinces. The major impetus to move, however, was that in Ontario the wine companies' purchases of grapes were restricted to those available through OGGMB. Outside Ontario, wine companies could consider other less expensive sources of supply, such as bulk wine and grape concentrate from Europe, the northeastern United States, and California.

COOPERATION AND CONFLICT IN THE INDUSTRY

In the early and mid-1970s the Ontario wine industry experienced substantial difficulties. One of the most critical problems was a shortage of hybrid grapes. Although Brights Wines had been experimenting with the production of nonlabrusca varieties since the early 1930s, by 1964 the hybrid constituted only 16 percent of the total grapes used in Ontario for winemaking. Even when a government-sponsored wine conversion program was implemented in 1975, only 40 percent of its target was achieved by 1977. As a result preliminary figures for 1977 indicated that hybrids and vinifera grapes were still just a little more than 50 percent of all the grapes delivered to wineries.

Many charges were laid by the growers and the wine companies against each other for the slow changeover to new varieties. The grape growers complained that, because of the wine industry's slowness to shift to nonlabrusca table wines, they did not have the confidence to invest in the new varieties that required 5 years to mature. The wineries, on the other hand, rebutted that their ability to innovate was hampered because of the growers' resistance to hybrids. The wineries also argued that, without a free market for grapes (as there was in the United States), they were continuing to subsidize the purchasing of unwanted labrusca varieties.

Whatever the reason, growers' resistance to change was strong, and formal cooperation between the two groups was, at best, tenuous. Although there were long-term contracts between the growers and the wineries, many industry observers agreed that these contracts fell far short of a guarantee to purchase agreed quantities of grapes at agreed prices.

The Ontario Wine Industry Assistance Programme

In 1975 the wine companies, the growers, and the government briefly joined forces to help implement the Ontario Wine Industry Assistance Programme. The OWIAP directed LCBO stores in major centers to carry all Ontario wines regardless of sales volume and to create room for these wines by delisting poor-selling imports. The program permitted point-of-purchase wine displays, liberalized the regulations governing "life-style wine advertising," and allowed for the expansion of winery-operated stores.

Prior to the program, prices of Canadian table wines were generally kept low by competing imports. Because the managers of LCBO retail outlets were assessed on the basis of the gross revenues of their stores, they naturally preferred to restrict the shelf space given to domestic wines since liquor and the higher-priced imports provided greater contributions to revenue. Since the program began in 1975, Ontario wineries had increased prices somewhat but had not been able to recapture lost market share.

OGGMB and LCBO Policies

The OGGMB and LCBO were sources of both help and hindrance to the wine producers. For the most part the regulatory bodies tended to help preserve the grape growers' position. For instance:

1. The OGGMB persistently resisted wine industry proposals to alter the rigid classification of grapes without regard to quality — although this position was modified in 1978.

2. In 1975 and 1976, when 16 percent and 19 percent respectively of the labrusca grapes produced went unharvested, the OGGMB obtained low-interest loans from the federal and provincial governments to purchase the surplus. These governments later forced the wine companies to purchase the grapes from the OGGMB.

3. The OGGMB also regulated the supply of imported grapes and concentrates used for blending or bottling. Yet when this agency decided to allow bulk wine imports of up to 15 percent of a winery's annual domestic production volume, the growers rendered this proposal ineffective by obtaining restrictions from the LCBO regarding the wineries' ability to add water and other additives to the output of one ton of grapes.

4. The wine producers' plans for a major advertising campaign were cut short when a LCBO markup reduction was passed on to the consumer rather than to the wineries.

Government Policies

Because of the actions and policies of the regulatory agencies, many people believed that the government's attitude toward the wine industry was becoming increasingly dispassionate. Even the province's price structure of reduced markups for domestic Ontario wines was no longer regarded as sacrosanct. In fact, in a March 1978 budget speech, the treasurer of Ontario hinted at the possible unconstitutionality of the discriminatory markups on out-of-province Canadian wines and suggested that such protection might be discontinued in the near future.

The federal government seemed equally unconcerned about the future of the Canadian wine industry. During the 1960s and early 1970s, for example, Canadian manufactured goods were traded for wine from Spain and some Eastern Bloc countries.

COMPETITION IN ONTARIO

Four companies, Jordan, Andres, Brights, and Chateau-Gai, dominated the domestic sector of the wine market in Ontario, accounting, in 1976–1977, for some 82 percent of domestic sales. With the exception of the 7 percent alcohol sparkling and dessert wines, where there were segment leaders, the domestic sector was fragmented among the leading companies and other smaller entrants. In the table wine sector, in particular, there was no Ontario producer in a strong market share position. A price comparison of selected Ontario and imported wines for the 1976–1977 period is given in Exhibit 11.

Andres Wines Ltd

Andres was founded in 1961 in Port Moody, B.C., by the Pellar family and became an Ontario producer in 1970. Its expansion from sales of under $1 million in 1967 to over $21 million in 1977 was the result of innovative promotion, marketing, and financial strategies. Anticipating that Canada would follow U.S. trends, the company concentrated its major effort in 7 percent alcohol sparkling wines and reaped the benefits, through economies of scale in advertising and production, of a dominant market share in the most rapidly growing sector. In creating its major brand, Baby Duck, Andres had broken with wine-marketing tradition. Although other wineries had similar 7 percent products, none had adopted the attitudes and spending levels essential to match Andres' proprietary brand/consumer packaged goods approach. One industry source estimated that Andres, for example, spent as much on promotion as the rest of the industry combined.

Andres was also one of the first companies to adopt a strategy of locating wineries by market rather than raw material source. By 1975 Andres operated six wineries from Nova Scotia to British Columbia. Finally, the company backed its expansion

EXHIBIT 11
Canadian and imported listings compiled from provincial liquor authorities' price lists, 1977

Category	Canadian	Imported
Sherry	53	34
Port	22	15
Apertif wine	3	10
Vermouths	11	19
White table wine	56	200
Red table wine	90	250
Rosé table wine	31	25
Crackling wine	21	16
Champagne	23	21
12% sparkling wine	6	24
7% sparkling wine	59	—
Cider	11	6
Other	21	27
Total	407	647
% share	39%	61%

Source: LCBO listings, March 31, 1977.

strategy with an aggressive financial policy, mortgaging all assets as soon as they were acquired and accepting a debt/equity ratio considerably above that of the other major wineries.

More recently, with the decline in growth rate of the pop wine sector in the mid-1970s, Andres began to explore the possibility of licencing its products overseas. It also purchased Chateau-Richelieu, and started to sell table wines with labels featuring both the Andres and the Richelieu names. The emerging branding strategy focused the Andres label on the 7 percent alcohol sparkling wines and introduced the Richelieu name for varietal table wines. Also, in the belief that the current generation of pop wine drinkers were the greatest potential market for its leading brand, Andres attempted to ''age'' the image of Baby Duck to retain consumer loyalty.

Chateau-Gai Wines Ltd.

Chateau-Gai was founded in 1928 and became a wholly owned subsidiary of John Labatts in 1973. Chateau-Gai was a full-line producer and had well-equipped research facilities for developing new types of wine. After acquiring Chateau-Cartier in 1976, the company attempted to create two different images. Low-priced products were associated with Chateau-Cartier, while higher-priced products were linked to Chateau-Gai. In an attempt to turn the company around, Labatts introduced a new top management team with considerable experience in consumer marketing and cost control. The company operated production facilities in Ontario, British Columbia, and New Brunswick.

Jordan & Ste-Michelle Cellars Ltd.

Jordan was founded in Niagara Falls in 1920, and in 1972 became a subsidiary of Carling O'Keefe, the brewing company, which in turn was controlled by Rothmans, the international cigarette manufacturer. Jordan was also a full-line producer, but its marketing emphasis had been on the low-priced pop wines sector. The company was known to be interested in increasing its position in the table wines sector and to be considering acquisitions as a means of gaining faster access to this market. In 1977 Jordan was the largest Canadian winery with national sales of nearly $30 million. The company had wineries in Ontario and each of the western provinces.

T. G. Brights & Co. Ltd.

Brights was founded in Toronto in 1874. In 1933 control passed to the late Harry C. Hatch, head of the Windsor-based distillery, Hiram Walker and Sons Ltd., and a group of associates. Although the company is no longer the largest producer, it dominated the Ontario wine industry for many years. The company enjoyed excellent relations with the growers and pioneered research into the growing of vinifera and hybrid grapes in its own vineyards in Ontario. Brights operated a large winery in Niagara Falls, Ontario, and two smaller wineries in Quebec. Between June 1977 and June 1978, all the senior executives of Brights, except the director of viticulture, changed.

Brights' marketing strategy was traditionally split between the champagne and the dessert wine segments. The general decline in the dessert segment resulted in considerable excess of inventory and serious overcapacity. Brights did not try to go after the growth in the pop wine segment. In spite of prolonged experimentation with table wines, the company had not succeeded in capturing a major portion of that segment either. The recent changes in the senior management were believed, by industry observers, to indicate a further effort to change from the dessert wine emphasis.

PROFITABILITY AND INVESTMENT

The domestic wine industry operated at profit rates substantially below those of the brewing or distilling industries (Exhibit 12). Comparatively, the wine industry was marked by a high investment level per production employee and a low rate relative to investment. These characteristics, combined with the market shift to table wines, created serious profit difficulties.

Historically, most wineries were set up to produce and market either dessert or pop wines. These facilities were not easily convertible to table wine production, and thus, as the market changed, the traditional facilities operated under capacity. Andres and Brights, for example, with Ontario wineries of 3.2 and 7 million gallon capacities, operated in 1976 at 60 percent and less than 50 percent capacity, respectively. Furthermore, a shift in production to table wines required new investment in plant and machinery.

These inflexible investment problems were compounded by the fact that product line profit margins were much lower for table wines than for dessert and pop wines.

EXHIBIT 12
Capital investment comparison of Canadian wineries with breweries and distilleries, 1974

	Wineries	Breweries	Distilleries
Sales to tangible net worth	1.20	1.52	2.29
Value of shipments ($ million)	79.8	612.9	488.4
Tangible net worth ($ million)	66.5	403.2	213.3
Fixed assets to tangible net worth (%)	49.9	51.9	95.0
Fixed assets ($ million)	33.2	209.3	202.6
Number of production-related workers	606	6,709	3,424
Plant investment/production employee	$55,000	$31,000	$59,000
Profit on sales (%)	6.3	6.6	13.9
Profits on tangible net worth (%)	8.2	15.1	20.6

Source: Dun & Bradstreet.

In fact, the industry estimated the average net profit on table wine production in 1976 to be 3.8 percent of sales as compared to 19 percent for sales of dessert wines and 30 percent for pop wines.[4]

Finally, the pricing policies of the cheaper imports placed constraints on the ability of Ontario producers to raise prices. As a result, industry selling prices increased at a compound rate of only 6 percent during the period 1973–1976, while costs increased at the rate of 9 percent annually.

PROBLEMS FACING NEW ENTRANTS

Perhaps the major barrier to entry in the mid-1970s was the industry's disappointing recent performance. New investment capital was simply not attracted. Given the overcapacity in the industry and the declining market share of Ontario wines, it would seem that acquiring large and established wineries at depressed prices would have been the best way for a potential entrant to enter the market. Significantly, however, no one stepped forward to purchase Turners, which closed in 1977.

It is also conceivable that a new entrant might have followed Andres' example of selecting the right market segment and then expanding production. Initial entry to the 14 percent-plus alcohol-content segment, however, was almost impossible. This segment of the market had been declining steadily, giving rise to surplus capacity. Since dessert wines were aged for several years, working capital requirements were high. Furthermore, the dessert wine producers had accumulated very high inventories as a result of "forced purchases" of surplus grapes in the early 1970s. Thus, the existing producers had considerable power to prevent a potential entrant from establishing a foothold in this segment.

Although the minus-percent alcohol-content sector experienced better growth, it was dominated by Andres which was prepared to react aggressively to any attempt

[4] Wine Council of Ontario, "Ontario Industry Profit Structure," 1976.

at encroachment on its markets. Morever, the growth rate in this segment was slowing and, if U.S. experience was a reliable guide, would stagnate in another 3 or 4 years.

The table wine market, on the other hand, was growing rapidly and was expected to constitute about 75 percent of all wine sales by volume within 8 years. The opportunity for new entrants here was that by operating on a small scale, they could specialize in a market segment with a potentially large volume of sales.

Since 1975 two of the three new entrants have begun producing table wines. Yet, it is too early to judge the success of this strategy. Given high variable costs (about 63 percent of net sales) and relatively high capital investment per gallon, small producers face a formidable challenge, particularly if they compete in the low-priced segment. A break-even analysis for a new winery entering the table wine sector is presented in Exhibit 13, and suggests that the best opportunity, from a financial standpoint, is in the above-average-quality segment. Exhibit 14 summarizes the cost components of an imported wine and a domestic wine to the Ontario consumer.

EXHIBIT 13
Typical break-even volume for an average- and above-average-quality winery with 1,140,000 ℓ capacity, 1977

	Average quality[a]	Above-average quality[a]
Shelf price ($/liter)	2.90	4.65
Revenue from LCBO ($/liter)	1.61	2.64
Variable costs ($/liter)	1.13	1.67
Contribution margin ($/liter)	0.48	0.97
Fixed costs		
Depreciation[b]	$ 65,000	$ 65,000
Interest[c]	57,000	98,500
Administrative and selling	210,000	210,000
Total fixed costs	$332,000	$373,500
Break-even sales volume (liters)	691,667	385,052

[a] *Average quality* and *above-average quality* are subjective terms used to arbitrarily define the taste characteristics of table wines in the "low-price" (less than $3.33/ℓ) and "medium-price" wine categories, respectively. "High-price" corresponds to "superior-quality." See Exhibit 5.
[b] Based on an estimated cost of $1.6 million for a 1,140,000-ℓ winery, with $1.3 million being amortized over 20 years.

Land	$ 300,000
Building	600,000
Equipment	500,000
Storage tank and oak casks	200,000
	$1,600,000

[c] Interest charge at 9 percent based on a working capital requirement for 9 months of $1,460,000 for an above-average-quality winery and $1,270,000 for 6 months for an average-quality winery operating at full capacity. However, working capital requirements will vary with production. For example, when production equals 334,000 liters in an above-average-quality winery, working capital requirements are only $0.814/ℓ. At full capacity, the working capital requirement increases to $1.28/ℓ for the entire output.
Source: Author's estimates.

EXHIBIT 14 Cost comparison

Derivation of cost of 26.4-ounce (750-ml) bottle of imported wine (1977) to consumer		Derivation of cost of 26.4-ounce (750-ml) bottle of Ontario wine (1977) to consumer
Selling price from producer	$2.00	$2.00 Selling price from producer
Freight	.19	— Freight (included in selling price)
Federal customs ($0.20/Imperial gallon)	.03	— Federal customs
Federal excise tax ($0.50/Imperial gallon)	.08	.08 Federal excise tax ($0.50/Imperial gallon)
Federal glass tax $\frac{26.4}{160} \times 15\%$	.02	— Federal glass tax
Subtotal	2.32	2.08 Subtotal
Federal sales tax (12%)	.24	.24 Federal sales tax (12%)
Subtotal	2.56	2.32 Subtotal
LCBO markup (115%)	2.94	.86 LCBO markup (37%)
Subtotal	5.50	3.18 Subtotal
Ontario retail sales tax (10%)	.55	.32 Ontario retail sales tax (10%)
Price to consumer	$6.05	$3.50 Price to consumer

Note: A 7–14 percent alcohol content assumed for both the imported and domestic wines. Note the leverage effect of a $0.05 increase in selling price from producer. With imported wine, cost to consumer increases $0.15 and, with domestic wine, $0.10. (LCBO rounds to the nearest $0.05.)

INNISKILLIN WINES INCORPORATED

In 1971, Hugh Johnson, the noted British wine authority, completely omitted Canadian wines from his famous *Wine Atlas*, explaining later that: "The foulness of taste is what I remember best — an artificially scented, soapy flavour." The criticism incensed Canadian vintners, especially from Ontario, who challenged Johnson to take part in blind taste tests. But the doyen of Canadian wine detractors left these challenges unanswered. Then, in a 1975 tasting session, organized in London, England, the same Hugh Johnson confessed to surprise with the Canadian wines which, he said, "bore no resemblance whatsoever to wines I tasted several years ago. My favourite without doubt was the Inniskillin 1974 Marechal Foch."

Obviously a lot of wine, Canadian wine, had passed under the bridge since 1971. The praise was particularly significant to Inniskillin because the Marechal Foch was one of only three table wines made by the company during its first fiscal year. Subsequently, the company's growth accelerated from the 23,000 liters of table wine made from the 1974 harvest crush (1974–1975 fiscal period) to 334,000 liters from the 1977 crush (1977–1978 fiscal period). So successful was the winery's product that the entire output had sold each year within several months of availability.

Industry observers agreed that Donald Ziraldo, the twenty-nine-year-old president of Inniskillin, and his partner-winemaker Karl Kaiser, had taken a huge gamble with Inniskillin. With the company showing its first profit in fiscal 1977, the partners were beginning to feel the gamble was paying off.

DONALD ZIRALDO

Donald Ziraldo was a confident, good-looking, Canadian-born individual of Italian descent. He had gained early experience in agriculture working while a boy on his family's farm near St. Catharines, Ontario. Later, while he was a student at Denis Morris High School, his father died and Donald assumed responsibility for the business aspects of the farm operation.

Case prepared by Joseph N. Fry with Christopher J. Bart and Paul W. Beamish. © The University of Western Ontario. Reprinted by permission.

When he graduated from the Ontario College of Agriculture in Guelph in 1971, Ziraldo converted the family property into a housing development, Ziraldo Estates, and purchased a new location for the farm and nursery just west of the town of Niagara-on-the-Lake, Ontario. The 100-acre farm was situated on the scenic Niagara Parkway and was considered part of Ontario history because a colonel in the Inniskillin regiment stationed at Niagara-on-the-Lake during the War of 1812 had formerly made his home on the farm. The main business of the farm was growing grape vines, especially the European vitis vinifera and the new hybrids which were steadily replacing native North American varieties, such as the Concord and Niagara labrusca vines, in Ontario vineyards.

Starting Up   Sitting in his office, in the midst of bottles of the latest vintage Marechal Foch, Vin Nouveau, and Chelois, Ziraldo, dressed in an immaculate suit, leaned back in his chair and recounted the early beginnings of Inniskillin Wines:

One day, in 1972, Karl Kaiser came in asking for grapes to make wine. He had heard we were growing hybrids. Like a lot of Europeans, he made wine in his basement. He was persistent, but we were sold out.

Later I had a chance to taste a bottle of Karl's wine. It was terrific! I couldn't believe he had made it from local grapes. I drank a lot of wine and beer with Karl over his kitchen table during the next few weeks and we got to thinking. Why not start a "boutique" winery that would produce good table wines in small quantities? So a few weeks later, I set up a meeting with a Mr. Harris, the deputy commissioner of the LCBO [Liquor Control Board of Ontario]. Harris said that no licence to manufacture wine had been granted since 1929. Even Andrew Peller, the founder of Andres wines, couldn't get one in 1956 and was forced to start up in British Columbia.

I returned and told Karl that there was not much point in pursuing the idea. However, several months later, Major General Kitching, the board's chairman, heard about our inquiry and seemed keen about it. I had a meeting with the general and he suggested we prepare a sample batch for examination by the board's tasters.

Karl prepared a few barrels of wine in my home in St. Catharines, and we wrote a brief outlining the type of wine we envisaged. By fall 1974, we were ready. The LCBO examiners conducted chemical and blind taste tests and gave a score of 59, one point below the minimum passing standard. They were willing, however, to take into consideration the limited facilities and difficult preparation conditions. So we got our manufacturer's permit to produce up to 45,500 liters of table wine of 1974 vintage. Then, in June 1975, we were granted our Ontario winery licence. We could hardly believe it.

During the fall of 1974, Ziraldo moved to strengthen the company, bringing in three new shareholders — Peter Sullivan, Ted Ralfe, and Alain Regaud. Sullivan, a grape grower, was to provide Inniskillin with a secure supply of quality hybrid grapes, which were still in short supply. Ralfe, a lawyer and Sullivan's brother-in-law, was to represent the company in all legal matters. Rigaud, Sullivan's partner, had worked as a winemaker for Chateau-Gai wines, studied 2 years at the Institute of Oenology in Dijon, France, and spent 3 years as a lab technician at the French

Institute Cooperatif de Vin. It was felt that he would supply the commercial experience that Kaiser lacked.

Thus Inniskillin began its first season in 1974 with Rigaud as oenologist and Kaiser as cellar master. Capital was supplied primarily through shareholder's loans with Ziraldo as the major source of shareholder capital and guarantor of the company's loans. Ziraldo, Sullivan, Kaiser, Ralfe, and Rigaud held 30 percent, 15 percent, 20 percent, 15 percent, and 20 percent, respectively, of the common shares. Trade suppliers and the banks were skeptical of the new venture and demanded personal guarantees for all debts. "Everybody who looked at the project told us it was one of the riskiest ventures they had ever seen," said Ziraldo. "Today they look at us and say 'What a great company' but they had no idea what was going on behind the scenes."

To be sure, the new management team experienced difficulties from the beginning. Rigaud and Ziraldo disagreed over equipment purchases. Rigaud demanded the most modern equipment available while Ziraldo, conscious of the difficulty of financing, was content to purchase secondhand equipment at bargain prices. There were also constant clashes of personality and philosophy between Rigaud and Kaiser. Matters finally came to a head in the fall of 1975 during the grape-crushing season. Differences over production and types of wine forced Ziraldo to buy out Rigaud and Sullivan and to reorganize the company with Ziraldo, Kaiser, and Ralfe holding 55 percent, 30 percent, and 15 percent of the outstanding shares, respectively.

Building Sales

Promotion was Ziraldo's most conspicuous flair. He was sometimes called a wine "evangelist," but his manner was one of relaxed warmth and enthusiasm. "He gets more publicity per gallon than the rest of the industry put together," one competitor complained.

From the start, Ziraldo committed himself to creating a following for his wines. He set out to convert opinion leaders in the industry and the media. His first step was a personal selling effort to get Inniskillin on the wine lists of prestigious restaurants and wine bars in Toronto, Ontario.

> To sell a proprietor or manager, I'd offer to give him and his staff a tasting session. A number of times, however, I was asked to leave the restaurant before they had even tasted the wine. I remember one European restauranteur who told me that he had tried a Canadian wine 10 years ago and that he "wouldn't wash his feet in it." Boy, old myths die hard. But, if I got in the door, I'd personally see that the waiters, who serve the wine, and might persuade customers to order it, knew the story behind it.

His efforts succeeded in getting Inniskillin wines listed in some choice locations: Three Small Rooms, Fingers, Valhallah Inn, the Royal York Hotel, and the Ontario Art Gallery.

At the same time, Ziraldo pressed to enter Inniskillin wines in public tasting competitions. He achieved early success. A 1974 vintage Marechal Foch entered in the 1976 *Toronto Globe and Mail* competition and placed first against many European wines including a Chateau de la Perriere, Brouilly (one of the nine first growths of Beaujolais), much to the French judges' amazement. "And then there's the Hugh Johnson story," says Ziraldo with a smile. "I tell you, every journalist who writes about us uses it."

Inniskillin and Ziraldo, however, became news. Numerous stories appeared on Donald Ziraldo's gamble and how he was heading the quiet revolution in the Ontario wine industry. The C.B.C. filmed a documentary on the company during the 1977 crush. Ziraldo was elected chairman of the Niagara-on-the-Lake Industrial Development Commission. Inniskillin wines were served at Ontario government functions and at the 1977 Commonwealth Conference in Toronto. The winery buzzed with visitors from the business world, wine societies, and universities.

With growing public awareness, there also came increased commercial recognition. A major commercial food chain proposed distribution of Inniskillin wines through a series of wine "boutiques" in their food stores — an offer rejected by Ziraldo because Inniskillin did not have sufficient production volume and because he felt the promotion was not in keeping with the Inniskillin image. And, of course, there was the signal rite of passage for a young company, an offer to buy from a major Canadian firm. Ziraldo recounted the decision not to sell:

> *After meeting with the president, Karl and I stood out in the parking lot talking about their offer. We knew it wasn't for us. The buyer was too big and we'd lose control of our operations. You see, we have a big advantage over most wineries. With the size of our operations, its almost like making wine in a basement.*

Looking Ahead   Continuing, Ziraldo said:

> *Basically, we're a small company making very good wines. There're only four of us full-time right now. Karl makes it — he's a genius. He has a real talent to judge grapes and get the best out of them. I sell it. Marion is our secretary and bookkeeper and also helps me with the promo. And J. R. helps Karl out. Our biggest problem now is filling the demand for our wines.*
>
> *For me, the zest of this business has come from the challenges, the day-to-day crises. I guess when the challenges stop, that's when I'll think about moving on. I'd like to change the image of Canadian table wine and get the people's support so we can continue to do what we're doing. And it's Canadian. That's very important to me because we've got a long way to go in the table wine business. We are way, way behind. But right now it's a challenge. You know, when we take a break and sit down over a glass of wine, it sort of makes up for all the problems.*

KARL KAISER

About 300 yards from the administrative offices on the farm property stands a converted barn which houses the fermentation tanks, wine press, storage tanks, and rows of Portuguese white oak casks of the winery. From the outside, it looks like a milking shed at any dairy farm. Inside, Karl Kaiser, age thirty-five, the stocky Austrian-born winemaker, works in a cramped corner office behind a door with a sign that says, "Employees will please wash their feet before returning to work." Raised in a monastery, Kaiser was introduced to fine wines when he was nine years old. He came to Canada in 1969 with his Canadian wife and children and recalls his first exposure to Canadian wine with a grimace: "It was a dry red and it was horrible . . . harsh and bitter. I decided right there that I would have to make my own wine."

Kaiser enrolled at Brock University, where he earned his Honours B.Sc. in chemistry and was continuing work on a master's degree. Although he had learned wine making from his grandfather in Austria, he felt that a chemist's degree would give him the background to really combine the science and art of wine making. For one of his first class experiments, he made some champagne. He recalled:

> *Everybody at Brock knew that I was interested in wine. But getting the right kind of grapes was difficult then. Not only were the new hybrids in short supply, but no one wanted to sell them to a home winemaker like me. There was no money in it for them. I met Don when I heard that he was growing hybrids. When he tasted my wine, he couldn't believe I made it from local grapes. When I said to him half-jokingly, "I'll make the wine and you sell it," I didn't think Don was going to do anything about it. But he had the courage to act on it.*

Making Wine   Kaiser went on to explain the company's production process:

> *One doesn't have to be a wizard to make a good wine. There are no secrets, no magic recipes. I don't go around with little salt shakers putting stuff in here and there.*
>
> *We're small and so we're flexible. In California the best wines are always made by the smaller producers. Good judgment and instinct are important. You need a feel for the grapes. Each variety requires different care and everything really happens in about 2 months — September and October.*
>
> *Don's vineyard only supplies about 40 percent of our current needs. The rest of the grapes have to be purchased from outside sources. In the beginning, nobody wanted to deal with us, but now we have a bit of a reputation. More and more wineries are after the hybrids, however, so they are still pretty short in supply. The harvest itself lasts maybe 4 to 5 weeks and the grapes ripen on the vines very rapidly. Different varieties mature at different times, making our manpower-scheduling problems very difficult. Don's vineyard is harvested by hand which is quite costly. Most other farms do it by machine. Mechanical harvesting also pierces the grape and leaves it open to attack by wild yeasts and bacteria, so we have to crush the grapes as soon as possible. We try to minimize these problems by maintaining a close contact with the growers.*
>
> *The grapes usually arrive in standard one-ton bins. I inspect each load for defects and determine sugar content and acidity.*
>
> *While the grapes are being crushed, I add a small amount of sulphur dioxide to control fermentation and prevent spoilage by wild yeasts and bacteria. After the crush, the free-run juice is collected in a pan and pumped to one of our stainless steel fermentation/storage tanks.*

Once the juice is in the tanks, I assist to create the necessary conditions for fermentation. This primary alcoholic fermentation lasts 5 to 6 days on a red wine and ends when the sugar content is fermented.

The reds also require separate fermentation to extract the right color from the grape skins. I also encourage our reds to go through a malo-lactic fermentation lasting 4 to 6 weeks to reduce acidity and give a smoother tasting wine. The process is not well understood, and we received a PAIT grant from the Federal Department of Industry, Trade and Commerce to investigate it. Currently, we're one of the few who use malo-lactic fermentation.

After fermentation, the wine is very cloudy and the suspended particles have to be removed, so we clarify it by means of a centrifuge. Then comes perhaps the most critical part. Fining agents such as bentonite and gelatin have to be added to remove extraneous matter which might spoil the wine and impair its smell and taste. Too much and you strip the wine of its color and taste. Too little and harmful matter is left in the wine. You have to know what you're doing.

There is no guarantee against a bad batch. I worry about bacteria invading and destroying the wine, which could easily happen, since we don't pasteurize and since we don't have the most modern equipment.

Anyway, the wine is then further clarified by filtering through a cellulose filter press. It's then ready for aging. Here the wine simply sits in a tank while its color stabilizes and its bouquet develops. The reds are aged in oak cooperage for 3 to 6 months. The earliest the wine can be bottled is 6 to 8 months after the grapes have been crushed. Then it's loaded into a tanker truck and shipped for custom bottling, corking, and labeling.

From a maintenance standpoint, there are not too many problems with our machines because we keep them in good operating condition with regular cleanings, and careful storage during the rest of the year. Sure, some pumps break down, but our emergency repairs have always worked so far.

This year [1977 vintage], our production reached about 334,000 liters. The crusher and the wine press handled this quantity only because we worked 24 hours a day. In addition, this building we're in has no more room and the receiving facilities are inadequate. I also won't store wine in tanks outside because I'm not sure what effect the varying temperatures would have on it.

Right now I have one full-time assistant, J. R., who helps me in analyzing the wines. There're only the two of us full-time in production, so we both have to get involved in the messy jobs like cleaning out the tanks.

The Future

Kaiser outlined his ambitions for the future:

I want to make an outstanding Canadian wine which has been vinified in the old world tradition. I get a great deal of pleasure from my job because I enjoy total freedom to make production decisions. I wouldn't want to lose the personal control I have over the wines we make. We had a problem like this with Alain Rigaud. Don made him the winemaker here and Alain and I never got along . . . the whole thing pushed Don and me apart. Things are okay today though. We have a good business relationship and work well as partners.

We don't want to become too big, ever. You get too big and you lose control. Our wines are good because they have qualities that only we can deliver. Like all good wines, they are unique in that they reflect the skills and care of the particular wine maker.

POLICIES AND PROGRESS

Corporate Strategy

In his brief supporting the application for an Ontario wine license, Ziraldo set the broad outlines of Inniskillin's policy: (1) to produce a high quality Canadian wine from a "cottage" or chateau winery; (2) to make the wine in the Old World tradition with 100 percent grape juice (no water amelioration), cold pressing, barrel aging, and bottle aging; (3) to use only hybrid and pure vinifera grapes; and (4) to market through prespecified channels so as to maintain direct contact with customers whose comments would assist in improving quality.

Production

In fiscal year 1977–1978 (the 1977 crushing season), Inniskillin continued its line of vintage wines produced in the previous year — a Marechal Foch (red), a Rosé, a Seyval Blanc (white), a Chelois (red), and a blended wine called Vin Nouveau. This line was in keeping with the original strategy of developing entirely on varietals.[1] Inniskillin also began producing limited editions of Gamay and Chardonnay — small quantities of estate bottled wines (i.e., the grapes came from vineyards under the control of the winery) based on pure vitis vinifera grapes. These limited editions were sold exclusively through chosen outlets such as the LCBO Rare Wines store and the Prince of Wales restaurant in Niagara-on-the-Lake.

Both Kaiser and Ziraldo had originally hoped to age their wines. Cash shortages and the sheer demand for Inniskillin's wines had prevented them from so doing. Both hoped that if capacity was increased, this policy could be implemented. In the meantime, they had vintaged (i.e., at least 85 percent of the wine originated in the designated year) all their wines so that their customers might, if they wished, lay them down in their own cellars.

Pricing

Inniskillin wines were presented to the public as a Canadian wine of a quality comparable to that of the medium-priced European imports. A 1976 vintaged Marechal Foch, for example, retailed for $3.30 (750 ml) while the varietal wine of the same name marketed by Andres (not vintaged) or Brights (vintaged) sold for $2.20. In general, though, Inniskillin's prices were lower than those of French "appelation controlée" wines but about the same as those of the lower-priced French blended imports such as Momessin Export ($3.40) and Calvert Lion Rouge ($3.70). The popular Hungarian Szeksardi was available for only $2.65.

Distribution

Inniskillin had benefited from the LCBO's near monopoly on distribution. Government regulations required that any Ontario wine be listed in all high-volume A-designated

---

[1] A varietal is a wine made at least 80 percent from one type of grape, e.g., Chelois or Marechal Foch.

stores and in a specified number of medium-volume B-designated stores. This assured Inniskillin access to a distribution network at a very low cost. Inniskillin also obtained a license to sell wine from its winery on the Niagara Parkway — a lucrative tourist attraction. By having its own retail outlet, Inniskillin was able to keep for itself the 47 percent LCBO markup on selling price.

Accounting

Inniskillin employed a simple actual full-process cost accounting system. The system, at the end of the fiscal year, provided an average product cost which could then be used to relieve the work-in-process account and to determine the cost of goods sold.

At the end of the fiscal year, July 31, a physical count was made of the raw material inventory which was then valued using the latest cost price. By this time, Inniskillin had bottled most of its wine, except for a small quantity set aside for aging in oak casks.

Because the company's cash requirements were highly seasonal with peaks in November, when the growers were paid, and in May, when the bottling expense was met, these needs had to be covered by working capital bank loans.

Cost control was done on an informal basis. Daily records for posting to the ledger were kept by Ziraldo's secretary, Marion. The general ledger and the financial statements were prepared by Ziraldo's sister-in-law, Judy. Ziraldo, however, was beginning to feel the need for some data that tied costs to particular wine types so that he could make decisions about which wines to make and what prices to charge. Several attempts were also made to get Kaiser to keep costs records, which he had so far successfully resisted. In addition, no formal track was kept of yields per ton of grapes, spillage, labor productivity, or machine performance. Company financial statements are presented in Exhibits 1, 2, and 3.

Future Plans

After the 1977 crush, Inniskillin bought out Ralfe because the latter was exhibiting less interest in the operations of the winery. Both Ziraldo and Kaiser were unsure, however, about the steps Inniskillin should take for the future.

The company had just made its first profit in fiscal 1977. The demand for Inniskillin's wines appeared to be stronger than ever. Although it was still not regarded by industry observers as an established winery, the company had enjoyed generous publicity from its inception and Inniskillin now had a good reputation. Both Ziraldo and Kaiser wanted to see the operations grow. The two men were well aware of problems and frustrations associated with a small cottage winery in an industry rushing to adapt to a changing environment.

Ziraldo and Kaiser pondered the alternatives available to them. There seemed three choices or strategies which could be pursued. These were: to sell out to a willing buyer, to continue operations with the present production capacity of 334,000 liters, or to expand the winery's production facilities, probably to about 1,140,000 liters.

If they were to go ahead with the last alternative, they knew the decision would have to be made quickly in order to have the facilities for the 1978 vintage season. Otherwise, they would be delayed at least another year. The partners now felt that they were on the verge of another gamble but this time the stakes were even higher!

EXHIBIT 1
Balance sheet as of
July 31, 1977

	1977	1976
Production (in liters)	159,000	54,500
Assets		
Current		
Cash	$ —	$ 3,052
Accounts receivable	144,103	26,438
Inventory, at cost	104,151	85,190
Prepaid expenses	934	780
	249,188	115,460
Fixed (net)		
Leasehold improvements	10,053	3,134
Equipment	58,958	53,075
Vehicle	1,120	1,540
	70,131	57,749
Other		
Deferred development costs	—	11,608
Total assets	$319,319	$184,817
Liabilities		
Current		
Bank overdraft	$ 26,361	$ —
Bank loan	60,000	89,000
Accounts payable and accrued liabilities	72,444	20,582
Current portion of long-term	5,000	8,553
	163,805	118,133
Long-term		
Ontario Development Corporation	47,242	49,317
Shareholders' loans, postponed	97,075	61,838
	144,317	111,155
Current portion	5,000	8,551
	139,317	102,604
Deferred income taxes	3,200	—
Shareholders' equity		
Share capital		
Authorized		
40,000 common shares of no par value issued and fully		
paid 20 common shares	20	20
Retained earnings (deficit)[a]	12,977	(35,940)
	12,997	(35,920)
	$319,319	$184,817

Note: No sales in fiscal year 1975.
[a] Incorporation costs of $625 were written off in fiscal year 1975.

EXHIBIT 2 Statement of earnings for the year ended July 31, 1977

	1977	1976
Sales (no sales/fiscal year 1975)[a]	$300,859	$ 54,196
Cost of goods sold[a]	200,857	60,149
Gross margin (loss)	100,002	(5,953)
Expenses[b]		
Market. development, travel & promotion	7,539	5,740
Amortization of development costs	11,608	5,571
Administrative & general[b]	7,525	5,526
Interest & service charges	14,352	10,459
Professional fees	5,419	1,561
Vehicle operation	1,442	668
	47,885	29,525
Net earnings (loss) from operations	52,117	(35,478)
Other income	—	163
Net earnings (loss) before income taxes	52,117	(35,478)
Income taxes, deferred	3,200	—
Net earnings (loss) for the year	$ 48,917	$(35,315)

[a] Production by Line in '77–78

	Rose	White	Red	Vinifera
Liters produced	78,600	40,000	202,300	13,200
Grape cost/ton	$ 250	$ 380	$ 355	$ 509
Grape yield (liters/ton)	682	500	705	573
Price/liter to LCBO from Inniskillin	2.18	2.92	2.52	3.78
Grape cost/liter	0.37	0.76	0.50	0.89

[b] The president has taken no salary since the company's incorporation. The secretary-bookkeeper's salary is shared between Inniskillin and Ziraldo Nursery Farms Ltd. Full-time labor employees are paid $30,400 per year, part-time $4,900 per year. For every 227,000 liters increase one more full-time employee is needed. Employee costs may go up 15% per year for the next 5 years, while grape, bottling, and transportation may go up 10% per year, and production supplies 5%. Currently supplies are .02953/L, bottling materials .337/L, bottling charges .194/L, transportation and handling .032/L.

EXHIBIT 3 Statement of cost of goods sold for the year ended July 31, 1977 (with comparative figures for 1976)

	1977	1976
Work in progress, beginning of year	$ —	$ 34,767
Raw materials		
Inventory, beginning of year	891	7,138
Purchases[a]	232,527	56,305
Freight, duty & storage	11,131	3,238
Less inventory, end of year	(6,647)	(891)
	237,947	100,557
	32,713	21,752
Direct Labor	270,660	122,309
Factory overhead		
Laboratory, insurance, maintenance & utilities	17,540	14,558
Amortization of leasehold & depreciation	10,161	7,581
	27,701	22,139
	298,361	144,448
Work in progress, end of year	—	—
Finished goods inventory, end of year[b]	97,504	84,299
Cost of goods sold	$200,857	$ 60,149

Note: Production History, '77–78—(334,100 L); '76–77—(159,100 L); '75–76—(54,500 L); '74–75—(18,200 L).
[a] Purchases account in 1977 includes the opening finished good inventory from 1976.
[b] There was no finished goods inventory in 1975.

JOSEPH SCHLITZ BREWING COMPANY

In early May, 1981, Frank Sellinger, Vice Chairman and Chief Executive Officer of Joseph Schlitz Brewing Company, headed the management team of a struggling company in a highly competitive industry. Schlitz, once the number one brewer in the United States, had slipped to fourth place at the end of 1980, behind Anheuser-Busch, Miller and Pabst. Furthermore, massive advertising expenditures, technological changes, strengthened quality controls, and fiscal belt-tightening had not yet resulted in the turnaround which will return the company to its once proud position.

THE BREWING INDUSTRY IN 1981

Economic and Demographic Trends and Conditions

The United States economic recession of the 1980s, characterized by high price inflation and interest rates, had a noticeable impact on the brewing industry. The following problems were indicative of the economic dilemma of the 1970s:[1]

1. Declining real discretionary income and consumers' inclination to purchase high-priced goods in expectation of further price increases slowed sales increases of inexpensive consumer products. (See Exhibit 1.)
2. High interest rates discouraged wholesalers from building inventories too far in advance of anticipated sales.
3. Increasing costs of advertising, materials, fuel, labor, packaging, and equipment could not easily be passed on to the consumer, due to a highly competitive con-

---

[1] "Beverages and Tobacco: The Outlook," *Standard and Poor's Industry Surveys*, March 2, 1980, p. B-80–81; and "Beverages and Tobacco Current Analysis," *Standard and Poor's Industry Surveys*, November 6, 1980, p. B-54.

This case was prepared by M. Fenton, S. Taudman, R. Neiman, T. Merriman, and P. Norton under the supervision of Professor Sexton Adams (North Texas State University) and Professor Adelaide Griffin (Texas Woman's University). Copyright © 1981 by Sexton Adams. Reprinted by permission.

EXHIBIT 1
Selected U.S.
economic data

	Gross National Product	Disposable personal income[a]	Personal consumption expenditures				Consumer Price Index	
			Total	Durables	Non-durables	Alcoholic beverages	All items	Beer
1973	1235.0	854.7	767.7	121.8	309.3	9.4	133.1	115.6
1975	1202.3	859.7	774.6	112.7	306.6	—	161.2	140.3
1977	1340.5	929.5	861.7	138.2	332.7	—	181.5	145.9
1978	1436.9	981.6	904.8	146.3	347.7	—	195.4	154.0
1979	1483.0	1011.5	930.8	146.6	354.6	—	217.4	170.0
1980P	1481.8	1018.6	934.1	135.6	357.6	11.3	246.8	192.0
1985E	1803.3	—	1184.4	207.3	436.1	13.4	—	—
1990E	2112.8	—	1428.7	262.7	505.5	15.4	—	—

P = Preliminary figures.
E = Estimated by Bureau of Labor Statistics.
[a] Billions of 1972 dollars.
Sources: Department of Commerce's Bureau of Economic Analysis and Department of Labor's Bureau of Labor Statistics.

sumer beer market which made price competition and price promotion especially risky since beer consumers are largely price-sensitive, impulse buyers.

Standard and Poor's forecasted continuing inflation in a slowing economy for the 1980s, so expectations for stronger industrial performance were conservative.

Schlitz had concentrated on controlling internal costs, but according to Board Chairman Daniel McKeithan, ''The ultimate resolution must come through a more moderate federal spending policy.'' He further stated in Schlitz's 1979 Annual Report that:

Warnings that a recession is under way are of some concern to us, but ours is a product that is part of the fabric of American life and for which there is historically a moderately growing demand. In times of more moderate consumer spending, the true value of fine malt beverages becomes more apparent in the marketplace.

Volume growth in the beer industry had been a function of the development of new markets and demographic factors. Demographic factors had been significant due to the ''Baby Boom'' after World War II. As a result, the eighteen to forty-four year-old primary beer-drinking group had grown much faster than other population segments. That growth, however, will begin to diminish as the end of the 1980s approaches (see Exhibit 2). To compensate for a smaller population of the beer-drinking age group, per capita consumption must increase to sustain growth. Thus far there is a definite trend of increasing per capita consumption (see Exhibit 3). Industry expectations were for continued growth in per capita consumption through broadening of product lines and successful marketing efforts. Some industry

EXHIBIT 2
U.S. population
projections

Age group	1980 Population (millions)	1980 Percentage of total	1985 Population (millions)	1985 Percentage of total	1990 Population (millions)	1990 Percentage of total
Under 5 years	16.0	7.2%	18.8	8.1%	19.4	8.0%
6–17 years	46.0	20.7	43.5	18.7	45.3	18.6
18–24 years	29.5	13.3	27.9	12.0	25.1	10.3
25–29 years	18.9	8.5	20.6	8.8	20.2	8.4
30–34 years	17.2	7.8	19.3	8.3	20.9	8.6
35–39 years	14.0	6.3	17.3	7.4	19.3	7.9
40–44 years	11.7	5.3	14.1	6.1	17.3	7.1
45–54 years	22.7	10.2	22.4	9.6	25.3	10.4
55–65 years	21.2	9.5	21.7	9.3	20.8	8.5
65+ years	24.9	11.2	27.3	11.7	29.8	12.2
All ages	222.2	100.0	232.9	100.0	243.5	100.0

Note: Includes Armed Forces abroad.
Source: U.S. Department of Commerce, Population Series P-25.

forecasters estimated annual per capita beer consumption of 27.6 gallons by 1990, an increase of 48 percent over twenty years.

Competing with malt beverages for consumer preference were distilled spirits, wines, and soft drinks (see Exhibit 3). All had experienced per capita consumption increases, but the most dramatic had been wine consumption. A significant change

EXHIBIT 3
U.S. per capita
consumption
of beverages
(in gallons)

	Wines	Beer	Distilled spirits	Total alcoholic	Soft drinks
1970	1.26	18.7	1.83	21.79	27.0
1971	1.43	18.6	1.85	21.88	28.7
1972	1.62	19.4	1.89	22.91	30.3
1973	1.66	20.2	1.93	23.79	31.9
1974	1.62	21.1	1.97	24.69	31.6
1975	1.70	21.6	1.98	25.28	31.4
1976	1.75	21.8	1.98	25.53	34.2
1977	1.80	22.7	2.00	26.50	36.3
1978	1.98	23.5	2.04	27.52	37.6
1979	2.02	24.3	2.04	28.36	38.9
1980 E	2.16	24.5	2.02	28.68	NA

E = Estimated.
NA = Not available.
Sources: Wine Institute, U.S. Brewers Association, Distilled Spirits Council of the U.S., *Beverage Industry*, and U.S. Department of Commerce.

EXHIBIT 4
Top ten beer brands

Rank	1980 market share	Brand	1980 production
1	19.4%	Budweiser	33.9%
2	13.6%	Miller High Life	23.8%
3	7.5%	Miller Lite	13.2%
4	6.5%	Coors	11.4%
5	6.4%	Pabst Blue Ribbon	11.2%
6	4.9%	Michelob	8.5%
7	4.3%	Schlitz	7.5%
8	2.3%	Old Milwaukee	4.0%
9	1.6%	Busch	2.8%
10	1.5%	Michelob Light	2.6%

Source: *Beverage Industry*, February 13, 1981.

in American drinking habits occurred in 1980 as wine displaced distilled spirits in consumption. Some analysts saw this as a trend toward lower-alcohol-content drinks. Others pointed to a growing preference for wine as an accompaniment to meals, and the availability of wines in food stores to account for increased consumption. Industry projections looked for a per capita consumption of 4.3 gallons by 1990, an increase of 250 percent over twenty years!

Standard and Poor's noted a shift in consumer preference toward domestic (as opposed to imported) wines. Imports were off 3.5 percent through the first eleven months of 1979, while data for the first three quarters of 1979 indicated California wines grew 5 percent. California is the dominant state supplying American wines: 68.5 percent of all wines in the U.S. market, 88 percent of all domestic wines in 1978, with white table wines predominant.

Industry Analysis

The brewing industry, characterized by an annual volume gain of 2.7 percent in 1980, was fiercely competitive. The industry leaders, Anheuser-Busch and Miller Brewing (owned by Philip Morris), dominated the market, as reflected in Exhibits 4 through 7. Their combined 1980 production was 50 percent of the entire industry.

EXHIBIT 5
Beer production
by brand

Brewer	1978	1979	1980	Change '79–'80
Anheuser-Busch				
Budweiser	27.0	30.0	33.9	13.0%
Michelob	7.5	8.0	8.5	6.3
Busch	3.6	3.2	2.8	(12.5)
Michelob Light	1.0	2.0	2.6	30.0
Natural Light	2.5	3.0	2.5	(16.7)
Total	41.6	46.2	50.3	8.9
Miller				
High Life	20.8	23.6	23.8	.8
Lite	9.5	11.2	13.2	17.9
Lowenbrau	1.0	0.9	1.2	33.3
Other	—	0.1	0.1	0
Total	31.3	35.8	38.3	7.0
Pabst				
Pabst	12.7	12.3	11.2	(8.9)
Old English (Malt)	0.5	0.7	1.0	42.9
Red, White & Blue	0.5	0.9	1.2	33.3
Blitz	0.3	0.5	0.8	60.0
Pabst Light	0.6	0.7	0.6	(14.3)
Other	0.8	—	0.2	—
Total	15.4	15.1	15.0	.7
Schlitz				
Schlitz	13.0	10.5	7.5	(28.6)
Old Milwaukee	3.6	3.7	4.0	8.1
Schlitz Malt	1.8	1.9	2.2	15.8
Schlitz Light	0.8	0.6	0.4	(33.3)
Erlanger	—	—	0.4	—
Other	0.4	0.1	0.2	100
Total	19.6	16.8	14.7	(12.5)
Coors				
Coors	12.4	11.3	11.4	.9
Coors Light	0.5	1.6	2.3	43.8
Total	12.6	12.9	13.7	6.2

Note: Figures in millions of barrels.
E = Estimate.
Source: *Beverage Industry*, February 13, 1981.

Indeed, trends toward greater concentration were evident. For example, production by the top six brewers in 1980 accounted for 82 percent of the industry total compared with 73 percent in 1975 and 59 percent in 1971.

The performance of the two industry leaders was quite different from that of the remaining competitors. Anheuser-Busch and Miller faced a problem meeting demand for their products due to a lack of capacity. Thus, Anheuser-Busch acquired Schlitz's 5.4 million-barrel Syracuse, New York, brewery in 1980, in an attempt

EXHIBIT 6 Brewers' production and estimated year-end 1980 capacity

Brewer	1971	1972	1973	1974	1975	1976	1977	1978	1979	1980	Change 1979–1980	Year-end capacity 1980E
Anheuser-Busch	24.3	26.6	29.9	34.1	35.2	29.1	36.6	41.6	46.2	50.3	8.9%	53.5
Miller	5.1	5.4	6.9	9.1	12.9	18.4	24.2	31.3	35.8	38.3	7.0	45.0
Pabst	11.8	12.5	13.1	4.3	15.7	17.0	16.0	15.4	15.1	15.0	(.6)	17.5
Schlitz	16.7	18.9	21.3	22.7	23.3	24.2	22.1	19.6	16.8	14.7	(12.5)	25.0
Coors	8.5	9.8	10.9	12.3	11.9	13.5	12.8	12.6	12.9	13.7	6.2	15.0
Heileman	9.4	9.9	10.5	9.5	10.0	9.6	10.6	10.5	11.3	13.3	17.7	14.5
Stroh	3.7	4.2	4.6	4.4	5.1	5.7	6.1	6.3	6.1	6.2	1.6	7.3
Olympia	4.2	4.4	4.7	5.3	6.6	7.3	6.8	6.7	6.1	6.1	0.0	9.0
Schaefer	5.6	5.5	5.6	5.7	5.9	5.2	4.7	3.9	3.5	3.6	2.9	5.0
Genesee	1.6	1.7	1.9	2.1	2.4	2.5	2.8	3.0	3.4	3.6	5.9	4.0
Schmidt	3.2	3.2	3.5	3.5	3.3	3.5	3.5	3.8	3.8	3.5	(7.9)	4.3
General	5.1	6.2	6.0	5.8	6.1	4.2	4.0	3.5	3.0	2.6	(13.3)	8.8
Pittsburgh	1.2	0.9	0.9	1.0	1.0	0.9	0.7	0.6	0.7	1.0	42.9	1.5
All others	29.2	24.2	20.5	17.6	10.9	11.2	8.2	6.0	6.0	3.2	(46.7)	3.5
Total	129.6	133.4	140.3	147.4	150.3	152.3	159.1	164.8	170.7	175.1	2.6	213.9
Less tax-free exports and military	2.2	1.6	1.8	1.9	1.7	1.9	2.2	2.6	2.6	2.6	0.0	
Total	127.4	131.8	138.5	145.5	148.6	150.4	156.9	162.2	168.1	172.5	2.6	
Imports	0.9	0.9	1.1	1.4	1.7	2.4	2.5	3.5	4.4	4.6	4.5	
Total U.S. consumption	128.3	132.7	139.6	146.9	150.3	152.8	159.4	165.7	172.5	177.1	2.7	

Note: Figures in millions of barrels.
Source: *Beverage Industry*, February 13, 1981.

to gain additional capacity. Other principal additions to Anheuser-Busch's capacity included a 4.4 million-barrel expansion of its Williamsburg, Virginia, plant in 1980 and 6.2 million-barrel expansion in Los Angeles in 1981.

Miller, the nation's second-largest brewer, had opened breweries in California and Georgia in 1980 which increased its capacity another 15 million barrels. Miller also planned to open a 10-million-barrel brewery in Trenton, Ohio, in 1982, which would bring its capacity even with that of Anheuser-Busch.

Assuming Anheuser-Busch and Miller were able to sell the additional production of the expansion, Standard and Poor's believed their combined market share could be 60 percent by 1983. Anheuser-Busch's stated goal was 40 percent market share by the end of the 1980s, while Miller's was, of course, to overtake Anheuser-Busch.

The second-tier brewers faced a stiff uphill climb against Anheuser-Busch and

EXHIBIT 7 Estimated market share by region for the top six brewers, full year 1979

	Anheuser-Busch	Miller	Schlitz	Pabst	Coors	Heileman	Total top 6	All other	Total industry
New England	33%	33%	9%	4%	—%	2%	81%	19%	100%
Mid-Atlantic	25	18	4	7	—	3	57	43	100
Total Northeast	27%	22%	5%	6%	—%	3%	63%	37%	100%
East North Central	16%	20%	5%	18%	—%	17%	76%	24%	100%
West North Central	23	19	9	15	12	13	91	9	100
Total North Central	18%	19%	6%	17%	3%	16%	80%	20%	100%
South Atlantic	35%	26%	16%	10%	—%	2%	88%	12%	100%
East South Central	28	41	12	7	—	5	92	8	100
West South Central	21	23	23	2	21	1	89	11	100
Total South	29%	27%	18%	7%	7%	2%	89%	11%	100%
Mountain	32%	13%	8%	3%	29%	4%	89%	11%	100%
Pacific	36	11	7	4	18	6	81	19	100
Total West	35%	12%	7%	3%	21%	5%	83%	17%	100%
Total all regions	27%	21%	10%	9%	8%	7%	81%	19%	100%

Note: Discrepancies due to rounding. 1980 data not available.
Source: U.S. Brewers Association, Beer Marketer's Insights, Inc., and Sanford C. Bernstein & Co.

Miller. Schlitz and Pabst had dropped volume in 1980, Stroh and Olympia held ground, and Coors and Heileman posted above-average gains. Stroh announced merger plans with F. M. Schaefer (ninth ranked) to be complete by 1985. Olympia, although holding volume steady, experienced a 59 percent earnings drop in 1980.

In 1981, Coors planned to expand into three more states (Arkansas, Louisiana, and Tennessee, which would bring its total to twenty), but also was diversifying into non-brewing business such as coal mining, and gas and oil exploration. Also, the successful 1980 marketing strategies of Coors *Light* helped boost its volume 6.2 percent, which, in turn, led to industry speculations that an East Coast brewery might be forthcoming.

Heileman was the fastest growing brewer in 1980 with a volume increase of 17.7 percent over 1979. During the 1970s, Heileman developed a strategy of acquiring a large number of troubled brewers at very low cost and turning them around quickly, as it did with Carling and Rainier, bought in 1979 and 1977, respectively. With more than forty labels, Heileman used many strategies to promote its beer. Six brands were sold nationally and the remainder, regionally, as Heileman capitalized on the regional demand for acquired brands, its excess capacity, and its wholesaler relationships.

Industry analysts predicted a shift away from an emphasis on volume growth to

EXHIBIT 8 Percentage distribution of barrelage by region for the top six brewers (full-year 1979)

	Anheuser-Busch	Miller	Schlitz	Pabst	Coors	Heileman	Total top 6	All other	Total industry
New England	7%	9%	5%	3%	—%	2%	6%	6%	6%
Mid-Atlantic	15	13	6	12	—%	8	11	34	16
Total Northeast	22%	22%	11%	15%	—%	10%	17%	40%	21%
East North Central	12%	18%	10%	40%	—%	49%	18%	23%	19%
West North Central	6	7	7	13	12	15	9	3	8
Total North Central	18%	25%	17%	54%	12%	64%	27%	26%	27%
South Atlantic	20%	19%	25%	18%	—%	4%	17%	10%	15%
East South Central	5	10	6	4	—	4	6	2	5
West South Central	8	12	26	2	30	2	12	6	11
Total South	34%	41%	57%	24%	30%	10%	35%	17%	31%
Mountain	7%	4%	5%	2%	22%	4%	6%	3%	6%
Pacific	20	8	10	6	36	13	15	14	15
Total West	26%	11%	15%	8%	57%	16%	21%	17%	20%
Total all regions	100%	100%	100%	100%	100%	100%	100%	100%	100%

Note: Discrepancies due to rounding. 1980 data not available.
Source: U.S. Brewers Association, Beer Marketer's Insights, Inc., and Sanford C. Bernstein & Co.

profitability improvement by Anheuser-Busch and Miller even though price-sensitive consumers were expected to make price escalation risky.

Overall, then, the pricing outlook for 1981 was uncertain. Higher costs for malt, barley, advertising, and packaging had to be offset by an 8 to 9 percent price increase according to Joseph Doyle of Smith Barney Harris Upham and Company, Inc. On the other hand, since 1975, beer prices had risen at only two-thirds the rate of increase for the Consumer Price Index (CPI), and analysts expected the 1981 rate of increase in beer prices to be less than the CPI.

Industry experts agreed with analyst Harold Davidson that: ''the dominant parameter in marketing scale economy is not the total number of different markets a brewer is in, nor even his total volume. It is the share of the market he holds in his areas. Thus, it is possible for a strong regional to have more favorable marketing scale economies than a weak national.''[2]

As Exhibits 7 and 8 indicate, all brewers except Anheuser-Busch and Miller showed a highly regional sales pattern which made them quite vulnerable to concen-

[2] Harold Davidson, ''The Bell Doesn't Toll for All Small Brewers,'' *Beverage World,* March, 1981, p. 31.

trated assaults by the top two. A particularly competitive area was the West South Central region (see Exhibit 9). Texas was the largest market in this region with the top four competitors holding the following market shares in 1979:

Brand	Share
Schlitz	25%
Coors	23
Anheuser-Busch	20
Miller	18

The significance of Texas sales to Coors and Schlitz is easily understood by the fact that 23 percent of Coors' 1979 total sales volume and 20 percent of Schlitz's were from Texas.

Market Expansion

In an effort to compete successfully in the malt beverage market, domestic brewing companies had tried during the preceding two decades to grow through acquisitions, introduction of new products, and increased advertising. Growth into non-malt beverage production had also been seen as brewers entered container manufacturing, other alcoholic and non-alcoholic beverage industries, snack food sales, and even the energy field.

As a result of acquiring smaller, regional breweries and maintaining the local brands, the number of brewing companies continue to fall. Thus, in 1979 the total was forty-two, just half of the 1969 total. The number of breweries has also continued to decline as well, as shown in Exhibit 10.

Product line expansion had been characterized by the introduction of low-calorie, super-premium, and imported beers, plus cream ale, malt liquor, and "dark" beer. With the introduction of Miller's *Lite* into the beer market in 1975, the low-calorie beer segment increased drastically in popularity. This product was less costly to produce and yet could be sold at a premium price. Consequently, all of the major brewers competed in this segment by 1981.

Super-premium products were led by Anheuser-Busch's *Michelob*. However, entries were also made by Schlitz (*Erlanger*), Pabst (*Andeker*), Heileman (*Special Export*), and Coors (*Herman Joseph's*). Industry sources predicted that Miller would introduce a super-premium (probably named *Frederic Miller*) in 1981.

In 1979, the imported beer market grew 25 percent (400 percent since 1970), but continued to amount to only 2 to 3 percent of the total U.S. market. This market was shared by over one hundred brands and dominated by few. The growth rate in the imported beer market had not gone unnoticed by the domestic brewers, though. Most domestic brewers competed with imports using their super-premium product, but recognized the appeal in foreign beers. Consequently, some brewers had obtained the rights to produce and market foreign-brand beers domestically (as Miller had with *Lowenbrau*), while others simply distributed foreign beers for foreign

EXHIBIT 9 West South Central region barrelage and market share by major brewer

	1974	1975	1976	1977	1978	1979	1980E	1984E	
Barrels shipped (millions)									
Anheuser-Busch	3.0	3.0	2.3	3.0	3.5	3.9	4.4	4.9	6.5
Miller	0.8	1.6	2.0	2.7	3.5	4.4	5.0	5.5	7.0
Schlitz	4.8	5.0	4.8	5.1	4.7	4.3	3.9	3.5	2.8
Pabst	0.2	0.2	0.2	0.3	0.3	0.3	0.3	0.3	0.4
Coors	2.4	2.6	3.7	3.7	3.7	3.9	4.6	4.6	5.3
Heilemen	0.2	0.2	0.2	0.2	0.2	0.2	0.2	0.2	0.2
Total top 6	11.4	12.6	13.2	15.0	15.9	17.0	18.0	19.0	22.2
All others	3.4	2.9	2.7	2.2	2.2	2.0	1.9	1.8	1.5
Total all brewers	14.8	15.5	15.9	17.2	18.1	19.0	19.9	20.8	23.7
Market share									
Anheuser-Busch	20%	19%	15%	17%	19%	21%	22%	24%	29%
Miller	5	10	13	16	19	23	25	26	32
Schlitz	32	32	30	30	26	23	20	17	11
Pabst	1	1	1	2	2	2	2	1	2
Coors	16	17	23	22	20	21	21	22	20
Heileman	1	1	1	1	1	1	1	1	1
Total top 6	77%	81%	83%	87%	88%	90%	90%	91%	95%
All others	23	19	17	13	12	10	10	9	5
Total all brewers	100%	100%	100%	100%	100%	100%	100%	100%	100%
Barrelage growth (annualized compounded growth rate)									
Anheuser-Busch		0 %	(23)%	30 %	17 %	11 %	13 %	11 %	10 %
Miller		100	25	35	30	26	14	10	8
Schlitz		4	(4)	6	(8)	(9)	(9)	(10)	(7)
Pabst		n/m	n/m	n/m	n/m	n/m	n/m	n/m	10
Coors		8	42	0	0	5	8	10	5
Heileman		n/m	n/m	n/m	n/m	n/m	n/m	n/m	n/m
Total top 6		11 %	5 %	14 %	6 %	7 %	6 %	6 %	5 %
All others		(15)	(7)	(19)	0	(9)	(5)	(5)	(6)
Total all brewers		5 %	3 %	8 %	8 %	5 %	5 %	5 %	5 %

Note: Discrepancies due to rounding.
n/m = not meaningful.
Pabst barrelage includes Blitz-Weinhard brands beginning April 1, 1979. Heileman barrelage includes Falls City and Carling-National Brands beginning January 1, 1979 and April 1, 1979, respectively.
Source: U.S. Brewers Association, Beer Marketer's Insights, Inc., and Sanford C. Bernstein & Co.

EXHIBIT 10
Number
of breweries
authorized
to operate
in the United States

Year	Number of breweries
1968	163
1969	158
1970	154
1971	148
1972	147
1973	122
1974	111
1975	102
1976	97
1977	94
1978	89
1979	90
1980	88

Source: U.S. Department of the Treasury,
Bureau of Alcohol, Tobacco, and Firearms.

firms. Thus, Anheuser-Busch marketed a German beer, importing *Wurzburger Hofbrau* in bulk and bottling it in the United States.

In the battle for market share, advertising expenditures had risen dramatically over the past decade, as shown in Exhibits 11 and 12. Rates for advertising in the broadcast and print media had escalated along with inflation, forcing brewers to re-examine these marketing expenditures in light of profitability. Industry analysts predicted a peaking of these costs in relation to revenues in 1981 and an emphasis toward non-media marketing programs designed to improve sales in specific, targeted markets.

Non-brewing endeavors like container manufacturing had grown as a result of rising packaging costs. Self-manufacturing of cans by brewers had shown an increasing trend with Anheuser-Busch participating not only in the production of cans for its own needs, but also in the development of advanced aluminum technology with Alusuisse, a Swiss aluminum company. Several brewers were also involved in recycling efforts as well. Glass containers were becoming more popular too. Cans

EXHIBIT 11
Media advertising
expenditures
for brewers

Company	1976	1977	1978	1979
Anheuser-Busch	$25.2	$45.0	$63.1	$87.1
Miller	29.0	42.1	64.0	75.0
Pabst	9.1	10.8	18.0	18.3
Schlitz	33.4	40.7	40.6	48.2

Note: Figures in millions of dollars.
Source: Leading National Advertisers, Inc. and Sanford C. Bernstein &
Co., Inc.

EXHIBIT 12
Brewer's
expenditures
per barrel

Company	1976	1977	1978	1979
Anheuser-Busch	$0.89	$1.24	$1.52	$1.89
Coors	0.11	0.31	0.65	1.16
Miller	1.58	1.74	2.06	2.10
Pabst	0.54	0.68	1.17	1.22
Schlitz	1.38	1.85	2.08	2.87
Industry average[a]	0.97	1.28	1.61	1.92

[a] Weighted by estimated sales volume
Source: Goldman Sachs Research based on Leading National
Advertisers, "Ad $ Summary" (six measured media).

represented 64 percent of beer packaging in 1978 (latest available data), with that percentage expected to decrease as the costs for glass bottles continued to become more favorable.

Expansion into soft drinks by Anheuser-Busch (*Root 66* root beer), wine by Schlitz (Geyser Peak Winery), snack foods by Anheuser-Busch (*Eagle* snack line), and energy exploration by Coors (gas and coal) further indicated diversification opportunities for brewers. Philip Morris, of course, added to its diverse holdings with its acquisition of Miller Brewing Company in 1970.

Industry Financing

The maturity of the beer market had created intense competition which was also the position of the overall beverage industry. Exhibit 13 shows performance indicators for the overall beverage industry. Earnings predictions for the top five brewers by industry analyst Andrew J. Melnick appear in Exhibit 14.

The brewing industry was a capital-intensive business with a high percentage of fixed costs. As indicated in the composite statistics of the brewing industry in Exhibit 15, the average operating margin was 10.5 percent, with an average net profit margin of 4.1 percent. The *Value Line* projections for 1982–85 (shown in Exhibit 15) indicated a rise in the industry operating margin to 11 percent and a rise in the net profit margin to 4.5 percent.

Labor

The labor force in the brewing industry was largely unionized. Consequently, strikes in the industry could seriously hamper competitive strategies. For example, a 100-day strike of Anheuser-Busch production workers in 1976 resulted in a 17 percent loss of volume. At the same time, Miller gained 43 percent.

The average salary of production workers employed in the industry jumped 88.1 percent between 1970 and 1977, making brewing workers the highest paid employees in the beverage business with an average annual wage of $18,942 according to the U.S. Department of Commerce. Nonproduction employees' wages rose 72 percent for a 1977 average of $20,806. Government figures placed the average annual salary for *all* beer industry employees for 1979 at $19,493.

EXHIBIT 13 Beverage industry yardsticks of management performance

| | Profitability | | | | | | | Growth | | | |
| | Return on equity | | | Debt/ equity ratio | Return on total capital | | | Net profit margin | Sales | | Earnings per share | |
	5-year average	5-year rank	Latest 12 months		Latest 12 months	5-year rank	5-year average		5-year average	5-year rank	5-year average	5-year rank
G. Heileman Brewing	30.2%	1	33.7%	0.3	23.9%	2	22.3%	4.8%	26.2%	1	30.3%	1
Coca-Cola	23.6	2	21.6	0.0	20.2	1	22.3	7.4	14.1	4	11.9	4
Pepsi	21.9	3	22.1	0.5	15.3	3	16.0	4.9	19.6	2	16.5	2
Brown-Forman Dist.	16.8	4	23.9	0.4	17.1	5	13.0	8.2	11.7	7	16.2	3
Heublein	16.2	5	16.8	0.5	12.0	7	11.7	4.1	9.7	9	9.3	9
Anheuser-Busch	15.6	6	18.1	0.5	11.5	9	10.0	5.2	13.7	5	9.3	8
Royal Crown	15.0	7	12.5	0.6	9.3	4	13.0	2.9	13.6	6	3.4	11
National Distillers	12.9	8	10.5	0.3	8.4	8	10.2	5.0	8.2	11	10.8	5
Adolph Coors	12.8	9	10.8	0.0	10.0	6	12.1	8.2	11.5	8	7.9	10
Seagram	10.8	10	11.8	0.4	9.8	10	8.4	5.7	6.3	12	10.3	6
Olympia Brewing	8.5	11	4.3	0.2	4.1	11	7.4	0.8	17.1	3	10.1	7
Pabst Brewing	6.8	12	4.1	0.1	3.7	12	6.2	1.3	8.4	10	-4.3	12
Schlitz	0.7	13	def	0.3	def	13	1.4	def	5.4	13	-44.4	13
Industry medians	15.0		12.5	0.3	10.0		11.7	4.9	11.7		10.1	
All industry medians	15.8		16.1	0.4	11.0		11.1	5.0	14.3		13.9	

Source: *Forbes*, January 5, 1981, p. 216.

502

EXHIBIT 14
Brewers' earnings
projections

	Earnings per share			P/E ratio	
	1980	*1981E*	*1982E*	*1981E*	*1982E*
Anheuser-Busch	$3.80	$4.50	$5.00	7.9	7.1
Coors	1.86	2.20	2.70	6.6	5.4
Heileman	3.98	4.70	5.40	7.1	6.1
Pabst	1.55	1.30	1.65	13.1	10.3
Schlitz	0.93	0.90	0.90	11.3	11.3

Note: E = Estimate.
Source: Andrew J. Melnick, "Brewing Industry Review," for Drexel Burnham Lambert, Inc., March 17, 1981, p. 819.

While wages have increased between 1970 and 1977, the number of employees has dropped by 23.2 percent during the same period. This includes an 18.2 percent drop among production workers and a 33.2 percent drop among nonproduction workers. Cost-cutting efforts, production slumps, technological improvements, and industry consolidation were cited as the principal reasons for the drop, which has resulted in average annual percentage increases in output per employee hour and output per employee of between 6.3 and 8.8 for the 1973–1978 period.

The Brewing Process

In the 1970s and early 1980s the actual brewing process involved the production of beer from malted barley, hops, and water, with or without the addition of other carbohydrate materials. Malted barley or malt was the principal brewing ingredient. The brewing functions outlined in Exhibit 16 were typical of the basic brewing process. The following is a brief description of that process:

Production stage	*Description*
Mashing	The brewer grinds the malt, producing a liquid grain residue.
Lautering	The grain is passed through a straining device which removes insolubles, creating a clear liquid called wort.
Kettle boil	Hops or extracts are added to give aroma and taste.
Wort cooling	The wort is sent through a hop strainer to remove protein-like semisolids by settling, filtration, and centrifugation.
Yeast pitching	Yeast is added to the wort and it is allowed to grow and ferment. (Active growth of the yeast takes forty-eight hours.)
Lagering	At the end of primary fermentation, lasting four to seven days, the yeast settles to the bottom of the fermenter. (Note: brewers vary the length of time they age beer, varying from a few days to a few months. Lagering is done in an environment of 0–10 degrees Centigrade.)
Finishing and packaging	The new beer is given a brief, chill-proofing treatment, filtered, carbonated, and packaged. (Note: In the 1980s, over 80 percent of packaged beer was put into cans or bottles, which were then pasteurized.)

EXHIBIT 15 Beer industry composite statistics

	1976	1977	1978	1979	1980E	1981E	1983–1985E
Sales ($mil)	6,327.8	6,487.4	7,235.8	8,412.7	9,700	11,200	16,300
Operating margin	12.9%	12.3%	11.1%	10.6%	10.5%	10.6%	11.0%
Depreciation ($mil)	205.6	230.2	254.8	273.8	305	340	475
Net profit ($mil)	292.2	281.5	265.1	290.5	400	370	740
Income tax rate	46.3%	43.3%	44.8%	36.6%	40.0%	41.5%	43.5%
Net profit margin	4.6%	4.3%	3.7%	3.5%	4.1%	4.2%	4.5%
Working capital ($mil)	666.6	736.6	739.3	692.2	800	880	1,650
Long-term debt ($mil)	938.7	906.0	965.9	1,064.6	1,325	1,525	1,400
Net worth ($mil)	2,424.3	2,556.9	2,659.9	2,887.2	3,260	3,660	5,400
% earned total capital	9.8%	9.1%	8.4%	8.4%	10.0%	10.5%	12.0%
% earned net worth	12.1%	11.0%	10.0%	10.1%	12.5%	13.0%	14.0%
% retained to common eq.	8.4%	7.3%	6.1%	6.8%	9.5%	10.0%	10.5%
% all divds. to net profit	32%	35%	40%	34%	25%	25%	25%
Avg. annual P/E ratio	12.4	10.3	10.6	9.9	—	—	14.0
Avg. annual divd. yield	2.5%	3.3%	3.7%	3.4%	—	—	1.8%

Note: E = estimate.
Source: *Value Line*, March 6, 1981, p. 1553. Reprinted by permission of the publisher. Copyright 1981, Value Line, Inc.

EXHIBIT 16
Schematic of the
brewing process

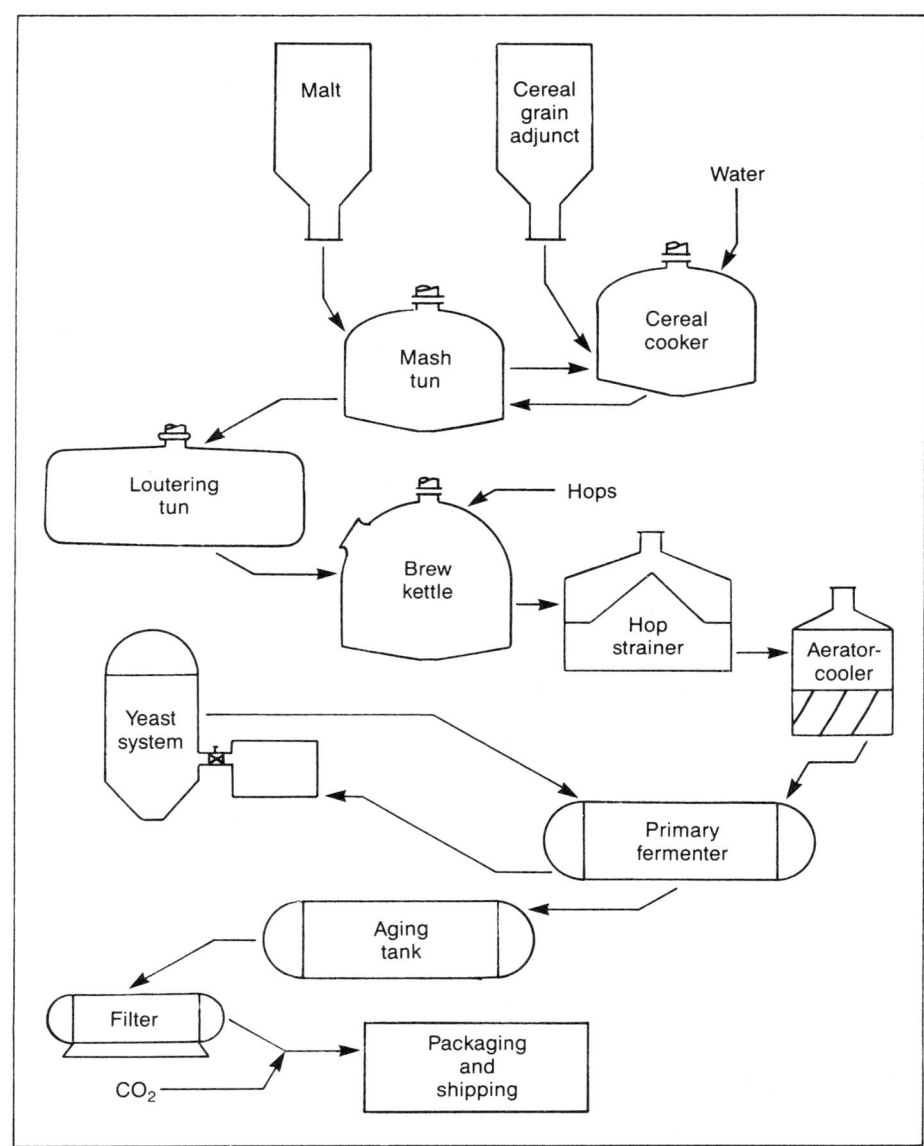

Source: Clifford F. Gastineau, William J. Darby, and Thomas B. Turner, eds., *Fermented Food Beverages in Nutrition* (New York: Academic Press, 1979), p. 247.

At the brewery, all product was shipped within twenty days of production, with the average time in inventory of two to three days. Only full truck, railcar, or container loads were shipped from the brewery. Thus, wholesalers were required to order sufficient product to fill a vehicle. However, if packaged beer is not consumed within ninety to one hundred days after packaging, a noticeable degradation in quality takes place.

Technology

In 1981, the latest development in achieving a nitrosamine- (known carcinogen) free beer consisted of the removal of most organic compounds, color, and heavy metals through the use of ozone, which replaced the chemical treatment of water, which was considered the source of the nitrosamine problem. Some advantages of ozonation over chemically treated water included: bacterial disinfection, color removal, odor removal, viral inactivation, taste removal, and algae removal. The largest application for ozone was the cooling water and boiling water, since algae growth and scaling were the largest problems in the industry. Recent studies of ozone treatment by the Jet Propulsion Laboratory indicated savings of 55 percent on operating costs, via savings on water and chemicals.

Government Controls and Litigation

Federal, state, and local governmental actions have also provided opportunities and threats to the brewing industry. Restrictions, implemented from 1980 until May 1981, on grain sales to the Soviet Union had a leveling effect on grain costs. With the discovery that many beers contained traces of nitosamines, a potent carcinogen, the Food and Drug Administration (FDA) ordered brewers to adjust production methods to reduce the level of nitrosamines to less than five parts per billion by the beginning of 1980. Schlitz made the necessary adjustments and according to Chairman McKeithan's comments at Schlitz's 1980 Annual Stockholder's Meeting: "All of our beer products are within the FDA guidelines . . . in short, nitrosamines are not a problem with any Schlitz malt beverage."

The federal Bureau of Alcohol, Tobacco, and Firearms (ATF) continued to consider and reconsider regulatory requirements regarding alcoholic beverage advertising, trade practice regulations, and ingredient labelling requirements. Topics covered in proposed regulations in 1981 included delineation of the use of the terms "light" and "natural," definitions of false and disparaging advertising covering rules for comparative taste tests, and bans on the use of "active" athletes or athletic events where participants consume alcoholic beverages before or during the event.

Statistics indicated an increase in alcohol abuse and the dangerous characteristics of alcohol (e.g., for pregnant women, highway safety, teenager abuse, etc.) prompted the federal government to begin efforts to curb alcohol abuse. Although warning labels were discussed, no statutory or regulatory action was initiated by 1982. Public awareness and education efforts were under way via television and radio media, schools, and social agencies, however. Also, some local jurisdictions began taking action to ban alcohol consumption on public property in order to combat crime and civil disturbances, and to promote highway safety.

Related to the above has been a slowly developing, yet accelerating emphasis on changes in state laws raising the minimum drinking age. During the turbulent sixties when eighteen-year-olds were drafted into military service for Vietnam, many states lowered the age of majority (drinking, voting, etc.) to eighteen. Since then, however, alcohol abuse by teenagers has prompted several states to initiate and/or finalize legislation to raise the legal drinking age to nineteen, twenty, or twenty-one.

Several states and local jurisdictions also enacted legislation concerning beverage containers and packaging. Included were bans on pull-tabs, nonbiodegradable plastic connecting devices, and nonreturnable bottles, and mandatory deposits on beer and soft drink beverage containers. Another approach known as a "litter tax" imposed a percentage tax on gross sales for all industries in which products contributed to litter (newspapers, bottlers, canners, supermarkets, brewers, etc.). A summary of such legislation and pending legislation is contained in Exhibit 17.

Although Schlitz opposed all attempts to restrict packaging and to require deposits, management supported the "litter tax" because it was a broad-based tax on all components of the solid waste stream. Thus, according to Schlitz's 1977 Annual Report: "Such a tax would finance resource recovery and community-wide litter programs which deal more completely with the problem. . . ." Schlitz's management also believed that further enactment of deposit bills and packaging restrictions laws would not materially affect its relative position in the brewing industry "since the impact will fall on all members of the industry" (1977 Annual Report).

At a time when most American industries were actively advocating reducing governmental influence in their affairs, brewers were actually inviting governmental inquiries in efforts to seek competitive advantages.

Some examples of such strategies included:[3]

The Miller Brewing Company's request to the Federal Trade Commission (FTC) to prohibit Anheuser-Busch from using the word "natural" in reference to its products

The Miller Brewing Company's challenge of Anheuser-Busch's promotion of *Michelob Light* as a light beer because it contained more calories than certain other light beers

Miller also contested as a trademark infringement several brewers' (including Schlitz's) use of the term "light" and "lite" in marketing low-calorie beer

Miller's dispute of Anheuser-Busch's advertising claim that dark bottles were better than clear ones

Miller, in turn, was questioned for marketing its domestic product as *Lowenbrau*, a foreign beer name

The Justice Department and FTC were also carefully monitoring the industry trend toward greater concentration and consolidation. Some greater leniency has

---

[3] "Beverages and Tobacco: The Outlook," p. B-71.

EXHIBIT 17
Litter control
legislation at the
state level

	Mandatory deposits	Litter/ recycling laws	Bans metal pull tab tops	Bills pending	
				Restrictive container	Litter/ recycling
Alaska					●
California		●	●		
Colorado		●			
Connecticut	●	●	●		
Delaware	●a		●		
Georgia		●c			
Hawaii			●		
Iowa	●		●		
Kentucky		●			
Louisiana				●	●
Maine	●		●		
Massachusetts			●	●	
Michigan	●b		●		
Minnesota			●		
Montana				●	
Nebraska		●			
New Jersey				●	
New York				●	
Ohio					●
Oregon	●b		●		
Pennsylvania				●	
South Carolina		●	●		
Vermont	●		●		
Virginia		●	●		
Washington		●			

Note: Table shows laws either enacted or passed, but not effective as of June 1980.
a Laws contingent upon enactment by Md. and Pa.
b Two-tier deposits.
c Voluntary program.
Sources: Can Manufacturers Institute, Glass Packaging Institute, and National Can Corp.

been seen in the approval of mergers, as evidenced by the approval of Heileman's acquisition of Carling in 1979, since the same acquisition by Pabst had earlier been discouraged.

SCHLITZ'S BACKGROUND AND HISTORY

The Joseph Schlitz Brewing Company was incorporated in Wisconsin in 1920, growing out of a company established in Milwaukee in 1849 by August Krug. Joseph Schlitz took over at Krug's death in 1856. At Schlitz's death in 1875, the company was willed to August Krug's four nephews, the Uihleins, with the stipulation that the name remain unchanged. At the end of 1980, the Uihlein family retained an estimated 60 to 75 percent of the stock of the company. Until 1976, the Joseph Schlitz Breweries had been headed by a Uihlein for four generations, when Chairman Robert Uihlein died of leukemia at the age of sixty. Daniel McKeithan, the present Chairman, was previously married to a Uihlein and had served as a director of the company. The family had such respect for his abilities that they made him Chairman after Robert Uihlein's death, despite the fact he was divorced and there were other Uihleins available to take over the position. In 1981 Schlitz was one of the largest U.S. corporations still under family control.

The Joseph Schlitz Brewing Company had grown from a one-brand, single-plant brewery to a six-brand, multi-plant company. Its product line included *Schlitz* (a premium beer), *Schlitz Light, Old Milwaukee* (popularly priced), *Old Milwaukee Light, Schlitz Malt Liquor,* and *Erlanger* (a super-premium beer). In addition to its six brands, Schlitz operated five aluminum can manufacturing plants through its container division. Other subsidiaries of the company included Geyser Peak Winery, a wholly owned subsidiary in Geyserville, California, acquired in 1972, which produced and sold twelve different wines under the brand labels *Voltaire* and *Summit*; and Murphy Products Company in Burlington, Wisconsin, a wholly owned subsidiary acquired in 1971, which processed and marketed animal feeds and feed concentrates from by-products of brewery grains. C & D Foods, a subsidiary of Murphy Products Company, grew and processed ducklings, which were sold to food wholesalers and major food chains. Schlitz also had investments in two Spanish breweries (La Cruz del Campo and Henninger Espanola) which did not contribute significantly to Schlitz's operations.

SCHLITZ'S CURRENT OPERATIONS

Organization and Management

Schlitz's organization structure as of May 1, 1981, is shown in Exhibit 18, with further detail on the organization of its marketing and operations departments shown in Exhibit 19. The container division, as well as the wholly owned subsidiaries reported directly to the president, as did the areas of finance, sales, government and legal, purchasing and materials services, and general counsel. The average age of all Schlitz officers on March 1, 1980, was fifty. Over the past several years, Schlitz had attempted to strengthen its management by recruiting marketing executives from the beverage industry. As noted, the Uihlein family owned a significant portion of the stock in Schlitz and the family continued to be involved in the operations of the company. Thus, a former president of Schlitz, Roy C. Satchell, said he left the company because he would never feel free to run it. "There were not many family members in management, but the family did influence the company behind the scenes."[4]

---

[4] Charles G. Burck, "Putting Schlitz Back on the Track," *Fortune*, April 24, 1978, p. 46.

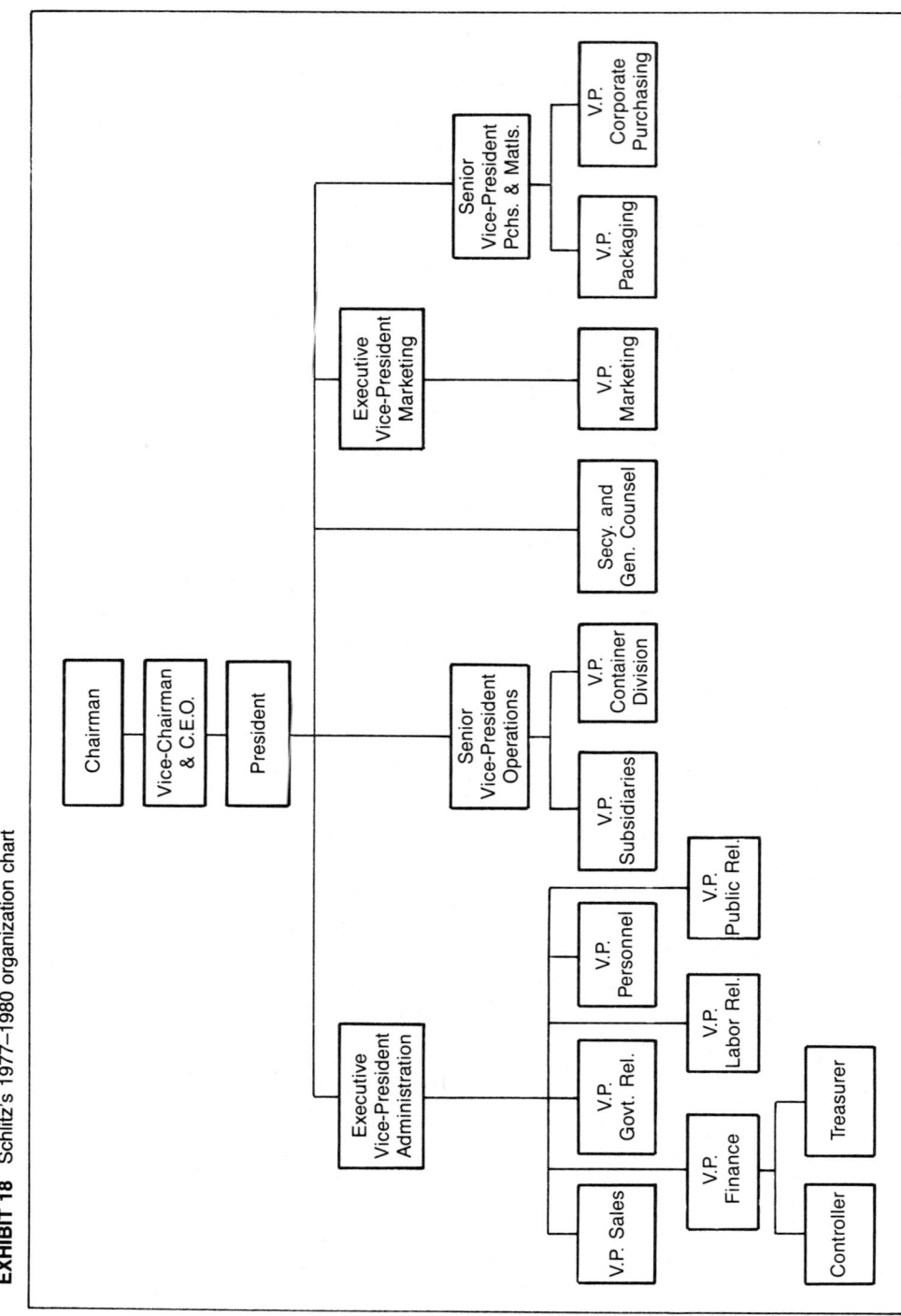

EXHIBIT 18   Schlitz's 1977–1980 organization chart

Source: Joseph Schlitz Brewing Company Annual Reports, 1977–1980.

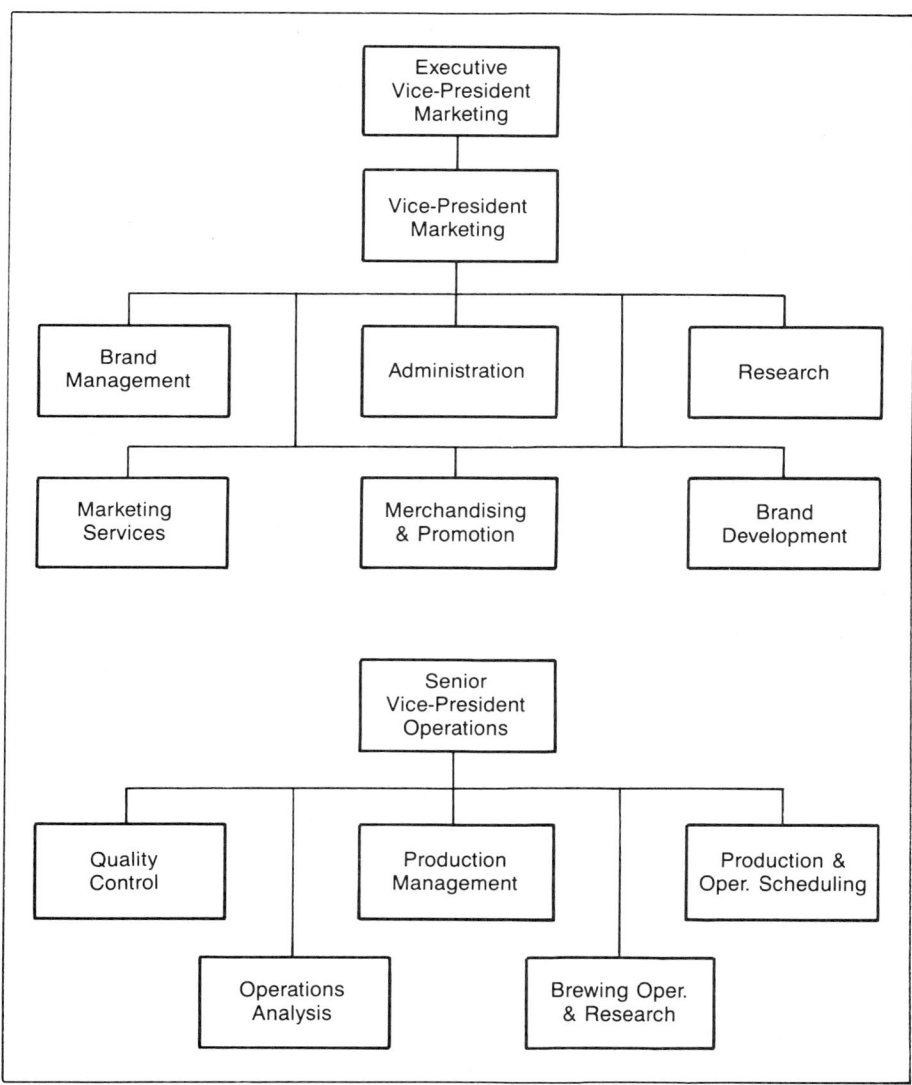

EXHIBIT 19
Schlitz's marketing and operations departments, 1977–1980

The major problems facing Schlitz in 1981 began in the early 1970s, when competition from Miller began affecting the entire brewing industry because of the large amount of funds Philip Morris was investing in Miller. By 1976, Schlitz completed the expansion of its plant capacity just as its sales began dropping because of the competition from Miller. This sales decline was aggravated by a change in Schlitz's brewing process which resulted in a loss of a large number of loyal Schlitz-brand drinkers. In addition, management at this time was faced with a cloud of indictments alleging improper payments to distributors, while constant feuding among the two-hundred-plus descendents of Uihleins perpetually diverted management from more important things. After Frank J. Sellinger joined the company in 1977, Schlitz mounted an aggressive internal campaign to increase efficiency and spur new product development. The end result was an increase in 1980's profits and vigorous activity with new products such as *Erlanger*, an all-barley malt beer, and *Old Milwaukee Light* beer. Publicity releases from Schlitz in 1981 characterized Sellinger as follows:

> *In his forty-four years in the brewing industry, Frank J. Sellinger has become one of the most knowledgeable figures in the industry. There is no major part of the beer business with which he is not personally familiar.*
>
> *Today, at age sixty-six, Frank J. Sellinger could be in sunny retirement. Instead, he's battling with gusto in the much publicized beer wars and, as Chief Executive Officer of Joseph Schlitz Brewing Company, is a pivotal member of the new management team that is leading the firm out of the trenches and into the attack.*

Operations

As of May 1981, Schlitz maintained five breweries and five canning facilities in the United States. Prior to 1981, Schlitz had also operated a brewery in Syracuse, New York and a brewery in Honolulu, Hawaii. However, the sale of these breweries was necessary according to management, because the company was operating at only 54 percent of its capacity in 1979. This divestiture left Schlitz with a brewing capacity of 25.6 million barrels (see Exhibit 20 for a breakdown by brewery). Thus, in 1980, the five remaining breweries operated at a capacity of 58 percent, compared to Schlitz's prior capacity utilization of 54 percent in 1979, 62 percent in 1978, and 75 percent in 1977. This decline in capacity utilization occurred because Schlitz's volume had dropped from a high of 24.2 million barrels in 1977 to 15.7 million barrels in 1980, an overall decline of 35 percent.

EXHIBIT 20
Schlitz brewery capacities

Location	1977	1978	1979	1980
Milwaukee	6.8	6.8	6.8	6.8
Memphis	5.5	5.5	5.5	5.5
Syracuse	2.0	5.4	5.4	—
Winston-Salem	5.0	5.0	5.0	5.0
Longview	3.8	3.8	3.8	3.8
Los Angeles	3.0	3.0	3.0	3.0
Tampa	1.5	1.5	1.5	1.5
Honolulu	0.4	0.4	—	—
Total	28.0	31.4	31.0	25.6

Note: Data in millions of barrels.
Source: Schlitz Annual Reports.

In 1978, *Fortune* observed that: "[Schlitz's] breweries as a group are still the most efficient in the industry."[5] Schlitz continually studied methods to improve the efficiency of its breweries. One typical study involved Johns-Manville, its filter aid supplier. Jointly Schlitz and Manville studied filtration at Schlitz breweries, with the result that Schlitz instituted standardized filtration procedures at all breweries which increased filter run times 20–25 percent and simplified maintenance schedules. Hours of labor per barrel filtered were also reduced, and purchasing and invoicing were simplified.

In 1970, Schlitz entered the container industry by constructing a can manufacturing plant in Oak Creek, Wisconsin, with a capacity of two billion cans per year. By 1980, Schlitz had constructed four more canning plants located in Winston-Salem, North Carolina; Longview, Texas; Tampa, Florida; and Los Angeles, California, with a total capacity of over three billion cans and lids per year. Production in 1980 amounted to 4.6 billion cans, utilizing approximately 92 percent of Schlitz's capacity and 3 percent of the total aluminum used in the United States. In addition, the self-manufacture of cans and lids provided approximately 90 percent of the company's requirements in 1980.

In the mid-1970s, Schlitz also phased in a more efficient brewing process which saved money, but as noted, customers did not like the new beer. Schlitz completed this conversion after eight years of research and a large capital investment. The change, known as "Accurate Balanced Fermentation," kept the yeast in active suspension for the exact time necessary to complete fermentation. In a further effort to cut costs, Schlitz also put in more corn syrup and less barley malt, the relatively expensive ingredient commonly used to give beer its flavor and body. To address this problem and get uniform quality and taste from each brewery, Sellinger imposed strong central controls on all plants shortly after he joined the company in 1977. Among other things, he required that Schlitz's tasting department get daily samples from each plant. Quality control was also improved by having test control personnel report directly to Milwaukee and by giving them final say over what left each plant.

Marketing

In 1977, Schlitz marketed four of the nine American beers in national distribution, more than any other brewer. Since that time, Schlitz's two major brands, premium-priced *Schlitz* and popular-priced *Old Milwaukee*, have both lost market share. (Market share in Texas dropped 4 percent in 1979, with the gain to Anheuser-Busch and Miller.) In addition, *Schlitz Light*, introduced in 1975, has continually fallen below sales expectations, despite reformulations and repackaging to improve its image. Also, in 1979 Schlitz entered the fast growing and highly profitable super-premium category with *Erlanger* to compete with earlier introductions by Anheuser-Busch (*Michelob*) and by Miller (*Lowenbrau*). Only one year later it was expanded nationally. This is an impressive statistic for any product, but *Erlanger*

---

[5] Charles G. Burck, p. 50.

still had a long way to go to catch up. Schlitz also test marketed another light beer in 1979, *Tribute*, later renamed *Old Milwaukee Light*, and its expansion to full nationwide distribution was planned for the summer of 1981.

The one area where Schlitz led the industry was with malt liquor, specifically the *Schlitz Bull* brand. Sales of this malt liquor represented about 3 percent of the total beer market and, according to company executives, aggressive advertising had been responsible for its success. Schlitz's strength in each region of the United States is indicated in Exhibit 21.

According to Schlitz representatives, Schlitz conducted major segmentation studies on a periodic basis to determine how to properly position its brands in the marketplace. These studies identified need segments of beer drinkers, including both those with physiological needs and those with psychological needs. Schlitz also conducted a major consumer tracing study each year to determine to whom commercials should be targeted from a media standpoint. These studies aided Schlitz in developing demographic profiles of its target drinkers as well as brands that were bought by different demographic groups. It also allowed Schlitz to determine the target groups it should attempt to reach via different media, such as television, radio, print, and outdoor advertising.

In 1981, advertising agencies which handled the Schlitz account included: J. Walter Thompson (Chicago) for the *Schlitz* and *Erlanger* brands; Della Fermina, Travisano, and Partners (New York) for *Schlitz Light*; Benton and Bowles (New York) for *Schlitz Malt Liquor*; and B.B.D. & O. International (New York) for *Old Milwaukee*.

For most of the 1970s, the *Schlitz* (premium beer) brand accounted for over 60 percent of Schlitz's sales. Schlitz's famous advertising campaign for its premium, ''Go for the Gusto,'' had been very successful for many years. By 1977, however, *Schlitz's* advertising began to lose its edge. To revive itself, Schlitz introduced a series of formidable beer drinkers who responded to a suggestion that they abandon *Schlitz* for another beer. The beer drinker would glower into the camera and demand, ''You want to take away my gusto?'' The commercials did not receive a good reception from most viewers, though, and were dropped in the fall of 1977 and replaced by the traditional ''gusto'' commercials.

In January 1978, Schlitz invited a select group of advertising agencies to prepare bids for acquisition of the Schlitz account since it was dissatisfied with the directions of advertising strategy being pursued by Burnett, Ted Bates, and Company. Even so, many in the advertising industry felt Schlitz had created the advertising problem itself by pressuring Burnett to drop the ''gusto'' campaign. Eventually, Schlitz selected the J. Walter Thompson Agency to coordinate the Schlitz premium account. Thompson had been the agency which handled the Schlitz account previously (1956–61).

In August 1979, J. Walter Thompson initiated a *Schlitz* premium marketing program featuring strenuous activities and people who reached for the gusto. This was the so-called ''Go for it'' campaign. Packaging for *Schlitz* premium was also changed at this time to a tapered ''classic'' bottle, with slim lines and a gold foil

EXHIBIT 21 Schlitz barrelage by region (millions)

	1974	1975	1976	1977	1978	1979	1980	1981E	1984E
New England	2.3	2.2	2.1	1.7	1.2	0.9	0.7	0.6	0.3
Mid-Atlantic	1.3	1.2	1.7	1.7	1.5	1.0	0.8	0.7	0.4
Total Northeast	3.6	3.4	3.8	3.4	2.7	1.9	1.5	1.3	0.7
East North Central	3.2	3.1	2.9	2.5	2.1	1.7	1.4	1.2	0.9
West North Central	1.9	2.0	2.0	1.7	1.4	1.2	1.0	0.8	0.5
Total North Central	5.1	5.1	4.9	4.2	3.4	2.9	2.4	2.0	1.4
South Atlantic	5.0	5.1	5.5	4.8	4.7	4.2	3.9	3.6	2.7
East South Central	2.3	2.3	2.3	1.9	1.4	1.0	0.9	0.8	0.6
West South Central	4.8	5.0	4.8	5.1	4.7	4.3	3.9	3.5	2.8
Total South	12.1	12.4	12.6	11.8	10.8	9.5	8.7	7.9	6.1
Mountain	0.7	0.8	0.9	0.9	0.9	0.8	0.7	0.6	0.5
Pacific	1.2	1.6	2.0	1.8	1.8	1.7	1.6	1.5	1.2
Total West	1.9	2.4	2.9	2.7	2.7	2.5	2.3	2.1	1.7
Total all regions	22.7	23.3	24.2	22.1	19.6	16.8	14.9	13.3	9.9

Note: Discrepancies due to rounding.
E = estimate.
Source: U.S. Brewer's Association, Beer Marketer's Insights, Inc., and Sanford C. Bernstein & Company.

label, and distribution to bars and restaurants was given major importance in the overall effort.

In 1980, Thompson shifted the Schlitz advertising from the revised "Gusto" campaign to one involving the use of Schlitz's president Frank Sellinger. This type of advertising was begun in the beer industry in March 1979 when Pittsburgh Brewing introduced the first such ad. They were followed shortly thereafter by the F. X. Matt Brewing Company, and then by Schlitz. Both Pittsburgh and Matt were regional brewers and the president concept was highly successful for them. Schlitz also felt the president concept had improved sales, but no conclusive figures were available by early 1981. These campaigns received positive responses from beer wholesalers, however, a very important group in the industry. In 1981 Schlitz planned to film yet another commercial with Frank Sellinger, who had appeared in its two previous presidential commercials.

During 1980, Schlitz also initiated a taste test during National Football League playoff games. In this context, the 1980 *Schlitz Annual Report* stated: "More than one hundred million Americans watched the Super Bowl (1981) which included the fifth of Schlitz beer's Great American Beer Tests. In these unique live television commercials, beer drinkers compared the taste of Schlitz and their regular brand of beer — with impressive results for Schlitz." During these taste tests, the participants identified themselves as drinkers of a competing beer brand. The highest percentage of drinkers selecting their regular beer brand in preference to Schlitz in these taste tests was 54 percent for Budweiser. Schlitz also placed among the top three brands in several regional taste tests conducted by various news media during this period. Some industry observers expressed skepticism about the results and effectiveness of these tests, however. They noted that most American beers, unlike most European brands, were subtly flavored and that a trained palate was required to distinguish among such beers. They also noted that probably no more than one person in one hundred had such a palate so that the test was really like a coin flipping contest which should produce 50/50 results over the long run. In addition, one former Schlitz marketing executive expressed doubts that the tests would prompt anyone to try Schlitz. Schlitz beer's reputation was so bad, he contended, that many people were actually ashamed to be seen drinking it. He suggested that no matter how favorable the results may seem, television viewers would automatically reject them.

Despite those reservations, the Great American Beer Tests represented a major part of Schlitz's strategy of heavy television advertising for sports events. Thus, in 1980, Schlitz estimated that its commercials run during network sporting events were seen seven times per month in 91 percent of American households.

The remaining brands brewed by Schlitz each had its own advertising campaign and packaging strategy tailored to reflect its particular advantages. Among these brands, *Old Milwaukee* beer was second in sales volume for Schlitz. Its advertising strategy included point of sale advertising and radio and television commercials that reenforced its name with the following jingle: "Whenever you think of the town of Milwaukee, you think of beer — and *Old Milwaukee* tastes as great as its name.''

Schlitz Malt Liquor, the largest selling malt liquor in the U.S. and third largest volume seller for Schlitz, utilized an advertising campaign centered around the famous *Schlitz Malt Liquor* bull. *Erlanger*, Schlitz's new super-premium beer which went national in April 1980, featured advertisements emphasizing its unique bottle and the slogan, ''Taste the Moment.''

Old Milwaukee Light, introduced in August 1980, debuted with the slogan: ''We got the taste of light right.'' The *Old Milwaukee Light* advertising campaign for the first quarter of 1981 featured a discount in price of *Old Milwaukee Light* and *Old Milwaukee*, accompanied by the slogans ''The price of great taste just went down'' and ''It doesn't get any better than this.''

Since the mid-1970s Schlitz had not been able to match Anheuser-Busch and Miller in total advertising dollars; on a per barrel basis, however, Schlitz led the industry (see Exhibit 12). Furthermore, in 1977 Schlitz executives in their Annual Report announced that ''[We will be] striving to develop advertising that is more cost effective than that of our competition.'' Frank Sellinger summarized Schlitz's advertising opportunities for the future as follows:[6]

> *The brewing industry has become a marketing battleground with the continuing barrage of advertising. It must confuse the consumer. Sometimes I'm not sure if people know whether they're buying a good beer or clever advertisement. We're trying to cut through that confusion with a simple message: we brew superior beer; try it and judge for yourself.*

Litigation

Legal battles have continually plagued Schlitz. A six-year-old antitrust lawsuit filed by the Pearl Brewing Company of San Antonio, Texas, and seven of its independent wholesalers was finally settled in 1977 with Schlitz agreeing to pay Pearl $2.6 million.

The same year, a Securities and Exchange Commission (SEC) civil suit was filed which alleged violations of the antifraud, proxy, and reporting provisions of federal securities law, particularly in regard to the company's domestic marketing practices and relationship with Spanish brewing investments designed to evade Spanish tax and exchange control laws. The suit was settled in 1978. Schlitz, without admitting or denying any of the allegations, consented to:

1. A permanent injunction prohibiting future violations
2. The appointment of a Special Review Person by the SEC to review Schlitz's procedures followed in its internal investigation, accounting, and bookkeeping practices in the Export Marketing Division, disclosures, and to make recommendations regarding past and future disclosures

---

[6] Brooker, p. 3.

3. The establishment of an Audit Committee of the Board of Directors, comprised of three outside directors, to review the company's financial controls and accounting procedures

In 1978, Schlitz was also indicted (on March 15) on three counts of felony tax fraud, one misdemeanor charge of conspiracy, and seven hundred individual misdemeanor counts allegedly in violation of the Federal Alcohol Administration Act (FAAA) following a three-year federal grand jury investigation assisted by the Treasury Department's Alcohol, Tobacco, and Firearms (ATF) division and the Internal Revenue Service (IRS). These charges stemmed from questionable marketing practices including the furnishing of products, equipment, services, and possible cash payments by Schlitz to retail accounts to induce the purchase of Schlitz company products. Settlement was reached in November 1978, with all but one count dismissed, including the felony tax fraud counts. Schlitz, although again not admitting any wrongdoing, agreed to pay $761,000 and to refrain from any questionable marketing practices in the future.

In 1979, the United States Court of Appeals Seventh Circuit upheld the dismissal of claims filed by the Miller Brewing Company against Schlitz in 1975. Miller had alleged trademark infringement in the way Schlitz used the term "light" in distributing *Schlitz Light* beer. The court reaffirmed an earlier determination that the word "light" and "lite" may not be exclusively appropriated by Miller as a trademark. The appeals court remanded for trial Miller's claim against Schlitz for unfair competition.

During this same period, Schlitz faced various other allegations and suits (both criminal and civil) in the antitrust areas of price fixing, monopolization, and illegal trade promotions. These allegations were all resolved by 1980 with no material erosion of Schlitz's position.

Finance

After nearly three decades of growth, Schlitz's sales began falling in the late seventies. Consequently, the company logged five straight quarters of red ink beginning with the fourth quarter of fiscal 1978. However, as of December 31, 1980, four straight quarters of profits had been reported, even though barrel shipments continued to decline. Despite these reported profits, Schlitz clearly faced a challenge in turning around the sales of its *Schlitz* brand (see Exhibits 22–25). Stock prices declined with sales (see Exhibit 26).

In 1980, Schlitz's earnings from operations were $30.1 million compared to a $77 million loss in 1979 and earnings of $36.0 million in 1978. In 1980, sales increased slightly to $897 million from $894 million in 1979. Sales of cans and lids to outside parties amounted to $78.9 million in 1980, $76.5 million in 1979, and $36.9 million in 1978. The key factors in the company's 1980 earnings performance included higher beer selling prices, lower production costs, and higher interest income. Thus, beer selling prices increased approximately 10 percent in 1980, while lower production costs and higher interest income were related to the closing of

EXHIBIT 22
Schlitz's
consolidated
balance sheets
for years ended
December 31

Assets	1979	1980
Current assets		
Cash	$ 10,661	$ 8,097
Marketable securities, at lower of cost or market	30,525	134,525
Accounts receivable, less reserves of $913 in 1980 and		
$891 in 1979	25,011	31,049
Receivable from sale of assets	30,000	30,000
Refundable income taxes	24,292	—
Inventories, at lower of cost or market	55,491	54,571
Prepaid expenses	5,501	3,756
Total current assets	181,481	261,998
Investments and other assets		
Notes receivable and other noncurrent assets	63,028	38,621
Investments	16,407	14,514
Land and equipment held for sale	6,711	6,710
	86,146	59,845
Plant and equipment at cost	661,305	663,176
Less accumulated depreciation and unamortized		
investment tax credit	319,783	346,056
	341,522	317,120
	$609,149	$638,963

Liabilities		
Current liabilities		
Notes payable	$ 2,084	$ 920
Accounts payable	47,393	49,833
Accrued liabilities	44,495	39,790
Federal and state income taxes	157	10,284
Total current liabilities	94,129	100,827
Long-term debt	131,032	119,767
Deferred income taxes	85,439	92,834
Shareholders' investment		
Common stock, par value $2.50 per share, authorized		
30,000,000 shares, issued 29,373,654 shares	73,434	73,434
Capital in excess of par value	2,921	2,921
Retained earnings	228,822	255,808
	305,177	
Less cost of 310,672 shares of treasury stock	6,628	6,628
Total shareholder's investment	298,549	325,535
	$609,149	$638,963

Note: Dollars in thousands except per share data.

	1978	1979	1980
Sales	$1,083,272	$1,042,583	$1,027,743
Less excise taxes	172,431	148,427	131,076
Net sales	910,841	894,156	896,667
Cost and expenses			
Cost of goods sold	729,854	746,415	721,278
Marketing, administrative, and general expenses	144,939	155,439	145,304
	874,793	901,854	866,582
Earnings (loss) from operations	36,048	(7,698)	30,085
Other income (expense)			
Interest and dividend income	3,311	4,485	21,796
Interest expense	(15,359)	(12,784)	(11,508)
Gain on repurchase of debentures	114	1,175	4,153
Gain (loss) on disposal of assets	(3,045)	(86,076)	596
Miscellaneous, net	(299)	54	734
	(15,278)	(93,146)	15,771
Earnings (loss) before income taxes	20,770	(100,844)	45,856
Provision for income taxes	8,809	(50,199)	18,870
Net earnings (loss)	$ 11,961	$ (50,645)	$ 26,986
Net earnings (loss) per share	$.41	$(1.74)	$.93

Note: Dollars in thousands except per share data.

	Retained earnings	Capital in excess of par value
Balance, December 31, 1977	$286,978	$2,921
Net earnings, 1978	11,961	—
Cash dividends declared, $.47 per share	(13,660)	—
Balance, December 31, 1978	285,279	2,921
Net loss, 1979	(50,645)	—
Cash dividends declared, $.20 per share	(5,812)	—
Balance, December 31, 1979	228,822	2,921
Net earnings, 1980	26,986	—
Balance, December 31, 1980	$255,808	$2,921

Note: Dollars in thousands except per share data. The statement of accounting policies and accompanying notes to consolidated financial statements are an integral part of these statements.

EXHIBIT 25 Schlitz's five-year financial summary

	1976	1977	1978	1979	1980
Sales including excise taxes	$1,214,662	$1,134,079	$1,083,272	$1,042,583	$1,027,743
Net sales	999,996	937,424	910,841	894,156	896,667
Earnings (loss) from operations	112,645	60,855	36,048	(7,698)	30,085
Net earnings (loss)	49,947	19,765	11,961	(50,645)	26,986
Depreciation of plant and equipment	35,685	41,127	45,946	44,516	34,445
Working capital provided from operations	101,178	85,423	68,179	41,638	63,307
Capital expenditures	111,234	35,670	14,461	11,426	9,778
Total assets	737,843	726,762	691,935	609,149	638,963
Net working capital	36,070	47,694	40,254	87,352	161,171
Current ratio	1.4 to 1	1.6 to 1	1.4 to 1	1.9 to 1	2.6 to 1
Plant and equipment, net	585,785	564,620	526,596	341,522	317,120
Long-term debt	223,195	196,506	140,362	131,032	119,767
Long-term debt to total capital ratio	38.5%	35.5%	28.3%	30.5%	26.9%
Average number of shares outstanding	29,063	29,063	29,063	29,063	29,063
Per-share data:					
Net earnings (loss)	$1.72	$.68	$.41	$(1.74)	$.93
Dividends	.68	.68	.47	.20	—
Shareholders' investment	12.27	12.27	12.22	10.27	11.20
Barrels of beer sold	24,162	22,130	19,580	16,804	14,954
Brewery capacity in barrels	27,000	29,500	31,400	31,000	25,600

Note: Amounts in thousands except per share data.

	1979		1980	
	High	Low	High	Low
First quarter	12⅜	9⅞	9¼	5
Second quarter	13⅜	9	8¼	6¼
Third quarter	12⅛	9⅛	9⅛	7
Fourth quarter	13⅜	7⅞	9⅞	7¼

Stock listed — New York Stock Exchange.
As of February 13, 1981, there were 17,622 holders of record of Schlitz common shares.

the Syracuse brewery, sold in February 1980. Also, the success of Schlitz's cost-cutting efforts, evident in Exhibits 27 and 28, were due to cutbacks of personnel over the previous four years, a gradual decrease in expenditures in Schlitz's capital improvements program, and discontinuation of quarterly dividends since the third quarter of 1979. Specifically, during the period 1977–81, Schlitz's staff was cut by 20 percent.

At the time of the sale of the Syracuse brewery, Anheuser-Busch agreed to a purchase price of $100 million, payable in three installments over a two-year period. The $30 million payable in January 1981 was received and the last payment of $35,714,000 plus interest, was due in January 1982.

Plant and equipment was carried at cost and included expenditures for improvements to existing facilities as well as expenditures for new facilities. Plant and equipment totals as of December 31, 1980 and 1979, are shown in Exhibit 27. Operating and per barrel results are shown in Exhibit 29.

Plant and equipment	1979	1980
Land	$ 9,007	$ 8,754
Building	114,177	114,782
Machinery and equipment	459,032	463,516
Cooperage and pallets	44,932	42,977
Construction in progress	4,157	3,147
	661,305	663,176
Accumulated depreciation	(305,420)	(334,431)
Unamortized investment tax credit	(14,363)	(11,625)
Total	$341,522	$317,120

Provision for depreciation was calculated using the "Straight-line Method."
Source: Joseph Schlitz Brewing Company, *1980 Annual Report*, p. 14.

EXHIBIT 28 Schlitz's cash flow, 1976–1981 (millions)

	1976	1977	1978	1979	1980	1981 est.
Internal sources						
Net income	$ 49.9	$19.8	$ 12.0	$(50.6)	$ 30.0	$ 30.0
Depreciation	31.9	36.4	41.1	39.5	33.0	30.0
Deferred tax	19.1	20.9	14.1	(23.4)	3.0	5.0
Other (mostly ITC)	15.8	3.5	—	—	—	—
Total	$116.7	$80.6	$ 67.2	$ 34.5	$ 66.0	$ 65.0
Internal uses						
Dividends	$ 19.8	$19.8	$ 13.7	$ 5.8	—	—
Capital expenditures, net	110.1	24.5	9.5	(95.2)[b]	11.0	12.0
Debt repayment	34.5	26.7	70.8	9.3	12.0	10.0
Other	(5.8)	(2.0)	(4.7)	(1.6)	—	—
Increase in working capital[a]	(2.4)	19.1	(12.0)	32.6	10.0	5.0
Total	$156.2	$88.1	$ 77.3	$ 49.1	$ 33.0	$ 27.0
Net internal cash	$ (39.5)	$ (7.5)	$(10.1)	$ 14.6	$ 33.0	$ 38.0
External sources						
Equity, net	—	—	—	—	—	—
Debt	$ 45.0	—	$ 14.6	—	—	—
Other[c]	—	—	—	—	$ 40.0	$ 30.0
Total	$ 45.0	—	$ 14.6	—	$ 40.0	$ 30.0
Net change in cash	$ 5.5	—	$ 4.5	$ 14.5	$ 73.0	$ 68.0
Year-end cash	29.5	22.1	26.6	41.2	114.2	182.0

[a] Excludes cash and equivalents.
[b] Largely the disposal of the Syracuse Brewery.
[c] Receivable from sale of brewery.
Source: Emanuel Goldman, "The Brewing Industry," *Bernstein Research*, 1980.

THE FUTURE

In 1981, Schlitz's top management felt that they were operating in a capital-intensive business where inflation and price changes could hit particularly hard. Nonetheless, Schlitz had identified two keys to its planned future growth: demographic factors and the ability to develop new markets. Specifically, the company felt that with the right combination of marketing strategies and new products, per capita beer consumption should increase. Consequently Schlitz planned to continue to make major commitments in all areas of marketing support, especially to advertising designed to generate positive images for new and established brands. In this context, Frank Sellinger stated in 1980: "I think that this opportunity to run Schlitz is probably the biggest thing I've ever done. I knew the problems when I came here three years ago. I felt then . . . and I continue to feel — that I can help correct them."[7]

[7] "Is the Gusto Forever Gone?" *Forbes* (126:12) 34.

EXHIBIT 29 Selected Schlitz operating results, 1976–1981 (millions)

	1976	1977	1978	1979	1980	1981 est.
Barrels sold	24.16	22.13	19.58	16.80	14.70	13.20
Sales	$1,214.7	$1,134.1	$1,083.3	$1,042.6	$1,040.0	$1,030.0
Net sales	$1,000.0	$ 937.4	$ 910.8	$ 894.2	$ 910.0	$ 910.0
Cost of goods sold	755.7	726.4	723.2	740.2	740.0	730.0
Marketing, general, and administrative expenses	131.6	150.1	151.6	161.6	135.0	150.0
Earnings from operations	$ 112.7	$ 60.9	$ 36.0	$ (7.7)	$ 35.0	$ 30.0
Interest and other expense, net	16.0	25.8	15.3	93.1[a]	(15.0)	22.0
Pretax income	$ 96.7	$ 35.0	$ 20.8	$ (100.8)	$ 53.0	$ 52.0
Tax rate	48.4%	43.6%	42.4%	—	42.0%	43.0%
Net income	$ 49.9	$ 19.8	$ 12.0	$ (50.6)	$ 30.7	$ 29.6
Net per share	$ 1.72	$ 0.68	$ 0.41	$ (1.74)	$ 1.05	$ 1.00
Per barrel						
Sales	$ 50.27	$ 51.25	$ 55.33	$ 62.04	$ 70.74	$ 78.03
Net sales	$ 41.39	$ 42.36	$ 46.52	$ 53.21	$ 61.90	$ 68.94
Cost of goods sold	31.28	32.82	36.94	44.05	50.34	55.30
Marketing, general, and administrative expense	5.45	6.78	7.74	9.62	9.18	11.36
Earnings from operations	$ 4.66	$ 2.75	$ 1.84	$ (0.46)	$ 2.38	$ 2.27
Interest and other expense	0.66	1.17	0.78	5.54	(1.02)	(1.67)
Pretax income	$ 4.00	$ 1.58	$ 1.06	$ (6.00)	$ 3.60	$ 3.94
Net income	$ 2.06	$ 0.89	$ 0.61	$ (3.01)	$ 2.09	$ 2.24

[a] Loss on sale of Syracuse Brewery.
Source: Emanuel Goldman, "The Brewing Industry," *Bernstein Research*, 1980.

THE ADOLPH COORS COMPANY

Coors had been very profitable and grew by emphasizing a single, premium brand of beer. It was the only major brewer located in the Rocky Mountains, with one large production facility in Golden, Colorado. While it had expanded into other states and was the sixth largest brewer in 1982, it was still a regional brewer.

In the 1980s, Coors faced increasingly stronger competition from two national brewers, Anheuser-Busch and Miller. Given the slow industry growth rate for beer sales in recent years, some industry analysts felt that an industry shake-out would occur. Regional brewers would be the most susceptible to going bankrupt or being acquired during such a consolidation. While Coors had been strong up through the 1970s, could it remain successful as just a regional brewer in the 1980s? Thus, two distinct strategic alternatives presented themselves to the Coors family who held tight control of the firm. Should the firm remain a regional brewer or go nationwide in the production and marketing of beer?

HISTORY

Adolph Herman Joseph Coors, a German immigrant, and Jacob Schueler, a Denver businessman, began brewing in an old tannery in the Clear Creek Valley of Golden, Colorado, in 1873. They called it the Golden Brewery. Coors was attracted to the area because of the numerous springs flowing from the Rocky Mountains. He realized the importance of water in the brewing process. In 1880, Coors bought out Schueler and renamed the successful venture Coors Golden Brewery.

The company thrived until Prohibition, but managed to survive through it by selling near beer and malted milk. It also developed several manufacturing operations for producing cement and porcelain during that same period. While Coors did well, such was not the case for breweries in general. From 1910 to 1933, the number of breweries was cut in half from 1,568 to 750.

This case was prepared by Jeffrey M. Miner (M.B.A. in finance) and Larry D. Alexander (assistant professor of strategic management), Department of Management, College of Business, Virginia Polytechnic Institute and State University. Copyright © 1985 by Jeffrey M. Miner and Larry D. Alexander. Reprinted by permission.

After Prohibition, Coors Company experienced phenomenal growth. Still, it remained a regional brewery which produced only one type of beer from a single brewery. Its beer was sold in eleven western states in 1970, with California being its largest market. By that same year, this regional brewer also became the nation's fourth largest brewer.

Coors beer began to develop a mystique in the early 1970s, perhaps because it was the only beer brewed with pure Rocky Mountain spring water. Many people thought it was of higher quality than other beers. Coors conveyed environmental purity and a western image, which were important at that time. Also, Easterners could not get the beer except at very high prices, which added to its mystique. The movie *Smokey and the Bandit* had as a plot the degree to which some people would go to get Coors beer. Celebrities such as Paul Newman and Clint Eastwood regularly drank Coors beer on movie sets. Even President Ford carried the beer on board Air Force One.

Coors, the market leader in nine of the eleven states it served including California, then turned to geographic expansion. The company began selling beer in Texas and other nearby states where it quickly gained market share. Its 1975 sales of $520 million represented a $270 million increase over 1971. Operating margin was 28 percent in 1975, the highest in the industry, and profit per barrel averaged almost $9, almost twice that of the industry leader, Anheuser-Busch. As a Coors marketing vice-president put it at that time, "You could have sold Coors beer in Glad bags."[1]

Coors' tremendous success, however, did not last. The company began to lose market share in many of its sales territories. There were several reasons why this occurred. First, Coors suffered from a negative public image. A brewery workers' union strike in 1977 led to a boycott of Coors beer by numerous AFL-CIO unions. Second, Joe Coors' ultraconservative philosophy alienated a number of groups, including women, Blacks, Hispanics, and gays. Third and most important, Coors failed to realize that the industry was changing. Miller Brewing, which was acquired by Philip Morris in 1970, was the first to recognize that beer drinkers were not a single market, but rather a number of differentiated segments. Whereas Anheuser-Busch used price and lower costs to compete with Schlitz in the 1960s, Miller shifted that emphasis toward heavy advertising and promotion and development of new products to appeal to specific segments in the 1970s. This new strategy helped Miller jump from eighth at the start of the decade to second by 1977.

Unfortunately, Coors ignored the signs for quite a while, continued with its production orientation, and brewed only one beer, Coors Premium. Coors' advertising expenditures were the lowest in the industry. In 1977, they were only about $.25 per barrel compared to an industry average of over one dollar. A marketing battle ensued as Miller attempted to unseat Anheuser-Busch from the number one spot, and Coors suffered from it.

Coors' loss in market share was most dramatic in California, its traditional stronghold. Share dropped from 40 percent in the mid-1970s to under 20 percent by 1982. The loss for Coors was a gain for Anheuser-Busch which then controlled about 47 percent of that market. Coors also lost share to Miller in Texas, another former stronghold. Overall, Coors dropped from being fourth-place brewer in the early 1970s to sixth place in 1982. Volume was 13.5 million barrels in 1976, a 9.1 percent market share, and earnings were $76 million on sales of $594 million. In 1982, however, volume dropped to 11.9 million barrels, which represented only a 6.6 percent share, while earnings were only $40 million on sales of $915 million.

MANAGEMENT

Adolph Coors Company had sustained itself for over one hundred years as a family-owned and -managed business. The Coors family had a pervasive influence over all aspects of company operations. Since 1970 the top spot had actually been shared by two brothers, William and Joseph Coors. Their late brother, Adolph Coors III, would have been chief executive had he not been killed in 1960. Adolph Coors II retained control of the company until he died in 1970, when control was passed on to Bill and Joe. In the early 1980s, Joe's two oldest sons, Jeff and Peter, were added to the management team, supposedly to provide a transition between the two generations of management.

Bill Coors, age sixty-six, was the elder of the two. His official position was chairman and chief executive officer. He handled the technical side of the business and had a reputation for being a genius in the brewing industry. Joe Coors, age sixty-five, was the president and chief operating officer and oversaw the financial and administrative functions. In reality, each brother acted in any capacity he wanted and there were no formal lines of authority. Their apparent lack of rivalry amazed outsiders. Both men were lean, tall, rugged Westerners who were very open and personal with employees. In fact, each was referred to as Bill and Joe by all employees, rather than by their famous last name.

The brothers devoted themselves to brewing the finest-quality beer that they could. Bill and Joe did not put much faith in that mystique bit. They genuinely believed they simply made a better product and that was why it sold so well. Bill was well respected for his technical know-how and was chairman of the United States Brewers Association. The brothers had shunned the public eye in the past; however, the company's more recent unfavorable public image had forced them to be more open with the public. Joe, a longtime conservative, was very outspoken and his views tended to alienate a number of minority groups.

The brothers realized that in the new competitive brewing industry of the 1980s, maintaining market share and survival were key goals. This was one reason that they decided to infuse fresh thinking in the management team when they brought Jeff and Peter into top management in 1982.

Peter Coors, age thirty-six, and Jeff, age thirty-eight, were named division presidents in 1982 when an expanded four-man office of the presidency was created. They both had engineering degrees from Cornell. Peter also had an M.B.A. degree and was involved in the sales and marketing aspect of the company. He initiated the company's first market research in the early 1970s, which his father disapproved of at the time. However, since he realized that the low-calorie beer market segment was growing rapidly, he proved instrumental in developing Coors Light. Both Joe and Bill opposed this move at first. Peter was heir apparent to the presidency and more easily handled the pressures of being a public figure. Jeff oversaw research and development operations and was a one-man research team in the early 1970s. By the early 1980s, that department had grown significantly in size and importance. Jeff also headed up all new product development efforts at Coors in the 1980s.

Both were responsible for shifting the emphasis toward advertising, price competition, and new product introduction. These actions probably helped the company to survive. The pair disagreed with each other and also with Bill and Joe, but the differences tended to be constructive.

PRODUCTION

Coors was considered a maverick among brewers because its brewing process defied industry norms. However, the company was very highly regarded in the industry as a quality and technologically superior brewer. With Coors' single brewery, which had a 20 million barrel capacity, uniformity and quality were easier to maintain. The drawback, however, was that transportation costs were quite high and there were significant logistics problems in producing and packaging different kinds of beer in the same brewery.

All raw materials and finished products were constantly monitored for uniformity and quality. Coors used the highest-quality ingredients possible. The water was pure Rocky Mountain spring water from over forty springs located on the brewery grounds. Rarely was water in its pure form suitable for brewing, but no chemical alterations of this water were necessary. Coors supplied its own special barley seed, Moravian III, to contract farmers in the West. Coors bought hops from growers in Washington and Idaho and imported two types from Germany. Coors also had its own malt house to ensure that proper aging of the barley was adhered to. Rice, grown for Coors in California and Arkansas, was used to give the beer its light body. A computer was used extensively to monitor many steps in the brewing operation, and flavor checks were performed regularly at each step. In addition, trained personnel routinely evaluated the quality of all ingredients and the final product.

Coors' brewing process was unique because it was entirely natural. No artificial ingredients were used. Since all biochemical processes were allowed to occur naturally, Coors had one of the longest brewing processes in the industry. It took an average of 68 days to brew and package the beer. Coors Light took even longer to produce because extra time had to be allowed for enzymes to dissolve the sugars.

In keeping with its natural brewing philosophy, Coors approached the problem of germ control in a unique way — the beer was not pasteurized. In 1959, company scientists discovered a better way which involved a series of filters combined with controlled conditions. The filling process was so germ-free that it was likened to a sterile operating room.

Coors' filling process was designed to keep the beer cold at all times. This was supposed to enhance the flavor since heat was thought to take away some of the beer's body and flavor. Packaging was a completely computerized operation to maintain Coors' goals of uniformity and quality. The computer told the forklift drivers which pallets to pick up and where to put them. Because of this system, Coors did not require a warehouse. Beer that came off the line was sent almost immediately to trucks and railcars for distribution.

Coors was trying to minimize pollution caused by its packaging materials. The company was the founder and leader of used aluminum can recycling. In 1979, 80 percent of its aluminum cans used in packaging were recycled. Coors paid out over $33 million for them. The major source for these cans were the recycling centers located at Coors' distributorships. Also, fifty can banks, which were reverse vending machines for aluminum cans, were being test marketed. This approach helped to make recycling more convenient for consumers. This program also enabled the company to be less dependent on the aluminum market. Recycling was not only cost-effective for the company, it also provided consumers with supplemental income.

Brewery wastes were always a problem, but Coors had developed a method to transform much of this waste into animal feed. An average of 4 million gallons of industrial wastes were processed daily at Coors. The company was a leader in the efficient use of waste water, yielding only 3.5 barrels of it per barrel of beer, compared to 8 for most brewers.

Coors was also committed to energy conservation. The company began converting to coal in 1976 and by 1980 was virtually 100 percent coal-dependent. This move was relatively risk-free since Coors sat in the middle of America's most plentiful coal supply. Also, recycling saved about 95 percent of the energy required to produce new aluminum from bauxite.

Clearly, Coors was the most energy-efficient brewer in America, with the lowest B.T.U. per barrel ratio in the industry. Its engineering capabilities enabled the company to become nearly energy self-sufficient while maintaining rigid pollution-control standards. For example, Coors had been able to remove 99.5 percent of the pollutants caused by burning coal.

MARKETING

In the 1980s, Coors' marketing capabilities were improving, but still did not compare to many of its major competitors'. However, it had come a long way since the midseventies when the company brewed only one product, did no market research, and spent next to nothing on advertising. By the early 1980s, Coors was trying to remedy this through extensive advertising, promotion, and development of new products to cater to different segments of the beer-drinking population.

Coors switched its emphasis from producing one beer of superior quality to producing assorted products of superior quality. Until 1978, Coors Premium was the only beer that the company produced. Management felt that this was a superior beer and they simply did not need another brand. Coors Premium was considered to be a rich and light-bodied beer and contained 138 calories per 12 ounces. This beer was still the staple for the company and the fourth best selling brand of beer in the nation. The company sold 8.4 million barrels of Premium in 1982, but this was down some 19 percent from 1981, mainly due to increased competition and the recession. By 1983, however, Coors also marketed other brands of beer to different market segments.

Coors Light was introduced in 1978 in response to the fast-growing light beer segment. The company had earlier insisted that Coors Premium was light enough, but later realized the importance of developing a new product for this important growth segment. Coors Light contained 105 calories per 12 ounces. In an effort to provide a light beer with quality taste, Coors spent a great deal of time developing this product. Not surprisingly, it also used all natural ingredients. The brand grew substantially since its introduction, but remained far behind the leader, Lite beer from Miller. The company sold 3.2 million barrels of Coors Light in 1982, an increase of 2.1 million over 1980. However, many analysts felt that this growth had been at the expense of Coors Premium, which was another reason for Premium's sales decline.

In 1983, Coors started test marketing a new premium brew called Golden Lager 1873 because the company recognized that both Coors Premium and Light appealed to basically the same type of beer drinkers. Company research showed that many drinkers wanted a heartier-tasting beer. Coors hoped that Golden Lager would compete effectively with the national leaders in this category, Anheuser-Busch's Budweiser and Miller's High Life. The company tried to add credibility to the brand by linking it with its Rocky Mountain heritage. Initially, it was tested in selected cities in the South and West. Coors also hoped that the new beer would help fill the brewery's excess capacity.

Coors had also tried to appeal to the growing import and superpremium beer market segment. George Killian's Irish Red Ale from France had been sold to Coors, which began testing the product in 1980. Successful results prompted a marketwide rollout in 1982. The company claimed that high initial sales indicated that the product had already developed a strong following.

Earlier in 1980, Coors began testing its first superpremium brand, Herman Joseph's 1868. It was very rich and full-bodied, which was achieved through a longer brewing and aging cycle. Coors hoped that the beer would be able to compete with Anheuser-Busch's Michelob, the leader in that segment. In 1982, the beer was still being tested in six states, but it had not yet been very successful. As a result, Herman Joseph's was periodically reformulated, repackaged, and readvertised, but it had never topped 100,000 barrels.

In an industry as competitive as brewing, it was important for Coors to generate a strong following for its products. Advertising and promotional skills were a great concern, probably because the firm had grown complacent in its century of operation. Fortunately, Coors management realized that it could no longer rely on its product's mystique to cure marketing problems. Since 1975, advertising expenditures increased dramatically as shown in Exhibit 1. However, Coors made frequent ad theme changes over the past few years, which gave the company a branding identity problem.

To complement its own marketing department, Coors also enlisted the aid of two top advertising agencies. Advertising for Coors Premium emphasized its purity, freshness, and superiority. The campaign was supported by in-store point-of-purchase displays which cost much less than television and were probably fairly effective. On television, Coors depicted its beer being drunk in traditional beer-drinking settings, such as bars and parties; ads were targeted at those who drank three or four beers at a time. Coors Light had an energetic new campaign to attract more consumers in the low-calorie segment. It focused on the unsurpassed taste in informal active settings.

Coors used outdoor billboards as a secondary medium, which was not standard for the industry. Billboards were used to depict the image of the snow-covered Rockies. This medium was used mainly for Coors Premium. While Coors previously used radio advertising to a rather limited extent, it was used more extensively in the 1980s for Coors Light.

Advertising and promotional efforts were increased in 1982 to the young-adult segment which, while declining in absolute numbers, was usually where brand loyalty was established. Campaigns to improve Coors product awareness among Blacks and Hispanics, who accounted for a significant proportion of the target market, had been initiated. Corporate messages aimed at these groups tried to persuade

EXHIBIT 1
Coors advertising expenditures, 1975–1983

Year	Expenditure (in millions)
1975	$ 1.2
1976	2.0
1977	15.5
1978	33.5
1979	46.4
1980	66.8
1981	85.8
1982	88.1
1983	over 88.1

Source: *Adolph Coors Company: 1980 Annual Report* and *Adolph Coors Company: 1982 Annual Report.* Also see Robert F. Hartley's "Coors — We Are Immune to Competition," in his *Management Mistakes* (Columbus, Ohio: Grid, 1983), pp. 139–53.

them to give the company a chance and dispel Coors' negative image, which still lingered on. Coors felt, however, that its new, open, straightforward public relations efforts would help win these consumers over to its side.

Perhaps the most important way in which brewers advertised their products was through sports promotions, especially on television. Coors focused on both participative and spectator sports events, selecting these events based on a sports activity study performed by the company. Its recent sports emphasis had been on motor sports and cycling. In 1980, many Coors distributors registered sizeable sales increases before, during, and after various Coors-sponsored sporting events. Sports promotion also helped Coors gain valuable national exposure. However, it should be pointed out that Coors and other smaller brewers had some difficulty finding available spots on nationally televised sports due to exclusive arrangements that Anheuser-Busch and Miller had established with the networks.

Coors had over 350 distributors in its marketing territory. These distributors usually had to be large because Coors insisted that its products be refrigerated during distribution. This required both the company and its distributors to undertake added expenses and pains to keep the beer cold so that the flavor of the beer was preserved until it got to retailers. All beer was shipped from Coors in insulated railcars or refrigerated trucks. Distributors in turn were required to keep the beer refrigerated in their warehouses. Coors thus usually only took on veteran wholesalers who could make the necessary investments in refrigeration and insulation. The beer was placed in special vaults and kept at a constant 35 degrees. Because of this requirement, distributors had to pay an additional $100,000 or more each year just to keep Coors beer cold.

Retailers were encouraged to keep Coors beer refrigerated at all times, but because of increased promotions, there were often floor displays at room temperature. The company claimed that it would not harm Coors beer or cause it to lose its flavor any faster than any other beer on the market. To further ensure that flavor was preserved, the distributors were required to rotate retailer stocks every 60 days. This 60-day rotation rule was the strictest in the industry.

The distributors also played a vital role in marketing the product. They set up point-of-purchase displays in retail outlets, prepared local advertising, and developed customer relations. In order to maintain better relations with its distributors, Coors established its own television network, Second Century, in 1980. Stories were periodically done on different wholesalers. Distributors had to purchase the equipment to view the films, but over 90 percent had already done so. Brewery employees also viewed what the distributors were doing on this network.

The company also owned six of its own distributorships, not to compete with the independent wholesalers, but to give Coors' management firsthand knowledge of actual conditions in the field. It also enabled the company to analyze local and regional consumer patterns, train management in marketing and sales, and test new programs before they were introduced everywhere.

Approximately 78 percent of Coors' products were shipped by rail. The remaining 22 percent were shipped by truck. Of this, 14 percent went by common carrier or trucks owned by Coors distributors, and 8 percent went by the Coors Transportation

Company. This wholly owned subsidiary had grown in the past couple of years since only 3 percent of Coors' products used it in 1980. The company was formed in 1971 to provide hauling flexibility. It operated 132 temperature-controlled trailers and 52 tractors. Each truck traveled about 215,000 miles a year. The purpose was to reach distributors who did not have rail service, to handle emergency loads, and to haul to areas where profitable backhauls were available. Backhauls usually brought food products into the Denver area. The company was also formed as a reaction to rising railroad rates.

The advantage of having this flexibility was exemplified in 1980, when Coors was entering Arkansas. Thousands of extra cases were needed because demand had been underestimated. It could have turned into embarrassing shortages just when the company was trying to establish itself in a new territory. Fortunately, it turned into extra sales because of quick, back-up trucking by Coors' trucks.

Coors had recently begun a two-pronged approach to gain market share. One way was to expand further into the East, and the other was to reverse share losses in its traditional twenty-state territory, most notably in California and Texas. Neither way promised to be an easy task. The effort would mean head to head competition with leaders Anheuser-Busch and Miller and would require huge marketing expenditures. Coors had been trying to meet advertising expenditures, but aggressive marketing was still a relatively new experience for Coors.

In 1983, Coors' biggest expansion campaign yet was undertaken to enter the Southeast market. This region was considered to be a growth area by many brewers. It appeared that the mystique was still alive in the Southeast, where there had been strong initial customer acceptance of Coors Premium and Light. Initital sales were going well in 1983 for both brands in this region. While competition in this area was intense, Coors had selected large distributors who were well established in their markets to help implement this effort.

This expansion was also supported by heavy advertising on radio and television which stressed the fact that Coors could finally be purchased in the region. With that expansion, Coors marketed its products in twenty-six states and the District of Columbia. However, the good news was tempered by two points. First, some analysts feared that perhaps the sales in the Southeast increased so very rapidly because of the novelty factor. Thus, they suggested that more time would be needed to determine if Coors' success would be maintained. Second, Coors' transportation costs to the Southeast were very high. One estimate was that the cost of shipping from Golden, Colorado, to the Southeast was $7–8 per barrel, compared to an industry average of $3 per barrel.

Coors had purchased land options for the possible erection of another brewery in Virginia or Tennessee. However, there were no plans to begin building any time soon. If the company were to acquire or build another plant, a marketing problem could arise, since Coors' identity was associated with pure Rocky Mountain spring water. Jeff Coors remarked, ''Now, you can make good water out of anything. We haven't crossed the hurdle of what impact we'd suffer if we dropped the Rocky Mountain water theme. But you never know. We might produce an entirely different beer for the East.''[2] However, one analyst suggested that the delaying of the plant would only allow the competition time to solidify their hold even further on eastern and southeastern markets.

FINANCE

Coors had always been strong financially. Exhibits 2 and 3 show the consolidated balance sheets and consolidated income statements for the years 1980–1982. The

EXHIBIT 2
Adolph Coors
Company
consolidated
balance sheets

	December 28, 1980	December 27, 1981	December 26, 1982
Assets			
Cash	$ 87,883	$ 76,614	$ 71,251
Accounts and notes receivable	57,930	66,667	64,909
Inventories	149,504	115,677	118,658
Prepaid expenses	28,856	34,282	34,614
Income tax prepayments	6,036	2,215	4,236
Total current assets	330,209	295,455	293,668
Properties, net	556,419	652,090	702,769
Excess of cost over net	2,649	2,567	3,029
Other assets	5,108	6,272	8,448
Total assets	$894,385	$956,384	$1,007,914
Liabilities and equity			
Accounts payable	$ 48,923	$ 40,033	$ 45,601
Salaries, vacation	25,677	27,488	25,543
Taxes (not income)	19,872	18,494	17,252
Income taxes	3,427	9,922	2,789
Accrued expenses	18,195	21,577	28,820
Total current liabilities	116,094	117,514	120,005
Deferred income taxes	60,149	75,968	95,097
Other long-term liabilities	6,042	9,335	9,600
Capital stock:			
Class A common, voting	1,260	1,260	1,260
Class B common, nonvoting	11,000	11,000	11,000
Total	12,260	12,260	12,260
Paid-in capital	2,011	2,011	2,011
Retained earnings	724,284	765,751	795,396
Total	738,555	780,022	809,667
Less treasury shares	26,455	26,455	26,455
Total equity	712,100	753,567	783,212
Total liabilities and equity	$894,385	$956,384	$1,007,914

Note: Dollar amounts in thousands.
Source: *Adolph Coors Company: 1982 Annual Report*, pp. 12–13.

EXHIBIT 3
Adolph Coors
Company
consolidated income
statements

	December 26, 1980	December 27, 1981	December 26, 1982
Sales	$1,012,198	$1,060,345	$1,032,297
Less excise taxes	133,301	130,429	117,039
Net sales	887,897	929,916	915,258
Costs and expenses			
Cost of goods sold	629,758	659,623	659,033
Marketing, general, and administrative	146,293	181,348	185,076
Research and development	14,256	16,848	15,230
Total	790,307	857,819	859,339
Operating income	97,590	72,097	55,919
Other			
Interest income	(16,514)	(13,788)	(10,411)
Interest expense	1,563	1,601	2,480
Miscellaneous	6,764	4,651	(1,298)
Total	(8,187)	(7,536)	(9,229)
Income before taxes	105,777	79,633	65,148
Income taxes	40,800	27,663	25,000
Net income	64,977	51,970	40,148
Beginning retained earnings	668,939	724,284	765,751
	733,916	776,254	805,899
Cash dividends	9,632	10,503	10,503
Ending retained earnings	$ 724,284	$ 765,751	$ 795,396

Note: Dollar amounts in thousands.
Source: *Adolph Coors Company: 1982 Annual Report*, p. 10.

company went public in 1975, only because it needed to raise money to pay inheritance taxes on the estate of Adolph Coors II. These public shares were traded over the counter and there were some 9,000 shareholders in 1983. However, this public stock was class B nonvoting, so outsiders did not have a say in management decisions. The Coors family owned 35 percent of the class B shares and 100 percent of the 1.26 million shares of class A voting stock. Thus, the Coors family controlled their stock so much so that no other firm would be able to acquire it unless management allowed it. That did not appear very likely given the history of this maverick brewery.

Another aspect of Coors' financial approach was the company's refusal to borrow money. This was a family tradition which dated back to the company's beginnings. Coors' capital structure consisted almost entirely of common stock. Also, since the company did not plan to issue any more stock, all future expansion would have to be financed through internally generated cash. Its normal cash balance was around $70 million, but Coors planned to increase this. Although lack of debt was a sign of financial strength, this avoidance of debt financing altogether sometimes caused the company to bypass attractive opportunities. One was the addition of an eastern plant, which the company agreed was necessary to offset huge transportation costs of shipping to eastern markets. Another example related to Coors' can-manufacturing facility, which developed the technical process for making the two-piece aluminum can. However, the company sold the process to Continental Can Company and American Can Company because Coors would have had to borrow money to begin production.

RESEARCH AND DEVELOPMENT

Coors was often considered to be the most technically advanced brewery in the world. The company had Colorado's single largest engineering crew for any private-sector firm. R&D was concerned with developing new products, brewing techniques, and packaging techniques. Coors had developed technical superiority in ceramics and aluminum cans. There was an extensive barley R&D program, which had genetically developed Coors' own special variety called Moravian III. Yeast cells, used in the brewing process, were specifically selected for testing to develop new and better strains to upgrade the quality of its beer. Farmers wanted a higher yield for their crops and Coors wanted reliable sources of supply, so much of the company's research dealt with counseling farmers on how to get higher yields while maintaining Coors' standards. The company also did research on how to get more out of the grain in the production process. They were now reusing many things that used to be thrown away.

Not all R&D efforts had been successful, however. The press-tab can was developed to stop pollution from ring-pull tabs. The idea was good, but it failed because the can was hard to open and consumers often cut their fingers in the process.

Jeff Coors, who was responsible for R&D, became the first American in a quarter-century to present a technical paper at the European Brewing Convention in 1979. R&D was a relatively minor part of the company's operations before Jeff became involved in the early 1970s. While many advancements in the industry occurred in the 1960s and 1970s, Jeff did not see any major technical breakthroughs on the horizon in the 1980s. Research appeared to have taken a distant back seat to marketing; however, Coors remained committed to R&D. Bill Coors' credo was, "If technology exists, use it. If it doesn't, develop it."[3]

HUMAN RESOURCES

Coors employed about 8,600 people in 1983, down some 850 from 1981. Company officials blamed the layoffs on the recession, which reduced industry demand. Coors tried to develop its own personnel so they could later be promoted from within. This required extensive education and training programs. The company's television network, Second Century, had also been used to produce in-house training programs.

Coors was committed to equal employment opportunity and supported an active affirmative action program. Minority employment agencies were used to recruit minorities, which represented 13.4 percent of the work force in 1979. Coors also had an employee opportunity training program which hired exconvicts, disabled veterans, and the disadvantaged and trained them for responsible positions within the firm.

An average salary for a Coors production worker was $20,000 a year and Coors offered fringe benefits totaling an additional $5,800 per employee per year. Clearly, these wages and benefits were considered higher than the average for Golden, Colorado, a city of approximately 11,000 people.

Coors' management maintained that business should operate as a free enterprise; thus, the company was philosophically opposed to unions. Unfortunately, Coors' brewery workers were unionized and represented a large proportion of the work force. They went out on strike in 1977. The issue was not money but rather that the company was forcing employees to take lie detector tests. A boycott of the company's products ensued, but Coors management stood its ground, replaced many of the striking workers, and rehired those who wanted to return.

In 1978, Coors' brewery workers voted out the union and the boycott's effect diminished. In 1982, the "60 Minutes" television show did a story on Coors to try to uncover human rights violations. The show, often noted for its revealing stories, found no such violations, which somewhat helped to ease Coors' negative image. As of 1983, Coors was still operating without a union.

Coors was very concerned about employee health and well-being. The American Center for Occupational Health, a Coors subsidiary, was committed to safer working conditions. The company provided healthcare tests and services to Coors' employees and other businesses, and in 1982 was completing the development of a light-weight, compact health-testing machine.

Coors opened a wellness center on its brewery property in 1981. All employees, retirees, spouses, and dependents were allowed to use the facility, which contained a track, trampolines, weight sets, stationary bicycles, and other equipment. The center also sponsored programs in physical fitness, nutrition, stress management, weight control, stopping smoking, and alcohol education. The staff was comprised of experts in each field. Thus far, it had been very successful. Bill Coors was not worried whether the center could be cost-justified; he simply wanted it to promote health and happiness. Coors also funded participation in various sports for a number of employees and many were sent to survival training courses. In sum, management regarded physical fitness as very important.

COORS' VERTICAL INTEGRATION AND DIVERSIFICATION EFFORTS

In keeping with Coors' philosophy of independence in all aspects of operations, it became the most vertically integrated firm in the industry. Exhibit 4 shows Coors'

EXHIBIT 4

Coors operations

Ceramic Manufacturing Plants
Benton, Arkansas
El Cajon, California
Golden, Colorado
Grand Junction, Colorado
Hillsboro, Oregon
Norman, Oklahoma

Foreign Operations Not Shown
Singapore
Glenrothes, Scotland
Rio Claro, Brazil

Rice Mill
Weiner, Arkansas

1983 Expansion
Alabama
Florida
Georgia
North Carolina
South Carolina
Eastern Tennessee
Virginia
District of Columbia

Grain Elevators
Burley, Idaho
Delta, Colorado
Huntley, Montana
Longmont, Colorado
Monte Vista, Colorado
Worland, Wyoming

Paper Converting Plants
Boulder, Colorado
Lawrenceburg, Tennessee
Main Offices
Golden, Colorado (largest single brewery
    and aluminum can manufacturing plant
    in the United States)

Company-Owned Distributorships
Boise, Idaho
Denver, Colorado
Omaha, Nebraska
Spokane, Washington
St. Louis, Missouri
Tustin, California

Glass Bottle Manufacturing Plant
Wheat Ridge, Colorado

Source: *Adolph Coors Company: 1982 Annual Report*, p. 26.

operations throughout the United States. Coors had attempted to control its raw materials supply by having contract farmers grow its barley and rice and by maintaining its own malt house. Coors also had its own supply of packaging materials. It owned a can-manufacturing plant (the largest single such plant in the industry), a glass-manufacturing plant, and a paper mill. Coors Energy Company owned a coal mine and 249 natural gas and oil wells; it also leased rights to 330,000 acres. Coors owned its own truck fleet and waste-treatment facility, and company engineers designed and constructed most of its own machinery and equipment. This was all very important for cost control, stability, and independence from supplier price hikes and shortages. Clearly, Coors believed in vertical integration, both forward and backward.

Coors had also diversified into companies not directly related to brewing, though they complemented the primary product. Coors Porcelain Company was one of the world's foremost suppliers of technical ceramics, mainly for the computer industry and energy firms. The company was trying to decide whether to compete in the $1 billion a year dental restoration industry. Coors Food Products Company did well in 1982, acquiring a snack food company which made potato chips. The Coors subsidiary also packaged rice and competed in the rice flour and cereal markets. They were experimenting with bread products made from brewers grain 28, a high-protein by-product of the brewing process. Variety breads were growing by 15 percent yearly. They also made cocomost, a cocoa substitute derived from brewer's yeast.

COORS' COMPETITION

Since Miller Brewing's effect on the industry was discussed earlier, only Anheuser-Busch, Stroh, and Heileman are profiled here. While Anheuser-Busch was the industry's giant, the two second-tier brewers were similar to Coors in size but followed different strategies. Exhibit 5 contains a list of the top six brewers and their major products in order of volume sold. Exhibits 6 and 7 show market share by company and brand.

Anheuser-Busch   Anheuser-Busch was the number one brewer in the United States ever since it took over that spot from Schlitz in the late 1950s. The giant lumbered along until the 1970s, when an onslaught by Miller to knock it out of its top position caused August Busch III, the company's chief strategist, to rethink his game plan. In large part, he began to copy Miller's methods. He determined that Miller's success was a direct function of heavy advertising in sports media, product diversification, and a switch in emphasis to the beer-drinking young adult segment. This strategy change occurred in 1977 and has often been seen as the turning point in the industry. From then on, Anheuser-Busch steadily pulled away from Miller. It was the best-performing brewer in 1982, with a market share of 32.7 percent. Its 59.1 million barrels sold topped Miller's by almost 20 million.

By 1983, the firm was pursuing a total marketing effort, continuing to focus on the young adult segment with a well-balanced line of quality beers. The Budweiser brand, by far the nation's best-selling beer and leader in the premium segment, represented an amazing 40.7 million of total barrels sold. Michelob was the leader in the superpremium segment. While Miller controlled 60 percent of the light-beer segment with its best-selling Lite, Anheuser-Busch had set its sights on taking over that market. It marketed three light beers with different tastes, prices, and images, and controlled 28 percent of the segment. Budweiser Light, introduced in 1982, had become the second best-selling light beer already. This brewing giant also had its sights on international expansion. Budweiser was already the best-selling import in Japan, and it was also strong in Canada.

The firm was the nation's biggest sponsor of sporting events. It had the twenty-second largest advertising budget among all U.S. firms, and it far outdistanced all competitors in television advertising. Furthermore, Anheuser-Busch was locked into many exclusive contracts as was Miller. The company's operating efficiency was outstanding, and it boasted the highest profit per barrel in the industry. It had the best distribution system in the industry and its plants were located strategically throughout the United States. It was committed to new capacity increases, especially in Los Angeles. Like Coors, the company had vertically integrated to better control

EXHIBIT 5
Top six brewers
and their major
brands, 1982

1. Anheuser-Busch
   Budweiser
   Michelob
   Busch
   Michelob Light
   Bud Light
   Natural Light

2. Miller
   High Life
   Lite
   Lowenbrau

3. Stroh/Schlitz
   Old Milwaukee
   Stroh's
   Schlitz
   Schaefer
   Schlitz Malt Liquor
   Old Milwaukee Light
   Stroh Light
   Goebel
   Schlitz Light
   Erlanger

4. Heileman
   Old Style
   Schmidt's
   Blatz
   Black Label
   Colt 45 Malt Liquor
   Old Style Light
   Blatz Light
   Black Label Light

5. Pabst
   Pabst
   Red, White & Blue
   Olde English Malt
   Blitz
   Pabst Light
   Jacob Best
   Andeker

6. Coors
   Coors Premium
   Coors Light
   George Killian's Ale
   Herman Joseph's 1868

Source: Paul Mullins. "Brewing Industry Has Flat Growth in '82," *Beverage Industry*, January 28, 1983, p. 31.

EXHIBIT 6
Brewers' estimated
market shares

	1979	1980	1981	1982E
Anheuser-Busch	26.8%	28.2%	30.0%	32.3%
Miller	20.8	20.9	22.2	21.8
Stroh/Schlitz	15.3	13.9	12.9	12.8
Heileman	6.6	7.5	7.7	7.9
Pabst	8.8	8.5	7.4	6.8
Coors	7.5	7.8	7.3	6.6
Olympia	3.5	3.4	3.1	2.8
Genesee	2.0	2.0	2.0	1.9
Schmidt	2.2	2.0	1.6	1.8
General	1.7	1.4	1.2	1.0
Pittsburgh	0.4	0.6	0.5	0.5
Others	4.4	3.8	4.1	3.8

Source: Paul Mullins. "Brewing Industry Has Flat Growth in '82," *Beverage Industry*, January 28, 1983, p. 34.

EXHIBIT 7
Top ten beer brands
in 1982

	Market share	Volume (millions of barrels)
Budweiser	22.0%	40.0
Miller High Life	11.0	20.0
Miller Lite	9.6	17.5
Coors Premium	4.6	8.4
Michelob	4.6	8.3
Pabst	4.5	8.1
Old Milwaukee	3.1	5.7
Stroh's	3.0	5.6
Old Style	3.0	5.5
Schlitz	2.6	4.7

Source: "Many Top Brews Give Ground to Other Brands," *Beverage World*, April 1983, p. 33.

raw material supplies and costs. The firm's growth was expected to continue and recent capacity expansions would increase pressure to capture more market share. Some industry observers felt that Anheuser-Busch might control 40 percent of the market by 1990.

Stroh Brewing Company

Stroh saw merger as the only way to survive against the two industry giants. The company acquired Schlitz in 1982, which had been suffering vast market declines. The merger put Stroh in the third spot in the brewing industry. Management was quite strong and had done a good job with its Stroh brand. However, the company had put itself at a disadvantage because it had leveraged itself so heavily with debt. Key problems for Stroh were how to successfully integrate its acquisitions into the company and how to reverse the sales decline of its Schlitz brand.

Stroh was not advertising the Schlitz brand very much in 1983, although there were plans to step it up in the near future. The company appeared to be using cash flow from the brand to finance marketing expenditures for its best-selling brand, Old Milwaukee. It was being promoted with heavy television advertising and cents-off coupons, which were fairly new to this industry. Many analysts attributed the success of Old Milwaukee, a popular-priced brand, to the 1981–1983 recession.

G. Heileman Brewing Company

Heileman, like Coors, had been very successful as a regional brewer. It was targeted for markets in the Midwest and Northwest, but was presently the fourth largest brewer in the United States. The company had increased barrelage dramatically over the past few years, from 4.5 million barrels in 1975 to 14.9 million in 1982. It was the only major brewer besides Anheuser-Busch to register a sales gain in 1982.

In 1982, Heileman took a big step toward long-term viability by acquiring Pabst and its 49 percent share of Olympia. However, due to objections raised by the Department of Justice, a new Pabst entity was spun off to the remaining Olympia shareholders. Heileman strongly believed that continued consolidation of second-tier and small brewers was needed to more effectively compete. (As a side note, seven of the top eleven brewers were involved in acquisitions or attempted acquisitions in 1982.)

Heileman also had very good management. The company was unusually adept at being able to market more than three dozen regional beers, of which Old Style was the best-selling. It also had a very good cost structure which was quite competitive with that of Anheuser-Busch. To remain competitive, Heileman knew it had to expand into new markets. But having regional products might have helped the company to target some of its products to local market conditions.

There were two potential problems for Heileman. First, it served only the popular-priced market segment. This was one of the reasons that the company did so well in the face of a recession. Lack of brand loyalty may be in Heileman's favor, however, if people continued to trade down from higher-priced brands. Second, Heileman tried to remain well under Anheuser-Busch's prices; unfortunately, the industry giant had not raised prices in Heileman's market for about 2 years. If an increase did not come shortly, profit margin pressures might reduce Heileman's profitability.

LEGAL AND POLITICAL ISSUES

A number of legal and political issues were becoming more prevalent in the brewing industry. First, the vast number of traffic deaths related to alcohol had increased dramatically. There had been numerous bills introduced in the U.S. Congress to raise the legal drinking age nationally to twenty-one, and such bills were gaining increasing support. Raising the age would cause a decrease in beer sales. Perhaps substitutes, such as near beer, would crop up. Also, a number of consumer groups were asking the Consumer Protection Agency to look into the advertising practices of brewers. They claimed that brewers were encouraging the consumption of alcohol by highly vulnerable younger groups, which brought about heavy drinkers.

The company was now distributing counter cards and posters to bars throughout its marketing area with a message from E.T., the extraterrestrial. E.T. advised, "If you go beyond your limit, please don't drive. Phone home."[4] Coors had a long-standing policy against alcohol abuse. It sponsored alcohol awareness classes at its wellness center and supported many organizations that dealt with alcohol abuse.

Another major issue was the threat of mandatory deposits for bottles and cans. This would increase the price of beer and decrease customer convenience, possibly affecting demand. The difficulties in handling, shipping, and selling beer under this law were well known, as 18 percent of the beer sold in the United States in the early 1980s was covered by such laws. The law's rationale was to cut down on litter along the roadside, in the city, or out in the country. However, recycling might be an alternative means to accomplish this. Coors had a vigorous program for recycling both bottles and cans.

A third issue was excise taxes. Various state legislatures currently had bills to raise the excise tax on beer. There had also been some activity at the federal level. A number of groups had advocated taxing all alcoholic beverages by their alcohol content, which would result in drastically higher taxes on malt beverages. This, too, would result in increased prices for the consumer.

PRODUCT/MARKET OPPORTUNITIES

Under market penetration, Coors could more heavily advertise its products on television. Radio might also be a promising medium for beer advertising. One survey revealed that beer drinkers spent only about 33 percent of their media time watching television, while 47 percent of their time was spent listening to radio, which was less expensive for advertisers.[5] Another method could be increased price competition through such means as price cuts, cents-off coupons, and rebates. Coupons might attract more women who then did not buy much beer. Finally, Coors could merge with other brewers, which could help it penetrate existing markets with a wider selection of products.

Under market development, Coors could continue to expand nationally. This could be done by expanding its own facilities or by acquiring another brewery to give it additional capacity. A list of the top forty breweries in the United States is shown in Exhibit 8. Expansion abroad might also be a viable alternative, especially since Anheuser-Busch was doing well in Japan. Clearly, this latter option would require additional plants to make it feasible.

Under product development, Coors could develop near beer or other nonalcoholic beverages in response to a raising of the mandatory drinking age. Near beer was one product that helped Coors survive during Prohibition. It could also sell bottled spring water. Coors could also develop plastic containers for beer products, which would be a response to the threat of mandatory deposits and a way to lower transportation costs with lighter plastic containers. Another alternative would be to develop a beer product for the popular-priced segment for a more complete line of products. Coors could also import a name brand to compete more effectively in that segment. Coors' engineers could do consulting jobs for area firms. Finally, Coors Porcelain Company could accelerate its plans to get into the lucrative billion dollar a year dental restoration market.

Finally, under diversification, Coors could consider other glass products, such as test tubes. Also, the company could get into areas related to the beverage industry, such as soft drinks and distilled spirits.

EXHIBIT 8 Top forty U.S. commercial brewers

	1983 sales (31-gallon barrels)	Percent gain or loss over 1982	Headquarters
1. Anheuser-Busch, Inc.	60,500,000	2.4%	St. Louis, MO
2. Miller Brewing Co.	37,500,000	−4.6	Milwaukee, WI
3. The Stroh Brewery Co.	24,300,000	6.1	Detroit, MI
4. G. Heileman Brewing Co.	17,549,000	20.9	LaCrosse, WI
5. Adolph Coors Co.	13,719,000	15.1	Golden, CO
6. Pabst Brewing Co.	12,804,000	—[c]	Milwaukee, WI
7. Genesee Brewing Co.	3,200,000	−5.9	Rochester, NY
8. Christian Schmidt & Sons	3,150,000	0.0	Philadelphia, PA
9. Falstaff Brewing Co.	2,704,884	−15.1	Vancouver, WA
10. Pittsburgh Brewing Co.	1,000,000[a]	1.0	Pittsburgh, PA
11. Latrobe Brewing Co.	700,000[a]	0.0	Latrobe, PA
12. Champale Products Corp.	450,000[a]	4.7	Trenton, NJ
13. Hudepohl Brewing Co.	400,000[a]	0.0	Cincinnati, OH
14. The F. X. Matt Brewing Co.	400,000[a]	0.0	Utica, NY
15. Eastern Brewing Co.	350,000[a]	0.0	Hammonton, NJ
16. The Schoenling Brewing Co.	315,000[a]	5.0	Cincinnati, OH
17. Joseph Huber Brewing Co.	272,000	−1.1	Monroe, WI
18. The Lion Inc. — Gibbons	230,000	0.0	Wilkes-Barre, PA
19. D. G. Yuengling & Son	143,000	0.0	Pittsburgh, PA
20. Jones Brewing Co.	122,000	−2.9	Smithton, PA
21. Dixie Brewing Co., Inc.	113,000	−24.7	New Orleans, LA
22. Jacob Leinenkugel Brewing	67,000	−1.5	Chippewa Falls, WI
23. Fred Koch Brewery	60,000	−7.7	Dunkirk, NY
24. Stevens Point Brewery	48,900	0.8	Stevens Point, WI
25. Cold Spring Brewing Co.	40,000[a]	0.0	Cold Spring, MN
26. Spoetzl Brewery, Inc.	36,000	−3.0	Shiner, TX
27. August Schell Brewing Co.	35,000	0.0	New Vim, MN
28. Straub Brewery, Inc.	35,000	0.0	St. Mary's, PA
29. Anchor Steam Brewery Co.	33,500	16.6	San Francisco, CA
30. Walter Brewing Co.	26,800	−3.9	Eau Claire, WI
31. Dubuque Star Brewing	5,400[b]	−75.3	Dubuque, IA
32. Old New York Beer Co.	3,629[a]	—	New York, NY
33. Geyer Brothers	3,500	−12.5	Frankenmuth, MI
34 Redhook Ale Co.	3,000	—	Seattle, WA
35 William S. Newman Brewing	2,800	12.0	Albany, NY
36. River City Brewing Co.	2,500	108.3	Sacramento, CA
37. Sierra Nevada	2,200	25.7	Chico, CA
38. Yakima Brewing	1,400	—	Yakima, WA
39. Boulder Brewing Co.	500	25.0	Longmont, CO
40. Thousand Oaks Brewing	232[a]	—	Berkerly, AZ

[a] Estimate.
[b] Less than a full year's production.
[c] Due to Pabst-Olympia merger, 1983 figures are not comparable to 1982.
Source: *Modern Brewery Age Blue Book, 1984* (Stamford, Conn.), pp. 6, 8, 10, 168.

THE FUTURE

The Coors family remained confident of their firm's success in the future. Bill and Joe Coors felt their firm had survived because of the superior quality of its product. But, would quality and its Rocky Mountain mystique be enough to survive a changing industrial structure?

It appeared that slow growth would continue to plague the U.S. brewing industry. This meant that any significant increase in sales by one brewer would be at the expense of other competitors. In addition, increased concentration among brewers — via acquisitions, mergers, and bankruptcies — would continue and it was predicted that the top three firms could have up to 80 percent of the market by 1990.[6] As a result, a major strategic decision faced Coors management in the mid-1980s. Could Coors remain a regional brewer and be successful? If so, what would it need to do differently as a regional brewer to compete against the national breweries and other regional firms. Conversely, should Coors go into nationwide production and distribution? These two clear strategic alternatives presented themselves to the Coors family members in top management.

Over the years, Coors had increased its territory to twenty-six states and Washington, D.C. It had announced that it would add Alaska and Hawaii by the end of 1983, and move into Maryland in early 1984. But would this be enough to compete against the two national giants, Anheuser-Busch and Miller? Could one production facility serve a nationwide distribution or would Coors have to operate additional breweries? The alternative — remain regional or go nationwide — that Coors management would select remained undetermined as 1983 came to a close.

REFERENCES

1. "A Test for the Coors Dynasty," *Business Week*, May 8, 1978, p. 69.
2. Bob Lederer. "Can Coors Survive its Image?" *Beverage World*, April 1979, p. 49.
3. Bob Lederer. "Coal Power," *Beverage World*, September 1978, p. 58.
4. *Ibid.*, p. 47.
5. "Industry News," *Beverage Industry*, April 10, 1983, p. 58.
6. Michael C. Bellas. "Beer Wholesaler Sales Concentration: Implications for the 80s and Beyond," *Beverage Industry*, January 28, 1983, p. 30.